D1803634

The Redbook

A Manual on Legal Style

FOURTH EDITION

Electronic Exercises

REGISTER THE CODE below to access over 350 multiple-choice questions created by Bryan A. Garner. The sophisticated user interface provides students with many useful options:

- Track progress through questions.
- View results after completing a quiz.
- Mark specific questions for further review.
- Retake a quiz any number of times.
- Follow links to explanations within the book.

Visit eproducts.westacademic.com to register your code and get started today!

CODE:

9C17-5QZ1-E0KI-9OLA-E2Z1

The Redbook

A Manual on Legal Style

FOURTH EDITION

Bryan A. Garner

with

Jeff Newman
Tiger Jackson

ISBN: 978-1-64242-268-9

Library of Congress Cataloguing-in-Publication Data
Garner, Bryan A.
The Redbook: A Manual on Legal Style / Bryan A. Garner

Includes bibliographical references and index.
1. Legal composition. 2. English language—usage.
3. English language—style. 4. Law—United States—terminology.
5. Law—United States—language. 6. Law—United States—methodology.
7. Printing, practical—United States—style manuals.

© 2019 LEG, Inc. d/b/a West Academic
444 Cedar Street, Suite 700
St. Paul, MN 55101
1-877-888-1330

Earlier editions:
© 2002 West, a Thomson business
© 2006 Thomson/West
© 2013 LEG, Inc. d/b/a West Academic Publishing

West, West Academic Publishing, and West Academic are trademarks of West Publishing Corporation, used under license.

The publisher is not engaged in rendering legal or other professional advice, and this publication is not a substitute for the advice of an attorney. If you require legal or other expert advice, you should seek the services of a competent attorney or other professional.

Printed in the United States of America.

In memory of

Charles Alan Wright

1927–2000

Other Books Written by Bryan A. Garner

Black's Law Dictionary (all recent editions)

Garner's Modern English Usage

The Chicago Guide to Grammar, Usage, and Punctuation

Garner's Dictionary of Legal Usage
foreword by Judge Thomas M. Reavley

Reading Law: The Interpretation of Legal Texts
with Justice Antonin Scalia

Making Your Case: The Art of Persuading Judges
with Justice Antonin Scalia

Nino and Me: My Unusual Friendship with Justice Antonin Scalia

The Law of Judicial Precedent
with 12 judicial coauthors, including Justice Neil Gorsuch; foreword by Justice Stephen Breyer

Guidelines for Drafting and Editing Legislation
foreword by Judge Harriet Lansing

Garner on Language and Writing
foreword by Ruth Bader Ginsburg

The Elements of Legal Style
foreword by Charles Alan Wright

The Winning Brief: 100 Tips for Persuasive Briefing in Trial and Appellate Courts

The Winning Oral Argument

Legal Writing in Plain English

The Chicago Manual of Style "Grammar and Usage" (ch. 5)

Quack This Way: David Foster Wallace and Bryan A. Garner Talk Language and Writing

Securities Disclosure in Plain English

Ethical Communications for Lawyers

Guidelines for Drafting and Editing Court Rules

The Oxford Dictionary of American Usage and Style

A Handbook of Basic Law Terms

A Handbook of Business Law Terms

A Handbook of Criminal Law Terms

A Handbook of Family Law Terms

HBR Guide to Better Business Writing

The Rules of Golf in Plain English
with Jeffrey S. Kuhn

Board of Editorial Advisers

David A. Anderson
University of Texas School of Law
Austin, Texas

Owen L. Anderson
University of Texas School of Law
Austin, Texas

Pamela J. Armstrong
Albany Law School
Albany, New York

Tammy Brown Asher
Western Michigan University
Cooley Law School
Lansing, Michigan

Gary M. Bishop
New England Law School
Boston, Massachusetts

Josh Blackman
South Texas College of Law
Houston, Texas

Brooke J. Bowman
Stetson University College of Law
Gulfport, Florida

Mary Nicol Bowman
Seattle University School of Law
Seattle, Washington

D. Ruth Buck
University of Virginia School of Law
Charlottesville, Virginia

J. Dean Carro
University of Akron School of Law
Akron, Ohio

Bradley G. Clary
University of Minnesota Law School
Minneapolis, Minnesota

Beth D. Cohen
Western New England School of Law
Springfield, Massachusetts

Charles Dewey Cole Jr.
Newman Myers Kreines Gross Harris, P.C.
New York, New York

(the late) Richard A. Danner
Duke Law School
Durham, North Carolina

Edward C. Dawson
Southern Illinois School of Law
Carbondale, Illinois

Ward Farnsworth
University of Texas School of Law
Austin, Texas

Kelly M. Feeley
Stetson University College of Law
Gulfport, Florida

(the late) Monroe H. Freedman
Hofstra University School of Law
Hempstead, New York

Willa E. Gibson
University of Akron School of Law
Akron, Ohio

Stephen Gillers
New York University School of Law
New York, New York

(the late) Geoffrey C. Hazard Jr.
U.C. Hastings College of the Law
San Francisco, California

Kevin L. Hopkins
John Marshall Law School
Chicago, Illinois

Elisabeth Keller
Boston College Law School
Newton Centre, Massachusetts

H. Dennis Kelly
Texas A&M University School of Law
Fort Worth, Texas

Sandra J. Kerber
Cleveland-Marshall College of Law
Cleveland, Ohio

Joseph Kimble
Western Michigan University
Cooley Law School
Lansing, Michigan

Kenneth S. Klein
California Western School of Law
San Diego, California

Susan M. Lauer
Contract Wrangler, Inc.
San Mateo, California

Board of Editorial Advisers

Pamela Lysaght
University of Detroit Mercy School of Law
Detroit, Michigan

Ruth Ann McKinney
UNC School of Law
Chapel Hill, North Carolina

Brian Melendez
Barnes & Thornburg
Minneapolis, Minnesota

Kathryn S. Mercer
Case Western Reserve School of Law
Cleveland, Ohio

Jane Moul
Washington University School of Law
St. Louis, Missouri

Teresa Godwin Phelps
American University
Washington College of Law
Washington, D.C.

Norman E. Plate
University of Missouri–Kansas City School of Law
Kansas City, Missouri

Diana V. Pratt
Wayne State University
Detroit, Michigan

Leslie Rose
Golden Gate University School of Law
San Francisco, California

Judith A. Rosenbaum
Northwestern University
Pritzker School of Law
Chicago, Illinois

Wayne Schiess
University of Texas School of Law
Austin, Texas

Stephen M. Sheppard
St. Mary's University School of Law
San Antonio, Texas

Steven R. Smith
California Western School of Law
San Diego, California

Sophie M. Sparrow
University of New Hampshire School of Law
Concord, New Hampshire

Michael L. Spekter
University of Baltimore School of Law
Baltimore, Maryland

Mary Rose Strubbe
Illinois Institute of Technology
Chicago-Kent College of Law
Chicago, Illinois

Julian C. Swearengin
Bessemer Trust
New York, New York

Heidi Thompson
Louisiana State University Law Center
Baton Rouge, Louisiana

Randall M. Tietjen
Robins Kaplan
Minneapolis, Minnesota

Judith B. Tracy
Boston College Law School
Newton Centre, Massachusetts

Cara L. Cunningham Warren
University of Detroit Mercy School of Law
Detroit, Michigan

Henry T. Wihnyk
University of Florida Levin College of Law
Gainesville, Florida

Mark E. Wojcik
John Marshall Law School
Chicago, Illinois

Frederick E. Woods
Catholic University of America
Washington, D.C.

(the late) Richard C. Wydick
U.C. Davis School of Law
Davis, California

Table of Contents

(For detailed contents, see page xvii.)

Part 1: Mechanics

Part 2: Grammar, Usage, and Editing

Part 3: Specific Documents

Part 4: Scholarly Writing

Preface to the Fourth Edition

This book had its genesis in repeated requests from law firms for me to prepare a style manual tailored for them—but of course such an undertaking proved uneconomical. Hence the thought: Why not prepare a style manual for the profession as a whole? Such guides are commonplace within specialties: book publishers have *The Chicago Manual of Style*; newspapers have the *Associated Press Stylebook and Briefing on Media Law*; dissertation writers have *The MLA Style Manual and Guide to Scholarly Publishing*; and so on.

The benefit of a style manual is to ensure consistency by codifying the stylistic choices that reflect the judgment of professional editors. Once learned, the stylistic guidelines spare writers and editors from the handwringing that takes place when a fastidious writer or editor must deal with any one of the thousands of knotty questions that occur to an alert mind. Seemingly only alert minds even bother with these matters—hence, only alert minds write well or edit well. Style manuals are for those who seek to do that.

This fourth edition of *The Redbook* builds on the first three as a kind of "restatement" of legal style. The widespread adoption of the book has been gratifying. But even more gratifying has been the willingness of so many professional legal writers to act as contributors of ideas. The board of editorial advisers (see p. vii–viii) is not just a list of people willing to lend their names. They lent their talent and hard work by carefully vetting any of several versions of the manuscript and offering voluminous suggestions for improvement. I'm grateful to them all.

What I think of as being the most useful part of the book—Part 3, with chapters on particular types of documents—has been expanded with the addition of new chapters on resolutions, statements of work, and letters relating to engagement. If you're working on any type of document treated there (or in Part 4, for that matter), you might be tempted to think that there is a locally established form that you must follow. But you'd be well advised to read the applicable section: undoubtedly you'll find ways of improving whatever document you're working on.

The Redbook is intended to be the definitive guide for considering the soundness of your choices in legal writing and editing. If you're editing, you ought to know why your edits make sense. You should be able to justify every edit you make, even if it's just a punctuation mark. You'll do well if you learn to know what you're doing and why.

B.A.G.

Preface to the First Edition

"The law," as William Prosser once said, "is one of the principal literary professions." If that is so, you might expect that lawyers would have a comprehensive style manual to help govern the decisions they make in their writing. Yet that has not been so until now.

It is true, of course, that there are many books on legal style. I have written more than one myself. But there has never been, for example, an exhaustive guide to capitalization, to punctuation, to bias-free language, to the use of numbers and symbols, and the like—to the thousands of sentence-level quirks that arise in legal writing.

The law has been blessed (a curmudgeon would say cursed) with citation manuals: the guides on how to cite authority. *The Bluebook* has held the field for many years, and recently the *ALWD Guide to Legal Citation* has come boldly onto the scene. They are both serviceable guides, even if they can lead the more obsessive-compulsive personalities in the profession to fret endlessly over which commas get italicized and which ones remain roman.

But the citation manuals deal almost exclusively with citing authority, and the question inevitably arises, What about the stuff that comes in between the citations? How the sentences read is surely as important as whether the citations are in proper form. That leads us to this book, which is concerned with the form of legal sentences and their relationship to the authorities cited.

The Redbook was more than a year in the making. I began by occasionally asking practicing lawyers and law students in my advanced legal-writing courses to note three or four points that they would like answered in a manual on legal style. In a year, I had about a thousand responses. My colleagues and I grouped these into categories and began working through all the various points of style, formulating blackletter rules and supporting comments. The book gradually became something of a restatement of legal style.

Rulebooks can fossilize thinking on questions of style. In a sense, that is their purpose and their virtue. But that virtue can turn into a vice if users stop thinking about the reasons for stylistic decisions. Undoubtedly every user of this book will encounter a situation in which the better course is to depart from a rule. But the acknowledgment of this fact hardly means that the rules can be tossed aside: you need to know the rules before you can decide when to depart from them. Only then is there any hope of using the language skillfully. And that is something that everyone concerned with law should want to do.

Bryan A. Garner
Dallas, Texas
February 2002

Acknowledgments

Many superb writers and editors contributed to this book—most importantly two of my colleagues at LawProse, Inc.: Jeff Newman and Tiger Jackson, both of whom researched and drafted major segments of the book. Capitalizing on many years of experience as a journalist and graphic designer, Jeff also laid out the pages and designed the cover. Tiger, meanwhile, took the lead on our two indexes—which are helpfully thorough.

Several other LawProse colleagues proved indispensable. As lawyer-editors, Becky R. Moler and Karolyne H.C. Garner made innumerable suggestions and read page proofs. Becky took the lead in managing the editorial team. Our multitalented paralegal, Ryden McComas Anderson, similarly improved many a page and made major contributions to the chapter on e-mail messages.

Many law professors and practitioners closely reviewed the manuscript and offered important suggestions. For a full roster, see pp. vii–viii. I am grateful to the entire board of editorial advisers.

Several erudite readers offered helpful comments. In particular, I'm grateful to Joe Adams, David A. Battaglia, Darby Dickerson, David Hercher, Osler McCarthy, Brian Melendez, Joseph Sanderson, and Randall M. Tietjen. For the sections on scholarly writing, several esteemed law professors offered suggestions: David A. Anderson (Texas), Josh Blackman (South Texas College of Law), Ward Farnsworth (Texas), the late Monroe H. Freedman (Hofstra), Stephen Gillers (NYU), the late Geoffrey C. Hazard Jr. (U.C. Hastings), Kenneth S. Klein (California Western), Stephen M. Sheppard (St. Mary's), and Steven R. Smith (California Western).

At the West Education Group, Pamela Siege Chandler and Louis Higgins once again proved indispensable in the production of the book. My heartfelt thanks to them both.

As with so many of my books, Karen Magnuson copyedited the page proofs with uncanny skill. She brings polish and professionalism to every page she touches.

This book is dedicated to the memory of one of the greatest legal writers ever: Charles Alan Wright. He cared almost as much about the correct use of commas and capital letters as he did the law of federal courts, and his incomparable work was the inspiration for this book.

B.A.G.

Contents in Detail

Part 1: Mechanics

Part 2: Grammar, Usage, and Editing

Part 3: Specific Documents

Part 4: Scholarly Writing

Part 1: Mechanics

§ 1
Punctuation

1.1 Punctuation marks are like traffic signs that guide readers through sentences. Although many marks are mandatory (depending on the construction), others are optional: they can enhance clarity or shade the meaning. Some marks may substitute for others—this clause, for example, could as easily be separated from the previous one by a colon, a semicolon, or even parentheses. Each choice would result in a slightly different feel for the sentence. The em-dash may suggest drama; the colon may suggest a cause–effect relationship; the semicolon may suggest that the clauses are equally important; parentheses may suggest that what they contain is less important.

With such possible variety, punctuation marks help impart style. With them, you can influence where the reader will pause and for how long, or how the reader will put the parts of a sentence together logically. Like well-placed traffic signs, they can also prevent accidents—that is, misreadings that make a reader stop for an instant to figure out the meaning.

Anyone who has trouble with punctuation should concentrate first on learning the mandatory rules, one by one. Then, after laying that foundation, learn to use marks that add voice and flourish.

Commas

1.2 For many writers, the comma is the most troublesome punctuation mark. While some comma rules are mandatory—for example, always use them in pairs to set off midsentence parenthetical matter—others are discretionary. Even the well-known rules have a subjective element about them. When is an introductory phrase long enough to require setting off by a comma? When is a compound sentence short enough to dispense with the comma? In fact, using commas is sometimes a matter of taste. Styles generally fall into two schools: *closed* (heavy on the commas) and *open* (light on the commas). The modern trend is toward open style, but this is no license to ignore commas altogether. Use them for what they are: guideposts to help readers get through sentences smoothly and without miscues.

1.3 Use commas to separate words or phrases in a series of three or more, and include a comma before the conjunction.

(a) *Serial comma.* The serial comma, which is placed before the conjunction *and* or *or* connecting the last two items in a list, can prevent ambiguity. Generally speaking, it's always included in formal writing and often omitted in informal writing. While books and most magazines use the serial comma, most newspapers rarely do. Although some writers treat it as optional—and that seems to be the trend in popular writing—the safer practice is to use the serial comma consistently. It's never incorrect, but omitting it sometimes results in awkwardness, miscues, or even ambiguities.

Ex.: red, white, and blue

Ex.: Can you help me research this memo, draft a pleading, and schedule depositions?

Ex.: The pizzeria's trade dress includes menu content, prices, pizza ingredients, and "style" or preparation. (Without the comma, the end of the sentence would be confusing.)

Ex.: The enrollment fee is $100 for each class: domestic violence, bankruptcy, personal injury, and damages. (Without the comma, the total fee might be $300 or $400. The comma makes the meaning unambiguous.)

Not this: Overtime pay is exempted for the canning, processing, preserving, freezing, drying, marketing, storing, packing for shipment or distribution of agricultural produce, meat and fish products, and perishable foods. (Without the serial comma after *shipment*, it's unclear what is exempted: the *distribution* or the *packing for distribution*. This example comes from a famous federal case in Maine. The lack of the serial comma in a state law cost one dairy company millions of dollars.)

But this: Overtime pay is exempted for the canning, processing, preserving, freezing, drying, marketing, storing, packing for shipment, or distribution of agricultural produce, meat and fish products, and perishable foods.

(b) *Complex phrases.* If phrases in a series are long and complex, or if any of them contains internal punctuation or a conjunction, separate them with semicolons rather than commas (see 1.18).

Ex.: Among the children's chores were mowing the lawn, washing the car, taking out the trash, and feeding the dog.

But: Among the children's chores were mowing, raking, and edging the lawn; washing the car; taking out the trash; and feeding the dog.

(c) *Conjunction repeated.* No comma is needed if the items are all joined by conjunctions (a construction known as *polysyndeton*).

Ex.: The plaintiff and defendant and intervenors were all ready for trial.

(d) *With ampersand.* When the last element in a list is preceded by an ampersand instead of the word *and*, as in a law firm's or other business's name, omit the serial comma. Never put a comma before an ampersand.

Ex.: Emerson, Lake & Palmer

Ex.: Sturm, Ruger & Co.

1.4 Use a comma to separate two independent clauses joined in a single sentence by a coordinating conjunction (*and, but, or, nor, for, yet, so*).

(a) *Independent clause defined.* An independent clause is a subject–verb construction that could stand alone as a complete sentence.

Ex.: The judge entered the courtroom, and the defendant rose to his feet. (Compound sentence, with a subject and a verb in each independent clause. Each clause could stand alone: "The judge entered the courtroom. The defendant rose to his feet.")

(b) *Compound predicate distinguished.* Avoid using a comma to set off the second part of a compound predicate (two or more verbs sharing a single subject). In general, use a comma only if it's needed to avoid a miscue.

Not this: The study group called out for pizza, and took a quick break.

But this: The study group called out for pizza and took a quick break. (Compound predicate, with one subject and two verbs.)

Or this: The study group called out for pizza and salad, and took a quick break. (The comma helps distinguish the *and* that joins two objects [*pizza* and *salad*] from the *and* that joins two predicates [*called* and *took*].)

(c) *Choice between comma and semicolon.* If either of the clauses is complex or contains an internal comma, you may need to separate them with a semicolon instead of a comma to clarify the sentence (see 1.16).

Ex.: The mediation was successful thanks to the mediator's insight, persistence, and forceful personality; and at long last, the case settled.

(d) *Comma splice.* Don't join independent clauses with a comma alone. Grammarians consider that construction, called a *comma splice*, a form of run-on sentence (see 1.16–1.17). There are several ways to edit a comma splice: (1) replace the comma with a semicolon; (2) use a coordinating conjunction after the comma (see 11.47); (3) break the clauses into separate sentences; (4) make one of the clauses dependent by introducing it with a subordinating conjunction (see 11.49).

Not this: The mediation worked, the case settled. (comma splice)

But this: The mediation worked; the case settled. (semicolon)

Or this: The mediation worked, so the case settled. (coordinating conjunction)

Or this: The mediation worked. The case settled. (period)

Or this: Because the mediation worked, the case settled. (subordinating conjunction)

1.5 Use a comma to set off introductory matter unless the phrase is short and the verb follows it closely.

(a) *Types of introductory matter.* Introductory matter may be a single word of transition <Later,>, a phrase <Two days later,>, or a dependent clause <After two days had passed,>.

Ex.: Fortunately, there were no more surprises in the eyewitness's testimony.

Ex.: Two years earlier, a similar incident had occurred in a nearby town.

Ex.: Since we have to be in Chicago next week anyway, we can take the deposition then.

(b) *Exception.* At your discretion, a very short introductory phrase, usually no more than three words, may appear without a comma. Often it's preferable to omit the comma (as after the first word in this very sentence). Whether to use the comma depends on how you would want the sentence to sound if it were read aloud.

Ex.: In October another Court term will begin.

Also acceptable: In October, another Court term will begin.

Ex.: Soon we will all know the verdict.

Also acceptable: Soon, we will all know the verdict.

(c) *Inverted sentence.* No comma separates an introductory phrase in an inverted sentence if the verb immediately follows the phrase. Without the inverted syntax, the introductory phrase would be part of the predicate of the sentence.

Ex.: At the opposing counsel's table was my old mentor. (Without inversion: *My old mentor was at the opposing counsel's table.*)

Ex.: On the table was a Scalia bobblehead. (Without inversion: *A Scalia bobblehead was on the table.*)

(d) *Direct address.* Use a comma to set off a word or phrase of direct address (see 1.13; cf. 1.25)

Ex.: Your Honor, may I approach the bench?

Ex.: John, I appreciate your help.

Ex.: Good afternoon, Sally.

Ex.: Hi, George.

Ex.: Hello, Dolly.

Ex.: Thanks, Rich.

> "Punctuation is the notation in the sheet music of our words, telling us when to rest, or when to raise our voices; it acknowledges that the meaning of our discourse, as of any symphonic composition, lies not in the units but in the pauses, the pacing and the phrasing." —*Pico Iyer*

1.6 Use commas to set off a nonrestrictive phrase or clause from the rest of the sentence.

(a) *Defined.* A nonrestrictive phrase or clause is one that could be taken out of the sentence without changing the essential meaning. It gives additional description or information that is incidental to the gist of the sentence (see 11.20(b)).

Ex.: The morning meeting, which starts at 10 a.m., is about the Matthews case. (The time is incidental to the sentence's meaning because the writer has already identified the meeting being referred to. Nonrestrictive matter is typically introduced by *which* (or *who*) and set off from the rest of the sentence by commas, parentheses, or em-dashes.)

But: The meeting that starts at 10 a.m. is about the Matthews case. (The time is a necessary part of the sentence because it identifies which of several meetings. So *that starts at 10 a.m.* is a restrictive phrase that is not set off from the rest of the sentence. Restrictive matter is best introduced by *that* (or *who*).)

(b) *Nonrestrictive appositive.* When an appositive adds only nonessential information about the noun it attaches to, it is a nonrestrictive construction to be set off with commas. But use em-dashes or parentheses instead if the commas could be mistaken for serial commas—or to emphasize (dashes) or deemphasize (parentheses) the appositive.

Ex.: O'Neal, a well-respected public defender, surprised everyone by running for district attorney. (The phrase *a well-respected public defender* is not essential to the central meaning of the sentence: *O'Neal surprised everyone by running for district attorney* could stand alone without losing any essential meaning. Because *a well-respected public defender* is nonrestrictive, it is set off by commas.)

Ex.: Sometime in the month after the accident, Hilton suddenly moved to a neighboring state, Indiana. (Because *Indiana* is nonrestrictive, it is set off by a comma.)

(c) *Restrictive appositive.* When an appositive adds information that is essential to identify the noun it attaches to, it is a restrictive construction that isn't set off with commas.

Ex.: This gift is for my daughter Jane, and that one is for my daughter Sarah. (*Jane* and *Sarah* are restrictive appositives: each tells which daughter is meant. Without them, the sentence would lose essential meaning.)

Ex.: The great jurist Learned Hand never served on the Supreme Court. (*Learned Hand* is a restrictive appositive, so no commas should separate it from *jurist*.)

(d) *Dependent clause.* A dependent clause is a subject–verb construction that couldn't stand alone as a sentence. It may be restrictive (not set off with commas) or nonrestrictive (set off with commas), depending on whether it could be taken out of the sentence without changing the meaning.

Ex.: An attorney who conscientiously follows ethical rules is unlikely to be sued for malpractice. (*Who conscientiously follows ethical rules* is a clause because it contains a subject and a verb. It is dependent because it could not stand on its own as a sentence. And it is restrictive because it adds essential meaning to the sentence, specifying what type of attorney is unlikely to be sued for malpractice.)

Ex.: The new mayor, who won in a landslide, takes office on January 1. (The dependent clause *who won in a landslide* is incidental to the central meaning of the sentence: that the new mayor takes office on January 1. So it is nonrestrictive and must be set off by commas.)

(e) *Exception with procedural labels in legal pleadings.* The issue of punctuating appositives arises in almost every court paper. Whether to use commas depends on how you're using a label. If you're referring to a litigant in the very case in which you're involved, and you're coupling the name with a procedural label, the convention is to omit the commas regardless of whether two or more parties answer to that particular label, or just one.

Ex.: Defendant Marshall is a citizen of Texas. (There are five other defendants in the case.)

Ex.: Plaintiff Howard Stanton urges this Court to deny the motion to dismiss. (Stanton is the only plaintiff in the case.)

The commas are omitted even when there is only one such party (as in the second example above) because these procedural labels operate as quasi-titles rather than as traditional nouns in apposition.

In practice, whether to punctuate a procedural label as a title or an ordinary appositive comes down to whether you precede the label with the. (This point is allied to the rules for capitalizing such labels—see 2.15(f).) When using a procedural label before or in place of the name of a party to the present case, the convention in legal writing is to omit the and any commas. But when syntax requires a preceding the—say, when identifying a specific subset of a group of parties on the same side—follow the normal rules for punctuating appositives.

Ex.: At trial, Appellees Dogstar and Chronis denied the allegations in the complaint.

But: Two of the appellees, Gorenstein and Schmidt, failed to file their motions by the Court's deadline.

When referring to parties in cases other than the present one, as when discussing cited authority, you should use *the* and set off nonrestrictive appositives with commas.

Ex.: The defendant in that case, Hiram Hartenstone, owned and operated a fitness facility.

Ex.: Two of the plaintiffs in *Silva*, Hailstone Industries and Piltech, were Delaware corporations.

Likewise, when referring to coparties as such (almost always in possessive constructions), punctuate appositives according to the usual rules set forth in (b) and (c).

Ex.: Wheeler's codefendant, Sadri, was found guilty of assault in an earlier proceeding. (Sadri is Wheeler's only codefendant, and thus the name is a nonrestrictive appositive.)

Ex.: Spiegelman's codefendant Moss resides in New Jersey. (Spiegelman and Moss are two of four defendants: restrictive.)

1.7 Use a comma to separate coordinate adjectives and adverbs—that is, those that modify their target rather than each other.

(a) *Definition and tests.* Coordinate modifiers have similar meanings: together they shade the sense of the word being modified. To test whether modifiers are coordinate, either (1) reverse their order, keeping the comma, or (2) insert the word *and* between them. If the meaning remains clear and natural-sounding, the words are probably coordinate modifiers that require a comma.

Ex.: The robber coldly, methodically planned the heist. (The robber planned *methodically and coldly*, so a comma is needed.)

Ex.: The opposing counsel was a tenacious, arrogant, brilliant lawyer. (The lawyer was *brilliant and arrogant and tenacious*, so commas separate the independent but coordinate modifiers.)

Ex.: Don't step on my blue suede shoes. (It would be quite odd to write *blue and suede shoes* or *suede, blue shoes*. Rather, *blue suede* is a phrase that modifies *shoes*. So the phrasing must stand without a comma.)

Ex.: I had a little red wagon. (That the wagon is red has nothing to do with its being little—so no comma.)

Ex.: They lived in a first-floor apartment in a six-story rent-controlled, union-subsidized housing development. (The fact that the building is six stories has nothing to do with its being rent-controlled. But *rent-controlled* seems related to *union-subsidized*, so those two modifying phrases need the intervening comma.)

(b) *Not coordinate.* Don't use a comma between two adjectives if the first adjective modifies a noun phrase consisting of an adjective plus a noun.

Ex.: The panel will include Linda Greenhouse, the respected legal reporter for the *New York Times*. (Here, *respected* modifies the noun phrase *legal reporter*.)

Ex.: For several weeks, the parties engaged in intense collective bargaining. (Here, *intense* modifies the noun phrase *collective bargaining*.)

1.8 Use a comma to set off a direct quotation of fewer than 50 words unless the quoted matter is woven into the sentence itself or is introduced by a colon (see 1.24(a)).

(a) *Placement.* Use a comma between a direct quotation and its attribution.

Ex.: Judge Duggan asked, "How do you plead?"

Ex.: "If you can't afford a lawyer, the court will appoint one for you," Judge Duggan told the defendant.

Ex.: "Your trial," Judge Duggan said, "is set for July 19."

(b) *Colon as a substitute.* If the quotation follows the attribution and is set up by a more formal device such as *the following*, use a colon instead of a comma.

Ex.: Judge Meir asked a single question: "How do you plead?"

Ex.: In her review of the new book, Ms. Sanders wrote the following praise: "It is a literary treasure that everyone should own."

Ex.: The most popular name for independent political movements in this country has always been these three words from the preamble to the Constitution: "We the People."

(c) *In context.* Don't use a comma to set off a quotation that is made part of the syntax of the main sentence. Don't use a colon to introduce a block quotation that begins with words similarly woven into the sentence.

Ex.: John swears that he "didn't see the red light."

Ex.: The judge believed, as the Federal Circuit once wrote, that "[i]t is sometimes more important that a close question be settled one way or the other than which way it is settled."

Ex.: Judge Combs said that she agreed with the jury's decision to deny punitive damages because

> the defendant presented no evidence that the plaintiff's conduct was intentional, and no amount of punitive damages can deter unintentional behavior.

1.9 Don't place a comma where it interferes with the flow of the sentence.

(a) *Before the predicate.* Don't use a comma to separate a subject from its verb. A comma may appear in the same position in the sentence, though, if it sets off a nonrestrictive element.

Not this: The issue whether the incorporation of such rules evinces a "clear and unmistakable" intent to arbitrate arbitrarily, was never decided by the New York Court of Appeals.

But this: The issue whether the incorporation of such rules evinces a "clear and unmistakable" intent to arbitrate arbitrarily was never decided by the New York Court of Appeals.

Ex.: This question, which has been the subject of much debate, has sharply divided circuit courts. (The commas are required here to set off the nonrestrictive *which*-clause after *question*.)

(b) *Between a verb and its object.* Don't place a comma between a verb and its object. If an intervening adverbial phrase appears between the two, relocate it either before the verb or after the object.

Not this: Before he struck, at 65 mph, Donnalson's retaining wall, Stevens tried to apply the brakes.

But this: Before he struck Donnalson's retaining wall at 65 mph, Stevens tried to apply the brakes.

(c) *Phrase after conjunction.* Don't use a comma after a conjunction that is immediately followed by an adverbial phrase or adverbial clause. Although the closed punctuation style (see 1.2) uses the comma, the open punctuation style doesn't.

> Not this: Michigan's long-arm statute may or may not grant jurisdiction, but, if there is a conflict of laws, Ohio law controls. (Closed punctuation style)
>
> But this: Michigan's long-arm statute may or may not grant jurisdiction, but if there is a conflict of laws, Ohio law controls. (Open punctuation style)
>
> Not this: The court ruled that, if there is a conflict of laws, Ohio law controls. (Closed punctuation style)
>
> But this: The court ruled that if there is a conflict of laws, Ohio law controls. (Open punctuation style)

(d) *Sentence-starting conjunctions.* Don't use a comma after a conjunction that starts a sentence. Despite the widespread misconception to the contrary, it has always been perfectly acceptable to begin a sentence with a coordinating conjunction (*and*, *but*, *or*, *nor*, *so*, *yet*—see 11.48). In much high-quality writing, some 10% to 20% of sentences begin with conjunctions. If a coordinating conjunction begins a sentence, no comma should follow.

> Ex.: This process is not a trial in the strict sense: it's an inquisition ex officio. And according to Sir Matthew Hale, an inquisition might be taken on whether the accused was in fact a cleric. (Initial *And*.)
>
> Ex.: The executive was empowered to fill all the major civil and military offices. But in neither case could the executive act unilaterally. (Initial *But*.)
>
> Ex.: The unconscious memory may be comfortably enfolded into conscious thought, even if it remains outside conscious attention. Or the relationship may be adversarial—with offstage memory banished from the center of conscious attention but unreconciled to exile. (Initial *Or*.)
>
> Ex.: No individual enjoyed arbitrary power in the natural state—hence none could be surrendered to the sovereign. Nor could the sovereign itself rule by arbitrary decree. (Initial *Nor*.)
>
> Ex.: Never during this development were judges themselves conscious of the change. So they continued to talk, as they still talk, using the language of the past. (Initial *So*.)
>
> Ex.: Kelsen predicted that Schmitt's excessive reliance on Article 48 of the Weimar Constitution would ultimately spell the end of parliamentary democracy. Yet when Schmitt's appointment came up before the Cologne faculty, Kelsen voted in favor. (Initial *Yet*.)

> "Most errors of punctuation arise from ill-designed, badly shaped sentences, and from the attempt to make them work by means of violent tricks with commas and colons . . . ." —*Hugh Sykes Davies*

(e) *Not before parentheses.* Don't put a comma before an opening parenthesis. Usually the comma belongs after the closing parenthesis.

Not this: Many of her staunch supporters even consider the campaign "a moral imperative," (in the words of one) a chance to make tough-minded reforms.

But this: Many of her staunch supporters even consider the campaign "a moral imperative" (in the words of one), a chance to make tough-minded reforms.

(f) *With nominal abbreviations.* Don't use a comma before or after *Jr.*, *III*, or the like with a personal name or *Inc.*, *L.L.P.*, or the like with a business name unless that is the person's or business's preference. But do use a comma before and after an academic-degree abbreviation such as *M.D.* or *Ph.D.* with a personal name.

Not this: Dr. Martin Luther King, Jr., delivered his "I Have a Dream" speech from the steps of the Lincoln Memorial on August 28, 1963.

But this: Dr. Martin Luther King Jr. delivered his "I Have a Dream" speech from the steps of the Lincoln Memorial on August 28, 1963.

Not this: In a single year, Enron, Inc., went from being the seventh-largest company in sales on the Fortune 500 list to being the biggest bankruptcy filing in U.S. history.

But this: In a single year, Enron Inc. went from being the seventh-largest company in sales on the Fortune 500 list to being the biggest bankruptcy filing in U.S. history.

Not this: John Smith, M.D. is not a committee member.

Not this: John Smith M.D. is not a committee member.

But this: John Smith, M.D., is not a committee member.

True, many people with a *Jr.* appended to their names prefer a comma. But it's both illogical (since the *Jr.* is restrictive) and ungainly (since, traditionally, a second comma is required after the *Jr.* except at the end of a sentence). The omission of the comma should be considered a matter of house style, not personal preference.

(g) *Law-firm short form.* Abbreviate the name of a law firm with three or more name partners by using the first two names with no comma or ampersand. For a firm with only two name partners, use whatever style the firm prefers, but don't use bullets or other symbols that appear on a firm's logo.

Ex.: The Boston firm of Mintz Levin negotiated the merger. (Referring to Mintz, Levin, Cohn, Ferris, Glovsky, and Popeo. The firm uses the word *and*, not an ampersand.)

Ex.: Isaac clerked for Carrington Coleman last summer. (Referring to Carrington, Coleman, Sloman & Blumenthal of Dallas.)

Ex.: Weil Gotshal conducted the environmental audit. (The firm's full name is Weil, Gotshal & Manges.)

But: The reporter was represented by two firms, O'Melveny & Myers and Locke Lord. (The first firm mentioned uses an ampersand in its name;

the second, even though there are only two name partners, does not. A firm's preference controls.)

1.10 In a full date that is written month–day–year, put a comma between the day and the year. Unless the date is being used as an adjective (see 11.37), place a comma after the year if the sentence continues. Don't use a comma with the day–month–year or month–year style.

(a) *American style.* In the standard American format, month–day–year, separate the day from the year with a comma. Unless the date is used adjectivally (see 11.37), use another comma after the year (which is treated syntactically as parenthetical).

Ex.: They fought the cold and the crowds in Times Square on December 31, 2018, waiting for the New Year's ball to drop.

Ex.: Your memo of April 14, 2018, has been very helpful.

(b) *Military and British style.* Don't use a comma within the day–month–year format (although a comma may appear before or after it if otherwise called for by the syntax).

Ex.: They fought the cold and the crowds in Times Square on 31 December 2018, waiting for the New Year's ball to drop.

Ex.: Your memo of 14 April 2018 has been very helpful.

Ex.: The accident occurred on the same day Mr. Jarvis saw his therapist, 15 November 2018.

(c) *Month–year.* Don't use a comma in the month–year format. Although it is possible to write *December of 2018*, the preferable form is *December 2018*. Even if the day is given as an ordinal, no comma goes between the month and year <dated this 21st day of May 2018>.

Ex.: The Florida re-count controversy raged throughout the remainder of November 2000 and long into December.

(d) *Holidays.* Don't use a comma when writing about a holiday or other specific day.

Ex.: Mr. and Mrs. Walker were married on Valentine's Day 2018.

Ex.: He signed the contract on Good Friday 2018.

1.11 Use commas to set off certain geographic place names.

(a) *With place names.* Use a pair of commas to separate a more general geographic place name from a more specific one (as with a state from a city, or a country from a city or state).

Ex.: Chicago, Illinois, is on the shore of Lake Michigan.

Ex.: President Obama spoke in Toyko, Japan, last night.

(b) *With two-letter postal designations.* In an address, don't use a comma between a state's USPS designation and a ZIP code (see 1.72(d)).

Ex.: Ship the materials to the Omni Chicago Hotel, 676 N. Michigan Ave., Chicago, IL 60611.

1.12 Use a comma to break down a number of 1,000 or more into sets of three digits.

(a) *Separating by threes.* Use commas to break whole numerals (not decimals) of four or more digits into groups of three. Although some writers omit the comma in four-digit numbers, the better practice is to include it. For one thing, this practice maintains a consistent style. After all, the comma is always used with four-digit numerals in columns of figures.

Ex.: 1,000

Ex.: 99,999

Ex.: 24,945,372

(b) *Exceptions.* Don't use commas in statute numbers, telephone numbers, house numbers, page numbers of fewer than five digits, years, and other serial numbers (see 5.12(b)).

Ex.: Rule 9002(a)

Ex.: 555-1212

Ex.: 6822 Magnolia Blvd.

Ex.: *Id.* at 1537

Ex.: *Id.* at 15,442

1.13 Use a comma (never a semicolon) after the salutation in a personal letter.

(a) *Informal salutation.* The comma is appropriate after the salutation in correspondence between friends and relatives. It is appropriate also for all handwritten notes. By contrast, a semicolon after a salutation, no matter how informal the correspondence may be, is always wrong.

Ex.: Dear Mom,

Ex.: Dear Sally,

(b) *Business correspondence.* For more formal uses, and especially business correspondence, use a colon (see 1.25).

Ex.: Dear Mr. Gillespie:

Ex.: Dear Chief Justice Roberts:

Never this: Dear Mr. Lochridge;

But this: Dear Mr. Lochridge:

1.14 Consider using a comma where one or more words are omitted but understood in context.

(a) *Understood words.* A comma pause can signal the reader that an obvious word or phrase, commonly the verb from the previous clause, is to be understood at this point.

> Ex.: Democrats won governorships in Maine and Delaware; Republicans, in South Carolina and Nevada.
>
> Ex.: Palestinians want statehood; Israelis, security.

(b) *Dramatic pause.* The comma can supply a dramatic pause for effect.

> Ex.: Pat had thousands of "friends" while she held office; afterward, none.

(c) *Often optional.* When the meaning is clear, the comma may be omitted.

> Ex.: California has 55 electoral votes, Florida 27, Vermont 3.
>
> Ex.: Candidates are few but propositions many in Tuesday's election.

Semicolons

1.15 Though similar in appearance, the semicolon isn't a colon at all. You might think of it as a "king comma," doing the work that a comma might ordinarily do if it weren't for some need for a stronger break in the sentence. When that need exists, what might have been a lowly comma before gets crowned like a checker reaching the eighth row. It's stronger than before; it has a more powerful impact on the reader. The pause is more pronounced than a comma would deliver, though of course it still doesn't have the punch of a period. And unlike a comma, a semicolon may join two independent clauses without a conjunction. Although some writers shun the semicolon, it's a versatile device in a skillful writer's hands.

1.16 Use a semicolon to separate independent clauses that are not joined by a conjunction.

(a) *Semicolon alone.* Use a semicolon between independent clauses that aren't linked by any transitional word or phrase.

> Ex.: Demeanor is typically a sum total of traits and appearance; change any one and you may change the witness's credibility.

> "In the hands of one who has mastered its principles, punctuation may become a means of revealing subtle shades of thought that can be revealed in no other way."
>
> —*Raymond Woodbury Pence*

(b) *Exception.* In informal writing, a comma alone may join two short and closely related independent clauses despite the general grammatical disfavor toward the comma splice (see 1.4(d)). Although this use is traditional and defensible, avoid it in legal writing.

Ex.: The time was right, the cause was just.

Ex.: Try it, you'll like it.

(c) *Strength of connector.* When one of the clauses contains an internal comma, another comma may not be strong enough to separate them; a semicolon may be needed, even if the linking word is a conjunction that would usually take only a comma.

Ex.: Our client took great pains to answer all interrogatories quickly, honestly, and completely; and in light of the goodwill we have shown, we were all upset that the other party answered our interrogatories so inadequately.

Ex.: Our client took great pains to answer all interrogatories quickly, honestly, and completely; so we were upset that the other party answered our interrogatories so inadequately.

(d) *Coordinating conjunction.* A semicolon may serve instead of a comma to separate independent clauses connected by a coordinating conjunction. The semicolon may be useful to help the reader understand a complex sentence or to indicate more of a break than a comma suggests.

Ex.: True, the President did stress in his message the need for more judges to help the federal courts catch up with their calendars of pending cases and to cut down the frequent delays in handling litigation; and this argument, while quite warranted with respect to many lower federal courts, let Chief Justice Hughes enter the fray a little later by allowing publication of a letter in which he rather indignantly stated that the Supreme Court was "fully abreast of its work."

Ex.: Courts relying on legislative history often make no pretense that they have developed and are using a theory derived from it; and history often seems to be used only when it supports a conclusion arrived at by other means.

Ex.: The defendant's long wait was finally over; and ever so deliberately the jurors filed back into the courtroom.

1.17 Use a semicolon to separate independent clauses if the second clause begins with a conjunctive adverb or transitional expression rather than a conjunction.

(a) *Common conjunctive adverbs.* Some common conjunctive adverbs are *accordingly*, *also*, *besides*, *consequently*, *further*, *furthermore*, *hence*, *however*, *indeed*, *instead*, *later*, *likewise*, *meanwhile*, *moreover*, *nevertheless*, *now*, *still*, *then*, *therefore*, and *thus*.

Ex.: Back then, tokens had legal-tender effect only if the law said they should have it; likewise, law might legitimize the circulation of designated kinds of tokens as money without making them legal tender.

(b) *Transitional expressions.* A transitional expression is a phrase that functions as an adverb and introduces a sentence or an independent clause. Examples: *on the other hand*, *in much the same way*, *by the same token*, and *in general*.

(c) *With comma.* Use a comma after a conjunctive adverb or transitional expression.

Ex.: It was almost quitting time; nevertheless, most workers planned to stay late to work on the project.

Ex.: We want the law to apply the same to everyone; on the other hand, we don't want it to be so rigid as to give harsh and unfair results.

1.18 Use semicolons instead of commas to separate items in a series if any of the items contains an internal comma or if semicolons would make the sentence clearer. See 1.3(b).

(a) *Internal commas.* Use semicolons to separate elements of a series of phrases or clauses if one or more of the elements contains an internal comma.

Ex.: The United States has three so-called historical bays: Chesapeake Bay, with an entrance 12 miles wide; Delaware Bay, with an entrance 10 miles wide; and Monterey Bay, with an entrance 19 miles wide.

Ex.: The campaign will stop tomorrow in Sacramento, California; Denver, Colorado; Tempe, Arizona; and Albuquerque, New Mexico.

(b) *Complexity.* When elements in a series are particularly complex, the sentence may be clearer with semicolons instead of commas separating the elements.

Ex.: As commonly defined for the charge of murder, *malice* means the specific intent to kill; the specific intent to inflict serious bodily harm; the specific intent to commit a serious felony; or reckless indifference to human life.

(c) *To separate citations.* Use a semicolon to separate citations in a string.

Ex.: *United States v. United Mine Workers of Am.*, 330 U.S. 258, 303–04 (1947); *see also Norman Bridge Drug Co. v. Banner*, 529 F.2d 822, 827 (5th Cir. 1976); *accord Travelhost*, 68 F.3d at 961; *Petroleos*, 826 F.2d at 400.

Ex.: *Faragher*, 524 U.S. at 807; *Ellerth*, 524 U.S. at 765.

1.19 Use semicolons to separate items in a series when the items are set off separately, as in a statute or contract.

(a) *Series lists.* In the drafting of statutes, contracts, and other legal documents, sound practice requires enumerating elements in separately numbered or lettered paragraphs, with a semicolon between every paragraph.

Ex.: 6.1 A model or exhibit will not be admitted as part of the record of an application unless it:
(A) substantially conforms to the requirements of § 1.52 or § 1.84;
(B) is specifically required by the Office; or
(C) is filed with a petition under this section including:
(1) the petition fee as set forth in § 1.17(B); and
(2) an explanation of why the model or exhibit is necessary.

(b) *"Whereas"-clauses.* In a resolution or similar document, follow each of a series of *whereas*-clauses with a semicolon. Still, more modern drafting style is to avoid *whereas*-clauses altogether by making them into simple declarative sentences, introduced by a heading that reads "Background" or "Recitals."

(c) *Advantages.* This "tabulated" style helps prevent various problems in legal drafting, not the least of which is unreadability.

Not this: **Failure to Attend or to Serve Subpoena; Expenses.** If the party giving the notice of the taking of a deposition fails to attend and proceed therewith and another party attends in person or by attorney pursuant to the notice, the court may order the party giving the notice to pay such other party the reasonable expenses incurred by that party and that party's attorney in attending, including reasonable attorney's fees. If the party giving the notice of the taking of a deposition of a witness fails to serve a subpoena upon the witness and the witness because of such failure does not attend, and if another party attends in person or by attorney because that party expects the deposition of that witness to be taken, the court may order the party giving the notice to pay to such other party the reasonable expenses incurred by that party and that party's attorney in attending, including reasonable attorney's fees.

But this: **Failure to Attend or to Serve Subpoena; Expenses.** The court may order the party giving notice of a deposition to pay another party's reasonable expenses in attending, including attorney's fees, if the party giving notice fails to:
(1) attend and proceed; or
(2) serve a subpoena on the witness, who consequently does not attend.

1.20 Use a semicolon to separate an appositive or elaboration at the end of a sentence if the matter is introduced by *that is, for example, namely,* or a similar device.

(a) *Appositive matter.* When a sentence ends with an appositive or other elaboration—particularly one beginning with an introductory word or phrase followed by a comma—you may separate it from the rest of the sentence with a semicolon. Or you may put it in parentheses or set it off by a dash. If it's short, a comma or even a colon may suffice.

Ex.: Tenant fixtures generally fall into one of three categories; namely, trade fixtures, agricultural fixtures, and domestic fixtures.

Ex.: Tenant fixtures generally fall into one of three categories (that is, trade fixtures, agricultural fixtures, and domestic fixtures).

Ex.: Tenant fixtures generally fall into one of three categories—specifically, trade fixtures, agricultural fixtures, and domestic fixtures.

Ex.: A trade fixture is used for one purpose, namely, business.

(b) *No signal.* If appositive matter at the end of the sentence isn't introduced by such a word or phrase, it should be preceded by a colon or dash instead (see 1.24(d), 1.54(c)). A semicolon would not work in this circumstance.

Ex.: Tenant fixtures generally fall into one of three categories: trade fixtures, agricultural fixtures, and domestic fixtures.

Ex.: Tenant fixtures generally fall into one of three categories—trade fixtures, agricultural fixtures, and domestic fixtures.

Ex.: A trade fixture is used for one purpose: business.

Colons

1.21 The colon both separates items and suggests some sort of relationship between them. As a separator, it creates a pause roughly equivalent to that of the semicolon. But unlike a semicolon, the colon points to what follows it, telling the reader that "here's a quotation," for example, or "here's something that reinforces what was just said," or "here's something that results from what was just said." Think of it as an arrow or a pointing finger. It's especially appropriate (and helpful) in legal writing to draw conclusions from inferences or to lead the reader down a chain of reasoning. In some situations it is equivalent to an em-dash, which may be substituted for stronger effect where appropriate.

1.22 Use a colon to join two separate but directly related clauses or phrases.

(a) *As a pointer.* A colon tells the reader that what follows the mark explains, supports, amplifies, or in some other way logically flows from what precedes it.

Ex.: Things got worse in a hurry: our codefendant turned state's evidence.

Ex.: The epidemic is showing signs of abating: only four new cases were reported in the last week.

(b) *Optional nature of use.* The colon is a helpful signal to readers, but its use as a link between independent clauses is never mandatory. A semicolon could be used in either of the examples above, and all that would be lost is stylistic nuance.

Ex.: Things got worse in a hurry; our codefendant turned state's evidence.

Ex.: The epidemic is showing signs of abating; only four new cases were reported in the last week.

(c) *Phrase after colon.* What follows the colon may be either a complete clause or a simple phrase.

Ex.: Here's where we part company: over ethics.

1.23 If what follows the colon isn't a complete sentence, don't capitalize the first word; if it is a complete sentence, you may choose to capitalize or not. Whatever style you choose on that point, be consistent.

(a) *With a phrase.* Unless some other rule of capitalization applies, never capitalize the first word of a phrase after a colon.

Ex.: Two distinct tests of constitutionality potentially apply to Act 257: a state-law test and a federal test.

(b) *With a sentence.* There are arguments for and against capitalizing the first word of a complete sentence that follows a colon. When the second clause is left uncapitalized, the colon does a better job of relating the two parts of the sentence. Also, that construction parallels the form that the sentence would take if a semicolon had been used instead of a colon. Neither style is wrong, but be consistent in the style you use.

Ex.: The deponent was starting to show signs of irritability: she was tired and just wanted to go home. (slightly preferred)

Ex.: The deponent was starting to show signs of irritability: She was tired and just wanted to go home. (also acceptable)

(c) *With a direct quotation.* Always capitalize a direct, freestanding quotation, whether it is set off by a comma or a colon.

Ex.: Objecting, Bilks said, "That question calls for an opinion."

Ex.: Bilks objected: "That question calls for an opinion."

(d) *With a direct question.* Sometimes, a direct question will appear within another sentence without enclosing quotation marks, introduced by a colon or a comma (or occasionally an em-dash). Always capitalize a direct question contained within another sentence (see 2.5(a)).

Ex.: This raises the fundamental question: Exactly what constitutes proof of an informal marriage?

(e) *With a series of sentences.* When a colon introduces a series of independent clauses, capitalize the first word of each clause, including the one after the colon.

> Ex.: Here are your options: You can take the settlement offer. You can make a counteroffer. You can take your chances at trial and maybe walk away with nothing.

(f) *In dialogue.* Capitalize after a name and colon in dialogue such as that reported in a transcript (see 1.24(b)).

1.24 Use a colon to set up a quotation, a formally introduced list, or a self-contained statement.

(a) *Choice of punctuation.* A quotation may be introduced by a colon (formal style) or by a comma (less formal; see 1.8). Or it may be worked seamlessly into the sentence (least formal). The colon is especially appropriate for introducing self-contained block quotations, statutes, transcripts, and similar material. Though not mandatory, an introductory term such as *following*, *as follows*, or *here* frequently accompanies the use of a colon. If the introductory term doesn't serve a useful function, omit it.

> Ex.: The court allowed the action to proceed, announcing the following rule adopting Restatement (Second) of Torts § 433B:
>
> > Where the conduct of two or more actors is tortious, and it is proved that harm has been caused to the plaintiff by only one of them, but there is uncertainty as to which of them has caused it, the burden is upon each such actor to prove that he has not caused the harm.

(b) *In transcripts.* Use a colon to set off the speaker's name from the text in a transcript.

> Ex.: BLAIN: Mr. Bergin, did you perform the repairs to Mr. Wilson's boat?
>
> BERGIN: Yes, I remember it well.
>
> BLAIN: Can you describe the nature of the damage it sustained in the storm?
>
> BERGIN: Well, it was pretty bad.

(c) *Numbered or bulleted list.* Use a colon to set off a numbered list that is formally introduced or a list that is broken down into numbered or bulleted subparagraphs, as opposed to one that is blended into the syntax of the sentence (see 1.28). Again, separate the items with semicolons.

> Ex.: Congress identified four factors as especially relevant in determining whether the use was fair: (1) the purpose and character of the use; (2) the nature of the copyrighted work; (3) the substantiality of the portion used in relation to the copyrighted work as a whole; and (4) the effect on the potential market for or value of the copyrighted work.

(d) *Appositive list.* Use a colon to introduce an appositive list at the end of a sentence—that is, a list that further explains the predicate of the sentence. If there are more than two elements in the list, separate them with commas.

If the list is complex or contains internal commas, use semicolons instead of commas.

Ex.: The CBEST is a pass–fail examination consisting of three sections: reading, writing, and mathematics.

Ex.: Relief from liability is justified when the consenting participant meets three tests: awareness of the risk; appreciation of the nature of the risk; and voluntary assumption of the risk.

(e) *Interrupting colon.* Use a colon only after (1) an independent clause or (2) introductory matter such as *the following*, *as follows*, or *namely*.

Not this: That afternoon Sanders had to: make a bank deposit, pick up a loaf of bread, and get in a few sets of tennis.

But this: That afternoon Sanders had to make a bank deposit, pick up a loaf of bread, and get in a few sets of tennis.

Or this: That afternoon Sanders had "chores" to do: make a bank deposit, pick up a loaf of bread, and get in a few sets of tennis.

Or this: His "chores" were as follows: make a bank deposit, pick up a loaf of bread, and get in a few sets of tennis.

Not this: Procedural safeguards are essential to assure all parties that the technical adviser is: unbiased, impartial, and qualified.

But this: Procedural safeguards are essential to assure all parties that the technical adviser is unbiased, impartial, and qualified.

(f) *Formal quotation.* Use a colon to introduce a quotation formally. Since the quotation stands alone (and isn't woven into the syntax of the sentence itself), capitalize the first word after the colon. If the original material was not capitalized, bracket the initial letter (see 1.43(a)).

Ex.: The accused showed no emotion, speaking only to enter a plea: "Not guilty."

Ex.: The sign read: "No trespassing."

Ex.: Retorted Holmes: "This case is decided upon an economic theory that a large portion of the country does not entertain."

Ex.: The Constitution explicitly instructs Congress to limit the term of copyright protection: "[P]romote the . . . Arts by securing *for limited Times* to Authors . . . the exclusive Right to their respective Writings" (emphasis added).

1.25 Use a colon after the salutation in a formal letter and after each tagline in a memorandum.

(a) *Formality.* Although a comma is proper after the salutation in a personal letter (see 1.13), a colon is standard for business letters. A semicolon (;) is always wrong after a salutation.

Ex.: Dear Mrs. Davis:

Ex.: Dear Mom,

(b) *British style.* Although American style is invariably to use a comma or a colon after a business salutation, British style is to use a comma for formal and informal letters—or, often, no punctuation at all.

Ex.: Dear Professor Tapper

(c) *In a memorandum.* Use a colon after each tagline in a memorandum (*To:*, *From:*, *Date:*, *Re:*, and the like), report, or business letter.

Ex.: To: All employees
From: Management
Re: Reserving vacation dates

Ex.: cc: TPM (recipients of a copy in business letter)

Ex.: Encl: Annual report

1.26 Use a colon to designate a ratio or analogy.

(a) *Ratio.* In a ratio, the colon stands for the word *to.* Don't put a space after the colon.

Ex.: Mix concentrate and water in a 1:4 ratio. (Reads "1-to-4 ratio.")
Ex.: Current ratio (*deviant behavior* vs. **deviate behavior*) in current print sources: 185:1

(b) *Analogy.* In an analogy, a single colon stands for *is to* and a double colon stands for *as.* In this construction, use a space before the colon or colons.

Ex.: preponderance of the evidence : negligence :: beyond a reasonable doubt : criminal culpability

1.27 Use a colon in the several ways prescribed for citations and references, including citing the case record.

(a) *Citations.* By convention, a colon is used between elements in a variety of constructions. In legal writing, it is used between the page number and line number (if available) in citations to the case record.

Ex.: (R. 38:12) (page 38, line 12 of the record)

Ex.: Trial Tr. vol. 1, 15:8 (June 23, 2018) (first volume of a multivolume trial transcript, page 15, line 8)

(b) *Miscellaneous uses.* Use a colon in bibliographic citations between the title and subtitle of a book or article, and between the city of publication and the publisher; put one space after the colon.

Ex.: *Sexual Harassment: A Practical Guide to the Law, Your Rights, and Your Options for Taking Action*

Ex.: St. Paul: West Education Group, 2018 (academic citations)

Also use a colon—without a following space—between the hour, minute, and second in times; between chapter and verse in traditional biblical citations; between the initials of the writer and the typist in business

*An invariably inferior form.

correspondence; and elsewhere as directed by a specialized style or citation manual to find its correct use in a specific field.

Ex.: 11:27 a.m.

Ex.: a record time of 3:47:21

Ex.: Matthew 7:7

Ex.: BAG:jwn (writer and typist in business correspondence)

1.28 Although in most contexts a colon is considered incorrect between a subject and its verb or a verb and its object, use one in legal drafting to introduce any separately demarcated subpart, whether it represents the entire predicate or the object of the verb.

(a) *The usual writing convention.* In normal prose, a colon must follow an independent clause, one that could stand alone as a sentence. So it would be quite wrong to write, for example, "Jake stated that he: (1) did not go to the theater that evening; (2) had no reason to go to the theater that evening; and (3) can name three alibi witnesses who were with him elsewhere that evening." By convention, however, the colon is considered a necessary anchor when enumerated items are set off (as they preferably should be) in legal instruments of all types.

(b) *Introducing the predicate in legal drafting.* The colon may appear after the subject (and perhaps a modal verb) to introduce various verbs in a conjunctive or disjunctive list.

Ex.: Elkin Management will:
  (1) cooperate fully with Roychem's broker and its agents regarding Roychem's efforts to sell the Livingston plant;
  (2) refer all inquiries about buying the Livingston plant to Roychem's broker;
  (3) furnish Roychem's broker with any information it requests about the Livingston plant; and
  (4) conduct all negotiations between prospective buyers and Roychem's broker.

(c) *Introducing the object of the verb in legal drafting.* The colon may appear after the verb as an introduction to various objects in a conjunctive or disjunctive list:

Ex.: An applicant must present:
  (1) a photo ID;
  (2) a recent utility bill in the applicant's name showing a Potter County residence; or
  (3) a letter of introduction from a member in good standing.

Quotation Marks

1.29 Quotation marks come in four flavors: double and single, opening and closing. On typewriters, a set of straight marks served for both opening and closing quotations (" . . . "), so the *straight quotes* used to be ubiquitous. Today, computers can automatically use the correct curly marks called *typographer's quotes* or *smart quotes* (“ . . . ”). There's no excuse for still using the ugly straight quotes, which are typographic blemishes that don't match any font. Yet they still show up. Worse, many documents mix the two styles almost at random. The single and double closed-quotation marks are sometimes improperly used as the symbols for *foot* and *inch*, respectively, but this gives a document an amateurish look. The correct symbols—the prime (′) for *foot* and the double-prime (″) for *inch*—are special characters available on word processors. An acceptable alternative is to use straight quotes in italics.

1.30 Use double quotation marks around a run-in quotation shorter than 50 words or five lines, but not around a block quotation.

(a) *Generally.* Enclose short quotations in double quotation marks. This is the standard and most familiar use of these marks.

Ex.: Russell said, “That delivery date is fine with me.”

Ex.: Here's what Irene said: “I don't have to pay if it's not what I ordered.”

Ex.: “Where do we go from here?” the mediator goaded the recalcitrant plaintiff. (The question mark takes the place of a comma at the end of the direct quotation.)

(b) *Admonition against overuse.* Many writers repeatedly use quotation marks around short phrases or even single words to show that the phrases or words used derive from a quotation, such as the text of a statute or contract. They aren't usually necessary. After quoting the source document in its fuller context, simply use the word or phrase as an integral part of your analysis or argument. The misuse or overuse of quotes around short phrases or single words can confuse readers into thinking that you're either trying to be snarky (see 1.34(e)–(f)) or using the word or phrase in some unusual way.

Not this: There is no “substantial evidence” to suggest that the Energy Commission's findings will result in a “net increase” in “greenhouse gas” emissions.

But this: There is no substantial evidence to suggest that the Energy Commission's findings will result in a net increase in greenhouse gas emissions.

(c) *Multiple paragraphs.* If the material inside quotation marks continues for more than one paragraph, don't use a closing quotation mark until the end of the matter, but place another opening mark at the beginning of each subsequent paragraph in the quotation.

> Ex.: "He has abdicated Government here, by declaring us out of his Protection and waging War against us.
>
> "He has plundered our seas, ravaged our coasts, burnt our towns, and destroyed the lives of our people.
>
> "He is at this time transporting large Armies of foreign Mercenaries to compleat the works of death, desolation, and tyranny, already begun with circumstances of Cruelty & Perfidy scarcely paralleled in the most barbarous ages, and totally unworthy of the Head of a civilized nation."
>
> (No closing quotation mark until after the last paragraph, but an opening mark repeated at the start of each paragraph.)

(d) *No marks for block quotations.* Don't use quotation marks around a block quotation. Instead, introduce the material with the proper lead-in, usually followed by a colon. Set it off from the previous text, indent it on both sides, and single-space it.

> Ex.: Parts of Brandeis's concurrence emphasized the need to show incitement:
>
> > But even advocacy of [law] violation[,] however reprehensible morally, is not a justification for denying free speech where the advocacy falls short of incitement and there is nothing to indicate that the advocacy would be immediately acted on. . . . [N]o danger flowing from speech can be deemed clear and present, unless the incidence of the evil apprehended is so imminent that it may befall before there is opportunity for full discussion.

(e) *Other set-off matter.* Use a block-quotation style—without quotation marks—for other set-off matter such as lines of a poem or song, or an epigraph.

1.31 Place other punctuation marks correctly in relation to quotation marks: periods and commas go inside; semicolons and colons go outside; and question marks and exclamation marks go inside only if they are part of the quoted matter.

(a) *With period or comma.* Place final periods and commas inside quotation marks. (British style is to place them outside.)

> Ex.: To grant the defendant another advantage, in nonreciprocal discovery rights, would make the prosecutor's task "almost insurmountable."
>
> Ex.: High-sounding phrases, such as "the public interest," "economic democracy," and "free enterprise," were to him mere propaganda clichés.

(b) *With semicolon or colon.* Place final semicolons and colons outside the quotation marks, even if the quoted material happens to have a semicolon or colon in that position.

Ex.: To formulate precise factual issues, a pleader had to state "facts," not "conclusions"; and in order that the issues be material according to the substantive law, the stating of "evidence" was condemned.

Ex.: As Archibald Cox noted, "The validity of the reporters' claim of a First Amendment privilege not to disclose sources of information was decided on the results of two inquiries": (1) were fears of sources drying up justified; and, if so, (2) does that loss outweigh the benefits of the testimony?

(c) *With question mark or exclamation mark.* A question mark or exclamation mark may go inside or outside the quotation marks, depending on whether it is part of the original quotation.

Ex.: Does the parol-evidence rule play a similar role in excluding evidence of prior negotiations to interpret contract language that is "clear on its face"?

Ex.: As Judge Fernandez asked in *Dagher*, "What could be more integral to the running of a business than setting a price for its goods and services?"

Ex.: The court session opens with the traditional cry, "Oyez! Oyez! Oyez!"

(d) *Amendment exception.* Punctuate the text of a statutory or contractual amendment exactly as it is to appear in the amended document. The usual rules of punctuation and capitalization do not apply: if a period is part of the amendment, it must go inside the quotation marks even if the main sentence continues, and it cannot itself serve as the terminal punctuation of the main sentence.

Ex.: In Rule 9027, replace "If a case under the Code is pending when a claim is asserted in another court," with "If a claim is asserted in another court after the commencement of a case under the Code,". (The comma inside the closing quotation mark is part of the amendment. The sentence period cannot go inside the quotation marks, as the usual rules of punctuation would require, because it is not in the text of the amendment. *If* must be capitalized even though it is not part of a complete sentence and would not be capitalized under the usual rules of capitalization.)

Ex.: In Rule 3, strike "Upon receipt of the motion and having ascertained that it appears on its face to comply with rules 1 and 2, the" and insert "The". (The main-sentence period goes outside the quotation marks because it is not part of the amendment.)

> "Language conventions are more akin to common law than to statutory law. For they are not the result of legislative action, not recorded in carefully drafted statutes; they are accretional, the product of accumulated behavior, clear at the core but blurred at the edges." —*John E. Jordan*

Ex.: Amend Fed. R. Crim. P. 32(d)(1) by replacing "The judgment must be signed by the judge and entered by the clerk." with "The judge must sign the judgment, and the clerk must enter it.". (The period must stay with the text inside both quotations, even though it does not end the main sentence after the first quotation. And a second period must go after the second quotation to terminate the main sentence.)

1.32 Use single quotation marks around a quotation within a marked quotation, and alternate double and single quotation marks for more deeply nested quotations.

(a) *Awkwardness.* Nested quotations are awkward but sometimes unavoidable. The need for them arises more often in legal writing than elsewhere, as writers quote courts that in turn quote other courts or statutes.

Ex.: "In this case, there is no life expressly mentioned who can be a 'life in being.'"

Ex.: The *Chapa-Garza* court noted that "8 U.S.C. § 1101(a)(43) provides, in relevant part: '[T]he term "aggravated felony" means . . . a crime of violence for which the term of imprisonment [is] at least one year.'"

(b) *In block quotations.* If the main quotation is unmarked (i.e., a block quotation), use double quotation marks around a quotation within it, and single quotation marks around a quotation nested inside that.

Ex.: As Glanville Williams notes in *Learning the Law*, the British Interpretation Act codifies the canon

> that the plural includes the singular, and the singular the plural, unless a contrary indication appears. Also, by virtue of the Act, if not independently of it, "words importing the feminine gender include the masculine" and vice versa.

(c) *Alternative style.* An acceptable alternative style uses smart double marks for the main quotation nesting smart single marks at the second level, straight double marks at the third, and straight single marks at the fourth. Rarely, if ever, should you need to use a fourth level of nesting.

Ex.: The *Chapa-Garza* court noted that "8 U.S.C. § 1101(a)(43) provides, in relevant part: '[T]he term "aggravated felony" means . . . a crime of violence for which the term of imprisonment [is] at least one year.'"

> "I myself have learned by experience that if the ideas that are difficult to understand are properly separated, they become clearer; and that, on the other hand, through defective punctuation many passages are confused and distorted to such a degree that sometimes they can only with difficulty be understood, or even cannot be understood at all." —*Aldus Manutius*

1.33 Use quotation marks around a word or phrase that is being referred to as a term, or else italicize it.

(a) *Generally.* A word used as a term (rather than for its actual meaning) is traditionally set off by quotation marks or italicized (see 3.4). This device is more common in legal writing than in general writing, largely because of its frequent use in defining terms and in using terms of art.

Ex.: The statute does not apply to honest differences of opinion. To leave no doubt on this point, Congress deliberately used the words "false" and "fraudulent."

Or: The statute does not apply to honest differences of opinion. To leave no doubt on this point, Congress deliberately used the words *false* and *fraudulent*.

Ex.: The meaning of "malice" depends on whether you're involved in a murder case or a libel suit.

Or: The meaning of *malice* depends on whether you're involved in a murder case or a libel suit.

(b) *Italics as alternative.* Italic type is a better alternative for this use of quotation marks, since there is no punctuation to slow the reader's pace (see 3.4(a)).

Ex.: In later years *among* in this context has carried the connotation of *between*, but it has also meant *intermingled with*.

1.34 Use quotation marks to mean "so-called" or (more negatively) to mean "so-called-but-not-really."

(a) *Odd or informal use.* Quotation marks can signal that a term is somehow odd, informal, or perhaps adopted by necessity.

Ex.: Although the primordial desire for vengeance is an understandable emotion, it is a testament to the constantly evolving nature of our social and moral consciousness that the law has, in recent decades, come to regard this "eye-for-an-eye" philosophy as an improper basis for punishment.

(b) *With "so-called."* The quotation marks alone serve to signal the meaning of "so-called." When that term is explicitly used, the quotation marks are generally superfluous, and the better practice is to leave them off.

Not this: The court further held that relief would require manual re-counts in all Florida counties where so-called "undervotes" had not been subject to manual tabulation.

But this: The court further held that relief would require manual re-counts in all Florida counties where "undervotes" had not been subject to manual tabulation.

Or this: The court further held that relief would require manual re-counts in all Florida counties where so-called undervotes had not been subject to manual tabulation.

(c) *With phrasal adjectives.* Don't use quotation marks around phrasal adjectives. Instead, hyphenate (see 1.62).

Not this: The defendant asked the court to lower the award, citing the "mitigation of damages" doctrine.

But this: The defendant asked the court to lower the award, citing the mitigation-of-damages doctrine.

(d) *Nicknames.* Use quotation marks around a nickname when it is unfamiliar or when it is used as an appositive of the formal name. Use no quotation marks when the nickname is familiar and isn't used with the formal name. Usually, the nickname should appear between the given name and the surname in the name's first use.

Ex.: Richard "Racehorse" Haynes (but *Racehorse Haynes*)

Ex.: William Jefferson "Bill" Clinton (but *Bill Clinton*)

Ex.: Theophilus Eugene "Bull" Connor (but *Bull Connor*)

(e) *Connoting irony.* Use quotation marks around a word or phrase that is used in an ironic sense, implying that the thing it refers to isn't really this thing at all. Used in this way, quotation marks are a signal of jest.

Ex.: Our first "Christmas tree" was a potted plant with a tin-foil star on top.

Ex.: In the past, Scholastic's best-selling product was *Goosebumps*, a series of "scary" children's books.

(f) *For sarcasm.* Avoid using quotation marks for sarcasm or ridicule. This rhetorical device can backfire if the reader finds it snide or disrespectful.

Ex.: The only "damage" this plaintiff suffered was a bruised ego.

Parentheses

1.35 Parentheses are frequent fliers in legal writing: it's rare to find a page without a few pairs on it. They are required in legal citations and often show up for subordinate matter in the text. In general, they are used in pairs to enclose matter that is helpful but not essential. They therefore tend to suggest to the reader, "Take me or leave me." If your purpose is to make the parenthetical content stand out rather than hide, a pair of em-dashes is probably the better tool. In

> "It is bad form to wear a flannel shirt with a dress coat, or a white lawn tie with a sack suit. It is quite as bad form to punctuate badly, to misspell, or to make mistakes in grammar, even if the clearness of your writing is not seriously impaired. Actually, of course, misspelling, grammatical errors, and bad punctuation do usually affect clearness, sometimes utterly changing the sense. But from either point of view, they are fatal to writing."
>
> —*Henry Seidel Canby*

legal writing, don't shrink from "nesting" parentheticals (one inside another), or even "kissing" ones (parentheticals placed back-to-back). And despite the practice in other styles of writing, don't use brackets as "subparentheses" in legal writing.

1.36 Use parentheses to set off extraneous matter (such as an explanation, reference, support, or comment) in a sentence or paragraph.

(a) *Incidental matter.* Parentheses tell the reader that the matter enclosed (called a parenthetical) is incidental to the central topic of the sentence or paragraph itself. A parenthetical in a paragraph may include more than one sentence. Parentheses are always used in pairs to begin and end the parenthetical matter.

> Ex.: Only two states, Nevada (1956) and Utah (1957), had enacted statutes that specifically permitted homeschooling. (The parenthetical matter gives extra information about the content.)
>
> Ex.: These include, among others, the opinion rules (Rules 701 and 702), the firsthand- or personal-knowledge rule (Rule 602), and the rule requiring authentication of documents (Rule 901). (The parenthetical matter refers the reader to a source.)
>
> Ex.: The Government simply relied on two affidavits by State Department officials attesting to the general (and undoubted) importance of maintaining the United States' leadership in the international war on drugs. (The parenthetical matter comments on the content.)

(b) *Minimizing effect.* Parentheses minimize their content (unlike em-dashes, which focus attention on what they set apart—see 1.53). The information may be important in its own right, but the words themselves could be removed without changing the meaning of the sentence.

> Ex.: In the single carton opened for examination (taken from the top tier of the last row), we noted no apparent heavy ice or frost inside the plastic bags.
>
> Ex.: Credit-card customers (like Schnall) were invited to use "the attached Line of Credit checks to consolidate other credit-card balances."

1.37 Use parentheses to define a quick reference for a longer name.

(a) *Quick reference.* It is customary in legal writing to use shorthand references for parties, and often for statutes and other subject matter that can be abbreviated for convenience without being ambiguous.

> Ex.: Columbia Gas Transmission Corporation (Columbia Gas) appeals the district court's dismissal of its declaratory-judgment action against the property owner, Deana Drain, for lack of subject-matter jurisdiction.
>
> Ex.: The defendants, including The David J. Joseph and Sons Co. (the Company), ...

(b) *Often not necessary.* The shortened reference may be so obvious that no parenthetical definition is needed at all. This often happens with names and with abbreviations that closely follow the first appearance of the words they stand for, and with well-known acronyms like FBI, NAACP, and NASA. These unnecessary definitions can be distracting or even irritating to some readers. They are especially perplexing when the defined terms aren't used again in the document.

Ex.: Plaintiff-appellant Daniel Reed was severely injured in the early-morning hours of September 2, 2017, when a car ran over the tent in which he was sleeping. Reed was attending an event known as the Burning Man Festival, held on federally owned land.

Ex.: David H. Marlin appeals the district court's grant of summary judgment to the District of Columbia Board of Elections and Ethics (Board). Marlin brought this action alleging the Board's enforcement of polling-place regulations . . . . (The writer thought it necessary to note the shortened reference to *Board*, but not to *Marlin*.)

(c) *With quotation marks.* Most legal writers use quotation marks inside the parentheses. Quotation marks may signal that what is inside them is a defined term. But if the definition stands alone inside the parentheses, the quotation marks usually add nothing to that signal and may be omitted without sacrificing clarity. If the reference might be ambiguous without the quotation marks, then use them. If, for example, the parentheses contain other words besides *the* (e.g., *collectively*), the quotation marks are often needed for clarity. By the way, if you use quotation marks with one reference, use them for all references to maintain a consistent style.

Ex.: Sterling manufactures and sells prescription drugs and over-the-counter ("OTC") medicines. (The quotation marks are correct but not necessary.)

Ex.: Rodger Smith worked as a technician for Longview Cable Company ("Longview"), which provided cable television service in the Longview, Texas, area. (Without the quotation marks, the short name of the defendant could be confused with the city where it's located.)

Ex.: In this putative class action, the plaintiffs assert various state-law claims based on an alleged scheme by the defendants, GTE Corporation and GTE South, Inc. (collectively, "GTE"), to defraud their customers into leasing telephones and paying exorbitant lease charges. (Quotation marks are needed for clarity with *collectively*.)

> "Punctuation should primarily prevent misunderstanding of thought or expression and should secondarily facilitate reading: the best punctuation is that which the reader is unaware of." —*Words into Type*

(d) *Avoiding surplusage.* The sense of parenthetical defined terms is usually clear without the use of surplusage such as *hereinafter.*

Not this: Appellant attempted to introduce evidence of battered women's syndrome (hereinafter referred to as BWS) to show that because of BWS, she believed that threats made to her by Rubio would be carried out immediately, even though an objective view of the threats would not show that to be the case. (Omit *hereinafter referred to as.*)

Not this: Janice Lee Brimberry White, as successor in interest for Susan Ann Brimberry Katzberg (hereinafter collectively referred to as "Mother"), appeals from an order granting the motion of the respondent, Richard W. Katzberg ("Father"), to modify his child-support obligations.

But this: Janice Lee Brimberry White, as successor in interest for Susan Ann Brimberry Katzberg (collectively, "Mother"), appeals from an order granting the motion of the respondent, Richard W. Katzberg ("Father"), to modify his child-support obligations. (Omit the phrase *hereinafter referred to as*, but retain *collectively* with a comma for clarity.)

1.38 Use parentheses to set off numbers and letters that denote subparts.

(a) *Generally.* Whether written in sentence form or table form, items in a list are separated by numbers or letters in parentheses.

Ex.: A lawyer who is not competent to handle a particular legal problem has three options: (1) decline to accept the client or withdraw from representing the client; (2) become competent through study and training, if it can be done without unreasonable delay or expense; or (3) associate with counsel experienced in the area, if the client consents.

Ex.: The common-law profits were (a) turbary, the right to remove turf for use as a fuel; (b) piscary, the right to fish; (c) estovers, the right to cut timber for fuel; and (d) pasture, the right to have animals graze.

Ex.: All states, both coastal and landlocked, have the right to exercise the freedom of the high seas. This freedom includes (but is not limited to):

(1) freedom of navigation;
(2) freedom of overflight;
(3) freedom of fishing;
(4) freedom to lay submarine cables and pipelines; and
(5) freedom of scientific research.

(b) *In pairs.* Use a set of parentheses—not a single end-parenthesis—around a number or letter used in a list.

Not this: The common-law profits were:

a) turbary, the right to remove turf for use as a fuel;
b) piscary, the right to fish;
c) estovers, the right to cut timber for fuel; and
d) pasture, the right to have animals graze.

But this: The common-law profits were:
(a) turbary, the right to remove turf for use as a fuel;
(b) piscary, the right to fish;
(c) estovers, the right to cut timber for fuel; and
(d) pasture, the right to have animals graze.

(c) *Special conventions.* Place each subsection designation of a statute, regulation, or rule in parentheses, with no space between them.

Ex.: 50 U.S.C. § 1702(a)(1)(B)
Ex.: Colo. Rev. Stat. § 38–10–117(1)
Ex.: Treas. Reg. § 301.6901–1(b)

(d) *Exception.* Follow the style of the source you're citing. Some treatises, for example, use brackets rather than parentheses for subparts.

Ex.: § 1.01[a][2].

1.39 Use parentheses in citations as prescribed by the citation manual you follow.

(a) *Idiosyncrasies.* Legal-citation style differs from academic style. In law, use parentheses for the name of the court and the date when citing a case. You may also use parentheses after the citation to quote from the cited case, to explain briefly how the case relates to the issue being discussed, or to point out any change made from the original, such as using italic type for emphasis. Use a space between sets of parentheses.

Ex.: *United States v. Shelton*, 66 F.3d 991, 992 (8th Cir. 1995) (per curiam) (upholding, on a similar basis, the prohibition in § 922(g) against possession of firearms by a felon).

(b) *Nesting parentheses.* In legal writing it is permissible to nest several levels of parenthetical material, and it is also permissible for parentheses pointing the same way to "kiss."

Ex.: (*But see New Rock Asset Partners, L.P. v. Preferred Entity Advancements, Inc.*, 101 F.3d 1492, 1496 (3d Cir. 1996) (quoting *Nat'l Iranian Oil Co. v. Mapco Int'l, Inc.*, 983 F.2d 485, 489 (3d Cir. 1992)).)

(c) *Space between parentheses.* Never have two parentheses pointing in different ways abut each other. When you have an end-parenthesis followed by a beginning-parenthesis, as often occurs in citations, always use a space between them (see 9.15(a)).

Not this: *Accord Childress v. City of Richmond*, 134 F.3d 1205, 1209 (4th Cir. 1998)(en banc) (Luttig, J., concurring)("Congress may, if it chooses, override prudential standing limitations and authorize all persons who satisfy the Constitution's standing requirements to bring particular actions in federal court.").

But this: *Accord Childress v. City of Richmond*, 134 F.3d 1205, 1209 (4th Cir. 1998) (en banc) (Luttig, J., concurring) ("Congress may, if it chooses, override prudential standing limitations and authorize all persons who satisfy the Constitution's standing requirements to bring particular actions in federal court.").

1.40 Punctuate and capitalize parenthetical matter correctly.

(a) *Terminal punctuation.* Terminal punctuation goes outside the closing parenthesis unless (1) the entire sentence is in parentheses, or (2) the parenthetical matter requires a question mark or exclamation mark. In the latter situation, if the sentence takes the same mark, place it outside the parentheses; but if the sentence takes a period, place the question mark or exclamation mark inside the parentheses and a period outside.

Ex.: Griggs was a longtime employee of DuPont. (He was hired in 2002.)

Ex.: Griggs was a longtime employee of DuPont (having been hired in 2002).

Ex.: The trial lasted three months (as I had predicted).

Ex.: The trial lasted three months (and what a hair-puller it was!).

Ex.: The trial lasted three months (didn't I tell you it would?).

Ex.: Did you know that the trial lasted three months (and didn't I tell you it would)?

(b) *Capitalization.* Don't capitalize the first word in parenthetical matter—even if standing alone it would form a complete sentence—unless (1) the entire sentence is in parentheses, or (2) it is capitalized for another reason, such as a proper noun or the pronoun *I.*

Ex.: The Court applied the clear-and-present-danger test (the test was first announced by Holmes and refined by Learned Hand) to a judge's power to gag news reporters covering a trial.

Ex.: The Court applied the clear-and-present-danger test to a judge's power to gag news reporters covering a trial. (The test was first announced by Holmes and refined by Learned Hand.)

Ex.: The Court applied the clear-and-present-danger test (Holmes's legacy) to a judge's power to gag news reporters covering a trial.

Brackets

1.41 Brackets are squarish parentheses, but they have their own personalities. This is especially true in legal writing, where they carry heavier editing burdens than they do elsewhere in the literary world. Brackets signal minor deletions, changes, and interpolations inside quotations, and because legal writers quote with such rigor in preserving the original text, pages can become peppered with the marks.

Don't italicize brackets. No such character as an italic bracket exists in classical typography. The mere fact that computers can make them is no reason to accept them now.

1.42 Bracket an editorial remark or clarification inside a quotation.

(a) *Editorial comment.* Brackets are used the same way in legal writing as in academic and business writing when the purpose is to comment on or add to the matter being quoted.

Ex.: As the court reasoned, "This approach recognizes that all activities and property require funds and that management has a great deal of [a word choice far short of "absolute"] flexibility as to the source and use of funds." (editorial comment)

Ex.: "The [2006] Act fundamentally restructures local telephone markets." (addition)

Ex.: The Clean Air Act's judicial-review provision provides that a petition for review of any "final action of the [EPA] Administrator . . . may be filed only in the United States Court of Appeals for the appropriate circuit." (clarification)

Ex.: Sometimes, as lawyers used to say, "*necessitas vincit legem* [necessity overcomes the law]." (translation)

Ex.: Doctors testified that Odham probably suffered from an organic brain disorder, which causes "defects in the way [a person] functions intellectually, socially, and emotionally." (substitution)

(b) [*Sic*]. Use "[sic]" to indicate that an error or oddity in quoted matter appeared in the original. The device should be used when rigorous accuracy is required, as when quoting the exact words of a statute. As a matter of etiquette, it should never be used as a snide way to highlight the errors of another writer; instead, it is better to correct those minor mistakes using brackets. An interpolated "[sic]" should not be italicized (it appears in italics above only as a tagline, to maintain an internally consistent style).

Ex.: The city ordinance in effect at the time required innkeepers to "make all reasonable accomodations [sic] for wheelchair-bound guests."

For avoiding "[sic]" by means of a cleaned-up quotation, see 8.5.

1.43 Use brackets in quoted matter to indicate that part of a quoted word has been omitted or that one or more characters or words have been changed.

(a) *Omissions and substitutions.* When quoted matter is altered in any way (as when *bracketed* becomes *bracket*[*ing*]), legal writing requires that the change be rigorously indicated—even to the point of using brackets to show a change in capitalization. Use brackets to mark omissions or substitutions of characters in words, especially to make the quotation agree in number, tense, or gender with the rest of the sentence. Use a pair of empty brackets (abutting the word being altered) to show that one or more characters at the end of a word have been left out.

Ex.: The regulations in question were 14 C.F.R. §§ 121.1(a)(5), (d), and 135.1(a)(2) (1965), which applied to "commercial operator[s]," who were defined as persons operating aircraft "for compensation or hire."

Ex.: We agree with the district court that the "deemed paid" language of § 904(c) can be inferred to "relate[] . . . to the year in which the foreign tax credit will be applied."

Ex.: She noted that it was her "obligation to make certain that people receive accurate information regarding the proceedings over which [she] preside[s]."

Ex.: The Constitution "indisputably entitle[s] a criminal defendant to 'a jury determination that [he] is guilty of every element of the crime with which he is charged, beyond a reasonable doubt.'"

Ex.: "[I]t is not inappropriate to allow § 1981 claimants to avail themselves of Title VII discriminatory treatment standards in proving a prima facie case."

(b) *Ellipses distinguished.* Don't use a set of empty brackets to mark the omission of a whole word or more; use ellipsis dots instead (see 1.47).

Not this: "When Burr lost [], he challenged Hamilton to a duel." (The word *again* is omitted.)

But this: "When Burr lost . . . , he challenged Hamilton to a duel."

(c) *Placement of brackets.* When brackets mark the alteration of a word—rather than marking the interpretation of words to clarify the text—don't put any space between the brackets and the word they go with. In other words, one of the brackets should always touch part of that word.

Ex.: The report stated that "[w]hen Burr lost again, he challenged Hamilton to a duel." (The capital *w* in the original has been made lowercase in the quotation.)

Ex.: "When [Aaron] Burr lost again, he challenged [Alexander] Hamilton to a duel." (Whole words—first names—that did not appear in the original have been added to clarify the quoted matter.)

(d) *Overuse.* Use brackets sparingly. A heavily bracketed passage is typically better paraphrased. Too many empty brackets and bracketed substitutions clutter a quotation and dull its impact. Reword instead.

(e) *Bracketing only as required.* No change in the case of a letter should be made if it isn't required. Some legal writers see examples of "[h]e did . . ." and don't recognize what this form represents to the informed reader: that *he*, in the original source, was *He* (capitalized)—and that it needed to become lowercase because the quoter blended it into the syntax of the quoter's sentence. The opposite, of course, also occurs: "[S]he did . . ." tells the informed reader that the quoter took a lowercase *she* and made it uppercase to begin the quotation, as a self-contained sentence. So the mistake that errant writers make is to bracket and change characters that don't require bracketing. The blunder appears to occur primarily in the writing of those who also misunderstand the correct methods of introducing quotations (see 1.8, 1.24(a)).

1.44 If brackets proliferate to the point where they're burdensome or unsightly, consider a cleaned-up quotation.

For an elegant method of eliminating brackets that are either coupled with ellipses or excessive in themselves, see 8.5.

1.45 In legal writing—as opposed to in other types of writing—don't use brackets as subordinate parentheses inside parenthetical matter.

(a) *As "subparentheses."* Although brackets are used as subordinate parentheses in other types of prose, in legal writing it is acceptable—in fact expected—to nest parentheses within parentheses instead. Indeed, in legal citations, so-called kissing parentheses—typically two consecutive end-parentheses thus:))—are commonplace.

Not this: (When the bill was debated [1964], the ban on "sex discrimination" was considered a killer amendment that no one could accept.)

But this: (When the bill was debated (1964), the ban on "sex discrimination" was considered a killer amendment that no one could accept.)

And this: The argument relied heavily on a holding in an oil-and-gas case (*Cenergy Corp. v. Bryson Oil & Gas P.L.C.*, 662 F.Supp. 1144 (D. Nev. 1987) (no obligation to produce information not in the company's possession)).

(b) *Rephrasing or paraphrasing.* If your parenthetical contains a quotation with omissions or substitutions, consider paraphrasing to eliminate the need for brackets.

Instead of: *See* Fed. R. Bankr. P. 9006(b)(3) ("The court may enlarge the time for taking action under Rule[] . . . 4003(b) . . . only to the extent and under the conditions stated in [that] rule[].").

Try this: *See* Fed. R. Bankr. P. 9006(b)(3) (allowing the court to extend the time provisions of Rule 4003(b) only so far as allowed under that rule).

Ellipsis Dots

1.46 Like brackets, ellipses get more use in legal writing than elsewhere. Lawyers quote a great deal (often way too much), and quotations often need editing and excising if they're to be effective. For example, transitional words that refer to some previous sentence or paragraph often make no sense when the quoted passage is standing alone. Properly used, ellipses are perfectly respectable, even necessary, and don't raise suspicions that the writer has tampered with the meaning. In fact, their very presence bespeaks care.

Many writers have trouble remembering the rules on how many dots to use, and how to space before, between, and after the dots. Help is on the way . . .

1.47 Use three ellipsis dots to indicate the omission of one or more words inside a quotation.

(a) *Midsentence.* Use three ellipsis dots to indicate that something has been omitted within the quoted sentence. Omit any punctuation that appeared on either side of the elided matter, unless it is grammatically needed in the restructured sentence.

> Ex.: "An accommodation party may sign the instrument as maker, drawer, acceptor, or indorser and . . . is obliged to pay the instrument in the capacity in which the accommodation party signs."

> Ex.: "Once a plaintiff establishes a prima facie case, . . . the burden shifts to the defendant to produce rebuttal evidence." (Note the retained comma.)

(b) *Paragraph omitted.* If a full paragraph or more has been omitted, center three widely spaced ellipsis dots on a separate line, and then indent and continue the quotation. Use five to seven spaces between the dots. Note that there are other styles as well. The current edition of *The Bluebook*, for example, uses four ellipsis dots, indented as a paragraph; older editions of *The Bluebook* handled the issue differently. The recommendation here—with three centered dots—reflects the dominant form in scholarly writing generally.

> Ex.: Section 8. The Congress shall have Power to lay and collect Taxes, Duties, Imposts and Excises, to pay the Debts and provide for the common Defence and general Welfare of the United States; but all Duties, Imposts and Excises shall be uniform throughout the United States;
>
> .   .   .
>
> To make all Laws which shall be necessary and proper for carrying into Execution the foregoing Powers, and all other Powers vested by this Constitution in the Government of the United States, or in any Department or Officer thereof.

> "Punctuation marks first came into systematic use in the fifteenth and sixteenth centuries when the printing press began to make written material available to a wide audience for the first time. The basic forms—commas, periods, apostrophes, quotation marks, etc.—have changed very little in the last 400 years."
>
> —*Lane Jennings*

Warning: you must be fair with your omissions. Don't use an ellipsis to denote a large jump across massive amounts of material.

1.48 Use four dots (three ellipsis dots and a period, all identical) to indicate the omission of either (1) the end of a sentence, or (2) matter after a completed sentence when the quotation continues after the elided matter.

(a) *When the elision precedes the period.* If the omitted matter includes the end of a sentence, follow the last word with a hard space (see 4.13) and then four dots—three ellipsis dots plus the sentence period, with hard spaces before and between the dots. Remember: ellipsis dots always come in threes.

Ex.: "The world will little note nor long remember what we say here . . . ." (Since *here* was not the last word of the quoted sentence, it is followed by a space, three ellipsis points, another space, and then the sentence period as the fourth dot.)

(b) *When the elision follows the period.* If the last word ends the quoted sentence, no ellipsis is needed unless the quotation continues. If the quotation does continue, the first dot is the sentence period, so don't use a space between the last word and the first dot. Follow the period with the three ellipsis dots, using hard spaces between all four dots.

Ex.: As Lincoln reminded the audience at Gettysburg, our founders were "dedicated to the proposition that all men are created equal." (The quotation does not continue after *equal*, so no ellipsis follows the period.)

Ex.: As Lincoln memorialized the cemetery, he said, "We are met on a great battlefield of that war. . . . The brave men, living and dead, who struggled here have consecrated it far above our poor power to add or detract." (The first sentence of the quotation ends with *war*, so there is no space between *war* and the period. Some text is omitted before the quotation continues, so three ellipsis dots follow the period, with hard spaces between all four dots.)

1.49 Don't use ellipsis dots at the beginning of a quotation or where the quoted matter is worked into the syntax of the main sentence.

(a) *Start of sentence omitted.* Although the practice is common outside law, in legal writing it is never permissible to begin a quotation with an ellipsis. Instead, a bracketed capital letter (if the word has been changed to uppercase or lowercase) will often signal that something has been left out.

Ex.: "[G]overnment o f the people, by the people, and for the people shall not perish from the earth."

(b) *Run-in syntax.* If the quoted matter is a fragment that is worked into the structure of the main sentence, don't use ellipsis dots before or after the quotation.

Ex.: It was only "[f]our score and seven years" since the founding of the republic.

Ex.: It was hardly fair—in fact, it was scandalously unfair—to say that the book was "rife with rumor-mongering."

1.50 Keep the ellipsis dots standard by using hard spaces and the correct typographic elements—or else use the special ellipsis character.

(a) *Hard spacing.* Use a nonbreaking ("hard") space to prevent the ellipsis dots from being separated by a line break. Use a hard space (see 4.13) between the dots and also between the last quoted word and the punctuation if the quoted sentence continues in the original source from which it is drawn.

(b) *Asterisks.* At one time, asterisks and bullets were commonly used to mark omitted text. This style persists in some places: some casebook editors still use it, and until recently it was the preferred style of the U.S. Government Printing Office. But in general, writers today should use only periods as ellipsis dots.

Not this: "The offering to distribute copies * * * to a group of persons for purposes of further distribution * * * constitutes publication."

But this: "The offering to distribute copies . . . to a group of persons for purposes of further distribution . . . constitutes publication."

(c) *An alternative: the ellipsis character.* Word-processing applications give you the option of inserting an "ellipsis character" into your text. The great advantage of it is that it takes a single keystroke (plus the Alt or Option key) rather than as many as nine (four dots and five spaces—all but one space being nonbreaking, which also requires the Alt or Option key). The disadvantage is that it's too tight (it doesn't have true word spaces between the dots) and too inflexible (where used, the fourth dot isn't evenly spaced with the ellipsis dots). All in all, the safest and most usual course is to stick to the traditionally spaced ellipsis dots, taking care to mind the "hard" spaces where needed. But as software becomes more sophisticated and nuanced, the special character may eventually prove the easier and better choice.

1.51 Ellipsis dots can be used to indicate that an unfinished sentence trails off.

(a) *Trailing off.* The ellipsis dots may indicate that a partial statement was followed by silence. Three (not four) dots are always appropriate: the sentence doesn't really terminate, so there is no period.

Ex.: The last time I saw Charlie . . .

(b) *Interruption.* In legal transcripts, terminal ellipsis dots are used to show that a speaker has been interrupted. In other styles of writing, an em-dash more often serves this purpose.

Ex.: Detar: I think that this was probably just an accident, okay. But there's a question . . . .
Dubria: But detective . . . .
Detar: Wait, wait, wait . . . let me finish, let me finish.

1.52 If ellipses become burdensome or unsightly, consider a cleaned-up quotation.

For an elegant method of eliminating ellipses that are either coupled with brackets or excessive in themselves, see 8.5.

Em-Dashes

1.53 The em-dash (also called a *long dash* or just a *dash*) is a forceful and conspicuous punctuation mark. Although you may have once heard a stern warning against em-dashes, they're an important part of your toolbox. Just look at almost any page of first-rate published prose and you'll see one or more irreplaceable dashes.

Roughly as wide as the font is tall—and twice as long as the en-dash—the em-dash stands out on the page. It highlights what it either contains (when used in pairs) or separates from the main sentence. The same matter inside parentheses would be de-emphasized. As a separator, the em-dash often performs the same pointing function as a colon. When that is so, the two marks are interchangeable.

On a computer, the em-dash is a special character, and applications differ about how to insert one. Although spaces are not inserted before or after an em-dash in most professional printing, that practice often gives terrible results in office documents. Faced with two words (often long words) joined by a long em-dash, an office computer will often produce awkward hyphenation and either short lines or (especially with right-justified type) gaping horizontal spacing—or perhaps both. For legal documents, use a nonbreaking space before the em-dash and a regular word space after. That will prevent the em-dash from showing up at the left margin.

Since em-dashes—like parentheses—so often work in pairs, avoid using more than two of them in a single sentence.

1.54 Use an em-dash—or a pair of em-dashes as required by sentence structure—to give emphasis to matter that is independent of the main sentence.

(a) *Setting off words at beginning or end of sentence.* Use an em-dash to separate an element that is placed at the beginning or at the end of a sentence to expand on or explain another part of the sentence. In this construction, the dash is similar in function to a colon (at the beginning) or parentheses (at the end), but more emphatic.

Ex. Paul McCartney—he was everybody's favorite.

Ex.: Principle—that's what's at stake here.

Ex.: The most common problem of extra-record evidence occurs when there are ex parte contacts—communications outside the hearing and off the record from an interested party to a decision-making official.

Ex.: Role models are not a wholesale matter—we select piecemeal aspects of their behavior and attitudes to develop ourselves as unique, self-defined, and determined to be not copies but our own selves.

Ex.: Airbags—Who would have imagined they could take lives instead of saving them?

(b) *In midsentence.* Use a pair of em-dashes instead of parentheses to set off important parenthetical matter—even an independent clause—inside the main sentence. While parentheses minimize what they enclose, em-dashes emphasize it. Don't use a comma, semicolon, or colon before or after an em-dash, even if one would be necessary without the interrupting matter.

Ex.: Because an assignment for the benefit of creditors places the debtor's property out of the reach of creditors—legal title passes to the assignee—it might seem that creditors would be able to void the assignment under a fraudulent-conveyance statute. (The comma that would have been required where the first em-dash appears is no longer necessary.)

Ex.: The court relied on an abridged, outdated, nonscholarly dictionary—the 1980 edition of the Oxford American Dictionary—which defined escape as to get oneself free from confinement. (The comma that would have been required where the second em-dash appears is no longer necessary.)

Ex.: Our discussion of dictum so far has mostly been about only one type—the major one—obiter dictum. (The colon or comma that would have been necessary where the second em-dash appears is no longer needed.)

> "The pauses that mark the sense . . . are the same in verse as in prose. They are marked by the usual stops, a comma, a semicolon, a colon, or a period, as the sense requires."
>
> —*Noah Webster*

Ex.: OpenType is based on Unicode character coding (international 2-byte character coding). This means that the usual assignment restrictions—PostScript fonts were restricted to 256 characters—no longer apply.

Ex.: If your college professor or your child's professor said LY-ber-ee—or *per*fessor for that matter—wouldn't you raise a concerned eyebrow?

(c) *With appositive.* In setting off an appositive, use a pair of em-dashes instead of commas to either (1) emphasize it or (2) clarify the sentence if the appositive is a phrase containing internal commas.

Ex.: The prediction must come from "reference to a law of general application"—a state statute or the state constitution—that will deny the defendant's civil rights. (emphasis)

Ex.: Aid to any element of the traditional learning process—institution, teachers, or students—is an educational purpose. (internal commas)

1.55 Use an em-dash—or consecutive em-dashes—in several conventions to indicate missing information.

(a) *In a transcript.* An em-dash may be used instead of ellipsis dots in a transcript of dialogue to indicate an interruption or abrupt change of thought.

Ex.: Q. Did there come a point when you decided you couldn't take it any longer?
A. I explained to him that I was and he wouldn't—like I said, he wouldn't approve anything.

(b) *Expunction.* Use two em-dashes with no space between them to replace part of a word or name. This device is most often used to elide all but the first letter of a word or a name, usually either to expunge an obscenity or to preserve a person's anonymity.

Ex.: "How do I get this d—— thing to work?"

Ex.: "Mr. H—— informed the police of the robbery plans."

(c) *In citations.* For extremely recent decisions for which no official citation is yet available, two consecutive em-dashes with no space between them may be used to stand in for the volume number of the reporter together with the page numbers. Underscores are also used for this purpose, and are recommended in *The Bluebook* and *ALWD.*

Ex.: *Florida v. Jardines,* —— U.S. ——, 133 S. Ct. 1409 (2013). (Each blank consists of two em-dashes.)

Or: *Florida v. Jardines,* ____ U.S. ____, 133 S. Ct. 1409 (2013). (Each blank consists of four underscores.)

(d) *Same author.* In academic style, use three consecutive em-dashes with no spaces between them to indicate the repetition of an author's name in an alphabetized bibliography.

Ex.: Kilpatrick, James J. *The Ear Is Human: A Handbook of Homophones and Other Confusions.* Kansas City: Andrews, McMeel & Parker, 1985.
———. *The Writer's Art.* Kansas City: Andrews, McMeel & Parker, 1984.

(e) *To be supplied.* In a transcript, use three closed em-dashes to indicate a speaker's pause while waiting for another person to "fill in the blank."

Ex.: Q. So the ship sailed on the ninth of ———? When was it?
A. March.
Q. The ninth of March. Thank you.

(f) *Elision of words.* Very occasionally, a dash can signal the omission of a word to be mentally supplied by readers <senior colleagues usually have negative reactions to Rambo theatrics: the thugs and bullies I've seen in action are usually rejected; thoughtful egalitarian listeners—accepted>.

En-Dashes

1.56 The en-dash is longer than the hyphen but half the length of the em-dash. It's helpful where a hyphen is too short to do the job. Today, outside publishing, the en-dash often goes unused, its duties having been overtaken by the hyphen. But meticulous writers still use it as described below.

1.57 Use an en-dash to designate a span from one value to another, but avoid it to stand for *to* if the word *from* is used.

(a) *To show year ranges and page ranges, etc.* The en-dash typically connects dates, page numbers, and the like.

Ex.: The American Civil War (1861–1865)

Ex.: *Schneider Nat'l Carriers, Inc. v. National Emp. Care Sys., Inc.*, 469 F.3d 654, 658–59 (7th Cir. 2006).

(b) *To show an unfinished range.* Use an en-dash to show an ongoing number range. For example, use an en-dash after the birth year in a biographical reference to indicate that the person is still alive.

Ex.: Justice Elena Kagan (1960–).

Or: Justice Ellen Kagan (b. 1960)

(c) *Ranges of amounts.* When using an en-dash with large numerals, as with a range of monetary or other amounts, always write both numerals in full to avoid confusion.

Not this: Paralegals at the firm typically earn $30–$50,000 per year.

But this: Paralegals at the firm typically earn $30,000–$50,000 per year.

(d) *Not mixed with words.* When spanning two numerals, an en-dash stands in for the phrase *from . . . to* or *between . . . and.* When the word *from* or *between* is used with an en-dash, the construction doesn't "read" correctly if the understood word *to* or *and* is mentally voiced.

Wrong: From 1779–1782 Randolph served in the Continental Congress. (Make it *From 1779 to 1782 . . . .*)

Right: Randolph served in the Continental Congress 1779–1782.

1.58 Use an en-dash to express scores and votes.

(a) *Scores and votes.* An en-dash should join two or more numerals representing the result of a vote or other tally, such as a win–loss record or scores in a sports game or other competition. To ensure that the reader won't mistake the figure for a numerical range, always be sure that the context makes it clear what the numbers represent. When the tally or score doesn't immediately precede a noun or follow a verb or preposition, it should usually be set off by commas.

Ex.: The Court voted 6–3 to uphold the lower court's ruling.

Ex.: The prosecutor's 19–2 trial record speaks for itself.

Ex.: Barack Obama was reelected with an electoral vote of 332–206.

Ex.: Republicans maintained control of the House of Representatives with a 233–200 majority.

Ex.: The Senate narrowly approved the bill, 51–47, with two senators abstaining.

(b) *Order of numbers.* Always arrange the numbers so that their order follows logically from the syntax. But whenever possible, structure the sentence to place the higher number first to better distinguish the tally from a numerical range (usually presented from lowest to highest). When referring generally to a win–loss record, a for–against vote, or the like, the order of the numbers should always mirror those of the words.

Ex.: Kentucky beat Tennessee, 97–82.

But: Tennessee was devastated by its 82–97 loss to Kentucky.

Or: Tennessee was devastated by its loss to Kentucky, 97–82.

1.59 Use an en-dash to join two terms of equal weight.

(a) *To show equality.* The en-dash signals that the two things joined are of equal importance.

Ex.: The Taft–Hartley Act

Ex.: attorney–client privilege

(b) *To show duality.* The conjunctive en-dash works better than a slash (which is more often disjunctive) to join two equal roles or offices held by one person.

Ex.: a talented playwright–director

Ex.: the newly elected secretary–treasurer

Ex.: the attorney–client privilege

(c) *Encroachment of the hyphen.* Admittedly, hyphens are increasingly being used for all the examples in (a) and (b) above. For example, *The Chicago Manual of Style* (17th ed. 2017) declares that most readers won't distinguish an en-dash from a hyphen when the en-dash joins two words, so en-dashes can usually be replaced by hyphens. The *AP Stylebook* doesn't even acknowledge that the en-dash exists and uses hyphens exclusively to connect words. But careful readers recognize that en-dashes provide an important emphasis that hyphens obscure.

1.60 Follow the established convention within a given publication or jurisdiction to use the en-dash to join sections or chapters and their subparts.

(a) *By convention.* Usage varies greatly on how en-dashes are incorporated into legal-numbering systems.

Ex.: 42 U.S.C. § 2000e–5(e)(1)

Ex.: Pub. L. No. 99–508

(b) *To distinguish.* If a designation is alphanumeric (e.g., 42 U.S.C. § 1396a), use an en-dash to distinguish the subparts.

Ex.: 42 U.S.C. § 1396a–2

(c) *Ambiguity.* If a designation already contains an en-dash or hyphen, use the word *to* rather than an en-dash to indicate a range.

Ex.: N.M. Stat. Ann. § 30-18-13(a) to (g)

Hyphens

1.61 Apart from the comma, the hyphen gives writers more trouble than any other punctuation mark. And like the comma, the hyphen generates some controversy. Fortunately, finding out when to hyphenate within a word is easier than finding out when to use a comma: just look up the word in a dictionary. Unfortunately, a dictionary is of no help when trying to master the phrasal adjective: after all, the number of such phrases is practically boundless.

1.62 Hyphenate a phrasal adjective that appears before a noun or pronoun unless it falls within one of several narrow exceptions.

(a) *Basic rule.* A phrase functioning as an adjective in front of a noun or pronoun should ordinarily be hyphenated (hence, *a failure-to-warn claim* but *a claim based on failure to warn*). Otherwise, some readers won't instantly know which noun in the phrase is really functioning as a noun (in the example above, *claim*) and which one is functioning as an adjective (in the example above, *failure*).

Ex.: A third-year associate is handling the breach-of-warranty case. (Writing *a third year associate* would cause a brief miscue; so would *the breach of warranty case*.)

Ex.: From the flag-salute cases to the released-school-time cases to the peddling-of-religious-propaganda cases, the Court usually came out, in a close vote, on the side of free religion.

Ex.: Even more than his go-right-ahead encouragements to Congress and his stop-right-there strictures to state legislatures, the assured audacity with which Marshall lifted his own branch of the federal government from neglect and contumely to respect and power helped fashion a cohesive, consolidated nation.

(b) *Need for clarity.* Some style guides recommend hyphenating phrasal adjectives only when needed for clarity. But while some phrasal adjectives may be clear to you and to most of your readers, the absence of hyphens will inevitably cause some readers to misstep midway through the sentence. Hence the better practice is to hyphenate uniformly.

Ex.: The defendant made an assumption-of-the-risk argument. (Without the hyphens, a reader would at first think the defendant made an assumption.)

Ex.: Our claim falls into a well-settled area of law. (Without the hyphen, the reader would at first see the claim falling into a well.)

Ex.: The court employed a likelihood-of-confusion test.

(c) *After the noun.* If a phrasal adjective doesn't precede the noun it modifies, do not hyphenate it unless it is a standard phrase that is invariably hyphenated, such as *cost-effective*, *drug-free*, *risk-averse*, and *short-lived*. In general, these hyphenated fixed phrases will be listed in a dictionary, but most other phrases needing hyphens won't be.

Ex.: The defense of assumption of the risk requires proof of actual notice of the danger.

Ex.: The rule of law we base our claim on is well settled.

But: Our exhilaration was short-lived.

And: A portion of each donation is tax-exempt.

(d) *"-ly" adverbs.* Don't hyphenate a phrasal adjective that begins with an *-ly* adverb unless the phrase is longer than two words.

Ex.: Our case got a badly needed boost when a corroborating witness came forward.

Ex.: A poorly prepared brief can mean the difference between winning and losing.

But: A poorly-thought-out argument can be worse than no argument at all.

And: A not-so-highly-regarded advocate can sometimes make stunningly good arguments.

(e) *Proper nouns.* Don't hyphenate a proper noun used as an adjective. If the phrase contains an additional word besides the name, hyphenate between the name and the other word; but if the construction is awkward, recast the sentence.

Ex.: The *State Street Bank* decision paved the way for business-method patenting. (No hyphens for *State Street Bank*.)

Ex.: The rookie litigator wore a Brooks Brothers suit to a Malibu Beach reception.

Ex.: Our firm was defending a Pulitzer Prize-winning reporter against a $10 million libel suit.

(f) *Foreign phrases.* Don't hyphenate an obviously foreign phrase used as an adjective.

Ex.: The defendant challenged the court's in rem jurisdiction.

Ex.: A hearing is set for Wednesday on McFadden's habeas corpus petition.

Ex.: The judge threw out the case, saying that the plaintiff had failed to state a prima facie case.

Ex.: Any retroactive enhancement statute would amount to a constitutionally prohibited ex post facto law.

(g) *With multiple elements.* When a phrasal adjective or a compound word contains an "understood" word, because it is paired with a similar phrase, use a hyphen with the other element.

Ex.: The Court found that the statute was both over- and underinclusive.

Ex.: More to the point are the numerous early- and mid-nineteenth-century decisions expressly sustaining warrantless arrests for misdemeanors not involving any breach of the peace.

Ex.: The rookie was a Nebraska-born and -raised athlete.

(h) *Common legal wordings that contain phrasal adjectives.* The following representative list illustrates the best practice for hyphenation. Professional writers and editors prefer strict hyphenation to forestall readers' miscues. So does the U.S. Supreme Court. Yet many legal writers don't fully appreciate the value of the phrasal-adjective rule.

adequate-state-grounds doctrine
administrative-expense reimbursement
advance-sheet errors
alternative-means doctrine
arbitration-specific rules
automobile-accident case
bar-association periodicals
best-evidence rule
best-interests test
breach-of-contract claim
cessation-of-production clause
child-support obligations
choice-of-law rule
civil-rights law
class-action rules
collective-bargaining agreement

"Call it precious and go to hell, but I believe a story can be wrecked by a faulty rhythm in a sentence—especially if it occurs toward the end—or a mistake in paragraphing, even punctuation. Henry James is the maestro of the semicolon. Hemingway is a first-rate paragrapher. From the point of view of ear, Virginia Woolf never wrote a bad sentence. I don't mean to imply that I successfully practice what I preach. I try, that's all." —*Truman Capote*

common-law action
conflict-of-laws hornbook
conflict-resolution factor
contagious-disease researcher
court-supervised buyback
criminal-justice coordinator
custodial-interrogation holdings
data-processing services
day-to-day basis
declaratory-judgment action
delegation-of-powers doctrine
district-court cases
dollars-and-cents injury
domestic-relations law
drug-trafficking crime
due-process limitations
eminent-domain case
external-act requirement
fact-dependent question
federal-courts text
federal-question jurisdiction
firm-specific human capital
four-year terms
grand-jury proceedings
gun-control ordinances
high-net-worth individual
high-water mark
immediate-release policy
impelled-perpetration doctrine
intellectual-property dispute
involuntary-termination-of-parental-rights issue
jurisdictional-amount requirement
law-firm politics
law-review editors
legal-certainty test
local-rule requirements
long-awaited decision
low-income housing
low-level flights
mail-order seller
material-purpose trust
medical-malpractice case
mirror-image rule
mixed-motive cases
mortgage-backed securities
mutual-defense treaty
no-impeachment rule
on-point authority
out-of-state service
parallel-citation requirement
past-due wages
pat-down search
pendent-party jurisdiction
pocket-part updates
political-question doctrine
popular-name table
pork-barrel politics
power-of-sale foreclosure
property-division decree
property-rights symposium
property-tax levy
public-housing project
public-safety exception
public-utility rates
rational-jury test
real-estate agent
real-party-in-interest requirement
real-property tax
replacement-cost depreciation method
resource-constrained judges
restrictive-covenant case
right-to-work state
safe-harbor provision
same-sex marriage
sentence-package rule
separation-of-powers principles
shopping-center lease
show-cause procedure
single-component product
single-creditor petition
slip-opinion review

social-security claims
state-court contempt
state-created claim
state-law claim
statute-based claims
subject-matter jurisdiction
substantial-evidence test
sue-and-be-sued clause
tax-exempt institution
term-limited relationship
third-party defendant
transferred-intent rule
two-dimensional art
two-person team
ulterior-motive argument
ultimate-interest test
under-color-of-state-law argument
undue-influence argument
unjust-enrichment claim
unlawful-act criterion
unpublished-opinion rule
voting-stock rights
well-pleaded complaint
would-be plaintiff
wrongful-life claim

1.63 Use a hyphen with numbers to join two-word spelled-out numbers from 21 to 99 and to write fractions unless one of the numbers is already hyphenated.

(a) *With numbers.* Use a hyphen between the tens place and the ones place when spelling out two-word numbers from 21 to 99.

> Ex.: The Twenty-sixth Amendment lowered the voting age to 18.

(b) *With fractions.* Use a hyphen to separate the numerator from the denominator when writing out fractions (when using numerals, see 1.87(a)).

> Ex.: Constitutional amendments require ratification by three-fourths of the states.

(c) *An exception.* But when the fraction being written out contains a hyphenated number, omit the hyphen that separates the two parts of the fraction.

> Ex.: Ninety-nine and forty-four one-hundredths percent pure.

1.64 Use a hyphen to break a word between syllables at the end of a line.

(a) *For line breaks.* When necessary, a word may be broken between lines. Avoid awkward breaks, which can occur when one of the parts is a separate word standing alone; avoid leaving fewer than three letters on each line; and avoid hyphenating at the end of more than two consecutive lines.

> Ex.: The policy's Coverage A provides comprehensive general liability insur-
> ance for bodily injury and is here extended to cover malpractice claims.

(b) *Between syllables only.* The break must always be between two syllables. If you're not confident, use a current dictionary to check where to break words.

1.65 Use a hyphen to show that you're referring to a prefix, suffix, letter, or letters in a word; to indicate syllabification; and to show that a word is being spelled out.

(a) *Part of a word.* Use a hyphen to show how part of a word or number relates to the omitted part.

> Ex.: In law, the prefix *quasi-* often describes a judicial fiction; a quasi-contract is not really a contract at all.

(b) *For syllabification.* Use hyphens to indicate where a word breaks into syllables.

> Ex.: The word breaks di-ver-si-fi-ca-tion.

(c) *For spelling.* Use hyphens to indicate that a word is being spelled out.

> Ex.: The word s-u-p-e-r-s-e-d-e stumps many legal writers.

1.66 Avoid using a hyphen after a routine prefix—but note the exceptions.

(a) *Generally.* Modern usage omits most hyphens after prefixes, even when it results in a doubled letter.

> Ex.: misspell, nonstatutory, overindulgence, preempt, reelect

(b) *With proper nouns.* Include a hyphen when the root word is a proper noun or a noun phrase (see 7.6(b), (g)).

> Ex.: un-American, anti-Semitic, pre-Columbian
>
> Ex.: pro-free-trade

(c) *With certain prefixes.* Use a hyphen with almost all words starting with the prefixes *all-*, *ex-*, and *self-*, and with the various legal terms formed with *quasi-*.

> Ex.: all-encompassing, ex-convict, self-serving, quasi-contract

(d) *Other exceptions.* There are no inflexible rules about hyphenating other prefixed words. In general, use a hyphen when it's needed to avoid a miscue or ambiguity. Use a hyphen with a compound that would otherwise look like another word or be awkward to pronounce.

> Ex.: anti-intellectual, co-op, pre-judicial, pro-abstinence, re-sign.

1.67 Use a hyphen to join dual proper nouns in ethnic and national identifications and in surnames according to the person's preference.

(a) *Ethnic identifications.* The dominant practice is to hyphenate combined designations of ethnic or national origin.

> Ex.: Boston's Irish-American heritage
>
> Ex.: Hispanic-American voters

(b) *Surnames.* When a married couple (or one spouse) adopts dual surnames, the names may or may not be hyphenated. Where no hyphen is used, the maiden name effectively becomes a middle name.

Ex.: Chris Evert-Lloyd

Ex.: Andrew Spindler-Roesle

Ex.: Hillary Rodham Clinton

Periods

1.68 The period was the earliest and is today the most common punctuation mark. (It's not abundant enough in much legal writing.) It is one of three terminal punctuation marks, the others being the question mark and the exclamation mark. Besides its use to end a sentence, the period also marks abbreviations, separates list designators from contents, and acts as the decimal point in numbers. A period is identical to an ellipsis dot.

1.69 Use a period to end a declaratory statement, an indirect question, or a request.

(a) *Generally.* The period is the standard terminal punctuation unless the sentence requires a question mark or an exclamation mark.

Ex.: Wong's mere access to the website is not proof that he was a "party" to its contents. (declaratory statement)

Ex.: For the first time, we must consider whether the Americans with Disabilities Act requires an employer to violate the seniority provisions of a collective-bargaining agreement to accommodate a disabled employee. (indirect question)

Ex.: Please speak louder. (request)

(b) *Matter of interpretation.* Sometimes, deciding which terminal punctuation mark is appropriate can be a close call. For example, a period may be more appropriate than a question mark for a polite vocal request that is stated in the form of a question. That is especially true if the request is spoken without a questioning tone and doesn't seek an answer.

Ex.: Would you hand me the dictionary.

Ex.: Will you look at the neighbors' new Corvette.

(c) *With exclamation mark.* It is a judgment call when the intensity of a sentence rises to a level justifying an exclamation mark (see 1.78–1.79).

Ex.: Stop it.

Ex.: Stop it!

(d) *With declaratory sentence.* Note that either a declaratory statement or, more commonly, a command may merit an exclamation mark. But the use of that mark is rarely appropriate in legal writing except when quoting a writing that contains one in the original.

1.70 Use periods after letters or numbers in an outline or list.

(a) *Outline style.* In traditional outline style, a period should always follow the letter or number.

Ex.: I. Introduction
A. First theme
1. First support for first theme . . .

(b) *Decimal numbering system.* In a decimal numbering system, avoid a period after the last number.

Ex.: 1.1 Term of Employment

(c) *Parentheses or period.* In a list, prefer parentheses around the letter or number to set it off from the text; otherwise, use a period after the letter or number. Don't use both.

Ex.: Limitations on involuntary bankruptcy petitions:
(1) Creditors may not file under Chapter 9, 12, or 13.
(2) Insurance companies, banks, farmers, and charities are protected.
(3) The petition must usually be filed by three creditors.

1.71 Use a period after a heading only if the heading is run in with text or is a complete sentence.

(a) *No period with tags.* If the heading is a simple tag or label, rather than a complete sentence, don't end it with a period.

Ex.: Statement of Facts (no period unless the heading is run in with text)

(b) *Period with sentences.* If the heading is a complete sentence, end it with a period or other terminal punctuation.

Ex.: The plaintiff suffered no physical injury, and this state does not recognize a tort for negligent infliction of emotional distress. (Period after the heading. In context, the heading would be set in boldface.)

(c) *Read-in tags.* Use a period after a read-in tag (such as the one that precedes this sentence) to separate it from the following sentence, even if the tag itself isn't a complete sentence.

(d) *Consistency.* Be consistent: make each heading at the same level either a phrase or a sentence.

1.72 Use a period after most abbreviations, but not after most contracted abbreviations.

(a) *Generally.* An abbreviation is a shortened version of a word formed by omitting some of its letters, usually at the end of the word.

Ex.: "Co." for "Company" in *Thompson Coal Co. v. Pike Coal Co.*

Ex.: "a.m." for *ante meridiem* (or "in the morning") in "9 a.m."

Ex.: "Ph.D." for "Doctor of Philosophy"

(b) *No periods.* By convention, some abbreviations don't take periods.

Ex.: "mm" for "millimeter" in "35 mm camera"
Ex.: "mph" for "miles per hour" in "55 mph"
Ex.: "PDF" for "portable document format"

(c) *Contractions contrasted.* A contracted abbreviation is made by substituting an apostrophe for one or more missing letters (see 1.84). But some contracted forms (such as *Mr.* and *Mrs.*) are traditionally spelled with a period (although in British English *Mr* and *Mrs* predominate).

Ex.: "it's" for "it is"
Ex.: "can't" for "cannot"
Ex.: "ma'am" for "madam"
But: "Dr." for "Doctor"

(d) *With state names.* Use a period after an abbreviated state name in text. Don't use a period after the two-letter postal designation, which should be capitalized (both letters) and used only in addresses.

Ex.: We moved from Fargo, N.Dak., to Nashville, Tenn., in 2018.
Ex.: Send the package to me at 3201 State Street, Nashville, TN 37221.

(e) *With personal names.* Use a period and no space between initials that stand for a personal name. But omit the periods and spaces when abbreviating the entire name. See 4.17(c).

Ex.: J.R.R. Tolkien (not J. R. R. Tolkien)
Ex.: E.D. Hirsch (not E. D. Hirsch)
Ex.: JFK (for John Fitzgerald Kennedy)
Ex.: FDR (for Franklin Delano Roosevelt)

1.73 Avoid periods after letters in an acronym or initialism unless a different style is required by your court's citation rules or some specific convention.

(a) *Modern style.* Don't use periods after acronyms (initial letters pronounced as a word, e.g., NASA) or initialisms (those pronounced as the letters themselves, e.g., IBM).

Exx.: LSAT / EPA / AFL–CIO / SCOTUS / WWW / USCA / Nasdaq

(b) *Conventions.* Demands of style, such as citation conventions, may dictate using periods.

Exx.: U.S. (United States) / U.S. (*United States Reports*)

> "In all composition, . . . the punctuation is as integral and as important a part of what is written as are the words."
> —*Arlo Bates*

Question Marks

1.74 The question mark gives writers little trouble. The only problems may be its use with a rhetorical or indirect question (where it is not appropriate) and inside a sentence to flavor a word, phrase, or clause (where it is). But both constructions are generally too casual for legal writing anyway.

1.75 Use a question mark to end an interrogative sentence.

(a) *Interrogative mood.* A question mark generally signals that the sentence is in the interrogative mood, as opposed to the usual indicative mood.

Ex.: Why should this fact matter?

Ex.: Where is venue proper?

(b) *Interrogative tag.* A tacked-on question at the end of a declaratory sentence requires a question mark to end the entire sentence.

Ex.: It's hot in here, isn't it?

Ex.: You're going to answer my questions, aren't you?

(c) *Declaratory form.* Note that a sentence may have an interrogative meaning but a declaratory form. It is the meaning that matters, not the form.

Ex.: You went back to the office the morning after being fired?

(d) *Multiple endings.* Use a question mark after multiple endings to a question; don't capitalize the beginnings of subsequent ending phrases.

Ex.: Does the biggest share of the blame go to Congress? the President? the people?

(e) *Compound sentence.* In a compound sentence, the nature of the second clause decides the terminal punctuation.

Ex.: I asked you once, is this your gun?

Ex.: Is this your gun?—tell me the truth.

(f) *Indirect question.* Use a period after an indirect question—which is really a type of declarative sentence with an embedded question.

Ex.: Is this your gun? (interrogative)

Ex.: I asked you if this is your gun. (declarative)

1.76 Use a question mark after a questioning word, phrase, or clause contained in the main sentence but separated from it by parentheses or em-dashes.

(a) *Capitalization.* Don't capitalize the first word unless it is a proper noun, the pronoun *I*, or the first word of the main sentence (see 2.4(e), 2.5(b)).

Ex.: This improper (illegal?) activity must end.

Ex.: The easement—you know it's a legal easement, don't you?—gives your neighbor the right to use that road across your property.

Ex.: When?—that's all my client wants to know.

(b) *No second terminal punctuation.* When the independent matter falls at the end of an interrogative sentence, the question mark of the main sentence serves to mark the inserted matter as well.

Ex.: Who will be next to fall for the illegal scheme (will the pyramid collapse before then)?

1.77 Use a question mark in parentheses to indicate uncertainty about what immediately precedes it.

(a) *Dates.* The most common use of the parenthetical question mark is to show that the writer is unsure about what precedes it, especially a name, date, or figure.

Ex.: Murray was born on July 17(?), 1757, in Swatara, Pennsylvania.

If the questionable fact itself appears in parenthetical matter, no parentheses are needed.

Ex.: Harry S. Dent Sr. (1930?–2007) was an architect of the Republican Party's Southern Strategy.

(b) *Not terminal punctuation.* The parenthetical question mark cannot serve as terminal punctuation for the main sentence (see 1.40).

Ex.: The doctrine today is recognized only in Louisiana(?).

Exclamation Marks

1.78 An exclamation mark is rarely justified in legal writing except in a direct quotation. When using one, keep the following conventions in mind.

1.79 Use an exclamation mark to end a sentence that expresses a demand, surprise, danger, stress, or some other intense emotion.

(a) *Generally.* The following examples illustrate the use of exclamation marks (see also 1.69(c)).

Ex. (demand): Police! Open up!

Ex. (surprise/danger): To arms! To arms! The British are coming!

Ex. (stress): You've got to be kidding!

(b) *In place of question mark.* An exclamation mark is sometimes appropriate instead of a question mark after an emotional question.

Ex.: How dare you say that!

1.80 Use an exclamation mark after an exclamatory interjection.

(a) *Generally.* Common exclamatory interjections are *Oh!*, *Hah!*, *Whew!*, and the like, as well as countless profanities. But phrases may be interjections as well.

Ex.: So! Now you're changing your story?

Ex.: For the love of Pete! Why didn't you tell me that before?

(b) *No mark with vocative "O."* The vocative *O*—used to call or invoke something—doesn't take an exclamation mark by itself, although it may be part of an exclamation that does.

Ex.: O Canada

Ex.: O Rising Dawn

Ex.: O tempora! O mores!

1.81 An exclamation mark in parentheses may indicate feigned shock at or mockery of what immediately precedes it.

(a) *Reference.* The relative position of a parenthetical exclamation mark indicates what it refers to: if it abuts a word with no intervening space, it refers only to that word; otherwise, it refers to the whole preceding phrase or clause.

Ex.: The defendant was too generous(!) not to share the opportunity with friends. (The exclamation mark suggests that the writer did not think the defendant's true motive was generosity at all.)

Ex.: Because the environmentalist plaintiffs had not bought tickets to the endangered territories they sought to defend (!), the Supreme Court ruled that they did not have standing to sue. (The exclamation mark suggests that the writer found the Court's reasoning to be absurd; it refers to the preceding clause, not just to the word *defend*.)

(b) *Editorial protest.* An exclamation mark is sometimes used, especially in nonlegal writing, following an oddity or misspelling in a quotation. In legal writing, use "[sic]" instead.

Not this: "I heard footsteps cranching(!) in the snow."

But this: "I heard footsteps cranching [sic] in the snow."

Apostrophes

1.82 Like the hyphen, the apostrophe punctuates a word rather than a sentence. It has two main purposes: to form a possessive and to indicate omitted letters in a contracted abbreviation. It is also sometimes used to form the plural of letters, numbers, abbreviations, and words used as words (rather than for their meaning). In form, it is identical to the single closing quotation mark. It is improperly used as the symbol for the measurement *foot*, which should be designated by a prime (′). Note that many word processors' smart-quote feature will incorrectly insert an opening single quotation mark instead of an apostrophe at the beginning of a word or number; one way to trick it is to type a dummy letter first, type the correct apostrophe, and then delete the dummy letter.

1.83 Use an apostrophe to form the possessive case.

(a) *Generally.* The formation of possessives is dealt with more extensively elsewhere (see 7.11–7.15). In general, if the word doesn't end in *-s*, form the possessive by adding *-'s*. If it is singular and ends in *-s*, add *-'s* unless the result would be truly hard to pronounce. If it is plural and ends in *-s*, add *-'* alone.

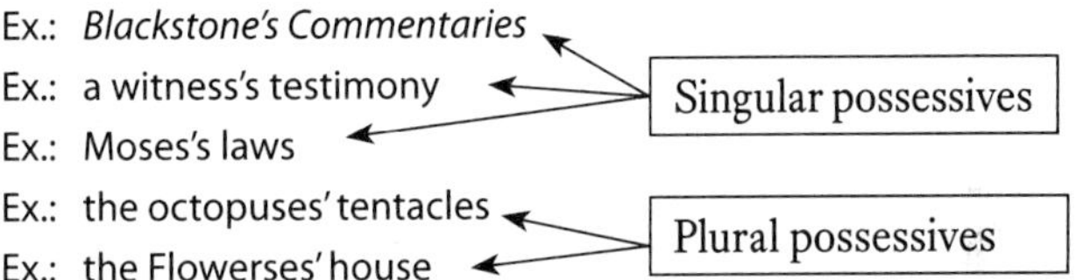

Ex.: *Blackstone's Commentaries*
Ex.: a witness's testimony
Ex.: Moses's laws
Ex.: the octopuses' tentacles
Ex.: the Flowerses' house
Singular possessives
Plural possessives

(b) *Possessive pronouns.* Don't use an apostrophe to form the pronoun possessive *hers*, *its*, *theirs*, *ours*, *yours*, or *whose*. And watch for the misuse of sound-alike contractions *it's* ("it is"), *there's* ("there is"), and *who's* ("who is").

1.84 Use an apostrophe to mark a contraction: it represents omitted letters or numbers.

(a) *Generally.* Contractions are common in case-name citations, and for that reason alone, they are often used in legal writing (see 1.84(c)). For example, *Department* is contracted to *Dep't* in *Bluebook* and *ALWD* style.

> Ex.: *D.C. Fed'n of Civic Ass'ns v. Volpe*, 520 F.2d 451 (D.C. Cir. 1975). (The apostrophes replace *-eratio-* in *Federation* and *-ociatio-* in *Associations* in this *Bluebook*-style citation.)
>
> Ex.: *Nat'l Alt. Fuels Ass'n v. EPA*, 546 U.S. 1025 (2005). (The apostrophes replace *-iona-* in *National* and *-ociatio-* in *Association.*)
>
> Ex.: *Metro. Dev. Comm'n of Marion Cty. v. Pinnacle Media, L.L.C.*, 836 N.E.2d 422 (Ind. 2005). (The apostrophe replaces *-issio-* in *Commission.*)

(b) *In dates.* In informal writing, an apostrophe marks the elision of numerals in a year, where the century is understood.

> Ex.: The senator was first elected in '16. (The apostrophe replaces 20 in 2016.)
>
> Ex.: The Americans with Disabilities Act of 1990 retained and expanded many of the provisions of a '73 statute, the Rehabilitation Act.

(c) *In formal writing.* Contractions (e.g., *it isn't*) have long been shunned in formal prose. But that taboo is fortunately disappearing. Consider how stilted the interrogative *Is it not?* sounds. Because contractions enhance readability and lighten tone, many writers of lawbooks and articles now use them—and some of the most influential judicial stylists also use them routinely.

> Ex.: Contractions aren't the taboo they once were in formal writing. (The apostrophe replaces the *o* in *are not*.)

(d) *Patent references.* Patents are conventionally shortened, after the first reference, to a three-digit form, such as *the '123 patent* (referring to U.S. Patent 6,543,123). Unfortunately, software often converts the apostrophe into a single open quotation mark—*the ‘123 patent*—as if you were going to have a matching end-quote mark. You must override this automated change. Try Shift-Alt-Close Bracket (or Shift-Option-Close Bracket on a Mac) to make a hard apostrophe. Some applications will let you type two apostrophes (the first will be a single open-quote mark, the second a close-quote mark, a.k.a. an apostrophe); then backspace, delete the first mark, forward-space, and continue typing.

1.85 Use an apostrophe (followed by *s*) to form the plural of letters, single-digit numbers, symbols, and some abbreviations.

(a) *Incorrect and correct uses.* The *-'s* is commonly misused to pluralize names (e.g., **the Smith's* should be *the Smiths*). But this form is correct in those limited instances when you need to form the plurals of lowercase letters, capital letters when necessary to avoid a miscue, and single-digit numerals.

> Ex.: Mind your *p*'s and *q*'s.
>
> Ex.: Her reports received A's, the top honor from the law-review awards panel. (The apostrophe distinguished As from the word *As*.) (But: Her report received As, Bs, and Cs from the panel.)
>
> Ex.: How many *0*'s are there in a million? (Better: *How many zeros . . . ?*)

(b) *With abbreviations.* This form is also used with lowercase abbreviations and capitalized abbreviations with periods. With other abbreviations, multiple-digit numbers, and dates, the preferred plural is a simple *-s*.

> Ex.: The speaker addressed the class of newly minted J.D.'s.
>
> Ex.: You will escort the VIPs to the head table.
>
> Ex.: The attorney general was a Detroit prosecutor in the 1980s.
>
> Ex.: The temperature that night was in the lower 20s.

Slashes

1.86 The slash (also called the *diagonal*, *virgule*, or *solidus*) has few uses in formal writing except with dates and fractions. It is best known as the star character in two grammatical abominations: *and/or* and *he/she*. It is especially unfit for

*An invariably inferior form.

legal writing because it is inherently ambiguous: its function may be conjunctive <secretary/treasurer> or disjunctive <a buy/sell decision>.

1.87 Use a slash in a limited number of grammatical conventions; where alternative punctuation is appropriate, avoid the slash.

(a) *Fractions.* Use a slash to separate the numerator from the denominator in a fraction when using numerals (but use a hyphen when the numbers are spelled out: see 1.63(b)).

> Ex.: Each of the eight grandchildren received 1/16th of the estate.

(b) *Dates.* Use a slash to separate the month, day, and year in the informal short-date style; a hyphen works just as well. Avoid using a period—it is harder to read.

> Ex.: The 11/7/2000 election would not be "over" for another month.
>
> Or: The 11-7-2000 election would not be "over" for another month.

(c) *Abbreviations.* Use a slash to denote an abbreviation when convention so dictates.

> Ex.: Recruiting Attorney, c/o Epstein, Honley & Burgess, Harvard Square, Cambridge, MA 02139 (*in care of*)
>
> Ex.: d/b/a (*doing business as*)
>
> Ex.: Do it w/o delay. (*without*)
>
> Ex.: $4,000/year raise (*per*)

(d) *Alternatives.* Use a slash in some paired words to indicate alternatives (*either/or*).

> Ex.: After two days of talking about the evidence, the jurors' guilty/not-guilty vote had not changed.
>
> Ex.: Under the program, students take some courses on a pass/fail basis.

(e) *Double offices.* Use a slash to indicate double roles (*both/and*); an en-dash works as well, and should be preferred.

> Ex.: Phelps was elected secretary/treasurer.
>
> Better: Phelps was elected secretary–treasurer.
>
> Ex.: Schwarz is the firm's top mediator/negotiator.
>
> Better: Schwarz is the firm's top mediator–negotiator.

(f) *Line breaks.* Use a slash to indicate a line break in poetry.

> Ex.: Yet, still we can turn inside out / Old Nature's Constitution, / And bring a Babel back of *names*— / Huzza! for REVOLUTION!

(g) *In examples.* Use a slash to separate examples of word usage.

> Ex.: Oxymorons—e.g., jumbo shrimp / soft rock / random order

Bullets

1.88 Bullets provide an attractive way to present a list of roughly equal elements. They work as well in legal writing as they do in journalism and elsewhere, as long as they're skillfully deployed—as specified in 1.89. Like other types of lists, a bulleted list may comprise single words, phrases, clauses, or sentences, as examples below illustrate. And like other lists, the elements must be parallel in form.

1.89 Use bullets to create visual appeal in setting out important lists.

(a) *With colon.* Unless the lead-in to a bulleted list is phrased as a question (ending, naturally, with a question mark), introduce a bulleted list with a colon. Bulleted items may end with periods or semicolons.

Ex.: Student publications that generate lawsuits fall into three categories:

- School-sponsored newspapers.
- Nonschool or underground newspapers written and distributed by students.
- Materials distributed by students at school but written and published by nonstudents.

(b) *Plain bullets.* For bullets, stick with solid round dots about the size of a lowercase *o*; avoid squares, triangles, diamonds, and Wingdings-type art.

(c) *Hanging indent.* Use hanging indents to make the bullets stand out, and set a small tab margin so that each bullet will be the equivalent of about two characters away from the text.

(d) *Indent list.* Indent the bullets to at least the point on the page where a paragraph indent is, or perhaps slightly to the right of that point.

(e) *Spacing.* Single-space within bulleted points. Add a little extra space between the points.

Ex.: In this factual setting, several policies supported the district court's dismissal without prejudice. The dismissal:

> "When there is no need for identifiers, a simple way to make the items of a list stand out is to separate them by proper spacing and indentation, and to introduce each item with a 'bullet' (•). You should avoid identifiers that serve no specific purpose because the reader instinctively looks for the purpose and may become disoriented when he doesn't find it. Also, unnecessary identifiers are nothing but clutter." —*Ernst Jacobi*

- removed the case from the district court's docket pending the agency appeal;
- preserved the resources of the court and the parties by preventing further discovery and litigation on claims that might not survive the reissue;
- eliminated any prejudice to the accused infringer from the bare existence of the infringement suit; and
- left undisturbed the patentee's opportunity to enforce any patent claims surviving the reissue process.

(f) *Capitalization and punctuation.* Two styles are acceptable. You may capitalize the first word in each bulleted item if the item ends with a period, or else make the first word lowercase and put a semicolon at the end of each item—except, of course, the last, which should end with a period.

(g) *Parallelism.* Keep your items grammatically parallel (all complete sentences, all noun clauses, all verb clauses, etc.).

1.90 Avoid bullets if the subparts marked by them will need to be cited.

(a) *Uncitability.* Bullets are often inappropriate in legal drafting because elements cannot be pinpointed in a later citation. But see Fed. R. App. P. 11(g) for an example of usefully bulleted items.

(b) *Numbers or letters instead.* Instead of a bulleted list, use a numbered or lettered paragraph form in legal drafting if there is a chance that anyone might later need to cite an item in the list (see 1.38).

Diacritical Marks

1.91 Diacritical marks (also called *diacritics*) are orthographical marks that indicate a character's special phonetic quality. They appear most often in foreign languages, but in English some borrowed words (also called *loanwords*) retain their marks. As the terms become fully naturalized, the marks will usually fall into disuse (see 1.92(d)). With borrowed words, you should always consult a current, reliable desktop dictionary to check if a term has retained its diacritical mark, foreign plural, or italics.

1.92 Learn the common diacritical marks, and for borrowed words, make a habit of consulting a reliable dictionary.

(a) *Most common marks.* To the extent that modern readers encounter diacritical marks, the ones they'll see most often are:

- **acute accent** (´): This mark generally indicates a stressed syllable or rising inflection. It sometimes shows that a final syllable is not silent, especially in words imported from French <flambé> <résumé>.
- **cedilla** (¸): This mark appears under the French and Portuguese *c* when the letter is to be pronounced as an *s* rather than as a *k* <façade>. Generally the cedilla is quickly dropped in English-language contexts.
- **diaeresis [umlaut]** (¨): The diaeresis sometimes appears in English over the second of two adjacent vowels to indicate that the vowel is treated as a separate syllable <Chloë> <naïve>. It appears in several Indo-European languages but is generally associated with German (in which it is termed an *umlaut*). An umlaut indicates that the vowel has a modified sound <Münster>.
- **grave accent** (`): In ancient Greek, this mark signaled a lower inflection, in contrast to the higher one called for by the acute accent. In English, the grave is rarer than the acute accent, but it does appear on occasion to indicate a falling inflection or that a final syllable is to be pronounced separately <cursèd> <blessèd>. The grave accent is used with all the vowels in Italian and sometimes used in French over the vowels *a*, *e*, and *u*.
- **tilde** (˜): This mark indicates that an *n* takes a palatalized sound <señor>. Tildes are common in Spanish but are not used in American English.

(b) *Other marks.* Other common marks include:

- **breve** (˘): This mark, used most commonly in pronunciations, indicates that a vowel is short or unstressed </ lĕt/>.
- **circumflex** (ˆ): This mark was used over vowels in ancient Greek to indicate a rising-falling tone. Today it appears most commonly over French vowels after which an *-s-* was once elided <côte (our *coast*)> <fête (our *feast*)>. The circumflex is now in retreat even in French print sources
- **macron** (¯): This mark, used most commonly in pronunciations, indicates that a vowel is long </bēt/>.
- **okina** (ʻ): This character (also called a *hamzah*) appears mostly in the Arabic and Hawaiian languages. It marks the glottal stop in the Hawaiian language and is sometimes carried over into English contexts <Hawaiʻi>.

(c) *With names.* Use diacritical marks in names in conventional ways—for example, in a person's name however the person prefers.

Ex.: Apollonia Poilâne

Ex.: Renée Zellweger

Ex.: Chloë Sevigny

(d) *Garner's Law of Loanwords.* The more arcane or technical a loanword (i.e., a word borrowed from another language), the more likely it is to retain a foreign plural, diacritical marks, and italics; the more common it becomes, the more likely it is to lose them. Corollary: if the loanword becomes widespread, it typically loses italics first, diacritical marks second, and a foreign plural last. In cases of real doubt, err on the side of anglicization.

Not this: hôtel; façade; coördinate

But this: hotel; facade; coordinate

> "Good writing seems to punctuate itself. That is because writing still derives much of its rhythm, word patterning, and emphasis from millennia of oral communication, during which commas, periods, and semicolons simply did not exist. Orators relied on breath patterns, inflections, and pauses of different lengths to group words into meaningful units."
>
> —*Cecilia Friend, Don Challenger & Katherine C. McAdams*

§ 2
Capitalization

2.1 The modern trend is toward less capitalization. Most commonly, capitals either (1) begin a sentence or (2) designate a proper noun or the pronoun *I*. But lawyers, like other specialized writers, capitalize some words by convention: *Court*, for example, to designate the U.S. Supreme Court, the high court of any jurisdiction, or the very court they are addressing.

Legal writing also makes liberal use of defined terms, typically designated in parentheses and perhaps quotation marks immediately after the first use of the full name. A contract may refer throughout to *Buyer* and *Seller*, for example. Once defined, the term is treated as a proper noun and is capitalized.

Capitalization is important in headings as well. The use of all caps in a short, centered heading might signal the beginning of a main section. (A competent stylist never uses all caps for a long heading.) The hierarchy of subheadings may be signaled in a variety of ways, and some writers like to use different styles of capitalization to signal subheadings. Even so, a coherent numbering system is easier for the reader to understand at a glance than variations in capitalization. The two techniques used together are most efficient.

Some writers overuse capitalization for emphasis. That's bad style. All-caps text is less legible than lowercase text, so the message (*"READ THIS!"*) conflicts with the medium (*"DON'T READ THIS!"*).

For rules on capitalizing names relating to race, religion, and national or geographic origin, see 13.5(n).

2.2 Use lowercase unless a rule calls for capitalization.

(a) *Down-style vs. up-style.* Although styles of capitalization have varied over time, the prevailing trend among professional editors is toward a down-style—one in which words are capitalized sparingly. Up-style, by contrast, capitalizes many words (even, in headings, most or all of them). Down-style is easier to read: it emphasizes only words that require emphasis, according to standards set by rule. In legal writing, there is an unfortunate tendency toward contagious capitalization. It is a reversible condition.

(b) *Quotations exception.* If a quoted passage contains an oddly capitalized word, reproduce it precisely as in the original (but see 1.43(a)). You may choose to note quirky capitalization in citing the source, though preferably without sarcasm.

> Ex.: "No Person shall be a Senator who shall not have attained the Age of thirty Years, and been nine Years a Citizen of the United States, and who shall not, when elected, be an Inhabitant of that State for which he shall be chosen." U.S. Const. art. I, § 3, cl. 3.

Ex.: "Dominguez urges the Court to 'order a Bifurcated Trial of Paulsen's affirmative defences of Laches and the Statute of Limitations.'" (Dom. Br. at 4 (capitalization in original).)

(c) *Consistency.* Make decisions about capitalization based on logic and established conventions. With names, take account of the preference of the person or company whose name it is. Once you've decided whether to capitalize, be consistent within each piece of writing and its related documents. If a term is capitalized in a contract, for example, don't make it lowercase in a related addendum or schedule.

2.3 Capitalize the first word in a sentence.

(a) *Names.* If a name that isn't usually capitalized <de la Rosa> or is idiosyncratically capitalized <iPad> appears at the beginning of a sentence, the first character should be capitalized.

Ex.: De la Rosa will race with Team Jaguar.

Ex.: IPad rumors were circulating before the trade show opened.

(b) *Sentence in a sentence.* The first word of a sentence inside a sentence may be capitalized for clarity, unless it is enclosed in parentheses (see 1.76(a)).

Ex.: We agreed to the settlement—It was more than we had expected, after all!—and shook hands.

But: We agreed to the settlement (it was more than we had expected, after all!) and shook hands.

(c) *Lines of poems.* Capitalize the first word in each line of poetry, even if the line breaks are indicated by slashes (see 1.87(f)).

Ex.: The woods are lovely, dark and deep.
But I have promises to keep,
And miles to go before I sleep,
And miles to go before I sleep.

Ex.: "Theirs not to make reply, / Theirs not to reason why, / Theirs but to do and die."

2.4 Capitalize the first word of a direct quotation if it is a full sentence and is formally introduced. Don't capitalize if it is a partial sentence, is grammatically woven into the main sentence, or is introduced by the conjunction *that*. Don't capitalize an indirect quotation.

(a) *Direct quotation.* The first word of a quoted sentence retains its initial capitalization. If the quotation is split by an attribution, don't capitalize the second part.

Ex.: When he was arrested, the defendant blurted out, "Man, some other dude did it!"

Ex.: "The only thing we have to fear," Roosevelt exhorted the nation, "is fear itself."

(b) *Partial sentence.* Don't capitalize a direct quotation that isn't a complete sentence.

Ex.: When arrested, the defendant said that "some other dude" did it.

Ex.: Fear itself, Roosevelt said, is "[t]he only thing we have to fear."

(c) *Sentence parts.* Don't capitalize part of a direct quotation that is woven into the syntax of the sentence, unless another capitalization rule applies.

Ex.: The manager was always "in a conference," or had "just stepped out of the office," according to the secretary.

(d) *Following "that."* Don't capitalize a quoted sentence if it follows the conjunction *that* in the main sentence.

Ex.: When he was arrested, the defendant blurted out that "some other dude did it!"

Ex.: Roosevelt told the nation that "[t]he only thing we have to fear is fear itself."

But: Roosevelt exhorted the nation: "The only thing we have to fear is fear itself."

(e) *Indirect quotation.* Don't capitalize an indirect quotation unless another capitalization rule applies.

Ex.: The secretary said that the manager was in a conference.

Ex.: My supervisor said I should reread both depositions.

(f) *Capitalization of original.* Use brackets to change the capitalization of the first word of a quotation if it is changed from the original (see 1.43(a)).

Ex.: Churchill warned: "[A]n iron curtain has descended across the continent."

2.5 Capitalize the first word in a direct question, rule, slogan, or motto, even if it does not begin the sentence.

(a) *Direct question.* Because a direct question is a sentence apart from the main sentence that contains it, always capitalize its first word. Set off the question with a comma, an em-dash, or a colon. If you use a colon, whether to capitalize depends on whether it introduces a direct question or a declaratory statement (including an indirect question) (see 1.23).

Ex.: And the petitioners' silence on this point raises another question: On what authority do they further ask for a setoff against the judgment?

But: And the petitioners' silence on this point raises another question, about on what authority they further ask for a setoff against the judgment.

Ex.: I need to call my lawyer—What's that number again?

Ex.: It makes you wonder, How can the State prove intent?

(b) *Indirect question distinguished.* Because an indirect question is a declaratory statement, it doesn't call for a question mark, so don't capitalize its first word.

Ex.: I need to ask my lawyer how I should plead.

Ex.: She asked whether we had been anywhere near the scene of the crime.

Ex.: He wondered whether anyone had seen him.

(c) *Rules, slogans, and mottoes.* Treat a rule, slogan, or motto appearing within another sentence as you would a direct question, capitalizing the first letter and setting it off with a comma, em-dash, or colon.

Ex.: Every child knows the Golden Rule: Do unto others as you would have them do unto you.

Ex.: When campaigns go into damage-control mode, they often forget the First Rule of Holes—When you're in one, stop digging.

2.6 Capitalize proper nouns—usually, the names of people and places or the titles of statutes, books, articles, and the like.

(a) *Common and proper nouns.* If a word or phrase may be either a proper noun or a common noun, capitalize it only when the context calls for a proper noun. Otherwise, make it lowercase.

Ex.: Oregon's legislature passed the Married Women's Property Act in 1866. (The article *the* signals that the phrase is being used as a proper noun, the name of a specific statute.)

Ex.: Seven states passed a married-women's-property act in that seven-year period. (The article *a* signals that the phrase refers to a class of statutes.)

(b) *Trademarks.* Trademarked names of products are capitalized proper nouns. Don't use trademark symbols in text (see 6.6).

Ex.: Coca-Cola

Ex.: Kleenex

(c) *Artwork.* Capitalize the title of an artistic work.

Ex.: Whistler's *Arrangement in Grey and Black: Portrait of the Painter's Mother*

Ex.: Bach's *Toccata and Fugue in D minor*

(d) *Midword capitals.* Use midword capitals if that is the style of a company or product name.

Ex.: PowerPoint

Ex.: ExxonMobil

(e) *Proper-noun phrases.* When two or more proper nouns that end with an ordinarily generic common noun are used in a series, don't capitalize the shared generic word. It can sometimes be advisable, however, to repeat the singular noun, in which case the noun must be capitalized.

Ex.: Main and Elm streets

Ex.: the Mississippi and Missouri rivers

Ex.: the Agriculture and Judiciary committees

Ex.: the Ways and Means and Rules committees

Better: the Ways and Means Committee and the Rules Committee

(f) *Old writings.* Formerly, as in the U.S. Constitution, important nouns were mostly capitalized at the writer's discretion. Today only proper nouns are capitalized in text, reflecting the modern trend toward less capitalization in general.

2.7 Capitalize short-form proper nouns.

(a) *Full and short names.* Legal writers frequently refer first to a full name and then to a shortened name. The shortened form may be a common noun that refers to a specific governmental entity or officer—or to a corporate entity. When that is so, capitalize the noun.

Ex.: Farmers Home Administration (on later reference, the Administration)

Following are some of the nouns that most frequently fall into this category:

Academy	Commissioner	District	School
Administration	Committee	Division	Secretary
Administrator	Commonwealth	Federation	Service
Association	Company	Foundation	State
Authority	Cooperative	Government	Subcommittee
Board	Corporation	Hospital	Superintendent
Bureau	Council	Institute	System
City	County	Institution	Township
College	Department	Partnership	Union
Commission	Director	Railroad	University

(b) *Specific governmental acts.* When you're referring to a particular governmental act that contains one of the following words, and you're using the word as a short form on a subsequent reference, capitalize:

Act	Charter	Pact	Resolution
Amendment	Code	Proclamation	Statute
Article	Doctrine	Regulation	Survey
Bill	Ordinance	Report	Treaty

(c) *The term "rule."* Capitalize *rule* when referring to a particular rule by number, but not when the number is absent.

Ex.: Rule 32

Ex.: The rule also specifies what type sizes are permitted.

2.8 Follow established conventions in capitalizing adjectives formed from proper nouns.

(a) *Exclusively proper nouns.* Capitalize adjectives derived from words that exist only as proper nouns.

Ex.: American

Ex.: Holmesian

Ex.: Marxist

(b) *Nonexclusive nouns.* When a word doesn't exist exclusively as a proper noun, don't capitalize the adjective derived from it.

Ex.: congressional (but *Congress*)

Ex.: constitutional (but *U.S. Constitution*)

Ex.: presidential (but *President Lincoln*)

(c) *Nonexclusive adjectives.* Some proper adjectives are used in phrases that have an independent common meaning; these are usually set in lowercase, depending on established usage. For example, one person may write *french fries* while another person writes *French fries*. Both are correct. Consult a current desktop dictionary to see whether a usage has become standard. If both capitalized and uncapitalized forms are in use, choose one and apply it consistently throughout your writing. When in doubt, use lowercase.

Ex.: brussels sprouts (often made *Brussels sprouts*)

Ex.: plaster of Paris (often made *plaster of paris*)

Ex.: diesel fuel

2.9 Capitalize defined terms.

(a) *Convention.* The established convention in legal writing is to capitalize defined terms to show that they've been defined and that they're being used with a specific meaning.

> "Absolute consistency in the use of capitals is impossible of achievement because of the many rules, the many exceptions to the rules, and the many instances when it is difficult to determine whether a rule or an exception applies." —*Paul M. Dwyer*

Ex.: George P. Whitley (Seller) agrees to sell John Inman (Buyer) a 1968 Volkswagen Minivan (Van) for the sum of $1,000. Buyer agrees that the Van is offered for sale "as is," with no warranties expressed or implied by Seller.

Ex.: In August 2018, the Agency's administrative law judge (ALJ) terminated the suspensions. But the ALJ declined to void the suspensions *ab initio*, and the Secretary affirmed this decision.

(b) *Syntax*. Define terms in a way that will preserve natural usage on subsequent references.

Ex.: First National Bank (the Bank) agrees to lend . . . . Further, the Bank agrees . . . .

Ex.: The Buyer further agrees to pay the Seller an additional $25 late charge if any payment remains unpaid ten days after the Due Date.

(c) *Emphasis and clarity*. Capitalization makes a defined term stand out. It may also help to avoid ambiguity if a similar term is used in the writing. Note, however, that abundant capitalization is off-putting.

Ex.: On Saturday the Developer promised that the house would be completed in the following week. (Here, *Developer* is a defined term. It may be a party or someone whose action is relevant to the facts of the case. The term will appear more than once in this document.)

Ex.: The developer lost photographs that would have documented the storm damage. (Here, the term *developer* refers to someone whose action is more incidental to the case. The term may not come up again in this document.)

2.10 Capitalize up-style headings—those not forming complete sentences (see 2.2(a)).

(a) *Styles*. Although some writers still prefer to capitalize every word in an up-style heading, the dominant modern style is to capitalize main words but to leave many other words lowercase (see 2.10(b)).

Old style: States And The Rights Of Citizens

New style: States and the Rights of Citizens

(b) *Uncapitalized words and exceptions*. Unless it is the first or last word in the heading, or immediately follows a colon, don't capitalize (1) an article, (2) a conjunction or preposition shorter than five letters, or (3) the word *to* in an infinitive. But do capitalize (1) prepositions when used adverbially in verb phrases, (2) prepositions at the beginning of hyphenated phrases, and (3) the preposition *with* if *without* also appears in the heading.

Ex.: False Statements on Stock-Performance Report
(*on* is a short preposition)

But: False Statements About Stock Performance
(*about* is longer than four letters)

Ex.: Going up the Mountain
(*up* is a short preposition)

But: Dissolution and Winding Up a Business Enterprise
(*up* in the term of art *Winding Up* is not a preposition)

Ex.: Walking off the Stage
(*off* is a short preposition)

But: An Off-the-Cuff Remark
(*off* is capitalized as part of the longer phrase *off-the-cuff*)

Ex.: Deciding to Proceed with Trial
(*with* is a short preposition)

But: Deciding to Proceed With or Without Counsel
(*with* is coupled with the longer *without*; both are capitalized)

(c) *Hyphenated and open compounds.* Always capitalize the first element. Capitalize each following element unless (1) it's an article or a short preposition or coordinating conjunction (shorter than five letters), or (2) the first element is a prefix and the second element isn't a proper noun or proper adjective. If a heading ends with a compound, other than one with a hyphenated prefix, capitalize the final element.

Ex.: Run-of-the-Mill Cases in Property Law

Ex.: Self-defense Arguments in Tort Cases
(*defense* is a common noun not capitalized after the prefix *self-*)

Ex.: In-House Counsel in Merger Negotiations
(*house* is capitalized because it's a compound word with *in*, and *in* is capitalized because it's the first word of the heading)

Ex.: Pre-Christian Legal Systems
(*Christian* is capitalized as a proper noun, even with the prefix *pre-*)

Ex.: Remedies for Quasi-contracts
(*contracts* is a common noun not capitalized after the prefix *quasi-*.)

Ex.: Strategic Run-Arounds to Be Dealt With
(*with* is capitalized here as the last word of the heading)

(d) *Not for point headings.* Don't—*don't*—use initial caps for point headings in briefs: use full-sentence headings in the argument section with the normal down-style. Although practicing lawyers commonly make the mistake of using initial caps, commonness doesn't make it correct. It's a mistake nevertheless. A competent set of point headings looks like this:

> The United States did not take petitioner's property. Any incremental flooding of the petitioner's floodplain lands caused by the Corps' operational decisions was not a taking because it was temporary, and this Court has consistently held that temporary flooding of riparian lands is not a taking.
>
> A. The court of appeals applied a test developed and settled by this Court nearly a century ago.
>
> B. This Court's flooding cases are foundational and have generated substantial reliance interests.
>
> C. This Court's distinction between temporary and permanent flooding is sound and practical.
>
> D. Petitioner's arguments for abandoning this Court's approach to temporary flooding are unpersuasive.

2.11 Make initialisms and acronyms (words and abbreviated names formed from the initials or parts of other words) all caps unless an exception applies.

(a) *Generally.* In American English, all-caps spelling is usual for terms such as *IRA* ("individual retirement account"). In British English, an initial cap is common (e.g., *Ira*).

Ex.: NATO (North American Treaty Organization, often written *Nato* in British English)

Ex.: DOJ (Department of Justice)

(b) *Proper-name acronyms.* In general, respect institutional preferences about capitalizing abbreviated names. It is permissible to use caps and lowercase to write a name that is an acronym (sounded as a single word), especially if the acronym is longer than four letters. Nevertheless, initialisms (sounded as individual letters) are uniformly written in all caps.

Ex.: UNICEF (or, less commonly, Unicef)—the acronym is sounded as a single word.

Ex.: Nasdaq—the acronym is sounded as a single word and commonly written with just the initial cap.

Ex.: NAACP—the initialism is sounded out letter by letter.

(c) *Generic common nouns.* Some acronyms have become common words. These are always lowercase unless a rule requires them to be capitalized (e.g., as part of a title).

Ex.: laser (light amplification by stimulated emission of radiation)

Ex.: radar (radio detecting and ranging)

(d) *State abbreviations vs. USPS designations.* Use all caps for states' two-letter postal codes in mailing addresses, but elsewhere use traditional abbreviations with only the first letters of each part of the name capitalized.

Ex.: Commonwealth Court of Pennsylvania
624 Irvis Office Building
Harrisburg, PA 17120

Not this: The hearing was held in Spokane, WA.

But this: The hearing was held in Spokane, Wash.

Better: The hearing was held in Spokane, Washington.

(e) *False acronyms.* Don't capitalize all the characters in so-called false acronyms—words in which the characters don't stand for other words.

Ex.: fax or Fax (if otherwise requiring a capital), never FAX.

2.12 Capitalize the word *court* in reference to (1) the United States Supreme Court; (2) the highest tribunal in the jurisdiction whose laws govern the outcome, such as a state supreme court; and (3) the court you're addressing, even if it is the lowest court within its jurisdiction.

(a) *Deference.* Capitalize the word *court* when addressing the tribunal that is handling the matter at hand.

Ex.: The Court will be deciding a question of first impression in this jurisdiction.

(b) *Lower courts.* When referring to any other court by a partial name, or to lower courts in general, don't capitalize the word *court.*

Ex.: the court below

Ex.: federal court

Ex.: probate court

Ex.: trial court

2.13 Capitalize a geographic term if it is part of a proper name or, by custom, if it denotes a well-defined region or area, but not if it merely denotes a direction or position.

(a) *Compass points.* Use lowercase for a compass point, unless it is part of a proper name or a regional term widely accepted and understood as an unofficial title or designation.

Ex.: north, south, east, west

Ex.: the American South

Ex.: Northwest Passage

Ex.: the West (i.e., the United States and western Europe)

Ex.: the south of France

(b) *Positions.* Capitalize a term that merely indicates position only if it is part of a proper name.

Ex.: Central Park

Ex.: Left Bank (Paris)

Ex.: right fork of the Colorado River

(c) *Descriptive or identifying terms.* Don't capitalize a term that doesn't apply to only one entity or isn't commonly used as a proper name.

Ex.: South American continent

Ex.: Brazilian rainforest

Ex.: polar region

(d) *Political divisions.* Unless it is part of a proper name, don't capitalize a political-division term such as *state*, *county*, *city*, or *republic*.

Ex.: the Chelmsford city limits

Ex.: New York City

Ex.: New England states

Ex.: State of Maine

(e) *Topographical names.* Don't capitalize a topographical name when it is used descriptively, but capitalize it when using it as part of a name or as a geographical denotation.

Ex.: Hudson River Valley

Ex.: the watershed valley of the Hudson River

Ex.: Florida peninsula

Ex.: Rocky Mountains

Ex.: Mississippi Delta

Ex.: the continent (referring to any continent)

Ex.: the Continent (referring specifically to the European Continent)

2.14 Capitalize calendar terms that are proper nouns, but not those that are generic terms.

(a) *Days and months.* Capitalize the proper names of the days of the week and the months of the year, but not generic terms.

Ex.: Tuesday, November 12, 2018

Ex.: a May–September romance

Ex.: working for the weekend

(b) *Seasons.* Lowercase the names of the seasons (but see 2.17(c)).

Ex.: the spring semester

Ex.: my winter coat

Ex.: in summer 2018

(c) *Holidays.* Capitalize the names of holidays, whether secular or religious.

Ex.: the Fourth of July

Ex.: New Year's Day

Ex.: Good Friday

Ex.: Passover

Ex.: Ramadan

2.15 Capitalize titles of honor or respect.

(a) *Title before name.* Capitalize a civil, religious, military, professional, or noble title that immediately precedes a person's name.

Ex.: Chairman Kaga

Ex.: President George Washington

Ex.: General Schwarzkopf

Ex.: King Faisal

Ex.: Justice Elena Kagan

Ex.: Assistant Secretary of State for Human Rights John Shattuck

Ex.: Representatives Kaptur and Granger

(b) *Title not before name.* Capitalize a title that immediately follows a person's name or that substitutes for a name only if it identifies a head or assistant head of state, a head or assistant head of an existing or a proposed national governmental unit, a diplomatic title, a ruler, or royalty. Don't capitalize other titles used similarly.

Ex.: the President is at Camp David (always capitalize *President* when referring to the U.S. President)

Ex.: Tony Blair, Prime Minister of the United Kingdom

Ex.: John Nance Garner, Vice President under Franklin Roosevelt

Ex.: Don Glazier, president of AdLuc Technologies

Ex.: John Shattuck, who was assistant secretary of state for human rights in the 1990s

Ex.: John Cornyn, senator from Texas

(c) *In addresses.* Always capitalize a title when it stands alone in an address.

Ex.: Mr. John Shattuck
Assistant Secretary of State for Human Rights
U.S. Department of State
2201 C Street NW
Washington, DC 20520

(d) *Titles in second person.* Capitalize titles, especially honorifics, when used in the second person or in direct address.

Ex.: Your Honor

Ex.: Madam Chair

Ex.: Mr. Secretary

(e) *Job titles.* Don't capitalize job descriptions, even when used before names.

Ex.: the basketball player LeBron James

Ex.: coach of the University of Texas football team

Ex.: LaWanda Anton, presiding juror

(f) *Parties.* In legal writing, the terms *plaintiff, defendant, appellant, appellee, petitioner, respondent,* and the like are sometimes used as quasi-titles for the litigants. If such a term is used before or instead of the party's name, and the term isn't preceded by *the*, capitalize it. Even so, the preferable style is to identify the party by name if possible.

Ex.: When Plaintiff Burke asked where the car was, Defendant McArthur claimed . . . .

Ex.: When Plaintiff asked where the car was, Defendant claimed . . . .

Ex.: When the plaintiff asked where the car was, the defendant claimed . . . .

Better: When Burke asked where the car was, McArthur claimed . . . .

But: Defendants are all liable for the damage to Burke's car. (With three or more parties on one side, naming each individually can be unwieldy.)

Generally, reserve capitalized procedural labels for litigants in the very case in which you're involved. When referring to the procedural roles of parties in other cases, as when discussing cited authority, use lowercase labels preceded by *the*. (Again, after establishing the party's role in the case, prefer the party's name to a procedural label in subsequent references.) Likewise, don't capitalize references to procedural roles generally, as when discussing rules or caselaw relating to matters of procedure.

Ex.: The respondent in *Magnut*, Gizmo Enterprises, ...

Ex.: California courts have consistently held that an appellee must not . . . .

(g) *Other cases.* When discussing a legal precedent, don't capitalize words such as *plaintiff*, *defendant*, and *court* (unless it is a court designated in 2.12).

Ex.: The court denied the defendant's motion for a judgment as a matter of law.

2.16 Capitalize a word or phrase that denotes an important epoch or historical event.

(a) *Generally.* Epochs and events can be historical, political, cultural, or economic; they're treated as proper names.

Ex.: the Renaissance

Ex.: Prohibition

Ex.: Roosevelt's New Deal

Ex.: South Sea Bubble

(b) *Numerical designations.* Unless it's part of a proper name, don't capitalize the numerical designation of a period.

Ex.: twentieth century

Ex.: Fourth Dynasty Egypt

(c) *Generic terms.* Don't capitalize common phrases with such words as *age* and *period* that frequently apply to more than one distinct era.

> "Never set headlines using capital initials and lowercase on every word—unless your intention is to create visual hiccups. This is a bad and outmoded convention left over from nineteenth-century newspapering days."
>
> —*Jan V. White*

Ex.: the golden age of film

Ex.: India's colonial period

But: the Bronze Age

2.17 Capitalize the name of anything personified.

(a) *Proper-name substitutes.* Capitalize common nouns and adjectives used in popular descriptive epithets for a person.

Ex.: the Old Pretender (James II of England)

Ex.: the Father of Our Country (George Washington)

Ex.: the Great Emancipator (Abraham Lincoln)

Ex.: the Great Dissenter (Justice Oliver Wendell Holmes)

(b) *Fictitious names.* A common noun may be combined with a human name to create a fictitious or unidentified person.

Ex.: Jim Crow

Ex.: John Barleycorn

Ex.: Jane Doe

(c) *Vividness.* Capitalize a vivid personification to distinguish it from its ordinary usage, especially if it is an abstraction that is given human qualities (see 2.14(b)).

Ex.: We are all architects of Fate.

Ex.: When Spring waves her wand, Winter is banished.

But: The spring semester begins after the winter break.

2.18 Capitalize to show irony or mockery.

(a) *Emphasis.* In some contexts, capitalize to give special stress to a word or phrase.

Ex.: After three years of intensely battling the law-school dragon, the lawyer-candidate is confronted by the Dreaded Bar Exam.

Ex.: The defendant wants to blame everything on the Big Bad Government.

(b) *Caution.* Use this device sparingly. A few instances heighten the effect, but overuse dulls the impact.

2.19 Avoid all-caps and initial-caps writing.

(a) *History.* Before computers became the ubiquitous office tools they are today, documents were prepared on typewriters with few or no type options. The only ways to make portions of a writing stand out were to underline them, to set them in all capital letters, or to use initial caps. Now, with computers that can readily produce boldfaced and italic type, all-caps text isn't necessary—or desirable.

(b) *All-caps unreadability.* A passage of text written in all caps is hard to read because the uniform height of the characters makes them indistinct. The ascenders and descenders of lowercase letters give common words distinctive shapes that help readers recognize them.

Not this: AS A SPECIFIC BARGAIN INDUCEMENT FOR CREDITOR TO EXTEND CREDIT TO DEBTOR, AND AFTER HAVING THE OPPORTUNITY TO CONSULT COUNSEL, EACH PARTY HEREBY EXPRESSLY WAIVES THE RIGHT TO TRIAL BY JURY IN ANY LAWSUIT OR PROCEEDING RELATING TO THIS AGREEMENT OR ARISING IN ANY WAY FROM THE OBLIGATIONS.

But this: As a specific bargain inducement for Creditor to extend credit to Debtor, and after having the opportunity to consult counsel, each party hereby expressly waives the right to trial by jury in any lawsuit or proceeding relating to this Agreement or arising in any way from the Obligations.

(c) *Initial-caps unreadability.* An extremely short passage, such as a title, may be marginally easier to read when written with initial capitals. But even capitalizing initial letters has drawbacks: the capitals are distracting, it becomes hard to identify defined terms (see 2.9), and a full sentence printed with initial caps becomes almost impossible to read as a sentence (one's eyes keep stopping). Reserve this style for headings of a few words—never for complete-sentence point headings.

Not this: Under Well-Settled Principles of Patent Exhaustion, Pharmagen's Authorized Sale of One Article Embodying a Patented Invention Does Not Exhaust the Patentee's Exclusive Right to Control the Creation of Other Articles Embodying the Same Invention.

But this: Under well-settled principles of patent exhaustion, Pharmagen's authorized sale of one article embodying a patented invention does not exhaust the patentee's exclusive right to control the creation of other articles embodying the same invention.

The inept legal writer not only uses initial-caps for point headings but also executes that style incorrectly—violating the established principles about lowercasing certain words (see 2.10(b)).

(d) *Limited capitals.* A similar passage written with some initial capitalization using the rules in this chapter is much clearer than full up-style.

Ex.: Under the Act and its well-settled principles of patent exhaustion as outlined by the Office, Pharmagen's authorized sale of one article embodying the patented Invention does not exhaust Patentee's exclusive right to control the creation of other articles embodying the Invention.

(e) *Different font.* Instead of using all caps, you might make a critical passage in a contract stand out by changing the font. For example, if you're using a serif font such as Times New Roman, try using a sans-serif font such as

Helvetica to draw attention to an important provision. You might also set it in boldface (but see 3.13). Or you might set the provision in a box.

Ex.: **As a specific bargain inducement for Creditor to extend credit to Debtor, and after having the opportunity to consult counsel, each party hereby expressly waives the right to trial by jury in any lawsuit or proceeding relating to this Agreement or arising in any way from the Obligations.**

Ex.:

As a specific bargain inducement for Creditor to extend credit to Debtor, and after having the opportunity to consult counsel, each party hereby expressly waives the right to trial by jury in any lawsuit or proceeding relating to this Agreement or arising in any way from the Obligations.

(f) *Limited all caps.* If you must use all caps, limit them to one line.

Ex.: STATEMENT OF FACTS

Ex.: BILSKY'S SUMMARY-JUDGMENT MOTION

2.20 Use caps and small caps (uppercase letters about as small as most lowercase letters) when a citation-system rule or other directive requires them or when the usage is conventional.

(a) *Dates and eras.* Some abbreviations are conventionally set in small caps with periods, though other styles are also common. For example, although the predominant style for times of day is lowercase with periods <a.m.; p.m.>, the traditional style for eras is small caps with periods <B.C.; A.D.; B.C.E.; C.E.>. But other styles are common for both types of abbreviations, with or without periods and, for eras, all caps. Follow an established style guide or your employer's preference, but be consistent.

Ex.: 9:30 a.m.

Ex.: A.D. 476

Ex.: 33 B.C.

Ex.: 2018 C.E. (C.E. and B.C.E. refer to the same eras as B.C. and A.D. The abbreviations stand for *common era* and *before common era,* respectively, and are common in historical and technical writing.)

(b) *Other abbreviations.* Styles used for other abbreviations also vary widely. In general, abbreviations of common-noun phrases are usually lowercase, while those of names are always capitalized <mpg; DOD>. But small caps are also used in some styles and for some purposes—for example, they are less obtrusive for academic and professional abbreviations after a person's name <Terry Shaw, M.D.>. Because capitalization and punctuation styles vary widely, rely on a current-edition dictionary for consistency.

(c) *Never in main text.* Most law reviews that follow *Bluebook* style use caps and small caps, roman type, and italics in citations. Don't use caps and small caps in text, except perhaps for short headings.

(d) *Periodical titles.* In a *Bluebook*-style and *ALWD*-style law-review citation, set the name of any periodical (e.g., newspaper, magazine, journal) in caps and small caps. Italicize the article's title (in caps and lowercase) but not the periodical's.

Ex.: 83 MINN. L. REV. 1337.

Ex.: NEWSWEEK, Jan. 8, 2018.

Ex.: 135 CONG. REC. H1811.

(e) *Book titles.* In a *Bluebook*-style and *ALWD*-style law-review citation, set a book's title and author's name in caps and small caps. Give the page number and, in parentheses, the year of publication, but don't include the publisher's name unless it is a work published by someone other than the original publisher. For an encyclopedia (such as *Corpus Juris Secundum* or *American Jurisprudence*), set the title in caps and small caps, with no publishing information other than the year. Italicize the title of a shorter work within a collection and set it in caps and lowercase.

Ex.: BLACK'S LAW DICTIONARY (10th ed. 2014).

Ex.: HANS J. WOLFF, ROMAN LAW 45 (1951).

Ex.: 60 AM. JUR. 2D *Patents* § 1003 (2013).

(f) *Authors.* In a *Bluebook*-style and *ALWD*-style law-review citation, set the name of a book's author in caps and small caps, even when citing a work within a larger book. But if the author of the shorter work isn't the author of the book, put the author's name in roman type.

Ex.: KARL LLEWELLYN, THE BRAMBLE BUSH 56 (1930; repr. 1951).

Ex.: CLARENCE DARROW, *The Skeleton in the Closet* 235, *in* VERDICTS OUT OF COURT (Arthur & Lila Weinberg eds., 1963).

Ex.: Felix Frankfurter, *The Case of Sacco and Vanzetti* 115, *in* 2 THE WORLD OF LAW (Ephraim London ed., 1960).

> "The first rule a child learns when beginning to write is, Start each sentence with a capital letter. Few other rules about capitalization are so simple to remember or so easy to apply. But sometimes a sentence has more than one 'first' word, the first sentence of this paragraph being one example."
>
> —*New York Public Library Writer's Guide to Style and Usage*

(g) *Codes, statutes, and rules.* In a *Bluebook*-style and *ALWD*-style law-review citation, set the titles of uniform acts, model codes, statutes, rules of evidence or procedure, and the like in caps and small caps.

Ex.: RESTATEMENT (SECOND) OF TORTS § 918 (1979).

Ex.: UNIF. PROBATE CODE § 2–706 (amended 1993).

Ex.: FED. R. CIV. P. 11.

2.21 Follow any special rules that may require caps and small caps.

(a) *Court rules.* Some courts prescribe caps and small caps for certain purposes. For example, one state's style guide recommends using caps and small caps when identifying the speaker in a transcript.

Ex.: ATTORNEY: Did you see the accident at the intersection?
WITNESS: I sure did.
ATTORNEY: Can you describe what you saw?
WITNESS: I'd just noticed the light was green so I could cross, when a truck raced across the intersection and then I heard the crash.

(b) *Government rules.* Some departments, agencies, and the like may have citation rules dictating the use of caps and small caps. For example, the first rule in the *Public Utility Commission of Texas Citation Guide* requires Texas statutes to be cited in caps and small caps.

(c) *Practitioners' usage.* Lawyers generally don't use caps and small caps for citations in legal memorandums or court documents. In fact, *The Bluebook* prohibits their use in any court document.

(d) *Judicial opinions.* Judicial writers sometimes use caps and small caps for citations, especially of statutes and rules of evidence and procedure. But no uniformly accepted stylistic rule exists. For example, although courts in Texas and Virginia use caps and small caps for the titles of periodicals, New York and Oregon courts do not. And although Texas courts use caps and small caps for rules of evidence and procedure, Virginia courts do not.

> "Adherence to conventions may be more important than you realize because violating them can irritate a reader who believes that adherence to the rules is a virtue, and that nonadherence is a vice. Such readers often view writers who fail to follow usage conventions as sloppy, ignorant, or both."
>
> —*Kenneth F. Oettle*

§ 3
Italics, Boldface, and Underlining

3.1 Writers use a variety of devices to make text stand out in a document: italic type, boldface type, underlining, even quotation marks and capitalization. There are only two possible reasons for making text stand out: to emphasize it and to comply with some style convention directing it.

In general, italic type is appropriate in text, while boldface type is appropriate for headings. Underlining and all-caps styles are holdovers from the typewriter era and should be avoided.

When it comes to using italics or any other device for emphasis, there is no greater rule than this: less is more. The sparing use of special type makes its appearance more special. Too-liberal use not only dilutes its impact but irritates readers as well. That's something you shouldn't risk.

In legal writing, italicize a word or phrase in a quotation for emphasis—to clarify to the reader that this particular part of the quotation is especially relevant to the issue at hand. And italicize case names just because that's the age-old practice.

Some word-processing applications automatically underline e-mail addresses and change the font's color to light blue. Avoid this style in formal writing. Either turn off the function in the program's preferences or manually remove the underlining and change the font color back to black.

3.2 Use italics (preferably not underlining) to show emphasis.

(a) *Styles compared.* For decades, office documents were produced on typewriters. When computers with word-processing software took over, the keyboard layout mostly remained the same. That made the transition easier, but it also tended to perpetuate some of the unfortunate shortcomings of typewriters. Some of those were easily overcome. "Straight quotes" (also called *typewriter quotes*) are still the only kind that appear on most keyboards, but word processors usually change them automatically to "curly quotes" (also called *smart quotes* or *typographer's quotes*). One thing that software can't correct is the holdover habit of using underlining (or all caps) for emphasis and other things such as differentiating a word used as a word, or a book title. Typesetting, such as that found in publications and books, always used italic type instead of underlining for those purposes <the word *word*> <*The Mac Is Not a Typewriter*>. Italic type is clean and legible. Underlining is ugly, both on-screen and in printouts. The line is typically too thick and too close to the type—in fact, it can make text harder to read by obliterating the descenders on the letters *f*, *g*, *j*, *p*, *q*, and *y*.

Not this: DeShaney v. Winnebago Cty. Dep't Soc. Servs., 489 U.S. 189 (1989).

But this: *DeShaney v. Winnebago Cty. Dep't Soc. Servs.*, 489 U.S. 189 (1989).

To the extent that *The Bluebook* specifies underlining case names in court papers, override that retrograde guidance and italicize. See 9.4(d).

(b) *Exception.* Break the rule only when necessary for unusual emphasis: that is, when a page is crammed with italicized citations, another word or two in italics wouldn't stand out. In that narrow circumstance only, underlining might be defensible. As a rule, though, never mix italics and underlining, such as underlining case names but italicizing signals. In the absence of an anomalous circumstance, be consistent with a single style throughout the document.

(c) *In quotations.* You don't usually have to follow the style of the source when quoting: if the original document used underlining for emphasis, for example, it's unobjectionable to substitute italics. Only if there is some question about what the styles mean (as when both italics and underlining appear in the source) must you either follow the style of the original or else explain the changes in a parenthetical note after the quotation. See 8.4(f).

3.3 Use italics for foreign words and phrases that have not been anglicized.

(a) *Uneven application.* Words and phrases borrowed from other languages should be italicized only if they haven't become so commonplace in English that they're said to be "anglicized," or assimilated into standard vocabulary. Unfortunately, there's no bright-line rule for determining just when a foreignism becomes anglicized and should no longer be italicized. The surest guide for legal terms is the most current edition of *Black's Law Dictionary*: check it to see whether phrases such as *de novo*, *habeas corpus*, *in loco parentis*, and *nunc pro tunc* should be italicized (the first two shouldn't; the last two should—all four are italicized here only because they're phrases being referred to as phrases [see 3.4]). The appearance of the dictionary's headword—the main entry—will tell you.

Ex.: "We review de novo the denial of Rhoads's request for judgment as a matter of law." *Rhoads v. FDIC*, 257 F.3d 373, 381 (4th Cir. 2001).

Ex.: The Roman lawyers' formulation was *De minimus non curat lex*: the law doesn't concern itself with mere trifles.

> "Good writers use italics for emphasis only as an occasional adjunct to efficient sentence structure. Overused, italics quickly lose their force."
>
> —*The Chicago Manual of Style*

(b) *General rule.* The determining factor is whether the word or phrase is commonly understood. But commonly understood by whom? A lawyer would know the meaning of many legal terms that most nonlawyers wouldn't. Again, the best practice is to consult a current legal dictionary.

Ex.: The district court granted Plaintiff *in forma pauperis* status and sua sponte dismissed his case as frivolous. (It would also be possible here—and perhaps preferable—to use the English phrase *pauper status* (without italics).)

Ex.: By definition, a dictum is an unnecessary statement made by a majority. An *ipse dixit* labeling of a statement as a "holding" does not make it so.

Ex.: This maxim is often cited by modern devotees of a turbulently changing common law—often in its Latin form (*cessante ratione legis, cessat et ipsa lex*) to create the impression of great venerability.

3.4 Use italics to signal that a letter, word, or phrase is being used as a term—when defining it, for example—rather than for its meaning.

(a) *Preferred to quotation marks.* Although quotation marks may show that you're referring to a word or phrase itself (see 1.33(b)), italics are preferable for this purpose. The reason is that quotation marks often interrupt the flow of a sentence or create confusion with the marks' other uses (see 1.34).

Ex.: The word *parody* denotes an imitation of a serious piece of literature, music, or composition for humorous or satirical effect.

Ex.: Finding the term *incentive compensation* ambiguous, the district court denied Bock's motion for summary judgment.

Ex.: The word *however* appears three times in the paragraph.

(b) *In contracts.* In legal instruments, defined terms are sometimes first capitalized and italicized and then just capitalized throughout the rest of the document to distinguish text-specific meanings from usual meanings.

Ex.: An *Establishment* is any place that sells your goods or services, including a store, a website, or some other outlet.

(c) *In hypotheticals.* In legal writing, the parties in hypothetical situations conventionally have the italicized names *A* and *B*, or *X*, *Y*, and *Z*.

Ex.: *A* conveys Blackacre to *B* "and his heirs forever."

3.5 Use italics for case names.

(a) *Legal convention.* Case names are invariably emphasized, either by italics or (less desirably) by underlining. Some practitioners and legal-writing professors still prefer underlining, arguing that it makes the case names stand out more than italicizing does. But for the reasons discussed in 3.2(a), italics are far preferable. Italicize the full case name, including the parties' names and *v.*, *In re*, or *ex rel.* (but not the comma following the parties' names—see 3.10). In later references, the case is usually referred to by one party's name alone, but the name is still italicized to show that a case and not a litigant is being referred to.

Ex.: *Allen v. United States*, 164 U.S. 492 (1896).

Ex.: South Carolina has adopted a statute that governs circumstances in which an *Allen* charge is prohibited.

Ex.: *In re Winship*, 397 U.S. 358, 361 (1970).

Ex.: The Court held that this instruction ran afoul of *Winship*.

(b) *Informal names*. Occasionally a notable set of cases developing a landmark doctrine is referred to collectively. Capitalize and italicize these phrases, including the word *cases*. But generally speaking, don't italicize names of pre-1800 British cases that have given their names to doctrines.

Ex.: The *Slaughter-House Cases* emasculated the Privileges or Immunities Clause of the Fourteenth Amendment.

Ex.: The *Civil Rights Cases* held that the Fourteenth Amendment reaches only state action.

But: Under the Rule in Shelley's Case, a grant in a single instrument of a freehold estate in *A* and a remainder to *A*'s heirs was considered a fee simple absolute in *A*.

(c) *In text*. Generally, follow the same italic style in text and in footnotes. If you're writing for a law review, follow its house rules, which may differ. But the law-review style of roman (nonitalic) case names in footnotes makes no sense in other documents—let alone law reviews themselves. See 9.4(f).

Ex.: In *Elkins v. United States*, the Supreme Court affirmed the Fourth Amendment prohibition of unreasonable searches.

Ex.: 4 The trial in *Bose Corp. v. Consumers Union* was not "just a few hours long"; it lasted six weeks.

3.6 Use italics for the titles of books and other publications, and (only in legal writing) for the titles of articles (but see 2.20).

(a) *Books*. Italicize titles of books, both in text and in footnotes.

Ex.: *Webster's Third New International Dictionary* 675 (1961).

Ex.: Copyright protection was sought for a work titled *Selden's Condensed Ledger of Bookkeeping Simplified*, which explained a new system of bookkeeping.

(b) *Articles*. In legal writing, italicize titles of articles. (This style differs from that in general writing, where article titles are set in roman and put inside quotation marks.)

Ex.: Hans Jonas, *Philosophical Reflections on Experimenting with Human Subjects*, 98 Daedalus 219 (1969).

(c) *Periodicals*. Don't italicize the names of periodicals.

Ex.: Jacob Jacoby et al., *Survey Evidence in Deceptive Advertising Cases Under the Lanham Act*, 84 Trademark Rep. 541 (1994).

3.7 Use italics for citation signals.

(a) *Purpose.* Italics draw attention to a signal and give it emphasis.

Ex.: *See* Peter T. Kilborn, *Feeling Devalued by Change, Doctors Seek Union Banner*, N.Y. Times, May 30, 1996, at A1.

Ex.: *Cf. Hill v. Lockhart*, 474 U.S. 52, 58 (1985).

(b) *Signals as sentence elements.* If the introductory signal is an ordinary English word or phrase used in syntax, don't italicize it.

Ex.: For a point-by-point analysis, see David L. Marcus, *Is the Submarine Patent Torpedoed?*, 70 Temple L. Rev. 521, 572–84 (1997).

3.8 Use italics to report subsequent history in a citation, but not for other information.

(a) *Subsequent history.* A complete citation includes a mention of actions taken on further appeals. The procedural information is italicized.

Ex.: *United States v. Valensia*, 222 F.3d 1173, 1182 (9th Cir. 2000), *cert. granted, judgment vacated, remanded*, 532 U.S. 901 (2001).

Ex.: *United States v. Alpine Land & Reservoir Co.*, 503 F.Supp. 877 (D. Nev. 1980) ("*Alpine Decree*"), *aff'd as modified*, 697 F.2d 851 (9th Cir.) ("*Alpine I*"), *cert. denied*, 464 U.S. 863 (1983).

(b) *Other information.* Don't italicize additional notes, such as the type of opinion (e.g., concurring, dissenting, en banc), the judge's name (per Buckley, J.), or the notation that italics have been supplied (emphasis added).

Ex.: "This case is decided upon an economic theory which a large part of the country does not entertain." *Lochner v. New York*, 198 U.S. 45, 75 (1905) (Holmes, J., dissenting).

Ex.: Our court has similarly observed that, in North Carolina, "allegations of ineffective assistance of counsel *generally* are properly raised on collateral review." *Smith v. Dixon*, 14 F.3d 956, 966 (4th Cir. 1994) (en banc) (emphasis added).

3.9 When a word or phrase within italicized matter should itself be italicized, make it roman instead.

(a) *Toggle between roman and italics.* The purpose of italic type is to make the word or phrase stand out from its surroundings. If the surrounding text is italic, switch to roman for contrast.

Ex.: Michael D. Cicchini & Vincent Rust, *Confrontation After* Crawford v. Washington, 10 Lewis & Clark L. Rev. 531, 540 (2006).

(b) *Context.* Show some flexibility with this rule. For example, if roman type doesn't adequately distinguish the word or phrase, quotation marks may occasionally be justified.

3.10 Do not italicize a punctuation mark after italicized matter unless it is a part of the matter itself.

(a) *Trailing punctuation.* Often in legal writing, a comma will follow italicized matter, as in a case citation. Always use roman type for a comma, closing parenthesis, or any other punctuation mark that isn't part of the italicized matter itself.

Ex.: A junior inventor "may be entitled to a patent even though an earlier inventor discovered it first if that earlier inventor is held to have abandoned it *without divulging the secrets of the invention.*" (The closing period and quotation mark are not italicized.)

Ex.: (*See, e.g., Dix-Seal Corp. v. New Haven Trap Rock Co.*) (The comma after *See* is italicized, but not the comma after *e.g.* or the closing parenthesis after *Co.* But the periods with *e.g.* and with the abbreviation *Co.* are italic because they are an integral part of the abbreviations.)

(b) *Exception.* Punctuation that is part of a title is italicized, even if it closes the citation or sentence as well.

Ex.: Timothy Jost discusses the dilemma in his article *The American Difference in Health Care Costs: Is There a Problem? Is Medical Necessity the Solution?*

3.11 Always italicize *Resolved* in resolutions, legislative acts, and the like.

(a) *The traditional norm.* In formal documents, individual resolutions are traditionally introduced by the word *Resolved*, which is uniformly set in italics for this purpose. For a thorough discussion of resolutions, see § 30.

(b) *Example.* The usual template of a corporate resolution is as follows.

Not this: WHEREAS, Hartsfield Industries wishes to adopt a tradename under which it may do business, be it:

RESOLVED, That Hartsfield Industries assume the tradename Street Dog Inc. for certain business activities; and be it further

RESOLVED, That Hartsfield Industries' president record with the appropriate entities this name's adoption and use.

But this: *Whereas* Hartsfield Industries wishes to adopt a tradename under which it may do business, be it:

Resolved that Hartsfield Industries assume the tradename Street Dog Inc. for certain business activities; and be it further

Resolved that Hartsfield Industries' president record with the appropriate entities this name's adoption and use.

3.12 Despite all the earlier rules, avoid overusing italics.

(a) *Effective when rare.* When used judiciously, italicizing for emphasis can be effective.

Ex.: In the first suit, Defendant Employer was nonsuited without prejudice, but the district court entered a final order dismissing Defendant Employee *with prejudice*. Under established caselaw, a final order against an employee acts as res judicata to a later suit against an employer.

(b) *Ineffective when overused.* Italicizing for emphasis is most effective when used in quoted matter to point out relevance to the issue at hand. It is also effective when used sparingly to emphasize your own words that, if delivered orally, would receive special stress. But it is ineffective—even counterproductive—when overused.

Not this: A *reasonable person* in the seller's position would provide a warning *after* the time of sale *only* when the seller *knows* that the product poses a *substantial risk of harm*.

But this: A reasonable person in the seller's position would provide a warning after the time of sale only when the seller knows that the product poses a *substantial* risk of harm.

Not this: But the interest that *can* protect a power of attorney *must* be an interest in the subject matter itself and *must be coupled in the same person* such that *agents may exercise his power in their own name*.

But this: But the interest that can protect a power of attorney must be an interest in the subject matter itself and must be coupled in the same person such that agents may exercise his power *in their own name*.

(c) *Rhetorical techniques.* Use rhetorical techniques that convey emphasis naturally without relying on artificial devices such as italicizing. Tighten a quotation to just the part that you want to emphasize, and then incorporate it into your own sentence. Use stronger words and leaner sentences. Use word order to take advantage of the strongest syntactical positions, at the beginning and (especially) the end of the sentence.

Instead of this: Statutory racial segregation bore the imprimatur of the United States Supreme Court for 58 years. "We consider the underlying fallacy of the plaintiff's argument to consist in the assumption that the enforced separation of the two races stamps the colored race with a *badge of inferiority*. If this be so, it is not by reason of anything found in the act, but solely because the colored race chooses to put that construction upon it." *Plessy v. Ferguson*, 163 U.S. 537, 551 (1896) (emphasis added).

Trim quotation: The Supreme Court sanctioned statutory racial segregation as no "badge of inferiority" for 58 years after *Plessy v. Ferguson*.

Strengthen words: The Supreme Court sanctioned Jim Crow laws as no "badge of inferiority" for 58 years after *Plessy v. Ferguson*.

Use word order: Jim Crow laws thrived for 58 years after the Supreme Court held in *Plessy v. Ferguson* that they were not a "badge of inferiority."

Or this: After holding in *Plessy v. Ferguson* that Jim Crow laws were no "badge of inferiority," the Supreme Court sanctioned racial segregation for another 58 years.

(d) *Explaining emphasis.* When italic type appears for emphasis in quoted matter, always append a parenthetical note explaining where the italics originated: were they in the source or did you add them? Although *The Bluebook* advises adding a notation only if emphasis has been added, an explicit comment removes any question about the source.

Ex.: Whether that service also includes a telecommunications "offering" "turn[ed] on the nature of the functions the *end user* is offered," *id.* at 4822, ¶ 38 (emphasis added).

Ex.: Of the criminal liability created in 18 U.S.C. § 111, the Supreme Court has found it "plain that Congress intended to protect *both* federal officers and federal functions . . . [and] [e]nsure a federal forum for the trial of offenses involving federal officers." *United States v. Feola*, 420 U.S. 671, 679, 683–84 (1975) (emphasis in original).

3.13 Reserve boldface type for headings.

(a) *For separation.* Because boldface type breaks up text, it is best used exclusively in headings to provide a vertical break between sections and subsections.

(b) *Not in text.* Using boldface type in text dilutes its functionality as a separator. It can also confuse the reader about what degree of emphasis you intended for bold and italic type.

3.14 Use italics for names of ships, spacecraft, and other vessels.

(a) *Name only, not class.* Always italicize a vessel's proper name, but leave in roman type any class designation appearing before the name.

Ex.: The SS *Ioannis P. Goulandris* had chartered to carry olive oil, cheese, and tobacco from the western Greek port of Piraiévs to the United States via the Strait of Gibraltar.

Ex.: The fiery crash of LZ129 *Hindenburg* in 1937 marked the end of airship passenger service.

(b) *Trains.* The names of noteworthy trains—especially passenger trains—are traditionally italicized <the *City of New Orleans*> <the *Orient Express*>. The practice is no longer universal, and today most train names are not italicized <the Downeaster> <the California Zephyr>.

§ 4
Document Design

4.1 Since the 1980s, computers have transformed lawyers' work environment. For better or worse, computer software has made a designer out of every user. Even following the same set of court rules and writing the same kind of document, two lawyers—one knowledgeable in document design and one not—will end up with documents that look quite different: one will be pleasant-looking, the other off-putting. So it's important for writers to know the basics of what makes for good (and bad) design in office documents, and why. This is far more than a mere matter of aesthetics: design affects readerly comprehension in all sorts of ways, many of them subliminal.

4.2 Follow court rules in formatting all documents to be filed in court.

(a) *Meticulous formatting.* Be rigorous about observing any applicable court rules on margins, spacing, font, type size, and page limits. Court clerks often check these elements before accepting briefs and other documents for filing.

(b) *Typographical tricks.* Never use tricks such as "squeezing" type to circumvent the court's formatting or page-limit rules.

(c) *Retrograde rules.* Some courts have issued briefing rules that result in crude-looking, unsightly pages—as by specifying Courier font (see 4.3(c)) or requiring footnotes to be double-spaced. Work within those rules as best you can, as by omitting footnotes entirely if they would have to be double-spaced. Then, if you're so inclined, do what you can to have the rules improved through amendment.

> "Fundamentally, it is good manners to take whatever measures are needed to see that the other fellow gets your point without unnecessary trouble. Remember that the reader uses a good bit of energy just in mechanically following your text."
>
> —*Gorham Munson*

Fonts

4.3 Choose a readable font appropriate for the document.

(a) *Definitions.* Fonts, traditionally called *typefaces* in printing, fall into three general categories: serif, sans serif (pronounced /**sanz sehr**-if/), and decorative. The letters of a serif font, such as the one used here, feature "feet" and other finishing strokes that make the type more readable. Researchers into readability find that the serifs subtly add to letters' distinctive shapes and also connect letters to give words recognizable looks. That's why almost every book and magazine publisher uses a serif font in body text. The letters of sans-serif type, such as that used in this book for examples and bold headings, have no such finishing strokes (*sans serif* simply means "without serifs"). Sans-serif type is considered more legible than serif type in single lines of type and in very short passages. It is appropriate in some headings and such callout graphics as pull quotes. It is also traditional in small sizes for classified ads and tabular matter such as stock prices and sports scores. For body text, however, serif fonts have traditionally been considered the better choice, especially for longer documents. Decorative fonts such as scripts, Old English, and fanciful faces serve a purpose in ads, posters, and the like, but they have no place in office documents. Keep it simple.

Exx. (serif):	Times New Roman	Garamond
Exx. (sans serif):	Arial	Gill Sans
Exx. (decorative):	MONTEREY	Comic Sans

(b) *Variations.* Typewriters once limited options for office documents: a legal writer could emphasize words only by underlining or capitalizing. Computers allow writers to change font size on the fly and choose the *italic*, **bold**, or ***bold italic*** version of most fonts. But you must use these tools with care, choosing an appropriate type style and using a variation only when it serves a good purpose. In general, use italics in text for special uses and boldface in headings to make them stand out from the text.

> "In the old days, you didn't have to spend much time designing your documents because all you had to work with was the Courier typeface. Paragraph indentations and margin widths were your only formatting concerns. But now that word-processing packages are becoming more like desktop-publishing software, expectations are higher."
>
> —*Catherine Kenny*

(c) *Courier.* The typewriter-style font Courier is *monospaced*, so that every letter takes the same amount of horizontal space, whether it's a lowercase *i* or a capital *W.* The visual effect is cruder than that of a proportionally spaced font—which explains why no publisher today would print a book with it. A proportionally spaced font such as Garamond or Palatino or Century Schoolbook is easier to read because the words form more recognizable units. These fonts allow more words to fit comfortably on a line, and therefore on a page, than Courier does (compare the type samples below). The only reason to use Courier today is that the judge to whom your document is addressed prefers the old typewriter style, as some do.

Ex.: This is set in 12-point Garamond.

Ex.: This is set in 12-point Palatino.

Ex.: This is set in 12-point Century Schoolbook.

Ex.: This is set in 12-point Courier.

4.4 Never use more than two fonts in a document.

(a) *Mixing styles.* A serif font is the better choice for body text because it enhances readability. For body text, stick to a single font throughout the document, using its italic variation appropriately but sparingly. For headings, a bold sans-serif font can provide more contrast with the body text and help make headings stand out.

Ex.: (both heading and body text in Times New Roman, a serif font):

STANDARD OF REVIEW

All the issues raised by this appeal are matters of law, to be reviewed de novo.

Ex.: (heading in Arial, a sans-serif font, and body text in Times New Roman, a serif font):

STANDARD OF REVIEW

All the issues raised by this appeal are matters of law, to be reviewed de novo.

(b) *Ransom-note effect.* Having too many different fonts on a page produces a piecemeal, cut-and-paste appearance that becomes distracting. In the example below, the heading is in Arial Bold, the body text in Times New Roman, and the quotation in Garamond Italic.

Not This: **History of the Boundary Line**

The boundary of the property in issue was established more than 250 years ago. By royal decree in 1740, King George II of England declared:

> *That the Dividing Line shall pass up thro the Mouth of Piscataqua Harbour and up the Middle of the River . . . . And that the Dividing Line shall part the Isles of Shoals and run thro the Middle of the Harbour between the Islands to the Sea on the Southerly Side . . . .*

Even though the United States achieved independence a few decades later, the courts have continued to recognize royal land grants in the chain of title.

But This: **History of the Boundary Line**

The boundary of the property in issue was established more than 250 years ago. By royal decree in 1740, King George II of England declared:

> That the Dividing Line shall pass up thro the Mouth of Piscataqua Harbour and up the Middle of the River . . . . And that the Dividing Line shall part the Isles of Shoals and run thro the Middle of the Harbour between the Islands to the Sea on the Southerly Side . . . .

Even though the United States achieved independence a few decades later, the courts have continued to recognize royal land grants in the chain of title.

4.5 Use an appropriate type size.

(a) *Readability.* Although many readers say that they prefer 12-point type, it is somewhat small for full-width lines of type on an 8½-by-11-inch page with margins of one inch or so. If you have a choice, use 13- or 14-point type instead. The national standard for federal appellate briefs is 14-point type (*see* Fed. R. App. P. 32(a)(5)). For headings, 14-point type is acceptable, but anything larger seems loud and aggressive. On the other hand, anything smaller than 10-point type looks like the proverbial "fine print," designed *not* to be read—unless you're working in a double-column format.

Ex.: **This Heading Shouts!** (16 point)

Ex.: **This heading is about right.** (14 point)

Ex.: This is the standard text size. (13 point)

Ex.: This type size is too small for full-width pages. (9 point)

Ex.: This fine print says, "Please don't read me." (7 point)

> "For large areas of text, it is usually better to use a serif type (that is, a type with tiny strokes or projections at the end of most of the letters). The serifs guide the eye horizontally and put light and shade on the page because the letters have thick and thin strokes. Serif types tend to look authoritative, classical, and official . . . . The sans-serif types (types without serifs) tend to be more useful as headings and in forms, catalogues, and flyers."
>
> —*Martin Cutts*

(b) *Size.* Fonts vary in apparent size, even if they're the same point size (see examples below). The difference is the *x-height* (referring to the lowercase *x*)—that is, the size of the middle zone of the letters. With two similar fonts, the one with the larger x-height is generally easier to read at small sizes, while the one with the smaller lowercase letters generally fits more characters on a line. Fonts also vary in how condensed the letters are. If you need to fit more text into a document, and if court rules permit, try changing the font.

Ex.: This is set in 13-point Garamond.

Ex.: This is set in 13-point Times New Roman.

Ex.: This is set in 13-point Palatino.

(c) *Headings.* The best practice is the easy one: adhere to one type size throughout the document. Main headings may be set in a slightly larger point size than text, but never larger than 14 point. Subheadings should be the same size as the text; if they are bold and in a contrasting font, they may even be slightly smaller. See 4.21.

(d) *Page numbers.* For most legal documents, page numbers should appear either centered about half an inch from the bottom of the page or flush right about half an inch from the top of the page. Set them in roman type, in the same font and size as the body text. Generally, no page number should appear on the first page unless the document has a table of contents or begins with Roman-numeral pages.

White Space

4.6 Use white space purposefully.

(a) *Definition and purpose.* White space is all the area on a page where no words appear. It includes not only the page margins but also the extra space around headings, block quotations, bulleted items, and other typographical devices that distinguish some things from the body text. (For this purpose it doesn't include the blank lines of double-spacing.) Meaningful white space enhances a document's appearance and readability.

(b) *Focal point.* White space directs the reader's eyes and gives them logical resting places. It works well in conjunction with appropriate headings to show readers the different sections of your document and how they fit together.

> "If you see errors in form, look for errors in content."
> —*Konstantin Fedin*

(c) *Contrast.* The empty space between text elements (headings, paragraphs, lists, and the like) separates the elements and makes them easier for the reader to distinguish. A little extra spacing between groups of text elements helps readers distinguish the different parts of the whole document and enhances its organization.

(d) *Comprehension.* Just as a long sentence or a long paragraph is difficult to read, so too is a long block of text. By using white space and subheadings to break up copy into smaller chunks, you can help your readers absorb the information better.

4.7 Leave a little more room in your margins than you're required to.

(a) *Readability.* When a court rule sets a margin width (e.g., one inch on all sides), the specified width is usually a minimum and not an absolute width. Greater margins enhance readability by creating more white space and preventing lines from becoming too long. Unless a rule disallows it, use 1.1-inch margins for 14-point type, or 1.3-inch margins for 13-point type.

(b) *Convenience.* Larger margins allow space for readers to make notes alongside the text. Some readers will appreciate the extra space. Also, photocopying tends to enlarge the text slightly—and therefore to shrink the margin. So the larger margins are especially important in a document to be photocopied.

(c) *Extra space at bottom.* When margins are equal on all four sides, the text may appear to slide down the page. Making the bottom margin a little bigger than the side margins avoids this effect.

(d) *Inside gutters.* If the document will be bound, add an extra half-inch to the appropriate margin. If the document is printed on one side of the paper only, add the extra space to the left side of each page. If the document is printed double-sided, add the extra space to the inside margin.

4.8 Use initial indents of a quarter of an inch or so; use the tab key or automatic paragraph formatting to keep them consistent.

(a) *Purpose.* Indents add white space and give shape and definition to a paragraph (see 4.14). They also make lists, long quotations, and other elements stand out better.

(b) *Width of indents.* An odd custom in legal writing is the use of an extremely wide paragraph indent, sometimes starting the first line nearly halfway across the page. Don't follow this weird practice. The wide indents serve no function and are unattractive. Indent the first line of paragraphs no more than half an inch, the default on word processors.

(c) *Block quotations.* Block quotations must have a left-margin indent. Unless they appear in a narrow column of type, they should also have a right-margin indent.

(d) *Uniformity.* Use the tab key, the indent function, or automatic paragraph formatting to keep indents uniform (see 4.15). With most fonts, the space-bar produces variable-width spaces, which can lead to alignment problems.

4.9 Use hanging indents on contracts, statutes, and other documents with numbered and lettered subparts.

(a) *Definition.* The paragraph style called *hanging indents* uses a full-spaced first line and left indents on all other lines. In a bulleted or numbered list, the beginning of the text on the first line will align with the left margin of the other lines. For an example of hanging indents, see 4.9(c).

(b) *Purpose of hanging indents.* Progressive indents on the left side neatly display the interrelationship of parts and subparts.

(c) *Length of indents.* To make this convention work, create small indents equivalent to only a space or two. This way, the progressive indents won't move so far to the right that too few characters will fit on a line.

Ex.:

(B) Under the Equal Credit Opportunity Act, a creditor's notification of adverse action must include:
  (1) a statement of the action taken;
  (2) notice of the provisions of the ECOA;
  (3) the name and address of the federal agency that regulates compliance; and
  (4) either:
    (a) a statement explaining why the action was taken; or
    (b) notification of the applicant's right to receive such a statement.

(d) *Examples.* For examples of the orderly appearance created by hanging indents in transactional documents, see § 27.

> "I'm not here to tell you that typography is at the core of a lawyer's work. It's not. But typography can optimize that work. All writing necessarily involves typography. And good writing is part of good lawyering. So good typography is, too. If you ignore typography, you are ignoring an opportunity to improve both your writing and your advocacy."
>
> —*Matthew Butterick*

Justification

4.10 Avoid full justification; set text flush left.

(a) *Definition. Full justification* refers to aligning type at both the left and the right margins by adding space between words as needed. Fully justified type contrasts with type set flush left (also called *ragged right*) with uneven line endings on the right side.

(b) *Readability.* Except in the hands of a skillful typographer, fully justified text can be harder to read than unjustified (*flush-left*) text. This is almost invariably true for office documents, especially when they are unhyphenated as well. Forcing the text to both margins may result in lines with word spacing that is too wide or, worse, unevenly distributed across the page. Rivers of white space may appear to flow down the type, requiring some editing of the copy to correct (see 4.10(c)). Text may even appear to be "sliding down the page" unless margins are then adjusted. Setting the copy flush left has its own advantages, too: the uneven right margin gives visual clues that help the reader find the beginning of the next line. Readers don't lose their place in the copy as often. If you must fully justify, use hyphenation.

(c) *Avoiding rivers.* A river is a vertical flow of white space produced by word spaces that appear near each other on consecutive lines of text. Rivers appear more often in fully justified text than in flush-left text because the word processor must increase the space between words to make the text stretch evenly between the margins. Rivers also appear when the line length is too long or too short. Rivers can be corrected either by changing the margin width (wider is usually better), by hyphenating the text, or by editing the copy so that the word spaces no longer align.

4.11 Reserve centering and flush-right alignments for special uses.

(a) *Centering.* Centering is sometimes appropriate for titles and captions of documents, for main headings, and for page numbers. Although some writers prefer to center all headings, the better and more common practice is to set all but major section dividers flush left.

> "The eye tends to jump, up or down, as it moves over a too-long line of copy. Spare the reader this exercise. The ideal length is 40 characters, although plenty of leeway is possible. If the type is larger, the lines well spaced, the paragraphs not too long, you can safely print up to 60, or even 70, characters."
>
> —*Walter Lubars & Albert J. Sullivan*

(b) *Flush right.* Flush-right style is aligned to the right margin, leaving the left ragged. There are few appropriate uses for flush-right alignment in office documents, although some legal writers set the court name and case number flush right in the captions of court documents, opposite the parties' names. Less often, the name and address of the attorney filing the document are set flush right, but tabs are better for this purpose so that the lines of the text block remain left-aligned. Page numbering is the only other appropriate use for flush-right text, although page numbers may also be centered.

Horizontal Spacing

4.12 Use even forward-spacing in your documents: one space between words and one space after punctuation marks (including colons and periods).

(a) *Typewriter limitations.* The custom during the reign of the typewriter was to insert two spaces between sentences and after colons. The reason was that letters on a typewriter are monospaced, as is the Courier font on computers: every letter takes the same amount of horizontal space, whether it's a lowercase *i*, a capital *W*, or a space. That's fine for lining up columns of numbers but lousy for creating readable text. Continue the custom only if you use a monospaced font such as Courier—which in any event you should avoid (see 4.3(c)).

Although it's true that 19th-century typesetters put a bit more space between sentences than between words within a sentence, it has been a settled convention for many decades in professional typesetting to put only one space between sentences. Many who learned to put two spaces in typewriting classes still cling to that practice, but the enlightened approach is to shed it.

(b) *Computers and flexibility.* On a computer, you have fonts with proportional spacing. Letters fit together snugly, words are more legible as discrete entities, and spaces stand out. Because double-spacing between sentences looks odd with proportionally spaced type, most word processors can automatically replace two spaces with one.

4.13 Use a hard (nonbreaking) space to avoid breaking lines at inappropriate places.

(a) *Hard space.* Get to know your word processor's hard-space function and use it in places where you don't want a line to break.

(b) *Importance.* The hard space is especially important in legal writing, where by convention a space separates citation symbols such as § and ¶ from the number that follows. The same is true of some abbreviations such as *cmt.* and *p.*

Ex.: § 1983

Ex.: cmt. a

Ex.: pp. 24–32

(c) *When to use.* Use a hard space to keep the following combinations together:

- *at* + a page number <*id.* at 14>.
- The first numeral in a citation (e.g., volume number) + the source abbreviation <66 S.W.2d . . .>.
- A numeral (outside citations) + the word it quantifies <180 days>.
- § + a letter or numeral <§ 7116(a)>.
- ¶ + a letter or numeral <¶ 3>.
- *Article* or *Section* + a letter or numeral <Section A>, <Article 47>.
- A letter or number in an in-line list + the following word <(1) allocate overtime assignments; (2) retain overtime records; (3) . . .>.
- The month + the day in a date <November 21, 2018> (a break between the day and the year is acceptable).
- The first word of a defined term containing letters or numerals + the letter or numeral <Employee 1>.
- The name of a circuit court in a citation + *Cir.* <D.C. Cir.>.
- A title + a last name <Judge Jones> (a break between a title and a full name is acceptable, but the full name must be kept intact).
- An inclusive number range <44–72> (since most word processors have no nonbreaking en-dash, you may need to insert a soft return before the first number to keep the range intact).

(d) *Ellipses.* Use hard spaces before and between ellipsis dots to ensure that the dots will be evenly spaced and will stay together on one line. If a period or other punctuation mark follows, make sure that it also stays on the line with those dots. This trailing punctuation mark should be spaced evenly with them, as if it were a fourth ellipsis dot.

Ex.: "in Order to . . . secure the Blessings of Liberty"

Ex.: "The monument sits in a large park containing 17 monuments and 21 historical markers . . . . The setting does not lend itself to meditation or any other religious activity."

Ex.: "The court was right about the result . . . , but it was the text and not the legislative history that made this so."

> "A little attention to the typographical details, while not absolutely essential to a good brief, goes a long way toward securing a careful consideration by the court."
> —*Roger W. Cooley*

4.14 Mark the beginning of a paragraph by tab-indenting the first line. In a single-spaced document, leave an extra line between paragraphs.

(a) *Indenting.* Indent the first line of each paragraph. Use the default setting of half an inch, or adjust the indenting to three- or four-tenths of an inch. Never use double-indenting.

(b) *New chapter or section.* You may choose not to indent the first paragraph of each chapter or section. The reasoning behind this book-style typesetting convention is that the purpose of the indent or extra space is to show readers where a new paragraph starts; at the beginning of a chapter or section, it's obvious where the paragraph starts. But this practice is more common in publishing houses than in law offices.

(c) *Intervening space.* Add a half-line or full line of space between paragraphs in a single-spaced document such as a letter or a memo. Word-processing programs can do this automatically, or you can add an extra hard return between paragraphs.

(d) *Block style.* Block-style formatting—with extra space between paragraphs but no indents—is discouraged in legal writing (other than e-mail messages). The style causes problems when some copy such as a long quotation is itself indented: it becomes impossible to tell whether what follows is a continuation of the previous paragraph or a new paragraph. Even without a block quotation, the same ambiguity can arise with a page break.

(e) *Below a block quotation.* Don't automatically start a new, indented paragraph below a block quotation just because it is set off from the text above it. If the text below the block continues the discussion of what came before the quotation, continue afterward just as you would have if the quotation had been a short, embedded one. It's still part of the same paragraph and shouldn't be separated by indenting.

4.15 To ensure that the indentation is consistent throughout the document, use a tab instead of the spacebar for indenting.

(a) *Paragraph indents.* With proportional fonts, the width of a spacebar's space is fixed in flush-left copy but variable in fully justified copy. Using the spacebar to indent paragraphs in justified copy will result in paragraph indents that vary noticeably. It wastes time and looks amateurish. Use the tab settings instead for ease and consistency.

(b) *Aligning columns.* Unless you're using a monospaced font (a practice to be discouraged), it is futile to try to align multiple columns using the spacebar. Even with Courier or some other monospaced font, any copy change will ruin the alignment. Instead, learn to use the word-processing tools: tab and table settings are there precisely to avoid alignment problems.

4.16 Avoid adjusting a font's spacing or width.

(a) *Spacing and width.* Word-processing software allows you to change the spacing between letters and between words. Reducing the space results in denser copy, while increasing it makes the copy airier. Word-processing software also lets the user compress and expand the horizontal width of a type's characters.

(b) *Limitations.* While it may at first seem tempting to use spacing and width to pack in more copy and still meet a court's page-limit rules, avoid that temptation. Text that is set too tight and letters that are condensed too much are hard to read. Besides, this practice violates the spirit (and possibly the letter) of court rules and risks annoying the judicial reader or even being sanctioned.

4.17 Don't put a forward space between consecutive initials.

(a) *Degrees.* The abbreviated forms of many degrees are consecutive initials (e.g., M.B.A., J.D., M.D.). These are traditionally never spaced out.

(b) *Business names.* Use the business's preferred name as shown in its signage, advertising, or registration. If the name has formal spaces between consecutive initials, retain them and use a hard space to prevent them from breaking at the end of a line. If an abbreviation for the business's legal form is included, don't add spaces (*L.L.C.* or *LLC*, not *L. L. C.*).

(c) *Personal names.* When a personal name contains two or more initials with periods in sequence, put a space only after the last period. Legal style differs from the advice in *The Chicago Manual of Style* (§ 10.12), which calls for a space after each initial. Keeping the initials together prevents them from being broken onto separate lines. See 1.72(e).

Vertical Spacing

4.18 Prefer single-spaced documents in-house, but for court filings always follow rules and customs that require double-spacing.

(a) *Advantages of single-spacing.* Surprisingly to some people, single-spaced copy is more reader-friendly than double-spaced copy. Not only will the document be about half as long, but the structure of the writing will show up better when the copy is single-spaced. Headings appear more frequently, and they stand out better because the extra spacing around them isn't diluted by extra white space between every line. Paragraphs are less intimidating: a double-spaced paragraph of 400 words can take up a full page.

(b) *Disadvantages of double-spacing.* Double-spacing prevents sentences from standing out. It results in fewer paragraphs and fewer headings on a page, making it harder to follow the writing's structure. While the extra white space is convenient for an editor (see 4.19), it hinders readability because it is dispersed throughout the page.

(c) *Paragraph spacing.* In most single-spaced documents, separate paragraphs with a single blank line. Do this also to set off bulleted lists and block quotations within paragraphs. Rather than creating this space by using hard returns, which can invite formatting problems, have your word processor do this automatically by adjusting the paragraph-spacing settings. Set the after-paragraph space to a height equal to or, ideally, slightly smaller than a line of normal text (e.g., a 10-point space with a 13-point type size). If your word processor has an option to suppress these spaces between paragraphs of the same style, you might disable this feature.

(d) *Court rules.* Despite the advantages of single-spaced copy, court rules often require that briefs and other filings be double-spaced. Strictly adhere to any such rules.

4.19 Double-space draft documents to make them easier to edit.

(a) *Editing ease.* Double-spacing leaves room for corrections and edits to be written between lines of type. A marked-up page will be much less cluttered than a page of single-spaced copy; the marks will be easier to follow, and only half as many will appear on a page.

(b) *Triple-spacing.* A draft that will be heavily edited may need to be printed out triple-spaced.

4.20 Avoid awkward page breaks.

(a) *Headings.* Make sure that a heading is followed by at least two lines of text before a page break, or else force a page break before the heading.

(b) *Widows and orphans.* Avoid any page break that puts the last line of a paragraph at the top of a page (called a *widow*). Less objectionable but still worth avoiding is a first line of a paragraph at the bottom of a page (called an *orphan*). This can be done automatically by setting the "widows and orphans" or "keep-together" preferences in your word-processing program.

Headings

4.21 Make the hierarchy of headings clear to the reader by using a combination of outlining tags, capitalization style, type style, and type size.

(a) *Outlining tags.* Use a simple and instantly recognizable system of tags to show the structure of your material. Make the tags and the text of the headings match your table of contents. The most functional system for court documents uses common Roman letters and Arabic numerals in the sequence I, A, (1), and (a).

(b) *One-level decimals.* In transactional documents and other types of legal drafting, use a modified decimal-numbering system in the order 1, 1.1, 1.1(A), 1.1(A)(1), 1.1(A)(1)(a). This system makes contract terms, statute provisions, and the like unambiguously citable by paragraph and subparagraph.

Though often seen, the continuation of decimals past one (1.1.1, etc.) is undesirable because it effectively creates a disincentive to tabulate lists: 5.1.3.2 is much more bulky before an enumerated item than (b).

(c) *Capitalization.* In general, all-caps style is acceptable only for a major section heading that is a short phrase of no more than one line. For other headings and subheadings, use up-style capitalization (see 2.10) with those that don't form complete sentences, and down-style sentence format for those that do.

(d) *Type style.* Using boldface type—or even a boldface sans-serif type with a serif body type—is a good way to make sure that headings stand out from the text.

(e) *Type size.* It is acceptable to set main headings in 14-point type, even if the body copy is smaller. But a change in type size smaller than 2 points is hardly noticeable to most readers.

(f) *Combining techniques.* Many writers combine both tags and different type styles to create a hierarchy of headings. Main headings may be further distinguished by using a slightly larger type size. A good choice is boldface initial caps for topical headings, boldface sentence-style for the next level, bold italics for the third level, and regular italics for the fourth level, all with outlining tags.

> "The truth is that nothing written is useful unless it is attractive enough to be read."
>
> —*Royal Bank of Canada*

Ex.: **I. The Contract-Interpretation Claims**

A. The word "vicinity" has no specialized meaning in this contract.

(1) *Parol evidence is admissible when a term is ambiguous.*

(a) *Whether ambiguity exists is a question of law.*

(g) *Number of levels.* Prefer two or three levels of headings, avoiding a fourth level if possible. The more levels there are, the harder it is for readers to recognize and follow the organizational structure.

(h) *Hybrid headings.* Avoid hanging, untagged headings: every part of your document should be citable. If a section heading would have only one subheading, combine the two into a hybrid heading using a colon. Treat the two parts of the new heading separately when applying the capitalization rules in 4.21(c).

Not this: **III. Analysis and Conclusion**
The award is contrary to law.

But this: **III. Analysis and Conclusion: The award is contrary to law.**

(i) *Progressive indents.* Beyond a single indent for a first-level subhead, avoid the practice—common but unnecessary in legal writing—of using wide and progressively large left-side indents to signify the hierarchy of headings. It is especially inappropriate because lower-level headings tend to become longer, yet with this technique they are forced into many short lines crowded onto the right-hand side of the page.

(j) *Cascading hanging indents in legal drafting.* Hanging indents in contracts, statutes, and other legal-drafting documents make individual provisions—each citable according to a hierarchical numbering system—easy to find. Cascading the subparts of each provision likewise makes finding provisions easier by showing at a glance where each one begins. For an example, see 4.9(c).

4.22 Except for short top-level section headings, which may be centered, prefer headings to be set flush left and single-spaced, with a tight hanging indent.

(a) *Centering.* Major section headings, such as "Statement of Facts," are best set centered on one line in boldfaced all caps.

> "The manner in which you physically present the brief has much to do with whether the brief will be read. . . . The brief should contain what is called the 'Psychologically Appealing Page.' It is the page that compels to be read and not to be ignored."
>
> —*William F. Causey*

(b) *Flush left.* Main headings are best set flush left, especially if they are longer than one line.

(c) *First-level subheads.* First-level subheads should be indented—with a hanging indent—to the extent of the text's paragraph indent.

(d) *Single-spacing.* Even if the text of a document is double-spaced, always single-space headings.

(e) *Hanging indent.* Use a narrow hanging indent between the outline tag and the text of a heading (see 4.9).

4.23 Use headings and subheadings to help the reader follow the structure of your document. Use a little extra space above breaks to help divide up the text.

(a) *Reader cues.* The white space around headings and subheadings makes the structure of your document more instantly visible. It helps readers see your organizational structure and gives them a moment to rest and think about the point they've just read before continuing to the next one.

(b) *Spacing.* Use an extra line or half-line of space above headings and subheadings; the distance will help cue readers to expect a change of subject. Headings and subheadings should be closer to the text they relate to—namely, what follows them—than to the preceding text.

(c) *Subheadings.* Easy-to-notice subheadings break long text blocks into smaller, bite-sized chunks. They make long messages easier to read. Use subheadings as appropriate—every few paragraphs or so—to help readers find what they're looking for. But don't allow them to chop up a series of individual paragraphs to the extent that they impede the flow of the text.

4.24 Study the techniques of effective document design.

(a) *Guidance.* The following publications will prove helpful if you wish to study matters of typography in greater depth:

- Philip Brady, *Using Type Right* (1993).
- Matthew Butterick, *Typography for Lawyers* (2d ed. 2015).
- Ellen Lupton, *Thinking with Type* (2d ed. 2010).
- Ilene Strizver, *Type Rules!* (4th ed. 2013).
- Colin Wheildon, *Type & Layout* (rev. ed. 2005).

> "If the form of information is difficult to assimilate, that affects our judgments about the substance of that information."
>
> —*Leonard Mlodinow*

(b) *Some contrasting examples*. Even when the so-called substance remains the same, the appearance of a document can make it dramatically more or less effective. The following pages demonstrate many of the *Redbook* techniques with a facing-pages redesign.

A Sample Redesign: The *Before* Version (page 1)

Nondisclosure and Confidentiality Agreement

This Nondisclosure and Confidentiality Agreement (the "Agreement"), effective as of ________________, 20__, is between Johnsonius Enterprises, Inc. (the "Company"), a California corporation, and ____________________________, whose address is ______________________________ (the "Recipient"). It is intended to protect confidential information in the Company's possession from being disclosed by the Recipient.

Background

The Company and the Recipient are considering entering into a business relationship for their mutual benefit. In consideration of the possibility of this relationship, the Company will disclose certain proprietary information about its business so that the two parties may assess whether such a relationship would be to their mutual benefit. To induce the Company to disclose sufficient information, the Recipient undertakes the nondisclosure duties outlined below.

Terms and Conditions

1. Limitations

1.1 Unprotected Information. The Recipient has no obligation to protect information that:

(A) was known or available to the Recipient before this Agreement without breach of a duty of confidentiality by the Recipient or a third party;

(B) is or becomes available to the public, other than by breach of this Agreement; or

(C) becomes known to the Recipient by a third party without restrictions as to disclosure.

A Sample Redesign: The *After* Version (page 1)

Nondisclosure and Confidentiality Agreement

This Nondisclosure and Confidentiality Agreement (this "Agreement"), effective as of __________________, 20__, is between Johnsonius Enterprises, Inc. (the "Company"), a California corporation, and ________________________________, whose address is ________________________________ (the "Recipient"). It is intended to protect confidential information in the Company's possession from being disclosed by the Recipient.

Background

The Company and the Recipient are considering entering into a business relationship for their mutual benefit. In consideration of the possibility of this relationship, the Company will disclose certain proprietary information about its business so that the two parties may assess whether such a relationship would be to their mutual benefit. To induce the Company to disclose sufficient information, the Recipient undertakes the nondisclosure duties outlined below.

Terms and Conditions

1. Duty Not to Disclose Confidential Information

Note that in the original, this critical provision appeared in § 3.3: the improved formatting entailed improving the organization.

1.1 Recipient's Duty. The Recipient must use its best efforts in taking precautions to safeguard the Confidential Information, including all precautions that the Company may, in its sole discretion, request. The Recipient may use Confidential Information only for the purposes contemplated by this Agreement. Before the Recipient discloses Confidential Information to any employee, the employee must first sign a nondisclosure agreement identical to the one in Schedule A.

A Sample Redesign: The *Before* Version (page 2)

1.2 Disclosure Required by Law. The Recipient may disclose Confidential Information to the extent required by law. But the Recipient must give the Company prompt written notice of the required disclosure and make a reasonable effort to avoid disclosure by seeking a protective order.

2. Nature of Relationship. The Recipient has no obligation to disclose any Confidential Information. This Agreement grants no rights of ownership, licenses, or any other intellectual-property rights. This Agreement does not create any agency, partnership, joint venture, or other business relationship.

3. Duty Not to Disclose Confidential Information

3.1 The Meaning of "Confidential Information." As used in this Agreement, "Confidential Information" means all proprietary information related to the Company, including:

(A) trade secrets and other intellectual property;

(B) financial information and pricing;

(C) technical information, including research, development, procedures, algorithms, data, designs, and know-how;

(D) business information, including operations, planning, marketing interests, and products;

(E) information collected or developed by the Company regarding its customers; and

(F) the terms of any agreement between the Company and the Recipient and the discussions, negotiations, and proposals related to that agreement.

3.2 Standard of Care. The Recipient must protect the Confidential Information from both unauthorized use and unauthorized disclosure by exercising the same degree of care that the Recipient uses with respect to information of its own of a similar nature, except that the Recipient must at least use reasonable care.

A Sample Redesign: The *After* Version (page 2)

1.2 **The Meaning of "Confidential Information."** As used in this Agreement, "Confidential Information" means all proprietary information related to the Company, including:

(A) trade secrets and other intellectual property;

(B) financial information and pricing;

(C) technical information, including research, development, procedures, algorithms, data, designs, and know-how;

(D) business information, including operations, planning, marketing interests, and products;

(E) information collected or developed by the Company regarding its customers; and

(F) the terms of any agreement between the Company and the Recipient and the discussions, negotiations, and proposals related to that agreement.

1.3 **Standard of Care.** The Recipient must protect the Confidential Information from both unauthorized use and unauthorized disclosure by exercising the same degree of care that the Recipient uses with respect to information of its own of a similar nature, except that the Recipient must at least use reasonable care.

1.4 **Protection Period.** The Recipient must protect the Confidential Information for two years from the last date that the Recipient received Confidential Information.

2. **Representatives.** The parties' representatives for disclosing or receiving information are:

Company: Jeffrey A. Gurlich

Recipient: ______________________________

A Sample Redesign: The *Before* Version (page 3)

3.3 Recipient's Duty. The Recipient must use its best efforts in taking precautions to safeguard the Confidential Information, including all precautions that the Company may, in its sole discretion, request. The Recipient may use Confidential Information only for the purposes contemplated by this Agreement. Before the Recipient discloses Confidential Information to any employee, the employee must first sign a nondisclosure agreement identical to the one in Schedule A.

3.4 Protection Period. The Recipient must protect the Confidential Information for two years from the last date that the Recipient received Confidential Information.

4. Representatives. The parties' representatives for disclosing or receiving information are:

   Company: Jeffrey A. Gurlich
   Recipient: ______________________________

5. Publicity. The Recipient must not, without the Company's prior written consent, make any news release, public announcement, denial, or confirmation of this Agreement or its subject matter.

6. Right to Enjoin Disclosure. The Recipient's unauthorized disclosure or use of Confidential Information may result in irreparable harm. The Company may therefore seek a temporary restraining order and other injunctive relief to protect its Confidential Information. The Recipient will not raise the defense of an adequate remedy at law. This provision does not alter any other remedies available to either party.

A Sample Redesign: The *After* Version (page 3)

3. Limitations

3.1 Unprotected Information. The Recipient has no obligation to protect information that:

(A) was known or available to the Recipient before this Agreement without breach of a duty of confidentiality by the Recipient or a third party;

(B) is or becomes available to the public, other than by breach of this Agreement; or

(C) becomes known to the Recipient by a third party without restrictions on disclosure.

3.2 Disclosure Required by Law. The Recipient may disclose Confidential Information to the extent required by law. But the Recipient must give the Company prompt written notice of the required disclosure and make a reasonable effort to avoid disclosure by seeking a protective order.

4. Nature of Relationship. The Recipient has no obligation to disclose any Confidential Information. This Agreement grants no rights of ownership, licenses, or any other intellectual-property rights. This Agreement does not create any agency, partnership, joint venture, or other business relationship.

5. Publicity. The Recipient must not, without the Company's prior written consent, make any news release, public announcement, denial, or confirmation of this Agreement or its subject matter.

6. Right to Enjoin Disclosure. The Recipient's unauthorized disclosure or use of Confidential Information may result in irreparable harm. The Company may therefore seek a temporary restraining order and other injunctive relief to protect its Confidential Information. The Recipient will not raise the defense of an adequate remedy at law. This provision does not alter any other remedies available to either party.

§ 5
Numbers

5.1 Deciding whether to use numerals or to spell out numbers in text is usually a matter of setting a style and sticking to it. There is no absolute right or wrong; consistency is all that any reader can ask for. But there are some general principles.

In the most formal writing, numbers are often spelled out: on a wedding invitation, for example, even the year, the date, and the time are traditionally spelled out. Legal writing tends toward the formal, and many lawyers follow the academic-writing convention of spelling out all numbers below 100.

But that style is in tension with modern trends toward space-saving simplicity. More and more lawyers now use numerals for all numbers higher than ten. This popular trend has one overwhelming advantage over the academic tradition: it's much easier to read numerals than spelled-out numbers.

Whatever style you decide on, there will still be some contexts in which only numerals are correct.

5.2 Use cardinal numbers for most purposes, but use ordinal numbers to indicate the position in a series and with some dates. Avoid superscripts with ordinals.

(a) *In general.* A cardinal number expresses amount (e.g., *one*, *two*, *three*). An ordinal number indicates the position in a series (e.g., *first*, *second*, *third*).

(b) *Day-month-year format.* Don't use an ordinal number when writing the full date in the day-month-year format.

Not this: May 29th, 2018

But this: May 29, 2018

(c) *Day precedes month.* When the day comes before the month, it may be either written as an ordinal number or spelled out.

Ex.: Sue mailed the letter on the 3rd of June.

Ex.: Sue mailed the letter on the third of June.

Better: Sue mailed the letter on June 3.

(d) *Day alone.* If the day of the month stands alone, it may be written as either an ordinal number or a spelled-out ordinal.

Ex.: The hearing was held on October 14, but the judge signed the order on the 27th.

Ex.: The parties reached a settlement on the ninth at the meeting in Chicago.

(e) *No superscripts with ordinals.* Some word-processing applications automatically make superscripts of *-nd*, *-rd*, *-st*, or *-th* after a number. Yet the convention in legal writing is to leave these suffixes on the baseline. So change the settings to avoid all superscripts with ordinals.

Not this: 9th Cir.

But this: 9th Cir.

5.3 Be consistent about when to use numerals and when to spell out numbers in text—preferably spelling out one to ten and using numerals for 11 and above.

(a) *Main conventions.* The two main style conventions in legal prose are to (1) use numerals for numbers higher than either nine or ten, and (2) use numerals for numbers 100 and higher. Unless court rules dictate otherwise, adopt a version of the former approach: spell out one through ten, and use numerals for 11 and above. The numeral *77*, for example, is tighter, easier to read, and faster to type than the phrase *seventy-seven*. Whatever convention you use, the practice applies to ordinal numbers (first, second, 24th) as well as cardinal numbers (one, two, 24). Exceptions exist, such as for days of the month (see 5.2, 5.3(e)).

Ex.: Edward Shelley had two sons: Henry was his first and Richard his second.

Ex.: An interest isn't any good unless it must vest, if at all, no later than 21 years after some life in being at the creation of the interest.

(b) *Other conventions.* Newspapers and other periodicals use numerals for numbers 10 and higher, spelling out one through nine. Many cities spell out the names of ordinal-numbered streets through Twelfth. And tabular matter such as election returns, stock-market figures, and sports statistics use numerals for all numbers. Some firms and companies adopt a specific style manual or maintain their own style guide for all official use. Be flexible enough to follow a specified style that may govern your writing.

(c) *Numerals in citations.* The style conventions in this section apply only to numbers in text; numbers in citations are always written as numerals unless they are part of a title. (See 5.10.)

(d) *In titles.* Repeat a title as it is written, regardless of what convention you use for your own text.

Ex.: She was reading *The 7 Habits of Highly Effective People.*

Ex.: Gabriel Garcia Marquez, *One Hundred Years of Solitude* 56 (1998).

(e) *Exception for like items.* For a major exception to this rule, no matter which specified threshold governs, see 5.4.

(f) *Exception for legislative drafting.* In legislative and contractual drafting, it is permissible to use a numerals-only policy for numbers: doing so makes them more immediately noticeable.

Ex.: up to 5 years' imprisonment

Ex.: from 1 to 5 years in prison

5.4 If one item of a kind should be in numerals, then use numerals for all items of that kind in the immediate context.

(a) *In series.* If one item in a series should be in numerals because the applicable threshold has been exceeded (see 5.3), use numerals for all items of the same kind.

Ex.: The convicted robber drew concurrent sentences of 5, 8, and 12 years for the three incidents.

(b) *In proximity.* Even if not strictly in a series, numbers that denote the same type of thing should usually reflect the same format (numerals trump spelled-out numbers). But be reasonable and ignore this guidance if the result would be absurd.

Ex.: In 1960 there were 5 lawyers in this county; today there are 125.

But: You can't see the next town, which is just five miles down the road, but you can see the sun, which is 93 million miles away.

5.5 If two numbers that are not of the same kind appear next to each other, one (usually the first) should be spelled out to avoid confusion.

(a) *First number.* When using two different kinds of numbers right together, you should generally spell out the first number and use numerals for the second.

Ex.: The package contained fifty $20 bills. (Normally, we would write *50*.)

Ex.: We are honoring fifteen 4.0-GPA graduates today.

(b) *Second number.* If the second number is an ordinal or part of an adjective phrase, it may be spelled out instead.

Ex.: The team's roster swelled with 17 second-round draftees.

Ex.: We have 256 one-L students this year.

But: We have three 1L representatives on the Student Bar Association. (*Three* should be spelled out anyway: see 5.3(a).)

5.6 Never begin a sentence with a numeral, even if it denotes a year—unless it's part of a proper noun; if you must use a number to start a sentence, spell it out.

(a) *Start of sentence.* No matter what numbering convention you use, always spell out a number at the beginning of a sentence.

Ex.: Eleven months and 29 days later, the plaintiff filed this suit.

Ex.: One hundred twenty-five students registered for the course.

True, in informal writing we increasingly see sentence-starting numerals. But apart from the exception mentioned in (c), the practice is widely considered improper in written English.

(b) *Years.* Avoid starting a sentence with a year; if you must, spell it out.

Not this: 1935 saw the passage of the Social Security Act.

Better: Nineteen thirty-five saw the passage of the Social Security Act.

Best: The Social Security Act passed in 1935.

(c) *Exception for proper nouns.* It's okay to start a sentence with a numeral if it's part of a proper noun.

Ex.: 21st Century Fox is based in New York City.

(d) *Citation.* The caveat against starting a sentence with a numeral holds even if the numeral is part of a citation. (But pure citations, either in text or in footnotes, that aren't part of a grammatical sentence are an exception.) Rewrite to avoid the problem.

Not this: 18 U.S.C. § 2511(2)(a)(i) authorizes the company's monitoring of employee e-mail traffic to enforce company policy.

But this: Title 18, Section 2511(2)(a)(i) of the U.S. Code authorizes the company's monitoring of employee e-mail traffic to enforce company policy.

Better: Federal law authorizes the company's monitoring of employee e-mail traffic to enforce company policy. 18 U.S.C. § 2511(2)(a)(i).

Or this: Federal law authorizes the company's monitoring of employee e-mail traffic to enforce company policy.[5] (Citation in footnote.)

Or this: Under 18 U.S.C. § 2511(2)(a)(i), the company may monitor employee e-mail traffic to enforce company policy.

5.7 Use numerals for statute, volume, chapter, section, and subsection numbers; in tables; in dates and times; for money; with units of measurement; in decimals; and in names of roads, military divisions, and the like.

(a) *General rule.* Whenever numbers are viewed more as mathematical symbols than as units of literary meaning, they are generally to be represented by numerals—as in citations, tables, dates, sums, calculations, and various official designations arrived at by counting.

Ex.: Title 28 of the U.S. Code

Ex.: § 1983

Ex.: Chapter 11

Ex.: 20th century

Ex.: July 4, 1776 (but *the Fourth of July* as the holiday)

Ex.: 5:15 p.m. (but *five-o'clock shadow*)

Ex.: $6.99

Ex.: 4 miles
Ex.: 6%
Ex.: 32°F
Ex.: 1.414
Ex.: I-95

(b) *Exceptions for names.* Some names contain numerals or spelled-out numbers; others are spelled out by convention. Use the preferred name despite any style rule to the contrary.

Ex.: 1st Infantry Division (but *The Big Red One*)
Ex.: First Division, Army of Northern Virginia
Ex.: the First Officers' Training Camp in San Antonio
Ex.: the Eleventh Circuit

(c) *Constitutional articles and amendments.* In text, spell out the ordinal designations of U.S. constitutional amendments (but use Roman numerals in citations—see 5.19(b)). Use Roman numerals in the names of articles.

Ex.: The Thirteenth Amendment abolished slavery.
Ex.: Questions about presidential succession were finally settled by the Twenty-fifth Amendment in 1967.
Ex.: Bankruptcies are overseen by Article I judges without lifetime tenure.

5.8 Spell out a large number that is used idiomatically or as an imprecise estimate or exaggeration.

(a) *Exactness not implied.* When words such as *hundreds* or *millions* are purposely loose or figurative, using numerals may falsely suggest precision. Spelling out the numbers minimizes this effect.

Ex.: Although the plaintiff claims that he was in great pain, he drove past a hundred doctors' offices before stopping at one.
Ex.: I've told you a million times.

(b) *Slogans.* With slogans, no sense of exactness is conveyed, so spelling out is more appropriate than using numerals.

Ex.: The first President Bush presented awards to many of the "thousand points of light" for their volunteer work.
Ex.: McDonald's boasts of "billions and billions served."

5.9 For a number in the millions or more (especially if precision is not required), round it off and spell out *million, billion,* etc.

(a) *Comprehension.* Because small numbers are easier to work with, for both reader and writer, the preferred practice is to replace a long string of zeros with the appropriate word, such as *million* or *billion.*

Ex.: A Middleton County jury awarded the plaintiff $210,000 in compensatory damages and slapped a $2 million punitive-damages verdict on the defendant.

(b) *Rounding off.* If more precision is called for, round the number to one or (at most) two decimal places.

Ex.: Congress allocated $2.6 billion for research on the secret project.

(c) *Dollar sign and word.* If the number denotes money, use either a symbol in front of the number or the corresponding word after the amount, but not both.

Not this: $1 trillion dollars
But this: $1 trillion
Or this: one trillion dollars

(d) *When precision counts.* If precision is required, give the exact number.

Ex.: The Franks sold the property in 2018 for $1,147,901.

5.10 In legal citations, spell the ordinal numerals *2d* and *3d*, not *2nd* and *3rd*—as high as the numbers may go.

(a) *Legal convention.* The proper practice for legal citations is to spell ordinal forms of numerals ending in *2* and *3* by adding only *-d.*

Ex.: *Lee v. Bankers Trust Co.*, 166 F.3d 540 (2d Cir. 1999).
Ex.: H.R. Rep. No. 92-1637, 92d Cong., 2d Sess.

(b) *General convention.* In all contexts besides legal citations—including text in legal documents—use the generally accepted spellings *2nd* and *3rd.*

Ex.: The musical is playing in a theater on 42nd Street.
Ex.: The 92nd Congress passed the act in 1972.

5.11 Avert ambiguities when writing numbers.

(a) *"K" and "M."* In business writing, $25K may be understood to mean $25,000 and 2M to mean 2 million. But in other trade usages, *M* stands for *thousand* (its value as a Roman numeral). Since there is a possibility of ambiguity, these numerical abbreviations should never be used in legal writing.

(b) *Billion and larger.* When referring to numbers of a billion and larger, keep in mind that the terms might be ambiguous to some readers, especially non-Americans. Today, the U.S. definition of terms such as *billion* (= a

> "It is a mistake to give an unnecessary amount of detail. The result is only confusing. It is also a mistake to give precise figures when round numbers serve equally well."
> —*Reginald O. Kapp*

thousand millions) and *trillion* (= a million millions) is universally recognized in international business, finance, and trade. But the traditional British understanding of the terms—and the meaning long accepted in most of the rest of the world—is that a *billion* is a million millions (what Americans call a *trillion*) and a *trillion* is a million times more than that (what Americans might call a *quintillion*). If there's any chance that a term you're using may not be clear to an intended reader, consider specifying on the term's first appearance that you're using the American system. Or simply use all numerals.

5.12 Use a comma to separate large whole-number digits into sets of three, from the right, but don't use commas in room numbers, telephone numbers, highway numbers, military time, years, or other serial numbers, or in page numbers shorter than five digits.

(a) *For thousands.* While some style guides make the comma in a four-digit number optional, it has to be used sometimes (e.g., to make the thousands column line up in a table that also contains numerals of five or more digits). To maintain a consistent style, the better choice is to use the comma all the time.

Ex.: 1,000 clowns

Ex.: 93,000,000 miles

(b) *Exceptions.* Don't use commas in serial-type numbers, such as addresses, military time, phone numbers, product serial numbers, radio-station frequencies, road numbers, room numbers, years, and the like (see 1.12(b)).

Ex.: 1600 Pennsylvania Avenue

Ex.: 1700 hours

Ex.: 800-555-1212

Ex.: 123-45-6789

Ex.: AM 1520

Ex.: Farm Road 2222

Ex.: Room 1408

Ex.: A.D. 2018

(c) *Page numbers.* Don't use a comma in a page number unless the number contains five or more digits.

Ex.: 299 F.3d 1219

Ex.: *Id.* at 1537

Ex.: *Id.* at 15,442

(d) *Not in decimals.* Never use commas within a string of numerals following a decimal point.

Ex.: 3.14159

5.13 Use an en-dash (or a hyphen) to signal an inclusive range of numbers; don't use the word *from* or *between* in front of numbers connected by an en-dash (see 1.57).

(a) *Using* "from" *and* "between." The en-dash often stands for *from . . . to* or *between . . . and*, and it includes both numbers. Use either the punctuation or the words, but not both: don't use *from* or *between* in front of two numbers joined by an en-dash.

Ex.: The discussion can be found on pages 25–27.

Ex.: Nixon's 1969–1974 tenure was marked by diplomatic achievements and domestic controversy.

Not this: The United States fought in World War II from 1941–1945.

But this: The United States fought in World War II from 1941 to 1945.

(b) *Avoiding multiple en-dashes.* Use *to* if the numbers being spanned themselves contain en-dashes.

Ex.: The statute's sanctions are set forth in subsections 84–4 to 84–11.

(c) *Word of measurement.* When expressing a range of numbers in legal writing, it is acceptable to use a unit of measurement once, after the numerals. But it is not acceptable to use a numerical term in the same way because the result is ambiguous.

Ex.: The plot was 140 by 210 feet.

Ex.: The project is expected to cost $30 million–$40 million. (Not *$30–$40 million* because the lower number could designate 30 dollars rather than 30 million dollars.)

(d) *Or hyphen.* Using an en-dash (–) shows attention to typographical style and is easy to do on computers. Although many people use the hyphen (-) for spans—and either mark is considered acceptable—the en-dash signals true fastidiousness.

5.14 Be careful about using apostrophes with numbers.

(a) *Plurals.* Form a numeral's plural by adding an *-s*; don't use an apostrophe.

Ex.: The top scorers included three 143s, four 157s, and one 161.

Ex.: 1920s

Ex.: The robber was described as being in his 40s.

(b) *Possessives.* Although the form is uncommon, possessive numbers must and do use apostrophes.

Ex.: We might look back at 1941's Day of Infamy for guidance.

5.15 Elide to two digits the second number in a range of pages if the numbers are three or more digits long. But don't elide numbers in a range of sections or paragraphs, a range of measurements, or a span of years (see 9.13).

(a) *Rules.* In legal style, don't elide two-digit page numbers. With larger page numbers, elide all but the last two digits if the other digits are the same in both numbers. But if more than two digits change, don't elide any digits.

Ex.: 893 F.2d at 1106–07 (not *1106–7* or *1106–1107*)

Ex.: 56 Fed. Reg. at 42,997–99

But: 56 Fed. Reg. at 42,997–43,000 (*00* alone would not be clear)

(b) *Not with measurements.* Unlike page numbers, which invariably proceed from the smaller number to the larger, measurements may go from the lesser to the greater or vice versa. Elision is never appropriate because of the possible ambiguities.

Ex.: The high temperatures reached 115–119 degrees. (Not *115–19 degrees.*)

(c) *Sections and paragraphs.* Retain all digits in ranges of sections and paragraphs.

Ex.: 42 U.S.C. §§ 12701–12714

Ex.: Miller Aff. ¶¶ 101–102

(d) *Not with years.* In legal style, don't elide the second number in a span of years. This practice differs from that of *The Chicago Manual of Style*, which allows elision if the range is within the same century.

Ex.: Andrew Johnson (1808–1875)

5.16 Use the simplest appropriate forms for times, dates, and money.

(a) *Minute amounts omitted unless needed for accuracy.* Don't include the minutes when writing an even hour—or the cents when writing an even dollar amount—unless the extra numbers are needed for accuracy or to match a related reference nearby.

Ex.: Krol left his house at 6 a.m. to drive to work.

Ex.: Krol was out of the house from 6:00 a.m. until he returned from work at 3:45 p.m.

Ex.: The 911 call was placed at 3:47 p.m.

Ex.: A $10 bill was left on the counter.

Ex.: The check was for exactly $10.37.

(b) *Relative time references.* When the date is important, make sure that the complete date is stated explicitly. But once it is established, avoid repeating the year, or even the month, on every later reference. To speed the narrative, relative references such as "the following week" are typically more helpful to the reader than a series of dates.

Not this: On April 7, 2018, the *Concord Monitor* used the Freedom of Information Act to ask the Nuclear Regulatory Commission for a copy of the safety report. On April 13, 2018, the Commission denied the request.

But this: On April 7, 2018, the *Concord Monitor* used the Freedom of Information Act to ask the Nuclear Regulatory Commission for a copy of the safety report. On April 13, the Commission denied the request.

Or this: On April 7, 2018, the *Concord Monitor* used the Freedom of Information Act to ask the Nuclear Regulatory Commission for a copy of the safety report. On the 13th, the Commission denied the request.

Or this: On April 7, 2018, the *Concord Monitor* used the Freedom of Information Act to ask the Nuclear Regulatory Commission for a copy of the safety report. Six days later, the Commission denied the request.

5.17 When spelling out numbers, hyphenate only the two-word numbers below 100; don't use the word *and* except when expressing cents.

(a) *Hyphen alone.* Don't use *and* to join parts of a whole number.

Not this: She wrote the check for one hundred and seventy-three dollars.

But this: She wrote the check for one hundred seventy-three dollars.

Ex.: Two hundred seventy electoral votes are needed to win.

(b) *With "and."* Use *and* to join the whole part of a number with a fraction.

Ex.: She wrote the check for one hundred seventy-three and 47/100 dollars.

5.18 Hyphenate spelled-out fractions unless one of the terms is itself hyphenated (see 1.63(c)).

(a) *Generally.* Hyphenate fractions regardless of whether they are serving as nouns or adjectives in the sentence.

Ex.: Two-tenths of a mile of skid marks led to the accident site.

Ex.: A two-thirds majority is needed to override a veto.

(b) *Exception.* Don't use a hyphen between a spelled-out numerator and denominator of a fraction if either of those terms itself contains a hyphen.

Ex.: One manufacturer famously claimed that its soap is "ninety-nine and forty-four one-hundredths percent pure." (No hyphen between *ninety-nine and forty-four* and *one-hundredths.*)

5.19 Use Roman numerals sparingly—and only according to convention.

(a) *Successors.* Roman numerals are used in names to differentiate successors. Don't use a comma to separate the name from the number.

Ex.: Loudon Wainwright III

Ex.: Pope John Paul II

(b) *Constitutions.* In citations, use Roman numerals for articles and amendments to the U.S. and state constitutions. (But see 5.7(c) for styles in text.)

Ex.: U.S. Const. art. III, § 1

Ex.: U.S. Const. amend. XIV, § 2

Ex.: Mo. Const. art. XIII, § 3.8

(c) *Outlines.* Roman numerals are traditional for main divisions in outlines.

Ex.: IV. Statement of Facts

(d) *Miscellaneous uses.* By convention, Roman numerals are used in various specific contexts.

Ex.: Super Bowl LXVII

Ex.: MMXIII (e.g., dates in movie credits)

(e) *Romanettes in legal instruments.* Although contracts and other legal instruments commonly contain romanettes to mark lists (i, ii, iii, iv, etc.), they are inferior to Arabic numbers or letters because of their variable length. The accordion-like swelling or shrinking from i to xxxviii makes tabulation difficult and awkward (see 27.3(e)). Romanettes typically indicate a less-than-ideal numbering system.

(f) *Front matter.* Use lowercase Roman numerals to number pages in the front matter of a book.

Ex.: The foreword begins on page ix.

5.20 Never use word-numeral doubling, as by writing "thirty (30) days."

(a) *Historical basis.* The only reason historically for word-numeral doubling was to prevent fraudulent alterations: *30* could, in the days of scribal legal instruments, be changed to *80*, or even *180*, without much difficulty. Hence

> "Roman numerals, especially when set in full capital letters, are large, cumbersome, and typographically unpleasant. . . . Some otherwise literate people cannot count up to C the Roman way."
>
> —*The Chicago Manual of Style*

the rule that words control over numerals in cases of discrepancy. It has always been impossible, or at least very hard, for a forger to alter a scrivener's *thirty* into *eighty*—or *ten* to *ninety*.

By the way, you will occasionally encounter various false explanations of the reasons for doubling numerical references—some having to do with carbon copies, others with early photocopiers, and others still with creating enough risk of error that it encouraged drafters to be more careful. They're all canards, and anyone who repeats such nonsense should be heard with serious skepticism.

(b) *The modern problem.* If you double up in modern legal instruments—apart from negotiable instruments such as checks, where fraud is still a concern—the doubling of numerals leads to the creation of possible discrepancies. In a contract, for example, there may be 50 or so numbers, now to be written 100 times because of doubling. The numbers that stand out visually are the numerals. If 99 numbers are subjected to change, and one change gets overlooked, it will probably be the spelled-out words that remain erroneously unchanged. Yet the words will govern. In modern documents, then, a medieval rule will usually yield the wrong result. So don't double up. Use numerals (subject to 5.3), and in any event check them all carefully.

Not this: Adkins must pay Tolleson two hundred thousand dollars ($200,000) within seven (7) days after this agreement is signed.

But this: Adkins must pay Tolleson $200,000 within 7 days after this agreement is signed.

> "Attorneys . . . have the habit of spelling out numbers next to the usual Arabic symbols for them, as in 'six (6) months in jail' or 'the sum of thirty-two (32) dollars.' This mannerism had a purpose when all documents were handwritten, as personal checks still are. . . . In typed and printed documents, however, the repetition of these figures serves no useful purpose."
>
> —*Ronald L. Goldfarb & James C. Raymond*

§ 6
Typographic Symbols

6.1 The section sign (§) and paragraph sign (¶—also known as a *pilcrow*) see more use in legal writing than anywhere else. Many symbols tend to be used less frequently in legal writing than elsewhere.

A symbol is effective only if the reader instantly recognizes it. For that reason alone, you would be hard-pressed to find a section or paragraph mark in the mass media. Yet lawyers see them every day.

It is this instant recognition that makes a symbol work for you. How much easier it is to recognize *$2.57* than *two dollars and fifty-seven cents*, *28%* than *28 percent* or *twenty-eight percent*, *75°F* than *75 degrees Fahrenheit* or *seventy-five degrees Fahrenheit.*

Some legal writers (and *The Bluebook*) insist that section and paragraph symbols should be restricted to citations only and should never appear in text. But where they help the reader and don't violate any other rule (such as appearing at the beginning of a sentence), they are helpful shortcuts. In a § 1983 action, do not hesitate to call it a *§ 1983 action*—no need to spell out the word *section* (see 9.4(c)).

6.2 When referring to a specific section or paragraph number, use the symbol § (section) or ¶ (paragraph) in text and citations, unless the symbol would start a sentence.

(a) *Legal convention.* In legal writing, the symbols § and ¶ are as recognizable as the symbols % and $ are in popular writing. Because their use facilitates rather than inhibits comprehension, the symbols are stronger than the spelled-out terms. Always use a nonbreaking space, or *hard space*, between the symbol and the number that follows (see 4.13).

> Ex.: The Cooperative contends, however, that despite the apparently absolute language of § 823(f), the statute is subject to additional, implied exceptions, one of which is medical necessity.

> Ex.: This dispute arises under ¶ 36 of the contract, governing periodic payments for supplies and materials.

(b) *Beginning sentence.* Always spell out the word when it begins a sentence.

> Ex.: Section 1983 was enacted by Congress as part of the Ku Klux Klan Act of 1871.

Ex.: Paragraph 52 is only a liquidated-damages clause, but ¶ 53 provides for injunctive relief.

Better: Although ¶ 52 is only a liquidated-damages clause, ¶ 53 provides for injunctive relief.

6.3 Because typographic symbols are typically pluralized by doubling them, use the double symbol §§ or ¶¶ when referring to two or more sections or paragraphs.

(a) *In citations.* Form the plural of a symbol used in a citation by doubling the symbol. If the symbol consists of a letter followed by a period (such as *p.* or *n.*), double the letter and retain the period.

Ex.: Weil contended that Jalyn's actions infringed its trademark rights in violation of §§ 32(1)(a) and 42 of the Lanham Act.

Ex.: p. 36 (singular); pp. 36–42 (plural)

Ex.: pp. 36 ff. (page 36 and the following pages)

Ex.: n. 14 (singular); nn. 14–15 (plural) (in *Bluebook* style, n.14 and nn.14–15)

(b) *Exception with subsections.* Use a single symbol to cite multiple subsections within the same section.

Ex.: § 42(1)(a), (2), (5)(b)

(c) *Exception with disjunctive "or."* Use a single symbol before a list of separate sections or paragraphs joined ultimately by the word *or*. Because *or* serves a disjunctive function, each reference in the list could be taken individually, so the singular is appropriate. Likewise, if such a list begins a sentence, write out the singular forms *Section* or *Paragraph*.

Ex.: This provision does not apply to the granting of a lien on a claim arising under § 544, 545, 547, 548, 549, 553(b), 723(a), or 724(a).

(d) *With page numbers.* If you also provide page numbers when citing nonconsecutive sections, list the sections separately and use a single symbol before each. (Do this even when citing subsections within the same section, and provide the full section number each time.) Place a comma after the section number, followed by *at* and the relevant page number or numbers. Use another comma before each subsequent section. If citing consecutive sections inclusively, follow the rules in (a) and (b) above, and then add a comma, the word *at*, and the page numbers.

Ex.: § 1332(a)(2), at 391, § 1332(c)(1)–(2), at 397–98, § 1404, at 472–85

Ex.: § 1332(a)(2)–(c)(1), at 391–97

Ex.: §§ 1332–1335, at 390–412

(e) *Et seq.* Because *et seq.* refers to multiple sections or paragraphs, it arguably requires the plural form §§ or ¶¶ <§§ 64 et seq.>. Then again, it might arguably refer to § 64 and the following sections <§ 64 et seq.>. But the use of *et seq.* is poor form that is forbidden by *The Bluebook* (Rule 3.3(b)) and disfavored by *ALWD* (Rule 6.2(b)). If possible cite the complete reference instead: find the ending point, and name it.

6.4 Use the symbols $, ¢, %, and ° with numerals in text; spell out the words when used alone.

(a) *Commonly understood.* When used with numerals, the symbols for dollars, cents, percentages, and degrees are more speedily comprehended than the spelled-out terms they stand for. The symbol is therefore preferable in text. Make the symbol flush with the numerals (that is, don't put a space between the symbol and the numerical figure).

Ex.: My torts casebook cost $70.

Ex.: I ate a 99¢ hot dog for lunch.

Ex.: Julie Kessler received 70% of the vote in the election.

Ex.: It must be 100° outside.

(b) *Spelling out.* When the number is spelled out for some reason, as when it falls at the beginning of a sentence or when it is purposely imprecise, the word that the symbol stands for must also be spelled out.

Ex.: Seventy dollars is a lot to pay for a schoolbook.

Ex.: Ninety-nine cents isn't cheap for a hot dog if you have to kick in another buck for antacids.

Ex.: Seventy percent of the vote went to Kessler to win the election outright.

Ex.: The locals say that hundred-degree temperatures are normal for this time of year.

(c) *Range.* When a range is expressed by two numerals, repeat the symbol.

> "**section,** n. . . . **2b.** A subdivision of a written or printed work, a statute, or the like. Often represented by the symbol § (preceding a numeral figure); also abbreviated sect. (rarely sec.). . . .
>
> "**6.** *Printing.* The sign §, originally used to introduce the number of a 'section' (sense 2b); subsequently used also as a mark of reference to notes in the margin or at the foot of a page. Also called **section-mark.**
>
> "The primary use of the sign seems to have become rare in the 18th c., and to have been revived in the latter part of the 19th c. under German influence. German printers give to this mark the name of *paragraph.*"
>
> —*Oxford English Dictionary*

Ex.: The company enjoyed a 15%–20% increase in sales in each of its first three years.

Ex.: Price cuts ranged from 25¢ to 40¢ per unit.

Ex.: The more powerful chip increased internal heat 2°–4°F.

(d) *Foot, inch marks.* Don't use smart quotes for *foot* and *inch* symbols. The correct marks are the prime and double-prime ([′] for *foot*, [″] for *inch*). As an acceptable substitute, you may use straight typewriter-style quotation marks, preferably in italic type ([*'*] for *foot*, [*"*] for *inch*). But the open and close quotation marks (single and double) are never acceptable for denoting measures in feet and inches.

Unacceptable: The skid marks were measured at 8'4".

Acceptable: The skid marks were measured at 8*'*4*"*.

Best: The skid marks were measured at 8′4″.

(e) *"At" symbol.* Use the @ (*at* symbol) only in e-mail addresses and social-media designations that call for it, such as Twitter handles.

Ex.: attorney@lawfirm.com

Ex.: @Username

6.5 Use an ampersand in a business name, in a case citation, and in a citation to a work by two or more authors.

(a) *In business names.* Use an ampersand when referring to a business that uses one in its formal name. Don't use an ampersand if the company's designation uses the word *and*.

Ex.: Procter & Gamble

Ex.: Pulaski Bank & Trust Co.

Ex.: Thompson & Knight, P.C.

Ex.: Sears, Roebuck and Co.

Ex.: Brown and Root Energy Services

(b) *In case names.* Regardless of a company's formal name, an ampersand may replace the word *and* in a case citation.

Ex.: Scrooge and Marley, L.L.P. (formal name)

Ex.: *Scrooge & Marley v. Cratchit, L.L.P.* (case name)

(c) *With multiple authors.* Use an ampersand before the final name in a citation to a work by two or more authors. If the work has three or more authors, you may name the first and use *et al.* to represent the others.

Ex.: Michael E. Tigar & Jane B. Tigar, *Federal Appeals: Jurisdiction and Practice* 114–15 (3d ed., West 1999)

Ex.: Jack H. Friedenthal, Mary Kay Kane & Arthur R. Miller, *Civil Procedure* 159 (4th ed., West 2005)

Or: Jack H. Friedenthal et al., *Civil Procedure* 159 (4th ed., West 2005)

6.6 Do not use a trademark or copyright symbol in text.

(a) *Purpose.* The purpose of intellectual-property symbols is to let the owner put the public on notice that the work is protected. There is no legal requirement that the symbol be reproduced every time the protected mark appears in copy, and to do so is distracting. The trademarked word should be capitalized, but no symbol should be used.

Ex.: Hard Rock owns the rights to a variety of Hard Rock trademarks.

Ex.: Handmacher–Vogel, Inc. owns Registration No. 554,949, comprising the word "Weathervane," coupled with the representation of a weathervane, for women's suits.

(b) *Significance.* The ® symbol signifies that the trademark or servicemark is federally registered. The ™ or ℠ symbol signifies a trademark or servicemark that is claimed but not necessarily registered.

(c) *Copyright notice.* The copyright symbol © should appear only in a copyright-notice line, not in text. Because the symbol stands for the word *copyright*, use a word space (nonbreaking) between it and the date. The U.S. Copyright Office accepts either of the following forms for the notice:

Ex.: © 2006 West Group

Ex.: Copyright 2006 by West Group

> "**paragraph,** n. . . . **2.** *Typogr.* A symbol or character (in later use usually ¶), originally used to mark the start of a new section of a text, later also used to introduce an editorial comment or as a reference to a footnote. Now chiefly hist.
>
> "The original use is common in Middle English MSS. . . . It was retained by early printers, and continued to be used to mark sections (usually several verses in length) in some bibles."
>
> "**pilcrow,** n. *Typogr.* Now chiefly hist. A symbol marking the start of a paragraph."
>
> —*Oxford English Dictionary*

§ 7
Spelling

7.1 The very thing that makes English such a rich language also makes its spelling so difficult. Words have entered modern English from many sources with different systems of spelling. Because words also bring their own pronunciations, phonetics is often an unreliable spelling aid.

The result of this mishmash is that for every "rule" of spelling there are usually many exceptions. Still, some basic rules come in handy again and again. The same is true for general guidelines about such matters as compounding words and hyphenating prefixes.

But when it comes to spelling, there is no alternative to looking a word up in a current desktop dictionary. No writer should hesitate to do so if there is any doubt about the spelling. After all, misspelled words in a legal document signal sloppiness, which explodes the writer's credibility.

General Principles

7.2 Always use your computer's spell-checker, but never rely on it alone.

(a) *Generally.* Get to know your computer's spell-checker, and especially how to add to and edit its custom dictionaries. Words and names that your computer flags over and over again—but that you know are spelled correctly—you should add to your custom dictionary.

(b) *Self-check.* Make a habit of checking your spelling every time you enter new text or edit existing drafts. The best routine is to save the file one last time (having saved regularly while working on the document), then run the spell-check, and finally close the file, saving changes.

(c) *Proofreaders.* Don't rely solely on the computer's spell-checker; it simply cannot substitute for perceptive human eyes. Invariably, the more eyes that see a draft, the better. Your work product reflects your level of professionalism, and neglectful errors suggest less-than-rigorous work habits.

(d) *Autocorrection.* Be careful about letting your computer make automatic corrections; be especially wary of such "time-saving" features as the global

> "Never use a doubtful word without investigation."
> —*Austin Phelps & Henry Allyn Frink*

find-and-replace at one fell swoop. There's a failure rate with automatic substitutions, and the practice will almost invariably introduce new errors.

7.3 Use an up-to-date dictionary. Preferably, everyone in an organization should use the same one.

(a) *Current edition.* One universal is that language changes, and change often occurs rapidly with compound words and new terms. Use the current edition of a good dictionary as your standard. *Merriam-Webster's Collegiate Dictionary* and *Webster's New World Dictionary* are the best. *The American Heritage Dictionary of the English Language* and *The New Oxford American Dictionary* are also first-rate. For legal terminology, consult the current unabridged edition of *Black's Law Dictionary*; each edition has thousands of significant updates. And get to know your computer's dictionary feature. Start adding to it the terms and names that you use often and that the spell-checker always flags.

(b) *Uniformity.* Law offices should adopt a standard dictionary for everyone to use. This is an inexpensive and easy way to ensure consistency in office writings.

7.4 Keep a list of the words you have trouble with; update it regularly and keep it handy.

(a) *Troublesome words.* We all have our own words that we struggle with every time we use them. Keep a list of your own troublesome words on your computer. If you have to look up a word more than once, add it to your list.

(b) *Ease of reference.* Sort the list in alphabetical order, and keep a printout handy beside your computer or in your desk. Not only is consulting your personal crib sheet faster than consulting a dictionary, but the effort you take to add a word to the list will itself help you learn the correct spelling.

7.5 Know the elementary spelling rules.

(a) *"I" before "e."* We all remember the rule: "*i* before *e*, except after *c*, or when sounded like *a*, as in *neighbor* and *weigh*" <feint>. But there are many exceptions: *codeine*, *counterfeit*, *either*, *feisty*, *foreign*, *forfeit*, *height*, *heir*, *leisure*, *neither*, *protein*, *seize*, *sovereign*, *weird*. Others include French words such as *caffeine*; and German words such as *braumeister*, *poltergeist*, and *stein*.

(b) *Silent "-e" and suffixes.* Drop the silent *-e* at the end of a word before adding a suffix that starts with a vowel <define–definable–defining>.

- By convention (and to keep the rule consistent), consider the silent *-e* dropped even if the suffix itself begins with *e-*, whether or not its replacement is still silent <refined–refinery>.

- If the silent *-e* is preceded by a vowel, the *-e* is dropped even if the suffix starts with a consonant <argue–argued–argument>.
- The most common exceptions to the rule crop up (1) where the silent *-e* is preceded by a soft *-c-* or *-g-*, to preserve the pronunciation <commence–commencement> <manage–management> (but the rule is preserved where the pronunciation is not threatened, as the *-dg-* accomplishes in *abridgment*, *acknowledgment*, *drudgery*, and *judgment*); (2) where the form might be confused with other words <dyeing> <singeing>; (3) where the word ends in *-ee*, *-ye*, or *-oe* <freeing (but *freed*)> <eyeing (but *eyed*)> <canoeing (but *canoed*)>; and (4) where the word ends in *-ie* <lie–lying (but *lied*) <die–dying (but *died*)>.

(c) *"-y" ending and suffixes.* When adding a suffix to a word that ends in *-y* preceded by a consonant:

- if the suffix is *-ing*, just add the suffix <burying>; but
- if the suffix is anything else, change the *-y* to *-i* <buried> <buries>.

(d) *Doubling consonants.* Double the final consonant before adding a suffix if:

- the word ends with a single consonant (other than *-w* or *-x*) preceded by a single vowel <omit–omitted–omitting>;
- it is a single-syllable word, or it is a multisyllable word and the final syllable is accented both before and after the suffix is added <cancel–canceled–canceling> (hence also *referred* but *reference*); or
- the suffix to be attached begins with a vowel, as with *-ee* or *-al* <commit–committee–commitment> <defer–deferral–deferment> but <travel–traveler–traveling> (accent on first syllable); <deal–dealer–dealing> (final consonant preceded by two vowels).

(e) *"-ic" ending and suffixes.* Add a *-k-* to a word ending in *-ic* before appending a suffix that starts with a vowel <trafficker> <panicky> <picnicking> <politicking>, but don't add one before a suffix that starts with a consonant <frolicsome>.

> "Spelling and pronunciation are not fully comparable .... People have been speaking English far longer than they have been writing it. And, of course, each of us learned first to speak and only later to write. Writing, though based on speech, is a somewhat artificial and stripped-down version of it." —*Barbara Wallraff*

7.6 Avoid hyphens with most prefixes and suffixes (but see 1.66).

(a) *Modern trend.* While there are exceptions, the modern trend is away from hyphenating prefixes. For most words, this principle applies even if the prefix ends with the same letter that begins the main word <neoorthodoxy> <nonnative> <posttrial> <preemption> <reelect>. An exception occurs with *anti-* combined with words beginning with *i-* <anti-inflammatory>.

(b) *Proper nouns.* A hyphen is always required when joining a prefix to a proper noun <pro-American> <pre-Columbian> <inter-European>.

(c) *Hyphenated prefixes.* A hyphen is almost always required with the prefixes *self-* <self-serving> (the exception to the exception is *selfsame*), *all-* <all-consuming>, *ex-* <ex-governor>, and *quasi-* <quasi-contract>.

(d) *For clarity.* A hyphen is sometimes needed to prevent a misreading <pre-judicial> <pre-sent> <re-lease> <un-ionized>.

(e) *With numerals.* Use a hyphen between a prefix and a date or other numeral <post-2000> <sub-0°F>.

(f) *With proper names.* Use a hyphen to combine two proper names into a single label <Italian-American>. But use an en-dash instead to indicate equal status <Taft–Hartley Act> (see 1.59(a), 7.19).

(g) *With hyphenated phrases.* Use a hyphen to join a prefix to a phrasal adjective <non-life-threatening injury> <pro-right-to-work state>. Although some typesetters use an en-dash after the prefix in such a phrasal adjective, the result looks overfussy and confuses some readers.

(h) *Suffixes.* Generally, don't use a hyphen between a word and its suffix. Two exceptions are: (1) when the result would otherwise repeat the same letter three times <childlike (but *quill-like*)>, and (2) with the suffix *-wise* in an adjective <penny-wise> but not in an adverb <otherwise>.

Plurals

7.7 Form the plural of most regular nouns by adding *-s* or *-es*.

(a) *Basic rule.* The simple plural form is the suffix *-s* <facts> <suits>.

(b) *Sibilant endings.* When the word already ends in *-s* or another sibilant sound (*-z*; *-x*; *-sh*; *-ch*):

- if the word ends in a consonant, add *-es* <boxes> <benches>; or

- if the word ends in a silent *-e*, drop the *-e* and add *-es* (the *-e* is now pronounced) <cases> <justices>.

(c) *"-y" ending.* If the word ends in *-y* preceded by a consonant, change the *-y* to *-i* before adding *-es* <jury–juries>. A common exception: *monies* is considered a passable but poor substitute for *moneys*.

(d) *"-o" ending.* If the word ends in *-o* and you're unsure of the plural form, check a dictionary because exceptions abound.

- Generally, if the final *-o* is preceded by a vowel, add *-s* to form the plural <trios> <zoos>; by a consonant, add *-es* <heroes> <tomatoes>.
- But many consonant-*o* words take *-s* alone <bozos> <silos>—many musical terms fall under this exception <pianos> <solos>.
- Many words can take either form <mottos–mottoes> <lassos–lassoes>, and some can even take a third form <buffaloes–buffalos–buffalo>.
- Words that appear in the plural as often as in the singular tend to take the *-es* ending <dominoes> <peccadilloes>.
- Foreign terms, proper names, and shortened terms tend to take the *-os* ending <gazebos> <Cheerios> <limos>.

(e) *"-f" or "-fe" ending.* If the word ends in *-f* or *-fe* (but not *-ff*), change that ending to *-v* and add *-es* <scarf–scarves> <knife–knives>. This rule also has many exceptions <roof–roofs> <safe–safes>, so unless you're sure of the spelling, consult a dictionary.

(f) *Irregular words.* If the word is irregular, the plural may be formed by changing vowels <foot–feet> <woman–women> and sometimes consonants <mouse–mice>; for a few words, by adding *-en* <ox–oxen> or *-ren* <child–children>; and, for even fewer words, by doing both <brother–brethren (even though the usual plural is *brothers*>.

(g) *Proper names.* For proper names, follow the rule for regular forms, but don't change a final *-y* to *-ie* <the Dalys> <four Marys in our family>. By convention, a few exceptions exist <the Rockies>. Don't make the common error of using an apostrophe to form the plural of a name.

7.8 Check the spelling of the plural forms of foreign terms; in most instances, prefer the anglicized form if one exists.

(a) *"-is" ending.* Many words from Latin that end in *-is* form the plural by changing the ending to *-es* <axis–axes> <neurosis–neuroses> <parenthesis–parentheses>.

(b) *"-um" ending.* Many foreign terms that end in *-um* form the plural by changing the ending to *-a* <bacterium–bacteria> <medium–media>. But most of these words have become anglicized and now have regular plural forms <forum–forums> <stadium–stadiums>. Many can take either form <curriculum–curricula–curriculums> <memorandum–memoranda–memorandums>, often according to the field they are used in. Prefer the regular English form ending in *-s*.

(c) *"-us" ending.* Many foreign terms that end in *-us* form the plural by changing the ending to *-i* <alumnus–alumni> <radius–radii>. But most of these words have become anglicized and now have regular plural forms <focus–focuses> <prospectus–prospectuses>. Many can take either form <cactus–cactuses–cacti> <fungus–funguses–fungi>, often according to the field they are used in. A few foreign terms that end in *-us* form the plural without any change in form <apparatus–apparatus>. Still others change the ending to *-era* or *-ora* <opus–opera> <genus–genera>. Of these, some are anglicized and accept the standard plural form as well <corpus–corpora–corpuses>. Avoid incorrect classical forms such as *octopi* (the correct English plural is *octopuses*, the classical plural being *octopodes*).

(d) *"-a" ending.* Many foreign terms that end in *-a* form the plural by changing the ending to *-ae* <alumna–alumnae> <alga–algae>. But most of these words have become anglicized and now have regular plural forms <cornea–corneas> <encyclopedia–encyclopedias>. Many can take either form <formula–formulas–formulae> <antenna–antennas–antennae>, often according to the field they are used in. Prefer the regular English form ending in *-s*.

(e) *"-on" ending.* Many foreign terms that end in *-on* form the plural by changing the ending to *-a* <phenomenon–phenomena> <criterion–criteria>. These words sometimes confuse writers because the plural form, which dominates in usage, looks like the singular form described in 7.8(d), so there is a mistaken tendency to add an *-s* to the already-plural form to derive, e.g., **phenomenas*, a nonword.

(f) *"-ex" or "-ix" ending.* Many foreign words that end in *-ex* or *-ix* form the classical plural by changing the ending to *-ices* <index–indices> <appendix–appendices>, but it is usually preferable to use the anglicized *-es* form <indexes> <appendixes>.

(g) *"-eau" ending.* A few foreign terms that end in *-eau* form the plural by changing the ending to *-eaux*, but they may take the regular anglicized plural form as well <bureau–bureaux–bureaus> <tableau–tableaux–tableaus>.

(h) *Retained forms.* Other foreign terms retain their form from the Italian <graffito–graffiti>, Greek <stigma–stigmata>, Hebrew <cherub–cherubim>, and other languages.

*An invariably inferior form.

7.9 In general, form the plural of a compound noun by pluralizing the main element.

(a) *Equivalents.* If both elements of the compound are nouns of roughly equal importance, and especially if the word is closed (not written as two words or hyphenated), pluralize the last element <county jails> <court documents> <handcuffs> <caseloads>.

(b) *Noun and modifier.* If the open compound comprises a noun followed by a modifier (also known as a *postpositive adjective*), pluralize the noun. Such open compounds occur frequently with legal terms taken from the French <attorneys-at-law> <attorneys general> <letters patent> <notaries public>.

(c) *Noun and particle.* If the compound fuses a noun with a preposition particle, the noun usually takes the plural form <hangers-on> <mothers-in-law> <passersby>.

(d) *Verb and particle.* If the compound joins a verb with an adverb particle, the plural form falls at the end of the word <runoffs> <sit-ins> <time-outs>.

(e) *Particle first.* If the particle precedes the noun or nominal verb, the plural falls at the end of the word <bystanders> <overruns> <undercurrents>.

(f) *"-ful" ending.* Pluralize words ending in *-ful* by adding *-s* to the end of the suffix <cupfuls> <handfuls>, but if the adjective *full* is used instead, pluralize the noun <cups full> <hands full>.

7.10 Follow a consistent style in forming the plurals of letters, words used as words (rather than for their meanings), numbers, and abbreviations.

(a) *Letters.* Form the plural of a single lowercase letter by setting the letter in italics and appending an unitalicized *-'s* <*p*'s and *q*'s>.

(b) *Words as words.* Form the plural of a word used as a word (rather than for its meaning) by italicizing the word and appending an unitalicized *-s* or *-es* <too many *of*s in a sentence make for bloated prose>.

(c) *Numbers.* Form the plural of numbers by adding *-s* without an apostrophe <the 1990s> <afternoon temperatures in the 70s>. While some older style manuals recommend using *-'s* in these constructions, the modern trend favors the simpler style.

(d) *Initialisms.* Add *-s* (with no apostrophe) to form the plural of initialisms <IRAs>, words that began as initialisms <lasers>, and capitalized unpunctuated abbreviations <CDs>.

(e) *Abbreviations.* Form the plural of abbreviations that are punctuated or all lowercase by adding *-'s* <LL.M.'s> <rpm's>.

(f) *Citations.* Form the plural of one-letter abbreviations in citations (*l.* for *line*, *n.* for *note*, *p.* for *page*, *v.* for *verse*) by doubling the letter <pp. 10–12> <nn.4–7>.

(g) *Measurements.* Don't change the form of spatial measurement abbreviations used in the plural <10 yd.> <4 mi.>, but do add *-s* to form the plurals of temporal measurements <30 mins.> <2 hrs.>.

Possessives

7.11 Add *-'s* to the end of a word to form the possessive of (1) a singular noun, or (2) a plural noun that does not end in an *s* or *z* sound (always an irregular plural).

(a) *Basic rule.* The general rule is to add an *-'s* to a word when forming the possessive of a singular noun <boy's> <girl's> <child's> or an irregular plural without a sibilant ending <men's> <women's> <children's>.

(b) *No exception for sibilant endings.* The rule applies to a singular noun even if the base word ends in *-s* <octopus's>, *-ss* <witness's>, or a double sibilant sound <princess's; nuisance's>. Admittedly, journalists follow a different rule, omitting the *-s* after the apostrophe , in accordance with the *AP Stylebook*. But the prevailing rule among nonjournalists of all kinds is to keep the *'s*.

(c) *Names.* The rules don't change for a proper noun <Chris's car> <the Cortezes' house>. If you're tempted to use a lone apostrophe rather than *-'s* on a singular possessive because the base word ends in a sibilant sound, try putting the word at the end of an answer with the noun understood. For example, if you're tempted to write, "This accident was caused by Mr. Jones' negligence," think how you would answer the question, "Whose negligence caused this accident?" Your answer would surely be, "Mr. Jones's." So write instead, "This accident was caused by Mr. Jones's negligence."

(d) *Ancient names.* In earlier practice, some ancient multisyllabic names ending in a sibilant sound took the apostrophe alone <Jesus'> <Moses'> <Socrates'>. This exception applied exclusively to classical and biblical names. It was an arbitrary "convention" and unwieldy—there was no list of names the exception applied to, only a few examples. The modern practice is to form these possessives in the usual, conventional way <Jesus's> <Moses's> <Socrates's>.

(e) *Singular name, plural form.* Singular names that are formed from a plural term take the apostrophe alone <American Airlines' profits (but *American's profits*)> <the Court of Appeals' decision>.

(f) *"For —— sake."* Idioms combining a word ending in a sibilant sound with the word *sake* use the apostrophe alone <for convenience' sake> <for goodness' sake>.

(g) *Postpositive exception.* Noun phrases that include a postpositive adjective cannot make a plural possessive. With such plurals as *attorneys general*, *notaries public*, and *professors emeriti*, it becomes necessary to use an *of*-genitive <the briefs of the attorneys general> <the signatures of seven notaries public>. No phrasal possessives are acceptable with these phrases.

(h) *The greengrocer's apostrophe.* Avoid the common but gross error of using an apostrophe to form a word's plural. The colloquial term *grocer's apostrophe* refers to the frequency of this error in shop signs.

Not this: Serving Minneapolitan's for 50 years
But this: Serving Minneapolitans for 50 years

Not this: Taco's—99¢
But this: Tacos—99¢

Not this: The Stevenson's live here.
But this: The Stevensons live here.

7.12 Add an apostrophe to the end of a regular plural to form a plural possessive, even if it ends in an *s* or *z* sound.

(a) *Basic rule.* The general rule is to pluralize first <boys> <women> <Smiths> <Joneses>, and then to form the possessive <boys'> <women's> <Smiths'> <Joneses'>.

(b) *Exception.* A very narrow exception arises with irregular-form plurals, even though they end in an *s* sound <mice's> <geese's>.

7.13 Don't use apostrophes with possessive pronouns or *who*.

(a) *Confused with contractions.* Apostrophes frequently cause misspellings when pronouns are confused with contractions—*its* (possessive) vs. *it's* (contraction of *it is*); *your* (possessive) vs. *you're* (contraction of *you are*); *whose* (possessive) vs. *who's* (contraction of *who is*).

(b) *Simple test.* One test is to always sound out the words that the contraction stands for when you use an apostrophe with these pronouns. If the contraction is wrong, use the other form instead.

> "Dictionaries are tools, and they are much more complicated and capable of many more uses than students suspect."
> —*Mitford M. Mathews*

7.14 With most phrases, form the possessive on the last word.

(a) *Last word.* The possessive form must go immediately before the word it modifies to prevent a misunderstanding <the school board's decision> <the Twin Cities' ball club>.

(b) *Contrasted with compound plurals.* Note how this rule differs from the rule for forming plurals of some compound words. For example, the plural of *attorney general* is *attorneys general*, but the singular possessive is *attorney general's*. Likewise, the plural is *sons-in-law*, but the singular possessive is *son-in-law's* (see 7.9(b)). These terms have no acceptable plural possessive (see 7.11(g), 11.8(b)). Use instead the *of*-genitive and write *the offices of the assistant attorneys general*.

7.15 Use the same rules for numbers and abbreviations.

(a) *Number examples.* The standards for singular and plural possessives hold true for numbers <2018's top story> <the 49ers' season>.

(b) *Abbreviation examples.* The standards for singular and plural possessives hold true for abbreviations <the NAACP's boycott> <the VIPs' table>.

Compounds

7.16 A compound word joins two or more words to express a single thing. Frequently used compounds become a permanent part of the language <rooftop> <farmhouse>, but many others are writers' temporary constructions that will probably never see widespread use <cyberlag> <waffle-textured>. These latter constructions can't be found in any dictionary, so how do we know whether to spell them as separate words ("open"), hyphenated, or as a single word ("closed")? A few principles can guide us, but there are no hard-and-fast rules.

Compound words tend to evolve over time and with general acceptance and familiarity, from the open form <whistle blower> to the hyphenated form <whistle-blower> to the closed form <whistleblower>. All three forms of *whistleblower* are currently in use (the one-word form being best).

A similar problem arises when words are strung together to modify another word. These strung-together-to-modify-another-word constructions are called *phrasal adjectives*. In this paragraph, for example, the *strung*-phrase poses no problem in the first sentence because the words are in natural word order. In the second sentence, though, they act as a single unit to modify the word *constructions*. Without the hyphens, the reader would have a hard time sorting out the sentence. No dictionary could anticipate every possible combination of words that could make up such a phrase, and lexicographers purposely omit most such nonce phrases.

Again, though, a writer may use certain guidelines in handling them.

7.17 A compound formed by two nouns of equal importance, especially those of one-syllable nouns and occasionally when one noun has two syllables, is likely to be closed.

(a) *Pronunciation clue.* One clue to the proper form of a compound is how it is pronounced. If the stress is clearly on the first word, the compound tends to be closed <workday> <bedspread> <classmate>. (Note that *caselaw* is preferably solid.) If the words carry the same stress, the compound tends to be open <ball game> <home page> <iron ore>.

(b) *Evolving use.* Watch for evolving use: from two words, to a hyphenated form, to a single compound. For example, in 1998–1999 *web site* was picked by writers 81% of the time (according to a Westlaw news survey). But by 2001 that open form was in a statistical tie with the single word *website.* The same evolution can be seen with other words, such as *database*, *fundraiser*, and *lawnmower.*

(c) *Human suffixes.* A compound formed with *man*, *woman*, or *person* is usually closed <fireman> <policewoman> <spokesperson> <busboy>, but there are exceptions <flower girl> (but see 13.5(p)).

7.18 The combination of an adjective and a noun is usually open.

(a) *Generally.* Since an adjective normally precedes the word it modifies, there is little reason to join the terms <red dog> <hot pad> <deep freeze>.

(b) *Distinct meaning.* On the other hand, when the two words take on a distinct meaning, they are often combined: a *hot bed* signifies something completely different from a *hotbed.* The same principle applies to many other words <blueprint> <shorthand> <drywall>.

7.19 Combine words of equal importance with an en-dash (see 1.59(a)).

(a) *Duality.* To show a double role or office, join the words with an en-dash <writer–philosopher> <secretary–treasurer>.

(b) *Measurement.* Also use this construction to join two unlike units of measurement when they are multiplied together <4 column–inches> <33 foot–pounds>. No en-dash is used where like units of measure are multiplied together <1,200 square feet> <4 cubic meters>.

(c) *Hyphen acceptable.* A hyphen is often used instead of the en-dash for these constructions, but the en-dash is stronger at showing equivalence between the joined terms.

7.20 When a noun is joined with a preceding preposition or adverb, the compound is usually closed.

(a) *Independent meaning.* Often preposition–noun or adverb–noun compounds have significance independent of their components and should be closed <upswing> <downtown> <overview> <underwear>.

(b) *No independent meaning.* But when the independent significance is weaker, the words are often open or hyphenated <down payment> <off-season>.

7.21 When a noun is joined to a gerund, it is usually hyphenated.

(a) *Temporary terms.* Hyphenate noun–gerund compounds, especially temporary phrases—those coined on the fly rather than established in common usage <wheat-growing> <trip-planning> <charity-giving>.

(b) *Permanent terms.* But hyphenation remains the rule with many permanent phrases as well <double-dealing> <ballot-stuffing> <house-raising>.

(c) *Closed terms.* Many such gerund phrases have become closed compounds <fundraising> <lawmaking> <housecleaning> <birdwatching>, especially terms that have secondary significance apart from their component terms <babysitting> <handwriting> <stonewalling>.

> "Borrowed words raise two questions: Should the words be italicized, and should they retain diacritical marks? . . . In general, the more widely used a foreign word becomes, the less need there is to italicize it. By the time a word appears in an American dictionary, italicizing is not only unnecessary but may seem somewhat pretentious.
>
> "The use of diacritical marks is more complex. Most modern languages written in the Latin alphabet use such marks; in only a very few cases, however, where confusion could result, does English retain them—*résumé* is one example."
>
> —*New York Public Library Writer's Guide to Style and Usage*

(d) *Open terms.* A few such phrases remain two words <data processing> <bill collecting> <lawn bowling>. But even such a phrase takes a hyphen when used as a phrasal adjective <data-processing department> (see 1.62(h)).

7.22 When a verb is coupled with a preposition or adverb, it is open, but a noun derived from the same form is either closed (usually) or hyphenated.

(a) *Phrasal verbs.* A verb comprising more than one word (usually a verb and an adverb or preposition) is called a *phrasal verb.* The term after the verb is called a *particle*, and it gives the verb a different meaning than the verb would have standing alone <hold up> <take off> <break down>.

(b) *As closed nouns.* Many of these phrasal verbs can be used as one-word nouns <holdup> <takeoff> <breakdown>. But some cannot <get over> <move on> <take up>.

(c) *Short particles.* When the particle is very short (two letters), the resulting noun is sometimes hyphenated <break-in>, sometimes not <breakup> <windup>. The determining factor seems to be whether the hyphenless form might create a miscue—as *breakin* could suggest *breakin'*.

7.23 When a verb is joined to a preceding preposition or adverb, the resulting word is closed; words formed this way don't serve as nouns.

(a) *Effect of closing.* Coupling a particle to a verb in that order creates a new word with a distinct meaning <uphold> <undermine> <oversee>.

(b) *Noun formation.* To form a noun, such a word must take on the *-ing* gerund ending <upholding> <undermining> <overseeing>.

7.24 A verb formed from a compound noun often takes the same form as the noun.

(a) *Closed.* If the noun is solid, the verb is almost always solid as well <rubberneck> <railroad> <handcuff>.

(b) *Hyphenated.* If the noun is open or hyphenated, the verb is usually hyphenated <rubber stamp (noun) vs. rubber-stamp (verb)>.

(c) *Adjective-noun phrase.* If an adjective-noun phrase is used as a verb, the verb is hyphenated even though the noun phrase would be open <strong-arm> <bad-mouth> <soft-pedal>.

7.25 For many other terms, no reliable principles apply; use a current dictionary to check the spelling.

(a) *Possessive noun–noun.* When a noun is joined with another noun in the possessive case, the result may be open <dead man's float>, hyphenated (more commonly) <bird's-eye>, or closed (rarely) <menswear>. When the words are joined, the apostrophe is lost <hairsbreadth>.

(b) *Agent noun.* When a noun is joined to a verb and used as an agent noun (with an *-er* or *-or* suffix), the result is usually hyphenated <page-turner> <pencil-pusher> <vote-getter>. These words seem to take awhile to close <bookkeeper> <copyeditor> <globetrotter>. And alternative spellings often continue to be common <copy editor>.

(c) *Verb–particle.* When the *-er* or *-ing* form of a verb is coupled with a trailing preposition or adverb, the resulting noun is usually hyphenated <looker-on (but *onlooker*)> <runner-up> <dressing-down>, and the first word usually takes the plural form <lookers-on> <runners-up>, but not always <dressing-downs>. Yet some similar terms don't follow these principles <passerby (or *passer-by*)–passersby (or *passers-by*)>.

(d) *Longer phrases.* Longer phrases may or may not be hyphenated when used as nouns <know-it-all> <son of a gun>.

(e) *Letter plus noun.* A noun coupled with a letter may or may not be hyphenated <A-line dress> <B movie> <C clef> <D-Day> <E-flat minor>.

American vs. British Spelling

7.26 Be aware of variations in American and British spelling. For the most part, the differences fall into one of several categories.

(a) *Scope.* Use of the British English spelling conventions extends well beyond the United Kingdom: they are also found in Canada, Australia, New Zealand, India, Nigeria, and all other Commonwealth countries. The spellings aren't erroneous just because they are quoted in an American document, so they never warrant a [*sic*] notation. Either keep the British spelling or paraphrase the quoted material.

(b) *"-ize" vs. "-ise."* In American spelling, the action suffix used in changing a noun into a verb is spelled with a *-z-*. British spelling often uses an *-s-* instead, although the *-z-* spelling is sometimes acceptable as well.

AmE: analyze	BrE: analyse
AmE: apologize	BrE: apologise
AmE: burglarize	BrE: burglarise
AmE: capitalize	BrE: capitalise

AmE: characterize	BrE: characterise
AmE: mobilize	BrE: mobilise
AmE: organize	BrE: organise
AmE: realize	BrE: realise
AmE: recognize	BrE: recognise
AmE: standardize	BrE: standardise

(c) *"-or" vs. "-our."* Some nouns that end in *-or* in American spelling end in *-our* in British spelling; this rule doesn't apply to agent nouns such as *payor* and *creditor.*

AmE: behavior	BrE: behaviour
AmE: demeanor	BrE: demeanour
AmE: honor	BrE: honour
AmE: labor	BrE: labour
AmE: misdemeanor	BrE: misdemeanour
AmE: neighbor	BrE: neighbour
AmE: rumor	BrE: rumour

(d) *Doubling the final "-l."* American and British spelling rules differ over how to add a suffix to a word that ends in a single vowel and the letter *l.* In American writing the *l* is doubled only if the word is accented on the final syllable <rebel–rebelled–rebelling>. In British spelling the *l* is almost always doubled.

AmE: canceled	BrE: cancelled
AmE: counselor	BrE: counsellor
AmE: labeled	BrE: labelled
AmE: libelous	BrE: libellous
AmE: traveling	BrE: travelling

Some words that end in *-ll* in American spelling end in a single *-l* in British spelling. When these words take on a suffix, it looks as though the spelling rule is turned on its head, but it is the spelling of the root word that accounts for the apparent anomaly.

AmE: enrollment (enroll)	BrE: enrolment (enrol)
AmE: installment (install)	BrE: instalment (instal)

Even that does not explain some forms, though.

AmE: skillful	BrE: skilful (skill)
AmE: willful	BrE: wilful (will)

> "Today British and American spellings diverge in some respects in consequence of the different lexicographical traditions handed down by Johnson and his revisers Todd and Latham in England, and by Noah Webster in the New World."
>
> —*Simeon Potter*

(e) *"-er" vs. "-re."* Many words that end in *-er* in American end in *re* in British.

AmE: caliber	BrE: calibre
AmE: center	BrE: centre
AmE: meter	BrE: metre
AmE: theater	BrE: theatre

(f) *"-dge" words.* In American, most words that end in *-dge* drop the final *-e* before adding a suffix. In British, the *-e* is retained.

AmE: abridgment	BrE: abridgement
AmE: acknowledgment	BrE: acknowledgement
AmE: judgment	BrE: judgement

(Note, however, that *judgment* is standard in British legal writing.)

(g) *Hyphenated forms.* Compound words and words with prefixes are more likely to be hyphenated in British than in American.

AmE: bookkeeper	BrE: book-keeper
AmE: cooperate	BrE: co-operate
AmE: neoclassical	BrE: neo-classical

(h) *"-ogue" words.* Many words that end in *-ogue* commonly drop the final *-ue* in American, but not in British. But it is never an error to retain the *-ue*, and that is the preferred form in legal writing.

Informal AmE: catalog	BrE: catalogue
Informal AmE: dialog	BrE: dialogue
Informal AmE: travelog	BrE: travelogue

(i) *Miscellaneous.* Many other words are spelled differently in American writing and British writing, but don't fall into easy categories. In legal writing, keep in mind particularly the American and British spellings of *offense* (*offence*), *defense* (*defence*), *specialty* (*speciality*), *pretense* (*pretence*), and the noun *license* (*licence*).

AmE: airplane	BrE: aeroplane
AmE: aluminum	BrE: aluminium
AmE: check	BrE: cheque
AmE: connection	BrE: connexion
AmE: draft	BrE: draught
AmE: fulfill	BrE: fulfil
AmE: gray	BrE: grey
AmE: jail	BrE: gaol
AmE: jewelry	BrE: jewellery
AmE: maneuver	BrE: manoeuvre
AmE: plow	BrE: plough
AmE: skeptic	BrE: sceptic
AmE: spelled	BrE: spelt
AmE: story	BrE: storey

Common Misspellings

7.27 Be wary of common misspellings. Below are the correct spellings of the most frequently misspelled words in the language.

absence
accessible
accidentally
acclaim
accommodate
accomplish
accumulate
achievement
acknowledgment
acquaintance
acquire
acquittal
address
admissible
adviser
align
all right
a lot
amateur
analogous
apparatus
appearance
arctic
argument
ascent
atheist
athletics
auxiliary
balance
balloon
barbecue
barbiturate
bargain
basically
battalion
beggar
beginning
belief
believe
beneficial
biscuit
bouillon
boundary
Britain
buses
business
calendar
camouflage
canceled
cancellation
cantaloupe
carousel
category
cemetery
changing
chief
cigarette
collectible
colonel
colossal
column
commingle
commission
commitment
committee
competent
conceivable
condemn
conference
conferred
connoisseur
conscience
conscientious
consciousness
consensus
consistent
continuous
controlled
controversy
coolly
corollary
correspondence
counseled
counselor
counterfeit
courteous
courtesy
criticize
deceased
decedent
deceive
deductible
defendant
deference
deferred
definitely
dependent
descendant
description
desiccate
desirable
desperate
develop
development
difference
dilemma
disappearance
disappoint
discernible
discipline
disingenuous
dissatisfied
dominant
drunkenness
ecstasy
efficiency
egregious
eighth
eligible
eliminate
embarrass
eminent
emperor
encouragement
enforceable
enroll
entirely
entrepreneur
equipped

equivalent
especially
exaggerate
exceed
excel
excellent
existence
exorbitant
expedite
expense
experience
fallacy
familiar
fascination
feasible
February
feisty
fiery
finally
financially
flammable
fluorescent
fluoride
forcibly
foreign
foresee
foreword
forfeit
formerly
forty
fourteen
fourth
frantically
fundamentally
gauge
generally
goodbye
government
governor
grammar
grandeur
gray
grievous
gruesome
guarantee
guerrilla
guidance
handkerchief
happily
harassment
height
heinous
hemorrhage
heroes
hierarchy
hoarse
homogeneous
hoping
hors d'oeuvre
humorous
hygiene
hypocrisy
hypocrite
ideally
idiosyncrasy
ignorance
imaginary
immediately
imminent
implement
imprimatur
inadvertent
incidentally
incredible
incumbent
independence
independent
indicted
indispensable
inference
innovate
innuendo
inoculate
insurance
intellectual
intelligence
interesting
interference
interrupt
irrelevant
irresistible
jealousy
jewelry
judgment
kaleidoscope
knowledge
labeled
laboratory
laid
led
legitimate
leisure
length
liaison
license
lieu
lieutenant
lightning
likable
likelihood
likely
limousine
liquefy
loneliness
lose
lovely
luxury
magazine
maintain
maintenance
manageable
management
maneuver
marriage
marshal
mathematics
maybe
medicine
medieval
mediocre
memento
mileage
millennium
millionaire
miniature
minuscule
minute
mischievous
missile
misspelled
mortgage
mosquito
mousse
movable
murmur
muscle
mustache
mysterious
narrative
naturally
necessary
necessity
neighbor

nickel
nineteenth
ninety
ninth
noticeable
nowadays
nuisance
obedience
obstacle
occasion
occasionally
occurred
occurrence
official
omission
opinion
opponent
opportunity
oppression
optimistic
origin
outrageous
overrun
paid
panicky
pantomime
parallel
paralyze
paraphernalia
parliament
particularly
pastime
pavilion
peaceable
peculiar
penetrate
perceive
performance
permanent
permissible
permitted
perseverance
persevere
persistence
personnel
physician
picnicking
piece
pilgrimage
pitiful
plagiarism
plaintiff
playwright
pleasant
poinsettia
possess
possession
possessive
possibility
possible
possibly
potato
potatoes
practically
prairie
precedence
preceding
preference
preferred
prejudice
preparation
prerogative
prescription
prevalent
primitive
principal
principle
privilege
probably
procedure
proceed
proceedings
prominent
pronunciation
propaganda
psychological
publicly
pursue
quandary
questionnaire
queue
quizzes
realistically
recede
receipt
receive
recognize
recommend
reconnaissance
reference
referral
referring
relevant
relieving
religious
remembrance
reminiscence
renaissance
repetition
rescission
resemblance
restaurant
restaurateur
rheumatism
rhyme
rhythm
ridiculous
sacrilegious
safety
salable
satellite
scary
scenery
schedule
scurrilous
secede
seize
seizure
sense
sentence
separate
separation
sergeant
several
severely
shepherd
sincerely
sizable
skiing
soliloquy
sophomore
souvenir
sovereign
specifically
specimen
specious
strategy
strength
stubbornness
subtle
succeed
success
sufficient

supersede
supplement
suppress
surprise
surreptitious
surround
surveillance
susceptible
suspicious
syllable
symmetrical
synonymous
temperature
tendency
themselves
therefore
thorough
though
threshold
through
tomorrow
totaled
tournament
tourniquet
trafficking
tragedy
transferable
transferred
traveled
treatise
tries
truly
twelfth
tyranny
ukulele
unmistakable
unnecessary
until
usable
usually
vacuum
valuable
vengeance
vilify
villain
violence
weather
Wednesday
weird
wherever
wholly
withhold
yacht
yield

"Nowhere are items more clearly right or wrong than in spelling. With a very few exceptions, all English words are correctly spelled in only one way. Like correctness in pronunciation, correctness in English spelling has no logical basis, but unlike pronunciation, spelling is uniform, and the agreed on system is knowable."

—*Paul Roberts*

§ 8
Quotations

8.1 Just as scholars in all fields must rely at least in part on the words and ideas of others, so must lawyers. You must give credit where credit is due, even if you're paraphrasing. (On the question of plagiarism, see 31.5(f).)

Among legal writers, there exist several schools of thought about quotations. Though seldom expressly stated, one holds that given our common-law system of precedent, if you seek to write authoritatively, you must maximize on each page the number of words deriving from an authoritative source such as governing caselaw. On this benighted view, the writer becomes little more than a quotation-gatherer, providing only small bits of connective tissue between the exalted words of others. Indeed, the view may actually be nothing more than a rationalization for those who are either hurried or lacking in effort. Another view, perhaps as a countermeasure to the first, holds that a brief should contain almost no quotations at all—apart from, say, the specific statutory, contractual, or regulatory text at issue. Hence some legal-writing professors require that their students, when learning the art of brief-writing, not use any quotations from caselaw: they must paraphrase accurately and provide meticulous citations. A third strain holds that quotations should invariably play supporting roles: they're used to buttress or illustrate a point but almost never to supply it wholesale. On this view, most of the prose on every page should be your own—not somebody else's. You may quote lightly, but only enough to show that you're accurately conveying the legal rules and caselaw. This technique requires artistry in weaving quoted matter into your own prose.

The first view mentioned above is responsible for reams of dreary legal writing that nobody has ever read. Although the second view is a defensible pedagogical technique, the third view is recommended.

8.2 Be cautious of overquoting. Quote a passage if (1) it's on point and authoritative, or (2) it's highly persuasive and you can't express the idea more clearly or forcefully.

(a) *Cultivating a reluctance to quote.* The criteria set forth above suggest a high standard for quotability. That's the right approach. Quotation-happy writers are lazy writers. But the judicious use of quotations can markedly enhance your credibility.

Perhaps from diffidence, law students and newish lawyers tend to think that they should quote as extensively as possible from authoritative sources, such as the U.S. Supreme Court. Legal writers who adopt this view essentially lower themselves from analysts and advocates to mere collectors of quotations, supplying meager links as they proceed from one quotation to another. The problem, of course, is that readers quickly tire of reading words about *other* matters by *other* writers, and they'll conclude that the writer has nothing to contribute to the discussion. In fact, there is no "discussion"—it's just a pastiche of other people's words about other matters, supposedly brought to bear on the present problem. If you debase your role in this way, your readers will inevitably (and understandably) rebel. They'll either start skimming or stop reading altogether. Overquoting makes it seem as if you don't have a full command of the material.

(b) *The desirability of close paraphrasing.* No matter how strong a quotation sounds on first reading, you should try to improve it by paraphrasing. This technique will test your comprehension of the quotation, and it will also ensure that you're in control of the material. If you can't readily explain what someone else has said, you probably don't understand it. Neither will your readers. And you don't want to suffer from the charge that you've provided too little of your own commentary and analysis.

(c) *Scrupulousness about controlling vs. persuasive authority.* Ideally, you'd be able to restrict yourself to quoting from vertical precedents—those delivered by higher courts within the same jurisdiction. Those are the strongest. So-called horizontal precedents—those from an appellate court you're writing to, if it's not the highest court within the jurisdiction—are less strong but still generally binding. Those from courts of other jurisdictions, or from nonjudicial sources such as law reviews or treatises, are compelling only to the extent that they reflect sound reasoning. Because it's unlikely that your sole support will be vertical precedents, you'll probably need to marshal other authorities. When you do so, you'll need to explain (in your own words, not theirs) why their reasoning is both sound and applicable to the matter at hand. For more on the hierarchy of precedents, see 9.7.

(d) *Topsy-turvy attributions.* If you're writing a brief to the Eleventh Circuit, don't cite an Eleventh Circuit case (especially an unpublished one) and then add that it was quoting the U.S. Supreme Court. Instead, quote the U.S. Supreme Court and then add that the passage quoted has been explicitly followed by the Eleventh Circuit.

(e) *No obscurities by way of support.* Never quote an obscure passage to support your position. You'll puzzle your readers, who probably won't pause to ferret out its meaning. Instead, fairly state the point without distorting the meaning, and allow your readers (if they're studious) to confirm—by checking your source—that you've summarized accurately. If they do that, and conclude that you've been fair in your approach, you'll have won points.

8.3 Avoid quoting dictum without acknowledging that it's dictum.

(a) *Understanding the difference between a court's holding and its dictum.* Of all the problems in jurisprudence, one of the trickiest—on close inspection—is the distinction between a court's holding and its dictum. Essentially, a holding is an appellate court's determination of a matter of law pivotal to its decision. Anything else said in an opinion is dictum—or, if you're enumerating instances, dicta (the plural noun). For a thorough discussion of the distinction between holdings and dicta, see Bryan A. Garner et al., *The Law of Judicial Precedent* § 4, at 44–75 (2016).

(b) *Knowing the value of dicta.* Although dictum is often dismissed as if it had no value at all, it can be highly persuasive. It may be the best indication about how the court would decide a case like yours. And the higher the court, the more sway dictum has.

(c) *Care in explaining.* Merely noting that a judicial statement you're quoting is dictum will tend to give you credibility: not only are you acknowledging that the statement isn't binding, but you're also signaling that you're a meticulous writer. If you tell your readers in advance what assumptions or different circumstances were at play in the court's statement, you're likely to enhance your credibility.

8.4 Make sure that every quotation you use is both correctly attributed and fully accurate, word for word and even character for character.

(a) *Attributions.* When quoting, make sure you've identified the source correctly. If it's a judicial opinion, make sure it's clear whether you're quoting the majority opinion, a concurrence, or a dissent. If it's a concurrence or dissent, of course, you must also note the writing judge.

(b) *Attention to detail.* To use a quotation is to borrow someone else's words. Presumably the previous writer chose them with great care. Otherwise, you probably wouldn't be using them. Avoid giving your readers an opportunity to question your punctilio; they will do that if you get things wrong. If you feel the urge to change the material in any significant way (more than a cleaned-up quotation would allow—see 8.5), then paraphrase.

(c) *Original sources if possible.* If possible—and admittedly it isn't always possible—review hard-copy print sources to verify quotations. Copies, even electronically generated duplicates, can introduce typographical errors, automatically "corrected" words, and elisions. So if you can readily do so, consult the books themselves during your fact-checking. Many online sources offer PDFs of published pages—the most reliable type of online source for quotations.

(d) *Using brackets and ellipses to indicate changes or omissions.* The traditional view of legal writing requires every alteration to be meticulously identified by bracketing (see 1.41–1.45) or ellipses (see 1.46–1.52), as well as all quotations within quotations to be marked as such. Unless you're using a cleaned-up quotation (see 8.5), and noting as much, you must adhere to the standards of showing each and every alteration.

(e) *Photographic reproductions of extracts from a governing legal instrument.* It's now possible to ensure absolute accuracy of the crucial legal instrument at issue by photographically reproducing, as a block quotation, the precise provision at issue. This technique works best with a provision in a statute, contract, will, or the like. It adds visual appeal: rather than retyping the words so that they take on the look and feel of the rest of your prose, you put the provision in high relief and instantly project its authenticity. The governing text is immediately foregrounded. If you use this technique, you must account for the words reproduced photographically against any word-count restrictions you might face.

Ex.: The spam provision of the forum's Rules of Conduct both defines *spam* and establishes the potential consequences for spamming:

> **1. SPAM IS NOT ALLOWED**
> Spamming is defined as either posting multiple times about the same issue or starting multiple topics about the same issue. Other actions are also considered spamming, such as continuous off-topic posting as well as the posting of unrelated links to a forum topic. Spam shall be deleted without warning and multiple acts of spamming under a member user name will be reviewed and access to the forum by such member user name may be restricted or banned.

It could not be clearer that "spam is not allowed," and undisputed evidence establishes that on several occasions, Choi posted messages meeting the Rules' definition of *spam*. WebbyServ was within its rights to ban Choi's access to the forum.

(f) *Unnoted corrections.* Is it ever permissible to fix a trivial mistake without noting it in your citation? Less so in legal writing than in other types—as most legal writers would insist. For nonlegal sources, it's said that "such obvious errors as a missing full point [period] or unclosed parentheses or quotation marks may be silently corrected." (*The New Oxford Style Manual* § 9.3.1, at 165 (2016).) Both the *New Oxford* and *The Chicago Manual of Style* allow writers to change, without note, a capital on the first word of a quotation to lowercase, or to change a lowercase letter to a capital. In law this practice is avoided—as the *Chicago Manual* explicitly notes (see § 13.18, at 715, of that book).

Yet a certain adherence to house style is allowed in law as elsewhere. (1) Double quotation marks can be changed to single, or vice versa, with a quote within a quote, as necessary according to house rules (see 1.32). (2) Punctuation relative to quotation marks should be adjusted (see 1.31). (3) Double hyphens (attempting to signal an em-dash) can be turned into a true em-dash. (4) Curly quotes can be imposed in place of straight ones (see

1.29). (5) En-dashes can be changed to hyphens, or hyphens to en-dashes, if the source material has printed them incorrectly. (6) The antiquated long *s* [ſ] (resembling the roman f, italic *f*) should be regularized to *s* (hence an 18th-century passage reading *with the kindneſs of your aſsuaging words* becomes *with the kindness of your assuaging words*). (7) Foreign forms of the question mark or quotation marks (such as « » or „ ") can be replaced. (8) If the original quotation uses underlining for emphasis, the underlined words may be changed to italics (see 3.2(c)).

8.5 Despite 8.4, consider a "cleaned-up" quotation if you're quoting something with embedded quotations, especially those larded with brackets and ellipsis dots.

(a) *Avoiding ostentatious pedantry when quoting something with embedded quotations.* In recent years, some legal writers have become so obsessed with noting every little bibliographic detail—for example, a parenthetical saying "brackets in original in second instance only" or "ellipsis in original source quoted within quotation"—that there has been an understandable backlash to this cumbersome equipment. Increasingly, we see quotes within quotes within quotes. Signaling such minutiae becomes both tedious and pointless. If a recent opinion quotes an earlier source, using ellipsis dots and brackets, and in quoting that opinion you need to add still more, it's fair to clean it up and signal that you've done so. The way to do that is to add "(cleaned up)" at the end of the citation. This signal solves a problem that is bound to grow worse as more and more opinions contain third- and fourth-generation repetitions of quotations.

You must not—*must not*—introduce any change in the substance. Only then does the method work.

The rationale behind the cleaned-up quotation is that when you use a quotation to draw on the authority of the court you're quoting, your reader doesn't need to know that the court itself was drawing on an earlier authority. In effect, the words of the quotation have become part of the new opinion.

Not this: The Ninth Circuit has noted that "[u]nder the Westfall Act, federal employees receive absolute immunity from suit 'for their "negligent or wrongful act[s] or omission[s] . . . while acting within the scope of [their] office or employment."'" *Jackson v. Tate*, 648 F.3d 729, 735 (9th Cir. 2011) (quoting *Green v. Hall*, 8 F.3d 695, 699 (9th Cir. 1993) (quoting 28 U.S.C. § 2679(b)(1))).

But this: The Ninth Circuit has noted that under the Westfall Act, "federal employees receive absolute immunity from suit for their negligent or wrongful acts or omissions while acting within the scope of their office or employment." *Jackson v. Tate*, 648 F.3d 729, 735 (9th Cir. 2011) (cleaned up) (referring to 28 U.S.C. § 2679(b)(1)).

Not this: Judge Bybee observed: "[A]dministrators must personally undertake 'a basic review of [patients'] file[s]' and monitor patients' bedroom decorations on 'walk[s] through the [hospital] facility,' to catch signs of burgeoning and illicit relationships between patients and staff, Maj. Op at 1033–34." *Ammons v. Dep't of Soc. & Health Servs.*, 648 F.3d 1020, 1037 (9th Cir. 2011) (Bybee, J., concurring in part and dissenting in part) (quoting, with bracketed alterations, the majority opinion of the same case at 648 F.3d 1020 at 1033–34).

But this: Judge Bybee observed that under the majority's holding, "administrators must personally undertake a basic review of patients' files and monitor patients' bedroom decorations on walks through the hospital facility to catch signs of burgeoning and illicit relationships between patients and staff." *Ammons v. Dep't of Soc. & Health Servs.*, 648 F.3d 1020, 1037 (9th Cir. 2011) (Bybee, J., concurring in part and dissenting in part) (cleaned up) (citing the majority opinion at 1033–34).

(b) *The precedent for "cleaned up."* Many state and federal courts have begun to use cleaned-up quotations—doubtless more than you might suspect. As the Pennsylvania Superior Court recently declared, "'Cleaned up' is a new parenthetical designed to tell readers that they have removed extraneous material for readability and guarantee that nothing removed was important. The superfluous material encompassed by the parenthetical includes brackets, ellipses, quotation marks, internal citations, and footnote references." *Commonwealth v. Diaz*, No. 1811 EDA 2016, 2018 WL 1443838, at *12 n.4 (Pa. Super. Ct. Mar. 23, 2018) (cleaned up). What was cleaned up in that citation? The attribution to the signal's innovator, who ought to receive credit here: Jack Metzler, a learned lawyer in Washington, D.C.

(c) *A means of avoiding "[sic]."* One justification for a cleaned-up quotation is to avoid the dreaded use of the bracketed *sic*—dreaded only because it often reflects poorly on the quoter who introduces it. If an opponent has misspelled a word or two, correct the words either without notation or with a "cleaned up" notation. If your adversary wants to complain about your tacit corrections—pointing out to the audience that in fact the words had originally been misspelled—then so be it. Your attempt at allowing the adversary to save face will have been for naught.

For more on [sic], see 1.42(b).

8.6 Avoid quoting in such a way that a foe might credibly say you're distorting the context.

(a) *Out-of-context quotations.* Never use a quotation if the fuller context undercuts your point. You must look at the entire passage—or, if it's a case, the entire case—to ensure that the overall import of the original supports your view. If, after finding a case online, you borrow a few words without ensuring that the holding supports your position, you'll almost certainly damage your credibility.

(b) *Ill-considered elisions.* Never omit contextual words and phrases to such a degree that you change the quotation's meaning. The quotation must fairly represent what the source stands for. If you don't obey this admonition, an opponent will be sure to point out your distortion.

8.7 Make every quotation as succinct as possible—ruthlessly omitting everything but the pith of what you need.

(a) *Support, not substitution.* You must present your points and your arguments to the reader. Nobody else's words, no matter how well expressed, can substitute for your own reasoning. Quotations play mere supporting roles, even if they're from the highest possible authority. If you quote too much, even with a few extraneous words, your readers will notice and start skimming them. You can't afford the loss.

(b) *Overlong quotations.* It's not uncommon to see legal writers using block quotations that occupy nearly a full page. Few readers will patiently slog through them. Instead, these should be broken up and accurately summarized, giving only the essentials for present purposes.

(c) *Blending.* Your prose will sound better and more natural if you embed quotations in your sentences without formal introduction. Weave them into your own prose. That way you own them.

Not this: Rule 1015 of the Federal Rules of Bankruptcy Procedure states as follows: "Prior to entering an order the court shall give consideration to protecting creditors of different estates against potential conflicts of interest." Fed. R. Bankr. P. 1015.

But this: Before a court orders joint administration of bankruptcy estates, the court must "give consideration to protecting creditors of different estates against potential conflicts of interest." Fed. R. Bankr. P. 1015.

(d) *Avoiding the source's transitional words.* Many quotations, when pulled from their context, have context-specific transitional words within them that make no sense in the newly made passage. You must excise them—even if you're generally averse to ellipsis dots. If you don't, you'll have a brutally distracting non sequitur.

Not this: The threat of poaching is a major incentive for companies to enforce noncompete agreements, as Edward H. Pappas has noted: "Alternatively, noncompete enforcement may be particularly critical because the employee's new employer has been raiding the client company." (The word *alternatively* has no place in this quotation.)

But this: Poaching creates a major incentive for companies to enforce noncompete agreements, as Edward H. Pappas has noted: "[N]oncompete enforcement may be particularly critical because the employee's new employer has been raiding the client company."

8.8 Never begin a paragraph with a quotation.

(a) *No borrowing a topic sentence.* The whole idea of "flow" in writing is that it's the result of the writer's train of thought—and the basic unit of discourse, for the mature writer, is the paragraph. Given this reality, you can't "borrow" a topic sentence. You must create the train of thought, and quotations must be subordinate matter, playing a supporting role—even if they're from the very highest court.

If you're tempted to borrow a topic sentence, you'll be better off paraphrasing and citing as opposed to quoting. The paragraph-starting quotation is yet another indicator of sluggish, unskillful writing.

Not this: "Arbitration is a matter of contract [and] the FAA's strong pro-arbitration policy only applies to disputes that the parties have agreed to arbitrate." *Klay v. All Defendants*, 389 F.3d 1191, 1200 (11th Cir. 2004). An exception to this rule is that a nonparty may force arbitration "if the relevant state contract law allows him to enforce the agreement" to arbitrate. *Board of Trustees v. Citigroup Global Mkts., Inc.*, 622 F.3d 1335, 1342–43 (11th Cir. 2010) (quoting *Arthur Andersen LLP v. Carlisle*, 556 U.S. 624, 632 (2009)). (Note that the first quotation is poorly punctuated, lacking a comma before the *and* in a compound sentence, and that the word *only* is misplaced within the sentence. Nothing about it is particularly well stated.)

But this: Because arbitration is a matter of contract, the FAA's strong pro-arbitration policy necessarily applies only to disputes that the parties have agreed to arbitrate. *Klay v. All Defendants*, 389 F.3d 1191, 1200 (11th Cir. 2004). Even so, the Supreme Court has recognized an exception to this rule: a nonparty may force arbitration "if the relevant state contract law allows him to enforce the [arbitration] agreement." *Arthur Andersen LLP v. Carlisle*, 556 U.S. 624, 632 (2009).

(b) *Epigraphs distinguished.* At the outset of a piece or one of its major divisions, it's possible to insert an epigraph—a choice quotation that beautifully capsulizes the thrust of the idea you're developing—usually right under the title or a heading. Normally, the epigraph is centered on the page, and the attribution is placed just below toward the right margin.

8.9 Never use back-to-back quotations without supplying your own connective words.

(a) *More on the flow of prose.* Because quotation marks show a reader where a borrowed thought starts and stops, each quotation stands independent. When you must use a series of quotations, especially from different sources, give the prose continuity by using your own voice to weave the quotations into a larger whole. Depending on the content, you may need to use only one or two words to show how a successive quotation builds on a preceding one, or you may need to provide your own transitional sentence or clause. Remember: quotations must be built into the discussion—not used as the equivalent of a string citation without conveying your points.

(b) *The crutch of in-line citations.* In assessing whether you've used back-to-back quotations, ignore in-line citations—which often become a crutch for the indolent writer who strings together quotation after quotation. Read as if the citations weren't there, and then you'll have a better sense of the relative degree of continuity or discontinuity in your writing.

Not this: This court concluded that "the arbitrator's conclusion that Mr. Weston's conduct was 'forgivable' . . . is not indicative of inattentiveness to the CBA and governing law." *Chevron Mining v. United Mine Workers of Am.*, 648 F.3d 1151, 1155 (10th Cir. 2011). "In determining whether or not the arbitration award 'draws its essence' from the CBA, a reviewing court looks to the award itself and not every phrase contained in the arbitrator's opinion." *Kennecott Utah Copper Corp. v. Becker*, 195 F.3d 1201, 1204 (10th Cir. 1999). "When an arbitrator is commissioned to interpret and apply the collective bargaining agreement, he is to bring his informed judgment to bear in order to reach a fair solution of a problem." *United Steelworkers v. Enter. Wheel & Car Corp.*, 363 U.S. 593, 597 (1960).

But this: The federal courts accord arbitrators broad discretion. In a 2011 case, for example, the Tenth Circuit concluded that the arbitrator's calling Weston's conduct "forgivable" was "not indicative of inattentiveness to the CBA and governing law." *Chevron Mining v. United Mine Workers of Am.*, 648 F.3d 1151, 1155 (10th Cir. 2011). The award had to be examined as a whole, as the court noted in relying on its own precedent: "In determining whether or not the arbitration award 'draws its essence' from the CBA, a reviewing court looks to the award itself and not every phrase contained in the arbitrator's opinion." *Kennecott Utah Copper Corp. v. Becker*, 195 F.3d 1201, 1204 (10th Cir. 1999). That is in keeping with the U.S. Supreme Court's admonition that "[w]hen an arbitrator is commissioned to interpret and apply the collective bargaining agreement, he is to bring his informed judgment to bear in order to reach a fair solution of a problem." *United Steelworkers v. Enter. Wheel & Car Corp.*, 363 U.S. 593, 597 (1960).

8.10 To introduce a block quotation most effectively, put a complete assertion right before it and allow the quotation to become support for your assertion.

(a) *Knowing that importance is almost never self-evident.* A quotation needs some context to inform readers about its purpose and the conclusion to be drawn from it. A good lead-in puts the reader in the desired frame of mind. So get in the habit of asserting something, and then quoting—as opposed to quoting and, afterward, stating what the reader should have concluded from reading it. The fairer assumption is that the reader will have skipped it if you don't lead into it informatively.

(b) *No stereotyped lead-ins.* Avoid lead-ins such as these: *The court stated:* . . . ; *The statute reads in pertinent part:* . . . ; *The witness testified as follows:* . . . . These phrases are the death knell to a good quotation. Once again, the point is to compose an independent clause (a stand-alone assertion) that precedes the colon before a block quotation.

Not this: The statute reads in pertinent part: . . .

But this: The statute specifies three considerations for weighing whether a claimant has standing in this context: . . .

(c) *More than mere repetition.* Your lead-in to a block quotation should be your own language—not words that needlessly regurgitate what the quotation is about to say. Somehow, you must find a way of making the reader want to see what's in the quotation.

Not this: Justice Bridget Mary McCormack of the Michigan Supreme Court has said that before the U.S. Supreme Court, advocates make mistakes with unsettling regularity:

> Lawyers make mistakes during oral arguments—even arguments before the Supreme Court of the United States. One might think that missteps would be relatively rare in that hallowed hall, given the quality of the lawyers, the importance of the issues, and the guiding interventions of the justices. But if you study Supreme Court arguments, you will likely find yourself grimacing—or, worse, imagining the Court doing so—with unsettling regularity.

(The error in this example is repeating the very words of the quotation.)

But this: Justice Bridget Mary McCormack of the Michigan Supreme Court notes the routine nature of blunders in U.S. Supreme Court advocacy:

> Lawyers make mistakes during oral arguments—even arguments before the Supreme Court of the United States. One might think that missteps would be relatively rare in that hallowed hall, given the quality of the lawyers, the importance of the issues, and the guiding interventions of the justices. But if you study Supreme Court arguments, you will likely find yourself grimacing—or, worse, imagining the Court doing so—with unsettling regularity.

8.11 Try not to end paragraphs or even entire pieces with block quotations: instead, when you can, create "quotation sandwiches" that follow up with your own transition to the next point.

(a) *The bottom layer.* If the advice in 8.10 creates the top layer of a quotation sandwich, this 8.11 creates the bottom layer. Using both layers ensures that you fully integrate quotations into your writing, as opposed to just plopping them down on the page and expecting them to do your work for you. In the example below, notice how the words *by contrast* in the follow-up to the quotation help the reader understand why the passage was quoted: the cited case is quite different from the present case, and the argument therefore runs that the present court should reach a different result. While the effective lead-in gives the reader a bridge to the quotation, the strong follow-up gives the reader a bridge back to the writer's thoughts.

Ex.: The *Central Airlines* court recognized that the facts before it involved a lawyer who neither willfully nor negligently misled the opposing party:

> We are compelled to affirm the judgment in this case because there was not fraud on the part of appellee or his attorneys which prevented appellant from making his defense; and there was no accidental act done or omission to act on the part of appellee or his attorneys, which prevented appellant from making its defense.

In the present case, by contrast, Kramer actively misled Sutherland in a manner that few officers of the court could find acceptable.

(b) *A rhetorical template for quotation sandwiches.* Essentially, the typical quotation sandwich goes something like this: "The statute establishes four requirements for [whatever you're talking about]: '[quotation].' The second and third parts of this enumeration are notably distinct: the one requires that ________, while the other requires that ________." Try a variation on this template to suit your own needs.

8.12 Avoid pockmarking a block quotation by boldfacing words within it. The judicious use of italics, however, is acceptable to show that you have emphasized text.

(a) *The desperation of boldfacers.* Ineffective writers frequently want all sorts of seemingly random words boldfaced within their quotations. Perhaps they mark these as they're reading, and do so without thinking about—much less understanding—how the same passage will read when various words are set in bold. Essentially, the prose becomes unreadable as certain words pop to the fore while others almost disappear, so that sentences can't really be read as sentences. The reader's eye is diverted to the bold words as soon as the page is turned, interrupting the reader's ability to follow the logic.

Not this: Under Rule 16(e) of the Federal Rules of Criminal Procedure, "[u]nless **these rules** or a **court order** provides otherwise, a deposition **must be taken** and filed in the **same** manner as a deposition in a **civil action**," with only three exceptions specified in Fed. R. Crim. P. 16(e)(1), 16(e)(2), and 16(e)(3).

But this: Under Rule 16(e), a criminal deposition must be both "taken and filed in the same manner" as a civil deposition—except that (1) a defendant cannot be deposed "without . . . consent," (2) the "scope and manner of the deposition" must be the same as in trial testimony, and (3) the government must provide to defense counsel "any statement of the deponent in the government's possession to which the defendant could be entitled at trial." Fed. R. Crim. P. 16(e).

(b) *Exception for headings.* If a boldface heading is reproduced, then of course the bolding should be preserved in the quotation.

Ex.: The applicable evidentiary rule creates an important exception in its second sentence:

> **Rule 411. Liability Insurance.**
>
> Evidence that a person was or was not insured against liability is not admissible to prove whether the person acted negligently or otherwise wrongfully. But the court may admit this evidence for another purpose, such as proving a witness's bias or prejudice or proving agency, ownership, or control.

(c) *Italic emphasis.* The traditional way of highlighting quoted text involves the staid use of italics. (But see 3.12.) If italic type appears in the original, some lawyers add the parenthetical tag "(emphasis in original)"—although *The Bluebook* disapproves this practice (Rule 5.2(d)(iii)). If you add the italic to make text stand out, you should add the parenthetical tag "(emphasis added)." Avoid the old-fashioned "(emphasis supplied)," which is ambiguous: are you saying that the italic type was already supplied or that you supplied it?

8.13 Once you have a draft, try to eliminate block quotations by cutting them in half—so that fewer than 50 words are quoted at a time.

(a) *The concept.* It's well known that readers tend to skip block quotations. This results partly from writers' habit of failing to introduce them properly, and partly from readers' skepticism about the applicability of others' words to the problem at hand, especially if those words are numerous. If you quote in chunks of under 50 words, and you don't block off the quotations, they're both less imposing and harder to skip. And you're more likely to integrate the points they're making into your commentary.

This isn't to say that you'll never again use block quotations. But you'll certainly reduce your reliance on them.

(b) *The technique.* You're to either radically shorten a block quotation or reduce it to a slimmer quotation. Start by locating your block quotations—you'll execute the method with each one. First, ensure that you've led into it properly, preferably with a full assertion in your own words preceding the colon (see 8.10). Then check to see whether every word in the quotation is necessary or helpful to your point. Excise those that aren't, either fore and aft (easily done) or in the middle (necessitating an ellipsis). Then see whether there's a natural breaking point in the middle of the quotation, perhaps where an ellipsis now appears. Look for an emphatic word that might end the first quotation, and put an end quote there. Finally, provide your own linking words to lead into the second part of the quotation—which now becomes a full-fledged quotation of its own. The linkage might be as simple as, "The court went on to observe that . . . ." Now you've completed a valuable task.

Not this: The whole question is whether leave of the appellate court is necessary. Rule 60(a) of the Federal Rules of Civil Procedure provides as follows:

> The court may correct a clerical mistake or a mistake arising from oversight or omission whenever one is found in a judgment, order, or other part of the record. The court may do so on motion or on its own, with or without notice. But after an appeal has been docketed in the appellate court and while it is pending, such a mistake may be corrected only with the appellate court's leave.

Fed. R. Civ. P. 60(a). Thus, leave is necessary.

But this: The whole question is whether the trial court can correct the error without leave of the appellate court. Under Rule 60(a), a district court may generally correct such a clerical error if it arises "from oversight or omission"—and it may do so either "on motion or on its own, with or without notice." Fed. R. Civ. P. 60(a). But this assumes, contrary to the present facts, that no appeal has yet been filed. The rule goes on to specify that "after an appeal has been docketed in the appellate court and while it is pending, such a mistake may be corrected only with the appellate court's leave." *Id.* This provision is dispositive here.

8.14 Punctuate in and around quotations appropriately, with the following marks as needed: quotation marks (see 1.29–1.34), colons (see 1.24), commas (see 1.8), ellipsis dots (see 1.46–1.51), and brackets (see 1.41–1.45).

See the sections cited.

> "Quotations are the bane of many a brief and the affliction of many an appellate judge."
>
> —*Ben W. Palmer*

§ 9
Citations

9.1 Citations identify original and supporting sources, show the significance of the information cited, and help readers find the sources either to verify or to conduct further research. Citations often demonstrate that a proposition has been thoroughly researched or that a principle of law is heavily supported by authority. But more is not always better. Overusing citations for no substantive legal reason merely clouds your point by burying it. And incorrect citations can impair your credibility and call an argument's validity into question. They may even lead to sanctions. Correct citations, on the other hand, can enhance your credibility by reflecting the care and attention to detail that went into preparing the document.

What follows here is not a comprehensive citation manual but rather some guidance on how to use citations most effectively.

9.2 Choose a citation system and stick to its essential conventions throughout a particular writing (but see 9.3 and 9.4).

(a) *The Bluebook.* The oldest and most comprehensive system available is *The Bluebook: A Uniform System of Citation*, which is widely used by law reviews, courts, and law firms. But *The Bluebook*'s comprehensiveness makes it complex. Explanations of some citation forms aren't clear, and many aren't illustrated. New editions, published every five years or so, sometimes include changes that seem arbitrary and illogical, often inconsistent with practices in earlier editions. Still, most judges and their clerks are accustomed to *The Bluebook*, albeit perhaps in its earlier incarnations.

(b) *ALWD.* A newer guide, introduced in 2000 by the Association of Legal Writing Directors and now having appeared in later editions, is the *ALWD Guide to Legal Citation.* Several law schools and law journals, some moot-court competitions, and some courts have adopted it. Written in plain English, it contains useful quick-format guides and informational sidebars. Rules have fewer exceptions than in the *Bluebook* system. Although *ALWD* is far easier to consult, it remains less comprehensive than *The Bluebook* (e.g., *ALWD* lacks detailed guidance on citing foreign sources of law). With each successive edition of *ALWD*, the differences between it and *The Bluebook* have become minimal—except that *ALWD* is more user-friendly.

(c) *Maroonbook.* Since 1989, Chicago's *Maroonbook* has offered brief guidance on citing legal materials. Less interested in prescriptive rules, the *Maroonbook* instead encourages flexibility. But this manual hasn't been widely adopted and is the least comprehensive system. The citation forms are unpunctuated, which produces a half-finished appearance and sometimes introduces ambiguity. The *Maroonbook* doesn't encourage consistency from one legal writing to another—even those by the same author.

(d) *State style manuals.* Some states, such as California, Michigan, New York, North Dakota, and Texas, have their own state-specific style manuals. These are usually mandatory for court documents and may be required by in-state legal publications. Other states, such as Delaware, let writers use either the state-specific citation manual or a general citation system.

9.3 If court rules, journal guidelines, or any other directives conflict with the citation system you use, follow those directives.

(a) *Courts.* Although some jurisdictions have their own citation rules (e.g., California, Michigan, Texas), many others (e.g., Delaware, Indiana) supplement the general systems with more detailed systems for citing that state's legal materials. Some courts strictly require attorneys to use a specific citation system. For examples of judicial strictness and consequences of disobedience, see *Trevarthen v. Treadwell*, 2012 WL 2552324, at *5 (N.C. Ct. App. 2012) (dismissing appeal "for substantial noncompliance and gross violation" of court's appellate rules); *Wade v. Gaither*, 623 F.Supp.2d 1277, 1280 n.2 (D. Utah 2009) (strongly encouraging adherence to *The Bluebook* "or some other widely used legal citation manual in future submissions to the Court"); *In re Raymond Prof'l Grp., Inc.*, 386 B.R. 678, 682 n.1 (Bankr. N.D. Ill. 2008) (stressing the importance of following citation "technicalities" consistently); *Hecht v. State*, 853 N.E.2d 1007, 1008 (Ind. App. Ct. 2006) (reminding attorneys to follow established citation conventions); *Ratts v. Bd. of Cty. Comm'rs*, 141 F.Supp.2d 1289, 1314 (D. Kan. 2001) ("encourag[ing] counsel to learn the established rules for legal citation"); and *Ilaian v. U.S. Dep't of Agric., Food & Nutrition Serv.*, 87 F.Supp.2d 1047, 1048 (S.D. Cal. 2000) (stating that "[p]apers not in substantial compliance [with local rules] will be rejected by the Court").

(b) *Law journals.* Law journals usually prefer one citation system and require its use for all submissions. For example, the *University of Chicago Law Review* prefers *Maroonbook* form but allows *Bluebook* form, while the *Harvard Law Review* requires *Bluebook* form only. But law journals may also have supplemental or even contradictory guidelines, especially for electronic

> "The citation forms in *The Bluebook* seek to provide the minimum amount of information necessary to lead the reader directly to the specific terms cited."
>
> —*The Bluebook*

submissions. For example, the *Michigan Law Review* uses a citation style that is more specific than ordinary *Bluebook* style. The *Fordham International Law Journal* requires citation forms for European Union law very different from those in *The Bluebook*. The *William Mitchell Law Review* expressly rejects *Bluebook* Rule 10.3.1(b) and requires parallel citations for Minnesota cases. And the *Baylor Law Review* requires citations for Texas cases to conform with the *Texas Rules of Form*.

9.4 Override *The Bluebook* on a few key points.

(a) *Generally.* Although it is widely followed, *The Bluebook* is hardly infallible. It has been prepared by successive generations of law students; each revisory cohort seems intent on leaving its imprint on the guide. Citations have gradually grown lengthier and more intricate. The following subsections note five *Bluebook* rules that should be ignored until reversed. Warning, however: this section shouldn't be construed in any way as instructing you not to learn *The Bluebook*. As with any complex system of rules (for example, those relating to English grammar), you must master the rules before occasionally breaking them. That's the only way to make informed decisions about which rules to ignore.

(b) *Numbers.* Spell out only *one* through *ten* (not 1 through 100)—and use numerals for 11 and above. If like items are being numbered, some above and some below the threshold of ten, then use numerals for all items referred to <3 citations to the first book and 17 citations to the second>. See 5.3, 5.4.

(c) *The section sign* (§) *and the percentage sign* (%). Whether in text or in a footnote, use "§" to refer to part of a legal instrument or statute <a § 1983 claim>—unless you're starting a sentence, in which case the word *section* should be spelled out <Section 23 is our standard indemnification clause> (see 6.2). Consider also how much more efficient it is to write 77% than *seventy-seven percent*—three characters as opposed to 20. If you want instant communication, you choose the shorter, less cumbersome route (see 6.1).

(d) *Underlining.* Never underline—well, almost never (see 3.2(b)). Use italics instead.

(e) *Citations in footnotes.* Ignore any *Bluebook* suggestion or prescription about placing citations in text in court papers. If court rules don't disallow footnoted citations, you may and probably should do so. You'll find that it eliminates the clutter of numerical pollution and that your line of argument—and even your sources—will be easier to follow. But avoid substantive footnotes.

To write effectively in this style, however, you must write in such a way that readers needn't glance down constantly at footnotes. This requires a modicum of skill. The idea is to compose above-the-line text in which nothing could or should be skipped, and below-the-line text in which nothing needs to be read except where to find the source material for verification or further research.

(f) *Roman case names in academic footnotes.* Oddly, in law reviews, *The Bluebook* has long prescribed italicizing case names in text but not in footnotes. There's no good reason for the difference. Use italics for case names regardless of where they appear. See 3.5.

9.5 Learn the fundamental rules of how to cite authority. But don't get so lost in the minutiae that you forget *why* they exist: to help the reader check your research.

(a) *Basics.* Among the essential rules that a legal writer needs to know are (1) the formats for citing cases, constitutions, statutes, regulations, rules of evidence and procedure, books, articles, and legal encyclopedias; (2) the rules about using signals; and (3) the methods of citing electronic materials (usually websites, legal databases, and materials in other electronic formats). Litigators also need to know how to cite evidence and case-related documents (especially those from the earlier stages of a case).

(b) *Trivia.* Although you want your documents to conform to a consistent style, don't obsess over the minutiae. For example, don't spend a lot of time trying to find out whether a period after an italicized abbreviation should be roman or italic. Don't let a citation manual dictate what font you use, especially if it seems to suggest Courier (see 4.3(c)). But *do* follow court rules, which may mandate type size. And although you want to produce the correct form of a citation, don't let a citation manual dictate whether you put citations in text or in footnotes. See 9.4(e).

9.6 Cite the record unobtrusively.

(a) *Basics.* Unless otherwise specified by court rules, a basic citation to the appellate record (or *transcript* or *appendix*) requires only the volume number (if the record consists of more than one volume), an abbreviation for *record*, and the page number. The citation may be offset with brackets or parentheses.

Ex.: R. 34 / (R. 34) / [R. 34] / R. at 34 / (R. at 34) / [R. at 34]
(All are ways to cite page 34 of the record.)

Ex.: 2 R. 34–35 / (2 R. 34–35) / [2 R. 34–35] / 2 R. at 34–35 / (2 R. at 34–35) / [2 R. at 34–35]
(All are ways to cite pages 34–35 in volume 2 of the record.)

(b) *Page and line.* If the page's lines are numbered, the precise line can be pinpointed after the page number and a colon.

Ex.: R. 34:28 / (R. 34:28) / [R. 34:28] / R. at 34:28 / (R. at 34:28) / [R. at 34:28]
(All are ways to cite line 28 of page 34 of the record.)

Ex.: R. 34:28–30 / (R. 34:28–30) / [R. 34:28–30] / R. at 34:28–30 / (R. at 34:28–30) / [R. at 34:28–30]
(All are ways to cite page 34, lines 28 to 30 of the record.)

Ex.: R. 34:28–35:2 / (R. 34:28–35:2) / [R. 34:28–35:2] / R. at 34:28–35:2 / (R. at 34:28–35:2) / [R. at 34:28–35:2]
(All are ways to cite line 28 of page 34 through line 2 of page 35 of the record.)

(c) *Overcitation.* Many legal writers write wordy and needlessly descriptive references to the record.

Not this: ABC's Memorandum in Opposition to Plaintiff's Motion for Judgment on the Pleadings and for Dismissal, January 30, 2018, record page 87.

But this: R. 87. (Pointing out where in the record the statement's supporting or documentary information can be found.)

9.7 Choose which precedents to cite based on authority, hierarchy, freshness, and clarity of reasoning. Avoid string citations.

(a) *Authority.* Always cite precedent from the jurisdiction you're writing for, if available. Controlling authority always outweighs authority from another jurisdiction, which can only be persuasive. (For more on this subject, see 8.2(c).) Be sure to follow ABA Model Rule of Professional Conduct 3.3(a)(2), requiring disclosure of adverse authority in the controlling jurisdiction.

(b) *Hierarchy.* Within the jurisdiction you're writing for, cite authority from the highest court, if available; citation to a higher court is always stronger than citation to a lower court.

(c) *Freshness.* Prefer more recent citations, if available. But if a seminal case is well known for developing the proposition you're arguing, cite that landmark case more prominently than its progeny.

(d) *Reasoning.* Regardless of its precedential value, discuss (don't just cite) a case that will give your reader a clear and well-reasoned understanding of an important doctrine, a public-policy consideration, a comparison of judicial approaches, or a point of law that is especially important to your argument.

(e) *Number of citations.* One or two citations suffice if the authority is controlling or well established. Citing a string of lower-court citations adds no weight to an appellate court's decision. Neither does citing a string of authorities that repeat a well-established point of law (e.g., the constitutional right to avoid self-incrimination).

(f) *No controlling authority.* If no controlling law exists but several authorities are in agreement, weave that information into the text and include exemplary citations in footnotes (e.g., "The First, Fourth, Fifth, Seventh, Tenth, and Eleventh Circuits have all held that . . .").

(g) *In-depth study.* For more on the use of precedents, see Bryan A. Garner et al., *The Law of Judicial Precedent* (2016).

9.8 Use abbreviations as required by your citation system in the first full citation.

(a) *First citation.* The first reference to an authority should always be a full citation.

(b) *Lists.* Each citation system provides a list of common abbreviations for state names, titles, frequently used words, and so on. Some of the abbreviations may differ slightly in *The Bluebook* and *ALWD*, so always double-check.

9.9 Use short-form citations after the first full citation.

(a) *Clarity.* Although less complete than its long form, a short-form citation must still clearly identify the source referred to. For example, *Wray v. City of New York*, 490 F.3d 189, 196 (2d Cir. 2007), in later citations becomes (in *Bluebook* style) *Wray*, 490 F.3d at 196.

(b) *Distinctive name.* Prefer the first party's name for the short-form citation. But if the first party (1) is a governmental entity, (2) is an institutional litigant, or (3) has a name similar or identical to that of a party in another citation, use the second party's name instead. So *General Motors Corp. v. Pappas*, 950 N.E.2d 1136, 1142 (Ill. 2011), becomes *Pappas*, 950 N.E.2d at 1143; *State v. Smith*, 920 N.E.2d 949, 953 (Ohio 2009), becomes *Smith*, 920 N.E.2d at 952; and *McDaniel v. Brown*, 558 U.S. 120 (2010), and *Brown v. Sanders*, 546 U.S. 212 (2006), become *McDaniel*, 558 U.S. at 122, and *Sanders*, 546 U.S. at 215.

9.10 Use pinpoint citations when quoting, paraphrasing, or referring to a specific part of an opinion.

(a) *Purpose.* Pinpointing the precise location of the information within the source, meaning the precise page and perhaps even the footnote number, enables researchers to locate the support for your position, especially if the source material is lengthy or the reference is to a footnote. Take, for example, *Hawaii v. Mallan*, 950 P.2d 178, 240 (Haw. 1998) (Levinson, J., dissenting). That opinion includes a 110-page dissent. If you cite the dissent without pinpointing the page, don't expect a researcher to take the trouble to find it.

(b) *Pinpoint citation to first page.* In legal writing, custom dictates showing the page number of the pinpoint citation even when it is the first page of the opinion itself.

Ex.: Richard A. Posner, *Against Footnotes*, 38 Ct. Rev. 24, 24 (2001).

Ex.: Maureen B. Collins, *Legal Writing Can Be a Scream*, 88 Ill. B.J. 725, 725 (2000).

(c) *Paragraphs.* If a decision has numbered paragraphs, and no rules direct otherwise, you may boost the pinpoint accuracy by citing the paragraph number.

Ex.: *Grand Casino Tunica v. Shindler*, 772 So. 2d 1036, 1038 ¶ 8 (Miss. 2000).

(d) *Credibility.* Failing to pinpoint a reference can hurt a writer's credibility by making it hard, even impractical for the researcher to evaluate the validity of an argument or proposition. A failure to verify one statement of support can undermine the researcher's confidence in the writer's other assertions. Good research is identified openly. Poor research is presented obscurely.

9.11 Use *id.* carefully.

(a) *Function of "id."* The term *id.* (the abbreviation for *idem*, "the same") is a special short-form citation. It means that the immediately preceding authority is cited again. If the authority is the same, but a different page is referred to, the short form becomes "*id.* at [page number]."

(b) *Multiple authorities.* If the preceding citation contains several authorities, it becomes unclear whether *id.* refers to the collective contents of the preceding citation or only a specific authority there. Is it the first case cited or the last? Rather than using *id.*, repeat the relevant citation in short form.

(c) *And "ibid."* The term *ibid.* (the abbreviation for *ibidem*, "in the same place") serves the same function as *id.* but appears mostly in nonlegal writing. Instead of *ibid.*, always use *id.*—the customary legal form.

9.12 Avoid *infra, supra, op. cit., loc. cit.,* and similar abbreviations to refer to a citation that appears elsewhere in the writing.

(a) *Definitions.* Cross-references direct the reader to a source cited elsewhere in the work. *Infra* tells the reader that the citation will be found later in the footnotes or text. *Supra*, *op. cit.*, *loc. cit.*, and others indicate that a reference has already been cited above. All these forms burden the reader with the necessity of hunting for other references at some indeterminate place. If cross-references don't adequately identify the source material, readers must go back and find the first full citation. For example, if a citation merely states, "*See* Solan, *supra* note 14, at 5," a reader must needlessly search the earlier pages of the document to find Lawrence M. Solan, *The Language of Statutes: Laws and Their Interpretation* (2010). It's usually better to cite the source again.

(b) *Footnotes.* When used in footnotes, internal cross-references to citations in other footnotes interrupt the discussion. They distract the reader, who is forced to flip through the document to find and read the other notes, search again for the original point, and only then rejoin the flow of the central argument or narrative.

(c) *Law reviews.* Most journals and law reviews allow cross-referencing in footnotes if (1) it avoids repeating a lengthy footnote, (2) it cross-references a nearby footnote, and (3) it's used sparingly. Some journals prefer that writers use English words (*below*; *above*) instead of the Latin signals *infra*, *supra*, and others—or simply identify the cross-referenced footnote (e.g., *See* n.52).

9.13 When citing sequential pages, sections, paragraphs, or similar elements, use an en-dash (see 5.15) to elide the numerals. If you elide page numbers of three or more digits, always show two digits after the en-dash.

Ex.: pp. 215–18
But: pp. 1089–1104
Ex.: § 34(a)–(d)
Ex.: ¶¶ 35–40

9.14 When citing a concurring, dissenting, en banc, or plurality opinion, include the type of opinion in parentheses immediately after the court and year but before any other parenthetical information. Identify the author of a concurrence or dissent.

(a) *Plurality opinion.* It is usually unnecessary (although it is permissible) to name the writer of a plurality opinion.

Ex.: *Bilski v. Kappos*, 561 U.S. 593, 596 (2010) (plurality).

Ex.: *Trop v. Dulles*, 356 U.S. 86, 89 (1958) (Warren, J., plurality opinion).

(b) *Concurrence or dissent.* In the citation of a concurrence or dissent, always identify the writer and the type of opinion in a parenthetical.

Ex.: *Brown v. Louisiana*, 447 U.S. 323, 339 (1980) (Rehnquist, J., dissenting).

Ex.: *Microsoft Corp. v. i4i Ltd. P'ship*, 564 U.S. 91, 114 (2011) (Breyer, J., concurring).

> "A signal prefaces a citation to indicate the type and degree of support or contradiction the cited authority provides for a proposition in text."
> —*ALWD Guide to Legal Citation*

(c) *Unsigned opinion.* A per curiam opinion—one issued by an entire court without attribution to an individual judge or justice—usually carries somewhat less weight than one authored by a specific judge. If the author is unidentified, append the parenthetical "(per curiam)."

Ex.: *Hernandez v. Thaler*, 630 F.3d 420, 425 (5th Cir. 2011) (per curiam).

Ex.: *Thornton v. Phillips Cty., Ark.*, 240 F.3d 728, 729 (8th Cir. 2001) (per curiam).

(d) *Full-court hearing.* If an opinion was issued after a hearing by a full court in a tribunal that usually hears cases in panels consisting of fewer than all the judges, append the parenthetical "(en banc)." *En banc* may be pronounced either /in bank/ or /on bonk/.

Ex.: *Nicini v. Morra*, 212 F.3d 798, 810 (3d Cir. 2000) (en banc).

Ex.: *Portalatin v. Graham*, 624 F.3d 69, 90 (2d Cir. 2010) (en banc) (stating that the court "must presume that the New York Court of Appeals meant what it said").

9.15 Space parenthetical explanations or quotations correctly in relation to the rest of the citation.

(a) *Spacing.* If a citation is followed by one or more sets of parenthetical information, leave a space between back-to-back parentheses (see 1.39(c)).

Ex.: *Metro. Coal Co. v. Howard*, 155 F.2d 780 (2d Cir. 1946) (involving warranty for barge).

Ex.: *Cowan v. Doering*, 545 A.2d 159, 168 (N.J. 1988) (Clifford, J., dissenting) (commenting on a mentally disturbed plaintiff).

(b) *Punctuation.* If a parenthetical doesn't contain a complete sentence, don't include terminal punctuation inside the parenthetical. Either a period or a semicolon (if another citation follows) always goes immediately after the citation's last closing parenthesis.

Ex.: *In re Oakwood Mobile Homes, Inc.*, 987 S.W.2d 571, 574 (Tex. 1999) (declaring that neither adhesion contracts nor arbitration clauses are per se unconscionable); *In re H.E. Butt Grocery Co.*, 17 S.W.3d 360, 371–72 (Tex. App. 2000) (considering procedural unconscionability of arbitration clause in adhesion contract).

Ex.: *MGM Studios v. Grokster, Ltd.*, 545 U.S. 913, 929 (2005) ("This very breadth of the software's use may well draw the public directly into the debate over copyright policy, and the indications are that the ease of copying songs or movies using software like Grokster's and Napster's is fostering disdain for copyright protection" (citations omitted).).

9.16 Parenthetical matter given with a citation should appear before the subsequent history.

(a) *History.* If a source (e.g., a case or statute) has been modified in any way after coming into existence, you must show its history and the effect on its value as authority. Never enclose the history in parentheses.

> Ex.: *W.J. Runyon & Son, Inc. v. Davis*, 605 So. 2d 38, 47 (Miss. 1992), *overruled on other grounds by Richardson v. APAC-Miss., Inc.*, 631 So. 2d 143, 152 (Miss. 1994).

(b) *Additional citation.* A case with a subsequent history often requires an additional citation to identify the source of the history.

> Ex.: *Conoco Inc. v. Dep't of Justice*, 521 F.Supp 1301, 1305–06 (D. Del. 1981) (declaring that FOIA exemption for "intra-agency" memorandums or letters was applicable to handwritten notes), *aff'd in part, rev'd in part & remanded on other grounds*, 687 F.2d 724 (3d Cir. 1982).

9.17 Use the correct signal to show the relationship between a textual statement and the material cited.

(a) *Basics.* Conventions for citation signals vary from system to system. Employ your signals consistently, following the guidelines of the citation system you're using. Here are the introductory signals and their customary meanings:

- *No signal.* If you're directly quoting authority, or if the cited authority either states the definition or proposition in the text or directly supports the stated proposition, don't use a signal.
- *See.* The cited authority implicitly supports the proposition in some way. For example, the supported proposition may logically flow from the cited authority, or the authority's dictum may suggest the proposition.
- *See also.* The cited authority, which is not mentioned in the text, provides additional supporting material. Because the authority might not directly support the proposition, you may need a parenthetical to explain its relevance. Ordinarily, a *see-also* citation must follow one introduced by *see.*
- *Cf.* The cited authority provides an analogy that indirectly supports the stated proposition. A parenthetical explaining the analogy is often necessary.
- *E.g.* The cited authority is one of many that similarly state or support the proposition. This signal is combined with other signals when the authorities do not directly support the proposition.

> Ex.: *E.g., Chisholm v. Georgia*, 2 U.S. 419, 478 (1793) (opinion of Jay, C.J.).

> Ex.: *See generally, e.g.*, Walter F. Murphy, *Elements of Judicial Strategy* (1964).

- *Compare . . . with.* Two possibilities: (1) The cited authorities support or illustrate the stated proposition but do so in different ways. (2) The authorities offer alternative analyses of the proposition and arrive at different conclusions. *The Bluebook* strongly recommends a parenthetical explanation for each authority.
- *Contra.* The cited authority directly contradicts the stated proposition.
- *But see.* The cited authority implicitly contradicts the proposition in some way. For example, the authority may show that the proposition is limited or contradicted by some factors or in some circumstances. Both *The Bluebook* and the *ALWD Guide* encourage a parenthetical explanation of the authority's relevance.
- *See generally.* The cited authority provides useful background information related to the proposition but does not necessarily support or contradict it.

Signals occasionally used:

- *Accord.* The cited authority, which is not mentioned in the text, states or directly supports the proposition. This signal usually introduces one or more case citations.

  Ex.: *McIlroy v. PaineWebber, Inc.*, 989 F.2d 817, 821 (5th Cir. 1993). *Accord Nat'l Post Office v. U.S. Postal Serv.*, 751 F.2d 834 (6th Cir. 1985).

  Ex.: *NSBA v. Rothery*, 619 N.W.2d 590, 593 (Neb. 2000). *Accord NSBA v. Howze*, 618 N.W.2d 663 (Neb. 2000); *NSBA v. Mefferd*, 604 N.W.2d 839 (Neb. 2000).

- *But cf.* The cited authority provides an analogy that contradicts the stated proposition. A parenthetical explaining the analogy is often necessary and strongly recommended by *The Bluebook.*

(b) *Older legal materials.* Because citation standards change, signals used in writings from earlier periods may prove unreliable. For example, *The Bluebook* redefined *cf.* six times in 39 years. In 1947, *cf.* signaled an authority containing parallel propositions but materially different facts. In 1955, it signaled an authority that expressed a proposition, possibly only analogous, that lent some support to the writer's statement, conclusion, or opinion of law. The current meaning is given in (a) above.

(c) *Modern resources.* Signals may not be identical across current citation systems. For example, under the *Bluebook* system, *but see* means that an authority "clearly supports" a contrary proposition; under the *ALWD* system, it means that the authority "implicitly contradicts the stated proposition."

(d) *Undefined signals.* Not all signals are used in all systems. For example, *The Bluebook* and *ALWD* both use *contra*, *e.g.*, and *cf.*; the *Maroonbook* does not. The *Maroonbook* uses *consider* and *contrast . . . with*, neither of which appears in *The Bluebook* or *ALWD.*

(e) *Order of use.* Both *The Bluebook* and *ALWD* specify how to arrange citations in a list that contains more than one.

9.18 Do what you reasonably can to condense citations.

(a) *Abbreviations.* As often as possible, use abbreviations for case names, judicial reporters, compilations of statutes and regulations, and other commonly consulted sources.

Not this: Federal Reporter (Third Series)
But this: F.3d

(b) *Short-form citations.* After the first full citation, use the appropriate short form (see 9.9). But be sensible. If that means a researcher would have to search back a dozen pages to find the reference, give the full citation again.

(c) *Redundancy.* If the reporter name identifies the deciding court, don't identify the court again in the parenthetical before the date. If the reporter name identifies the state, don't repeat that in the parenthetical.

Not this: *Waggener v. Leggett*, 246 Miss. 505, 509 (Miss. 1963).

But this: *Waggener v. Leggett*, 246 Miss. 505, 509 (1963).

Not this: *Howard v. Oakland Tribune*, 245 Cal. Rptr. 449, 451 n.6 (Cal. Ct. App. 1988).

But this: *Howard v. Oakland Tribune*, 245 Cal. Rptr. 449, 451 n.6 (Ct. App. 1988).

9.19 Avoid parallel citations unless local rules require them.

(a) *Generally.* If parallel citations aren't required, don't use them. Parallel citations bulk up the text with more numbers. They unduly separate sentences and parts of sentences. They inflate the number of authorities without adding weight. Choose just one form as dictated by your citation system or some other overriding directive. Although parallel citations can aid the researcher who primarily uses books, they have the drawback of seriously cluttering the paragraphs in which they appear.

Not this: *Estate of Braden v. State*, 266 P.3d 349, 288 Ariz. 323, 622 Ariz. Adv. Rep. 35 (Ariz. 2011).
But this: *Estate of Braden v. State*, 266 P.3d 349 (Ariz. 2011).

(b) *Punctuation.* Separate parallel citations with commas unless you must follow another style. The *Michigan Uniform System of Citation*, for example, requires semicolons.

Ex.: *Brown v. Bd. of Educ.*, 349 U.S. 294, 75 S. Ct. 753, 99 L. Ed. 1083 (1955).

9.20 Use a parenthetical note if an explanation would clarify something about the citation, such as how the source supports the argument.

(a) *Clarification.* If a source directly supports your statement or proposition, you don't generally need a parenthetical. But if several unrelated points are discussed on the page cited, a parenthetical may help make it clear what text you're citing as support.

(b) *Multiple sources.* If several sources support a single statement but on different grounds, use parentheticals to distinguish the citations.

> Ex.: *Peay v. BellSouth Med. Assistance Plan*, 205 F.3d 1206, 1211–12 & n.4 (10th Cir. 2000) (concluding that personal jurisdiction in ERISA case requires adequate contacts with the particular state); *Bd. of Trustees v. Elite Erectors, Inc.*, 212 F.3d 1031, 1035 (7th Cir. 2000) (deciding that personal jurisdiction in ERISA cases is established by adequate contacts with United States as a whole).

(c) *Specificity.* A narrow parenthetical can help pinpoint the specific information in a source.

> Ex.: *Addressograph-Multigraph Corp. v. Zink*, 329 A.2d 28, 33 (Md. 1974) (defining incidental and consequential damages resulting from a breach of warranty under UCC § 2–715). [The contextual information helps the researcher quickly locate the information on the page.]

(d) *Obscurity.* A vague or broadly worded parenthetical diminishes a citation's value. For example, a parenthetical stating "discussing contract law" isn't helpful to show, for example, that the source supports a textual proposition concerning the rights of a third-party beneficiary.

(e) *Form.* Although a parenthetical explanation may be as simple as a tagline (*telephone harassment*), most should (1) begin with a present participle (*holding, affirming, reversing, overruling*, etc.), (2) include a direct quotation, or (3) combine both approaches.

> Ex.: *Boos v. Barry*, 485 U.S. 312, 318 (1988) (recognizing public-issue signs to be classic examples of free speech).

> Ex.: *Schenck v. Pro-Choice Network*, 519 U.S. 357, 377 (1997) ("Leafletting and commenting on matters of public concern are classic forms of speech that lie at the heart of the First Amendment.").

> Ex.: Andrew Siegel, *"Steady Habits" Under Siege: The Defense of Federalism in Jeffersonian Connecticut*, in *Federalists Reconsidered* 199, 207 (Doron Ben-Atar & Barbara B. Oberg eds., 1998) (discussing the strong republicanism of the Connecticut Federalists on the eve of the "infamous" Hartford Convention).

(f) *Cleaned-up quotations.* If you omit internal quotations, brackets, or obtrusive ellipsis dots to use a cleaned-up quotation (see 8.5), note as much with the parenthetical "(cleaned up)."

Ex.: In 1495, Parliament enacted an anomalous (and void) provision: "If any act or acts or other process of law hereafter happen to be made contrary to this ordinance, then that act or acts or other process of law . . . should be void." 11 Henry 7, ch. 1 (cleaned up)." (What has been cleaned up? The spelling has been modernized, brackets omitted, and an ellipsis omitted.)

9.21 Never trust the citations in another document. Always verify from original sources.

(a) *Electronic shortcomings.* The citation forms provided by electronic legal databases typically include all the parallel citations. But never assume that the form in the electronic source conforms to a standard legal-citation system. For that matter, never assume the word-for-word accuracy of the electronic text. Although most online versions of print materials are fully accurate, there are inevitable lapses. Whenever possible, confirm electronic citations against print versions.

(b) *Inaccurate information.* Legal materials may be retitled, codified, renumbered, or amended. A citation in another document may no longer be a good one.

(c) *Older legal materials.* The older the source material, the less likely it is that the internal citations will be consistent with current citation norms.

Ex. (from a 1941 citation):
Anderson v. Dunn, 6 Wheat. 204, 227, 5 L.Ed. 242.

Ex. (as it would appear today):
Anderson v. Dunn, 19 U.S. (6 Wheat.) 204, 227 (1821).

(d) *Sanctions.* Improper citations and other errors can result in a range of sanctions.

- **Rebuke:** *DeLeon v. Beneficial Constr. Co.*, 998 F.Supp 859, 864 n.3 (N.D. Ill. 1998) (stating that both parties' pleadings were "so packed with erroneous citations and typographical errors that at certain points they [were] almost incomprehensible"); *Howard v. Oakland Tribune*, 245 Cal. Rptr. 449, 451 n.6 (Ct. App. 1988) (stating that the appellant's brief was unhelpful because it was "riddled with inaccurate and incomplete case citations").

- **Fine:** *State v. Gebhardt*, No. 41068-1-II, 2013 WL 1489449, at *5 (Wash. Ct. App. Apr. 9, 2013) (fining attorney $250 for failing to cite the record and failing to provide citations to authority); *Sobol v. Capital Mgmt. Consultants, Inc.*, 726 P.2d 335, 337 (Nev. 1986) (imposing $5,000 sanction on respondent for misrepresenting stipulated facts and wrongly representing that quoted language from a dissent was the court's holding).

- **Appeal dismissed:** *Han v. Stanford Univ.*, 210 F.3d 1038, 1040 (9th Cir. 2000) (dismissing plaintiff's appeal for completely disregarding rules about citing to the record).
- **Suspension:** *In re Shepperson*, 674 A.2d 1273, 1274 (Vt. 1996) (suspending attorney for six months for preparing incomplete and incomprehensible briefs with numerous citation errors, among other deficiencies).

9.22 Before you submit your writing to anyone else, double-check your citations to ensure that all citations and subsequent histories are correct.

(a) *Updates.* Cases, statutes, and regulations are especially likely to have been modified in some way that either needs to be reflected in a parenthetical or requires changing the citation's form.

Ex. (vacated decision, published just three months after the original):
United States v. Faasse, 227 F.3d 660, *opinion vacated*, 234 F.3d 312 (6th Cir. 2000).

Ex. (recodified statute):
Act of April 6, 1995, 74th Leg., R.S., ch. 20, § 1, sec. 152.006, 1995 Tex. Gen. Laws 113, 142–43 (amended and recodified 1999) (current version at Tex. Fam. Code Ann. §§ 152.206, 152.307 (Vernon Supp. 2001)).

Ex. (amended regulation):
1989, No. 68, §§ 4, 5 (amending 23 V.S.A. §§ 1203(d), 1205).

(b) *Proper authorities.* Cite the proper authorities. A court may impose sanctions for failure to cite good authority or controlling authority.

Ex.: *Smith v. United Transp. Local 81*, 594 F.Supp. 96, 101 (S.D. Cal. 1984) (attorney based entire argument on vacated authority).

Ex.: *Glassalum Eng'g Corp. v. 392208 Ontario Ltd.*, 487 So. 2d 87, 88 (Fla. Dist. Ct. App. 1986) (counsel neglected to shepardize questioned authority that would have led to controlling authority).

9.23 If no legal-citation manual explains how to cite some material, such as an electronic or Internet source, consult a current nonlegal style manual.

(a) *Nonlegal style.* For any issue addressed neither here nor in *The Bluebook* or the *ALWD Guide*, consult the leading text on matters of nonlegal style: *The Chicago Manual of Style*. Keep an up-to-date edition handy.

(b) *Clarity.* When special circumstances make legal-style conventions unworkable, choose clarity over convention. For example, if there is a commonly understood or otherwise logical abbreviation for a word in a lengthy citation, use that abbreviation.

§ 10
Footnotes

10.1 Footnotes are traditionally the mark of a scholar. They establish the foundation on which you've built new ideas and qualified or replaced old ones. A dearth of footnotes may suggest that the writer is unfamiliar with the literature on the subject, is afraid that readers will be repelled by too many footnotes, or is withholding due credit, perhaps to make the work seem more original. On the other hand, a spate of footnotes may suggest the folly of pedantry, the inability to leave items on the cutting-room floor—or perhaps something as simple as a desultory organization.

Because footnotes are also resources and stepping-stones for others who are investigating the subject, appearance and content are important. No magic ratio of footnotes to text exists, but guiding factors include the purpose of the writing, the intended audience, the subject matter, and the content. The more formal and academic the writing, the higher the ratio is likely to be—though indisputably many law journals greatly overdo the number and length of footnotes.

10.2 Follow whatever prescriptions are set down in court rules, journal guidelines, or any other controlling directives.

(a) *Court rules.* There is no consistency among courts' preferences for footnote style. For example, U.S. Tax Court Rule of Practice & Procedure 23(d) prescribes 12- or 14-point type for footnotes (depending on the font), but U.S. Supreme Court Rule of Practice & Procedure 33 prescribes 10-point or larger type. Some courts prohibit all footnotes on the assumption (not without experiential foundation) that lawyers might be using them to circumvent page limits. On that same assumption, other courts require double-spacing footnotes and using the same size type as in the text. Such fatuous rules are based on crude page-limit rules instead of word-limit rules. However ill-considered these rules may be, you must follow them.

(b) *Law reviews.* Some law reviews require footnotes to conform to a local system of citation (for example, the *Texas Law Review* and most other law reviews in that state follow the *Texas Rules of Form*). Others provide detailed guidelines to supplement a general citation system. For example,

> "I once asked a young dissertation writer whether her suddenly grayed hair was due to ill health or personal tragedy; she answered: 'It was the footnotes.'"
>
> —*Joanna Russ*

the *American Indian Law Review* advises writers to use *Bluebook* form while amending it to require some terms to be spelled out in the text but expressed as symbols in footnotes—contrary to *Bluebook* style.

10.3 Set footnotes in smaller type than the text, and single-space them.

(a) *Font.* Unless court rules, journal guidelines, or other directives state differently, follow the font conventions set forth in your chosen legal system of legal citation.

(b) *Type size.* Unless an express directive provides otherwise, a footnote should be about two points smaller than the body's text (11-point type for 13-point text, 10-point type for 12-point text). But avoid minuscule footnotes. They may create the impression that you're trying to hide your work, obscure poor research, or (again) evade page limits (see 10.8).

10.4 Use sequential numbering for footnotes throughout most documents—but renumber them for book chapters.

(a) *Documents and articles.* Footnotes in a brief or a law-review article must be consecutively numbered throughout the work whether the work contains hundreds of footnotes or just a few.

(b) *Books and treatises.* In a longer scholarly writing such as a book or treatise, restart the footnote numbers at the beginning of each chapter or section.

(c) *Arabic numerals.* Although nonlegal sources with very few footnotes may use a nonnumerical system, legal writers prefer numerals, even if only one footnote appears. (For a curious exception, a solitary footnote marked with only an asterisk, see *Westinghouse Elec. Corp. v. NLRB*, 809 F.2d 419, 425 (7th Cir. 1987).)

10.5 Put the superscript footnote number after all punctuation marks except a dash and, sometimes, a closing parenthesis.

(a) *Quotation marks.* Place the superscript outside closing quotation marks.

> Ex.: Paraphrasing Justice Oliver Wendell Holmes, the court declared that "it must be assumed that a jury does its duty, abides by cautionary instructions, and finds facts only because those facts are proved."[2]

(b) *Dash.* Separating the superscript from the related clause or sentence can cause confusion. The em-dash highlights what immediately precedes it. Separating the citation from the emphasized clause obscures the relationship between the sources listed in the footnote and the statements. For example, if both statements are supported by caselaw, a reader cannot distinguish whether a cited case supports both statements or only one.

Ex.: It is a well-established common-law principle that mere "fighting words" are not sufficient provocation to justify an assault[8]—yet some appellate courts have found that a victim's vaguely worded insults invite a defendant's violent response.[9]

(c) *Parentheses.* Place the footnote superscript outside an end-parenthesis if the superscript refers to what is before the opening parenthesis as well as the contents of the parentheses. If the superscript refers only to what is inside the parentheses, place it just inside the closing parenthesis.

Ex.: The monitor was visible to everyone in the courtroom (except for one juror who was asleep)[1] throughout the daylong hearing. (Reference is to everything before and within parentheses.)

Ex.: A reasonable consumer should be able to see that a bottle contains a foreign substance as large as a mouse (unless the bottle is opaque[7]), and complain to the vendor, not a court. (Reference is to contents of parentheses only.)

10.6 Never use more than one superscript in the same place.

(a) *Lack of clarity.* Avoid using two superscripts side by side: their purposes will be unclear. They may refer to different sources for different propositions or to the same proposition in multiple sources (see 10.7). Or they may refer to contradictory sources. They may also create a visual miscue—an adjacent *3* and *4* may look to the reader like *34.*

(b) *Contrary information.* Cite any contradictory source in the same footnote as the supporting citation. Use a signal to distinguish the sources cited and use explanatory parentheticals if necessary—as they often are.

Not this: 3 *Crawn v. Campo*, 643 A.2d 600, 605 (N.J. 1994) (holding that the standard for liability in recreational-sports-injury cases is recklessness, not ordinary negligence).

> "Perhaps no single implement of all the vast apparatus of scholarship is so thoroughly misused in the law as the footnote. There may be some justification in the manifold areas of the academic world for that formidable display of learning and industry, the thin stream of text meandering in a vale of footnotes, but such a technique is quite self-defeating in the law: it makes the writer's thoughts more difficult to follow—and hence far less likely to persuade the judicial reader."
>
> —*Frederick B. Wiener*

4 *But see Lestina v. West Bend Mut. Ins. Co.*, 501 N.W.2d 28, 33 (Wis. 1993) (adopting a negligence standard for liability of participants in recreational-sports-injury cases).

But this: 3 *Crawn v. Campo*, 643 A.2d 600, 605 (N.J. 1994) (holding that the standard for liability in recreational-sports-injury cases is recklessness, not ordinary negligence). *But see Lestina v. West Bend Mut. Ins. Co.*, 501 N.W.2d 28, 33 (Wis. 1993) (adopting a negligence standard for liability of participants in recreational-sports-injury cases).

10.7 Consolidate multiple sources into one footnote when possible.

(a) *Full support.* All sources that apply generally to a statement or proposition should appear in the same footnote, even if several are specifically referred to.

Ex. (in text): Many leading legal minds—Dworkin, Darrow, and Blackstone among them—have spoken out about capital punishment.[4]

Ex. (footnote): 4 Ronald Dworkin, *Freedom's Law* 300–01 (1996) (on how the Eighth Amendment bars capital punishment); Clarence Darrow, *Clarence Darrow on the Death Penalty* 39 (1991) (noting that although the defendant has killed, that itself is no justification for the state's taking life; stating, "I would hate to live in a state that I didn't think was better than a murderer"); 4 William Blackstone, *Commentaries on the Laws of England* 18–19 (1765) (calling for restrictions on the death penalty).

(b) *Paragraph footnotes.* If a series of footnotes requires several or many *id.* citations, all referring to the same page, you may collect them all at the end of the paragraph to eliminate the pesky interruptions that superscripts cause.

(c) *Distinctions.* If a clause in a cited sentence applies to some but not all of the cited sources, place one superscript at the end of the clause and another at the end of the sentence or make two sentences.

Ex.: Although one legal scholar has argued that a fine is sufficient punishment,[5] another asserts that confinement motivates offenders to reform.[6]

Ex.: One legal scholar has argued that a fine is sufficient punishment.[5] But another asserts that confinement motivates offenders to reform.[6]

10.8 Never use footnotes to evade page-limit restrictions.

(a) *Ethics.* Don't try to circumvent court rules by footnoting text. This ploy is easily detected, is widely frowned on, and can raise questions of integrity. Find other ways to come in under the page limit: start by tightening your argument and eliminating superfluous words. Of course, sensible readers will instantly perceive that footnoted citations don't squeeze more text onto the page—as long as the footnotes contain no independent sentences but bibliographic information only.

Ex.: *Bollea v. Clem*, 937 F.Supp.2d 1344 n.1 (M.D. Fla. 2013) (Whittemore, J.) (noting that the party's response "inexcusably contains extensive substantive footnotes in an apparent effort to circumvent the page limits prescribed by [local rules]").

Ex.: *See, e.g., Anderson v. Alpha Portland Indus., Inc.*, 836 F.2d 1512, 1521 (8th Cir. 1988) (caustically observing that plaintiff's counsel violated the spirit of the page-limit rules by overusing single-spaced footnotes).

(b) *Sanctions.* Ignoring or attempting to circumvent court rules can draw severe sanctions, such as:

- **A public reprimand.**

  Ex.: *Lake Cty. Riverboat L.P. v. Ill. Gaming Bd.*, 730 N.E.2d 524, 534 (Ill. App. Ct. 2000) (scolding attorneys for using voluminous single-spaced substantive footnotes in minuscule type).

- **Damages.**

  Ex.: *Cattellier v. Depco, Inc.*, 696 N.E.2d 75, 79 (Ind. Ct. App. 1998) (ordering attorney to pay opposing counsel's fees as damages and penalty for using smaller type than rules required).

- **A lost award.**

  Ex.: *Varda, Inc. v. Ins. Co. of N. Am.*, 45 F.3d 634, 640 (2d Cir. 1995) (denying usual award of costs on appeal because three-quarters of brief's facts and argument were contained in single-spaced, page-long footnotes).

- **Fines.**

  Ex.: *Westinghouse Elec. Corp. v. NLRB*, 809 F.2d 419, 425 (7th Cir. 1987) (unnumbered footnote) (levying a $1,000 fine on attorneys who used single-spaced footnotes to condense 70 pages into 50).

  Ex.: *Kano v. Nat'l Consumer Coop. Bank*, 22 F.3d 899, 899 (9th Cir. 1994) (imposing a $1,500 fine after noting that attorney was aware of rules and nonetheless used noncompliant footnotes in two briefs).

- **The striking of the footnote.**

  Ex.: *Lundy v. Farmers Grp. Inc.*, 750 N.E.2d 314, 318 (Ill. App. Ct. 2001) (striking footnotes containing substantive material that if integrated into the body of the brief would have caused the brief to exceed the page limit).

- **The striking of a brief.**

  Ex.: *TK-7 Corp. v. Estate of Barbouti*, 966 F.2d 578, 579 (10th Cir. 1992) (striking brief for compressing nine pages of text into illegitimately shrunken footnotes).

> "Every legal writer is presumed to be a liar until he proves himself otherwise with a flock of footnotes."
>
> —*Fred Rodell*

- **Waiver of appeal.**

  Ex.: *Tech. Solutions Co. v. Northrop Grumman Corp.*, 826 N.E.2d 1220, 1224 (Ill. App. Ct. 2005) (reprimanding counsel for putting substantive material in footnotes to evade page limitations and "admonish[ing] all counsels involved in preparing these briefs . . . to comply with supreme court rules in the future or face the possibility of dismissal of their clients' appeals").

10.9 Avoid substantive footnotes—those containing statements involving reason, argument, or assertions in sentence or paragraph form (as opposed to those merely containing bibliographic information coupled perhaps with properly formatted parentheticals).

(a) *Distracting and tiresome.* Especially in analytical and persuasive writing not directed to a scholarly audience, don't count on your busy readers to look at your substantive footnotes. Most find shifting their attention up and down the page tiring and distracting. And the very fact that the material is footnoted rather than in the body of the writing signals that the content is not considered to be of central importance. Some courts are explicit in their policy of not considering any issue raised only in footnotes (see 10.9(c)).

Writers who freely drop down to a footnote to continue a discussion or to embark on a sidebar discussion often reveal their failure to organize the material sensibly and to signpost their analysis. The cure is often simply to reinsert the footnoted text where the superscript had appeared and then to massage the surrounding paragraphs to ensure that they flow logically and smoothly.

(b) *Bad reactions.* If you use a great many substantive footnotes, readers may well conclude that you're lazily dodging the responsibility to organize a coherent discussion, self-indulgently exploring trivialities, or hedging your arguments.

Ex.: *M&M Metals Int'l v. Continental Cas. Co.*, 870 N.E.2d 167, 167 (Ohio Ct. App. 2006) (noting that with a combination of substantive and citational footnotes, "the brief declines into law-reviewesque unreadability").

(c) *Ignoring arguments in footnotes.* Many courts will disregard arguments raised exclusively in footnotes.

Ex.: *Otsuka Pharm. Co. v. Sandoz, Inc.*, 678 F.3d 1280, 1294 (Fed. Cir. 2012) (stating that arguments raised only in footnotes in appellate briefs are waived).

Ex.: *Americas Mining Corp. v. Theriault*, 51 A.3d 1213, 1264 (Del. 2012) (barring issue because argument was in a footnote).

Ex.: *Solis-Alarcon v. United States*, 662 F.3d 577, 584 (1st Cir. 2011) (declaring that an evidentiary claim developed solely in a footnote in the opening brief was forfeited for consideration on appeal).

Ex.: *Boston Edison Co. v. Mass. Water Res. Auth.*, 947 N.E.2d 544, 549 (Mass. 2011) (stating that arguments relegated to a footnote are waived).

Ex.: *Minto Grain, LLC v. Tibert*, 776 N.W.2d 549, 559 (N.D. 2009) (pointing out that the court does not condone using footnotes to make arguments).

Ex.: *Odd v. Malone*, 538 F.3d 202, 207 n.2 (3d Cir. 2008) (finding that the plaintiff waived state-law claims made only in a footnote).

Ex.: *NSTAR Elec. & Gas Corp. v. FERC*, 481 F.3d 794, 799–800 (D.C. Cir. 2007) ("[T]his argument is found in a single footnote in NSTAR's opening brief, and such a reference is not enough to raise an issue for our review.").

Ex.: *Fuji Am. Corp. v. United States*, 30 Ct. Int'l Trade 1991, 1993 (2006) (Musgrave, J.) (expressing doubt that an issue carried any weight because "it was 'raised' exclusively in a footnote" and not "fleshed out during the normal course of briefing").

Ex.: *SmithKline Beecham Corp. v. Apotex Corp.*, 439 F.3d 1312, 1320 (Fed. Cir. 2006) ("[A]rguments raised in footnotes are not preserved.").

Ex.: *City of Syracuse v. Onondaga Cty.*, 464 F.3d 297, 308 (2d Cir. 2006) (holding that argument made only in a brief's heading and footnote was waived).

Ex.: *United States v. Dairy Farmers of Am., Inc.*, 426 F.3d 850, 856 (6th Cir. 2005) ("An argument contained only in a footnote does not preserve an issue for our review.").

Ex.: *Lutwin v. Thompson*, 361 F.3d 146, 148 n.1 (2d Cir. 2004) ("We decline to consider this argument because '[a] contention is not sufficiently presented for appeal if it is conclusorily asserted only in a footnote.'" [quoting *Tolbert v. Queens Coll.*, 242 F.3d 58, 75 (2d Cir. 2001)]).

Ex.: *Equip. Mfrs. Inst. v. Janklow*, 300 F.3d 842, 848 n.2 (8th Cir. 2002) ("[T]his Court will not consider a claim improperly presented in a footnote.").

Ex.: *AAR Int'l, Inc. v. Vacances Heliades S.A.*, 202 F.Supp.2d 788, 796 (N.D. Ill. 2002) (noting that claims raised only in a footnote are waived).

Ex.: *People v. Crosswhite*, 124 Cal. Rptr. 2d 301, 306 n.5 (Ct. App. 2001) ("This argument is waived by raising it only in a footnote under an argument heading which gives no notice of the contention.").

Ex.: *Roberts v. Worcester Redev. Auth.*, 759 N.E.2d 1220, 1227 n.11 (Mass. App. Ct. 2001) ("We are not required to address an argument raised in a footnote.").

Ex.: *Sledd v. Lindsay*, 102 F.3d 282, 288 (7th Cir. 1996) ("Sledd relegated his . . . arguments to a footnote . . . . [W]e therefore consider it forfeited.").

(d) *Exception for scholarly prose.* In scholarly writing (see Part 4), "talky" footnotes admittedly have a place. In the hands of a skilled scholar who maintains a clear exposition or argument above the line, they can provide

> "The pseudo-scholarly approach of tackling substantive, sometimes quite subtle, themes and topics in the fine print of footnotes is a fierce distraction. Burying an argument in a footnote, and expecting the reader to excavate it, is simply inexcusable."
>
> —*Tom Goldstein & Jethro K. Lieberman*

important and even delightful commentary of secondary note. A good example appears in the hornbook by Charles Alan Wright, to whom this style manual is dedicated. In the last edition of *The Law of Federal Courts* to appear during his lifetime, the following note appears in reference to *Swift v. Tyson*:

> * Ironically the defendant's name, which was a household word to lawyers for a century, was apparently misspelled by the Supreme Court, and was in fact "Tysen." *See* Tenton, *The Story of* Swift v. Tyson, 35 Ill. L. Rev. 519, 530 n.2 (1941). This is not the only example of misspelling in Supreme Court cases. The bank cashier in the great case of *McCulloch v. Maryland*, 17 U.S. (4 Wheat.) 316, 4 L.Ed. 579 (1819), actually spelled his name McCulloh. Lewis, *Without Fear or Favor* 504 n.163 (1965). The defendants in *Cohens v. Virginia*, 19 U.S. (6 Wheat.) 264, 5 L.Ed. 257 (1821), were two men with the last name "Cohen." Jackson, *The Supreme Court, the Eleventh Amendment, and State Sovereign Immunity*, 98 Yale L.J. 1, 15 n.65 (1988). The defendant in Dred Scott's case was John F.A. Sanford, but the case has gone into the books as *Dred Scott v. Sandford*, 60 U.S. (19 How.) 393, 15 L.Ed. 691 (1857). *See* Latham, *The* Dred Scott *Decision* 26 (1968). The stubborn parents in *Minersville School District v. Gobitis*, 310 U.S. 586, 60 S.Ct. 1010, 84 L.Ed. 1375 (1940), were really named Gobitas. Harrell & Jones, *Equal Justice Under Law* 85 (1965).
>
> In *Ford Motor Credit Co. v. Milhollin*, 444 U.S. 555, 100 S.Ct. 790, 63 L.Ed.2d 22 (1980), the Court, in an introductory footnote, says that the respondents spell their name "Millhollin," but since it has been misspelled throughout the litigation and since "legal research catalogs and computers are governed by the principle of consistency, not correctness, we feel constrained to adhere to the erroneous spelling."

Notes like this one aren't necessary to understand the above-the-line text, but they're interesting notes that preserve useful information for posterity. And they're reasonably short.

When, however, below-the-line commentary feels bloated and scattered, it's time for curtailment. See 10.9(a) & 32.3(d).

> "One kind of note must always be excised: the defensive footnote. Scholars, especially when they are treading on new ground and are afraid of the reception of their ideas, tend to cover themselves with references, attempting to show that no book has gone unread and no issue ignored. This makes for boring and irritating reading."
>
> —*Jane Isay*

Part 2:
Grammar, Usage, and Editing

§ 11
Grammar

11.1 Grammar is the system of using words to build sentences. These sentence-builders are classified into parts of speech. A single word may act as a different part of speech in different sentences, depending on its role in the sentence. The word *name*, for example, may function as a noun <my name is Jordan>, a verb <name this tune>, or an adjective <name brand>. *More* may function as an adjective <get more exercise> or an adverb <study more diligently>. *Out* may be a noun <three outs retire the side>, a preposition <go out the side exit>, an adverb <it's nice out>, or an adjective <out-box>. In modern usage, *out* may also be a verb <you had no right to out him>.

The rules of grammar are entirely functional in their operation: the word's function in the sentence is what matters, not what part of speech the word is usually classified as. By understanding how the various parts of speech work together to convey an idea, writers develop the skills needed to express new ideas in new ways—and still be confident that the message will be communicated to the reader.

Unfortunately, grammar also bears a legacy of bad writing advice. The pedantic "rule" to never split an infinitive, for example, is a superstition that just won't die. So too that a preposition is a taboo part of speech to end a sentence with. And forget the idea that a conjunction should never start a sentence. Any writer can benefit from unlearning such baseless nonsense.

For a much more detailed statement of English grammar than can be given in the compass of this modest chapter, see Bryan A. Garner, *The Chicago Guide to Grammar, Usage, and Punctuation* (2016).

Nouns

11.2 A noun is a name. It may be generic (a *common noun*) <street> or specific (a *proper noun*) <Wall Street>. It may name a person <lawyer> <Clarence Darrow>, a place <courtroom> <Albany>, or a thing, either tangible (a *concrete noun*) <reporter> <Federal Reporter 3d> or intangible (an *abstract noun*) <public good> <Good Samaritan doctrine>.

A noun may serve as a subject or its complement, as an object or its complement, or as a possessive. But in English, only the possessive has a change in spelling.

A noun also has properties of number (singular or plural), gender (masculine, feminine, or neuter), and person (first, second, or third). Its spelling usually changes for number, rarely changes for gender, and never changes for person.

A participle, a phrase, or an entire clause may function as a noun in a sentence <seeing is believing> <the Old Man of the Mountain was in New Hampshire> <that we must act quickly should surprise no one>. For that matter, any word or even a letter or number is a noun when used as a word <the word *please* contains two *e*'s>.

A word that is ordinarily a noun may function as some other part of speech. For example, it may function as an adjective in a noun phrase <the litigation team>, and in the possessive case a noun is always adjectival in function <the judge's robe>. Or, especially in loose usage, it may function as a verb <to office downtown>. Some nouns used as verbs may become standard over time <to premiere on Broadway>, but unless they are well accepted you should avoid them in formal writing.

11.3 Related nouns should agree in number.

(a) *Concrete nouns.* Concrete nouns that relate to each other in the sentence must agree in number.

Ex.: Both lawyers played the negotiations close to their vests. (Not *vest.*)
Ex.: Each lawyer played the negotiations close to the vest. (Not *the vests.*)

(b) *Abstract nouns.* Use a singular abstract noun with a plural concrete noun if the use is idiomatic.

Ex.: Three witnesses promised to testify, and they all kept their word.

But: Family members gathered while the rescue went on; quietly they shared their fears.

11.4 With joint possession, only the final noun in the series is possessive; with separate possession, each noun in a series is possessive.

(a) *Joint possession.* When only the final noun in the series is possessive, the indication is that the thing is owned collectively by each of those named in the series.

Ex.: The study group will meet at Jim and Monika's house tonight to review for the final. (Jim and Monika share possession of the house.)

(b) *Individual possession.* When each noun in the series is possessive, the indication is that each owns a separate thing.

Ex.: The group looked at Jim's and Monika's class notes before discussing the model-exam question. (Jim and Monika have separate class notes.)

11.5 The possessive case often indicates a sense of measuring time or value.

(a) *As measurement.* When a possessive describes a noun in terms of measurement, the possessive is shorthand for an *of*-phrase.

Ex.: The tenant gave the landlord 30 days' notice. (The sense is *notice of 30 days.*)

Ex.: Carlton charged that there wasn't a dime's worth of difference between the two major parties. (The sense is *the worth of a dime.*)

(b) *Old-fashioned.* The possessive construction can sound archaic. Rewording the phrase usually involves a straightforward edit.

Ex.: Each party was required to give a 30-day notice.

11.6 Use the double-possessive construction (*of ——'s*) with a noun to shift perspective to the object: the focus is on the object's relationship to the subject of the preposition, not the other way around.

(a) *Redundancy.* The double-possessive construction (also known as the *double genitive*) is logically redundant: *of* is possessive and *-'s* is possessive. But it's deeply rooted in English idiom, and it's mandatory with personal pronouns—we might write about *a friend of Keisha* but never *a friend of her* (always *a friend of hers*) (see 11.18(a)).

Ex.: Jacob was a friend of Mike's. (The focus is on Mike's attitude toward Jacob, not the other way around.)

Ex.: This line of questioning of Mr. Clark's has nothing to do with any issue before this court.

(b) *To avoid ambiguity.* The construction can sometimes be useful to prevent ambiguity. But there is often a superior alternative to the double possessive.

Ex.: This is a painting of Helen's.
(Did she paint it, or does it belong to her?)
Distinguish: This is a painting of Helen.
(It's a portrait of her.)
Better: This is Helen's painting.
(She might have painted it, or it might belong to her.)
Or: This painting belongs to Helen.
(The ownership is now unmistakable.)

(c) *Reword.* Even when no ambiguity is possible, a simple edit may result in a more natural-sounding sentence.

Correct: A friend of Amy's stopped by.
Better: One of Amy's friends stopped by.

11.7 An appositive must agree with and directly follow the noun or noun phrase that it identifies or supplements; if it's nonrestrictive, set it off with commas, parentheses, or em-dashes.

(a) *Defined.* An appositive is a noun or noun phrase that further identifies or further describes another noun or noun phrase (its referent). A restrictive appositive is essential to the sentence and would leave its referent's identity unclear if removed. It should never be set off from the rest of the sentence by commas, em-dashes, or parentheses. A nonrestrictive appositive, by contrast, merely provides additional information about its referent without exclusively identifying it. It should be set off from the rest of the sentence.

> Ex.: Susan B. Anthony's father belonged to the Society of Friends, a religious group that recognized the equality of men and women. (The phrase *a religious group that recognized the equality of men and women* is the appositive of *Society of Friends*. It is nonrestrictive, so it is set off from the rest of the sentence, here by commas.)

> Ex.: The philosopher Jeremy Bentham is considered the founder of Utilitarianism. (*Jeremy Bentham* is the appositive of *philosopher*. It is restrictive, identifying precisely *which* philosopher, so it is not set off.)

> Ex.: Unless they represent the government, amici curiae must obtain the court's leave (permission) to file a brief. (*Permission* is the appositive of *leave*. It is nonrestrictive, so it is set off, here by parentheses.)

(b) *Agreement.* An appositive must agree in number, gender, case, and person with its referent.

> Not this: John C. Calhoun's career, Vice President under both John Quincy Adams and Adams's archrival Andrew Jackson, was unique in American history. (The possessive *Calhoun's* cannot properly serve as the referent to the nominative appositive *Vice President*.)

> But this: John C. Calhoun, Vice President under both John Quincy Adams and Adams's archrival Andrew Jackson, had a career unique in American history. (Both referent *Calhoun* and appositive *Vice President* are in the nominative case.)

> Ex.: Truman bypassed two sitting justices, Robert Jackson and Hugo Black, and nominated as chief justice his treasury secretary, Frederick Moore Vinson. (*Justices* and *Jackson and Black* agree in number, as do *secretary* and *Vinson*.)

(c) *If nonrestrictive.* If an appositive is nonrestrictive, set it off by commas (usually), parentheses (to decrease emphasis), or em-dashes (to increase emphasis).

> Ex.: John McCain, an Arizona senator, found unlikely allies among liberal Democrats.

> Ex.: John McCain (R-Ariz.) found unlikely allies among liberal Democrats.

> Ex.: John McCain—a conservative Republican senator—found unlikely allies among liberal Democrats.

> But: The conservative Republican senator John McCain found unlikely allies among liberal Democrats. (No commas or other set-off punctuation because *John McCain* is necessary to the meaning of the sentence: it restricts the universe of *conservative Republican senators* that the sentence may refer to.)

(d) *With possessive referent.* Appositive agreement becomes particularly problematic when the referent is in the possessive case. When the appositive is restrictive, the solution is simple: just add the characters *'s* (or *'* where appropriate) after the appositive, making the entire noun phrase possessive <my friend Davis's car>. When the appositive is nonrestrictive, however, the issue becomes more complicated—and is best avoided altogether.

Because the punctuation that separates the appositive from its referent breaks up the noun phrase, making the appositive possessive upsets its case agreement with its referent. (See 1.6.) And because making both possessive would sound awkward, it is permissible to omit the punctuation enclosing the appositive and treat it as if it were restrictive. When the punctuation is necessary for other reasons—for instance, the parentheses around a defined term in a legal document—or when the appositive itself is a noun phrase, the best course is to recast the sentence, perhaps using an *of*-genitive so that both the appositive and the referent remain in the same case.

Not this: my mother, Barbara's, birthday
Not this: my mother's, Barbara's, birthday
But this: my mother Barbara's birthday
Not this: We promised to have dinner at our in-laws', Chris and Diane.
Not this: We promised to have dinner at our in-laws, Chris and Diane's.
But this: We promised to have dinner at the home of our in-laws, Chris and Diane.

11.8 Master irregular plurals such as *attorneys general*, *dicta*, and *memoranda*.

(a) *Irregular forms.* Most English nouns form their plurals by adding *-s* or *-es*. But many words have irregular plural forms. Some change a vowel; some change a consonant; some add an *-en* or *-ren* (see 7.7(c)–(f)).

Ex.: foot–feet
Ex.: mouse–mice
Ex.: man–men
Ex.: woman–women
Ex.: life–lives
Ex.: child–children

(b) *Romance syntax.* Especially in law, many phrases that entered the language from Law French retain the noun–adjective syntax of Romance languages. The noun part of these phrases takes the plural form (see 7.8, 7.9(b)). The second word in such a phrase is called a *postpositive adjective*—that is, unlike most adjectives in English it is placed after the noun it modifies.

Ex.: attorney general–attorneys general
Ex.: court-martial–courts-martial
Ex.: notary public–notaries public

These terms have no acceptable plural possessive. Because you cannot really say **all the notaries public's records*, you must rephrase with an *of*-genitive: *the records of all the notaries public.* See 7.11(g), 7.14(b).

(c) *Foreign terms.* Many foreign words retain their original plural forms; others have been anglicized so that they take the English *-s* or *-es*; still others take both forms, sometimes for different meanings of the word (see 7.8).

Ex.: alumnus–alumni
Ex.: alumna–alumnae
Ex.: antenna–antennae (on insects)–antennas (on radios)
Ex.: dictum–dicta
Ex.: medium–media (journalistic outlets)–mediums (clairvoyants)

(d) *Same form.* Some words keep the same appearance for the singular and plural; this is especially true of game animals.

Ex.: deer–deer
Ex.: fish–fish
Ex.: caribou–caribou

(e) *Confused singulars.* Some words look plural in form but are actually singular; many of them are often mistakenly used with plural verbs. For example, *kudos* /**koo**-dahs/ and *bona fides* /**boh**-nə **fɪ**-deez/ are both singular nouns, not plural.

Pronouns

11.9 A pronoun is a word that stands in for a noun (or, sometimes, another pronoun). That noun is usually an antecedent—that is, a word that appears before the pronoun and that the pronoun refers to. A few pronouns—such as *you*, *I*, *everyone*, and *nobody*—don't require antecedents because the reference is obvious. Interrogative pronouns don't require antecedents because the reference is unknown—that's the purpose of the inquiry. Because indefinite pronouns are undefined, most do not take antecedents.

Pronouns are classified by their function as:

- personal (*I*, *me*, *you*, *he*, *him*, *she*, *her*, *it*, *we*, *us*, *they*, *them*);
- possessive (*my*, *mine*, *your*, *yours*, *his*, *her*, *hers*, *its*, *our*, *ours*, *their*, *theirs*);
- reflexive-intensive (*myself*, *yourself*, *himself*, *herself*, *itself*, *ourselves*, *yourselves*, *themselves*);
- demonstrative (*this*, *that*, *these*, *those*);
- interrogative (*who*, *whom*, *whose*, *which*, *what*);

*An invariably inferior form.

- relative (*who, whom, whose, what, when, where, why, which, that*, and many combined forms with the suffixes *-ever* and *-soever*);
- indefinite (*all, another, any, both, each, either, every, few, many, more, most, much, neither, nobody, none, no one, nothing, one, ones, oneself, other, others, several, some, such*, and compound forms with the suffixes *-one, -body*, and *-thing*);
- reciprocal (*each other, one another*); or
- adjective (other than nonpossessive personal pronouns [*I, me, you, he, him, she, her, it, we, us, they, them*], any pronoun may function as an adjective).

A pronoun has the same number, person, and gender as its antecedent, but its case is determined by its use in the sentence. In general, these properties matter more with pronouns than with nouns because pronouns can vary considerably in form according to those properties <they–them–their–theirs>.

Particular problems arise with agreement in number, person, and gender between the pronoun and its antecedent, and with confusion about where to use the nominative or objective case.

11.10 The grammatical antecedent of a pronoun is the noun that (1) precedes the pronoun most closely; and (2) agrees in number, gender, and person with that pronoun.

Number

(a) *Generally.* Use a pronoun that agrees in number with its antecedent.

> Not this: The *company* found that *they* could not meet the demand.
>
> But this: The *company* found that *it* could not meet the demand.

(b) *From antecedent.* A pronoun is singular or plural according to the number of the noun or pronoun it refers to.

> Ex.: The *parties* entered the mediation session reluctantly, but by early afternoon *they* appeared to be more cooperative.
>
> Ex.: The parties entered the mediation session reluctantly, but by early afternoon *each side* decided that *it* should cooperate.

(c) *Conjunctive compound antecedent.* A pronoun that refers to two or more antecedents joined by *and* is generally plural. But when two or more singular antecedents joined by *and* refer to the same thing—or are modified by *each, every*, or *no*—the pronoun is singular.

> Ex.: *The district attorney and the defense counsel* announced that *they* were ready for trial.
>
> Ex.: *The 12 jurors and the bailiff* developed a bond during *their* time together.

But: *The lawyer and human-rights activist* moved the audience with *her* impassioned speech.

And: *Every firm and bar association* is required to have *its* attorneys take continuing-education courses on ethical issues.

(d) *Disjunctive compound antecedent.* A pronoun that refers to two or more singular antecedents joined by *or* or *nor* is singular.

Ex.: Neither *the prosecution nor the defense* had *its* case ready for trial.

Ex.: Tell *Walter or Bill* to file the petition when *he* goes to the courthouse this afternoon.

(e) *Disjunctive with mixed antecedents.* If antecedents of mixed number are joined by *or* or *nor*, the pronoun should agree with the closest antecedent <neither you nor I am to blame>. That is the rule. Because it is jarring to encounter a singular pronoun with a potentially plural antecedent, it is much better to put the plural antecedent last, if possible (see 11.26(d)).

Ex.: If you find *my keys or my pen*, bring *it* to me.

Better: If you find *my pen or my keys*, bring *them* to me.

Ex.: Either *the trial judge or the three appellate judges* will decide this issue, so we will leave it up to *them*.

(f) *Two or more adjectives.* If a singular antecedent is modified by two or more adjectives denoting different varieties, the pronoun will be plural to reflect the plural sense of the multiple adjectives combining with the singular noun.

Ex.: The civil procedures of Scottish, French, Quebecois, and Louisiana law reflect their Roman roots.

Ex.: Criminal and tort law differ significantly in their definitions of *assault*.

(g) *Singular indefinite pronoun.* As an antecedent, a clearly singular indefinite pronoun (*another*, *each*, *either*, *every*, *much*, *neither*, *nobody*, *no one*, *nothing*, *one*, *other*, and combination forms) takes a singular pronoun.

Ex.: *Something* about our witness seemed to bother the jurors. I'm not sure what *it* was.

Ex.: *Everyone* is free to take *his or her* business elsewhere.

In recent years, a shift has occurred with *anybody*, *anyone*, *everybody*, *everyone*, *nobody*, and *no one*: in informal usage especially, these have come to be matched with *they*, *them*, *their*, and *themselves*. The reason is partly to avoid the choice between the generic masculine pronoun (seen as sexist) and the awkward use of *he or she*, etc. (seen as hopelessly clumsy). The constructions with *they*, *them*, *their*, and *themselves* aren't uncontroversial, though, so please understand that any visible choice you make is likely to bother some number of readers. Anything apart from invisible gender-neutrality will be seen by some as a political statement. For strategies to achieve gender-neutrality, see 13.5(o). For *they* in a singular sense, see also 11.10(o).

(h) *Plural indefinite pronoun.* As an antecedent, a clearly plural indefinite pronoun (*both*, *few*, *many*, *others*, *several*) takes a plural pronoun.

Ex.: Counsel clients thoroughly; *most* don't understand *their* rights, and *few* know all *their* options.

Ex.: In the jury room, *several* still held out. *They* didn't believe that the plaintiff was being honest.

(i) *Other indefinite pronouns.* Some indefinite pronouns may be singular or plural (*all*, *any*, *more*, *most*, *none*). Such a pronoun, as an antecedent, takes either a singular or a plural verb, depending on its context in the sentence. *None* is notable: as a historical melding of *not one* or *no one*, it would appear to be singular in form; but it's most often today construed as a plural. Both uses are correct (and have been for centuries), the rare singular being more emphatic.

Ex.: *Some* of the money *is* mine. I want *it.*

Ex.: *Most* of the coins *are* mine. I want *them.*

Ex.: *More* than one attorney *is* attending the deposition.

Ex.: *More* than five attorneys *are* billing for their services.

Ex.: *None* of the circuits *are* eager to extend the doctrine. (Normal usage.)

Or: *None* of the circuits *is* eager to extend the doctrine. (Emphatic usage.)

(j) *Collective nouns.* A collective noun poses a special problem: if the action or state expressed by the predicate is collective, with the members acting as a unit, the pronoun is singular; but if it is individual, with each member acting separately, the pronoun is plural. In British usage, a collective noun usually takes a plural pronoun regardless.

Ex.: The *crowd* rose to *their* feet as the ball-carrier broke into the clear.

Ex.: The *team* gave *its* all in the come-from-behind win.

(k) *Relative pronouns.* A relative pronoun takes on the number, person, and gender of its antecedent and passes them on to any pronouns that in turn refer to the relative pronoun.

Ex.: It is I who am responsible for my fate. (*Who* becomes first-person singular and takes the *be*-verb *am* and the personal pronoun *my.*)

Ex.: It is she who is responsible for her fate. (*Who* becomes third-person singular feminine and takes the *be*-verb *is* and the personal pronoun *her.*)

Ex.: It is they who are responsible for their fate. (*Who* becomes third-person plural and takes the *be*-verb *are* and the personal pronoun *their.*)

Gender

(l) *Generally.* A pronoun must agree in gender with its antecedent.

(m) *Third-person singular.* A personal pronoun in the third person may be masculine (*he*, *him*, *his*), feminine (*she*, *her*, *hers*), or neuter (*it*, *its*) in gender.

Ex.: President Taft never forgot *Learned Hand*'s "disloyalty," and many believe that this act cost *Hand his* first chance to serve on the Supreme Court.

Ex.: By this time, *she* was known as *Red Emma*, and *she* was followed by detectives wherever *she* went.

Ex.: The *Tractatus* played a crucial role in making the common law more uniform. In 14 books *it* covered each of the 80 distinct writs used in the king's courts.

(n) *Gender-neutral masculine.* It is no longer customary to use a masculine form as a gender-neutral inclusive (that is, with the understanding that the feminine is included as well). See 13.5(o)–(p) for tips on how to avoid constructions that readers may consider sexist.

Ex.: A respondent has 20 days to file an answer. (Preferably not *his answer.*)

(o) *Singular "they."* Traditionally, a singular antecedent has required a singular pronoun. But because *he* is no longer universally accepted as a generic pronoun referring to a person of unspecified gender, people commonly (in speech and in informal writing) substitute the third-person-plural pronouns *they*, *them*, *their*, and *themselves* (or the nonstandard singular **themself*). While this usage is increasingly accepted in speech and informal writing, it has only recently gained ground in more formal writing—including a few U.S. Supreme Court opinions. Yet despite the official approval in some style manuals of the singular *they*, a 2018 poll found that half of American readers consider it objectionable. So be forewarned.

Some writers try to avoid the plural form by (1) using the formal *he or she*, *him or her*, *his or her*, or *himself or herself*, or (2) employing an artificial form such as **s/he*, or (3) alternating masculine and feminine pronouns for generic references to a single person. Often these techniques can be ungainly and distracting—and they end up emphasizing the inherent problem of not having a generic third-person pronoun. Of those three, the first is most palatable if used sparingly.

In limited cases—when referring specifically to a hypothetical person of unspecified gender or (especially) to a real person who does not identify with a gender-specific pronoun—*they* and its forms are preferred by some writers. When possible, a person's stated preference for a specific pronoun should be respected. Still, if you can reword your sentence to avoid the issue altogether—that is, if you can achieve invisible gender-neutrality—that's the preferable course.

Ex.: The longer a leader is in office, the less likely they are to receive accurate information about policy-related crises. (Though some writers fearlessly use this generic singular *they*, it continues for the time being to be objectionable in the eyes of a traditionalist.)

Ex.: If a severely abused child is not removed from their home, they have an increased risk of suffering life-threatening injuries or death.

Better: If a severely abused child is not removed from the home, the child has an increased risk of suffering life-threatening injuries or death.

Better still: If a severely abused child is not removed from the home, the child's risk of suffering life-threatening injuries or death increases.

*An invariably inferior form.

Ex.: Donatto, the plaintiff's younger sibling, testified that they had often been the only person to visit Roy, who had always been polite to them. (Donatto does not identify as either male or female.)

For various strategies to achieve gender-neutrality short of resorting to the singular *they*—mostly in contexts not involving someone who is neither male nor female—see 13.5(o).

(p) *Neuter by default.* Where gender is indefinite or irrelevant, use neuter pronouns.

Ex.: The court has made its *decision*.

Ex.: It was as though *time itself* stood still.

But: It was as though *Justice herself* wept.

Person

(q) *Generally.* A pronoun must agree in person with its antecedent.

Not this: Every lawyer needs a good moral compass, or else you may well wind up facing disciplinary proceedings. (Shift from third-person antecedent to second-person pronoun.)

But this: As a lawyer, you need a good moral compass, or else you may well wind up facing disciplinary proceedings.

Or this: Lawyers need good moral compasses, or else they may well wind up facing disciplinary proceedings.

(r) *Distinguished.* A first-person pronoun refers to the speaker (*I*, *me*, *we*, *us*, *my*, *mine*, *our*, *ours*, *myself*, *ourselves*); a second-person pronoun refers to the person being spoken to (*you*, *your*, *yours*, *yourself*, *yourselves*); a third-person pronoun refers to someone or something else (*he*, *him*, *she*, *her*, *it*, *they*, *them*, *his*, *her*, *hers*, *its*, *their*, *theirs*, *himself*, *herself*, *itself*, *themselves*).

Ex.: *Tom Clark* had been a Texas Democrat all *his* life and a politician–prosecutor for most of *it*, *his* six years on the Court not excluded.

Ex.: *I* can't find *my* glasses.

Ex.: *Mr. Watson*, come here. I want *you*.

11.11 Make your pronoun references unambiguous.

(a) *Multiple antecedents.* If another noun of the same number, person, and gender comes between the intended antecedent and the pronoun, the sentence may be ambiguous; it will probably be awkward even if there is no reasonable misunderstanding.

Ex.: The plaintiff's attorney handed the affidavit to the clerk; she then asked the judge to enter it into evidence. (*She* might be either the *clerk*—the closer noun and the grammatical antecedent—or the *attorney*.)

Better: After handing the affidavit to the clerk, the plaintiff's attorney asked the judge to enter it into evidence. (The pronoun *it* is unambiguous since it could not refer to any of the three people that precede it in the sentence.)

(b) *Repeated pronoun.* Don't use the same pronoun to refer to more than one antecedent in close proximity, especially in the same sentence.

Not this: Ayoka had left her purse at the office, so Robin lent her $10 of her own money.

But this: Ayoka had left her purse at the office, so Robin lent her $10.

(c) *Explicit antecedent.* Be sure the pronoun's antecedent is actually used in the same sentence or the previous sentence. Some pronouns, however, rarely or never require antecedents: the first- and second-person pronouns, standing for the speaker and the addressee, respectively, almost never need antecedents since their referent is always clear. Pronouns used as expletives, such as *it* <it's cold outside> and *this* <this is no way to treat a client>, don't have antecedents. Similarly, *what* never takes one—nor do the interrogative pronouns (except *which*, which properly refers to one or more members of a specific group). The bottom line is that you should never require the reader to make a mental leap by implying what the antecedent should be.

Not this: Having grown up in a law-oriented family, Karen wanted to become one herself. (Karen does not want to become a *law-oriented family*; the reader is left to infer the meaning of *one* because it has no explicit antecedent.)

But this: Her grandfather, father, and brothers were all lawyers. Karen wanted to become one herself. (*Lawyer* is the explicit antecedent of *one*.)

(d) *Noun antecedent.* Possessive nouns function as adjectives. In formal writing, an adjective cannot serve as an antecedent; also, the noun it is modifying may be the grammatical antecedent in the sentence. Yet the possessive antecedent occurs frequently in colloquial speech, particularly when the noun it modifies would take a different pronoun. Some authorities even condone its use. But because the usage is grammatically illogical and can invite ambiguity, avoid it in legal writing.

Not this: The car's exhaust system needs work, but otherwise it runs fine. (The grammatical antecedent of *it* is *system*, not *car*.)

But this: The car's exhaust system needs work, but otherwise the car runs fine.

Not this: We took John's car because he was going to drive anyway. (Because *John's* is adjectival in the sentence, it can't grammatically serve as a noun antecedent for *he*.)

But this: John was going to drive anyway, so we took his car.

(e) *Antecedent first.* In formal writing, avoid using a pronoun before its antecedent in a sentence. Otherwise, it may be unclear what the pronoun refers to.

Not this: Because they were afraid of the expense and the uncertain outcome, the plaintiffs agreed to the settlement offer.

But this: Because the plaintiffs were afraid of the expense and the uncertain outcome, they agreed to the settlement offer.

Or this: The plaintiffs agreed to the settlement offer because they were afraid of the expense and the uncertain outcome.

11.12 Use the nominative case for a subject or a predicate nominative.

(a) *Generally.* The nominative-case pronouns are *I*, *we*, *you*, *he*, *she*, *it*, *they*, *who*, and *whoever.*

Ex.: They will make the first offer. (Subject.)

Ex.: Who am I? (*Who* and *I* are in the nominative case.)

Ex.: You! Get over here! (Direct address.)

(b) *As predicate nominative.* A predicate nominative is a noun or pronoun that follows a linking verb and refers to the subject. When a personal pronoun is used as a predicate nominative, the choice between the nominative and objective case can be tricky: the nominative case, while correct, sounds stilted. It is usually better to rephrase the sentence.

Ex.: This is she. (Predicate nominative.)

Better: Speaking.

(c) *As subject of dependent clause.* When a pronoun serves as the subject of a dependent clause that in turn serves as an object in the sentence, the choice of case can be especially difficult. Grammatically, the subject of the clause is always nominative, even though the clause itself, as a syntactic element in the sentence, may function as an object.

Ex.: Give it to whoever asks first. (*Whoever* is the subject of the clause *whoever asks first*, which in turn is the object of *to*.)

Ex.: Give it to whomever you choose. (*Whomever* is the object in the clause *you choose whomever*, which in turn is the object of *to*.)

Ex.: Give it to whoever you think earns it. (*Whoever* is the subject of the clause *whoever earns it*, which in turn is the object of *to*. The parenthetical idea in *you think* plays no grammatical role in the clause.)

11.13 Use the objective case for (1) the direct or indirect object of a verb, or (2) the object of a preposition.

(a) *Generally.* The objective-case pronouns are *me*, *us*, *you*, *him*, *her*, *it*, *them*, *whom*, and *whomever.*

Ex.: How will this ruling affect us? (Direct object.)

Ex.: Give me an example. (Indirect object.)

Ex.: To whom is the letter addressed? (Object of a preposition.)

Ex.: Let this be a lesson to you and me. (Not *you and I*.) (Compound object of a preposition.)

(b) *Determined by function.* When a pronoun appears in a clause, the pronoun's function in the clause—not the clause's function in the sentence—determines its case (see 11.12(c)).

Ex.: The contract will go to whoever submits the lowest bid. (Not *whomever*: *whoever* is the subject of the clause, so it is nominative even though the dependent clause itself is the object of the preposition *to*.)

11.14 Use the correct case and order when using a first-person pronoun with a noun or another personal pronoun in a compound phrase.

(a) *First person last.* By custom, the first-person pronoun comes last in such a phrase, whether it's nominative or objective.

Ex.: Ralph and I will take the deposition. (Not *I and Ralph*.)

Ex.: Just between you and me, I think they're ready to settle. (Not *between me and you*.)

(b) *Getting the pronoun case right.* In a compound phrase in which the last element is a pronoun whose case differs in nominative vs. objective uses, try the pronoun without its accompanying nouns.

Ex.: Please do stop by to confer with (John and) me.

Ex.: (Mary and) I would like to discuss your counteroffer.

Ex.: It's a letter addressed to (you and) me.

Ex.: Is that something that (he and) I should write about?

(c) *Hypercorrection in first person.* It's a common error to "overcorrect" and use the nominative case where the objective case is required in a compound construction with the first-person personal pronoun. One way to check is to speak the sentence using only the questionable pronoun.

Ex.: Just between you and me, I think they're ready to settle. (Not *between you and I*.)

Ex.: It's time for her and Abbie to get over their differences. (Not *for she and Abbie*.)

11.15 In formal writing, use the nominative case after *than* or *as . . . as* if the pronoun would be nominative in the understood clause that follows.

(a) *As a conjunction.* In formal writing, restrict *than* to its traditional use as a conjunction. The pronoun takes its case from its function in the resulting clause, even if most of the clause is understood rather than expressed. If the pronoun is the subject or the predicate nominative of the clause, it should be in the nominative case.

Ex.: You know that better than I. (The understood clause is *than I do*.)

Ex.: You know that as well as I. (The understood clause is *as I do*.)

Ex.: I regard her more highly than he. (The understood clause is *than he does*.)

Ex.: I regard her more highly than him. (The understood clause is *than I regard him*.)

(b) *As a preposition.* In speech and in informal writing, the idiomatic use of *than* as a preposition with a pronoun in the objective case is accepted.

> Ex.: You know better than me how patent law works.
>
> Ex.: I deserve to win this case more than her.

11.16 In formal writing, a pronoun used as a predicate nominative—renaming the subject after a linking verb—is in the nominative case.

(a) *Formal usage.* In formal writing, the rules of grammar are followed more strictly. If the wording sounds pompous, it's usually better to recast the sentence.

> Ex.: It was I who testified in your behalf. (Better: *I was the one who testified in your behalf.*)
>
> Ex.: The witness spoke with Mrs. Harrison almost every day; he knew right away that the caller was she. (Better: . . . *he knew right away that she was the caller.*)

(b) *Informal usage.* In speech and in informal writing, the use of the objective case is often idiomatic and unobjectionable.

> Ex.: This is me.
>
> Ex.: Is that her?

11.17 The possessive case of a pronoun shows not only ownership but also (frequently) attribution, measure, or some similar relationship.

(a) *Generally.* The possessive pronouns are *my*, *mine*, *your*, *yours*, *his*, *her*, *hers*, *its*, *our*, *ours*, *their*, and *theirs*.

> Ex.: Can a third party get its voters to the polls?
>
> Ex.: You have to get your facts right.

(b) *No apostrophe.* None of the possessive pronouns uses an apostrophe; confounding the possessive *its* with the contraction *it's* (meaning *it is*) is the most common spelling error in the language. Similarly, the possessive of *who* is *whose*, not *who's* (a contraction of *who is* or *who has*).

> Ex.: It's important that achievement receive its reward.
>
> Ex.: Who's the one whose cellphone rang?

(c) *Absolute possessives.* There are two ways to show possession with possessive pronouns: the simple possessive <that is *your* car> and the absolute (or *independent*) possessive <that car is *yours*>. The form is the same for some pronouns <his–his> <its–its> but different for others <my–mine> <our–ours> <your–yours> <her–hers> <their–theirs>. Unlike the simple form, the absolute possessive doesn't need an explicit object: the thing possessed may be merely understood. In this case, the absolute possessive may also function as a noun—as the subject or object of a verb or the object of a preposition. Used with *of*, the absolute forms a double possessive (see 11.18).

Ex.: That is *his* wallet. / That wallet is *his*. (Same form.)
Ex.: That is *her* briefcase. / That briefcase is *hers*. (Different forms.)

(d) *With a gerund.* Use the possessive case for a pronoun or noun that is paired with a gerund (i.e., an *-ing* verb functioning as a noun), but the objective case if it is paired with a present participle.

Ex.: There's no use in your testifying. (It is the *testifying* that is useless, not *you*.)
Ex.: Our schedule shows him flying to the convention on the 15th. (The entire clause *him flying to the convention on the 15th* is what the schedule shows.)

11.18 The double-possessive construction (*of* + absolute possessive) is fully acceptable with personal pronouns—as in *a friend of mine*.

(a) *Mandatory with pronouns.* In most possessive *of*-constructions, the use of a noun in the objective case is defensible (see 11.6) and even preferred by some authorities. Not so with personal pronouns: the use of the objective case is always a glaring error. When showing possession with *of* + a personal pronoun, always use the pronoun's absolute-possessive form.

Ex.: He was a friend of mine. (Obviously not *a friend of me*.)
Ex.: Math was never a strong point of yours.

(b) *To intensify.* This construction can have an intensifying connotation, frequently negative, when the prepositional phrase follows a demonstrative pronoun (*this*, *that*, *these*, *those*) and a class noun.

Ex.: That boy of hers is always getting into trouble.
Ex.: This interrogatory of yours is just a burdensome fishing expedition.
Ex.: Who could ever forget that moving speech of his?

> "When a relative pronoun is required, the rule is that defining clauses are introduced by *that*, and others, nondefining or informative ones, by *which*. If this sounds horrible, just keep repeating *This is the house that Jack built.*" —*Kingsley Amis*

11.19 The relative pronoun *who* refers to people only (although *whose* may refer to things as well); *which* to things or animals only; and *that* to either people or things (or both).

(a) *"That" with people.* While *who* is often the better choice when referring to people, *that* is perfectly proper as well, especially when referring to groups of people taken collectively. It is mandatory to use *that* when referring to people and things combined.

Ex.: The senators who had voted against the bill celebrated their victory.

Ex.: It was the Senate that killed the bill.

Ex.: It was the farm-state Republicans who killed the bill.

Ex.: It was a handful of lobbyists and their bankrolls that turned public opinion against the bill.

(b) *"Which" with things.* Don't use *which* to refer to people; if the clause is nonrestrictive, use *who.*

Ex.: The class of plaintiffs is composed of former customers of the bankrupt company, many of whom lost their entire savings. (Reference to people, so *of whom* rather than *of which.*)

Ex.: A bloc of East Coast senators who had supported the bill tried to bring it up for another vote. (Reference to people—*senators.*)

Ex.: A bloc of East Coast senators, which had supported the bill, tried to bring it up for another vote. (Reference to a thing—*bloc.*)

Ex.: The Capitol dome, which was built in 1882, will be restored next year. (Reference to a thing.)

(c) *"Whose" with things.* It is permissible to use *whose* to mean *of which.*

Ex.: The Capitol dome, whose completion was celebrated in 1882, was recently restored.

11.20 For relative pronouns referring to anything other than people, use *that* to introduce a restrictive clause and *which* (after a comma) to introduce a nonrestrictive clause.

(a) *Restrictive clause.* A restrictive (or defining) clause is one that is essential to the meaning of the sentence. In the preceding sentence, for example, the clause *that is essential to the meaning of the sentence* is essential to the meaning of the sentence, so it is a restrictive clause. It identifies the type of *one* (clause) that this sentence is about from the universe of all clauses. Use *that* or *who* to introduce a restrictive clause, and don't set off the clause from the rest of the sentence by commas, em-dashes, or parentheses.

Ex.: A union that did not allege any injury from the disqualification of its officer immediately upon conviction lacked standing to challenge the statute imposing the disqualification. (The clause *that did not … conviction* restricts the universe of *unions* that the sentence is about.)

Ex.: A defendant who claims mootness because it has stopped the challenged acts bears a heavy burden to show that the wrongful behavior will not recur. (The clause *who claims . . . acts* restricts the universe of *defendants* that the sentence is about.)

(b) *Nonrestrictive clause.* A nonrestrictive clause, which is also called a nondefining clause, can be removed without changing the essential meaning of the sentence. For example, in the preceding sentence, *which is also called a nondefining clause* is a nonrestrictive clause because the essence of the sentence is unchanged if the clause is removed. It doesn't restrict the number of *nonrestrictive clauses* that the sentence is about from the universe of all nonrestrictive clauses. Use *which* or *who* to introduce a nonrestrictive clause. Set off the clause from the rest of the sentence—usually by commas, but by parentheses to minimize the matter or by em-dashes to make it stand out.

Ex.: The plaintiff asked to substitute the state officer as a defendant in place of the state, which had been dismissed on Eleventh Amendment grounds. (The clause *which had been dismissed . . . grounds* does not restrict the universe of *states* that the sentence is about.)

Ex.: Lawyers—who are officers of the court—should never overlook jurisdictional questions that courts expect the parties to raise first. (The clause *who are officers of the court* does not restrict the universe of *lawyers* that the sentence is about.)

(c) *"That" as restrictive.* By rule, *that* is used to introduce a restrictive clause only; it is always an error to use *that* to introduce a nonrestrictive clause.

Ex.: Courts may attempt to control prejudicial publicity by restricting the information that (not *which*) trial participants can give to the press both before and during a trial. (Restrictive clause.)

Ex.: In *Nebraska Press Ass'n v. Stewart*, the Court held that pretrial gag orders on the press, which (never *that*) amount to prior restraints, are unconstitutional. (Nonrestrictive clause.)

(d) *"Which" as nonrestrictive.* By convention in American English, *which* is reserved for introducing a nonrestrictive clause. It's not an outright blunder to use *which* to introduce a restrictive clause. It's even necessary in the phrase *that which* and after a preposition, as in *by which* or *in which* <the field in which Radin specialized>. But when *that* is possible in place of a comma-less *which*, use it.

Ex.: The fighting-words doctrine, which (never *that*) is often relied on by governments to justify regulations, has not been a dispositive ground of decision in many Supreme Court cases. (Nonrestrictive clause.)

Ex.: Fighting words are words which (prefer *that*) by their very utterance inflict injury or tend to incite an immediate breach of the peace. (Restrictive clause.)

(e) *No commas with restrictive clauses.* Never use commas, em-dashes, or parentheses to set off a restrictive clause.

Ex.: Erroneous statements are inevitable in free debate and must be protected if free expression is to have the breathing space that it needs to survive. (Never a comma after *space.*)

11.21 Reflexive and reciprocal pronouns require care.

(a) *Reflexive for objective.* Don't use *myself* as a stuffy substitute for the simple *I* or *me.*

Not this: John and myself want you to draft our wills.
But this: John and I want you to draft our wills.

Not this: The letter was addressed to Jane and myself.
But this: The letter was addressed to Jane and me.

(b) *When object is also subject.* Use the reflexive pronoun for the object when the object is the same as the subject.

Ex.: You've really outdone yourself. (*Yourself* reflects *you.*)

Ex.: I cut myself while gathering the papers. (*Myself* reflects *I.*)

Ex.: They had to see it for themselves. (*Themselves* reflects *they.*)

Ex.: Keep it to yourself. (*Yourself* reflects the understood subject *you.*)

(c) *When subject is repeated for emphasis.* Use the reflexive pronoun as an intensive when the subject or object is mentioned twice.

Ex.: Abby herself wanted to try the case.

Ex.: Abby wanted to try the case herself.

Ex.: All we have to fear is fear itself.

(d) *"Each other" and "one another."* Use the reciprocal pronoun phrase *each other* to refer to two nouns, *one another* to refer to more than two.

Ex.: The twin brothers supported each other throughout law school.

Ex.: Members of the victim's family consoled one another as the detective testified.

Verbs

11.22 Verbs are words of action or linking. They form the basis for the sentence predicate: the word that either tells what the subject does or links the subject to a label or description. Many verbs we use in English today have been taken from German, Latin, Norse, French, and many other languages. The result is a diverse language, but also one lacking a rigorous grammatical uniformity and teeming with sometimes-perplexing exceptions to the general rules of grammar.

> "As the verb goes, so goes the sentence."
> —*William D. Andrews & Deborah C. Andrews*

Verbs have properties of voice (active and passive), mood (indicative, subjunctive, and imperative), tense (present, past, and future, with alternative perfect, progressive, and perfect-progressive aspects of each), number (singular and plural), and person (first, second, and third).

Verbs have five forms: the stem <work> and the third-person singular <works> (both present tense); the present participle <working>; the past tense <worked>; and the past participle <[had] worked>. Most regular verbs form the third-person singular by adding *-s* or *-es* to the stem <he works at Morgan Lewis>, the past tense and past participle by adding *-ed* to the stem <he worked at Morgan Lewis> <he has worked at Morgan Lewis and elsewhere>, and the present participle by adding *-ing* to the stem <he is working at Morgan Lewis>. But there are spelling variations according to the suffix attached to the stem. These examples show the forms for present-tense stem, present-tense third-person-singular, past tense, past participle, and present participle:

- normal <fold–folds–folded–[has] folded–folding>
- silent *-e* <race–races–raced–[has] raced–racing>
- consonant + *-y* <bury–buries–buried–[has] buried–burying>
- vowel + consonant <hop–hops–hopped–[has] hopped–hopping>

There are many exceptions to the last pattern. Words that are not accented on the last syllable, for example, usually do not double the final consonant before adding a suffix <travel–traveled–traveling>. And American and British spellings differ for many words <canceled–canceling (American English); cancelled–cancelling (British English)>.

Irregular verbs follow no standard rules in forming their past tense and past participle, although their present participle is formed in the same way as that of regular verbs. When in doubt, consult a dictionary. Here are a few of the irregular verbs in the English language (showing the traditional inflection of stem, past tense, and past participle):

- <begin–began–begun>
- <break–broke–broken>
- <bring–brought–brought>
- <eat–ate–eaten>
- <fly–flew–flown>
- <go–went–gone>
- <hurt–hurt–hurt>
- <lay–laid–laid>
- <lie–lay–lain>
- <mean–meant–meant>
- <set–set–set>
- <sit–sat–sat>
- <steal–stole–stolen>
- <swear–swore–sworn>
- <take–took–taken>

For an exhaustive list, see *Garner's Modern English Usage* 529–31 (4th ed. 2016); *see also The Chicago Guide to Grammar, Usage, and Punctuation* 74–81 (2016).

Some verbs have alternative past-tense forms <learned *or* learnt> <strived *or* strove> <sank *or* sunk> or past-participle forms <proved *or* proven> <sunk *or* sunken> <shrunk *or* shrunken>. A good dictionary will show the preferred form and also usage appropriate to the variants—e.g., differences between the past-tense verb <the plaintiff has proved negligence> and the past-participial adjective <the defendant's negligence is a proven fact>.

Tense, voice, and mood are indicated by using one of the four main verb forms, either alone or with one or more *be*-verbs (*am*; *are*; *is*; *was*; *were*; *be*; *being*; *been*), auxiliary verbs (*can*; *could*; *shall*; *should*; *will*; *would*; *have*; *has*; *had*; *may*; *might*; *must*; *do*; *does*; *did*>, or both. Quasi-auxiliary verbs may also add nuance <ought to> <used to> <need to> <dare to>.

Irregular forms and subject–verb agreement are two of the most common problems that writers have with using verbs.

11.23 Use a singular verb after a singular subject.

(a) *Generally.* Use a singular verb with a subject composed of a singular noun or a singular phrase or clause.

> Ex.: Nothing is forever.
>
> Ex.: To settle for less than my client has actually paid in medical bills is out of the question. (The entire infinitive phrase *to settle . . . bills* is the subject; it is singular in number.)
>
> Ex.: Denying aliens entry into the country is called *exclusion*. (The gerund phrase *denying aliens . . . country* is the subject; it is singular.)

(b) *Distractions.* Don't be distracted by a prepositional phrase that comes between the subject and verb, or by a predicate nominative or a complement of the other number.

> Ex.: A panel comprising seven lawyers, four judges, and three nonlawyers is going to study the community's pro bono needs. (*panel . . . is*)
>
> Ex.: Only one in six of the city's registered voters is expected to participate in the off-year election. (*one . . . is*)
>
> Ex.: Your audience is three judges on the appellate panel. (*audience is*)
>
> Ex.: Quick and painful comes the 12 jurors' decision. (*decision . . . comes*)
>
> Ex.: Furthermore, a faction on the committees that recommended the reforms—after five public hearings and four months of debate—is now talking about opposing the majority report. (*faction . . . is*)

(c) *Dependent clauses.* Don't be distracted by separate agreements within dependent clauses, whose subjects and verbs must agree independently of the main clause.

> Ex.: Not one of those people who think they know everything thinks very hard. (*Thinks* agrees with *not one*; *think* agrees with *who*, which in turn takes the plural attribute of *people*; and *know* agrees with *they*.)

(d) *Compound but singular in meaning.* When a compound subject is singular in meaning, it will take a singular verb. This occurs more often with compound phrases and clauses than with compound words because the construction more often describes steps in a singular process.

Ex.: Black tie and tails is the designated attire.

Ex.: Cream cheese and olive is her favorite sandwich spread.

Ex.: To forsake my client and to settle for less than my client has actually paid in medical bills is out of the question. (The two infinitive phrases refer to the same action, so the sense is singular in number.)

(e) *Compound referring to one thing.* When the compound words refer to a singular thing, the verb is singular.

Ex.: The hammer and sickle was the Communist Party's insignia. (The singular determiner *the* before *hammer* is a clear signal that the phrase is singular in meaning.)

Ex.: A philanthropist, author, and scholar is with us tonight. (*Philanthropist*, *author*, and *scholar* all refer to the same person.)

(f) *Illusory compounds.* When a singular subject is joined with other nouns or pronouns by phrasal connectives such as *together with*, *as well as*, *along with*, *but not*, and the like, the subject is still singular and the matching verb should also be singular. The resulting phrase is nonrestrictive and set off with commas, em-dashes, or parentheses. You can avoid the sometimes-awkward result by replacing the prepositional phrase with *and*, thereby making the subject and its matching verb plural.

Ex.: Senator Briley, along with several colleagues, continues to oppose the redistricting plan.

Ex.: The attorney general, not to mention the secretaries of state and defense, supports using the military tribunals.

Ex.: Tawana, but no other students, insists that class never end early.

(g) *Idioms with indefinite pronouns.* Use a singular verb with a compound construction of the singular indefinite pronouns *anyone and everyone*, *anybody and everybody*, and *anything and everything.*

Ex.: The sergeant said that anything and everything is being done to locate the suspects.

Ex.: Anyone and everyone who calls in to the new phone system gets put on hold immediately.

(h) *Idioms with "each" and "every."* Use a singular verb with compounded singular subjects modified by the indefinite pronoun *each* or *every*; these pronouns relate individually to the verb, so the use of a singular verb is idiomatic (but see 11.24(c)).

Ex.: Every Tom, Dick, and Harry who applies is accepted. (The phrase *every Tom, Dick, and Harry* takes the singular verbs *applies* and *is accepted*, even though the phrase *Tom, Dick, and Harry* alone would take the plural verbs *apply* and *are accepted.*)

(i) *Idiom with "many a."* Use a singular verb when the subject is the plural indefinite pronoun *many* followed by *a* and a singular noun.

Ex.: Many a young lawyer has gone into public service.

(j) *"Either" or "neither" as subject.* The terms *either* and *neither*, when acting as the subject of a sentence, take a singular verb.

Ex.: Has either of our clients arrived yet?

Ex.: Neither of these arguments is a winner.

(k) *Phrases of measurement.* Use a singular verb with a noun phrase that is plural in form or appearance but singular in meaning; especially watch out for mass-noun phrases of measurements, names and titles in plural form, and similar traps.

Ex.: Ten blocks is too far to walk in this rain.

Ex.: A hundred dollars is more than I am willing to pay.

Ex.: Thirty minutes is the standard lunch break here.

Ex.: The Boy Scouts of America has taken a lot of criticism lately.

Ex.: "Seventy-six Trombones" is always a fitting selection for any parade.

Ex.: The United States is a common-law nation.

Ex.: General Motors is up 3%.

Ex.: Politics makes strange bedfellows.

11.24 Use a plural verb after a plural subject.

(a) *Generally.* Use a plural verb with a plural subject and most compound subjects.

Ex.: People demand justice.

Ex.: First-year property and torts were my strong suits.

(b) *Conjunctive compound.* A conjunctive-compound subject (joined by *and*) will usually be plural (but see 11.23(d)–(e)).

Ex.: The plaintiff and the defendant agree to the continuance.

Ex.: What your client wants and what my client wants are two different things. (The two phrases joined by *and* make a plural subject, agreeing with the plural verb *are*.)

(c) *With "each" in apposition.* Use a plural verb with a plural subject even if the subject is followed by the singular indefinite pronoun *each* in apposition. This placement of *each* after the subject doesn't create the singular-sense idiom described in 11.23(h). Instead, *each* functions as an adverb.

Ex.: The candidates each have two minutes for an opening statement.

(d) *Plural indefinite pronouns.* Use a plural verb with the plural indefinite pronoun *both*, *few*, *many*, *others*, or *several* as the subject.

Ex.: We have two options. Both are problematic.

Ex.: Many are called, but few are chosen.

(e) *With class adjectives.* Use a plural verb with an adjective that is used as a noun to represent a class with the adjective's attribute. Unlike a collective noun (which denotes a singular entity that comprises individual members), a collective adjective represents no singular entity but the assemblage of individual members.

Ex.: The meek stand to inherit the earth.

Ex.: The fragile are protected by the eggshell-skull doctrine.

(f) *Plural-form nouns.* Use a plural verb with a noun that has a plural form and sense.

Ex.: Were these scissors the murder weapon?

Ex.: The scales of justice are a powerful symbol.

Ex.: The odds are against us.

11.25 With certain types of subjects, use the context of the sentence to determine whether a singular or plural verb is required.

(a) *With quantifying or partitive subjects.* Use the context of the sentence to determine the number of the verb when the subject is a noun of multitude <bunch> <number> <variety> or partition <fraction> <part> <portion>, a numerical fraction, or an indefinite pronoun of count <all> <any> <more> <most> <some>. When the meaning is a part of a singular whole or a mass noun, use a singular verb. When the meaning is a number or a share of more than one thing (a count noun), use a plural verb.

Ex.: Most of the new law students study hard for finals.

Ex.: Most of the first-year class studies hard for finals.

Ex.: Two-thirds of the students who study hard perform well.

Ex.: Two-thirds of that group performs well.

The article is often a reliable indicator of whether the subject takes a singular or plural verb. A subject with an indefinite article (*a* or *an*) is usually plural, while a subject with the definite article (*the*) is almost always singular.

Ex.: A variety of study aids are available.

Ex.: The variety of study aids available is impressive.

(b) *With collective nouns.* Use the context of the sentence to determine the number of the verb when the subject is a collective noun; use a singular verb if the action itself is collective, but use a plural verb if the action is individual. The American preference is to use collective nouns <committee> <staff> <team> as singular, and to specify individuals <committee members> when individual action is implied. In some sentences the distinction between group and individual action will be clear. But often the meaning will be susceptible of either interpretation, and the word choice will be based merely on which form sounds better. When that is so, consistency of choice within the document is more important than which choice is made.

Ex.: The jury deliberates on a verdict. (A singular, collective action.)

Ex.: The jury order individual lunches. (Plural, individual actions.)

Ex.: The band plays *The Star-Spangled Banner*. (Clearly collective.)

Ex.: The band warm up their instruments. (Clearly individual.)

Ex.: The court issues its decisions daily. (Always singular.)

Ex.: The faculty (*is*? *are*?) divided on the issue of affirmative action. (The action can be construed as collective or individual.)

(c) *With singular-form nouns.* Some nouns have the same form in the singular and the plural <aircraft> <counsel> <trout>. When a noun has the same form in both numbers, use the correctly numbered verb according to the subject's number.

Ex.: The series on the history of common law runs on Wednesday nights.

Ex.: Two series on the history of common law run simultaneously.

Ex.: A leaping fish breaks the surface.

Ex.: Two leaping fish break the surface.

(d) *With foreign nouns.* With a foreign-derived noun, match the verb's number according to the subject's number. Foreign-derived nouns ending in *-a* can be especially troublesome because they may be singular <amoeba> <encyclopedia> <minutia> or plural <criteria> <data> <media>. *Data* and *media* are often treated as singular "mass" nouns even in formal writing, though some persist in making them strictly plural in sense. To further complicate matters, the singular terms may form plurals with the Latin *-ae* <minutiae>, the English *-s* <encyclopedias>, or both, alternatively <amoebae *or* amoebas>. And the plural nouns may take the singular ending *-um* <medium> or *-on* <criterion>. When in doubt, check a dictionary.

Ex.: Local media are covering this case closely.

Ex.: The Yale alumna is taking a job with Dow Chemical.

Ex.: The data are clear on this point.

Ex.: The minutiae of the disputed facts of this case make the legal principles hard to extract.

(e) *With "-ics" words.* Use the context of the sentence to determine the number of the verb when the subject is the name of a science or discipline ending in *-ics*. Words such as *economics* and *statistics* may refer in the singular to the discipline itself, or in the plural to the practical application of the discipline.

Ex.: Economics is central to any management curriculum.

Ex.: The economics of this project are going to require some public funding.

Ex.: Ceramics is a great hobby.

Ex.: These ceramics are from the pre-Columbian era.

(f) *In relative clauses.* Use the antecedent of a relative pronoun to determine the number and person of the verb in the relative clause.

Ex.: The book that contains the story is checked out. (*That* is third-person singular, properties that it assumes from *book*, so it takes the corresponding verb, *contains*.)

Ex.: The books that contain the story are checked out. (*That* is third-person plural, properties that it assumes from *books*, so it takes the corresponding verb, *contain*.)

Ex.: Wasn't it you who were responsible? (*Who* is second person, a property that it assumes from *you*, so it takes the corresponding *be*-verb, *were*.)

11.26 If the subject is a disjunctive compound (joined by *or* or *nor*), the verb should agree with the element of the compound closest to the verb; if the compound contains both singular and plural elements, try to place the plural subject closest to the verb.

(a) *With singular subjects.* Use a singular verb with two or more singular subjects joined by *or* or *nor.* It doesn't matter whether the subject is composed of words, phrases, or clauses.

Ex.: Neither the prosecution nor the defense is ready for trial.

Ex.: Either trade-secret law or patent law protects any single invention.

(b) *Singular in meaning.* If the compound subject denotes a thing that is singular in meaning, or describes the same thing, use a singular verb.

Ex.: To plead it or to try it is the decision you face. (It's a singular decision with two options.)

Ex.: To be or not to be is Hamlet's dilemma. (It's a singular dilemma.)

(c) *With mixed elements.* If the compound subject contains singular and plural elements, use a verb that agrees with the closest subject.

Ex.: Neither the jurors nor the judge seems sympathetic to our argument.

Ex.: Neither the judge nor the jurors seem sympathetic to our argument.

Ex.: Either two new associates or I am responsible for taking Stone's deposition tomorrow. (The verb *am* agrees in both number and person with the nearer subject, *I*.)

Ex.: Neither they nor he was at the meeting. (The verb *was* agrees in both number and person with the nearer subject, *he*.)

(d) *Plural element last.* If possible, put the plural subject last to make the sentence less jarring (see 11.10(e)).

Ex.: Neither the judge nor the jurors seem sympathetic to our argument.

> "Laziness is a major reason for writers' using the passive voice."
> —*Ernst Jacobi*

11.27 Minimize the passive voice.

(a) *Recognizing it.* The passive voice consists of a *be*-verb (or sometimes a form of *get*) combined with the past participle of a transitive verb. Intransitive verbs (those that don't take a direct object) cannot form the passive voice. The *be*-verb may be understood rather than expressed, as in the first two examples below. A *by*-prepositional phrase often accompanies the construction; when it doesn't appear, it can be understood from the context (see 11.44(c), 14.3(b)).

Ex.: Consider it done. (Either *to have been* or *as having been* is understood before the past participle *done* in this oblique passive construction.)

Ex.: I heard it suggested that we raise our offer. (Some *be*-verb is understood before *suggested*.)

Ex.: State immunity cannot *be abrogated* under the Fourteenth Amendment unless it *is shown* that the states have engaged in a pattern of patent infringement. (The sentence has two passive constructions: *immunity cannot be abrogated* and *it is shown*.)

Ex.: Before the 1976 Act, sound recordings had no copyright protection and could *be reproduced* by "pirates" with relative immunity from federal copyright laws. (The *could be reproduced* construction is followed by a *by*-prepositional phrase.)

(b) *Editing it.* The structure of the passive voice makes the subject the recipient of the action or state that the verb expresses. The actor is often (not always) identified in a *by*-prepositional phrase. When appropriate, then, you can rewrite the sentence, making the object of the *be*-phrase the subject of the new sentence and the subject of the old sentence an object in the new sentence.

Passive: When the arcade *was checked*, it *was determined* that a video game *had been broken into* and the money changer *removed*. (Italics indicate passive voice.)

Active: When police *checked* the arcade, they *found* that someone *had broken into* a video game and *removed* its money changer. (Italics indicate active-voice edits.)

Passive: If the human trials *are satisfactorily completed* and the new drug *is still considered* both safe and efficacious, an application *is made* to the FDA for permission *to get the drug marketed*. (Italics indicate passive voice.)

Active: If the new drug *proves* safe and efficacious after human trials, the company *applies* to the FDA for permission *to market* it. (Italics indicate active-voice edits.)

(c) *When it's appropriate.* Stylists often criticize the passive voice as weaker than the active voice. This weakness shows in the active–passive comparisons in the examples with (b) above. The criticism is justified by general overuse of the passive voice. Writers should watch for it and prefer the active voice unless there is good reason not to. But the passive voice is appropriate in some places, especially (1) when the emphasis is on the recipient of the action instead of the actor, and (2) when the actor is unknown or unimportant.

> Ex.: A Boston jury convicted Crittenden of fraud. (Active voice: focus is on what the jury decided.)
>
> Ex.: Crittenden was convicted of fraud by a Boston jury. (Passive voice: focus is on what happened to the defendant.)
>
> Ex.: The cemetery has been vandalized four times in the past year. (Passive voice: the actor is unknown and unimportant.)

11.28 Use the subjunctive mood to express a wish, a demand, a requirement, an exhortation, or a statement contrary to fact—as well as in a number of fixed idioms.

(a) *Generally.* The subjunctive mood is peculiar in both form and function. It is rarely used except in a few fixed phrases. A verb in the subjunctive mood has no third-person-singular (*-s*) variation; *be* is used rather than *am*, *are*, and *is* <if that be true>; and *were* is used instead of *was* <if he were honest>. The present tense may be used to express would-be conditions in the past <truth be told, their objection should have been sustained>, and the past tense to express would-be conditions in the present <I would not do that if I were you>.

> Ex.: Be that as it may, the suit has already been filed. (*Be that as it may* is a fixed phrase in the subjunctive mood.)
>
> Ex.: If you be honest, you will admit liability for the accident. (The stilted sound of *if you be honest* reflects the archaic nature of the subjunctive mood. But changing it to *if you were honest* changes the tone from "you can be honest" to "you are dishonest.")

(b) *"That"-clause of need.* Use the subjunctive mood in *that*-clauses of request, demand, and requirement. If a *be*-verb is required, use *be* (regardless of person and number) and the past or present participle, regardless of when the action takes place. If no *be*-verb is required, use the present-tense stem alone, regardless of when the action takes place.

> Ex.: We insist that we be allowed to review the document before it is admitted into evidence. (*Be allowed to review* is subjunctive, expressing a request.)
>
> Ex.: Rule 11 requires that lawyers use good faith in making and responding to discovery requests. (*Use* is subjunctive, expressing a requirement.)
>
> Ex.: The retiring judge told about being a first-year law student whose torts professor insisted that he study harder or face certain failure. (*Study* is present-tense subjunctive, expressing a demand.)
>
> Ex.: The foundation requires that a scholarship recipient be enrolled full-time to maintain eligibility. (*Be enrolled* is subjunctive, expressing a requirement.)

(c) *Expressing a wish.* Use the past-tense subjunctive mood with the word *were* (regardless of person and number) to indicate a wish. Use the past tense to indicate a present-time wish.

Ex.: I wish Maria were more certain about her decision. (*Were* is subjunctive; the indicative verb would be *was*. The past-tense form attains a present-time meaning in the subjunctive mood.)

Ex.: Don't you wish you were a fly on the jury-room wall?

Ex.: I wish I were in Dixie.

(d) *Exhortations and things contrary to fact.* Use the subjunctive mood in clauses starting with *if*, *as if*, or *as though* to express exhortations and things contrary to fact (including suppositions and illusions as well as impossible things).

Ex.: If we were to offer $75,000, would you take it?

Ex.: The cross-examination seemed as though it were never going to end. (An illusion: *were going to end* is subjunctive.)

Ex.: Long live rock 'n' roll! (An exhortation: *may* is understood, so the meaning is *may rock 'n' roll live long*.)

(e) *In fixed idioms.* Use the subjunctive mood as it occurs in many fixed phrases.

Ex.: May it please the Court . . .

Ex.: Suffice it to say . . .

Ex.: Be that as it may . . .

Ex.: If I were you . . . .

Ex.: If need be . . . .

Ex.: So help me God . . . .

11.29 Connect every participial phrase to its subject.

(a) *At start of sentence.* When a participial phrase begins a sentence, its subject should be the noun, pronoun, or noun phrase that most closely follows. A participial phrase that modifies any other potential subject is called a *misplaced participle* or *misplaced modifier*. One that has no subject at all in the sentence is called a *dangling participle*.

Ex.: In keeping with constitutional policy, the Supreme Court has defined a "writing" as any physical rendering of fruits of creative intellectual or aesthetic labor. (The subject of *in keeping with constitutional policy* is *the Supreme Court*.)

Ex.: Described in dissent as "the *Dred Scott* decision of copyright law," *Williams & Wilkins Co.* appears not to have given serious consideration to the effect of defendants' practices on plaintiff's potential market. (The subject of *described . . . law* is *Williams & Wilkins Co.*)

Not this: If convicted, the jury could give Parham up to 10 years.
But this: If convicted, Parham could receive up to 10 years.

(b) *Close to subject.* If a participial phrase doesn't start a sentence, it should modify the noun, pronoun, or noun phrase that most closely precedes it.

Ex.: The Court has held there to be no First Amendment immunity for a television station charged with misappropriating a performer's human-cannonball act by videotaping the entire act and broadcasting it on a news program. (The subject of *charged . . . program* is *television station*.)

Ex.: Because "malice" is a term of such variable meaning, some courts, influenced no doubt by the prima facie tort theory, have abandoned the concept of malice altogether and speak rather of justifiable and unjustifiable interference. (The subject of *influenced . . . theory* is *courts*.)

(c) *Misplaced and dangling modifiers.* If the phrase is misplaced (not clearly connected to the word it modifies) or dangling (having no word to modify), edit the sentence. One solution is to rearrange the sentence so that the modifier is syntactically connected to the noun or phrase it modifies. But often the better option may be to reword the sentence to move the modifier.

Misplaced: Often used in early America, experts now suggest that shaming punishments may have a promising future in the modern criminal-justice system. (*Often used in early America* is misplaced because it does not modify the nearest noun, *experts*.)

After: Often used in early America, shaming punishments may have a promising future in the modern criminal-justice system, experts suggest.

Better: Experts say that shaming punishments, often used in early America, may have a promising future in the modern criminal-justice system.

Dangling: Faced with dwindling fertility, Chile's president, Sebastián Piñera, has implored his compatriots to have more kids. (Presumably, the fertility problem lies with Chile, not with its president as the dangling participle implies.)

11.30 Generally, if a present participle functions as a noun (that is, it's a gerund), and it is preceded by a noun or pronoun, put the noun or pronoun in the possessive case—which is to say, avoid fused participles.

(a) *The rule.* Generally speaking, prefer the possessive case for a noun or a personal pronoun that precedes an *-ing* verb acting as a noun.

Ex.: The driver's texting caused the accident.

Ex.: Our reaching a settlement will depend on their good-faith negotiating.

(b) *The exceptions.* The possessive-gerund construction can sometimes be unnatural or unidiomatic. You must use your ear to tell the difference.

Ex.: The chances of our settling are slim.

But: The chances of that happening are slim.

Ex.: The former volunteers' criticizing the new campaign manager infuriated the candidate.

But: The candidate was mad at former volunteers criticizing the new campaign manager.

11.31 In a compound predicate, if an auxiliary verb grammatically matches all the main verbs, omit it after its first use.

(a) *Style benefits.* Omitting repeated words makes prose more concise and effective.

Ex.: In the last 60 years, the role of the common-law judge has been revolutionized in civil law and amplified in criminal law. (The auxiliary *has been* is understood before the second main verb *amplified*.)

Ex.: We can and should reform our judicial-selection process. (The main verb *reform* is understood after *can* as well as *should*.)

(b) *Parallel constructions.* Don't use this device if the auxiliary verb must be changed in any way to grammatically match one of the main verbs.

Not this: The invention must be refined to a point at which a prototype has or could be made.

But this: The invention must be refined to a point at which a prototype has been or could be made.

11.32 Use the past tense to describe what a court did in a particular case. Otherwise, when discussing the law, generally use the present tense.

(a) *Present tense as default.* Prefer the present tense for legal writing unless there is a good reason to use another tense.

Ex.: Clarence Darrow is a folk hero, an American legend.

Ex.: I argue that Cardozo was an authentic legal pragmatist in the tradition of Oliver Wendell Holmes and, especially, John Dewey.

(b) *Past tense for case history.* Use past tense in narratives such as events in a statement of facts or the procedural history of a case, both of which happened in the past. But use the present tense when discussing the law generally.

Ex.: Abdille, a Somali national, was orphaned at an early age. He never learned his parents' identity or his clan lineage. [Past tense to discuss history.] Clan lineage is a central feature of social and political life in Somalia, and a lack of clan identification can be life-threatening. [Present tense to discuss law or custom.] Abdille sought asylum and withholding-of-removal relief from Somalia and South Africa. [Past tense to discuss procedural history.]

Adjectives

11.33 An adjective is a word that describes, specifies, or in some other way modifies a noun. (Grammatically, an adjective may also attach to a pronoun, but it is still detailing the person, place, or thing that the pronoun is standing in for.) It may describe the noun <flowery meadow> <mellow wine> <persnickety neighbor> or delimit the noun <three pigs> <the legislature> <Paul's briefcase>.

Many adjectives are words in their own right, such as *good*, *bad*, *red*, *green*, *short*, *tall*, *fast*, and *slow*. But many others are produced by adapting a noun (or, less often, a verb) with a suffix such as *-able* <laughable>, *-al* <critical>, *-ary* <monetary>, *-ed* <zippered>, *-en* <golden>, *-esque* <picturesque>, *-ful* <youthful>, *-ial* <presidential>, *-ible* <defensible>, *-ic* <Icelandic>, *-ish* <boyish>, *-ive* <responsive>, *-less* <selfless>, *-like* <lifelike>, *-ly* <fatherly>, *-ous* <glamorous>, *-some* <burdensome>, *-ual* <spiritual>, and *-y* <toothy>. All participles are inherently adjectival <a perfected interest (*perfected* is the past participle of the verb *perfect*)> <a sitting judge (*sitting* is the present participle of *sit*)>. Nouns often serve as attributive adjectives <pilot training> <quality control> <court documents>.

An adjective typically precedes the word it details <red light>, but it can also serve as a predicate complement <the light was *red*>. A few adjectives may be used only in the predicate <I was *afraid*>. A few others, mostly French in origin, always follow the noun they modify <attorney general> <carte blanche> <court-martial>.

A number of words can serve in the same form as either an adjective or an adverb <better> <best> <much> <less> <near> <far>. A phrase or clause may also serve as an adjective in a sentence <the word *of the day*> < the thing *that matters most*>.

Adjectives lend color and texture to writing. But their overuse weakens prose: skilled writers rely on nouns and verbs to tell the story and make the argument.

> "It is the adjective, in fact, that supplies the descriptive and decorative matter . . . . Therefore, it is abundant in the richer styles, but the danger is that it should be too frequent, and then the effect is flamboyant. There lies the wisdom of Pudd'nhead Wilson's [Mark Twain's] advice—'as to the adjective; when in doubt, strike it out.'"
>
> —*Henry Bett*

11.34 Use the comparative form as a measure of quality between two things and the superlative form as a measure of quality among three or more.

(a) *Regular forms.* As a rule, for most one-syllable and many two-syllable adjectives, use the suffix *-er* to form the comparative and *-est* to form the superlative. If the word ends in *-e*, drop the *e*. If the word ends in *-y*, change the *y* to *i*. If the word ends in a *-d* or *-t* preceded by a single vowel, double the final consonant.

Ex.: mean–meaner–meanest

Ex.: eerie–eerier–eeriest

Ex.: toothy–toothier–toothiest

Ex.: mad–madder–maddest

(b) *Irregular forms.* Watch for irregular words, which form their comparative and superlative in unpredictable ways.

Ex.: good–better–best

Ex.: bad–worse–worst

Ex.: many–more–most

Ex.: much–more–most

(c) *With "more–most," "less–least."* For other two-syllable and longer adjectives (including those formed with suffixes other than *-y*), form the comparative by using the adverb *more* or *less*, and the superlative by using the adverb *most* or *least*. While many two-syllable adjectives ending in *-er*, *-le*, *-ow*, *-ure*, or *-y* can use either the *-er* suffix or *more/less* to form the comparative, they generally form their superlative with the adverb–positive-adjective construction.

Ex.: maroon–more maroon–most maroon

Ex.: youthful–more youthful–most youthful

Ex.: condescending–less condescending–least condescending

(d) *Class comparison.* Use *other* or *else* when using the comparative form to rank something against the rest of its class; otherwise, you're making an illogical comparison.

Ex.: Tamesha made better grades than anyone else in her class. (Without *else* the illogical comparison is between Tamesha and, among others in her class, Tamesha herself.

Ex.: Tamesha made better grades than any other first-year law student in the school. (Without *other* the sentence implies that Tamesha is not a first-year law student.)

(e) *Double comparatives.* Never use a double-comparative or -superlative construction—that is, the comparative or superlative form with *more*, *most*, *less*, or *least*.

Not this: Isn't there a more superior authority?

But this: Isn't there a higher authority?

11.35 Use an adjective, not an adverb, as a subject complement (predicate adjective) after a *be*-verb or other linking verb, a verb of perception, or a verb of becoming.

(a) *With linking verbs.* Some writers who would never be tempted to write *she is prettily* trip over *be*-verbs and other linking verbs.

Ex.: The brief turned out good. (Not *well*.)

Ex.: The deal went bad when one backer reneged. (Not *badly*.)

(b) *With verbs of sense or becoming.* Verbs of sensory perception (such as *appear*, *feel*, *look*, *smell*, *sound*, and *taste*) call for a predicate adjective. But sometimes an adverb sounds tempting, as in the common error *I feel badly for you*. A test for whether an adjective or an adverb is needed is to substitute a *be*-verb to see whether the sentence makes sense: *I am badly* fails the test, so make it *I feel bad*.

Ex.: I feel bad about your loss.

Ex.: A cup of coffee sounds good about now.

11.36 Don't use an adverb of comparison with a noncomparable adjective.

(a) *No qualifiers.* A noncomparable (or *absolute*) adjective is one whose quality cannot be changed. The best example is *unique*: something either is or is not "one of a kind." Nothing can be more or less "one of a kind" than something else, so *more unique* and *less unique* are illogical. Other examples of noncomparable adjectives are *absolute*, *complete*, *false*, *fatal*, *final*, *irrevocable*, *sufficient*, and *void*.

(b) *"Almost" and "nearly."* Something may be closer to a noncomparable quality than another thing. So it's not wrong to say that an edited manuscript is "more nearly complete," for example, or that an injury is "almost fatal."

11.37 Use dates as adjectives sparingly.

(a) *Full dates as adjectives.* Using all three elements (month–day–year)—plus a comma—can become unwieldy, so use the construction sparingly. An *of*-phrase is traditionally preferred to using a date as an adjective—that is, *meeting of Jan. 5, 2018* instead of *Jan. 5, 2018 meeting*. When a date is used as an adjective, omit the otherwise-mandatory comma after the year. A second comma would halt the reader between the adjective and its noun even though no pause occurs when the words are spoken.

Ex.: your July 23, 2018 letter

Not this: the April 12, 2018, accident

But this: the April 12, 2018 accident

Better: the accident of April 12, 2018

(b) *Short dates as adjectives.* Using a short date—such as a year or a month and day—as an adjective may tighten a sentence.

Ex.: the 2016 campaign

Ex.: the May 3 hearing

11.38 In some phrases and idiomatic constructions, the adjective follows the word it modifies.

(a) *Legal terms.* Several legal terms, mostly from Law French, retain their Romance "postpositive" syntax in which the adjective follows the noun. Even terms whose words have been replaced with their English counterparts retain that arrangement. (For more on the plurals of terms like these, see 7.9(b).)

Ex.: court-martial

Ex.: notary public

Ex.: attorney general

Ex.: the body politic

Ex.: the city proper

(b) *Pronouns.* The compound indefinite pronouns formed by joining *any-*, *every-*, *no-*, and *some-* to *-body*, *-one* (including *none*), *-thing*, *-time*, *-where*, and others often take a postpositive adjective.

Ex.: Are you looking for someone special?

Ex.: Nothing good can come of this.

But: They whispered sweet nothings to each other.

(c) *Stilted phrasing.* The words *things* and *matters* may take postpositive adjectives, but the result may sound stilted.

Ex.: In matters procedural, Professor Wright admitted of no equal.

Ex.: She urged her students to fight for all things just and true.

11.39 Use the definite article *the* to signal a specific person, place, or thing; use the indefinite article *a* or *an* to signal a generic reference.

(a) *Placement.* Place the article first in any noun phrase, ahead of any adjective. It isn't hyphenated as part of a phrasal adjective unless it falls in the middle.

Ex.: the middle-class voters

> "No exact and determinate rule can be given for the placing of adverbs on all occasions. The general rule may be of considerable use; but the easy flow and perspicuity of the phrase are the things that ought to be chiefly regarded." —*Charles M. Ingersoll*

Ex.: a middle-of-the-road candidate

(b) *Deciding between "a" and "an."* Use *a* before a word beginning with a consonant sound, *an* before a word beginning with a vowel sound.

Ex.: a humbling wait to hear a one-hour talk at a historical society (The *h*'s in *humbling* and *historical* are sounded.)

Ex.: an unambiguous statement about a universal truth

Ex.: an SEC position offered to a UCLA graduate (SEC starts with a vowel sound (/ess/), so it takes *an*. UCLA starts with a consonant sound (/yoo/), so it takes *a*.)

Adverbs

11.40 If nouns are the *who*-words of a sentence, and verbs are the *what*-words, adverbs are the *when-*, *where-*, *why-*, and *how*-words. They modify verbs to explain more about the action <we must move *quickly*>, adjectives to clarify that attribute <we need a *fully* developed theory>, and other adverbs to calibrate their degree of modification <we must move *very* slowly>. They also join with prepositions and verbs to form phrases that alter the meaning of the base word in some idiomatic way <chalk *up* another victory> <get *down* to brass tacks>.

As with adjectives, a phrase or clause may also serve an adverbial function in a sentence. This often occurs with introductory temporal phrases <On Monday,> and clauses <Once we select a jury,>. But mid- and end-sentence phrases are also common <we drove to the capital [*where?*] in Julia's car [*how?*] Wednesday [*when?*] to testify [*why?*] at a hearing [*where?*]>.

An adverb is typically formed by adding the *-ly* suffix to an adjective <madly> <insanely>, changing *-y* to *-i* as needed <sleepily> <toothily>. But many adverbs do not end in *-ly*, and it is wrong to add the unnecessary suffix <thus (never *thusly*)> <doubtless (never *doubtlessly*)>.

Often, an adverb could fit into a sentence in more than one place (as with *often* in this sentence). At other times, there is only one proper position for the adverb (as with *only* in this sentence). Placement can have rhetorical effect or even change substantive meaning.

A simple (*adjunctive*) adverb modifies a single word in the sentence <May I speak *frankly*?>. A sentence (*disjunctive*) adverb modifies the sentence itself <*Frankly*, my dear, I don't give a damn>. A *conjunctive* adverb joins two clauses and indicates the relationship between them <Kym got the papers signed; *afterward*, she filed them with the clerk>. Many kinds of relationships can be expressed this way: *likewise*, *otherwise*, *therefore*, *however*, *for instance*, *in other words*, and *meanwhile*, to name a few. An *interrogative* adverb likewise modifies the entire clause <*Where* did that come from?>.

11.41 Place an adverb in its strongest position, often at the beginning of a sentence or inside a verb phrase.

(a) *With the modified word.* The general rule is that an adverb should appear as near as possible to the word it modifies. This placement ensures that the relationship and the intended meaning are clear. A misplaced adverb can obscure or wholly alter a sentence's meaning.

(b) *After first auxiliary.* The strongest position for an adverb that modifies a verb phrase is right after the first auxiliary verb (see 11.22). Since 1762, grammarians have consistently held that this is the most natural and robust placement for an adverb. (Notice *have consistently held* in the preceding sentence.)

Ex.: We *should not have let* Duckworth testify.

Ex.: Harlan *may yet prove* not so orthodox a Justice as many suppose.

Ex.: Mental derangement sufficient to invalidate a will *is generally said* to consist in one of two forms.

Not this: Congress specifically and repeatedly has addressed the matter at hand.

But this: Congress has specifically and repeatedly addressed the matter at hand.

(c) *Split infinitive.* When the verb phrase containing the adverb is an infinitive (*to* plus a verb, as in *to dismiss*), the result is what has sometimes been condemned as a "split infinitive" (e.g., *to summarily dismiss*). Avoid this construction if you're not comfortable with it, but use it if the word order strengthens both the infinitive and the adverb—or if avoiding the split results in an awkward-sounding sentence.

Ex.: In the proposed budget, the President wants *to more than double* spending on domestic security.

Ex.: *To boldly go* where no one has gone before.

(d) *With intransitive verb.* An adverb modifying an intransitive verb should usually come immediately after the verb. But adverbs describing the frequency of an action—such as *always*, *sometimes*, *never*, *often*, *generally*, *typically*, *usually*, *rarely*, and *seldom*—often sound better before the verb (as in this sentence: *sound often better* sounds unnatural).

(e) *Temporal adverbs.* The strongest position for a temporal adverb or adverbial phrase that precedes the action of the main verb in time or logic is at the beginning of the sentence.

Ex.: *After developing a useful, nonobvious, and new invention,* the inventor may claim a patent.

Ex.: *Before distributing the estate,* most jurisdictions authorize relatively liberal periodic payments of cash to the surviving spouse, dependent children, or both.

(f) *Contrast at start of sentence.* The strongest position for an adverb or adverbial phrase that contrasts the sentence with what came before is at the start of the sentence. This provides a transition between sentences.

Ex.: *On the other hand,* a broad construction of "relatives" would encompass a group too broad to be ascertainable as a private trust.

Ex.: *Conversely,* the promise must be made and accepted as the conventional motive or inducement for furnishing the consideration.

Ex.: *Still,* there was a strong trend at work: New York passed its first law in 1848, and by 1850 about 17 states had granted married women some legal capacity to deal with their property.

(g) *Emphasis at end of sentence.* Sometimes the strongest position for an adverb is at the end of the sentence, for emphasis.

Ex.: If the plaintiff could prove any actual monetary damages that resulted from this minor incident, my client would pay them *happily.*

Ex.: While that routine evaluation might have justified some disciplinary action against Mrs. Holtzen when it was issued, today it doesn't look like anything more than a pretext for her discriminatory firing *a year later.*

11.42 Place emphatic adverbs such as *only, so, very, quite,* and *just* immediately before whatever they modify.

(a) *Placement of "only."* The word *only* is probably misplaced more often than any other modifier in English writing. It emphasizes the word or phrase that comes immediately after it; therefore, when it comes too early in the sentence, it actually plays down what it should emphasize.

Ex.: The "sweat-of-the-brow" doctrine only demanded (read *demanded only*) that the author demonstrate the investment of some "original work" into the final product.

Ex.: The prankster intended only to scare the victims, not to hurt them.

(b) *Idiomatic placement.* The idiomatic use of *only* before the verb, regardless of what it is modifying, works in spoken English because the meaning is usually clear from the speaker's inflection. But in writing that placement is often ambiguous.

Not this: The statute only covers imported goods.

But this: The statute covers only imported goods.

Or this: The statute covers imported goods only.

Prepositions

11.43 A preposition is so named because it is usually positioned before its object, which may be a noun, pronoun, phrase, or clause. The name's origin may be largely to blame for the superstition that a preposition should not end a sentence (that is, because it must come *before* its object). In fact, though, not only can a preposition end a clause (especially a relative clause) or a sentence, but the result often sounds far more natural than the convoluted syntax that the superstition would demand. A preposition also follows the relative pronouns *which* and *whom*, and it always follows its object when used with *that*.

Whatever its placement, a preposition's role is to relate its object to another word in the sentence. The relationship is commonly one of space <in> <on> <under> <beside> or time <before> <after> <during> <until>, but it may also express possession <of> <for> <by>, description <with> <like> <as>, or circumstance <about> <against> <aboard>. The resulting prepositional phrase may serve as an adjective or adverb (or, less commonly, a noun), depending on its function in the sentence.

Prepositions can be simple <in> <of> <for> or complex <in accordance with> <on behalf of> <with respect to>. Complex prepositions are often a source of wordiness and overblown style: prefer the simple forms when possible (see 12.2(c)). At other times they are unavoidable <across from> <out from under>.

In addition to the common prepositions, several prepositions have the form of a verb's present participle <considering> <regarding> <barring>.

The use of prepositions is highly idiomatic: there are no infallible rules to guide you in deciding which preposition to use with a particular word. See 13.4 for a list of terms that take specific prepositions. For other terms, check a dictionary.

11.44 To combat verbosity, minimize prepositional phrases.

(a) *Zombie nouns.* Verbs are often buried in so-called zombie nouns ending in *-tion*, *-ment*, *-ance*, *-ity*, *-sure*, and the like. Restoring the verb typically eliminates a stuffy prepositional phrase and adds action to the sentence (see 14.3(c)).

Before: If the parties had agreed upon a specified method of making *the determination*, such as by *computation*, the *application* of a formula, or the *decision* of an arbitrator, they could have agreed upon whatever rent figure emerged from *utilization* of that method. (Italics indicate zombie nouns.)

After: If the parties had agreed on how *to set* a rent figure—for example, *to compute* it, *to apply* a formula, or to let an arbitrator *decide* it—they could have agreed on the figure reached by *using* that method. (Italics indicate active-verb replacements.)

Before: The employer had an *obligation* to make *contributions* to the pension fund's *endowment*. (Italics indicate zombie nouns.)

After: The employer was *obliged* to *contribute* toward *endowing* the pension fund. (Italics indicate active-verb replacements.)

> "Two prepositional phrases in a row turn on the warning light, three make a problem, and four invite disaster."
>
> —*Richard A. Lanham*

(b) *One-word replacements.* Some prepositional phrases can be replaced with an adverb <with all diligence = quickly>, an adjective <with blue eyes = blue-eyed>, or a term of possession or agency <of the company = the company's>. In all such cases, the sentence will be shorter and cleaner (see 14.3(d)).

> Before: Some are convinced that punishments of the scarlet-letter type have the potential for more effectiveness than prison sentences for many offenders, especially for offenders who are nonviolent.
>
> After: Some are convinced that scarlet-letter punishments could have more effect than prison sentences for many offenders, especially nonviolent ones.

(c) *Active voice.* Eliminate *by*-prepositional phrases by changing from the passive to the active voice where appropriate; the sentence will be stronger and shorter (see 11.27, 14.3(b)).

> Before: The legislation was fiercely debated by both sides, each offering its own bill.
>
> After: Both sides fiercely debated the legislation, each offering its own bill.

(d) *As a cause of bloat.* Some prepositional phrases are necessary. But their overuse—especially in *of*-phrase strings—is a leading cause of clogged prose. Some can be simply eliminated without losing any meaning.

> Ex.: Although the automaker recently reported a second-quarter loss of $1.3 million, the CEO of the company expects to end the year with a modest profit. (*Of the company* adds nothing to the sentence and should be omitted.)
>
> Before: "Maximizing profits" means terminating the employment of any physician whose use of ancillary services cuts too deeply into the profit margin.
>
> After: "Maximizing profits" means terminating any physician whose use of ancillary services cuts the profit margin too deeply.

11.45 When possible, omit a repeated preposition or object in favor of a compound construction, but don't if the omission would make the construction unparallel.

(a) *Compound object.* If a preposition might be repeated with a different object, the better style is to use the preposition once with a compound object—unless a miscue might otherwise occur.

> "And the idea that *and* must not begin a sentence, or even a paragraph, is an empty superstition. The same goes for *but*. Indeed either word can give unimprovably early warning of the sort of thing that is to follow."
>
> —*Kingsley Amis*

Ex.: Commercial speakers have extensive knowledge of the market and their products. (Rather than *of the market and of their products.*)

Ex.: The creditor may use the note to pay its own debts, sell to another creditor, or post as security for its own obligations. (Rather than repeating *to* before each infinitive phrase.)

Not this: The creditor may use the note to pay its own debts, sell to another creditor, or as security for its own obligations.

But this: The creditor may use the note to pay its own debts, to sell to another creditor, or as security for its own obligations.

Ex.: He insisted that textualism is preferable both to purposivism, with its amorphous boundaries, as he called them, and to consequentialism, which invites judges to engage in freewheeling policy-making. (This is an example of desirable repetition: the second *to* helps signal the parallel phrasing.)

(b) *Ambiguity.* If a compound object may confuse the reader, repeat the preposition instead.

Ex.: The defendant may meet the burden of coming forward with evidence by an independent showing or by reference to the presentence report. (Not *by an independent showing or reference to the presentence report* because a misreading would result.)

(c) *Compound prepositions.* When the object is repeated, it is usually better style to use compound prepositions with the single object.

Ex.: An easement of necessity gives the plaintiff the right to get on and off the landlocked property.

Ex.: The indictment charges the defendant with shoplifting a shirt from Wal-Mart on or about the night of July 3.

Conjunctions

11.46 A conjunction joins two or more words, phrases, clauses, or sentences. It may coordinate one element with another as equals <her LSAT score was high, *but* her GPA was average>, or subordinate one element to another <*although* her GPA was average, her high LSAT score got her accepted>.

Correlative conjunctions are used in pairs to introduce equal or alternative elements <both–and> <either–or> <neither–nor> <not only–but also>. Adverbs and adverbial phrases may also be used as conjunctions <consequently> <with the discovery phase of the lawsuit complete>.

11.47 Use a coordinating conjunction to join like elements.

(a) *Definition.* The main coordinating conjunctions are *and*, *but*, and *or*; also common are *nor*, *for*, *yet*, and *so*. They join words, phrases, clauses, and sentences of equal stature.

(b) *Punctuation.* Follow punctuation rules (see 1.3–1.4, 1.16(d)) when a coordinating conjunction joins like elements.

Ex.: "Last Words" is not vulgar, lewd, obscene, or plainly offensive. (Joining equal words.)

Ex.: Analysis of the "substantially limits" prong requires an individualized inquiry, guided by three independent considerations articulated by the EEOC: (1) the nature and severity of the impairment; (2) its duration; and (3) the expected long-term impact. (Joining equal phrases.)

Ex.: Felix explained that a § 1031 permit was conditioned on the provision of adequate insurance and bond, and that in light of Steele's recent bankruptcy, the City was concerned with his ability to provide adequate security. (Joining equal clauses.)

Ex.: A coowner may waive the right to refuse to join a suit to enforce a patent. But Holland never waived that right. (Equal sentences.)

11.48 When appropriate, begin a sentence with a coordinating conjunction to emphasize contrast (*but, yet*), additional support for a proposition (*and*), an alternative (*or*), or a logical conclusion (*so*).

(a) *Start of sentence.* The occasional use of a coordinating conjunction to begin a sentence is an effective rhetorical device. Avoid putting a comma after it (see 1.9(d)).

Ex.: But if appellants alleged that such a mandatory policy actually existed—without knowing whether it did or not—they would risk violating Rule 11.

Ex.: Yet those bargains would not be void. At most, they would be voidable if the buyer chose to challenge the seller.

Ex.: And thus we are confronted with the question, "What possible analogy could have been found between a wrongful act producing harm and a failure to act at all?"

(b) *Stuffiness.* The use of *for* in the same construction is archaic and sounds stuffy.

Ex.: For to hesitate is to lose.

11.49 Use a subordinating conjunction to join a dependent clause to the main clause of a complex sentence.

(a) *Definition.* In a complex sentence, a dependent (or *subordinate*) clause typically stands at the beginning or end of the sentence and serves an adverbial function by specifying when, where, or why the main clause takes effect <*after the house alarm went off*, neighbors reported hearing a car speed off down the street>. A dependent clause cannot stand alone as a sentence <after the house alarm went off> but depends on the main clause to complete its meaning. It may function in the complex sentence as a noun <when they settle is anybody's guess> or an adverb <call me when they settle>.

Ex.: Although Jarvis invested the money in legitimate mutual funds, he knew that he was potentially endangering Hagen's solvency by encouraging Hagen to invest with Penn Central. (*Although . . . funds* cannot stand on its own, but only because of the subordinating conjunction, *although*.)

(b) *To show relationships.* The conjunction shows a time, place, or manner relationship to the main clause, or a logical connection to the main clause.

Ex.: "Blue Laws" came to life in part thanks to labor, because unions wanted a shorter workweek and Sunday laws were a useful instrument. (The second, subordinate clause explains why (*because*) the first, main clause is true.)

Ex.: When a case came before Holmes in which he had to choose between the realist critique of his youth and his settled judicial doctrine, he chose orthodoxy. (The first, subordinate clause tells *when* the second, main clause is true.)

11.50 Make sure that correlative conjunctions frame sentence parts that match each other grammatically.

(a) *Definition.* Correlative conjunctions operate in pairs to show the relationship between matching elements or to join parallel clauses that together form a complete idea. These pairs may express concurrence <both–and> <neither–nor> <where–there> <not only–but also>, alternatives <either–or> <whether–or> <not–but>, comparison <as–as>, degree or extent <so–that>, a logical connection <although–yet> <if–then> <since–therefore>, or a sequence in time <once–then> <when–then>.

Ex.: These examples indicate the controversy that exists *both* between *and* within states as to the permissibility of scarlet-letter punishments.

(b) *Parallelism.* The elements must be the same part of speech, and if they are phrases or clauses they must be parallel in structure as well. One way to check for parallelism is to ensure that the same part of speech follows each half of the correlative pair.

Not this: We plan to either recoup our investment in the first three years or to sell the assets and move on.

But this: We plan to either recoup our investment in the first three years or sell the assets and move on.

Or this: We plan either to recoup our investment in the first three years or to sell the assets and move on.

"Interjections are among the least important of speech elements. Their discussion is valuable mainly because it can be shown that even they, avowedly the nearest of all language sounds to instinctive utterance, are only superficially of an instinctive nature."

—*Edward Sapir*

Not this: Under the Open Meetings Law, the public is *not only* entitled to attend governmental meetings, *but also* to be given notice of the time, place, and subject matter of those meetings.

But this: Under the Open Meetings Law, the public is entitled *not only* to attend governmental meetings, *but also* to be given notice of the time, place, and subject matter of those meetings.

Or this: Under the Open Meetings Law, the public *not only* is entitled to attend governmental meetings, *but also* must be given notice of the time, place, and subject matter of those meetings.

Interjections

11.51 Use interjections sparingly, if at all.

(a) *Definition.* Interjections are words or phrases that are, by definition, "thrown into" a sentence. They function absolutely—that is, with no connection to any other word or phrase in the sentence. They most often express exclamation <Oh!> <Now!> <Damn!> and stand alone with an exclamation mark or appear at the beginning of a sentence. But they may also be placed within a sentence, set apart by commas <oh> <uh> <well>.

(b) *Limited use.* Except for *Oyez! Oyez! Oyez!* and direct quotations, interjections have little place in most legal writing.

> "Nobody who thinks or writes can be above grammar. It is like saying, 'I'm a creative genius, I'm above concepts'—which is the attitude of modern artists. If you are 'above' grammar, you are 'above' concepts; and if you are 'above' concepts, you are 'above' thought. The fact is that then you are not above, but far below, thought. Therefore, make a religion of grammar."
>
> —*Ayn Rand*

§ 12
Stuffy Words and Legalese

12.1 Just because you know what *malum prohibitum* means or what a *habendum clause* does is no reason to use such language at the dinner table. A lawyer should keep in mind that the purpose of communication is to communicate, and this can't be done if the reader or listener doesn't understand the words used.

Some lawyers also tend to use words in peculiar ways, using *same* as a pronoun <plaintiff accepted the deed and signed *same*> and *said* as an adjective <driver struck *said* pedestrian>. Some pepper contracts and resolutions with *whereas*es and *wherefore*s. Harsher critics suggest that the impenetrable language serves the same purpose that mumbo-jumbo always has: to keep the public in the dark and protect a trade monopoly. Less severe critics chalk it up to professional inertia.

Fortunately, the trend today is toward plain language and away from the stuffiness and jargon-laced prose that characterized so much legal writing in the past. It's a welcome trend, and one that writing coaches universally encourage.

12.2 Use the simplest, most straightforward words that you can.

(a) *Plain English.* Language lovers often go through predictable phases of growth: first learning exotic new words and later avoiding them in favor of plain and clear terms. Using simple words and phrases instead of stuffy ones results in a more natural style.

(b) *Simple substitutes.* Choose simple words over fancy ones. Below is a necessarily limited list of dressed-up words and their simpler alternatives.

Instead of this:	**Try this:**
abutting	next to
accede to	allow; grant
accordingly	so
acquainted with	know
acquire	get
additional	more; extra; added; other
adjacent to	next to
administer (medicate)	give
administer	run; operate; manage; handle
advantageous	useful; helpful
advert to	refer to; note
advise	tell [unless you're giving advice]
afford	allow
all or part	any; some or all

Instead of this:	**Try this:**
alter	change
ameliorate	improve
apparent	plain
appellation	name
append	add; attach; enclose
approximately	about
ascertain	find out; make sure
assist; assistance	help
attain	reach; get; win; make
attempt	try; seek
attributable to	because of
augment; augmentation	increase
authored	wrote
automobile	car
cognizant	aware
commence	start; begin
comment	say
conceal	hide
concept	idea; plan
concerning	on; about; for
condign	fitting; deserving
conflagration	fire
conjecture	guess
consequently	so; thus
constitute	make up; form; be
consummate	utmost; best; top
contiguous to	next to
contumacious	contemptuous
converse	talk
couched	phrased
demonstrate	show
desideratum	wish; aim; goal
deteriorate	get worse; run down
determine	decide
dichotomy	split
directive	order
disadvantage	drawback
discontinue	stop
divers	various; several
domesticate	tame
dwell	live
dynamic	forceful
educator	teacher
elapse	pass; go by
elect to	choose to
elucidate	explain
eminently	highly

Instead of this:	Try this:
emphasize	stress; point out; highlight
endeavor	try
enthused	enthusiastic; excited
envisage	foresee; see; predict; look for
equanimity	poise
erroneous	wrong; incorrect; mistaken
erstwhile	former; formerly; once; one-time
eschew	avoid
essayed	tried; did
eventuality	event; possibility
eventually	in the end
evidencing	showing
evince	show
examination	exam; test; check; checkup
exceedingly	highly
excessively	too; unduly
exclusively	only
expenditure	cost; expense; payment
experiment	test
extended	long
extinguish	put out
facilitate	help; ease; make easier
favorable	good
following	after
fore	beginning; front
forward	send
frequently	often
fundamental	basic; main
furthermore	further
gainsay	deny
gratuitous	needless; free
impact	affect; influence
implement	carry out; set up
inaugurate	begin; start
inception	start; beginning
incongruous	unfitting; incoherent
inconsiderable	slight; small; little
indebtedness	debt

"Simple prose is clear prose. And simple prose, if smooth and rhythmical, is readable prose. Let your ideas alone do the impressing. If they look banal to you, there's only one remedy: upgrade them. Don't try to camouflage their weakness with razzle-dazzle rhetoric. You'll razzle-dazzle yourself right into a bog of bull." —*John R. Trimble*

Instead of this:	Try this:
indicate	say; mention; write; hint; suggest
indication	sign
indisposed to	reluctant to
individual	person
inform	tell
infringe on	infringe
inimical	adverse; hostile
initial	first; early
injudicious	unwise
instant [adj.]	this
intimate [vb.]	hint
intransigence	stubbornness
inundate	flood
inure (get used to)	adjust; accustom
inure (of a benefit)	mature; vest
kindly	please
lengthy	long
locality	place; town; city; village; county
modify; modification	change
multitudinous	many
narrate	tell
necessitous	needy
nevertheless	even so; still; but
notwithstanding	despite
numerous	many
obligate	bind
occupation	job; work; business
occur	happen
odor	smell
oftentimes; ofttimes	often
opportune	convenient; handy; proper
*orientate	orient
originate	start; come from
outcome	result
overall	whole; entire; total
overly	unduly; too
paradigm	model
partially	partly
participate	take part; go along; be one of
possibility	chance
practically	almost; nearly
precede	go before; come before
predecease	die before
presently	now; soon; in a moment
proceeded to (call)	called
procure	get

*An invariably inferior form.

Instead of this:	**Try this:**
prosecute (a business)	do; carry on; conduct (business)
purchase	buy
regarding	about
relocate	move
render	make; leave
request	ask
requisite	needed; required
reside	live
residence	house; apartment; address
respecting	for
schism	split
segment	part
significance	meaning; point
simultaneously	at the same time
subsequent	later
subsequently	later; after that; afterward; then
substantial	large
substantially	largely; much
supposition	belief; thought; idea
surmise	guess
susceptible of (a meaning)	open to; capable of
susceptible to (a threat)	prone to; vulnerable to
thrice	three times
transmit	send
ultimately	in the end
unto	to
utilize	use
vend	sell
wherewithal	means; money; ability

(c) *Paring down phrases.* By trimming your sentences you will make your prose tighter, more forceful, and more persuasive (see 14.3(e)). Wordy phrases are the biggest source of surplusage and can make your prose less clear, even confusing. For those reasons, these phrases are the first things to look for when you trim your drafts. Below are some common phrases used in legal writing and their simpler substitutions.

Instead of this:	**Try this:**
acquire knowledge	learn
adequate number of	enough
a large amount of	a lot of; much
a large number of	many
along the lines of	like; such as
am in receipt of	have
append a signature to	sign
as a consequence of	because of
as a matter of fact	in fact

Instead of this:	**Try this:**
as a means of ——ing	to ——
a small amount of	some; a little
a small number of	a few
as previously stated	again
as regards	about
at all times	always
at no time	never
at that point in time	then
at the place where	where
at the present time	now; today
at the time that	when; once
at the time when	when
at this juncture	now
at this point in time	now
because of the fact that	because; since
be determinative of	determine
by means of	by
by necessity	necessarily
by reason of	because of
by virtue of the fact that	because
cause injury to	injure
commensurate with	equal to; appropriate for
despite the fact that	although
due to the fact that	because
during such time as	while
during the course of	while
enclosed please find	enclosed is/are; I enclose; here is/are
excessive amount of	too much
excessive number of	too many
for the purpose of ——ing	to ——
for the reason that	because; since
for this reason	so; thus
have knowledge of	know
in a —— manner	——ly (with many adjectives)
in accordance with	under; according to
in addition to	besides; plus
inadequate amount of	too little
inadequate number of	too few
in an effort to	to
inasmuch as	because; since
in back of	behind
in conjunction with	with; along with
in connection with	regarding; about; for
in excess of	more than
in favor of	for
in furtherance of	furthering; to advance
in lieu of	instead of

Instead of this:	Try this:
in light of the fact that	because; since
in order that	so
in order to	to
in proximity to	near
in reference to	about
in regard to	about
in respect to	respecting
in spite of the fact that	although; though
in the amount of	for
in the course of	while; during
in the event of	if
in the event that	if
in the final analysis	finally
in the instant case	here; now
in the nature of	like
in the near future	soon
in the neighborhood of	around
in the vicinity of	near; around
is able to	can
is applicable	applies
is authorized to	may
is binding on	binds
is required to	must
is unable to	cannot
it is certain that	certainly; surely
it is probable that	probably
it would appear that	apparently
make a decision	decide
make an inquiry	ask
make an observation	comment; observe; watch
make reference to	refer to
notwithstanding the fact that	although
notwithstanding the foregoing	yet; but; nevertheless
on a daily basis	daily
on behalf of	for
on the ground that	because; since
on the part of	by
period of time	period; time
pertaining to	on; about
previous to	before
prior to	before
pursuant to	under
reach a resolution	resolve
subsequent to	after
sufficient amount of	enough
sufficient number of	enough
take into consideration	consider

Instead of this:	Try this:
the majority of	most
to the detriment of	harming; prejudicing
undertake an effort	try
under the provisions of	under
until such time as	until
with reference to	about
with regard to	about; regarding
with respect to	about; regarding
with the exception of	except for

(d) *Avoiding legalese.* Some legal writers cling to legalisms as if they were life preservers. The result is usually a confused client, and perhaps even an irritated judge as well. Good legal writers favor words that their intended readers—especially clients—will understand. Below is a list of legalisms and their plain-English translations.

Instead of this:	Try this:
ab initio	from the start
aforementioned	this; that; named earlier
aforesaid	this; that; named earlier
albeit	although; though
anent	about; concerning
antecedent to	before
anterior to	before
apprise	tell; inform
arguendo	for the sake of argument
aver	state
bestow	give
bona fide; bona fides	good faith
case at bar	here; this case
case sub judice	here; this case
cestui que trust	beneficiary (of a trust)
child en ventre sa mere	fetus; unborn child
de son tort	by (his or her) own wrongdoing
et al.; et alii	and others
ex contractu	in contract (law); contractual
ex delicto	in tort (law)
execution (will, contract)	signing
ex hypothesi	hypothetically
feral	wild
fora	forums
foregoing	above; previous
forthwith	immediately; now; at once
gravamen	crux; gist; burden
henceforth; henceforward	from now on
herein	here
heretofore; hitherto	up to now; until now; till now

Instead of this:	Try this:
in esse	in being
in haec verba	in these words; verbatim
instant case	this case
instanter	at once
inter alia	among other things
inter alios	among other people
inter partes	between parties
inter se	among themselves
lessee; leasee	tenant
lessor; leasor	landlord
mesne	intermediate
messuage	house, buildings, and land
negative [vb.]	negate
non compos mentis	insane
notwithstanding	despite; in spite of; even though
pray	request; ask for
pursuant to	under
remise	release; surrender
residue	rest; remainder
res nova	case of first impression
said [adj.]	the; this; that
same [pron.]	it [or the antecedent]
save	except
seisin	title; possession
shall	must
simpliciter	simply; considered by itself
style	name
subjoin	attach
such [adj.]	the; this; that
sui generis	one of a kind; unique
sui juris	legally competent
tabula rasa	clean slate
testament	will
testifier	witness
thence	from this; from that; from there
thenceforth; thenceforward	from then on
thereafter	afterward; from then on
thereat	there; at it
therefor	for it; for them
therefrom	away; from it; from that
therein	there; in it
thereof	of it
thereout	from it; from that; from them
theretofore	up to then; until then; till then
thereupon	then
these presents	this document
thitherto	up to then; until then; till then

This is one of the worst instances of legalese because it's the most common. → pursuant to

Instead of this:	Try this:
to wit	namely
vel non	or not; or the lack of it
vendee	buyer
vendor	seller
viz.	namely; that is
whence	from where
whensoever	whenever; at all
whereat	where
wherein	in which; where; when
whomsoever	whomever
whosoever	whoever

(e) *Useless verbiage.* Many terms and phrases continue to drift along in legal writing like so much deadwood in a stream. There is no reason anymore for writing "know all men by these presents." Watch out for the words and phrases below, and don't hesitate to dismiss them with prejudice.

It's needless in either form: *comes now* or *now comes.*

aforementioned
aforesaid
as a matter of fact
as such
as to
basically
clearly
comes now
for all purposes
for your information
further affiant saith [or *sayeth*] not [or *naught*]
hereinafter referred to as [*just place the defined term in parentheses*]
in any way
in connection with
in the above-styled and -numbered cause
in the final analysis
in the process of
it being the case that
it goes without saying that
it is apparent [clear] that
it is important to bear in mind that
know all men by these presents
needless to say
now comes
on the matters set forth herein
overall
the fact [of the matter] is
the fact that
veritable
whereas
wherefore, premises considered
witnesseth
would show that

(f) *Synonymia.* The doublet and triplet phrasing common in Middle English still survives in legal writing, especially contracts, wills, and trusts. That's probably the worst possible soil for it to grow in because those who interpret legal writing are impelled to strain for distinctions so that no word is rendered surplusage. Yet that is exactly what all but one word (and often *any* one word) in each of the following phrases is.

Doublets
act and deed
agree and covenant
agreed and declared
aid and abet
aid and comfort
all and singular
all and sundry
amount or quantum
annoy or molest
annul and set aside
answerable and accountable

any and all
appropriate and proper
as and for
attached and annexed
authorize and empower
betting or wagering
bills and notes
bind and obligate
by and between
by and under
by and with
canceled and set aside
cease and desist
cease and determine
chargeable and accountable
covenant and agree
custom and usage
deed and assurance
deem and consider
definite and certain
demises and leases
deposes and says
desire and require
do and perform
dominion and authority
due and owing
due and payable
each and all
each and every
ends and objects
escape and evade
exact and specific
execute and perform
false and untrue
final and conclusive
finish and complete
fit and proper
for and in behalf of
fraud and deceit
free and clear
from and after
full and complete
full faith and credit
full force and effect
good and effectual
good and tenantable
goods and chattels
have and hold
indemnify and hold harmless
keep and maintain
kind and character
kind and nature
known and described as
lay and levy
leave and license
legal and valid
liens and encumbrances
made and signed
maintenance and upkeep
make and enter into
make and execute
means and includes
messuage and dwelling-house
mind and memory
name and style
new and novel
nominate and appoint
null and of no effect
null and void
object and purpose
order and direct
other and further
over and above
pains and penalties
pardon and forgive
part and parcel
perform and discharge
power and authority

> "Simple English is no one's mother tongue. It has to be worked for."
> —*Jacques Barzun*

premeditation and malice aforethought
repair and make good
restrain and enjoin
reverts to and falls back upon
sale or transfer
save and except
seised and possessed of
sell or transfer
separate and apart
separate and distinct
set aside and vacate
shall and will
shun and avoid
similar and like
sole and exclusive
son and heir
successors and assigns
supersede and displace
surmise and conjecture
terms and conditions
then and in that event
title and interest
total and entire
touch and concern
true and correct
truth and veracity
type and kind
uncontroverted and uncontradicted
understood and agreed
unless and until
uphold and support
use and apply
various and sundry
will and testament

Triplets

cancel, annul, and set aside
form, manner, and method
general, vague, and indefinite
give, devise, and bequeath
grant, bargain, and sell
grants, demises, and lets
hold, possess, and enjoy
lands, tenements, and hereditaments
make, publish, and declare
name, constitute, and appoint
ordered, adjudged, and decreed
pay, satisfy, and discharge
possession, custody, and control
promise, agree, and covenant
remise, release, and forever discharge
remise, release, and forever quitclaim
repair, uphold, and maintain
rest, residue, and remainder
right, title, and interest
situate, lying, and being in
vague, nonspecific, and indefinite
way, shape, or form

> "With writers who use lofty language, people never *do* anything, they always *perform*. They don't *begin* a project; they *initiate* or *inaugurate* it; they don't *end* it; they *terminate* or *conclude* it. They don't *help*; they *render assistance*. And they don't *learn* or *find out*; they *ascertain*."
>
> —*Jerome H. Perlmutter*

12.3 For the sake of clarity and readability, avoid acronyms and initialisms that aren't well known.

Be slow and reluctant, not quick and eager, to adopt acronyms and initialisms with which readers are unlikely to be familiar.

12.4 Unless the context requires otherwise, use legal terms according to their specialized sense as terms of art.

(a) *Terms of art—Latin.* Some words are terms of art for lawyers—that is, they express specific legal ideas succinctly. Some are Latin terms such as *habeas corpus* and *res ipsa loquitur*, both of which have a rich legal history and aren't used outside law.

(b) *Terms of art—ordinary words with special legal senses.* Another type of term of art is an everyday word that takes on a new meaning when used in a legal context. Following is a collection of words that law students must relearn: they mean one thing to most people but often something completely different to a lawyer.

abstract. *Common meaning:* an adjective describing something theoretical rather than practical <abstract math> or interpretive rather than representative <abstract painting>. *In law:* a noun denoting a concise summary of a writing <abstract of title>.

acceleration. *Common meaning:* a speeding up. *In law:* the calling due of a mortgage or other loan, or the cutting off of an interest in property because of the failure of an estate.

accounting. *Common meaning:* the analysis of a company's financial condition. *In law:* also, a cause of action to settle accounts, recover money owed, or compensate for a breach of contract.

action. *Common meaning:* movement. *In law:* a legal proceeding <action to quiet title>.

adhesion. *Common meaning:* the sticking together of two things. *In law:* an adjective describing a contract that gives one party no bargaining power.

admiralty. *Common meaning:* a high rank in the navy. *In law:* maritime law, or an adjective describing any court that is hearing a suit in maritime.

affirmation. *Common meaning:* confirmation that something is true, or a motivational statement. *In law:* a secular counterpart to an oath, typically worded "do you swear or affirm . . . ?"

alibi. *Common meaning:* any excuse to avoid blame for something. *In law:* the specific defense of proving that the defendant was somewhere else when the crime was committed.

allowance. *Common meaning:* money, especially a weekly stipend from one's parents. *In law:* money set aside for a purpose; a court's compensation for the services of a fiduciary such as a trustee; or a tax deduction <oil-depletion allowance>.

alter ego. *Common meaning:* a second identity; a very close friend. *In law:* a business entity being used fraudulently to disguise the owner's dealings while protecting the owner from liability.

ancient. *Common meaning:* very old, as of the Roman Empire and earlier. *In law:* about 20 years old, for purposes of authenticating a writing to be introduced as evidence, or establishing an easement restricting both landowners from removing a shared stone wall.

answer. *Common meaning:* a reply to a question. *In law:* a response to either a pleading or a request for discovery <respondent has 20 days to file an answer>.

appearance. *Common meaning:* what you look like. *In law:* attendance in a courtroom, especially for purposes of establishing personal jurisdiction.

appropriation. *Common meaning:* money allocated for a certain purpose, especially by a legislature. *In law:* (1) private property taken away, especially by a court; (2) the privacy tort of making commercial use of another person's name or likeness; or (3) the acquiring of water rights in states that adhere to the appropriation doctrine.

artisan. *Common meaning:* a skilled craftsperson. *In law:* a contractor or mechanic <artisan's lien>; or, in patent law, "a person of ordinary skill in the art," be it industrial design or biochemistry.

assault. *Common meaning:* a physical attack. *In law:* at common law (but not under modern penal statutes), the act of putting someone in reasonable fear of a physical attack or offensive touching (i.e., battery).

assignment. *Common meaning:* a task or an appointment to a position. *In law:* the transfer of one person's legal interest in property to another person <assignment of account>, or an appellant's charge that the trial court made a mistake <assignment of error>.

assumption. *Common meaning:* something taken for granted. *In law:* the taking on of another person's debt or liability <assumption of a loan> <assumption of risk>.

attachment. *Common meaning:* one thing stuck to another thing, or affection for another person. *In law:* seizure of property to secure or satisfy a money judgment <attachment of wages>.

author. *Common meaning:* a person who writes a book, article, or the like. *In law:* for copyright purposes, the creator of almost any creative work, such as a painting, sculpture, choreography, or computer software.

avoid. *Common meaning:* to dodge or elude something. *In law:* to make something void, such as to make a contract unenforceable or to annul a marriage.

bankrupt. *Common meaning:* an adjective describing an insolvent person. *In law:* as easily, a noun for the debtor.

bargain. *Common meaning:* something bought at a discounted price; a good buy; to dicker over a price. *In law:* an agreement between two people for the exchange of promises or performances <benefit of the bargain>.

basis. *Common meaning:* the fundamental principle on which other things stand. *In law:* the amount that a taxpayer has invested in a capital asset, as used in calculating gains and losses for tax purposes.

bill. *Common meaning:* a statement of an amount owed. *In law:* a pleading to a court of equity, similar to a complaint or pleading in a court of law <bill of exceptions>; a proposed statute.

blackletter. *Common meaning:* (as two words) a thick Gothic or Old English typeface. *In law:* an adjective designating a well-settled principle of law <blackletter law>.

bona fide. *Common meaning:* genuine; real. *In law:* done in good faith <bona fide effort at mediation>.

camera. *Common meaning:* a device for taking photographs. *In law:* a judge's chambers, in the phrase *in camera.*

caption. *Common meaning:* text under a picture in a publication. *In law:* the identification of a lawsuit by the parties' names, the court, the docket number, and the cause of action.

chose. *Common meaning:* selected among alternatives. *In law:* (pronounced /shohz/) an item of personal property; also, a thing, whether tangible or intangible (such as a right).

churning. *Common meaning:* stirring up, as with water, or turning cream into butter. *In law:* the wrongful practice of a professional, especially a stockbroker, in performing unnecessary work for a client to pad the fee.

code. *Common meaning:* a system of encryption for transmitting secret messages. *In law:* an organized system of statutes or regulations <United States Code>.

color. *Common meaning:* a hue. *In law:* the appearance of authority or a right <under color of state law>.

colorable. *Common meaning:* capable of being colored. *In law:* apparently true and valid <a colorable claim on an estate>, or intentionally deceptive <a colorable transfer of property to avoid taxes>.

common. *Common meaning:* shared; familiar; inferior; vulgar. *In law:* a right to use the property of another, such as the common areas of a rental property.

community. *Common meaning:* collectively, people who live in a distinct area or who share a common interest. *In law:* also, in community-property states, the marriage itself <fraud on the community>.

competency. *Common meaning:* competence; an area of competence. *In law:* narrowly, the mental ability to understand one's circumstance and to make decisions to assist in one's own defense; a competency hearing determines whether a defendant can be put on trial.

complaint. *Common meaning:* a grievance. *In law:* the plaintiff's initial pleading in a civil lawsuit, or a formal charge against a criminal defendant.

composition. *Common meaning:* an arrangement of things, such as an essay or a piece of music. *In law:* an agreement by creditors to accept less than everything the debtor owes them.

compound. *Common meaning:* to increase in value, as interest on invested money; or to make worse, as an error. *In law:* also, to forgo prosecuting a criminal defendant in exchange for a bribe <compounding a felony is itself a felony>.

conclude. *Common meaning:* to finish; to deduce. *In law:* also, to formalize an agreement <conclude a contract>; to bar or estop <the admission concluded our main line of defense>.

condemn. *Common meaning:* to denounce. *In law:* to pronounce a criminal defendant guilty; to take private property for a public purpose; to declare a structure uninhabitable; to declare food or water unfit for human consumption.

connive. *Common meaning:* to conspire. *In law:* more specifically, to look the other way while a wrong is being done, while under a duty to stop or report it <the night manager connived at the pilferage of other employees>.

consideration. *Common meaning:* respect; kindness; thought. *In law:* something of value or a legal detriment promised in exchange for another person's contractual promise or performance.

consortium. *Common meaning:* a collection of companies working together toward a common goal. *In law:* a family member's companionship, love, help, and (of a spouse) capacity for sexual relations, the loss of which may provide a cause of action in tort for the other spouse.

construction. *Common meaning:* the building of a structure. *In law:* the construing of a writing, especially a statute, will, contract, or deed <the plaintiff offers a strained construction of the agreement>.

constructive. *Common meaning:* positive; promoting further development. *In law:* irrebuttably established by operation of law <constructive knowledge>; established by a legal fiction to craft a remedy <constructive trust>.

continuance. *Common meaning:* the state of remaining in the same state; a sequel. *In law:* postponement of a trial or other judicial proceeding until another date.

contort. *Common meaning:* (accent on the second syllable) to twist out of shape, especially one's body. *In law:* (accent on the first syllable) a cause of action that includes aspects of contract law and tort law.

contribution. *Common meaning:* a donation. *In law:* (1) the right of a tortfeasor who has paid more than a proportionate share of a judgment to recover the excess from other liable defendants; or (2) the right of a cotenant who has paid more than a proportionate share for upkeep to recover from other cotenants.

conversion. *Common meaning:* the changing from one form into another, or adopting a new religion. *In law:* the act of treating the property of another as one's own, as by possessing it or disposing of it.

conveyance. *Common meaning:* a means of transportation. *In law:* the transfer of interest in real property from one person to another, or the document by which the transfer is accomplished.

cover. *Common meaning:* a lid or blanket. *In law:* the purchase of goods to replace those not supplied because of a breach of contract, with the right to recover costs in excess of the contracted price.

coverage. *Common meaning:* reporting of an event, or the extent to which something is covered, such as by paint. *In law:* protection by insurance against risk.

curator. *Common meaning:* a museum manager. *In law:* (in some jurisdictions) a guardian or conservator.

cure. *Common meaning:* to restore physical health. *In law:* to restore legal "health," as by remedying defects in a title or by replacing nonconforming goods rejected by the buyer.

damages. *Common meaning:* more than one type or incident of damage. *In law:* the money that a defendant is ordered to pay a plaintiff to compensate for the harm caused.

dedication. *Common meaning:* commitment; the addressing of something (e.g., a book) to someone. *In law:* a gift of private property for public use, such as a public road or park.

defective. *Common meaning:* inoperable or dangerous because of a flaw in design or manufacture. *In law:* also, describing an insufficiency in a legal process <defective service of notice>.

demean. *Common meaning:* to debase someone or oneself. *In law:* in the term's original sense, as used in the lawyer's oath of office, "to behave" (here, to behave in an upright manner); that archaic sense lives on in the word *demeanor.*

demise. *Common meaning:* death. *In law:* a lease (either the document or the legal relationship); the conveyance of a decedent's property to another person, either through a will or by intestacy; or a conveyance by lease, as distinguished from a devise.

demur. *Common meaning:* to object, take exception, or decline (or confused with *demure,* the adjective meaning "coy"). *In law:* to admit all the facts in a plaintiff's petition while denying that they state a claim on which relief can be granted (today's demurrer is most often called a *motion to dismiss*).

depose. *Common meaning:* to dethrone a monarch. *In law:* to take someone's testimony in a sworn deposition; to testify.

determine; determinable; determination. *Common meaning:* all have to do with deciding something. *In law:* all have to do with ending (terminating) something, usually an interest in property <fee simple determinable> <cease and determine>.

detour. *Common meaning:* a rerouted street. *In law:* not a frolic (see below), but an employee's minor departure from business for personal reasons; the employer remains liable for the employee's torts on a detour.

devise. *Common meaning:* to think up a scheme for doing something. *In law:* to pass on property to someone through a will; or, as a noun, that property, the provision in the will, or the will itself.

digest. *Common meaning:* a book of articles and stories condensed from another source and republished. *In law:* a systematic collection of case excerpts, arranged by legal subjects and the propositions that the case holdings support.

> "If . . . we are to be governed by written instructions and regulations the time has come when we, as a public, should demand that they be written in the best and simplest English."
> —*B. Ifor Evans*

dignitary. *Common meaning:* a person of rank. *In law:* describing a type of tort that compensates the plaintiff for an insult or humiliation rather than for a personal injury or property damage <invasion of privacy is a dignitary tort>.

dilution. *Common meaning:* the watering down of a liquid. *In law:* a weakening by a variety of means, such as by gerrymandering (voting power), selling more stock (per-share value), or using a famous name for an unrelated product (trademark distinctiveness).

disability. *Common meaning:* a debilitating physical condition. *In law:* a legal incapacity, such as being a minor and therefore unable to contract.

discovery. *Common meaning:* the finding of something new. *In law:* (1) pretrial investigation of information held by the other party; (2) the means of carrying out that investigation, such as written and live questioning of parties and witnesses, disclosure of documents, physical and mental examinations, and on-site visits; or (3) the pretrial period set aside for the investigations.

disinterested. *Common meaning:* not interested (as many people understand the word). *In law:* having no personal or financial interest at stake, and therefore able to render a fair and impartial decision.

disposition. *Common meaning:* demeanor or inclination. *In law:* the distribution of an estate according to either instructions in a will or an intestacy statute; also, a final determination in a proceeding.

distress. *Common meaning:* anguish. *In law:* seizure of property to secure a debt; the property seized; a court order for such a seizure <distress sale>.

domicile. *Common meaning:* one's home. *In law:* the jurisdiction (especially the state) in which a person intends to stay, even if currently residing elsewhere, or where a corporation either is incorporated or has its main place of business.

entail. *Common meaning:* to require. *In law:* to limit the ability of heirs to divest real property by specifying that title pass to the offspring (or just sons or daughters) of the original owner and the heirs.

equity. *Common meaning:* ownership; the difference between the value of a property and the amount owed on it. *In law:* justice based on principles of fairness rather than statute and common law; remedies other than money damages.

execute. *Common meaning:* to carry out something; to put someone to death. *In law:* also, to sign a will or contract; to collect on a money judgment.

exemplary. *Common meaning:* serving as a good example to be emulated. *In law:* serving as a bad example to deter others from similar behavior <exemplary damages>.

expectant. *Common meaning:* pregnant. *In law:* contingent, said of an interest in property.

facial. *Common meaning:* of the face; a beauty treatment. *In law:* of a challenge to a statute on the basis that it is unconstitutional on its face (always unconstitutional); of an attack on a complaint as insufficient to state a claim; readily apparent.

fact. *Common meaning:* a true thing. *In law:* a thing that a jury or a judge (in a bench trial) has determined to be true, whether it really is or not <findings of fact>.

factor. *Common meaning:* a thing to be considered. *In law:* also, a commission merchant, a garnishee, or a discount buyer of accounts receivable.

fee. *Common meaning:* a charge for a service. *In law:* an inheritable and transferable interest in real property.

fixation. *Common meaning:* a preoccupation or obsession with something or someone. *In law:* the recording of a creator's work in tangible form, as is required by federal law for copyright protection.

foreign. *Common meaning:* of another country. *In law:* also, of another jurisdiction, especially another state <a judgment from a foreign court>.

fraud. *Common meaning:* loosely, anything false. *In law:* rigorously, a deception carried out deliberately and successfully to induce someone to do something to his or her own detriment.

frolic. *Common meaning:* merrymaking. *In law:* not a detour (see above), but an employee's major departure from business for personal reasons; the employer is not liable for an employee's tort on a frolic because the employee is outside the scope of employment.

garnish. *Common meaning:* something added to a plate of food to add color, ornamentation, or flavor. *In law:* to attach property being held by a third party (such as wages held by an employer), to pay the owner's debt (such as delinquent child support).

hearsay. *Common meaning:* loosely, a rumor. *In law:* rigorously, testimony about a statement, writing, or other assertion made outside court and offered into evidence to prove the truth of its content.

heir. *Common meaning:* loosely, anyone who inherits from an estate. *In law:* more precisely, someone who inherits by intestate succession rather than by will.

holding. *Common meaning:* of a court decision, the outcome; (pl.) a person's or company's assets. *In law:* of a court decision, a ruling on a question of law necessary for the outcome, as distinct from a finding of fact or a comment on a nonessential question of law (obiter dictum).

holograph. *Common meaning:* by error from *holography*, a hologram or three-dimensional image. *In law:* a writing done entirely in the maker's handwriting, especially a will or deed.

homicide. *Common meaning:* a crime of murder or manslaughter. *In law:* not necessarily a crime, but any killing of one human being by another, including a lawful killing such as one done in self-defense.

ignore. *Common meaning:* to deliberately disregard. *In law:* of a grand jury, to decline to indict an accused person (return a no bill), especially on the basis that the charge is groundless or the evidence insufficient.

impeachment. *Common meaning:* a formal charge against a government official, especially a president or judge (but not, as many believe, the removal from office). *In law:* a challenge to the veracity of a witness or the reliability of documentary evidence.

impertinent. *Common meaning:* rude. *In law:* irrelevant, especially said of matter contained in a pleading that does not pertain to any issue material to the cause of action.

implication. *Common meaning:* an inference from one truth of what else must necessarily be true. *In law:* an involvement or connection, especially with a scheme of misconduct or crime.

impossibility. *Common meaning:* inability to exist at all. *In law:* the doctrine in contract law that excuses a party from meeting an obligation because a presupposed condition has failed for any of a variety of reasons, some well short of physical impossibility.

indorse. *Common meaning:* an alternative spelling of *endorse*; to support. *In law:* to sign on the back, especially the back of a check or other negotiable instrument.

infant. *Common meaning:* a baby. *In law:* as easily, a strapping 17-year-old fullback; a minor (under 18 in most jurisdictions), with the legal disability of infancy.

infection. *Common meaning:* contamination by disease. *In law:* contamination by crime or contraband <a cargo infected by any amount of smuggled drugs subjects the entire ship to seizure>.

information. *Common meaning:* knowledge. *In law:* a charging instrument filed by a prosecutor without the need of a grand-jury indictment, often used for misdemeanors but also used by many states for felonies.

initiative. *Common meaning:* readiness to lead or start an activity. *In law:* a procedure, available in some states, that allows voters to propose a law and force a vote on it by the legislature or by the electorate at large.

injury. *Common meaning:* a physical bodily trauma. *In law:* any violation of a legal right, including one that results in property damage or economic loss <the breach of contract was a civil injury redressable by money damages>.

innuendo. *Common meaning:* a suggestive comment, usually with a sexual or derogatory connotation. *In law:* a statement in an indictment more fully explaining the charge, or in a pleading of defamation explaining why the words said by the defendant were actionable.

integrated. *Common meaning:* not separated, especially by race or gender. *In law:* of a contract, containing the final agreements between parties and, if fully integrated, all the agreements <the court will not hear extrinsic evidence to challenge a fully integrated contract>.

interference. *Common meaning:* the meddling in or obstruction of something. *In law:* also, a patent-office proceeding to determine which of two or more applicants claiming the same invention is the first inventor.

interrogatory. *Common meaning:* a question. *In law:* more specifically, a set of written questions addressed to the opposing party in the discovery phase of a lawsuit <rules of procedure govern how many questions may be asked in an interrogatory>.

intervention. *Common meaning:* a stepping in to stop or settle a problem. *In law:* more specifically, the entering of a lawsuit by a third party to protect that party's independent interests.

invest. *Common meaning:* to put money into something with an expectation of financial gain. *In law:* to confer a legal interest, right, or authority in someone <the will invests the spouse with sole title to the homestead>.

judgment. *Common meaning:* appraisal (of a situation), especially prudent appraisal. *In law:* a court's final ruling on the outcome of a lawsuit.

knowledge. *Common meaning:* actual awareness. *In law:* notice, whether perceived or not; sometimes a person will be deemed to have constructive knowledge regardless of subjective awareness, as when a public record exists that the person should have found.

lapse. *Common meaning:* a gap or termination. *In law:* also, the failure of a gift in a will because the beneficiary predeceased the maker of the will.

leakage. *Common meaning:* loss of a liquid from a faulty container. *In law:* the decline in value of a copyrighted work because of unauthorized copying <recording artists see leakage by Internet piracy as a major threat to their livelihood>.

legacy. *Common meaning:* the reputation one leaves behind; to a college or university, the child of a prominent graduate. *In law:* a gift in a will of personal property or, less frequently, money.

letters. *Common meaning:* written communications. *In law:* a document formally granting some authority or right <letters patent>.

liable. *Common meaning:* likely (to occur); apt (to happen). *In law:* legally responsible for damages.

lie. *Common meaning:* to recline; to tell a falsehood. *In law:* of a cause of action, to have merit in an area of law <a remedy will lie in tort for a customer injured because of a shopkeeper's negligence>.

limitations. *Common meaning:* restrictions or boundaries. *In law:* a period set by statute for a criminal offense or a cause of action, beyond which time any prosecution or lawsuit is barred <statute of limitations>.

malice. *Common meaning:* hatred, spite, ill will. *In law:* a term of art with different meanings in different areas of law, but generally meaning either intent to do harm or a reckless disregard of a known, high risk that harm would result.

mandate. *Common meaning:* a strong electoral victory. *In law:* an order from an appellate court to a lower court, directing it how to proceed with the case; a judicial command to a court officer to carry out a court order.

mayhem. *Common meaning:* rioting, bedlam, disorder, even rowdy merrymaking. *In law:* historically, the common-law felony of intentionally crippling someone or cutting off a limb so as to deny the king his services as a soldier; in modern times, maiming.

misadventure. *Common meaning:* an accident or misfortune. *In law:* the accidental killing of a person by someone acting lawfully and bearing no malicious intent.

moot. *Common meaning:* beside the point, so not worth debating. *In law:* unsettled, so worth debating as a hypothetical (archaic except in the term *moot court*); but also not debatable because another issue has already decided the outcome on other grounds <a moot point>.

notice. *Common meaning:* sensory awareness of something. *In law:* as easily, no awareness at all, but just a good reason why one should have become aware (*constructive notice*) because, for example, a public record existed or because a reasonable person would have thought to ask.

notorious. *Common meaning:* infamous; widely known for some evil or misdeed. *In law:* of common knowledge, so that anyone with an adverse interest is deemed to have been on notice <open and notorious possession>.

offset. *Common meaning:* a degree of separation between two things, or a thing, element, or agent that balances, counteracts, or compensates for something else. *In law:* a person's claim or potential right to something that in some measure counterbalances someone else's claim or right against that person, such as mutual liabilities in a pledge relationship.

option. *Common meaning:* a choice. *In law:* a contract to hold an offer open for a specified time.

paper. *Common meaning:* a document or report. *In law:* a negotiable instrument <bearer paper is payable to anyone with possession of it>.

partition. *Common meaning:* a room divider. *In law:* a dividing of two or more people's joint or common interest in a single property, either by splitting the land into tracts or by selling the property and splitting the proceeds.

party. *Common meaning:* a festive gathering. *In law:* a legal entity bound by a contract or subject to the outcome of a lawsuit.

perfect. *Common meaning:* to achieve something's final form. *In law:* to conform with a law by correctly finishing all steps necessary to secure a record, or to protect an interest.

perfection. *Common meaning:* the pinnacle of quality. *In law:* the validation of a security interest as against other creditors, usually by filing a financing statement or by taking possession of the collateral.

performance. *Common meaning:* an artistic presentation. *In law:* the carrying out of a contract obligation <a unilateral contract can be accepted only by the performance of the thing sought by the offeror>.

permissive. *Common meaning:* tolerant of behavior that others might object to. *In law:* permissible, especially of claims that may or may not be joined in a suit as the party wishes <permissive counterclaim>; wrongfully permitted <permissive waste>.

person. *Common meaning:* a human being. *In law:* a legal being, either a born human being or a legal entity such as a corporation.

personality. *Common meaning:* a person's unique demeanor, and especially a friendly disposition. *In law:* the status of being a person (born human, corporation, or other entity) as recognized by law.

pledge. *Common meaning:* a promise. *In law:* property put in a creditor's possession as security for a debt <pawn is the most common form of pledge security>.

positive. *Common meaning:* certain. *In law:* formally enacted or established, as opposed to customary or natural <positive law>; by an act, as opposed to by an omission <positive misprision>.

prefer. *Common meaning:* to favor one thing over another. *In law:* to bring a charge against a criminal defendant, or to present a case to a grand jury <prefer charges>.

preference. *Common meaning:* the tendency to favor one thing over another. *In law:* a transfer of money or property to a creditor by an insolvent person or company before filing for bankruptcy, to the detriment of other creditors.

prejudice. *Common meaning:* to evoke a bias, especially one based on emotions. *In law:* to put one at a legal disadvantage; to impair a legal right or a cause of action <disallowing this evidence will unfairly prejudice our case>.

prescription. *Common meaning:* an instructed course of action, especially a regimen of medicine. *In law:* a rule or set of rules; also, the gain or loss of title by long-term open and notorious possession or by prolonged nonuse <easement by prescription>.

presents. *Common meaning:* gifts. *In law:* [*pl.*] an instrument; the term is part of the archaic and meaningless clause "know all men by these presents."

presumption. *Common meaning:* an assumption, especially based on some evidence. *In law:* procedurally, an inference based on some evidence; a legal presumption carries some weight by shifting the burden of producing contrary or conflicting evidence to the other party.

privilege. *Common meaning:* a benefit granted, as opposed to a right. *In law:* a right (1) of immunity from forced testimony <attorney–client privilege>; (2) of immunity from tort liability <affirmative defense of privilege>; or (3) to a specially conferred exception to a duty <work-product privilege>.

privy. *Common meaning:* an outhouse. *In law:* a person with a legal interest in a transaction.

process. *Common meaning:* a way of doing something. *In law:* a writ or summons, especially to answer a petition or to appear in court <original process>.

profit. *Common meaning:* a net financial gain. *In law:* also, a nonpossessory interest in land, giving one the right to fish, cut timber, mine minerals, let animals graze, or in some other way remove things.

progeny. *Common meaning:* a person's descendants. *In law:* a line of court decisions stemming from and further developing a landmark holding <*New York Times v. Sullivan* and its progeny>.

prohibition. *Common meaning:* the banning of something, especially alcohol. *In law:* a writ from a higher court to a lower court ordering it to stop proceedings that exceed the lower court's jurisdiction.

publish. *Common meaning:* to put a writing or a musical composition on the market. *In law:* to declare a will to contain the maker's true intentions; to show the jury evidence during a trial; to make a defamatory statement to a third person.

puffing. *Common meaning:* blowing, panting. *In law:* hyping; in the law of false advertising, expressing an overblown opinion as contrasted with stating an unsubstantiated or misleading claim as a fact.

quiet. *Common meaning:* to silence. *In law:* to secure a title to property or another legal right by having potential challenges declared invalid <action to quiet title>.

quit. *Common meaning:* to resign. *In law:* to leave rented property <quit the premises>.

raise. *Common meaning:* to increase or to bring up. *In law:* also, to alter a check so that it purports to pay more than the maker intended <a raised check>.

real. *Common meaning:* actual, genuine. *In law:* of land and buildings; of the type of property that is fixed and immovable, in contrast with personal property (chattels) <real estate; real action>.

recall. *Common meaning:* to remember something, or a manufacturer's calling back of products to repair a defect. *In law:* a petition and election to remove someone from public office, or retraction of a court's judgment or mandate, usually to correct errors.

receiver. *Common meaning:* a telephone handset or a football player. *In law:* a neutral party assigned to take possession of assets that are being litigated or are involved in a bankruptcy proceeding.

recital. *Common meaning:* an artistic performance, especially by music or dance students; repetition of poetry or prose, especially to an audience. *In law:* a statement in a contract or deed, identifying the parties and summarizing the facts and circumstances surrounding the transaction (once introduced by *whereas* and *therefore*, but that usage is fading).

recover. *Common meaning:* to get over, as an illness; to get back, as a cost or a loss. *In law:* to win money damages in a lawsuit; to collect on a judgment.

rectify. *Common meaning:* to make right. *In law:* for a court: (1) to change ambiguous or misstated wording in a contract or deed to enforce the intent of the parties; or (2) to make minor textual changes in a statute to carry out its purpose.

reduction. *Common meaning:* the process of making something smaller. *In law:* as used in the patent-law phrase *reduction to practice*, the refinement of an inventive concept to the point at which a prototype or sample has been or could be made.

reform. *Common meaning:* to change a system to get rid of corruption or to bring it up to date. *In law:* to change the wording of a writing such as a contract or deed, to make it enforceable or to carry out the intent of the makers.

regress. *Common meaning:* to backslide; to revert to a lesser state. *In law:* the reentering of a place, or the right to do so <an easement of ingress, egress, and regress>.

rehabilitation. *Common meaning:* therapy for a dependency, a physical handicap, or criminal tendencies. *In law:* restoration of a witness's credibility after it has been impeached by the other side; reorganization of a bankrupt's finances.

relief. *Common meaning:* solace or charity. *In law:* a remedy, especially an equitable remedy such as injunction or rescission.

remainder. *Common meaning:* what's left over. *In law:* what's left after a will's specific instructions are carried out; also, a third party's future interest in real property, an interest that will become possessory upon the natural termination of the intervening estate.

removal. *Common meaning:* eviction. *In law:* the transferring of a lawsuit from a state court to a federal court, either for good cause and the petition of a defendant or because the suit involves a violation of civil rights.

repose. *Common meaning:* restful serenity, a nap. *In law:* a permanent cutoff period for lawsuits over a certain matter <statute of repose>, or the doctrine that a final judgment, plus any appeal, should bar all further legal proceedings.

repugnant. *Common meaning:* repulsive. *In law:* inconsistent, contradictory, not reconcilable <a race-based classification repugnant to the Fourteenth Amendment>.

return. *Common meaning:* generally, a coming back. *In law:* specifically, the return of a process, writ, or other court document, along with the server's report of what was found or done <return of writ>; a report <tax return; election returns>.

reversion. *Common meaning:* a return to a previous state or behavior. *In law:* the automatic return of an interest in property to a grantor who has conveyed less than the entire interest the grantor owns <the owner of a fee simple who grants a life estate retains a reversion>.

rider. *Common meaning:* one who rides something. *In law:* a supplemental writing attached to a proposed statute, an insurance policy, or some other document, adding further provisions to the main document.

ripeness. *Common meaning:* of a fruit or vegetable, the state of being fully matured and ready to pick. *In law:* of a dispute, the state of being developed to a point at which judicial intervention is warranted; the constitutional "case or controversy" doctrine of avoiding premature adjudication.

salting. *Common meaning:* seasoning. *In law:* a labor-union practice of getting a union member (the "salt") employed at a nonunion shop with the intention of organizing the workers and calling for a collective-bargaining election.

savor. *Common meaning:* to enjoy the taste or experience of something. *In law:* to take on the character of or to be closely associated with something <a death savoring of foul play; an interest in property savors of the realty>.

schedule. *Common meaning:* a timetable or itinerary. *In law:* an attachment to a document, itemizing things or detailing matters referred to in the main document <Schedule A is an inventory of business assets>.

seal. *Common meaning:* (1) to close tightly, or (2) an aquatic mammal. *In law:* a distinctive impression used to authenticate a document; at common law, a seal rendered contract obligations indisputable, but that distinction is gone today in most jurisdictions <contract under seal>.

seasonable. *Common meaning:* just right for the season. *In law:* timely; within the time specified in a contract or, if no time is specified, within a reasonable length of time.

secrete. *Common meaning:* to discharge, as a gland produces a bodily fluid. *In law:* to conceal and keep secret <the defendant secreted the documents to avoid their discovery>.

security. *Common meaning:* safety. *In law:* collateral for a loan; any interest or instrument relating to finances; a note, stock, bond, debenture, certificate of deposit, etc.

seduction. *Common meaning:* any person's nonviolent persuasion of another person to have sex. *In law:* at common law, a man's nonviolent persuasion of a previously chaste woman to have sex.

self-help. *Common meaning:* a genre of publishing centered on motivational and self-improvement tips. *In law:* a nonlegal remedy for a wrong; e.g., methods outlined in the UCC for merchants to deal with breaches of contract without going to court.

servant. *Common meaning:* a domestic employee; an employee with a high duty of loyalty and service <public servant>. *In law:* any employee <master–servant relationship>.

service. *Common meaning:* assistance; rite; repair. *In law:* the formal delivery to someone of a legal paper such as a pleading, a summons, or a writ <service of process>.

set aside. *Common meaning:* to put to one side; to earmark funds for some purpose. *In law:* to overturn a conviction or to vacate a judgment or court order <the appellate court set aside the damages judgment and remanded the case for relitigation on that issue>.

setback. *Common meaning:* a reversal of fortune. *In law:* a minimum distance that must be preserved between property lines and any building erected on the lot, as specified in a deed or a zoning ordinance.

setoff. *Common meaning:* a counterbalancing thing or quality, such as a complementary color in a room-decor plan or an auxiliary typeface in graphic arts. *In law:* a counterclaim in a lawsuit, as when a defendant or a debtor seeks compensation from the plaintiff or creditor, perhaps in an unrelated matter.

several. *Common meaning:* a few. *In law:* referring to the liability of multiple tortfeasors or contracting partners, separate rather than joint; severable, so that each defendant or party is responsible for only a share of the potential liability.

shrinkage. *Common meaning:* the process of shrinking. *In law:* loss of inventory that is due to things like pilferage, spoilage, breakage, and unavoidable loss.

sidebar. *Common meaning:* a supplemental and related article published along with a main article. *In law:* the side of a judge's bench where the judge and lawyers can talk but the jury can't hear; a conference held at that place.

signal. *Common meaning:* a sign. *In law:* in a legal citation, an introductory word or phrase that tells the reader how the citation relates to the statement in the text; common signals are *see*, *see also*, *but see*, *see generally*, *compare . . . with*, *cf.*, *accord*, and *contra*.

signature. *Common meaning:* a person's handwritten name. *In law:* as easily, under the UCC, a logo on a letterhead or fax cover sheet, an electronic signature, or any other mark used with the intention of authenticating a writing.

simple. *Common meaning:* easy. *In law:* of an estate, unconditionally inheritable and assignable <fee simple>; of a crime, not aggravated by use of a deadly weapon or other consideration <simple assault>; of a contract, not made under seal <simple contract>.

simultaneous. *Common meaning:* of two events, happening at the same time. *In law:* of two deaths, happening within 120 hours of each other, for the purpose of construing wills under the Uniform Simultaneous Death Act and the Uniform Probate Code.

specification. *Common meaning:* a detailed listing, as of materials, parts, steps, and the like. *In law:* the taking of title to property by innocently converting it to another form, such as wood into furniture or grapes into wine; in patent law, a detailed description of how an invention is made and used.

standing. *Common meaning:* status, rank. *In law:* the state of having enough of a stake in a controversy to support asking a court for a remedy; to have standing, a party must have suffered an actual injury related to the zone of interests that a law was intended to protect.

stay. *Common meaning:* to stop or remain. *In law:* more specifically, to suspend a legal proceeding or execution of an order, usually pending some further deliberation <stay of execution>.

strike. *Common meaning:* to hit; to stop work in a labor dispute. *In law:* to dismiss a potential juror; to expunge statements from a trial record <motion to strike the witness's last statement>.

style. *Common meaning:* fashion, flair, manner, rhetoric. *In law:* a case name <the complete style of the case is *Vanna White v. Samsung Electronics America, Inc.*>.

surcharge. *Common meaning:* an added tax, especially a steep one. *In law:* also, a second mortgage, a fiduciary's liability to a court for misconduct, and a number of other meanings of only historical significance.

surrogate. *Common meaning:* a stand-in. *In law:* a probate judge.

tail. *Common meaning:* a caudal appendage. *In law:* a limitation on the inheritability of an estate, specifying that only actual offspring or only specified offspring may inherit <fee tail>.

taint. *Common meaning:* to contaminate. *In law:* to corrupt <do large campaign contributions taint the electoral process?>.

taking. *Common meaning:* the acquisition of something. *In law:* the acquisition by a government or public utility of private property for a public purpose by condemnation and with compensation, or the property's drastic diminution in use or value because of a law or regulation.

toll. *Common meaning:* of a bell, to ring; a fee, especially to use a highway or make a phone call. *In law:* to suspend the running of a time period, such as under a statute of limitations; to take away a right, such as the right of entry.

traverse. *Common meaning:* to cross over or through a place, or to lie across something. *In law:* a detailed answer to an opposing party's pleading, denying the allegations it contains.

trespass. *Common meaning:* the entry onto someone else's property without permission. *In law:* also, historically and as used in the Bible, any wrongful act; and in the development of common law, any wrongful injury to a person or property, and the legal writ to remedy that injury.

trust. *Common meaning:* confidence and reliance, especially in someone. *In law:* an arrangement in equity whereby a settlor gives legal title to some property to a trustee

> "The kind of writing instruction most of us have gotten in school is exactly the reverse of what we need. Instead of teaching us how to communicate as clearly as possible, our schooling in English teaches us how to fog things up. It even implants a fear that if we don't make our writing complicated enough, we'll be considered uneducated."
>
> —*John L. Beckley*

who manages the property for the good of one or more beneficiaries; also, a business combination seeking to monopolize a market.

umpire. *Common meaning:* an official in baseball and other sports. *In law:* in arbitration, a person assigned to decide how to resolve a dispute after arbitrators have failed to agree.

unclean hands. *Common meaning:* dirty hands. *In law:* a metaphorical defense in equity, established by showing that the plaintiff acted in bad faith and therefore does not deserve equity ("he who comes into equity must come with clean hands").

undertake. *Common meaning:* to take on, as a task. *In law:* to guarantee something <the manufacturer undertakes that the product is free of defect> or to guarantee that someone else will do something <the father will undertake the son's car loan>.

use. *Common meaning:* function, operation, consumption, utility. *In law:* before the Statute of Uses (1536), equitable ownership and the right to possession of land that another person holds legal title to, for the purpose of rendering the interest inheritable.

utter. *Common meaning:* to speak. *In law:* to pass or attempt to pass a forged check; to hold out that an instrument is genuine, especially when it is not <utter a forgery>.

variance. *Common meaning:* variation. *In law:* variation between a pleading and proof, or a criminal charge and evidence; official permission to use land in a way that would otherwise violate a zoning ordinance.

veracity. *Common meaning:* the personal quality of honesty and truthfulness. *In law:* truth or accuracy of a statement.

verdict. *Common meaning:* loosely, the outcome of a trial. *In law:* rigorously, the finding of facts by the jury (or the judge in a bench trial), as distinguished from the final judgment or sentence.

vested interest. *Common meaning:* loosely, any personal interest. *In law:* rigorously, an interest—whether possessory or future—that is fixed in law and is not contingent on any event or condition.

waste. *Common meaning:* something left over or unusable; devastation; garbage; excrement. *In law:* actual damage, change, or legal encumbrance to property, caused by a tenant to the harm of someone with a future interest in the property; a common-law action to remedy waste.

work. *Common meaning:* to labor; to operate. *In law:* for patent-law purposes, to fully develop and market an invention <work the invention>.

writing. *Common meaning:* words on paper. *In law:* for purposes of copyright, "any physical rendering of the fruits of creative intellectual or aesthetic labor," including music, art, movies, even pantomime (*Goldstein v. California*, 412 U.S. 546, 561 (1973)).

wrong. *Common meaning:* an evil; an injustice. *In law:* something that causes a physical injury or detriment to a legal right; a tort, or an act that makes the wrongdoer liable to the other party.

§ 13
Troublesome Words

13.1 Jarring words are speed bumps on the road to comprehension. When your reader hits a term that is misused, is phrased incorrectly, or is somehow shocking to the sensibilities, your message becomes secondary for a moment. The reader becomes distracted, trying to figure out what is wrong with your expression or why you worded the idea so poorly. These distractions quickly affect the reader's opinion of your competence and credibility. Why did you word this so strangely? Don't you know what this word actually means? Etc. Anything you do to make the reader pause to consider your educational deficits, even fleetingly, is bad. This chapter contains tips for preventing these distractions.

13.2 Use words correctly and precisely.

(a) *Correctness.* Although the notion of linguistic correctness may seem absolute—right or wrong—it is mutable. Words change over time: they grow new meanings and shed old ones. Usually these changes are extremely gradual. Our language remains relatively stable, each generation understanding the language of those who came before. Occasionally, however, change is abrupt. Today, the progress of technology, especially communications technology, has stepped up the pace. New words—and new meanings for old words—now spring up almost overnight. But that doesn't mean we should abandon the idea of correctness in word usage. What is "correct" (some prefer to say "appropriate") is a word choice that, in a given age, has two characteristics: (1) it is consistent with historical usage, especially that of the immediate past, and (2) it preserves valuable distinctions that careful writers have cultivated over time. By meeting these standards, the legal writer achieves a greater degree of credibility with an educated readership.

(b) *Precision.* Often either of two words will suffice in a sentence, but the shades of meaning differ. There is, for example, a difference between saying that a doctrine is *old* and saying that it is *venerable*, between calling a treatise *compendious* and calling it *voluminous*; and between characterizing a person as *drunken* as opposed to merely *drunk* on a specific occasion. Careful writers make distinctions. They cultivate an awareness of words and their connotative differences. They would no more write *incidental to* when they mean *incident to* than a carpenter would try to drive a nail with the handle of a screwdriver.

(c) *Further guidance.* For a much fuller treatment of the wording issues discussed in the following glossary, see *Garner's Modern English Usage* (4th ed. 2016), the first usage guide ever to be based on a thorough canvassing of big data. For each disputed usage problem, it records ratios of frequency (standard form vs. nonstandard form) in English-language print sources—an unprecedented feature. The following resources are also useful:

- Theodore M. Bernstein, *The Careful Writer* (1965).
- Wilson Follett, *Modern American Usage: A Guide* (Erik Wensberg ed., 2d ed. 1998).
- H.W. Fowler, *A Dictionary of Modern English Usage* (Ernest Gowers ed., 2d ed. 1965).
- Bryan A. Garner, *The Chicago Guide to Grammar, Usage, and Punctuation* (2016).
- Bryan A. Garner, *Garner's Dictionary of Legal Usage* (3d ed. 2011).
- Pam Peters, *The Cambridge Guide to English Usage* (2004).
- Barbara Wallraff, *Word Court* (2001).
- Barbara Wallraff, *Your Own Words* (2004).

13.3 Consult the following glossary to find the correct uses of problematic expressions—words and phrases that are sometimes misused in legal writing.

If your work requires you to edit—and it almost certainly does—you'd be well advised to read and reread this 13.3 from time to time: all 72 pages. You must sensitize yourself to verbal distinctions. Even if you don't memorize the material here, you'll be alert to certain word choices that raise concerns. You'll therefore be prepared to look up guidance on the point. So browse this compendium periodically.

a; an. *A* precedes a word that starts with a consonant sound; *an* precedes a word that starts with a vowel sound. Note that it's the sound and not necessarily the letter that counts <an unimportant exception to a universal rule>. The word *historical* and its variants cause missteps, but usage authorities generally agree that since the *h* is pronounced, the word takes an *a* <an hourlong talk at a historical society>. Likewise, an initialism (whose letters are sounded out) may be paired with a different article from the one used with a similar-looking acronym (which is pronounced as a word) <an HTML website for a HUD program>.

abandon; desert. For the most part, these words overlap. But when it's a plan or an enterprise that is being left behind, use *abandon*. Cf. JUST DESERTS.

ability; capability; capacity. *Ability* refers to a person's physical or mental power or skill to do something <the ability to ride a bicycle>. *Capability* refers more generally to power or ability to do something challenging <she has the capability to play soccer professionally> or to the quality of being able to use or be used in a certain way <a jet with long-distance-flight capability>. *Capacity* refers especially to a vessel's ability to hold or contain something <a high-capacity fuel tank>. Used figuratively, *capacity* refers especially to a person's physical or mental power <an astounding capacity for

mathematics>. It can also be used as a synonym for *ability* <capacity to make a contract>, as a formal word for someone's job, position, or role <in an advisory capacity>, as a word denoting an amount that can be produced or dealt with <full capacity>, or as a means of denoting size or power <engine capacity>.

abjure; adjure. To *abjure* something is either to formally renounce it <the new leader abjured the palatial trappings of the old regime> or to refrain from it <both sides abjure violence>. To *adjure* someone to do something is to plead or to make the person swear to do it. It used to mean "to order someone to do something under threat of a curse." We don't do curses today (not that kind, anyway), but this obsolete meaning has not died out entirely: the word is occasionally used to mean "to require by law."

abolition; *abolishment. Stick to *abolition*, which is the more natural and more common term.

abrasion. See CONTUSION.

abrogate; arrogate. To *abrogate* something (usually a law, treaty, or other agreement) is to abolish it <the invasion abrogated a nonaggression pact signed just weeks before>. To *arrogate* something (usually a power or right) is to commandeer it to oneself or assign it to another <the regents fired the dean and arrogated that office's financial responsibilities to the president>.

absolve of; absolve from. To *absolve* is to wipe away. But there's a fine distinction: we are *absolved of* our debts and other obligations, but *absolved from* our crimes and other transgressions.

abstruse. See OBTUSE.

accept. See EXCEPT.

acceptance; acceptation. *Acceptance* is broad enough to handle most common meanings of these terms. *Acceptation* is marginally better to denote widespread public use of a word or phrase <these words are used as jargon, not according to their ordinary acceptation>.

accepter; acceptor. *Accepter* is the common spelling. In law, we use *acceptor* for one who *accepts* (pays) a draft or *accepts* an offer (to parallel *offeror*).

access, *vb.* As a verb meaning "to gain access," this word is well accepted in the context of computer use. In other fields, including legal writing, it still strikes some readers as jarring, which is reason enough to avoid it.

accessory. See PERPETRATOR.

accommodate; accommodable; *accommodatable. Repeat over and over: two *m*'s. Make it a mantra until it's second nature. **Accomodate* [spell *accommodate*] is a red flag of sloppy writing to the literate reader, who will be hard-pressed to resist the

> "The real reason for good usage in writing is that if you do not achieve it, your educated reader will be thinking of you, not of the point you're trying to make."
>
> —*John W. Velz*

*An invariably inferior form.

urge to *sic* you in any responsive brief. The adjective *accommodable* (preferred over **accommodatable*) is gaining use in employment law.

accomplice. See PERPETRATOR.

accord; accordance. An *accord* is an agreement. If you're *in accord* with someone, the two of you agree. *Accordance* is conformity. If you perform your obligations under that agreement, you've acted *in accordance* (not *in accord*) with its terms.

accord and satisfaction. See COMPROMISE AND SETTLEMENT.

accounting; bookkeeping. *Accounting* is the management of financial affairs, especially of a company. It entails making judgments about such things as tax deductions, acquisitions, and stock offerings. *Bookkeeping* is the clerical maintenance of financial records.

accuse; charge. A person is *accused of* but *charged with* a crime or other malfeasance. *Accuse* is informal; *charge* connotes official action, as by a prosecutor. Cf. ALLEGE.

acknowledgment; verification. The difference between these two legal terms is what is sworn to. An *acknowledgment* (so spelled) attests only that the attached signature is genuine. A *verification*, on the other hand, is an acknowledged writing containing a further sworn statement that the contents of the writing are true.

acquiesce. To *acquiesce in* something means "I'll do it, but I don't have to like it." It is a passive acceptance rather than an affirmative endorsement. For example, if a court interprets a statute a certain way, and Congress does not amend the statute to effectively overturn the court's decision, Congress is said to have *acquiesced in* that interpretation. The phrase *acquiesce to* is not as traditional or idiomatic. **Acquiesce with* is always wrong.

acquittal; acquittance. A criminal defendant walks after an *acquittal*. A debtor is freed from an obligation with an *acquittance* (a written release).

acquitted of; *acquitted from. Always the first—never the second.

***actual fact.** Avoid this redundant phrase. Either use *actually* or delete altogether.

acuity; acumen. Both words mean "sharpness" in a figurative sense, and both can also denote mental sharpness. But *acumen* applies only to mental sharpness <the nominee's legal acumen was never in question>, while *acuity* applies more often to the physical senses <visual acuity is a requirement for flight school>.

adapt. See ADOPT.

adequate; sufficient. Avoid using the qualitative *adequate* (good enough) to mean "quantitatively *sufficient*" (plenty or big enough). In contract law, a legal detriment or anything of economic value is *sufficient* consideration, but we compare the value of what each party brings to the table to decide whether the consideration is *adequate* (so that the bargain is fair). **Adequate enough* is a substandard redundancy.

adherence; adhesion. While *adherence* is usually figurative <adherence to a code of ethics>, *adhesion* is usually literal <adhesion of a window decal>. The exceptions in law are the contract of *adhesion* (a one-sided, take-it-or-leave-it contract) and a third-party nation's *adhesion* to some but not all of a treaty's terms.

adjure. See ABJURE.

*An invariably inferior form.

administer; administrable. Because *administrator* and *administration* appear so much in legal usage, we sometimes trip over the simple verb *administer.* Don't backpedal from those noun forms to arrive at the silly variant **administrate.* And an estate that can be distributed by this process is *administrable*, not **administratable* or **administerable.*

administrator; executor. A person distributing a decedent's estate is an *administrator* if appointed by a court, or an *executor* if named in the will. The feminine forms (*administratrix* and *executrix*) are becoming obsolete, since *administrator* and *executor* are considered gender-neutral.

admission; admittance. *Admission* is usually permission to enter, whereas *admittance* is physical entry only. *Admittance* is often misused where *admission* is meant <she received her notice of *admittance* [read *admission*] into college>.

admission; confession. In law generally, an *admission* is any concession or stipulation. But in criminal law, reserve *confession* for an admission of guilt.

admittance. See ADMISSION.

admonition; admonishment. Although both terms are correct, prefer *admonition*, the more common term.

adopt; adapt. You *adopt* something when you accept responsibility for it <adopt a child> <adopt a contract>. You *adapt* to a new situation <adapt to married life> or *adapt* something for a purpose different from that of the original <adapt an old farmhouse into a bed-and-breakfast>.

adopted; adoptive. The child is *adopted* (legally taken in as one of the family). The parents are not *adopted* by the child and are not traditionally so labeled—they are the *adoptive* mother and father. Unfortunately, the United States Code and many state codes do use the slipshod **adopted parents.*

adverse; averse. *Adverse* (think *adversary*) describes something we face that is opposed to us or blocks our way. In a lawsuit, that something is a person (the *adverse* party), but elsewhere it is more often a condition <the climbers faced adverse weather conditions>. *Averse* (think *aversion*) describes our negative reaction to something <the plaintiff was averse to any settlement offer>.

advert. See ALLUDE.

advise; advice. The first term is the verb, the second the noun. Trying to be formal (but sounding pompous), some writers use *advise* for *told*—when only information and no advice is communicated.

advocate. See BARRISTER.

affect; effect. These words are confused fairly often, but they are usually simple to straighten out: to *affect* something is to have an *effect* on it. If it's a verb meaning "to influence," use *affect*; if it's a noun meaning "result," use *effect.* Then watch for the exceptions. *Effect* as a verb meaning "to bring about" is common in legal writing <the *Brown* decision effected a profound change in society>. Less common are (1) *effect* as a noun meaning "possession" <personal effects>; (2) *affect* as a verb meaning "to put on airs" <affecting a British accent>; and (3) *affect* as a noun meaning "emotional response" (rare outside psychology). For more on *effect*, see EFFECT.

*An invariably inferior form.

affirmance; affirmation. Reserve *affirmance* for an appellate-court ruling upholding a trial-court decision. Use *affirmation* for all other meanings. In law, *affirmation* is also the term for an oath without any reference to religion.

affirmative (or negative), in the. The construction *answered in the affirmative* (or *negative*) has been roundly criticized as pompous jargon. In formal legal writing, the alternatives are not much better. But in all other contexts, ask whether you really want to use such stilted language. Then say no.

afflict. See INFLICT.

***after having [+ past participle].** Avoid this redundant phrasing. Use *after* [+ present participle] instead. That is, change **After having made law review, she was soon appointed managing editor* to this: *After making law review, she was soon appointed managing editor.*

afterward; afterword. *Afterward* is an adverb meaning "later." *Afterword* is a noun meaning "epilogue."

age of capacity; age of consent; age of majority; age of reason. All these phrases have developed separate doctrinal meanings; be careful to use the right one. *Age of capacity* is the age at which one may take legal action, such as signing a contract, writing a will, or bringing a lawsuit. *Age of consent* is the age at which one can agree to marry or to have sexual relations. *Age of majority* is the age at which the law considers one an adult and entitled to legal rights (beyond those of the age of capacity), such as voting. *Age of reason* is the age at which one is considered to know right from wrong, and so may be sued in tort or charged with a crime.

aggravate; irritate; annoy. Misusing *aggravate* (to worsen a condition, but not really to irk a person) can really *irritate* (annoy) some readers. And if you've *irritated* them by that misuse in conversation, you will only *aggravate* the situation if you commit the same error in writing.

agreement; bargain; contract. *Agreement* is the broadest term, meaning an understanding between parties. *Bargain* is the further agreement to exchange promises (or a promise for a performance), regardless of consideration. With sufficient consideration (and other legal requirements), a *contract* is formed.

aide; aid. *Aide* is the helper; *aid* is the help.

alibi. See EXCUSE.

all (of). Omit *of* after *all* whenever you can—except when *all of* precedes a nonpossessive pronoun <all of them>.

allege; accuse; contend. To *allege* something is to say that it's true before it has been proved, especially in court <the plaintiff alleges negligence on the part of the defendant>. Facts—not people—are alleged, so the common phrase "*alleged* robber" is not quite correct. *Allege* should not be used informally to mean "assert," "claim," "declare," "maintain," or the like. To *accuse* someone of something is to say that the person did it, and especially to bring formal charges <the accused slayer>. To *contend* something is to state a position <we contend that the witness is biased>.

allot. See A LOT.

allow. See PERMIT.

*An invariably inferior form.

all right. So written. Avoid the misspelling **alright.*

allude; advert; elude. To *allude* to something is to suggest it indirectly. To *advert* to it is to refer to it directly. To *elude* is to evade or escape. Be careful not to misuse *elude* for *allude.*

allusion; illusion. An *allusion* is an implied reference, especially an indirect evocation of a literary work. The near-homonym *illusion* is something that appears to be something that it is not, such as an optical *illusion*. See ILLUSION.

alongside. The word *of* does not belong after this word, which means "at the side of" <alongside the ship>.

a lot; *alot; allot. *A lot* is the correct term for "many" or "much." **Alot* appears a lot, but it's never correct. *Allot* is both an unrelated term meaning "to allocate" and an occasional misspelling of *a lot.*

already; all ready. *Already* refers to time <the statute of limitations has already begun running>. *All ready* refers to preparation <the witnesses are all ready>.

alternative; alternate. *Alternative* is the more frequently used term, meaning one of several options (not necessarily one of two, as the word's Latin root suggests). An *alternate* is a substitute.

altogether; all together. *Altogether* means "entirely" or "wholly" <his account was altogether unbelievable>. *All together* denotes a unity of time and place <the firm's lawyers were all together for that memorable CLE program>.

ambiguous; ambivalent. Communication that is unclear because it is open to more than one reasonable interpretation is *ambiguous.* A person who has mixed emotions about something is *ambivalent.*

amenable; amenity. To be *amenable* to process is to be subject to a court's jurisdiction <the foreign corporation was amenable to suit under the long-arm statute>. Loosely, then, to be *amenable* is to be subject to persuasion <the defendant may be amenable to a plea bargain>. *Amenity* has nothing to do with law, except maybe to denote one of the luxurious adornments in a conference room: it is a pleasant accommodation or a pleasant demeanor.

amend; amends; emend. To *amend* a document, law, or constitution is to correct or improve it, often by adding something new. To make *amends* is to correct a wrong done to someone. To *emend* text is to correct errors in it.

amenity. See AMENABLE.

amiable; amicable. Friendly people are *amiable.* A friendly relationship is *amicable.* The first is best used to describe people, the second dealings between people.

among. See BETWEEN.

amoral. See IMMORAL.

amount. See NUMBER.

amuse. See BEMUSE.

an. See A.

*An invariably inferior form.

and/or. If you wish to appear at least minimally competent as a legal writer, banish this unnecessary monstrosity. Prefer *and* or *or*—or, if necessary with a list longer than two items, *any one or more of the following*. Be assured that *and/or* is never a desirable adornment.

anecdote; anecdotal. These two terms regarding stories of real-life events carry different and somewhat contrary connotations. An *anecdote* is presumed to be true (and funny), while *anecdotal* evidence is usually considered unreliable because it has not been subjected to scientific scrutiny. Cf. ANTIDOTE.

angry. See MAD.

annoy. See AGGRAVATE.

antepenultimate. See ULTIMATE.

anticipate; expect. Although using *anticipate* to mean "expect" is common, careful legal writers should restrict *anticipate* to its original sense: to foresee or prepare for an event <we don't anticipate [read *expect*] any problems with the trial (but trials are unpredictable, and a good lawyer prepares for the unexpected)>. To *expect* something is to look forward to it.

antidote; anecdote. Laughter is the best medicine? Not here. *Antidote*, a potion that neutralizes a poison, is sometimes misused where the writer meant *anecdote*, a funny and supposedly true story. One who has been poisoned is probably in no mood for jokes. See ANECDOTE.

antinomy; antimony. *Antinomy* is the word that denotes contradicting authority, such as inconsistent caselaw or one judge's reasoning that is at odds with another's. *Antimony* is a metallic element.

anxious; eager. *Anxious* connotes an element of fear (think *anxiety*), so it should not be used as a synonym for *eager*. An *anxiously* awaited phone call is one you'd probably rather not answer, while an *eagerly* awaited call you'd pick up on the first ring.

appellate; appellant; appealer; appellor; appellee; petitioner; respondent. A court of appeals is an *appellate* court, despite some references outside legal writing to *appellant* courts. *Appellant* is the correct term for one who appeals a decision: *appealer* never caught on, and *appellor* is an archaic British term that has nothing to do with modern practice. *Appellee* is the party that answers the appeal. Some courts refer to the *appellant* and *appellee* as the *petitioner* and *respondent*, respectively.

appertain; pertain. Don't use *appertain* as just a fancy way to say *pertain*. To *pertain to* is to relate to <the clause pertains to assignment of risk>; this is the more common term. To *appertain to* is to belong to by right <the defendant's rights appertaining to the Fifth Amendment>.

apply; follow. Technically speaking, if a court is bound by precedent it will *apply* that law to the facts of the present case for a fairly mechanical outcome. If the court is not bound by the precedent but finds the reasoning persuasive, it may *follow* that precedent.

appraisal; appraisement. *Appraisal* is the general term for an objective assessment of value. In law, an *appraisement* is an appraisal of the value of a decedent's estate.

appraise; apprise; apprize. To *appraise* something is to estimate its value <the broker appraised the house at $250,000>. To *apprise* someone is to inform that person about something <please apprise me of the appraised value before putting the house on the market>. Writers occasionally misuse *appraise* when they mean *apprise.* To *apprize* something is to value it highly <the judge's apprized collection of colonial Spanish lawbooks>.

appraisement. See APPRAISAL.

apprise; apprize. See APPRAISE.

appropriate; expropriate. Both verbs mean "to take away" (but note that *appropriate* can also mean "to give to," as when a legislature appropriates funds for a project). Courts distinguish between the terms according to who's doing the taking: *appropriate* is the general term, but a government *expropriates* private land for public use by its power of eminent domain.

approve; endorse; approve of. To *approve* something means to formally accept it <approve a budget>. To *endorse* something indicates more active support for it <the mayor endorsed the governor's reelection bid>. To *approve of* something is less concrete; it denotes a favorable opinion <most Americans approve of free trade>. Cf. ENDORSE.

approximately. Prefer *about* to *approximately.*

apt; likely. In the best usage, things in general are *apt* to occur under certain circumstances <it's apt to be rainy in April>, whereas specific things are *likely* to occur under specific circumstances <it's likely to rain this afternoon>. *Apt* also means "appropriate" <an apt response>.

arbiter; arbitrator. *Arbiter* is the general term for someone who settles disputes, and especially someone authorized to do so, such as a judge. An *arbitrator* is someone who conducts an *arbitration.* (Use varies, though: in Scotland it is an *arbiter* who conducts *arbitration.*) The cliché is *final* or *ultimate arbiter* (not *arbitrator*).

arbitration. See MEDIATION.

arbitrator. See ARBITER.

arrogate. See ABROGATE.

as. See LIKE; SINCE.

***as per; per.** In the commercial world, *per* was once considered acceptable <per your request> and **as per* an illiterate barbarism. But as examples of commercialese, they're both bad. Instead of **As per your request* or (less bad) *Per your request*, write *As you requested.*

assault; battery. Most laypeople—and modern penal codes—do not distinguish *assault* from *battery.* But in criminal law and tort law, an *assault* is a threat or an attempt to

> "Archaic words thrust into a commonplace context to redeem its ordinariness are an abomination."
>
> —*H.W. Fowler*

*An invariably inferior form.

commit *battery* (a harmful or offensive touching), but only if the threat or attempt was perceived by and alarmed the other person.

assay; essay. To *assay* something is to analyze it. To *essay* something is to attempt it. The verbal use of *essay* is unduly formal, even obscure; so for clarity you should avoid it.

assembly; assemblage. Both words apply to a collection, especially of people. But *assembly* connotes organization and purpose and is more formal than *assemblage.* One might speak of the *assembly* of a model ship from an *assemblage* of parts, for example.

assent; consent. The first connotes a positive and voluntary agreement <assent to a proposal of marriage>, while the second is neutral in connotation and can apply even when the agreement is given reluctantly <consent to a strip search>.

assessment. See TAX.

assignment; assignation. What's the difference between being on *assignment* and being in an *assignation*? The first is a delegated mission, the second an illicit rendezvous. Actually, *assignation* could legitimately cover the other meanings of *assignment* (e.g., transfer of an interest), but you know your readers would snicker.

as such. The *such* in this phrase is a pronoun: "She's a lawyer. As such [i.e., as a lawyer], she owes fiduciary duties to her clients." Many writers today mistakenly consider *as such* to be equivalent to *therefore.* (Try *therefore* in the preceding example, and you'll see how the mistake occurs.) They erroneously write, "We risk being late. *As such* [read *Therefore*], we had better move for an extension of time." That makes no literal sense. Don't write *as such* unless you can replace it with "as [some noun or noun phrase just mentioned]" <Sources said that early indications pointed to a state-sponsored assassination attempt and that it was being treated as such by police and the CIA>.

assumption; presumption. An *assumption* is an unverified belief that something is correct. You can *assume* all you like, but it won't have any legal effect. A *presumption*, on the other hand, carries weight in the courtroom: it raises an inference that must be rebutted by the opposing party.

assure; ensure; insure. You *assure* a person (always a person as the object) that something will be done. You make preparations to *ensure* that it will be done. You call your underwriter's agent to *insure* yourself against financial loss if it doesn't get done.

as to. In legal writing, this two-word preposition commonly displaces *in*, *for*, *with*, *about*, and just about all the other simple prepositions. Often, *as to* is deadwood, as in the faulty phrasing **question as to whether*, which should be simply *question whether.* (See QUESTION WHETHER.) Reserve *as to* for one circumstance: at the beginning of a sentence <As to the fraud charges, Dr. Johnson claimed that he had never misrepresented any fact>.

***as yet; *as of yet.** Avoid these faulty phrases. Try *yet*, *still*, *so far*, or some other equivalent.

attachment. See SEQUESTRATION.

attain; obtain. To *attain* something is to accomplish it <the dieter attained his weight-loss goal>. To *obtain* something is to acquire it <the law-school graduate passed the bar exam and obtained her law license>.

*An invariably inferior form.

at the time when; at the time that. Intolerably verbose. Try *when* instead.

attorney's fees. Use the singular by default, the plural (*attorneys' fees*) only if more than one lawyer will in fact receive fees. The possessive-free *attorney fees* is a perfectly acceptable way to dodge the apostrophe issue altogether. But never, never, never write **attorneys fees*.

avenge; revenge. Motive is the message in this word choice. One *avenges* a wrong done to anyone by seeing that the wrongdoer pays. But *revenge* is not about high notions of justice; it's about settling a personal score. While the first term may have positive connotations, the second usually carries some negative ones.

averse. See ADVERSE.

avocation. See VOCATION.

avoid; void. Remember that *avoid* means something different to lawyers (to make legally *void*, as if the relationship never existed) than to laypeople (to evade). The general meaning is perfectly proper in legal writing, but the careful writer may prefer to *avoid* it (in the common sense) if its precise use might be ambiguous.

awhile; a while. The one-word form is correct as an adverb meaning "for a short period of time" <let's wait awhile>. But when it's part of a prepositional phrase, it's no longer an adverb: it's an article (*a*) plus a noun (*while*) <let's wait here for a while> <we'll go in a while>.

bail; bale. The first is the legal term for the security that gets someone released from jail. The second denotes a big bundle of hay, cotton, or the like.

bar; debar; disbar. To *bar* someone or something is to stop it <the statute of limitations bars this suit>, or to keep the person out of someplace <trustees voted to bar the fraternity from campus for two years>. *Debar* is a fading legalism meaning "to prevent someone from doing or having something" <this compulsory precedent debars the court from dismissing our suit>. To *disbar* a lawyer is to revoke the license to practice <disbar for misconduct>.

bargain. See AGREEMENT.

barrister; advocate; solicitor. In the United Kingdom, there are two types of lawyers: *barristers* (called *advocates* in Scotland), who argue cases in superior court; and *solicitors*, who counsel clients, prepare legal documents, and make limited court appearances (especially in lower courts).

battery. See ASSAULT.

because. See SINCE & *REASON . . . IS BECAUSE.

because of. See DUE TO.

begging the question. Traditionally, this phrase means "arguing in circles": while arguing, making an assumption about the very thing you're arguing about. For example, someone might defend a government's regulatory power by saying, "We license broadcasters so that we can regulate them; we can regulate them because we license them." Justice Kennedy noted this circular reasoning in oral arguments during *FCC v. Fox Television Stations, Inc.* on 10 January 2012. The old-fashioned term for this

*An invariably inferior form.

logical fallacy is *petitio principii*. Avoid using *beg the question* in the watered-down sense "to invite or prompt the question." Although the misusage has spread far and wide, lawyers ought to know better.

behalf. See ON BEHALF OF.

behest. See REQUEST.

bemean. See DEMEAN.

bemuse; amuse. These are not synonyms. One who is *bemused* is usually not at all *amused*, but rather confused or lost in thought.

benefactor; beneficiary. A *benefactor* is on the giving end of a gift, a *beneficiary* on the receiving end.

beneficent; benevolent. A person who is *beneficent* (disposed to doing kind deeds) performs acts that are *benevolent* (helpful, kind). *Beneficence* is the character trait; *benevolence* is the conduct.

beneficiary. See BENEFACTOR.

benevolent. See BENEFICENT.

bequest. See REQUEST; DEVISE.

beside; besides. A fairly common error is the use of *beside* (next to, compared to) to mean *besides* (except, also) <it will take something *beside* [read *besides*] money to get the plaintiff to settle>.

between; among. The old "rule" that *between* refers to two things and *among* to more than two isn't quite right—never has been. The distinction is the relationship between or among the various things. If it's distinctly one-to-one, use *between* even if there are more than two in total <personal bonds between senators>. If it's collective, use *among* <consensus among senators>.

bi-; semi-. *Bi-* means "two" <bicycle> <bifocal> <bilateral>. *Semi-* means "somewhat" and, specifically, "half" <semicircle> <semifinals> <semisweet>. But the literal meanings have been abused in practice when used as periodic prefixes: *biannual* has come to be synonymous with *semiannual*, meaning "twice a year" (*biennial* means "every other year"), and *biweekly* newspapers publish twice a week. To avoid confusion, spell it out to your reader <the board meets every other week>.

billion; trillion. The names of large numbers can be ambiguous. In the U.S. a *billion* is a thousand millions (9 zeros), but in most other countries a *billion* is traditionally a million millions (12 zeros, which is what Americans call a *trillion*). Further, in Great Britain a *trillion* is traditionally a million million millions (18 zeros)—what Americans would call a *quintillion*. Yet American meanings are now widely accepted in international finance and commerce.

black-letter; blackletter. The first term describes a Gothic or Old English typeface <a book's cover with black-letter type>. The second term describes well-settled legal principles <blackletter law>. Although *blackletter* law derives its name directly from *black-letter* type, by convention it is losing its hyphen.

blackmail; graymail; greenmail; feemail. *Blackmail* is the usual word for illegal extortion; the other terms are spinoffs. The CIA coined *graymail* to describe the effort of a criminal defendant to avoid prosecution by threatening to disclose classified information on the witness stand. *Greenmail* is the buying of stock in a target corporation, threatening a hostile takeover, and then selling back the stock at an inflated price. *Feemail* is the unethical practice of extracting a legal fee by duress, threat, or intimidation.

blameworthy; culpable. In law, a simple and useful distinction has developed between these two terms, which were formerly synonymous. Today, we use *blameworthy* in civil disputes and *culpable* in criminal cases. An exception might arise in a claim for punitive damages: a writer might find *blameworthy* too weak to describe the defendant's conduct. Shun the ambiguous *_inculpable_: it means "not guilty," but it can be misunderstood to mean "capable of being made guilty." Cf. GUILTY; NONCULPABLE.

blatant; flagrant. What is *blatant* is conspicuous <the videotape evidence exposed the defendant's alibi as a blatant lie>. What is *flagrant* is also conspicuous, but often with a stronger suggestion of shocking illegality or immorality <the mayor's junket to Tahiti was a flagrant waste of taxpayers' money>.

bombastic. Don't nibble at the word's bait: it has nothing to do with an explosive temper. Rather, a *bombastic* person is pompous in speech and manner, and unduly theatrical. It originally meant "stuffed with cotton padding" and still describes a stuffed shirt. A *bombastic* argument is pompously long-winded but substantively empty.

bona fide; real. In legal writing, *bona fide* is a term of art, its definition varying with the area of law, the relevant statutes, and caselaw <bona fide purchaser for value>. Outside legal writing, it just means "real" <a bona fide Grandma Moses> <a bona fide apology>. To avoid confusion, don't use it in legal writing.

bona fides; good faith. *Bona fides* is an inferior way of saying *good faith*; writers should much prefer the latter phrase. If *bona fides* is used, however, keep in mind that despite its appearance and pronunciation [**boh**-nə **fɪ**-deez], it is singular <the defendant's bona fides is not an issue>.

bookkeeping. See ACCOUNTING.

born; borne. Of the two past participles of *bear*, *born* applies only to birth in a passive sense <born in the U.S.A.> <native-born citizen>. *Borne* applies in other senses: "carried" <canister borne by ship> <with that doctrine borne in mind> and "given birth to" <she has borne three children>.

breach; broach; breech. Lawyers should have no trouble handling *breach* in its contract-law sense, meaning "to break." *Broach* means "to tap into": literally to put a hole in something (such as a keg) to let the liquid out, and figuratively to open up a subject for discussion. So you could either *breach* a dam or *broach* it—the first of those choices being the more usual one. *Breech* is the back part of something, especially a gun or the buttocks.

bribery; extortion. If you offer something of value in exchange for corrupt conduct, it is *bribery*. If you demand something in exchange for corrupt favors, it is *extortion*. But if the person on the receiving end is a public official, acceptance under color of public office is *extortion*, even if the gift was unsolicited.

*An invariably inferior form.

bring; take. If the movement is toward you, use *bring* <please bring me my glasses>; if it's toward someone or something else, use *take* <I need to take my dog to the vet>. Misusing *bring* and *brought* for *take* and *took* is surprisingly common.

broach. See BREACH.

building. See FACILITY.

burglarize. See ROB.

but. The ill-schooled incorrectly believe that this word should not begin a sentence. They are wrong: *But* as a sentence-starter is incomparably effective to introduce a contrast—much better, typically, than *however.* For a full essay on the subject, see *Garner on Language and Writing* 63–87 (2009).

can; may. We all know that *can* denotes ability and *may* permission. Most of us blatantly misuse the terms in speaking, at least on occasion, but in writing we *can* do better. The meanings almost merge when the context is whether one *can* legally do something—that seems like a question of permission, but it's still about ability: can it be done without breaking a law?

cannon; canon. Sometimes writers mistakenly pull out the big gun (*cannon*) for one of *canon*'s senses, especially a body of doctrines <canon of ethics>.

canvas; canvass. *Canvas* is the heavy cloth, used in such activities as painting. To *canvass* is to solicit votes, to count votes, to examine votes, or to debate.

capability. See ABILITY.

capacity. See ABILITY.

capitol; capital. You'll find the state *capitol* (the building where the legislature sits) in the *capital* city. With an *o*, the term always denotes a building for the legislature. In all other senses it's *capital.*

carat; karat; caret. The weight of a jewel is measured in *carats* <a 1-carat diamond>. The purity of gold is measured in *karats* <24-karat means pure gold> (but note that in British English it is also spelled *carat*). A *caret* is an insertion mark on a manuscript, usually marking an edit.

career; careen. A car that *careers* down the street travels at full speed. A sailboat that *careens* around a turn tips dangerously to one side. The comparatively recent use of *careen* to indicate high-speed and erratic movement, though it began as a corruption, is now too common to be called an error.

caret. See CARAT.

caselaw; case law; case-law. Although all three variants appear with great frequency, the unhyphenated *caselaw* is increasingly prevalent.

catalogue; catalog. Despite the increasing popularity of the shortened term, *catalogue* is still the preferred spelling.

cause célèbre; cause. At law, a *cause célèbre* is a trial or decision involving a famous person or a sensational event. In general use, it refers to a notorious person or event. But it does not properly refer to a *cause* or movement.

cede; secede; concede. To *cede* something is to give it up. To *secede* is to formally withdraw from an organization. To *concede* something is to admit it, especially a fact or defeat.

censor; censer; sensor. A *censor* is someone who reviews writings and art and excises offensive or otherwise objectionable content. Writers sometimes misspell it *censer* (an incense burner on a chain) or *sensor* (a mechanical detector).

censor; censure. To *censor* writings, art, and other works is to inspect them and excise objectionable (or merely embarrassing) content. To *censure* someone is to criticize or officially reprimand that person.

center on; *center around; revolve around. Since the center is a single point, it is illogical to say that something **centers around* anything. Rather, it may *center on* it or *revolve around* it.

certainty; certitude. A person may know something to a *certainty* (especially if it can be objectively proved), or know it with *certitude* (especially if it's a matter of faith). The thing that is known is a *certainty*, but never a *certitude.*

cession; session. *Cession* is the act of ceding (giving up); *session* is the act of sitting (meeting formally).

chair; chairman; chairwoman; chairperson. Since the mid-17th century, *chair* has been regarded as the best gender-neutral choice. Avoid *chairperson.* The sex-specific terms might seem acceptable to some. But when the sentence is "We need to elect a ——," you can understand how *-man* and *-woman* suffixes become objectionable.

character; reputation. What you really are, good and bad, is your *character*; what other people think you are, good and bad, is your *reputation.*

childish; childlike. These words carry opposite connotations: *childish* suggests a stubborn immaturity; *childlike* suggests innocence and purity.

cite; citation; site; sight. To *cite* a reference (never **cite to* a reference) is to relate its importance to the issue at hand and to identify its source <on this point, the brief cited *Palsgraf*>. In general use, the term also means "to point out," either for good <cited for bravery> or for ill <cited for speeding>. The colloquial use of *cite* as a noun meaning *citation* is inappropriate in formal writing <one footnote alone contained 24 *cites* [read *citations*]>. *Cite* and *site* (place) are sometimes confused, as are *site* and *sight* (to see or the thing seen).

citizen; subject. The distinction is to whom you owe political allegiance: the nation collectively or a monarch. If it's the former, you're a *citizen.* If it's the latter, you're a *subject.*

> "The pebble must be polished with care, which hopes to be valued as a diamond; and words ought surely to be laboured, when they are intended to stand for things."
> —*Samuel Johnson*

*An invariably inferior form.

citizenship; domicile; residence. *Citizenship* is one's status as a member of a nation, with the rights and privileges that status carries with it. *Domicile* is where one lives with the intent to stay; it refers particularly to a state, county, and city. *Residence* is, broadly, where one's home is, or the building itself. One may have many *residences* but only one *domicile*. Note that the U.S. Constitution refers to *citizens* of the states, so for purposes of federal diversity jurisdiction, *citizenship* and *domicile* are the same.

claim preclusion. See COLLATERAL ESTOPPEL.

clean; cleanse. The first term is literal, the second figurative: you *clean* your hands and *cleanse* your soul.

cleanliness; cleanness. Fastidious people (and their surroundings) are noted by their *cleanliness*. When not referring to people, the correct word is *cleanness*.

cleanse. See CLEAN.

clearly; obviously. As sentence adverbs <Clearly, this is true>, these weasel words are often exaggerators. They may reassure you but not your reader. If something is clearly or obviously true, prove it to the reader without resorting to the conclusory use of these words.

cleave; cleft; clove; cloven; cleaved. *Cleave* is really two verbs with nearly opposite meanings. To *cleave* in one sense is to split in two <lightning can cleave a mighty oak>; that word is inflected *cleft* (or *clove*)–*cloven*. To *cleave* in the other sense is to stick together <wet hair cleaved to the forehead>; that word is inflected *cleaved–cleaved*.

clench; clinch. Both words mean "to grasp or tighten," but *clench* is literal <clench fists>, while *clinch* is usually figurative <clinch victory>. Exceptions crop up in woodworking <clinch with a screw>, metalworking <clinch with rivets>, and boxing <tired and bloodied, he could only clinch his opponent and pray for the bell>.

climactic; climatic; climacteric. The adjective formed from *climax* (culmination) is *climactic*. The adjective formed from *climate* (prevailing weather) is *climatic*. *Climacteric* was once preferred over *climactic*, but its status today is anticlimactic.

clinch. See CLENCH.

closure; cloture. *Closure* is the act of closing something or the state of being closed; it is most commonly used today as vague psychobabble <seeking closure>. *Cloture* is a narrow term for the parliamentary procedure of forcing a cutoff of debate and a vote on a proposal.

clove; cloven. See CLEAVE.

coequal; equal. On rare occasions *co-* may add something that *equal* can't do alone. But the word probably would not exist today if it weren't for our "*coequal* branches of government."

cognoscenti. So spelled. The *cognoscenti* are the experts in a field, those in the *know*. **Cogniscenti* is one of many possible misspellings. It's an embarrassing word to misspell because the reader will view the writer as out of the *cognoscenti*. Prefer simpler terms such as *experts*. The singular form is *cognoscente*.

cohabit. An unmarried couple who live together *cohabit*. **Cohabitate* is a needless variant formed from the noun *cohabitation*.

*An invariably inferior form.

cohort; cohorts. *Cohort* is a singular mass noun that strictly refers only to an uncountably large group <the candidate's cohort of followers>. But it has been used as a synonym for *colleague* for so long that today this meaning is dominant <the candidate huddled with her closest cohorts>.

coin a phrase (term, word, etc.). To *coin a phrase* is to use it for the first time, not to repeat an old cliché.

collaborate; corroborate. To *collaborate* is to cooperate with someone in an endeavor <to be competent to stand trial, an accused person must be able to collaborate in the defense>. To *corroborate* something is to confirm it <an eyewitness corroborated the defendant's statement>.

collateral estoppel; res judicata. These two forms of preclusion have long been confused. *Collateral estoppel* (issue preclusion) bars relitigation of a material issue that has already been adjudicated. *Res judicata* (claim preclusion) bars relitigation of an entire dispute after a final judgment has been entered.

collegial; collegiate. *Collegial* corresponds to *colleague* <a collegial environment for all the lawyers—associates and partners alike>; *collegiate* corresponds to *college* <collegiate athletics>.

colloquy; colloquium. A *colloquy* is a discussion, especially with a judge; the verb form is *collogue.* A *colloquium* is an academic seminar.

commendable; commendatory. If you donate to a worthy cause, that is *commendable* (worthy of praise). The recipient may respond by presenting you with a *commendatory* plaque (one that expresses praise).

common. See MUTUAL.

commonwealth; commonweal. A *commonwealth* is a state, nation, or group of nations in which the people have a say in their own governance. The *commonweal* is the public well-being. Cf. TERRITORY.

compare with; compare to. *Compare with* is the usual phrase, meaning "to note similarities and differences" <the purpose of the colloquium is to compare the compensatory mechanism of the common law with that of the civil law>. *Compare to*, however, means to emphasize similarities; it often appears in a metaphorical or poetic construction <shall I compare thee to a summer's day>.

compel; impel. To *compel* an action or decision means to force it, to leave the actor no alternative <the justices knew their decision would compel an end to the re-count>. To *impel* an action or decision means to push the actor in that direction, especially by mental suasion <they should declare the causes that impel them to secede>.

compendious; voluminous. A *compendious* book is an abridgment (a *compendium*). A *voluminous* output fills a large book or many volumes. *Compendious* is often misused to denote "large," but in fact these words bear nearly opposite meanings.

competence; competency; competent. *Competence* is the general term for fitness or ability. *Competency* is the narrow legal term for fitness to stand trial or to give testimony, and for questions of sanity. For both words, the corresponding adjective is *competent.*

complacent; complaisant; compliant. A *complacent* person is comfortable and self-satisfied—even, by connotation, smug and foolhardy <the general warned budget-makers not to become complacent in peacetime>. A *complaisant* person is agreeable, often to the point of being a pushover <advisers worried that the President had been too complaisant at the summit>. A person who is *compliant* is obedient <the old-style CEO had expected a more compliant workforce>; a product or service that is *compliant* is in accordance with applicable regulations <the manufacturer replaced the out-of-spec goods with compliant ones>.

compliment; complement; supplement. *Compliment* (to praise, flatter, or bestow) is frequently misused for its look-alike, *complement* (to round out) <fine wine *compliments* [read *complements*] a fine meal>. To *supplement* something is to add to it, but without the nuance of completing. See COMPLIMENTARY.

complimentary; complementary; supplementary. A *complimentary* comment is a bit of praise; a *complimentary* ticket is free. A *complementary* accessory enhances an outfit. *Supplementary* income adds to a main source of support. See COMPLIMENT.

comprise; compose. The most frequent error in using these terms is signaled by the phrase **comprised of.* Strictly speaking, since *comprise* means "to include," the phrase makes no sense. John, Paul, George, and Ringo *composed* (*were comprised in*) the Beatles. The Beatles *comprised* (*were composed of*) John, Paul, George, and Ringo.

comprising. See INCLUDING.

compromise and settlement; accord and satisfaction. The first phrase can apply to the agreement to resolve any legal dispute. The second phrase is narrower, usually applying to contract law: the parties reach an *accord* (a substitute for the original contract obligation), and performance of the *accord* gives the formerly aggrieved party *satisfaction*.

compulsive; compulsory. The first term implies a psychological obsession <compulsive behavior>; the second means "mandatory" <compulsory-attendance laws>.

concede. See CEDE.

conclusory; conclusive. The appearance of *conclusory* in tens of thousands of legal opinions is *conclusive* proof that the word does in fact exist, despite its absence from many dictionaries. It describes a statement that puts forth a conclusion but not the reasoning behind it. *Conclusive* means "authoritative."

concurrence; concurrency. *Concurrence* in general usage denotes an agreement. In law it means a judge's agreement with the outcome of a decision, but for reasons different from the majority opinion. It also refers to that judge's separately written opinion. *Concurrency* means the simultaneous (*concurrent*) running of multiple criminal sentences (as contrasted with consecutive, cumulative, or "stacked" sentences).

concussion. See CONTUSION.

condemn; contemn. In legal senses, *condemn* means "to pass judgment against" <condemned to death>, "to take property by eminent domain" <the city condemned the lots for a runway-expansion project>, or "to declare a building uninhabitable" <the

*An invariably inferior form.

long-abandoned tenement building was condemned>. *Contemn* means "to show contempt"; in legal writing it is used in the context of contempt-of-court proceedings.

condemner; condemnor. The first is correct in the general sense of one who passes an adverse judgment. But when the government is taking property by eminent domain, it's the *condemnor* (the correlative term being *condemnee*).

condole. See CONSOLE.

conferral; conferment. Both terms mean the same thing: the act of *conferring* or what is *conferred*. But *conferral* predominates in legal writing, *conferment* in popular writing.

confession. See ADMISSION.

confident; confidant; confidante. To be *confident* is to be assured and determined. A *confidant* is a friend you can trust with your secrets; the word is also spelled *confidante*, although that feminine variant is disappearing.

conformity; *conformance. The first is Standard Written English; the second is a needless variant seen too often in legal writing.

congruous; congruent. *Congruous* and *congruent* both describe a good fit, harmony, or conformity between two things. But *congruous* is best used with people and qualities; *congruent* best deals with physical forms and geometry. The negative form *incongruous* is more common than either of the other terms; it means "inconsistent, unexplainable."

connive; conspire. If you *connive* at something, you look the other way when you should object. It is passive in that sense, whereas if you *conspire* with someone you take an active role.

connote; denote. Words often *connote* more than the literal meanings they *denote*. They pick up nuances that invite good or bad reactions. But remember that words alone carry *connotations*; acts do not <what does this protest *connote* [read *suggest*]?>.

consensus. So spelled—not **concensus*.

consent. See ASSENT.

consequent; subsequent. Both words describe something that follows another event. But *consequent* further describes something that happens as a result of the first event <speeding and the consequent accident>. *Subsequent* merely denotes time, not causation <subsequent Congresses acquiesced in the Court's interpretation>.

conservator; curator. As legal terms, both refer to the guardian appointed by a court to care for an incompetent person. The first term predominates, but the second is used in some states.

consist of; consist in. The first term is used with physical things <the flag consists of 50 stars and 13 stripes>. The second is preferred with abstract things <the driver's negligence consisted in speeding and not paying attention>.

console, v.t.; **condole.** To *console* someone is to comfort that person. To *condole* with someone is to express sympathy; it is more often seen in the noun form, *condolence*. *Condole* is intransitive, so while you may *console* a friend, you can't *condole* a friend.

consolidation. See JOINDER; MERGER.

*An invariably inferior form.

conspire. See CONNIVE.

constructive; constructional. In legal usage, the first term applies to something that is imposed by law <constructive notice> <constructive trust>. The second refers to construing writings, such as wills or statutes <constructional canons>.

consul. See COUNSEL.

contagious; infectious. These terms are distinguished in medicine. A *contagious* disease is easily spread by personal contact <influenza is highly contagious>. An *infectious* disease is spread by germs and viruses in the environment, or from person to person only by certain types of contact <although HIV is infectious, it is not spread by casual contact>.

contemn. See CONDEMN.

contemporary; contemporaneous. Both terms describe things that happen at the same time. But the first is used as an adjective or a noun, usually referring to people <Lord Coke and Shakespeare were contemporaries>. It can also mean "contemporary with us" (i.e., "modern") <contemporary fashions>. *Contemporaneous* is usually used with things and events <two theaters of war were raging contemporaneously>.

contemptuous; contemptible. If you feel contempt, you're *contemptuous* of some person or thing. If you're *contemptible*, you give others reason to feel contempt for you. Cf. CONTUMACIOUS.

contend. See ALLEGE.

contingent fee; contingency fee. The fee is *contingent* on success, not a charge for some *contingency.* The first phrase is better, but both are common.

continual; continuous. The first means "recurring," the second "uninterrupted." If you get *continual* calls from telemarketers, you may suffer a *continuous* headache.

continuance; continuation; continuity. To laypeople a *continuance* is going ahead with something now, but to a lawyer a *continuance* postpones a trial, so it means not going ahead till later. A *continuation* can be going forward without interruptions, or resuming after an interruption. *Continuity* is the absence of interruption.

continuous. See CONTINUAL.

contract. See AGREEMENT.

contravene; controvert. To *contravene* something is either (1) to conflict with or impair it <new fighting threatened to contravene peace efforts>, or (2) to violate it <this call contravened the gag order>. To *controvert* something is to speak against it or contradict it <our witness will controvert the plaintiff's version of what happened>.

contribution; indemnity. *Contribution* is a partial payment of a monetary award, made by one defendant to another. *Indemnity* is full payment under a legal duty, such as an insurance policy or a judgment.

contributory; contributive; contributorial; contributional. *Contributory* describes the contribution of money or physical things; *contributive* is an inferior way to say "conducive" <diligent outlining is *contributive* [read *conducive*] to success in law school>. *Contributorial* describes one or more contributors, and *contributional* describes one or more contributions.

controvert. See CONTRAVENE.

contumacious; contemptuous. The first is the legal term describing one who intentionally disobeys a court order and is therefore subject to punishment for *contempt* of court. The second is used for the same purpose, but less frequently. Outside legal usage, *contemptuous* dominates. See CONTEMPTUOUS.

contusion; abrasion; concussion. If you fall off your bicycle, you may get a *contusion* (bruise) or an *abrasion* (scrape or cut). But if you're wearing your helmet, you're not as likely to get a *concussion* (head injury from a hard hit).

convicted (of) (for). A hapless defendant is *convicted of* a crime or *convicted for* a criminal act, but is not *convicted in* anything.

convince; persuade. We hope to *convince* a jury to view the facts our way (mental state), and then to *persuade* them to return a favorable verdict (action). Watch the prepositions: one is *convinced of* or *convinced that*, but one is *persuaded to* do something.

copulate; fornicate. While both terms refer to the same act, they differ in their legal implications. The first can be used regardless of the marital status of the parties. The second refers only to an unmarried person's having sexual intercourse with another; it is still a crime in some places.

copy. See REPLICA.

copyrighted. This is the correct adjective; *copywritten* is not a proper word.

corespondent; correspondent. The first term is always a legal term, meaning either (1) one of two or more *respondents* (appellees), or (2) an adulterous spouse's paramour joined in a divorce suit (in the days before no-fault divorce). The second term covers all usual meanings, as in news reporter, letter-writer, or business representative.

corollary. See CORRELATION.

corporal; corporeal. *Corporal* describes something relating to the body <corporal punishment>. *Corporeal* describes *having* a physical body <corporeal manifestation>; it is sometimes misused for *corporal.*

corpse; corpus; corpus delicti; corpus juris. These are all terms for bodies of one sort or another. A *corpse* is a dead human body. A *corpus* is the body of assets held in a trust. *Corpus delicti* is literally "the body of the crime," the *actus reus* in modern law (not necessarily the dead body as popularly thought, but proof that a crime has been committed). Watch out for the humorous but distasteful misspelling, *corpus delecti.* *Corpus juris* is a body of law, the term used in the sixth century's Justinian Code and today's legal encyclopedia, *Corpus Juris Secundum.*

correctional; corrective. If there are problems in the *correctional* system (prisons), the legislature should take *corrective* (remedial) action.

correlation; corollary. When two facts, events, ideas, etc. are connected, esp. when one likely caused the other, they have a *correlation.* One thing that naturally follows another thing—esp. a proposition that follows another, proven proposition logically, with little or no additional proof—is a *corollary.*

correspondent. See CORESPONDENT.

*An invariably inferior form.

corroborate. See COLLABORATE.

***could care less.** The proper phrase is *couldn't care less* (or *couldn't possibly care less*). The illogical phrasing, dropping the *not*, occurred first among people who misunderstood the age-old idiom and didn't hear the second syllable of the contraction.

council. See COUNSEL.

counsel; counselor; council; councillor; consul. *Counsel*, as a noun, is an adviser (also *counselor*) or the advice itself. As a verb, it means "to give advice." A city *council* passes local ordinances; a person serving on a *council* is sometimes called a *councillor.* A foreign government's representative is a *consul.*

couple. Traditional phrasing requires *of*—hence *a couple of people*, not **a couple people.*

court-martial; courts-martial. The term is always hyphenated, never combined or separated into two words. Because *court* is the noun and *martial* the adjective, the plural form is *courts-martial.*

credible; creditable; credulous; incredulous. If you're an honest person, both you and what you say will be *credible* (believable). Honesty is a *creditable* (praiseworthy) trait. Those who will believe anything are *credulous* (gullible). And those who simply can't believe what they are hearing are *incredulous* (unbelieving).

crevice; crevasse. A *crevice* (accent on the first syllable) is a small crack, as in a plaster wall; a *crevasse* (accent on the second syllable) is a gaping chasm, as on a glacier.

criminal. See UNLAWFUL.

criteria. One *criterion*, two *criteria*. Never use *criteria* as if it were a singular noun.

culpable. See BLAMEWORTHY; GUILTY.

curator. See CONSERVATOR.

currently. See PRESENTLY.

curtesy. See DOWER.

curtilage; messuage. The area immediately surrounding a house is its *curtilage*, a term that is sometimes misspelled **curtilege* (perhaps through the influence of *privilege*). The house, curtilage, and outbuildings together are the *messuage.*

custody; possession. The first term applies to people and things <a suspect in police custody>, the second to things only <take possession of a new car>. In a master–servant (or employer–employee) relationship, the servant has *custody* of the master's chattels, but not *possession.*

damage; damages; injury. The first is the harm <the accident caused damage worth $50,000>, the second the compensation for that harm <the jury awarded $50,000 in damages>. What seems like an obvious distinction—that property sustains *damage* but a person sustains an *injury*—does not hold up in legal usage: people are *damaged* and property *injured* all the time.

data. Although *data* was long considered the plural of the singular noun *datum*, in recent decades it has shifted to be a mass noun that can take a singular verb <file encrypting ensures that your personal data is secure>. Ensure that *data* is consistently treated as either singular or plural throughout a piece of writing. See 11.25(d).

*An invariably inferior form.

deadly; deathly. A poisonous snake is *deadly* (it can kill you). A sudden ghostly silence might seem *deathly* (deathlike).

death statute; survival statute. A *death statute* lets the family recover the economic benefit they would have received but for the death. A *survival statute* lets a tort action survive the decedent so that the decedent's estate may recover damages.

debar. See BAR.

deceive; defraud. To *deceive* me is to mislead me into believing something that is not true. To *defraud* me is to get me to act in reliance on that misconception so that I suffer some detriment.

decided. See DECISIVE.

decide whether; *decide if. Prefer the former.

decimate; destroy. To *decimate* something is to damage it greatly, not to destroy it. Derived from the Latin word meaning "one-tenth," *decimate* was originally a repressive tactic in which every tenth person in a rebellious village or a defeated army was put to death. So to some readers it's an unintentionally funny word choice when it refers to some different percentage <the tornado *decimated* [read *destroyed*] half the town>.

decision; judgment; decree; opinion. Judges make and issue (but do not write) *decisions*, *judgments*, and *decrees*. The caselaw we read in law school is the judges' written *opinions*. In the past, a *judgment* came from a court of law, while a *decree* came from a court of equity, admiralty, probate, or divorce. Today there is no such distinction. Cf. VERDICT.

decisive; determinative; resolute; decided. A fact that compels a decision is said to be *decisive* or *determinative*. To lawyers, facts are *decisive*, but to others, this word more often describes people who are *resolute*. *Decisive* is frequently misused where *decided* (clearly identified) is intended <the Mets will start the Series with a *decisive* [read *decided*] advantage in pitching>.

declaim. See DISCLAIM.

decree. See DECISION.

deduce; induce; deduct; deduction; induction. We *deduce* an answer by applying general rules to specific facts. We *induce* an answer by collecting specific facts and looking for a general rule. *Deduct* (to subtract) is sometimes misused to mean *deduce*, perhaps because the noun form (*deduction*) is the same for both words. *Induction*, the noun form of *induce*, is much more common than the verb.

de facto; de jure. Something that is *de facto* is not authorized or mandated by law, but exists in fact <de facto government> <de facto segregation>. Something that is *de jure* is established by law <de jure custody rights>.

defamation; libel; slander. *Defamation* is the communication of a falsehood that damages the reputation of someone. If it is recorded, especially in writing, it is *libel*; if it is merely spoken and unrecorded, it is *slander*.

defective; deficient; deficiency; defect. A *defective* thing is faulty. A *deficient* number or amount is insufficient. *Deficient* may mean *defective* only in the sense that something

*An invariably inferior form.

is missing, not that the design is flawed. (When writing of due-process rights, for example, if notice is *deficient* it is also said to be *defective*.) Watch out for the noun forms, too: don't use *deficiency* (inadequate in number or amount) to mean *defect* (fault).

defense; defence. See OFFENSE.

deficient; deficiency. See DEFECTIVE.

definite; definitive. A *definite* answer is clear and exact. A *definitive* answer is final, conclusive, and authoritative. Supreme Court decisions are *definitive* but sometimes not so clear. The error comes when a writer tries to elevate the mundane word *definite* <the jury was visibly irritated at the witness for refusing to give a *definitive* [read *definite*] answer>.

defraud. See DECEIVE.

de jure. See DE FACTO.

delegate. See RELEGATE.

deliberate; deliberative. A *deliberate* act may be intended and planned <a deliberate act of terrorism> or slow and methodical <the deliberate pace of the rulemaking process>. *Deliberative* relates to debate <the Senate is a deliberative body>; it is misused when substituted for *deliberate* <the race went to the more *deliberative* [read *deliberate*] tortoise>.

delimit; limit. To *delimit* something is to refine its meaning by finding its limits <courts struggled to delimit the newfound right to privacy>. The word is misused when substituted for *limit* to mean "restrict."

delusion. See ILLUSION.

demean; bemean. The meanings of these words have shifted over time. To *demean* oneself originally meant "to behave" (hence, *demeanor*), and to *bemean* someone was to debase or belittle that person. Today, *demean* means what *bemean* once did, and *bemean* has faded into obscurity.

demur; demure. To *demur* in law is to file a *demurrer*, admitting the facts as the plaintiff has pleaded them but denying that they state a cause of action. More generally, to *demur* is to object (make a *demurral*), especially on moral grounds. The adjective *demure* describes a coy or restrained person.

denote. See CONNOTE.

denounce; renounce. To *denounce* is to accuse a person of engaging in criminal or reprehensible activity <the informant denounced the bookkeeper as an embezzler>. To *renounce* is to reject or to relinquish something <renounce an inheritance>.

dependence; dependency. *Dependence* is reliance on someone or something. *Dependency* is a much narrower term, meaning a land ruled by but not annexed by another country.

dependency. See DEPENDENCE; TERRITORY.

deport; deportment; deportation. *Deport* may mean either "to behave" in a particular way or "to expel from a country." In the first sense, the corresponding noun is *deportment*; in the second sense, *deportation*.

depository; depositary. At one time, a *depository* was a place (such as a bank) to deposit things, especially money; *depositary* was reserved for people. Then the Uniform Commercial Code used *depositary* to refer to banks. Outside UCC contexts, the old distinction is still a good one.

deprecate; depreciate. To *deprecate* someone or something is to express disapproval. To *depreciate* something is to belittle it; if something *depreciates*, it loses value. Although the traditional phrase was *self-depreciating*, *self-deprecating* is now well established and has become standard.

desert; dessert. See JUST DESERTS.

desirable; desirous. A *desirable* person or thing is alluring; seeing a desirable person or thing stirs *desirous* emotions in us.

despoliation; spoliation. *Despoliation* means "plunder and ruin," but so does *spoliation.* Be careful to avoid the misspellings caused by false association with *spoil.*

dessert. See JUST DESERTS.

destroy. See DECIMATE.

determinative. See DECISIVE.

determine whether; *determine if. Prefer the former.

detract; distract. Keep *detract* intransitive <grammatical errors detract from any brief's impact> and *distract* transitive <typos distract the reader's attention from the message>.

device; devise. The *-c-* spelling is the noun <an ingenious device>. The *-s-* spelling is the verb <surely we can devise a way to settle this>.

devise; bequest; legacy. As the common-law terms developed regarding wills, a *devise* was a gift of real property, a *bequest* was a gift of personal property, and a *legacy* was a gift of money. The terms have shifted somewhat: modern usage includes money as a *bequest*, and U.S. statutes consider items of personal property to be *devises.*

diagnosis; prognosis; prognostication. The doctor gives you a *diagnosis* (what is wrong with you), and then discusses your *prognosis* (what course the disease will take; what your chances of recovery are). *Prognostication* (a forecast or prophecy) connotes mysticism, so it's not entirely appropriate as a medical term. It's also a highfalutin word for a weather forecast.

dietitian; dietician. Although both spellings are acceptable, the first is preferred.

different from; different than. The first phrase is usually the better choice. The second can be smoother idiomatically when *than* substitutes for *from what* <in defamation law, after *New York Times v. Sullivan* "malice" meant something different than it did before>.

differ from; differ with. To *differ from* something is to deviate from it <your numbers differ from mine>. To *differ with* someone is to disagree with that person <I have to differ with you about those numbers>.

dilemma; Hobson's choice. If you face two bad options, you're in a *dilemma.* A *Hobson's choice*, strictly speaking, is a take-it-or-leave-it situation: no choice at all. But that literal

*An invariably inferior form.

meaning has been obscured in American usage, and today the phrase has come to mean, like *dilemma*, the choice between two evils.

diminution. So spelled—not **dimunition.*

disbar. See BAR.

disburse. See DISPERSE.

disc. See DISK.

disclaim; declaim. The word for disavowing a warranty is *disclaiming.* To *declaim* is to give a public speech <the Declaration was written to be declaimed in every town square>.

disclose; expose; divulge. All three words mean "to make (something) known." But *disclose* does not carry the connotations of scandal that *expose* does, nor the connotations of betrayal or confession that *divulge* does <disclose financial backing> <expose corruption> <divulge state secrets>. To *expose* something is also to place it in danger <expose to liability> <expose to the elements> or to reveal to view <the curtain rose, exposing an elaborate set> <the flasher was arrested for exposing himself in public>.

discomfort; discomfit. To feel *discomfort* is to feel uneasiness. To *discomfort* someone else is to make that person feel uneasy. Strictly speaking, to *discomfit* an enemy is to utterly destroy it or to dash its plans and leave it in a state of total confusion. But today about all that's left of that meaning is "to confuse." And since a confused person is usually uneasy as well, the distinction and the meaning have both become, well, confusing.

discrete; discreet. A *discrete* thing is distinct from others <the crime has five discrete elements>. To be *discreet* is to be either tactful <he discreetly declined> or circumspectly confidential <the reporter was discreet about the informant's identity>.

discriminatory; discriminating, *adj. Discriminatory* means "reflecting a biased, unfair treatment" <discriminatory employment policy>. *Discriminating*, as an adjective, means "analytically refined, discerning, tasteful" <a discriminating palate>.

disinformation; misinformation. Both words denote incorrect information. But *disinformation* means *misinformation* that is deliberately created or spread for some purpose, usually as propaganda.

disingenuous. See INGENIOUS.

disinterested; uninterested. A *disinterested* person is impartial in the sense of not having any legal or financial interest involved in the outcome of a dispute, nor any bias toward the parties or the facts. An *uninterested* person has no intellectual interest in the people or the controversy, and probably doesn't care how it is resolved. A judge must be *disinterested*, but should never be *uninterested.* The distinction is eroding in general usage, but it remains sharp in legal writing.

disk; disc. *Disk* is the correct spelling for most uses <computer disk> <a slipped disk in his back>. The exceptions are audio and video *discs*, *disc* brakes, and the parts of a plow that turn up the soil.

disorganized; unorganized. Something that is *disorganized* is usually chronically or inherently so <my desk is a disorganized mess>, or else thrown into disarray by events <the mayor's unexpected resignation left City Hall utterly disorganized>. *Unorganized*

*An invariably inferior form.

has no such negative connotations <the "blue flu" sick-out appeared to be spontaneous and unorganized>.

disperse; disburse. To *disperse* a crowd is to break it up; to *disperse* things is to distribute them. To *disburse* money is also to distribute it, but note that this word can be used only in connection with money.

disposal; disposition. The words share the same general meaning (the getting rid of), but the connotations are very different. *Disposal* connotes getting rid of unwanted things <garbage disposal>, while *disposition* connotes a planned distribution <disposition of the assets of an estate>.

distinctive; distinguishable; distinguished. Something that is *distinctive* is recognizable out of others of the same type <a distinctive birthmark>. *Distinguishable* is generally synonymous with *distinctive*, but in law it is the word used to argue why a rule in a precedential case should not apply to the facts in the present case <that case is distinguishable because no consent was involved>. Someone who is *distinguished* is held in high regard <a distinguished senior judge>.

distract. See DETRACT.

dive. This verb is traditionally inflected *dive* > *dived* > *dived*—the past form *dove* being considered regional dialect.

divorcé; divorcée. See FIANCÉ.

divulge. See DISCLOSE.

doctrinal; doctrinaire. *Doctrinal* is used to describe a *doctrine*; it's neutral in connotation. *Doctrinaire* describes a dogmatic person and connotes stubbornness and narrow-mindedness.

domicile. See CITIZENSHIP.

dominant; predominant; dominate; predominate. *Dominant* and *predominant* are adjectives <a dominant personality> <the predominant political party>. *Dominate* and *predominate* are verbs <dominate the game> <neither party predominates in the legislature>. Note that *predominate* does not take an object. One thing does not *predominate* another; rather, it *predominates* in its field. A common error is to use the verb forms as adjectives.

double jeopardy. See FORMER JEOPARDY.

***doubt if.** Prefer *doubt that* or *doubt whether* to convey a sense of skepticism.

doubtless; *doubtlessly; no doubt; undoubtedly. *Doubtless* is already an adverb, so it's incorrect to tack on *-ly*. *No doubt* says the same thing as *doubtless*, only more strongly. And *undoubtedly* is an even stronger word.

dower; curtesy; dowry. *Dower* (the right of a widow to a life estate in a third of her husband's land) and *curtesy* (the right of a widower to a life estate in all his wife's land) live on in some forms in a few U.S. jurisdictions. *Dowry* is the collection of assets that a wife brings into a marriage. *Curtsy* (a woman's bow made by bending the knees) and *courtesy* (politeness) are common slips for *curtesy*.

dowry. See DOWER.

*An invariably inferior form.

drag. This verb is inflected *drag* > *dragged* > *dragged*—never *drug* as a past-tense form in refined prose.

dream. This verb is preferably inflected *dream* > *dreamed* > *dreamed* in American English. *Dreamt* is a British English variant of the past tense and past participle.

drink. This verb is inflected *drink* > *drank* > *drunk*. Hence it is correct to write *He had drunk four energy drinks that morning*, not **had drank*.

drowned; was drowned. The first, in active voice, suggests an accidental death; the second, in passive voice, suggests foul play. **Drownded* is a dialectal variant.

drunk; drunken. If you're *drunk*, you are intoxicated. If you're a *drunken* sot, you are habitually drunk. The first term implies an instance of intoxication, the second a constant tendency toward intoxication. Also, people are *drunk*, but their behavior is *drunken* (with the idiomatic exception of *drunk driving*). Finally, remember that *drunk*—not *drank*—is the past participle of *drink* <have you drunk any coffee this morning?>.

dual; duel. *Dual*, an adjective meaning "two," is often misspelled *duel*. *Duel* is the noun and verb dealing with the formal two-way combat, traditionally with pistols or swords.

due to; because of. Strictly speaking, *due* is a noun <give them their due> or an adjective <due process>. That is why purists sanction its use (1) after a *be*-verb, as a predicate adjective <the delay was due to bad weather>, and (2) to modify a noun <the delay due to bad weather upset the whole schedule>. Sticklers object to using *due to* as a preposition <*Due to* [read *Because of*] bad weather, the trial was delayed>. Others think their scorn is undue. In any event, when a preposition is needed, *because of* is a stronger and safer choice.

duplicate. See REPLICA.

each other; one another. *Each other* requires that there be only two actors <the two advocates clearly respected each other>. *One another* takes three or more <the states that had enacted the model law all honored one another's child-support judgments>.

eager. See ANXIOUS.

ease. See FACILITY.

economic; economical. See FINANCIAL.

effect; effectuate. In legal writing at least, these terms can be distinguished. To *effect* a result is to bring it about <effect a change in trade policy>. To *effectuate* something is to give effect to the purpose behind it <regulations designed to effectuate the enabling legislation> <a good executor tries to effectuate the testator's wishes as closely as possible>. For more on *effect*, see AFFECT.

e.g.; i.e. The first is the abbreviation (for *exempli gratia*) that you want when citing examples <top-tier law schools, e.g., Yale, Harvard, and Michigan>. The second (short for *id est*, "that is") is used where further explanation is due <the Framers insulated Article III judges from the political fray, i.e., they are appointed for life and not easily subject to removal>. But *i.e.* is often misused to mean "for example." Despite their appearance to the contrary in this entry, *e.g.* and *i.e.* should not ordinarily be italicized,

*An invariably inferior form.

and they should each be followed by a comma. One exception is *e.g.* in legal-citation signals such as *see, e.g.*, which are italicized.

elicit; illicit. To *elicit* a reaction is to draw it out of someone <the question was intended to elicit an angry response>. Writers occasionally misuse *illicit* (illegal) when they mean *elicit* <fighting words may *illicit* [read *elicit*] more than the speaker bargained for>. Cf. UNLAWFUL.

elude. See ALLUDE.

e-mail. This and other *e*-words <e-commerce> are best typed with their hyphens. The *e-* is not a prefix but an abbreviated form of *electronic.*

embarrass. See HARASS.

embassy; legation. An *embassy* is the office of a foreign country's ambassador. A *legation* is the office of other diplomatic agents such as envoys and ministers.

emend. See AMEND.

emigrant; emigrate; émigré. See IMMIGRANT.

eminent. See IMMINENT.

empanel; *impanel. *Empanel* (meaning "to put on a panel; esp., to swear [a jury] to try an issue or case") is now the preferred spelling in both American English and British English <it's time to empanel the jury>. **Impanel*, though once the predominant form, might now be regarded as a needless variant.

empathy; sympathy. We feel *empathy* when we are mentally able to put ourselves into a work of art or another person's situation and get a deeper understanding of it, as if it were happening to us. We feel *sympathy* when we are sad at someone else's sorrow.

endemic. See EPIDEMIC.

endnote. See FOOTNOTE.

endorse; indorse. *Endorse* (meaning "to authorize" or "to support") is correct in every sense except one. To sign commercial paper is to *indorse* it, and the Uniform Commercial Code has effectively made that distinction inviolate. Also note that *indorse* means "to sign on the back," so the phrase *indorse on the back* is redundant. See APPROVE.

enervate; innervate. These terms have opposite meanings: to *enervate* is to sap of energy, while to *innervate* is to energize (or, in biology, to supply [tissue or an organ] with nerves).

enforceable. See FORCIBLE.

enhance; improve. A quality (never a person) that is *enhanced* is expanded or raised. The word in general use has positive connotations <a dash of salt to enhance the flavor>, but not always so in law <an enhanced sentence> <the enhanced-injury doctrine>.

> "Every time a usage distinction is wiped out, writers lose the ability to use that nuance. Just how much of a loss that is will have to be weighed case by case."
>
> —*Bill Walsh*

*An invariably inferior form.

If it is a person who is better than before, use *improve* <we go to college to improve ourselves>.

enjoin from; enjoin upon (to). Depending on whether the injunction is negative or positive in effect, the target is *enjoined from* doing something, or *enjoined upon* to take action. The first sense is prevalent in the United States.

enormity; enormousness. *Enormity* is often misused to denote *enormousness* (hugeness). In fact, *enormity* means "great evil, heinousness" <the enormity of the terrorists' attacks>.

ensure. See ASSURE.

***enthused.** Prefer *enthusiastic*, the traditional adjective. Avoid all uses of **enthuse* as a verb.

enumerable; innumerable. These words sound alike, but they designate almost opposite qualities. An *enumerable* number can be counted <our options are few and enumerable>, but an *innumerable* number is impossible or impractical to count, usually because it is too large <death by innumerable paper cuts>.

enure. See INURE.

envelop; envelope. To *envelop* something is to surround it. An *envelope* is an item of stationery.

envious; enviable. One who envies another is *envious* of that person. What one envies in another person is some *enviable* trait or asset. Cf. JEALOUS.

epidemic; pandemic; endemic. An *epidemic* is a local outbreak of a disease (or by extension, of anything, usually something bad). A *pandemic* is the spread of a disease across a large area, such as throughout a country or worldwide. A disease that is *endemic* to an area or a population is continuously present there; indigenous plants and animals are also *endemic* to their native area, and a quality that is *endemic* in a person occurs naturally or habitually.

equal. See COEQUAL.

***equally as.** This phrasing is almost invariably faulty. Use *equally* without *as*.

essay. See ASSAY.

estoppel. See WAIVE.

et al. This abbreviation stands for *et alii* ("and others"). Don't put a period after *et*, which is Latin for "and."

etc. This abbreviation for *et cetera* ("and other things") is often misused in two ways: (1) writers often use the faulty phrasing **and etc.*, and (2) they often erroneously tack on *etc.* to a list introduced by *for example* or *e.g.* Both misusages create redundancies.

evoke; invoke. To *evoke* is to draw something out of others <evoke memories> <evoke bittersweet tears>. To *invoke* is to call upon something, especially for help <invoked the Fifth Amendment> <invoked martial law>. A common error is using *evoke* where *invoke* is needed <the judge *evoked* [read *invoked*] the name of Solomon in handing down the decision>.

*An invariably inferior form.

exalt; exult. To *exalt* people or things is to lift them up (in esteem or rank) and honor them. To *exult* is to rejoice.

example. See EXEMPLAR.

ex ante; ex post. These two reader-unfriendly phrases describe what point of view is used to examine a matter. An *ex ante* examination asks what circumstances looked like to someone before an event—it is prospective and subjective. An *ex post* examination looks at all the circumstances of an event that has already happened—it is retrospective and objective.

except; accept. To *except* something is to leave it out. To *accept* something is to take it in. *Except* and *excepted* are sometimes misused for their near-opposites, *accept* and *accepted.*

exceptional; exceptionable. Something *exceptional* is out of the ordinary, and usually superior <the lawyer won over the jury with an exceptional closing statement>. Something *exceptionable* is objectionable <the lawyer's exceptionable mention of insurance triggered an angry rebuke from the judge>. The second term is sometimes used incorrectly when the writer means *exceptional.*

ex-convict; *ex-felon. A person released from prison is an *ex-convict* or, informally, an *ex-con*. But someone convicted of a felony remains a *felon* for life (unless pardoned), so **ex-felon* is incorrect.

excuse; justification; alibi. In criminal law, these terms are distinguished. We consider duress, for example, a valid *excuse* for most crimes (as if to say, "You did wrong, but it wasn't your fault"). We consider self-defense a legitimate *justification* (as if to say, "What you did wasn't wrong under the circumstances because it avoided a greater harm"). An *alibi* is not an *excuse* or a *justification*, and it is not just any defense. It is specifically a defense that the accused was somewhere else when the crime occurred.

executor. See ADMINISTRATOR; TRUSTEE.

executory; executorial. *Executory* describes something that will take full effect in the future <an executory interest in property>. *Executorial* describes an estate's *executor* or what the executor does <completed all executorial duties>.

executrix. See ADMINISTRATOR.

exemplar; example. An *exemplar* is a type of *example.* In law, it is a typical sample, as of handwriting, a signature, or a voice, that is used to identify the writer or speaker. In general use, it is an ideal example.

***ex-felon.** See EX-CONVICT.

expect. See ANTICIPATE.

explicit; implicit. What is *explicit* is detailed and obvious <the contract is explicit: time is of the essence>. What is *implicit* is suggested, assumed, or necessary to carry out the purpose <further powers necessary and proper to carry out the federal government's enumerated powers are implicit in the Constitution>.

expose. See DISCLOSE.

ex post. See EX ANTE.

*An invariably inferior form.

ex post facto; post hoc. *Ex post facto* means "after the fact." *Post hoc* is short for *post hoc, ergo propter hoc* ("after this, therefore because of this"). It is often misused to mean "after the fact" <that testimony is just *a post hoc* [read *an ex post facto*] rationalization>.

expropriate. See APPROPRIATE.

extension; renewal. These terms are distinguished in law: after a contract or lease expires, the parties may continue their relationship by an *extension* (under the same agreement) or by a *renewal* (under a new, often identical agreement).

extortion. See BRIBERY.

exult. See EXALT.

facility. Properly, *facility* is the ease with which something can be done <a double axel performed with facility> or the physical things that make something easier or possible <recreational facilities>. But the word has been so overused for *building* as to become meaningless <school *facilities* [read *buildings*]>; avoid that sense in formal writing.

fact; factual. Ambiguities can arise because to most people these terms refer to the truth <the fact is that any Supreme Court nominee will be grilled in the confirmation hearings> <a factual account of the campaign>. But in law they more often refer to events that the parties disagree about and that can probably never be known with certainty <the facts of the case are in dispute> <just because a jury made a factual determination doesn't make your lie true>.

farther; further. The best way to handle these terms is to use the first literally <from here it's farther to Paris than to London> and the second figuratively <the justices did not overturn the doctrine, but they refused to extend it any further>.

fax. Prefer *fax* over *facsimile transmission* (n.) or *send a facsimile transmission* (vb.). Don't use the all-caps version *_FAX._ It's *fax.*

faze; phase. To *faze* is to flummox or bother. Somebody can remain *unfazed*, but never *_unphased._ To *phase in* or *phase out* is to transition.

feel bad. Correct. *_Feel badly_ is wrong. If you're unsure about this point, read any grammar on the point of linking verbs or copulas.

feemail. See BLACKMAIL.

feign; feint. To *feign* something is to fake it <the driver feigned ignorance of the speed limit>. In boxing and fencing, to *feint* is to *feign* an attack to mislead the opponent <the challenger feinted a right jab, and then stunned the champ with a left uppercut>.

fewer; less. Use *fewer* when referring to numbers <the First Monday demonstrations drew fewer protesters this year>; use *less* when referring to volume, amount, or degree <the senior judge has less influence these days>. It is redundant to write or say *_a fewer number_ because the sense of number is included in the meaning of *fewer.* Make it *a smaller number* or simply *fewer.*

fiancé; fiancée; divorcé; divorcée. Concern over gender-neutrality has not reached these French loanwords for a man (one *e*) and a woman (two *e*'s) before getting married and after dissolving their marriage.

*An invariably inferior form.

fictional; fictitious; fictive. *Fictional* is generally neutral in connotation, referring to such things as literary novels and judicial constructions <a fictional story based on real characters> <that fictional person called "reasonable">. *Fictitious* connotes a sham, something either fraudulent or nonexistent <the rancher purported to collateralize the loan with a fictitious herd of cattle> <the teen's fictitious driver's license was nothing but trouble>. *Fictive* can but shouldn't be used as a synonym of *fictional.* It properly refers to one's power of imaginative creation <her renowned fictive ability> or a product of the imagination <his fictive creations>. In law, however, you'll most often use it to describe people treated as family members despite not being related by blood or marriage <fictive relative>.

figuratively. See LITERALLY.

financial; economic; economical. When writing about a company's or household's money, use *financial* <the Nasdaq collapse brought financial ruin to many dot-com companies>. When writing about managing resources (including money) on a large scale, regional or nationwide, use *economic* <rising energy prices often signal an economic downturn>. Reserve *economical* to mean "thrifty."

finding; holding. Strictly speaking, a court makes *findings* on questions of fact and *holdings* on questions of law. So it's incorrect to write, for example, that a court will *find* a statute unconstitutional. Rather, the court might *hold* that it is unconstitutional.

flagrant. See BLATANT.

flair; flare. A *flair* is a knack <a flair for words> or stylishness <the ballet was performed with flair>. A *flare* is a sudden flame-up or a bright fire used to provide light <the flares from burning oil wells marked Saddam's final blow against Kuwait>.

flammable; inflammable; nonflammable. *Flammable* has become the accepted term meaning "capable of burning," beating out the synonym *inflammable. Inflammable* can be ambiguous, since the intensive *in-* prefix can be mistaken to mean "not." And this is a word that we don't want people to confuse. The term for "not capable of burning" is *nonflammable.*

flare. See FLAIR.

flaunt; flout. To *flaunt* something is to show it off <if you've got it, flaunt it>. To *flout* something (especially a law or an order) is to disregard it with contempt <the ousted dictator openly flouted the arrest warrant until the new regime arrested him>. *Flaunt* is often misused as a substitute for *flout*, perhaps because it sounds similar and also suggests "taunt."

flounder; founder. To *flounder* is to flail about or struggle wildly (think *flounder = fish out of water*), not to fail. The word for the latter meaning is *founder.* In admiralty law, a ship or boat will *founder* if it sinks or runs aground.

flout. See FLAUNT.

follow. See APPLY.

footnote; endnote. If they are at the bottom of the page, they are *footnotes.* If they are collected at the end, they are *endnotes.*

forbear; forebear. To *forbear* is to refrain from doing some act <in the settlement the plaintiff agreed to forbear any future claims>. A *forebear* is an ancestor <the tribe's oral traditions perpetuated the stories of their forebears' wanderings>. Each term is often misused for the other.

forcible; forceable; enforceable; forceful. *Forcible* is standard only when the force is physical <DEA agents forcibly entered the warehouse>. *Forceable* has a passive sense, meaning "able to be forced" <the door wasn't forceable>. *Enforceable* is standard <despite the parties' minor breaches, the court held that the contract was fully enforceable>. *Forceful* is correct for literal or figurative force <a forceful reaction to the protesters' rock-throwing> <a forceful appeal for unity>.

forebear. See FORBEAR.

forego. See FORGO.

foreword; preface. The introduction to a book is a *foreword* only if it is written by someone other than the book's author. If the author wrote it, it's a *preface.* And although it does appear in a forward position in the book, it is always an error to call it a *forward* (read *foreword*).

forgo; forego. To *forgo* something is to do without it <let's forgo the chitchat>; to *forgo* a legal right is to waive it <the defendant agreed to forgo a jury trial>. To *forego* something is to go before it <in light of the foregoing discussion, this court should grant summary judgment>. The misuse of *forego* for *forgo* is lamentably widespread.

formality; formalism; formalistic. *Formality* is strict adherence to rules, manners, or customs. *Formalism* is also adherence to rules, but with the emphasis on procedural minutiae regardless of substance and fairness. Both *formalism* and its adjective form, *formalistic*, are usually pejorative terms.

formally; formerly. To do something *formally* is to do it either according to proper custom <formally attired> or in accordance with procedural requirements <a formally executed will>. Writers occasionally misuse *formally* when they mean *formerly* (previously).

former; latter. These terms refer only to the first and second of two things in a set. They are misused when they refer to the first three things in a series of nine, for example.

former jeopardy; double jeopardy. *Former jeopardy* means "prosecution by the same government for a crime that one has previously been convicted or acquitted of." *Double jeopardy* includes *former jeopardy*, but also describes a situation in which a defendant has been convicted of multiple counts, one of which is a lesser-included offense of another (as for robbery and assault).

formerly. See FORMALLY.

fornicate. See COPULATE.

fortunate; fortuitous; gratuitous. Something *fortunate* is lucky <you were fortunate to win the door prize>. Something *fortuitous* happens by chance, but it may be either good or bad luck <a fortuitous turn of events made me late for my interview>. *Gratuitous* means "free" <beverage is gratuitous with any meal> or "unwarranted" <the movie had too much gratuitous nudity>, but it is occasionally confused with *fortuitous.*

fortunately. See HOPEFULLY.

founder. See FLOUNDER.

from whence. See WHENCE.

fulsome. Traditionally, what is *fulsome* is overdone to the point of being disgusting; it especially applies to cloying flattery. Yet when the word appears, it is most often misused (with unintended irony) in the phrase *fulsome praise.*

funeral; funereal; funerary. *Funeral* is a noun and also an adjective <funeral procession>. *Funereal* describes a funeral-like mood <a funereal gloom fell on the campaign headquarters>. *Funerary* describes things that are used in a burial <the funerary canopy>.

further. See FARTHER.

***gantlet.** See GAUNTLET.

garnishment. See SEQUESTRATION.

gauntlet; *gantlet; gamut. The standard phrases are *run the gauntlet* (predominant over **run the gantlet* since about 1800) and *throw down the gauntlet. Run the gamut* means "to have a full range" <the buffet ran the gamut from soup to nuts>.

gender. See SEX.

generative; generational. *Generative* describes the creation of offspring. It is misused when discussing *generations*, as when counting *generational* steps to determine next of kin.

genericness; genericism. *Genericness* is the accepted noun form of *generic*, as used in trademark law. *Genericism* appears infrequently.

gibe; jibe; jive. A *gibe* is an angry taunt <gibes from the dissatisfied audience>, but today it is also a good-natured teasing <gibes among poker buddies>. The word is also a verb <to gibe one's opponents>. To *jibe* with something is to agree with it <these numbers jibe with our budget projection>. To *jive* is to deceive by fast talking, to taunt, or to dance the jitterbug. *Jive* is sometimes misused for *jibe.*

glance; glimpse. By idiom, these words for "a quick look" go with different verbs and prepositions. One takes (or gives) a *glance at* something, but gets a *glimpse of* it.

> "Because language is a living thing, there are processes of change always going on. Words alter slightly in meaning, and more in usage; some go out of use, and some that have gone out of use come into use once more; some gain and some lose in force and in dignity, and so on. Sometimes in the lapse of the years a word has lost caste through the commonplace usage of it, so that it cannot any longer be employed to express grave and lofty thoughts."
>
> —*Henry Bett*

*An invariably inferior form.

good faith. See BONA FIDES.

gorilla. See GUERRILLA.

gourmet; gourmand. These are similar words for a lover of food and drink, but they have wildly different connotations. A *gourmet* is a sophisticated connoisseur, while a *gourmand* is a glutton.

gratuitous. See FORTUNATE.

graymail. See BLACKMAIL.

greenmail. See BLACKMAIL.

grievous. Often misspelled **grievious*.

grisly; grizzly; grizzled. *Grisly* describes something bloody or horrifying. *Grizzly* describes a bear or gray hair; in the latter sense it is synonymous with the more common *grizzled.*

guarantee; warranty; guaranty. *Guarantee* looks to the future, as assurance that something will or will not be done. *Warranty* looks to the present and past, by accepting legal responsibility that things are as they were represented. *Guaranty* is mostly used as a noun, and is interchangeable with *guarantee.*

guarantor. See SURETY.

guerrilla; *guerilla; gorilla. A *guerrilla* is an irregular soldier engaged in surprise attacks and sabotage. This spelling is preferred over **guerilla*. A *gorilla* is a big ape and a big laugh when misused to mean *guerrilla.*

guilty; culpable. A jury (or the judge) decides whether the accused is *guilty* or *not guilty.* But that finding doesn't change how *culpable* (blameworthy) the accused truly is. Although the first term occasionally arises in civil suits <guilty of misrepresentation>, it is usually (and better) restricted to criminal contexts. Cf. BLAMEWORTHY; INNOCENT.

habitable; *inhabitable; uninhabitable. The first two terms are synonyms. Modern usage prefers *habitable* as the term for "fit to be occupied." As **inhabitable* has declined in use, it has become ambiguous (i.e., seen as a negative form) and ought to be avoided. The antonym is *uninhabitable.*

***hairbrained.** See HAREBRAINED.

hale into court; haul into court. These two phrases are correctly used to indicate a compelled appearance. *Hale into court* is the original phrase. *Haul into court*, which creates a mental picture of being physically dragged into the courtroom, is more evocative. **Hail into court* is a common error.

hallucination. See ILLUSION.

hand up an indictment; hand down a decision; hand down a verdict; return a verdict. A grand jury *hands up* (never *down*) an indictment, presenting criminal charges to the court. A judge *hands down a decision.* A petit jury *hands down a verdict* or, more properly, *returns a verdict.*

hanged; hung. *Hanged* is the correct past tense for an intentional killing by suspending a person by the neck, esp. as a form of suicide, murder, or capital punishment <convicted

*An invariably inferior form.

of murder and promptly hanged>. *Hung* (often misused to mean *hanged*) is the correct past tense for all other meanings <they all hung their coats>.

harass; embarrass. These terms *embarrass* those who misspell them (is it one *-r-* or two?). Think of it this way: *harass* has one *-r-* but two pronunciations (accent either syllable).

harebrained. This is the correct term for "silly" or "stupid"; **hairbrained* is a common error.

haul into court. See HALE INTO COURT.

havoc. See WREAK HAVOC.

healthy; healthful. In the best usage, what is *healthy* is itself in good health; the word should refer only to living things. What is *healthful* promotes good health <a healthful diet will keep you healthy>. Today the words are often used interchangeably.

help (to). Omit the *to* whenever you can <a treatise can help you locate the landmark cases>.

he or she. This gender-neutral alternative phrasing is acceptable only if seldom used—but it may be necessary every third page or so. It is certainly less objectionable than *he/she*, *s/he*, or *(s)he*, and similar makeshifts. On *they* as an alternative, see 11.10(o).

hesitancy; hesitation; *hesitance. Someone who *hesitates* has the quality of *hesitancy* (reluctance), while the act itself is *hesitation* (pause). **Hesitance* is an inferior variant of *hesitation.*

hijack. This is the correct spelling (not **highjack*). Robbers may *hijack* vehicles and their loads, but not people; people taken by force are *kidnapped.*

historic; historical. *Historic* refers to someone or something that significantly changed *history* <the historic D-Day invasion>. *Historical* means "of history" <a historical society> or "occurring in the past" <the clerk's records were full of historical details about the town's early families>. Since both words start with a consonant sound, they take the article *a* rather than *an.*

hoard; horde. A *hoard* is a hidden supply, especially of something valuable or scarce. A *horde* was originally a wandering tribe of barbarians, and today by extension it is a mob or an army.

Hobson's choice. See DILEMMA.

hodgepodge. See HOTCHPOT.

hoi polloi; hoity-toity. The *hoi polloi* is the masses. Perhaps because of *hoity-toity* (pretentious, and by extension a mocking pejorative to describe the upper crust), *hoi polloi* is sometimes misused to refer to high society.

holding. See FINDING.

home in; *hone in. *Home in* is the correct phrase for getting nearer and nearer the target <the carrier pigeon circled overhead, homing in on its cage>. The erroneous substitution of **hone in* is a later development.

homicide. See MURDER.

*An invariably inferior form.

***hone in.** See HOME IN.

hopefully; fortunately. Use of *hopefully* to mean "it is hoped" (rather than "in a hopeful manner") is widespread, even in legal writing. It is defensible as a sentence adverb similar to *fortunately* and *certainly* <fortunately, the jury agreed with us [which doesn't mean that the jury agreed in a fortunate manner]>. But *hopefully* used this way has been condemned for so long that writers use it at their peril. Its use is a distraction—and careful writers avoid distractions.

horde. See HOARD.

hotchpot; hotchpotch; hodgepodge. *Hotchpot* is the original term, derived from a meal in which all the ingredients are shaken together. By extension it applied to an estate whose assets were consolidated and then distributed. In U.S. community-property states, *hotchpot* also means "property belonging to the community." *Hotchpot* is still the preferred term in legal writing, but in ordinary use the term evolved into the reduplicative *hotchpotch* and then to today's dominant form, *hodgepodge.*

humanitarian. To promote human welfare is *humanitarian* <humanitarian aid>. Because the word isn't a synonym for *human*, avoid such phrases as **humanitarian crisis* or **humanitarian disaster.*

hung. See HANGED.

hypothesize; hypothecate. To *hypothesize* is to form a hypothesis about something. In admiralty and in civil-law jurisdictions, to *hypothecate* is to pledge something without delivering either title or possession. *Hypothecate* should not be misused for *hypothesize.*

ideal. See IDYLLIC.

idyllic; ideal. An *idyllic* place may be very nice, but it's not *ideal* (as some writers mistakenly believe). Rather, it may be rustic, charming, and picturesque <an idyllic alpine village>, or simple and stress-free <an idyllic childhood>. The word derives from *idyll*, a short poem, often with a pastoral theme.

i.e. See E.G.

ignorant; stupid. Even the smartest person is *ignorant* (unaware) of some things. And a person who is *stupid* (unintelligent) is not *ignorant* of all things.

illegal. See UNLAWFUL.

illegal alien; undocumented worker. *Illegal alien* is the traditional phrase for one who has entered the country illegally. *Undocumented worker* is a politically correct euphemism. *Illegal* should not be considered pejorative in the phrase because (1) it is true (unauthorized entry violates the law), and (2) *illegal* is not synonymous with *criminal*, so it is not a severe aspersion. *Illegal immigrant* is a milder equivalent.

illegible; unreadable. *Illegible* describes handwriting or printing that is not clear enough to be read <it was the victim's handwriting, but the words were illegible>. *Unreadable* refers to content that is so poorly written as to be almost impossible to understand <the judge dreaded the thought of opening another unreadable brief>.

illicit. See ELICIT; UNLAWFUL.

*An invariably inferior form.

illusion; delusion; hallucination. An *illusion* is a deceptive appearance <the company's "profits" turned out to be the illusion of a creative accountant>. A *delusion* is an illusion with added elements of danger, self-deception, and prolonged influence <delusions of grandeur>. *Delusion* refers to an erroneous mental belief, whereas *hallucination* is an erroneous sensory perception <the drug induced colorful hallucinations>. Cf. ALLUSION.

immanent. See IMMINENT.

immigrant; emigrant; immigrate; emigrate; émigré. A person who leaves one country to live in a second is an *immigrant* in the second and an *emigrant* in the first; the person has *immigrated to* the new country and *emigrated from* the old. An *émigré* is one who flees a country (or is expelled) for political reasons.

imminent; eminent; immanent. *Imminent* means more than just "near" or "probable"; it means "very close at hand and almost certain to happen" <imminent bodily harm>. *Eminent* means "distinguished" <the eminent justice> or "highest" <eminent domain>. *Immanent*, which is sometimes confounded with *imminent*, means "spiritually pervading the material world."

immoral; amoral; unmoral. An *immoral* person is affirmatively evil. An *amoral* person is indifferent to concerns of morality. An *unmoral* being (such as an animal) is incapable of having moral values.

immunity; impunity. *Immunity* is the exemption from some responsibility or liability <the senator could not be sued for the defamatory floor speech because the Speech or Debate Clause conferred immunity>. *Impunity*, a narrower term, means freedom from punishment for one's acts <enjoying diplomatic immunity, some embassy employees are flouting our traffic laws with impunity>.

impact, *vb.* Although it is a time-honored usage to refer to *impacted wisdom teeth*, all other uses of the verb are questionable. Avoid them.

impair. See IMPUGN.

impartable; impartible. Something *impartable* is capable of being made known or given (i.e., *imparted*). Something *impartible* is incapable of being divided into parts; the word is common in describing an estate.

impassable; impassible. See PASSABLE.

impeachment; removal from office. *Impeachment* is a charge of official wrongdoing, not a conviction. *Removal from office* is the penalty upon conviction.

impecunious. See PECUNIARY.

impel. See COMPEL.

impertinent. In common usage an *impertinent* person or remark is sassy and rude, especially to a superior. But in law, *impertinent* retains its original sense of "not pertinent" or "irrelevant to the issue at hand."

impinge; infringe. These similar terms, commonly used interchangeably, have different connotations. To *impinge* is to touch, bump up against, or strike; to *infringe* is to trespass onto, damage, or weaken. The intransitive *impinge* requires an *on-* or *upon-* phrase <impinge on your time>. *Infringe* is best used as a transitive verb <infringe

patent rights>, but it can also be intransitive <infringe on the neighbor's right to quiet enjoyment>.

implicit. See EXPLICIT; IMPLIEDLY.

implicitly. See IMPLIEDLY.

implied. See IMPLIEDLY.

implied contract; quasi-contract. At one time these terms were distinct: an *implied contract* was one "implied in fact" by the parties' actions, and a *quasi-contract* was (as it still is) one "implied in law" as a remedy for unjust enrichment. Today, the former phrase is used for both, making it confusing when it is used for either. It's best avoided altogether.

impliedly; implicitly; implied; implicit. *Impliedly* is an awkward substitute for *implicitly.* It's also something of a legalism, since most nonlawyers don't know what it means. *Implied*, on the other hand, is a more straightforward term than *implicit.*

imply; infer. You *imply* a subtle meaning without explicitly stating it. Your reader *infers* that subtle meaning by "reading between the lines." These two terms are confused less in legal writing than elsewhere, but missteps still occur.

impotence. See STERILITY.

improve. See ENHANCE.

impugn; impair; impute. To *impugn* something is to raise doubts about it <don't impugn your opponent's integrity>. To *impair* something is to weaken it <don't impair the investigation>. To *impute* something is to attribute it to someone or something <don't impute blame without proof>. *Impugn* is sometimes misused where the writer meant *impair* or *impute.*

impunity. See IMMUNITY.

impute. See IMPUGN.

inasmuch as. Use *because* or *since* instead.

inaugural; inauguration. The swearing-in ceremony for the President or a governor is the *inauguration.* Things pertaining to the inauguration are *inaugural* <inaugural ball> <inaugural gown>. The *inaugural address* is often shortened to the noun *inaugural.*

in behalf of. See ON BEHALF OF.

incidentally. This word means "pertaining to something other than the current main topic." It is sometimes misspelled **incidently.*

incident to; incidental to. If one thing is *incident to* another, both things are part of an inseparable whole <a deposition incident to the lawsuit>. If one thing is *incidental to* another, the two things are only loosely associated <a trade agreement incidental to the arms-control summit>.

including; namely; comprising. When laying out a list, introduce it with the term *including* only if the list is not exhaustive. Otherwise, use *namely* or *comprising*, both of which signal an exhaustive list. It is a maxim of judicial construction that *including* signals a nonexclusive list. But if your writing may be the subject of litigation, you should be explicit and use a phrase such as *including but not limited to* or *consisting only of.*

*An invariably inferior form.

incompetence; incompetency; incompetent. *Incompetence* is the general term for a lack of fitness or ability. In law, *incompetency* is the narrow term for unfitness to stand trial or to give testimony, and for questioning sanity. In both senses, the corresponding adjective is *incompetent.*

in connection with. This vague, fuzzy phrase is a favorite of legal writers who seek to be vague. Try *of*, *for*, *about*, *related to*, or *associated with* instead.

incredulous. See CREDIBLE.

inculcate; indoctrinate. The choice of words depends on the subject and object: you *inculcate* values into people, but you *indoctrinate* people with values. You don't *inculcate* people with values.

***inculpable.** See NONCULPABLE.

indemnity. See CONTRIBUTION.

indicate. This vague verb can often be advantageously replaced with *say*, *state*, or *suggest.*

indictment; information; presentment. These are all charging instruments. An *indictment* is a formal charge, usually of a felony, handed up by a grand jury after an investigation or presentation of evidence by the prosecutor. It is required in the federal system and in most states for serious charges, typically those punishable by a year or more in prison. An *information* is a charging instrument that is sworn by the prosecutor and requires no grand-jury action. An *information* is used for less serious offenses, and in some jurisdictions, such as California, for felonies as well. Historically, a *presentment* was a charge handed up by a grand jury on its own initiative. While the procedure is no longer used, the term lives on as part of the Due Process Clause of the Fifth Amendment.

indispensable; necessary; proper. Of parties joined in a lawsuit, an *indispensable* party is someone without whom the matter cannot be fairly tried, and whose absence requires that the suit be dismissed. A *necessary* party is someone who should be joined, but whose absence does not render the matter untriable. A *proper* party is someone who may be joined if the plaintiff chooses to do so.

individuals. See PERSONS.

indoctrinate. See INCULCATE.

indorse. See ENDORSE.

induce. See DEDUCE.

induction. See DEDUCE.

inequity; iniquity. Both beg for justice to be done, but *inequity* typically refers to civil justice and *iniquity* to criminal justice. *Inequity* is unfairness <the court conceded that the harsh bright-line rule would sometimes result in inequity>, while *iniquity* is evil <the defendant never showed regret over the fruits of his iniquity>.

in excess of. Use *more than* or *over* instead.

inexpert; nonexpert. To be *inexpert* at something is to be unskilled at it <the teen's inexpert driving kept his parents jumpy>. *Nonexpert* says nothing about skill; it merely

*An invariably inferior form.

designates a witness who is not an expert witness <a nonexpert witness may give opinion testimony about matters of common knowledge>.

infamous; infamy. See NOTORIOUS.

infant; infancy; minor; minority; nonage. To most people, a child ceases to be an *infant* at an early age, but in law *infancy* continues until the age of majority, usually 18. To avoid confusion, it is better to use the terms *minor* and *minority. Nonage* is a rarer term for legal infancy.

infected; infested. To be *infected* is to be contaminated, especially with disease but by extension with moral corruption. To be *infested* is to be overrun with vermin. Metaphorically, then, a bad neighborhood is *infected by* crime and *infested with* criminals. And any amount of contraband on a ship *infects* the whole vessel and subjects it to seizure.

infectious. See CONTAGIOUS.

infer. See IMPLY.

inference. One draws inferences (that is, makes deductions); one does not make an inference (readers might misread *inference* as if it meant "implication"). Better still, one *infers.* See IMPLY.

infested. See INFECTED.

inflammable. See FLAMMABLE.

inflict; afflict. You *inflict* (impose) bad things *on* people <this bill inflicts more burden on the taxpayer>. You can also *afflict* (torment) people *with* bad things <the dilatory defense lawyer afflicts adversaries with walls of discovery requests>. But *afflict* is most often used without the prepositional phrase <corruption afflicts even the noblest organization>. And as an adjective, *afflicted* can take the preposition *with* or *by* <afflicted with disease> <afflicted by an enemy>.

information. See INDICTMENT.

infringe. See IMPINGE.

ingenious; ingenuous; disingenuous. An *ingenious* person or idea is very clever <an ingenious invention>. An *ingenuous* person is naive and childlike <the witness seemed ingenuous, incapable of fabrication>. *Ingenuous* is more often seen in its opposite, *disingenuous,* meaning "falsely appearing to be open and honest" <the tipster stood to gain from our investment, so we worried that he was being disingenuous>.

inhabitable. See HABITABLE.

inherent. See INNATE.

iniquity. See INEQUITY.

injury. See DAMAGE.

innate; inherent. *Innate* (inborn) qualities and aptitudes are with you from birth <an innate gift for mathematics>. Nonliving things have *inherent* qualities and properties instead <the inherent malleability of gold>.

innervate. See ENERVATE.

innocent; guilty; not guilty; nolo contendere. *Innocent* is not an option for either a plea or a verdict. A defendant may plead *guilty*, *not guilty*, or *nolo contendere* (no contest). Verdicts are *guilty* or *not guilty*. In press accounts the term *innocent* is used to prevent the possible error of omitting *not* from the verdict when reporting an acquittal. Cf. GUILTY.

innumerable. See ENUMERABLE.

in order to; in order for. Try *to* or *for* instead.

inquiry. See QUERY.

in regard to. This is the phrase, not **in regards to.* But try instead *about*, *regarding*, or *concerning*.

insidious; invidious. These two types of unpleasantries differ in style. What is *insidious* is underhanded, sneaky, hidden, working slowly, or waiting to spring a trap <the "grassroots" movement turned out to be a well-planned, insidious power grab>. What is *invidious* is based on creating or spreading ill will <invidious racial discrimination>.

insoluble; unsolvable. See SOLUBLE.

instantly; instantaneously; *instanter. If something happens *instantly*, it happens immediately <the driver was killed instantly>. If it happens *instantaneously*, it happens in an imperceptible span of time <when the driver turned the ignition key, the bomb went off instantaneously>. **Instanter* is a pompous Latinism for *instantly*; ban it from your vocabulary instanter.

insure. See ASSURE.

insurgence; insurgents; insurgency. An *insurgence* is an uprising. *Insurgents* are the people rising up. *Insurgency* is the state of or tendency to revolt.

insurrection; revolt; rebellion; revolution. An *insurrection* is a public uprising against the government. If the insurrection seeks to overthrow the government, it is a *revolt.* If the revolt is widespread, it becomes a *rebellion.* And if an uprising succeeds in overthrowing the government, it is a *revolution.*

intense; intensive. *Intense* is the preferred term in most legal contexts, where *intensive* adds nothing new <when race is involved, state action receives more intense scrutiny from the courts>. *Intensive* is now customary in jargonistic phrasal adjectives such as *labor-intensive*, *time-intensive*, and the like.

intensely. See INTENTLY.

intent; intention; motive. *Intent* is the mental state of resolving to do something (especially, in law, to commit a crime). *Intention* is often used in place of *intent*; it has no connotations regarding crime, but it sometimes carries a sexual connotation <bad intentions>. *Motive* is the reason for doing something.

> "Correct English, as it is usually understood, is usage that conforms to the norms of the standard language."
> —*Sidney Greenbaum*

*An invariably inferior form.

intentional. See VOLUNTARY.

intently; intensely. Both adverbs describe a high degree of intensity. But acting *intently* shows intense concentration. One might act *intensely* with no concentration at all, as in a fit of rage.

interment; internment. *Interment* is a burial. *Internment* is confinement, especially of aliens during wartime.

internecine. The term originally described a war of extermination, and later a war in which both sides suffer great slaughter. Today it means "mutually destructive; deadly to both parties." It is often used far more loosely to describe any internal controversy.

internment. See INTERMENT.

interpretive. Although *interpretative* was the traditional form, *interpretive* is now fully accepted—and heavily predominant in print sources.

inure; enure. *Inure* is the standard spelling, *enure* a variant. The ordinary meaning is "to become accustomed to a bad situation" <the POW became inured to the squalid conditions>. In legal use, it means "to take effect," usually to benefit someone <the bond's maturity will inure to the bondholder's benefit>.

inveigh; inveigle. To *inveigh* against something is to rant on about it <protesters inveighed against globalization>. To *inveigle* is to beguile or cajole someone into doing something <the salesman inveigled the customer into taking a test drive>.

invidious. See INSIDIOUS.

invoke. See EVOKE.

***irregardless.** See REGARDLESS.

irrespective. See REGARDLESS.

irritate. See AGGRAVATE.

issue preclusion. See COLLATERAL ESTOPPEL.

its; it's. This basic spelling rule is still a common error: *its* is the possessive form of *it* <each court has its local rules>; *it's* is a contraction of *it is* <it's foolhardy to ignore local rules>. When you see the apostrophe, think "*it is*" to make sure that *it's* the right form.

jealous; envious; zealous. *Jealous* properly applies only in romantic relationships <a jealous suitor>. *Envious* applies to resentment over another person's good fortune <envious of the new partner's success>. A *zealous* person is ardent <a zealous young convert>; it is occasionally confounded with *jealous*, perhaps because a lover can be either or both. Cf. ENVIOUS.

jibe; jive. See GIBE.

joinder; consolidation. *Joinder* is the act of bringing additional parties into a lawsuit. *Consolidation* is the act of combining multiple lawsuits into a single suit. Cf. MERGER.

joint tenancy; tenancy in common. A *joint tenancy* is a property interest held by multiple owners with identical interests and rights of survivorship. A *tenancy in common* is an interest held by multiple owners with undivided (and not necessarily equal) shares and no rights of survivorship.

*An invariably inferior form.

judgment; judgement. *Judgment* is the preferred spelling in American English and in British legal writing. *Judgement* is standard in British general writing. Cf. DECISION; VERDICT.

judicial; judicious. *Judicial* has several meanings relating to courts <judicial restraint>, courtrooms <judicial sequestration>, decrees <judicial order>, and the law in general <judicial privilege>. But *judicious* touches the law only by analogy: it means "discreet; prudent; well thought out."

just deserts. So spelled—not **just desserts*. The rare noun *desert* (pronounced /di-**zərt**/ in this sense) is cognate with the verb *deserve*. The phrase has nothing to do with end-of-meal sweets.

justification. See EXCUSE.

karat. See CARAT.

knowledge; notice. *Knowledge* is awareness of a fact or condition. In law, *notice* does not require actual knowledge. It can be constructive knowledge: notice imputed to a person who had reason to know of a fact or condition (for example, because it was a public record). *Constructive knowledge* means *notice*, but *notice* is the better term.

laches. See WAIVE.

latent. See PATENT.

latter. See FORMER.

laudable; laudatory. Good deeds are *laudable*, i.e., they deserve praise. If someone praises them, those comments are *laudatory*, i.e., they express praise.

lay. See LIE.

leach. See LEECH.

lead; led. The past tense of *lead* (as in "to guide") is *led*. But there is a tendency to misspell it *lead*, perhaps because the metal *lead* is pronounced /led/, and the past-tense *read* rhymes with *led*.

lease; let. Both are correct verbs for the renting out of property. *Let* is not slang or substandard; in fact, its use goes back 300 years earlier than *lease*. Only the lessor *lets* the property, but either party may be said to *lease* it.

led. See LEAD.

leech; leach. *Leech* is a noun: the blood-sucking worm or the houseguest who won't go away. *Leach* is a verb: to percolate water to remove solids.

legacy. See DEVISE.

legation. See EMBASSY.

lend. See LOAN.

less. See FEWER.

lessor; lessee. *Lessor* and *lessee* are the correct terms—not **leasor* and **leasee*.

let. See LEASE.

*An invariably inferior form.

levee; levy. *Levee* is the spelling of the word for (commonly) a riverbank and (rarely) a state reception. *Levy* is the spelling of the noun and verb for laying and collecting taxes, drafting soldiers and sailors, and seizing property to satisfy a judgment.

libel. See DEFAMATION.

lie; lay. You *lay* down your book and *lie* down on the bed. Last night you *laid* down your book and *lay* down on the bed. Every night this week you *have laid* down your book and *have lain* down on the bed. Same with *lie low* (present)–*lay low* (past)–*lain low* (past participle).

life-and-death; *life-or-death. While it may be counterintuitive for an "either–or" phrase, *life-and-death* is the standard idiom <a life-and-death struggle>.

like; as. *Like* is a preposition, not a conjunction. It can precede a noun <in like Flynn> <it looks like a winner>. If what follows is a clause (with a verb), use *as* <steady as she goes> <she talks as if she means it>.

like; such as. Is it permissible to say *Universities like MIT and Stanford help set the government's policies in technical fields?* That is, should *like* be *such as*? Are the exemplars actually listed to be included in the genus denoted by the noun preceding *like*? Literalists say that only colleges similar to MIT and Stanford—but not those schools themselves—are included, so if MIT and Stanford are meant to be included, the reference should be to *Universities such as MIT and Stanford.* This hard-nosed literalism may be hard to shake. But there's nothing wrong with using *like* in this context—and to many it sounds more natural.

likely. See APT.

limit. See DELIMIT.

literally; figuratively. Something *literally* means exactly what the words say it means (think *literature*). *Literally* is sloppy when employed as an intensifier <the defendant *was literally sweating bullets* [read *was sweating bullets*] as the verdict was read>. In the example, the defendant was *figuratively* (metaphorically) sweating bullets, although you would never write it that way—just omit *literally* in such a phrase.

litigable; *litigatable. *Litigable* is the correct term for an issue suitable for trial.

litigator. See TRIAL LAWYER.

***loadstar.** See LODESTAR.

loan; lend. In best usage, *loan* is a noun and *lend* is a verb. But when what is being *lent* is money, *loan* as a verb is entirely acceptable.

loathe; loath; loth. To *loathe* is to detest <the plaintiff loathed the defendant>. To be *loath* to do something is to be reluctant <the lawyer was loath to let the hotheaded witness testify>; **loth* is a rare variant form. The usual error is to use the verb *loathe* where the adjective *loath* was intended.

locus; situs. Both refer to a place where an event happened or where property is located. But *locus* is more specific, referring, for example, to the piece of property itself <the locus passed to the decedent's son>. *Situs*, on the other hand, refers to the jurisdiction

*An invariably inferior form.

where the event happened or the property is located <the law of the situs governs foreign property belonging to the estate>.

lodestar. The guiding star (usually Polaris)—and by extension a guide for setting fees and damages—is so spelled. Avoid **loadstar.*

loose; loosen; lose. To *loose* something is to free it completely <the guards loosed the dogs at the first sign of a break>, while to *loosen* something is to partially unbind it <after supper Dad loosened his belt>. Writers sometimes misspell *lose* as *loose* <Dad should *loose* [read *lose*] some weight>.

loth. See LOATHE.

luxurious; luxuriant. What is *luxurious* is elegant and indulgent <luxurious accommodations>. What is *luxuriant* is fast-growing and abundant <a luxuriant flower garden>.

mad; angry. The use of *mad* to mean "angry" dates back to at least 1300, but there was a movement in the early twentieth century to limit its definition to "insane." Since it carries a negative connotation, its use in that sense is limited. It's a perfectly proper term for *angry*, but since it has been stigmatized it should probably be avoided in formal writing.

maelstrom. This term denotes a whirlpool and, by extension, a turbulent situation. It is often misspelled **maelstorm.*

majority; plurality. A *majority* is more than half—50% plus one or more <a bare majority at 51%>. A *plurality* is less than a majority but still the highest percentage among three or more figures <a plurality of 42% in a three-way race>. Of legal precedents, a *majority* opinion (one in which most of the judges join) is stronger than a *plurality* opinion (in which one or more swing votes determine the outcome, but for different reasons).

make do. The phrase meaning "to get by with what you have" is *make do* <we're going to have to make do>. **Make due* is a common error.

malfeasance; misfeasance; nonfeasance. *Malfeasance* is wrongful or illegal conduct, especially by someone in office. *Misfeasance* is either (1) conduct that, while not itself illegal, is done in a wrongful manner, or (2) a trespass or transgression. *Nonfeasance* is the failure to act when one has a duty to do so.

malice aforethought. See WILLFULNESS.

malodorous. See ODIOUS.

maltreatment. See MISTREATMENT.

mandate. See VERDICT.

manslaughter. See MURDER.

mantle; mantel. A *mantle* is a cloak or other loose-fitting cover. A *mantel* is an enclosure for a fireplace. Legal writers often figuratively cloak things with *mantles* <protected by the mantle of prosecutorial immunity>, but occasionally slip and use the wrong homonym.

marriage; wedding. *Marriage* is the wedded state, a legal relationship. A *wedding* is the ceremony at which two people are married.

*An invariably inferior form.

marshal; Marshall. *Marshal* is always spelled with one *-l* unless it is a name <the marshals protected John Marshall>.

masterful; masterly. Careful writers use *masterful* to describe domination, as of a master over a servant <the swaggering governor was a masterful presence in the statehouse>. The right term to describe artistic or professional mastery is *masterly* <a masterly performance by the young virtuoso>.

may. See CAN.

mean; median. The *mean* is the statistical average of a set of numbers <the mean of the set 1, 2, 999 is 501>. The *median* is the middle number in an ordered set <the median of the set 1, 2, 999 is 2>.

meantime; meanwhile. In common use, *meantime* most often appears in the phrase *in the meantime*, although the term can also stand alone. *Meanwhile* should always stand alone.

medal. See METTLE.

meddle. See METTLE.

media; medium; mediums. *Media* is plural and should take a plural verb <the news media are going to be all over this story>. But it has been used as a mass noun with a singular verb for so long that the usage is now considered standard <the media is overplaying this story>. A single type of mass-media outlet is still called a *medium* <the medium of television became popular after World War II>. *Mediums* is the plural only when referring to clairvoyants <two mediums attended the séance>.

median. See MEAN.

mediation; arbitration. These are the two standard forms of alternative dispute resolution. *Mediation* is nonbinding negotiation through a neutral third party in an attempt to reach a settlement. *Arbitration* is the submission of the parties' cases to one or more neutral third parties, who hand down a decision that is usually binding on the parties.

medium; mediums. See MEDIA.

meet out. See METE OUT.

memoranda; memorandums. Although both plural forms are correct, *memoranda* is far more common. Don't make the mistake of using *memoranda* as if it were singular.

meretricious; meritorious. *Meretricious* derives from the Latin word for "prostitute"; it means "alluring by deception." *Meritorious* generally means "praiseworthy," but in law it describes a claim or defense that has legal merit and a chance to succeed. Obviously, the writer who inappropriately describes a client's claim as *meretricious* does so at great peril: the judge may decide that the claim is unmeritorious.

merger; consolidation. When two companies combine by *merger*, the company that absorbs the other retains its corporate identity and structure. When two companies *consolidate*, they form a new corporate identity and structure and shed their previous ones. Cf. JOINDER.

meritorious. See MERETRICIOUS.

mesalliance; misalliance. *Mesalliance* is a marriage between people of different social positions. *Misalliance* is an incompatible marriage. By definition, a *misalliance* can't be a happy marriage, but a *mesalliance* may be.

messuage. See CURTILAGE.

metal. See METTLE.

mete out. This is the correct spelling of the phrase meaning "to allot" (as praise, pay, or punishment). **Meet out* is an error seen most frequently in the past tense <the commissioner *meeted out* [read *meted out*] fines to players on both teams>.

mettle; meddle; medal; metal. The first two, especially, can be tricky. *Mettle* is courage or inner strength <your first trial will test your mettle>; to *meddle* is to interfere <don't meddle in my business>. A *medal* is an award, often made out of *metal.*

militate. See MITIGATE.

millennium. So spelled. The roots are *mille* (thousand) and *annus* (year), so the word needs both *l*'s and both *n*'s.

minimize; minify; *minimalize. To *minimize* something is to hold it to a minimum. To *minify* something is to depreciate it or to hold out that it is smaller than it really is. **Minimalize* is not a word and should not be used where *minimize* is intended.

minor; minority. See INFANT.

minuscule. So spelled. The root of *minuscule* (very small) is *minus*, not *mini-*. *Minuscule* is one of the most commonly misspelled words in legal writing.

minutia; minutiae. *Minutia* is the singular, *minutiae* the plural of this word, which means "a petty detail." Writers often tend to treat the first as plural, and sometimes mistake the second as singular.

misalliance. See MESALLIANCE.

mischievous. Often misspelled **mischievious.*

misfeasance. See MALFEASANCE.

misinformation. See DISINFORMATION.

misprision. In law, *misprision* most often refers to the concealment of certain crimes by a nonparticipant <misprision of felony>. In common use it most often means "mistake" <a misprision of language>. The word is often misspelled **misprison.*

misquote; misquotation. See QUOTE.

mistreatment; maltreatment. *Mistreatment* is the general term for "abuse." It may be anything from neglect to physical abuse. *Maltreatment* involves rough physical treatment.

mitigate; militate. To *mitigate* something is to make it less severe or forceful <to mitigate the harshness of the bright-line rule, courts soon began carving out exceptions>. To *militate* is to influence strongly <the persuasive force of the foreign court's reasoning on the issue militated in favor of following suit>. Something can *militate for* or *against* (though not *toward*), but cannot *mitigate for* or *against.*

momentarily. See PRESENTLY.

*An invariably inferior form.

motive. See INTENT.

murder; manslaughter; homicide. One who unlawfully kills another person with malice aforethought commits *murder.* If the killing was not malicious, it was *manslaughter. Homicide* is the general term for any killing of another person. *Homicide* does not denote a crime: the carrying out of a death sentence is a homicide.

mutual; common. What is *mutual* is reciprocal <the partners' mutual respect>. What is *common* is shared <the parents' common love for their child>. Two people may have a *common* friend, but not strictly speaking a *mutual* friend. The use of *mutual* invites redundancies: agreement and cooperation, for example, are by definition *mutual.* In law, a *mutual mistake* should more properly be called a *common mistake*, but the phrase is carved in judicial stone and unlikely to change.

myself. Avoid using what is properly a reflexive <I hurt myself!> or intensive <I myself> pronoun in place of the simple *I* or *me.* Do not write **My wife and myself would like to invite you to dinner*, but *My wife and I . . . .*

namely. See INCLUDING.

naturalist; naturist. A *naturalist* is one who studies nature, such as a biologist, or one who paints or writes about nature and the outdoors. A *naturist* is a nudist.

naught; nought. Of these alternative spellings for the word meaning "nothing," *naught* is usually used in the general sense and *nought* is reserved for the mathematical zero.

nauseous; nauseated. To be *nauseous* is to cause nausea <the nauseous clams>. To be *nauseated* is to feel nausea <he felt nauseated after eating the clams>. The use of *nauseous* to mean *nauseated* may happen too often for it to be called incorrect, but careful writers will still use the right term. One easy solution is to avoid *nauseous* altogether and to use either *nauseating* or *nauseated* instead.

necessary. See INDISPENSABLE.

negative, in the. See AFFIRMATIVE, IN THE.

no doubt. See DOUBTLESS.

noisome; noisy. *Noisome* is etymologically related to *annoyance*, not *noise.* Something *noisome* is smelly, harmful, or offensive <a noisome swamp>—it offends the nose, not the ears.

nolo contendere. See INNOCENT.

nonage. See INFANT.

nonculpable; *inculpable. The meaning of *nonculpable* is clear: "not blamable." But the meaning of **inculpable* is not: it could mean either "not blamable" or "able to be blamed." Because of the ambiguity, avoid **inculpable* (which, in fact, traditionally means "blameless"). Cf. BLAMEWORTHY.

none. Either *none are* or *none is* is correct <all the candidates have been subjected to exceptional scrutiny, and none have escaped unscathed> <each candidate has been subjected to exceptional scrutiny, and none has escaped unscathed>. The singular use is more emphatic—and less common.

nonexpert. See INEXPERT.

*An invariably inferior form.

nonfeasance. See MALFEASANCE.

nonflammable. See FLAMMABLE.

not guilty. See INNOCENT.

notice. See KNOWLEDGE.

notorious; notoriety; infamous; infamy. All four terms can carry negative connotations of a bad reputation. But *notorious* and (especially) *notoriety* may also be neutral; *infamous* and *infamy* always reek of evildoing.

notwithstanding. Try *despite* instead.

nought. See NAUGHT.

number; amount. If you can count them, you have a *number* of them <she handles a large number of civil-rights cases>. Otherwise, you measure the *amount* <a large amount of her time is spent on civil-rights cases>.

numerous. Prefer *many.*

observation; observance. An *observation* is a perception of something, or a pertinent comment based on observation and analysis. An *observance* is the adherence to a law or custom.

obtain. See ATTAIN.

obtuse; abstruse. Anything *obtuse* is dull or blunt. Anything *abstruse* is hidden or hard to discover. So the first can describe a dull-witted person, and the second an esoteric idea.

obviously. See CLEARLY.

odious; odorous; malodorous; odoriferous; *odiferous. *Odious* (hateful) and *odorous* (smelly) are sometimes confounded. Of the variants of *odorous*, *malodorous* is quite bad-smelling and *odoriferous* is good-smelling. **Odiferous* is a mistaken variant of *odoriferous.*

off. Never write **off of.*

offense; defense; offence; defence. *Offense* and *defense* are the American English spellings. *Offence* and *defence* are the British English spellings; they sometimes appear in older American texts.

officious; official. An *officious* person is pushy and meddlesome. An officer may or may not be *officious* but is by definition *official.*

old. See VENERABLE.

on; upon. The simple preposition *on* is almost always better than its dressed-up sibling *upon.* Avoid using *upon* just to affect a tone of formality. It is useful, however, to introduce a causal or temporal event <the banker called police immediately upon discovering the embezzlement> <please respond upon receipt>.

> "In legal affairs . . . it is often possible as well as necessary to insist that particular words be used in particular ways."
> —*Irving Lee*

*An invariably inferior form.

on behalf of; in behalf of. To act or speak *on behalf of* someone is to act as that person's representative <counsel entered a not-guilty plea on behalf of the defendant>. To act or speak *in behalf of* someone or something is to do so in praise or defense <five students spoke in behalf of the suspended professor>.

one another. See EACH OTHER.

oneself. So written—not **one's self*.

operable; operational; operative. Something *operable* is capable of being operated <the old tractor was still operable>. Something *operational* is able to function <the collector hoped to have the computer network operational by tax season>. Something *operative* is either in effect <the new ordinance was not yet operative> or most relevant <the penal code, not the highway code, had the operative definition>.

ophthalmologist; oculist; optometrist; optician. An *ophthalmologist* and an *oculist* are medical doctors specializing in the treatment of eyes. An *optometrist* is a licensed practitioner who conducts sight exams and writes prescriptions for eyeglasses. An *optician* is a person who makes eyeglasses.

opinion. See DECISION.

oppress; repress. To *oppress* a people is to subjugate them through persecution and other inhumane treatment. To *repress* a people is to control or subordinate them. *Oppress* is the stronger term.

oral. See VERBAL; PAROL.

oration. See PERORATION.

ordinance; ordnance. An *ordinance* is a law of narrower scope than a statute, especially a municipal regulation <a zoning ordinance>. *Ordnance* is artillery, ammunition, and other military weaponry <resupply ordnance to advance troops>.

orient; *orientate. To find east is to know all directions, so to *orient* yourself is to get your bearings <the judge read the statement of facts to get oriented to the parties and the controversy>. **Orientate* adds an extra-syllable irritant but adds no meaning to the word.

***overly.** Use *unduly* or *too* instead.

overrule; overturn; reverse; set aside; vacate. A judge may *overrule* an objection, and an appellate court may *overrule* a precedent. The court may also *overturn* the precedent, in whole or in part. *Overturning* may also be a gradual process of eroding an old doctrine. The last three terms usually apply to what an appellate court does to a trial court's decision: to *reverse* it is to change the outcome, but to *set* it *aside* or *vacate* it is to erase the judgment so that no one wins and the parties go back to the trial court.

overturn. See OVERRULE.

pair. One *pair*, two *pairs*.

pallet; palette; palate. A *pallet* is a makeshift bed or a short crate that items are stacked on for shipping and storing. A *palette* is an artist's board for mixing colors. A *palate* is the roof of the mouth and, by extension, the sense of taste.

*An invariably inferior form.

palming off. See PASSING OFF.

pandemic. See EPIDEMIC.

parameter; perimeter; periphery. A *parameter* (usually plural) is a number or variable in a mathematical equation, and by extension a factor in any consideration <narrow your web search by using more specific parameters>. Outside math and science, it is jargon to be avoided. *Perimeter* is the outer boundary of a space <perimeter fence>. *Periphery* is also the outer boundary, but whereas *perimeter* is a clear line, *periphery* can be of uncertain reach <the periphery of the town>.

parol; oral; parole. In law, *parol* is often used to mean *oral.* But in contracts, *parol* evidence can also be a writing other than the contract itself. It is sometimes spelled *parole*, but that should be discouraged to avoid confusion with the conditional release of prison inmates.

parricide; patricide. Both denote either the murder of one's father or the person who commits such a murder. But *parricide* is more general: it applies to the murder of any close relative, and also to the murder of a ruler.

partake in; partake of. To *partake in* (and sometimes *of*) is to take part in <partake in a public forum>. To *partake of* is to get a share of <partake of the cake and ice cream> or to suggest a certain attribute <a crime that partakes of racism>.

parties. See PERSONS.

partly; partially. If the parts are physical or the measure is of an extent, use *partly* <a partly finished building>. If speaking of a quality or the measure is of degree, use *partially* <partially recovered from an illness>. If either word works in the context, choose *partly* as less ambiguous: *partially* also means "showing favoritism" <the shares were partially divided among the children [incompletely divided, or unfairly divided?]>.

passable; impassable; passible; impassible. *Passable* and *impassable* refer to whether something can be passed <the coalition's work made the legislation passable> <the blizzard made the road impassable>. *Passible* (rare) and *impassible* refer to whether someone can feel pain or emotions <a passible God has human qualities> <an impassible old codger>. The *-ible* terms are common misspellings where the *-able* terms are meant.

passed. See PAST.

passible. See PASSABLE.

passing off; palming off; *pawning off. The first two phrases mean "selling goods or services under circumstances in which the buyer is misled about the source." *Passing off* is standard in law, but both phrases are common in lay usage. **Pawning off* is a fairly common error.

past; passed. When writing of time, it is surprisingly easy to misuse *passed* when *past* is the right word—after all, the *past* has *passed* <reminiscing about years *passed* [read *past*]>. At other times, the *passing* itself is referred to, so *passed* is the right choice <days passed in quiet reverie>.

pastime. So spelled—it's a compound of *pass* (not *past*) and *time.*

*An invariably inferior form.

patent; latent; patent. A *patent* thing is open and obvious <that's a patent lie>. A *latent* thing is hidden <discover a latent talent>. Both terms are pronounced with a long *a*. The noun *patent*, with a short *a*, is a limited-term monopoly granted to an inventor.

patricide. See PARRICIDE.

***pawning off.** See PASSING OFF.

peaceful; peaceable. To be *peaceful* is to be serene or not involved in armed conflict; to be *peaceable* is to be disinclined toward war or confrontation.

peak; peek; pique. A *peak* is a mountaintop, a *peek* is a surreptitious look, and a *pique* is a fit of resentment. *Pique* is also a verb meaning "to arouse" or "to annoy." *Peak* and *peek* are sometimes switched in pure blunder. And *peak* also sometimes appears where the writer meant *pique* <the First Amendment argument *peaked* [read *piqued*] the judge's interest>.

pecuniary; pecunious; impecunious. *Pecuniary* means "concerning or consisting of money" <the schedule listed the plaintiff's pecuniary damages>. *Pecunious* means "wealthy" <a pecunious financier>. *Impecunious* means "poor" <a judgment against an impecunious defendant is worthless>.

peddle; pedal; soft-pedal. To *peddle* something is to sell it. To *pedal* is to pump with the foot, as in riding a bicycle or operating the *pedals* on a piano. One of those piano pedals muffles the sound, so by extension to *soft-pedal* something is to tone down the intensity. In this sense the phrase is sometimes misspelled **soft-peddle.*

peek. See PEAK.

pejorative. This word, meaning "disparaging," is so spelled—not **perjorative.*

penal; punitive; penological. *Penal* relates to punishment <a penal institution>. *Punitive* means "intended to punish" <punitive damages>. *Penological* relates to the study of punishment and rehabilitation <penological research>. *Penological* is misused when applied as a five-syllable substitute for *penal*.

pendant; pendent. A *pendant* is a piece of jewelry. *Pendent* is an adjective meaning "suspended"; in law it refers to an associated but subordinate state claim allowed in a federal suit <pendent jurisdiction>.

penological. See PENAL.

penultimate. See ULTIMATE.

people. See PERSONS.

per. See *AS PER.

percent; per cent; %. The one-word spelling is better, but the symbol is best.

perimeter. See PARAMETER.

period of time; time period. These phrases are redundant. Try *period* or *time* instead.

periphery. See PARAMETER.

permit; allow. While these are used synonymously, there is a connotative nuance. To *permit* something is to give it some form of approval <overruling the objection, the

*An invariably inferior form.

judge permitted the question>. To *allow* it to happen connotes no approval, just the lack of opposition <hearing no objection, the judge allowed the question>.

peroration; oration. The conclusion of a speech is the *peroration*, and in best usage the term is restricted to that meaning. Some writers misuse the word to denote a rousing *oration* (speech) or writing.

perpetrator; accomplice; principal; accessory. Participants in a crime are sorted out by two schemes: (1) *perpetrator* and *accomplices*, and (2) *principals* and *accessories*. In the first scheme, the *perpetrator* carries out the crime, while *accomplices* aid in its preparation and execution. In the second scheme, the *principals* carry out the crime. *Accessories* are not present at the scene but help prepare (*accessories before the fact*) or help elude arrest (*accessories after the fact*). In most jurisdictions, an *accessory after the fact* is not considered an *accomplice* but is guilty of obstructing justice.

perquisite; prerequisite. A *perquisite* is a job benefit; the term is often shortened to *perk*. A *prerequisite* is a condition that must be met to qualify for something.

per se. In general usage, *per se* can mean "as such" <there is no "bond exchange" per se> or "by itself" <planning per se is less a problem today than underfinancing>. At law it carries this latter meaning, describing a legal status that exists without the need of additional evidence <the doctrine of negligence per se requires no proof of fault>. If the phrase modifies a noun, it almost always follows the noun. With other parts of speech, it may precede the word it modifies.

persecute; prosecute. To *persecute* a people (especially a religious minority) is to oppress them. To *prosecute* is to press criminal charges against someone or to pursue a patent application.

persevere. So spelled—not **perservere*.

persons; people; individuals; parties. The choice between the words *persons* and *people* is best made by ear. The traditional advice is that *persons* usually refers to small numbers of identified people, but *people* is more natural in most contexts. *Persons* sounds stuffy, as does *individuals*. *Parties* should be restricted to its legal sense, referring to separate sides in a dispute.

perspicuous; perspicacious. Clear and lucid reasoning is *perspicuous*. The person whose acute discernment and shrewdness led to the perspicuous reasoning is *perspicacious* (wise).

persuade. See CONVINCE.

pertain. See APPERTAIN.

petitioner. See APPELLATE.

phenomenon. This is the singular form. The plural is *phenomena*.

picaresque; picturesque. A *picaresque* story tells the adventures of a rogue. A *picturesque* scene is one that would make a nice picture. And *picturesque* language paints a vivid picture.

pique. See PEAK.

*An invariably inferior form.

pitiful; pitiless; pitiable. To be *pitiful* was originally to be full of pity, but in modern usage to be *pitiful* is to be detestable. To be *pitiless* is to show no compassion, and to be *pitiable* is to deserve the pity of others.

playwright. So spelled—not **playwrite.*

pleaded; *pled; plead. A century of pleas to use the correct past tense (*pleaded*) has had little effect: **pled* is at least minimally acceptable in American legal usage. Still, *pleaded* is dominant in print sources generally and is best in legal writing. The variant past-tense *plead* is objectionable because it looks like a present-tense verb (like *read* or *lead*).

plurality. See MAJORITY.

populace; populous. The *populace* is the population. *Populous* is an adjective describing a heavily populated area.

pore. The verb meaning "to read carefully" is *pore* (over), but in writing it is frequently misspelled *pour.*

possession. See CUSTODY.

post hoc. See EX POST FACTO.

pour. See PORE.

practical; practicable. What is *practical* is either (1) realistic, not just theoretical <the new formbook made a practical difference for litigators>, or (2) advantageous <it wasn't practical to pay so much more for little added benefit>. The noun form is *practicality.* What is *practicable* is feasible <the budget increase made the hiring of another clerk practicable>. The noun is *practicability.*

precede; proceed; *preceed. *Precede* and *proceed* are switched surprisingly often. To *precede* is to go before <her husband preceded her in death>, while to *proceed* is to go ahead <you may proceed, counselor>. *Precede* is sometimes misspelled **preceed.*

precedent; precedence. A *precedent* is a previous event that may guide the way through a present, similar event. At law, it is a judicial decision that is binding or persuasive on an issue at hand. The plural, *precedents*, is a homonym (at least in American English) of *precedence*, meaning "priority." The two words are sometimes confounded.

precipitate; precipitous. Actions and demands are *precipitate* (sudden; with unrestrained speed; rash) <a simple phone call might have prevented the precipitate filing of this lawsuit>. Steep slopes are *precipitous*; any use of this term with an action should convey the metaphor of a fall <the Internet rumor caused the company's stock to go into a precipitous decline>.

***precondition.** Use *condition* or *prerequisite* instead.

predominant; predominate. See DOMINANT.

preface. See FOREWORD.

preliminary to. Try *before* or *in preparing for* instead.

premise; premises. The first word is a proposition from which a conclusion is drawn <a faulty premise leads to an unreliable conclusion>. The second, always plural, is the space inside the boundaries of a piece of property <leave the premises at once>.

*An invariably inferior form.

prerequisite. See PERQUISITE.

prescribe; proscribe. To *prescribe* something is to order or direct it, especially a rule or treatment <the legislature prescribed a policy favoring mediation over litigation>. To *proscribe* something is to ban it <the new statute proscribes open containers of alcohol in the passenger compartment>.

presently; currently; momentarily. *Presently* may mean "immediately" or "soon," but in modern usage it has come to mean "now"; careful writers choose a more precise term. *Currently* means "now" and causes no problems. But *momentarily* is another ambiguous term, strictly meaning "lasting for a moment" but loosely meaning "in a moment."

presentment. See INDICTMENT.

prestigious. See PRODIGIOUS.

presumption. See ASSUMPTION.

presumptive; presumptuous. *Presumptive* is the term to use when writing of a legal *presumption* <the senior party to an interference is the presumptive first inventor>. *Presumptuous* means "arrogant and pushy" <the presumptuous summer clerk was blowing any chance for a job offer>.

preventive; *preventative. Although **preventative* is common, *preventive* is the correct term.

previous to. Try *before* instead.

prideful. See PROUD.

principal. See PERPETRATOR.

principal; principle. *Principal* is usually the adjective meaning "main"; *principle* is the noun meaning "tenet." But *principal* is a noun when it stands for a main person <the high school principal> or primary funds <principal and interest>.

***prior to.** Instead of this bloated phrase, use *before* or *until*.

probity; probative. *Probity* is integrity and honesty <the judicial nominee had a solid reputation for probity>. Something *probative* either (1) tends to prove something <the autopsy photos were disallowed because their prejudicial nature far outweighed their probative value> or (2) explores new territory <the lawyer slipped a few probative questions into the interrogatories>. The noun corresponding to *probative* is *probativeness*.

problem. See QUANDARY.

proceed. See PRECEDE.

prodigious; prestigious. Something *prodigious* is exceptional in size or extent <preparation for the trial required a prodigious effort from everyone>. Something *prestigious* is esteemed <selected for the prestigious Order of the Coif>.

profit. See PROPHESY.

prognosis; prognostication. See DIAGNOSIS.

*An invariably inferior form.

promulgate; propagate. To *promulgate* is to announce or declare, especially a law or rule <regulations promulgated by agencies are first published in the Federal Register>. Writers sometimes slip up by using *propagate* (to reproduce or disseminate) instead.

proper. See INDISPENSABLE.

prophesy; prophecy; prophet; profit. To *prophesy* is to predict <critics prophesy disaster>. *Prophecy* is the prediction <but their last prophecy proved wrong>. *Prophet* is the one predicting <there will always be a prophet of doom>. *Profit* is a net financial gain <as long as there's a profit to be made in scaring people>.

proscribe. See PRESCRIBE.

prosecute. See PERSECUTE.

prostrate; prostate. To *prostrate* yourself is to lie facedown on the ground; it denotes total surrender or exhaustion. The *prostate* is the gland at the base of a male's bladder; it is a common error to refer to the *prostrate* (read *prostate*) gland.

protrude; protuberance. At first glance these words with similar looks and meanings appear to have the same root. But they don't. To *protrude* is to stick out; a *protuberance* bulges out. Sometimes writers mistakenly want to put the second *-r-* of *protrude* after the *-t-* in *protuberance.*

proud; prideful. Both mean "with pride," but *prideful* connotes arrogance to a moral fault.

proved; proven. *Proved* is the past participle of the verb *prove*, except in the catchphrase *innocent until proven guilty* and the Scots verdict of *not proven.* In other contexts, use *proved* <no motive has yet been proved>. *Proven* is an adjective <the defendant's presence was a proven fact>.

punitive. See PENAL.

purposely; purposefully. Something done *purposely* is done with intent, on purpose <the defendant purposely ran the red light>. Something done *purposefully* is done with a definite purpose in mind <the stalker purposefully collected information about the model>.

quandary; problem. A *quandary* is a confused mental state <the low settlement offer left the plaintiff in a quandary>. The term is misused when referring to the puzzle or problem itself <the clash of precedents presents a problem [not a quandary] for the court>.

quasi-contract. See IMPLIED CONTRACT.

query; inquiry. A *query* is one question, not an investigation. An *inquiry* may be a single query or a course of questioning, such as an investigation.

question whether; question of whether; *question as to whether. The first phrase is refined; the second is common but unrefined; the third is inept.

quote; quotation; misquote; misquotation. Traditionally, *quote* is a verb, *quotation* a noun. But the casual use of *quote* as a noun appears often, even in otherwise formal writing. The analogous points apply to *misquote* and *misquotation.*

rack. See WRACK.

*An invariably inferior form.

rare. See SCARCE.

ratiocination; rationalization. *Ratiocination* is the process of reasoning. *Rationalization* is the process of making something rational, but more often the term denotes false reasoning, used after the fact to explain away or justify something that otherwise does not make sense.

real. See BONA FIDE.

***reason . . . is because.** This construction is unacceptably redundant, *reason* and *because* each implying the sense of the other word. Make it *reason is . . . that.*

rebellion. See INSURRECTION.

rebut; refute. To *rebut* something is to offer evidence or arguments to counter it. To *refute* something is to disprove it beyond doubt. The words are not interchangeable: to *rebut* an argument is to try to *refute* it. A *refutation* is a resoundingly successful *rebuttal.* Perhaps because the *-t-* is doubled in *rebuttal* and other forms, *rebut* is occasionally misspelled **rebutt.*

recension. See REPUDIATION.

reciprocity; reciprocation. *Reciprocity*, the more common word, is the mutual respect by two entities of each other's interests or policies <the states' reciprocity statutes allow an attorney from either state to participate in lawsuits in the other state>. *Reciprocation* is an act done in reciprocity <since the other party did not object to our minor motion, in reciprocation we will not object to theirs>.

recital; recitation. In a contract or deed, a *recital* is an introductory statement of who the parties are, some background of the transaction, and what the document purports to accomplish. In a pleading it is an allegation. In general it is a statement of facts. *Recitation* is an act of reciting, not the recital itself; it connotes a public statement before an audience.

recklessly. See WANTONLY.

recover back. See RELATE BACK.

re-create; recreative; recreate; recreational. The hyphen makes quite a difference. To *re-create* something is to create it again; its adjective form is *recreative* (no hyphen). To *recreate* is to enjoy a leisure activity; its adjective form is *recreational.*

recur; reoccur. If something *recurs*, it happens repeatedly with some regularity <a recurring nightmare>. Something that *reoccurs*, on the other hand, merely happens a second time; there is no connotation of its continued repetition <if this situation ever reoccurs, call me at once>.

recuse; recusal; recusation; recusement; recusancy. To *recuse* oneself is to remove oneself as a judge or juror, usually because of a conflict of interests. *Recusal* is the corresponding noun, although *recusation* is standard in civil-law jurisdictions and is sometimes used elsewhere. *Recusement* is rarer but also appears. *Recusancy* is an unrelated word that means "refusal to submit to authority."

reek; wreak. To *reek* is to stink (or, as a noun, a *reek* is a bad odor). To *wreak* is to inflict something bad on someone. Cf. WREAK HAVOC.

*An invariably inferior form.

referable. So spelled—not **referrable.*

referendum. Both *referendums* and *referenda* are acceptable plurals. Prefer *referendums.*

referral; reference. Both correspond to *refer* (to someone or something), but *referral* has acquired the special meaning of sending a client to a specialist or passing a client's information to a third person.

re-form; reform; reformation. The hyphen affects meaning. To *re-form* is to form again; the noun is *reformation.* To *reform* is to change law, policy, or procedures for the better, and especially to make them fairer; its noun is *reform.*

refractory; refractive. Something *refractory* is hard to manage, as an unruly child or a stubborn disease. Something *refractive* bends light rays; the term is restricted to the field of optics.

refrain; restrain. You *refrain* from doing something yourself, whereas other people *restrain* you.

refute. See REBUT.

regardless. This is the correct form. Use of the nonword **irregardless*—probably a confounding of *regardless* and *irrespective*—is a badge of illiteracy.

register; registrar. In reference to one who keeps records, a *register* is usually a public official <register of wills>, while a *registrar* usually works for an educational institution <transcripts are available in the registrar's office>.

regrettable; regretful. Unfortunate incidents are *regrettable* (worthy of regret); the people who are sorry about their role in those incidents are *regretful* (feeling regret). *Regretfully* is often misused for *regrettably.*

rein; reign. A *rein* is a bridle strap, used to control a horse. By extension it is the means of controlling other things <the Senate usually gives a new President free rein to pick a cabinet>. *Reign* is the rule of a sovereign <England flourished during Elizabeth I's reign>. Perhaps because of the connotation of control, people sometimes write **reign in* when they mean *rein in.*

relate back; recover back. Although *re*-verbs are usually incorrect when used with *back*, these phrases are not redundant. *Relate back* refers to the doctrine of *relation back* <the amendment relates back to the date of the original pleading>. And common law distinguishes *recover*, meaning "to collect" <recover damages>, from *recover back*, meaning "secure return of" <the plaintiff sought to recover back the loan collateral>.

relater; relator. A *relater* is a narrator. A *relator* is a party seeking mandamus or quo warranto to force a public official to perform a legal duty.

relegate; delegate. To *relegate* someone originally meant to send the person into exile, the essence of the word being "to send away." Today we may *relegate* someone to a lesser assignment <the DA relegated Pat to misdemeanors> or *relegate* a matter to some other authority to make or enforce a decision <the board relegated the grievance to a subpanel>. To *delegate* also means "to send away," but with the authority to act as one's agent or representative <the senior partner delegated Robin to negotiate the merger>.

relevance; *relevancy. Prefer the first.

*An invariably inferior form.

relic; relict. A *relic* is something that survives from the past <relics from a Phoenician shipwreck>. *Relict* is an obscure, legalistic, and much inferior term for a widowed spouse.

relief. See REMEDY.

reluctant. See RETICENT.

remedial; remediable. *Remedial* describes a corrective measure <remedial English> and, in law, a legal remedy <the remedial device of a resultant trust>. *Remediable* describes something that can be remedied <the storm damage was severe but remediable>.

remedy; relief; remediation; remediate. Historically, a *remedy* was what one sought from a court of law <a legal remedy> and *relief* was what one sought in a court of equity <equitable relief>. *Remediation* is the process of remedying <environmental remediation>. *Remediate*, a back-formation from *remediation*, is used in the context of environmental cleanups.

remit; remission; remittance. *Remit* has several meanings in the sense of "to transfer something" or "to ease up." The noun for all senses but one is *remission*—when it is money that is sent, the funds are a *remittance.*

removal from office. See IMPEACHMENT.

renewal. See EXTENSION.

renounce. See DENOUNCE.

reoccur. See RECUR.

repellent; repulsive; repugnant. Something *repellent* wards off or drives away (people, insects, etc.). Something *repulsive* has the same effect, but only because it is truly disgusting. To most people, *repugnant* means the same thing as *repulsive* (disgusting). To lawyers, it retains its original meaning of "contradictory." So when we write that a proffered interpretation of a will is *repugnant* to the testator's intent, we can do so without holding our noses.

repetitive; repetitious. To describe something that happens again and again, *repetitive* is usually neutral in connotation (although "repetitive stress syndrome" may change this), while *repetitious* often connotes that the repetition is tiresome.

replica; copy; duplicate; reproduction. In best usage, a *replica* is a precisely detailed copy. Originally, the term denoted a copy made by the original artist, but that sense is lost in American English. It has come to denote a model, especially on a smaller scale <a replica of the Empire State Building>. A *duplicate* is an exact copy. A *reproduction* is a close copy, and especially one made after the original is no longer available.

repress. See OPPRESS.

reprise; reprisal. A *reprise* is a repetition, as of an artistic performance or, in law, an annual payment from an estate or manor. A *reprisal* is a hostile act taken in retaliation for a previous wrong.

reproduction. See REPLICA.

republication; revival. In the law of wills, *republication* is the repetition of execution formalities for a previously revoked will, thereby making it valid again. *Revival* is the restoration of a revoked will by revoking the superseding will. In most jurisdictions revoking a will that revoked a previous will does not *revive* the previous will, but *republication* always does.

repudiation; rescission; recension. In contract law, *repudiation* is behavior or words indicating a party's clear intent not to perform future obligations. *Rescission* is a party's cancellation of a contract for good reason, such as the other party's material breach. *Rescission* is also an abrogation or repeal, as of a statute. The word is misspelled many ways (**recision*, **recission*, **rescision*). *Recension* is the revision of a writing.

repugnant. See REPELLENT.

repulsive. See REPELLENT.

reputation. See CHARACTER.

request; behest; bequest. If people ask you to do something, you act at their *request*. If you promise them you'll do it, or if they order you to do it, you act at their *behest*. *Bequest*, which some confuse with *behest*, is a gift in a will and nothing else.

rescission. See REPUDIATION.

residence. See CITIZENSHIP.

residue; residuary; residual. *Residue* is that which is left behind; in law it is that part of an estate or trust left over after all other distributions have been made. *Residuary* is the best adjective to use in this legal sense, although *residual* is used as well. In nonlegal usage, *residual* is universal.

res judicata. See COLLATERAL ESTOPPEL.

resolute. See DECISIVE.

respondent. See APPELLATE.

restive; restful. *Restive* (restless) is almost the opposite of *restful*, which describes a peaceful condition. *Restive* can also mean "stubborn."

restrain. See REFRAIN.

retainer; retainage. A *retainer* is what a client pays a lawyer to take a case, or the client's authorization to act as legal representative. *Retainage* is money withheld by a property owner from a contractor's payment pending completion of the work and release of all liens.

reticent; reluctant. *Reticent* is often misused to mean *reluctant* (unwilling to act). But its real meaning is much narrower: it means "reluctant to speak," "unable to speak freely," or just "quiet by nature."

retract. See REVOKE.

return a verdict. See HAND UP AN INDICTMENT.

revenge. See AVENGE.

reverse. See OVERRULE.

reverse; reversal; revert; reversion. To *reverse* is to turn around; its noun form is *reversal* <a reversal of fortune>. To *revert* is to go back to a previous condition; its noun is *reversion* <reversion of a contingent estate>.

*An invariably inferior form.

revival. See REPUBLICATION.

revoke; retract. Both mean "to take back," but in contract law one *revokes* an offer and *retracts* an anticipatory repudiation.

revolt. See INSURRECTION.

revolution. See INSURRECTION.

revolve around. See CENTER ON.

rob; steal; burglarize. A criminal *robs* you (takes your goods from your person with real or threatened bodily harm), *steals* your goods (from anywhere, whether you're around or not), and *burglarizes* your house or car (breaks in with the intent to commit a felony, usually *stealing*).

roll; role. *Roll* (in its meaning as "roster") and *role* (in its meaning as "a part in a play," literally and metaphorically) are commonly confused <the firm's *role* [read *roll*] of clients was impressive> <even though he played only a bit *roll* [read *role*] in the bank robbery, it was his third felony>.

sacrilegious. The functional opposite of *religious* does not believe in orthodox spelling; the correct term is *sacrilegious*, which corresponds to the noun *sacrilege*. **Sacreligious* is a fairly common misspelling.

salvager; salvor. The common term for one who rescues property from a shipwreck is *salvager*. But in admiralty law it is *salvor*.

sanction. This word can bear opposite meanings, both as a noun and as a verb. It can mean "penalty" (or "to penalize") <the bar association's sanctions for commingling a client's funds range from suspension to disbarment>, or it can mean "approval" (or "to approve") <the charity sanctioned the fundraising event>.

scarce; rare. Both adjectives describe something that is hard to come by. But a common object may be *scarce* at times <vine-ripened tomatoes are scarce in winter>, whereas in best usage a *rare* item is always in short supply, and usually of high cost and quality <collecting rare stamps>.

seasonal; seasonable. What is *seasonal* relates either to the seasons <a seasonal display of spring fashions> or to something that happens in a particular season <the seasonal nature of the sugaring>. What is *seasonable* is either timely <a seasonable appeal> or (more often in the negative) in the right season <seasonable temperatures for August>.

secede. See CEDE.

sedition; treason. *Sedition* denotes plotting to incite action against the government. *Treason* denotes actual acts taken against the government.

semi-. See BI-.

sensor. See CENSOR.

sensuous; sensual. *Sensuous* (related to or stimulating any of the five senses) has no indecent overtones. *Sensual* (pleasing to the five senses, and especially relating to sexual gratification) does. The terms are often confounded.

sequestration; attachment; garnishment. *Sequestration* is the court-ordered seizure of property at issue in a lawsuit. *Attachment* is court-ordered seizure of property as

*An invariably inferior form.

security for the payment of a judgment. *Garnishment* is a proceeding in which a judgment creditor seeks to have property owned by the judgment debtor, but in the possession of a third party, turned over to the creditor.

servicemark. See TRADEMARK.

session. See CESSION.

set aside. See OVERRULE.

sewer; sewage; sewerage. A *sewer* is a pipe carrying wastewater. *Sewage* is what the sewer carries. *Sewerage* is the sewer system or the act of removing sewage.

sex; gender. Although these terms are often used as synonyms, there is a trend in academic circles to restrict *sex* to the biological differences between man and woman, and use *gender* to refer to psychological and sociological dispositions.

shall. Although *shall* commonly appears in statutes, rules, and contracts, it's an ambiguous word with as many as five senses. In its most defensible use, it can be replaced by *has a duty to*—but few legal drafters exercise the self-discipline to use it exclusively in that way (and in any case, *must* conveys the same meaning with no ambiguity). Otherwise, it may be permissive, or indicate a future action, or even mean nothing at all. *Shall* has been widely litigated, resulting in vastly different interpretations. It's better to use plain words and phrases with narrow meanings, such as *must*, *is*, *will*, *may*, and so on. See 27.3(b); 29.3(h).

shares. See STOCK.

sheer; shear. *Sheer* is the spelling for the adjective describing a steep cliff or a transparent fabric, or the verb meaning "to swerve" or "to change direction." *Shear* is the verb for cutting (especially, fleecing a sheep) and (in the plural form) the noun for scissors or some other cutting instrument.

sight. See CITE.

since; as; because. *Since* can mean "because" or "from that time on"—that's a linguistic fact dating back over a thousand years. Still, be aware that *since* is occasionally ambiguous: in "the father hasn't made support payments since he was denied visitation," was the denial his motive or just the time the payments stopped? *As* can also carry two similar meanings, "because" or "during that time." In the first sense, *as* is weaker than *because* or *since*. *Because* is typically the best pick, both for strength and for always being unambiguous. But sometimes *since* is just the word to express causation more mildly <since I've got you on the phone anyway . . .>.

site. See CITE.

situs. See LOCUS.

slander. See DEFAMATION.

sneak. The past-tense form is preferably *sneaked*. The dialectal **snuck* is unfortunately common.

social; sociable; societal. *Social* relates to living among other people <social skills>. *Sociable* means "friendly; interactive with other people" <a sociable guest>. *Societal* deals with society itself <societal breakdown>.

*An invariably inferior form.

soft-pedal. See PEDDLE.

solicitor. See BARRISTER.

soluble; insoluble; solvable; unsolvable. *Soluble* and *insoluble* can apply to physical solutions <the material must be soluble in water> and mental solutions <most mathematicians today believe that the old conundrum is insoluble>. But *solvable* and *unsolvable* can apply only to mental solutions <without the missing clues, the crossword puzzle was unsolvable>. *Unsolvable* is the preferred negative form, not **insolvable.*

sometime; some time. *Sometime* means "at some time," but just when is uncertain <the break-in occurred sometime last night>. *Some time* means "for some time," but the duration is uncertain <the new rules will take some time getting used to>.

species; specie. *Species*, meaning a specific type of plant, animal, or other general category of living thing, is both singular and plural, so it is erroneous to write of one *specie* in this sense. *Specie* is coined money. It takes a plural form only when writing of the coins of more than one country.

specious. See SPURIOUS.

spiritual; spirituous. Something *spiritual* relates to the spirit world or is concerned with religious things. Something *spirituous* contains alcoholic spirits.

spoliation. See DESPOLIATION.

spurious; specious. Both words mean "false." But *spurious* best describes people and things that are superficially attractive but ultimately fake <a spurious autograph>, while *specious* applies to reasoning <a specious argument>.

stationary; stationery. What is *stationary* is standing still. *Stationery* is writing paper and related supplies (think *stationer*).

staunch; stanch. A *staunch* supporter is loyal and zealous. To *stanch* a flow is to stop it, especially to stop bleeding.

steal. See ROB.

sterility; impotence. *Sterility* is the inability to conceive or sire offspring—for example, because of a male's low sperm count or a female's blockage of the fallopian tubes. *Impotence* is a male's inability to perform sexually because of erectile dysfunction. Rarely, it also refers to a female's inability to engage in sexual intercourse.

stock; shares. *Stock* is the proportional part of a corporation's capital or principal fund owned by one who buys *shares.* While *stock* is a mass noun <some stock>, *shares* is a count noun <20 shares of IBM>.

strait; straight; straitjacket; straitlaced. A *strait* is a tight spot, literally a narrow passage between two large bodies of water <Strait of Hormuz> and figuratively a precarious situation <in dire straits>. *Straight* means "linear" and, by extension, "upright." It is *strait* (not *straight*) that forms words implying tight constraint, such as *straitjacket* and *straitlaced.*

strategy; tactics. Both words have Greek military roots, *strategy* relating to a general and *tactics* to the arrangement of battle forces. *Strategy* is the long-range plan for winning a

*An invariably inferior form.

campaign of some sort <Nixon's Southern strategy>. *Tactics* are short-term maneuvers for winning individual battles <strong-arm tactics>.

stupid. See IGNORANT.

subject. See CITIZEN.

subsequent. See CONSEQUENT.

subsequently. Use *later*—or, better yet, a more specific time <*the next afternoon*>.

subsequent to. Use *after* instead.

such. If by *such property* you mean "property of that kind," you're fine. But if you mean "the property just mentioned," you're engaging in legalese. Never use *such* in place of *this*, *that*, *these*, *those*, or *the*.

such as. See LIKE; SUCH AS.

sufferance; *suffrance; suffrage. *Sufferance* is the correct spelling, **suffrance* a common error. *Suffrage* is the right to vote; its spelling may influence some to misspell *sufferance*.

sufficient. See ADEQUATE.

sui generis; sui juris. If something is *sui generis*, it is in a class by itself, unlike others <if databases can't be copyrighted, perhaps we need to devise some form of sui generis protection>. A person who is *sui juris* is of legal age and capacity or has full civil rights <all parties to the suit being sui juris>. As with other Latinisms, each phrase should be avoided whenever a suitable English substitute would work.

sumptuous; sumptuary. What is *sumptuous* is extravagant and expensive. What is *sumptuary* is meant to regulate someone's extravagant and expensive purchases, and also to curb bad habits.

supersede; supersession. *Supersede* (to take the place of) may be the most misspelled word in legal writing: it appears as **supercede* in almost a thousand federal-court opinions. It derives from the Latin *sedeo* (sit), not *cedo* (yield). *Supersession* is the noun.

supplement. See COMPLIMENT.

supplementary. See COMPLIMENTARY.

surety; guarantor. Both pledge to accept responsibility for another person's debt, but a *surety* takes primary responsibility on an equal level with the principal, whereas a *guarantor* takes secondary responsibility and becomes liable only if the principal defaults.

surplus; surplusage. *Surplus* is anything left over—an excess. In law, *surplusage* is text that adds no meaning and serves no purpose in the document. In all other senses, *surplusage* is a poor variant of *surplus*.

survival statute. See DEATH STATUTE.

suspicious; suspect. *Suspicious* can describe someone who arouses suspicion <a suspicious loiterer> or someone who suspects <the officer became suspicious>. As an adjective, *suspect* means "untrustworthy" <with no chain-of-custody foundation, the blood-sample evidence was suspect>. As a verb, *suspect* connotes a more fully formed belief than does the noun *suspicion* <I suspect that you're hiding something from me>.

*An invariably inferior form.

As a noun, *suspect* denotes the person under suspicion <police arrested a suspect in the robbery>.

sympathy. See EMPATHY.

systematic; systemic. What is *systematic* is either done as part of a formal system <Jim Crow laws were systematic racism> or methodical <a systematic review of the literature>. An affliction that is *systemic* is not isolated but affects multiple organs.

tactics. See STRATEGY.

take. See BRING.

talisman; talismanic; talesman. A *talisman* is a charm believed to have magic powers. The term is used as a pejorative by judges to suggest that a doctrine being relied on is not above scrutiny. The plural is *talismans*, not **talismen*. The adjective form is *talismanic*. *Talesman* is a rare term for a person available to replace a dismissed juror.

tantalizing; titillating. What is *tantalizing* is alluring but always just beyond our grasp. What is *titillating* tickles or excites.

taut; taught. *Taut* means "tight," as a tightrope, a stressful emotion, or discipline. *Taught* (the past tense of *teach*) is sometimes misused in its place <the bodybuilder's *taught* [read *taut*] abs>.

tax; assessment. A *tax* is a levy on the general population to raise funds that will be spent for the benefit of an entire community <a tax to support highway construction>. An *assessment* is (1) a special levy just on those who will benefit from the expenditure of those funds <an assessment to pay for curbs and sidewalks in one neighborhood>; or (2) the determination of a tax rate <residential assessments rose 3% last year>.

tax evasion; tax avoidance. *Tax evasion* is escaping payment of taxes by illegal means, such as hiding income or claiming fictitious dependents. *Tax avoidance* is escaping payment of taxes by legal means, such as buying tax-exempt securities or investing in a tax-deferred pension plan.

tenancy in common. See JOINT TENANCY.

territory; dependency; commonwealth. U.S. *territories* and *dependencies* are part of the United States but not a part of any single state; *territories* (e.g., Guam) have their own legislatures, while *dependencies* (e.g., the Philippines, formerly) are governed by U.S. law. A *commonwealth* (e.g., Puerto Rico) is an autonomous nation voluntarily affiliated with the United States. Cf. COMMONWEALTH.

testamentary; testimonial. *Testamentary* refers to wills, *testimonial* to oral evidence. It is surprising how often *testamentary* is erroneously used for *testimonial* in judicial opinions, perhaps because the context is often "documentary and *testamentary* [read *testimonial*] evidence."

that; which; who. *That* introduces a restrictive clause, one that can't be left out without changing the meaning of the sentence <all businesses that violate antitrust laws

> "The better we understand our words, the less we will want to change them." —*T.W.H. Holland*

*An invariably inferior form.

should be shut down [not all businesses, just some]>. *Which* introduces a nonrestrictive clause, one set off by commas and whose omission would not change the meaning <the statute, which was signed yesterday, will take effect on September 1>. *Who* can be restrictive or nonrestrictive; it follows the same rules <the candidate who spoke at the school won the election> <you, who disagreed with me, voted for the loser>. Cf. WHO.

their. See THERE.

there; their; they're. Basic but still misused homophones: *there* is the direction <over there> or place <where there is life>, *their* is the possessive of *they* <all their worldly belongings>, and *they're* is the contraction of *they are* <they're on the way>.

therefore; therefor. *Therefore* is the common term for "consequently" <the plaintiff did not appear; the suit was therefore dismissed>. *Therefor* is used in legal writing to mean "for that" or "for it" <I bought a car, paying $22,000 therefor>—but it's clunky and easily avoided by better wording.

they. On the use of *they* in reference to a single person, see 11.10(o). See also 11.10(g) and 13.5(o).

they're. See THERE.

third party; third-party. As a noun, use two words <the third party in the suit>, but hyphenate the phrase when used as an adjective <a third-party defendant> or an informal verb <the defendant third-partied two other companies>.

threshold; withhold. Although *threshold* does not derive from *hold*, it is often misspelled as if it did <across the *threshhold* [read *threshold*]>. *Withhold* does contain the word *hold*, hence the double-*h*. *Withhold* is sometimes used incorrectly to mean "deny" <as punishment, she was *withheld* [read *denied*] phone privileges>.

thus; *thusly. *Thus* is already an adverb; it does not need the *-ly* ending.

till. This preposition is Standard Written English <open till 8 o'clock>. Do not make the mistake of thinking it is an abbreviation of *until*—that is, *'*til* is a mistake.

timber; timbre. *Timber* is the correct spelling for all meanings except the musical term meaning "tonal quality" (*timbre*).

time period. See PERIOD OF TIME.

titillating. See TANTALIZING.

tolerance; toleration. *Tolerance* is the attribute of being tolerant; *toleration* is an act of tolerance.

torpid. See TURBID.

tortious; tortuous; torturous. *Tortious* refers to acts that give rise to actions in tort <tortious battery>. *Tortuous* means "full of twists and turns" <a tortuous mountainside road>. *Torturous* means "involving torture" <a torturous interrogation>.

toward; towards. There is no distinction between these two words. *Toward* is universally preferred in American English; *towards* is preferred in British English.

toxology; toxicology. *Toxology* is the study of archery; *toxicology* is the study of poisons.

*An invariably inferior form.

trademark; tradename; servicemark; trade dress. A *trademark* is a name, phrase, logo, or other graphic element that identifies a company's goods or services. It is always one word. By custom, a *tradename* identifies the company itself, although in law it is not distinguished from a trademark. A *servicemark* is a trademark on services. *Tradename* and *servicemark* both are frequently rendered as two words, but the one-word forms are increasingly dominant. *Trade dress*, the overall appearance of a product or business, may also be protected by trademark laws.

treason. See SEDITION.

treble; triple. As verbs, these terms are usually interchangeable. As adjectives, they are distinguished. What is *treble* is three times as much as something else <treble damages>; what is *triple* is composed of three parts <triple play>.

trial lawyer; litigator. An attorney who takes part in a trial, on either side, is a *trial lawyer* and a *litigator.* But increasingly, the term *trial lawyer* denotes plaintiff's attorneys who specialize in suits for personal injuries, medical malpractice, and other torts. An earlier distinction was a connotation that *trial lawyers* enjoyed the front-line advocacy of trials, while *litigators* preferred behind-the-scenes discovery and pleadings.

trillion. See BILLION.

triple. See TREBLE.

triumphal; triumphant. *Triumphal* describes a thing associated with a triumph <the conquerors erected a triumphal arch at the city's gate>. *Triumphant* describes how the victors feel after a triumph <triumphant shouts of joy>.

trustee; trusty; executor. A *trustee* is a fiduciary designated to hold legal title over trust property and to use it for the good of one or more beneficiaries. A *trusty* is a trusted prisoner who is given special privileges and may perform some tasks for prison guards. An *executor* is one who collects the property of an estate and distributes it according to the wishes of the testator. Nonlawyers sometimes call this person a *trustee.*

turbid; turgid; torpid. What is *turbid* is unclear: literally, dark with stirred-up mud or smoke <turbid waters>; figuratively, confused <the statute seemed to be deliberately turbid>. What is *turgid* is literally swollen <a river turgid from heavy rains> and figuratively pompous <a turgid but empty speech>. What is *torpid* is literally numb <a torpid bear in hibernation> and figuratively sluggish <the mind torpid in old age>.

ultimate; penultimate; antepenultimate. Counting backward from the end, *ultimate* means "the last," *penultimate* means "next-to-last," and *antepenultimate* means "the one before the next-to-last."

undocumented worker. See ILLEGAL ALIEN.

undoubtedly. See DOUBTLESS.

unequivocal. So spelled. **Unequivocable* is not a legitimate word, but it appears quite often nonetheless.

unexceptional; unexceptionable. An *unexceptional* thing is ordinary. An *unexceptionable* thing is inoffensive or, in law, not cause for an objection.

uninhabitable. See HABITABLE.

*An invariably inferior form.

uninterested. See DISINTERESTED.

unique; unusual. Strictly speaking, *unique* is an absolute term meaning "one of a kind." In common usage it can't take an intensive modifier <a very unique [read *unique*] experience>. Using *unique* loosely to mean *unusual* is not normally acceptable in formal writing. But in contract law, the term is used in a less-than-absolute sense when addressing the adequacy of money damages in a prayer for specific performance <the location is so unique that no alternative site would be an adequate remedy>.

unlawful; illegal; illicit; criminal. These appear in order of increasing stigma. An *unlawful* act is one not approved by law, but not necessarily against the law, either. It could be a civil wrong, or an offense that no one would consider particularly blameworthy, such as overparking. An *illegal* act is a violation of law, but even this term can apply to civil offenses. *Illicit* carries a strong connotation of immorality, and *criminal* denotes punishable wrongdoing. Cf. ELICIT.

unmoral. See IMMORAL.

unoccupied. See VACANT.

unorganized. See DISORGANIZED.

unreadable. See ILLEGIBLE.

unusual. See UNIQUE.

unwritten. See VERBAL.

upon. See ON.

use; usage; utilization; utilize. Always *use* the simple term unless there's a reason not to. *Usage* is a separate term altogether, meaning "a custom or practice." *Utilization* and *utilize* connote using something to its best advantage; the words are appropriate only when that meaning applies.

v.; vs. In case citations, *versus* is abbreviated *v.* <*Bush v. Gore*>. In all other contexts, use *vs.*

vacant; unoccupied. For insurance purposes, a building is *vacant* if it has nothing in it, and *unoccupied* if no one lives there.

vacate. See OVERRULE.

variance; variation. In law, *variance* refers to a difference between what was pleaded or charged and what is proved at trial. It also refers to a permit to use land in a way that would otherwise violate zoning laws. The phrase *at variance* also means "in disagreement" <the holding was at variance with the rule in most circuits>. A *variation* is any departure from the norm or the past; this general term should not be used where the specific meaning of *variance* is needed.

venal; venial. *Venal* describes a person (or, rarely, a thing) who is for sale—corrupt and disposed to accepting bribes <a venal code-enforcer>. *Venial* means "minor" and "forgivable" <a venial sin>. But while the adjectives are almost opposite in effect (very corrupt vs. slightly corrupt), they look and sound close and are often confused for each other.

venerable; old. *Venerable* should not be used to mean merely *old.* It describes one who is worthy of great respect and reverence.

venial. See VENAL.

veracity; voracity. *Veracity* is the human characteristic of truthfulness <the rabbi had a reputation for veracity>. It is sometimes used loosely as an equivalent of *accuracy* <challenge the veracity of the witness's statement>, but this use should be avoided. And the mistake of using *voracity* (gluttony) in error is a frightening prospect.

verbal; oral; unwritten. *Verbal* means "of words"; *oral* means "spoken." In the best usage, *verbal* should not be used in place of *oral* to mean "unwritten" <verbal contract [read *unwritten contract*]>, since writing and speech both comprise words. But it's a common slip-up that legal writers seem especially prone to.

verbiage. This best means "wordiness," a stylistic fault. It is less often used with neutral connotations to mean *wording* <the actual *verbiage* [read *wording* or *text*] of the contract>. But since it has always had connotations of bad writing, this use is often confusing and should be avoided.

verdict; judgment; decision; mandate. A *verdict* is handed down by a jury (or a judge, in a bench trial); then the trial judge issues a *judgment.* The losing party may appeal the *judgment* (not the *verdict*). An appellate court reaches a *decision* and issues its *judgment.* If more action is required of the trial court, the appellate court will issue a *mandate* instructing the lower court what to do. *Judgment* is the preferred spelling in American English. Cf. DECISION.

verification. See ACKNOWLEDGMENT.

vilify. So spelled. **Villify* is a common error.

vocation; avocation. The first is what you do for a living; the second is what you do for relaxation. Your *vocation* is your career; your *avocation* is your hobby.

void; voidable. In law, a *void* contract (or marriage) is not a contract at all and never was. A *voidable* contract is a contract until a party with justification declares it void. Cf. AVOID.

voluminous. See COMPENDIOUS.

voluntary; intentional. An act can't be inculpatory unless it was *voluntary* (done consciously), so one can't be held accountable for acts done while sleepwalking, for example. But whether the actor consciously intended a wrongful consequence of a *voluntary* act—whether the outcome was *intentional*—goes to the degree of culpability. The first term looks at the nature of the act itself, the second at the motive behind the act.

voracity. See VERACITY.

vs. See V.

waive; waiver; laches; estoppel. To *waive* a right is to give it up. A *waiver* must be voluntary, so the word is misused when substituted for *laches* (the equitable doctrine that unreasonable delay can bar relief) or *estoppel* (the equitable doctrine that bars a party from contradicting a previous stance). *Waive* is sometimes misused for the common verb *wave*. Also, *waiver* is sometimes used where *waver* (to vacillate) is intended.

*An invariably inferior form.

wangle. See WRANGLE.

wantonly; recklessly. In criminal law, a person acting *wantonly* acts with malice (intent), while a person acting *recklessly* does not.

warranty. See GUARANTEE.

wave; waver. See WAIVE.

wedding. See MARRIAGE.

whence; from whence. *Whence* means "from where" or "from which," so *from whence* is considered redundant <go back *from whence* [read *whence*] you came>. Even so, it has been used that way for five centuries, by the likes of Shakespeare and Dickens. *Whence* sounds stilted anyway and should be avoided.

whether; whether or not. *Whether* does not usually need *or not* because that sense is included in the word itself <the issue is *whether or not* [read *whether*] the statute applies to resident aliens>. The one exception occurs when the phrase means "regardless of whether" <the bill's supporters have the votes to override a veto, so it will become law whether or not the President signs it>.

which. See THAT.

while away; *wile away. Both of these synonymous phrases for leisurely passing time are accepted and have long been used. But the second was originally a corruption of the first, which is preferred and predominant.

who; whom. *Who* is the subject, *whom* the object. If the sentence is so complex that it is hard to tell whether the term is subjective or objective, you should probably rework the sentence. Cf. THAT.

who's; whose. Pronoun contractions and possessives can require a second look to be sure you've picked the right form. But as with *it's* and *its*, the apostrophe always marks the contraction. *Who's* is the word for *who is* <Who's there?>. *Whose* is the possessive for *of whom* <a man whose identity is still unknown>.

whosever; whoever's. The strictly correct possessive form is *whosever*; it should be used in formal writing. The more common *whoever's* (also a contraction for *whoever is*) is acceptable only in casual use.

***wile away.** See WHILE AWAY.

willful; wilful; *willfull. The first is the American spelling. The second is British. The third is always wrong.

willfulness; malice aforethought. An act done *willfully* is done voluntarily, intentionally, and with the specific intent of accomplishing the outcome. *Willfulness* is an element of a number of crimes, while *malice aforethought* is an element only of murder. The latter does not imply *malice* in the everyday sense of hatred or ill will, but rather means the specific intent to kill, to inflict serious bodily harm, or to commit a dangerous felony, or the total disregard for human life ("depraved heart").

withhold. See THRESHOLD.

workers' compensation; workmen's compensation. The phrases are always plural (not *worker's* or *workman's*). The gender-neutral first phrase has become standard.

*An invariably inferior form.

worse comes to worst; worst comes to worst. The second phrase is the original form, but the first phrase now dominates. It's also more logical, suggesting as it does a worsening (from the comparative *worse* to the superlative *worst*).

wrack; rack. *Wrack* is seaweed or kelp. In all other senses, *rack* is the word. To *rack* is to torture by stretching on a *rack*. When something completely falls apart, it "goes to *rack* and ruin." When you search your memory for an answer, you *rack* (stretch) your brain.

wrangle; wangle. *Wrangle* (to argue heatedly) is sometimes mistaken for *wangle* (to get by scheming or to succeed despite obstacles) <he tried to *wrangle* [read *wangle*] an invitation to the Inaugural Ball>.

wreak. See REEK.

wreak havoc. The past tense of this phrase is *wreaked havoc*, not **wrought havoc* (a common error). Aggravating circumstances may also *play havoc* or *create havoc*. Avoid **work havoc*. Cf. REEK.

wreath; wreathe. *Wreath* is the noun for an ornamental circle made of plants. *Wreathe* is the verb meaning "to encircle."

wrong; wrongful. What is *wrong* may be either incorrect <the wrong trousers> or evil <stealing is wrong>. What is *wrongful* may be either (1) without legal right <a wrongful beneficiary> or (2) illegal or immoral <a wrongful assault>.

your; you're. Basic but still misused homophones: *your* is the possessive <it's your right>; *you're* is the contraction for *you are* <you're right about that>.

zealous. See JEALOUS.

13.4 Use the correct preposition for the meaning you intend.

(a) *Idiomatic phrasing.* Legal idiom, no less than English idiom generally, consists of characteristic ways of saying things. Among the trickiest of these are prepositional constructions. For example, the legal stylist knows that a party may be either *estopped from* doing something or *estopped to* do something, but is never *estopped in* or *for* doing it. This type of knowledge comes very gradually, through wide reading of legal texts.

(b) *List of prepositional pairings.* Some wordings cause even the most experienced writers to pause. For example, should it be *conform to* or *conform with*? As it happens, they're both perfectly proper. This illustrates, though, that careful writers often need assurance on a tentative choice of a preposition. What follows is a listing of the prepositional pairings that legal writers most commonly pause over. In the list, angle brackets contain the object or type of object that goes with a certain preposition; *inf.* indicates that the word goes with an infinitive (*to* plus a verb, e.g., *act*) and, in some instances, a specific infinitive; and ~ stands in for the word itself where it commonly follows a preposition.

abandoned, *adj.* by <a spouse>; to <foreclosure>; for <another plan>; in <a year; a place>.

*An invariably inferior form.

abetted, *vb.* in <a crime>; by <an accomplice>.

abide, *vb.* by <an agreement; a law>; with <a person; a condition>; in <the truth>; for <a time>.

abscond, *vb.* with <a stolen item>; from <a place>; to <a place>; for <fear of something>.

absolved, *vb.* of <a debt; an obligation>; from <guilt>; by <the verdict>.

abstain, *vb.* from <voting>; in <the vote>; on <certain grounds>; for <a time>.

abstention, *n.* from <voting>; in <a vote>; on <principle>; by <members>.

abstract, *n.* of <title>; from <a writing>; in ~.

abuse, *n.* of <discretion; power>; in <childhood>; heap ~ on <a person>; hurl ~ at <a person>; take ~ from <a person>.

abut, *vb.* on, upon, *or* against <a property>; at <one side>.

accede, *vb.* to <a demand>.

acceleration, *n.* of <payment>; in <growth>; at <the surface>; to <the center>.

acceptance, *n.* of <a settlement>; by <the recipient>; from <a donor; a colleague>; in <the community>; for <honor>; toward <a colleague>; on *or* upon ~.

accessory, *n.* to <a crime>; before *or* after <the fact>; of <a machine>; in <felony>.

accomplice, *n.* to <a crime>; of *or* with <a coconspirator>; in <crime>.

accord, *n.* over *or* about <an issue>; with, between, *or* among <another party>; in ~.

accord, *vb.* with <a policy>; to <the people>; by <law>; in <a place>.

account, *vb.* to <a person>; for <an action; a person>; of <great importance>; by <a historian>.

accusation, *n.* of *or* about <an offense>; by <an accuser>; against <an accused>; in <writing>.

accuse, *vb.* of <an offense>.

accused, *adj.* of <an offense>; by <an accuser>.

accused, *n.* in <the case>; to <be tried>.

acquiesce, *vb.* in <an action; a policy>; to <demands>.

acquit, *vb.* of *or* on <a charge>; from <an obligation>; [oneself] by <redemption>.

acquitted, *adj.* of *or* on <a charge>; by <a judge or jury; redemption>.

act, *n.* of <a legislature; God; aggression>; against <an opponent>.

act, *vb.* on <a proposal>; toward *or* with <another>; to <*inf.*>; against <an opponent>; as <a role>; like <a role model>; for <another person>.

adherence, *n.* to <a rule>; in ~.

adhesion, *n.* to <a surface>; contract of ~.

adjourn, *vb.* for <an interval; a purpose>; to <a place>.

administration, *n.* of <an enterprise; an estate>.

admissible, *adj.* in <court>; into *or* as <evidence>; for <a limited purpose>; against <a party>; over <an objection>; of <another explanation>.

admission, *n.* of *or* about <a fact>; by *or* from <the admitting person>; to <another person>; against <one's interests>; to *or* into <a place>.

admit, *vb.* to <doing something>; into *or* to <a place; a group>; to <a person>; of <a state or condition [e.g., failure]>.

adoption, *n.* of <a child; a contract; a cause>; by <the one adopting>; up for ~.

adversary, *n.* of <an opponent>.

adverse, *adj.* to <a situation; an interest>.

advert, *vb.* to <a reference>.

advise, *vb.* about *or* on <an issue>; against <a decision; an act>; of <a right; a situation>; in <a lawsuit>; to <*inf.*>.

advisement, *n.* about *or* of <a development>; under ~.

affirmation, *n.* of <truth>; by *or* from <the affirming person>; in ~.

agent, *n.* of *or* for <a principal>; in <a transaction>.

aggravated, *adj.* by <an intensifying factor>.

aid, *vb.* for <a need>; against <an enemy>; in *or* with <an undertaking>.

alibi, *n.* for <the time a crime was committed>.

alienation, *n.* from <a person; a group; society>; of <a relationship; property>.

allegation, *n.* of <a charge>; by <an accuser>; against <an accused>; about *or* over <a fact>.

ambiguity, *n.* about <a fact>; of <a communication>.

ambivalent, *adj.* toward *or* about <a person; a situation>.

analogous, *adj.* to *or* with <another thing>.

annotation, *n.* of <a writing; an issue of law>; by <the author>; about <the subject>.

annulment, *n.* of <a marriage>.

answer, *vb.* for <a misdeed>; to <a person wronged; an authority>; by <an atonement; a punishment>.

appeal, *n.* to <a higher court; a person>; of *or* by <the appellant>; from <the judgment>; for <a change in the judgment>; before <the higher court>; on ~.

appeal, *vb.* to <a higher court; a person>; from <the judgment>; for <a change in the judgment>.

appearance, *n.* of *or* by <a party in court>; for <a client>; through <a lawyer>; in <a jurisdiction>; before <a court>.

apprise, *vb.* of <information>.

arbitrate, *vb.* between <parties>; in <a dispute>.

arraignment, *n.* of <an accused>; on *or* for <an offense>; by *or* before <a magistrate>; in <a courtroom>.

arrest, *n.* of <an accused>; for <an offense>; by <an officer>.

assault, *n.* on *or* of <a victim>; for <a motive>; by <an attacker>; with <a weapon>.

assignment, *n.* of <an interest>; by *or* from <an assignor>; to <an office; a task>; on ~.

assimilate, *vb.* into *or* with <a community>.

assumption, *n.* about <a fact>; of <a risk; a role>; by *or* of <the assumer>.

asylum, *n.* in <a place>; from *or* against <oppression>; grant ~ to <a person>; for <a refugee>; seek ~ from <a nation>.

attachment, *n.* to <a document; an interest>; of *or* on <property>; by <a court; a sheriff>; for, to, *or* toward <satisfying a judgment>.

attempt, *n.* at <an act>; by <the actor>; on <a person's life>; to <*inf.*>.

attest, *vb.* to <the truth>.

attorney, *n.* at <law>; in <fact>; of <record>; for <a client>; with *or* of <a firm>; power of ~.

authenticate, *vb.* as <genuine>.

authentication, *n.* of <genuineness>; as <genuine>; by *or* from <a warrantor of genuineness>.

authority, *n.* over, in, *or* for <a domain>; of <an officer>; from <a delegator>; to <*inf.*>; on ~ of <a grant of power>; person of ~; in ~; on good ~; an ~ on <a subject>; <submit, surrender, yield, etc.> to ~.

averse, *adj.* to <a thing; a situation>.

award, *n.* to <an honoree>; of <an honor>; for <an accomplishment>; by *or* from <an honorer>.

badge, *n.* of <a state, condition, or position [e.g., slavery, honor]>.

bail, *n.* post ~ for <a person>; release on ~.

bail, *vb.* out of <jail; a plane>; out <water from a leaking boat>.

bailee, *n.* of <property>.

ban, *n.* on <a thing; an activity>.

ban, *vb.* from <a place>.

banish, *vb.* to *or* from <a place>.

bar, *n.* to <an action>; of <a material [e.g., gold, chocolate]; a state or nation [e.g., the state bar of Arizona]; an area of law [e.g., the public-law bar]>; case at ~.

bar, *vb.* from <a place>.

bargain, *n.* with *or* between <people>; from <a seller>; on <a thing>.

bargain, *vb.* with <people>; for <a price; an agreement>; over <a thing>.

barratry, *n.* of <a person>.

barter, *vb.* for <a thing>; with <a person>.

battery, *n.* of <a person>.

bearer, *n.* of <a thing>.

behalf, *n.* on ~ of <a client; a principal>; in ~ of <a person or cause that the actor supports>.

beneficiary, *n.* of <a gift>.

benefit, *n.* of *or* from <an advantage>; for *or* to <a person>; of ~ to; to *or* for the ~ of.

benefit, *vb.* from *or* by <an advantage>.

bequest, *n.* from <a benefactor>; to <a beneficiary>; of <a gift>; of ~ to; to *or* for the ~ of.

bias, *n.* against, toward, *or* for <a person; a class of people>; on *or* about <an issue>; of <a person>.

bill, *n.* of <rights, lading, etc.>; for <goods; services>; from <a creditor>.

bill, *vb.* for <goods; services>; to <a debtor>.

binding, *adj.* on <a person>.

boilerplate, *n.* of *or* in <a contract>.

bona fides, *n.* of <a person; a claim>.

bond, *n.* for <a thing ensured>; of <a relationship>; with, between, *or* among <people>.

boycott, *n.* of *or* on <an enterprise>; by <patrons>.

boycott, *vb.* for <a reason>; by <a tactic>.

breach, *n.* of <a duty>; in ~.

bribe, *vb.* to <*inf.*>; into <doing something>; by *or* with <an inducement>.

bribery, *n.* of <a person>.

broker, *n.* for <a principal>; of <goods; services>.

burden, *n.* of <proof, persuasion, production, etc.>; on *or* to <a person>; to <*inf.*>.

burden, *vb.* with *or* by <a load>.

burglary, *n.* of *or* at <a place>; by <a perpetrator>.

bylaw, *n.* of <an organization>.

cajole, *vb.* into <doing something>; by <a means>.

camera, *n.* [*judge's chambers*] in ~.

capacity, *n.* of <a room; a container>; for <learning>; to <*inf.*>; at full ~; fill to ~; as *or* of <a position>.

capital, *n.* of <a place>.

capitulate, *vb.* to <an adversary>; on <an issue>.

care, *n.* of <a caregiver; a dependent>; for <a dependent>; against <a danger>; in <an action>.

care, *vb.* for <a dependent>; about <something; someone>.

case, *n.* of <a person; a thing; a legal action>; about *or* over <a situation>; against <a person>; in <chief>; make a ~ for *or* against.

cause, *n.* of <action; a result>; for <a reaction>; for ~.

cause, *vb.* by *or* with <an action; a thing>; to <*inf.*>.

cease, *vb.* to <*inf.*>; from <an action>.

cede, *vb.* to <another person>.

censure, *vb.* for *or* over <an act>; as <a criminal, perjurer, etc.>.

chain, *n.* of <command, custody, etc.>.

challenge, *n.* of <a difficulty; a dispute>; for <a prize>; by <a contest>; from <a contestant>; about *or* over <an issue>; to <*inf.*>.

change, *n.* of <venue, heart, etc.>; for <money; the better/worse>; by <a cause>; from <an old form>; into <a new form>; in <form>.

character, *n.* of <a quality; a person>.

characterize, *vb.* as <one of two or more possible types>.

characterized, *adj.* by <a quality>.

charge, *n.* of <an accusation>; for <goods; services>; on, to, *or* against <an account>; at *or* against <a person or thing>; in *or* take ~ of; judge's ~ to the jury.

charge, *vb.* with <an accusation>; for <goods; services>; on *or* to <an account>; to <*inf.*>; with <a responsibility>; at <a person; a thing>; into *or* out of <a place>.

citation, *n.* of *or* from <a reference>; for *or* against <an assertion>; for <a distinction; a petty offense>; by <a superior; a police officer>.

civil, *adj.* to *or* toward <a person>.

claim, *n.* of <an allegation; a person>; for *or* against <a person; a disputed thing>; on *or* to <a thing>; by *or* from <a claimant>.

claim, *vb.* for <a person>; to <*inf.*>.

claimant, *n.* to <property>; in <an action>.

clerk, *n.* of, at, *or* in <an institution>.

clerk, *vb.* for <a judge>; for *or* at <a court; a law firm>.

closing, *n.* of <a thing; a case>; on <property>.

cloud, *n.* on <a title; a patent>; of <a complicating quality>; over <a troubled person>; under a ~.

coalesce, *vb.* into <a whole; a union>; around <a common concern>.

coalition, *n.* of, between, *or* among <partners>; with <another partner>; for <a purpose>.

code, *n.* of <conduct, statutes, etc.>; for <an encryption>; in ~.

codicil, *n.* to <a will>; of *or* by <a testator>.

coerce, *vb.* into <doing something>; to <*inf.*>.

coercion, *n.* of, by, *or* from <other people>; to <*inf.*>; under ~.

coincident, *adj.* with <another event>.

coincidental, *adj.* to <another event>.

collaborate, *vb.* with <another person>; in, on, *or* over <an enterprise>.

collateral, *adj.* to <the main proceeding; the main issue>.

collateral, *n.* for *or* on <a loan>; as *or* for ~.

colloquy, *n.* with *or* between <two people [esp., a judge and a criminal defendant]>.

collude, *vb.* to <*inf.* [esp., defraud]>; with, between, *or* among <someone to defraud a third person>; in <a scheme to defraud>; against <the victim of a fraud>.

collusion, *n.* to <*inf.* [esp., defraud]>; by, with, between, *or* among <someone to defraud a third person>; in <a scheme to defraud>; against <the victim of a fraud>; in ~.

comity, *n.* of, between, *or* among <cooperating entities>; to <a foreign court's proceedings>.

commitment, *n.* to <an enterprise; an institution>; of <a participant; an institutionalized person>; for <a purpose; a term>; by <a participant; a person instigating an institutionalization>; against <one's will>; in <an institution>; to <*inf.*>.

compare, *vb.* with <something else [an objective comparison]>; to <something else [a metaphorical exaltation]>.

compensate, *vb.* for <a loss>; by <an atonement>.

competence, *n.* of <a person [to do something]>; in *or* with <a skill>.

competency, *n.* to <*inf.* [esp., stand trial]>.

compliance, *n.* with <an order; a law; a policy>; of, from, *or* by <people>; by <a means>; in ~ with.

complicity, *n.* in <a crime>; of <a participant in a crime>.

comply, *vb.* with <an order; a law; a policy>; by <a means>.

conclusion, *n.* of <law; a proceeding or event>; by <the person reasoning or proceeding>; about <a question>; of <an event>; to <*inf.*>; in ~.

conclusive, *adj.* of <a decision>.

concur, *vb.* with <another person>; in <a decision>.

concurrence, *n.* of *or* by <a person in agreement>; in, on, to, with, *or* about <a judicial opinion>; with the ~ of; in ~ with.

concurrent, *adj.* with <a contemporaneous event; an additional penal sentence>.

condemn, *vb.* to <a punishment>; for <a public use>; as <a criminal, traitor, etc.>.

condition, *n.* of <a state or quality>; for <a reciprocal promise>; on ~ <that>.

> "Phrasal verbs remain idiomatic, too: 'in' and 'out' are antonyms, but 'fill in' and 'fill out' (a blank or form) are virtually synonyms; while to be 'all set up' is the opposite of 'all upset'. Older 'fall down' gives 'downfall' but newer 'melt down' and 'fall out' give 'meltdown' and 'fallout'; likewise 'breakthrough' and 'kickback'. The verb/noun is 'shoot out' but 'shoot off' gives 'offshoot'. The verb 'take out' gives two nouns, 'takeout' if it is food but 'outtake' if it is edited film."
>
> —*W.F. Bolton*

condition, *vb.* on <a requirement>; to *or* for <an undertaking; a changed situation>; to <*inf.*>.

conflict, *n.* of <interest, laws, authority, etc.>; over *or* about <an issue>; with, between, *or* among <adversaries>; in ~ with.

conform, *vb.* to <social expectations>; with <specifications>.

connive, *vb.* with <another person>; at <wrongdoing>; to <*inf.*>.

consecutive, *adj.* to *or* with <another event; an additional penal sentence>.

conservator, *n.* of, for, *or* to <a minor; an incompetent person; a failed business>.

consider, *vb.* for <a position>; as <one aspect of a person>.

consideration, *n.* of *or* for <a contract obligation; a mitigating circumstance>; by *or* from <a person>; to <an offer; a suggestion>; on further ~; take into ~; in ~ of; out of ~ for.

consignment, *n.* of <goods>; to <a seller>; for <an owner>; on ~.

consistent, *adj.* with <another consideration>.

conspiracy, *n.* to <*inf.*>; of *or* by <participants>; against <a target>.

conspire, *vb.* to <*inf.*>; with <one or more other people>; against <another person>.

constrain, *vb.* from <doing something>.

construe, *vb.* as <a characterization; an interpretation>.

contempt, *n.* of <authority [esp., a court or Congress]>; for *or* toward <a person; a thing>; by *or* from <a person>; in ~; beneath ~.

contingent, *adj.* on *or* upon <a condition>.

contingent, *n.* of <supporters; people>; from, to, *or* in <a place>.

continuance, *n.* of <a trial>.

contract, *n.* to <*inf.*>; of <nature of contract>; for <terms of contract>; with <the other party>; under ~.

contract, *vb.* with <another party>; to <perform some obligation>.

contribution, *n.* to <an enterprise; a fund>; for <a purpose>; by *or* from <a contributor>; toward <a fundraising goal>.

conveyance, *n.* of <property to a new owner>; by *or* from <the previous owner>; to <the new owner>.

convict, *vb.* of *or* for <a crime>.

conviction, *n.* of *or* for <a crime>.

copyright, *n.* of, in, on, *or* for <a work>; under ~.

corpus, *n.* of <a trust>.

counsel, *n.* of *or* from <an adviser>; for <a purpose>; to <*inf.*>; of ~.

counsel, *vb.* to <*inf.*>; about <an issue>.

course, *n.* of <dealing, conduct, etc.>; for <a destination>; through <a subject, field, etc.>; in *or* on <an academic subject>; on *or* off ~; as a matter of ~; in the ~ of; of ~.

covenant, *n.* to <*inf.*>; of <warranty, etc.>; by, with, *or* from <a promisor>; between <two people>.

credit, *n.* of *or* to <a person>; for *or* against <an amount>; by *or* from <a creditor>; on ~.

credit, *vb.* to <an account>; with *or* for <an accomplishment>.

crime, *n.* of <offense, passion, omission, etc.>; against <persons, property, humanity, etc.>.

custody, *n.* of *or* over <a dependent; property>; [take *or* award ~] from *or* to <a person>; [in the ~] of <a custodian>; [in ~] under <legal authority>; [in ~] for <a charge; a conviction>; [in ~] at <a jail, prison, etc.>; into ~; in ~.

damages, *n.* of <an amount>; for <an injury>; from <a tortfeasor>; to <a person>; in <a judgment>; sue for ~.

deal, *vb.* in <goods>; with <customers>; about *or* over <terms of a sale>; from <a deck of cards>; to <card players>.

debt, *n.* of <a person; an amount>; to <a creditor>; [impose a ~] on <a person>; in *or* out of ~; go into ~.

deceive, *vb.* into <doing something>.

decide, *vb.* to <*inf.*>; for *or* against <a party>; against <doing something>; between *or* among <alternatives>; on <a selection>; about <an issue>.

decision, *n.* of, from, *or* by <a person>; about *or* on <an issue>; in <a case>; for *or* against <a party>.

declaration, *n.* of <a status [e.g., default, intent]>; of, by, *or* from <a person>; to <*inf.*>.

deed, *n.* to *or* for <property>; in <a person's name>; of <trust, etc.>.

deed, *vb.* to <a person>.

defamation, *n.* of <character, etc.>.

default, *n.* of <an obligation>; in ~; by ~.

default, *vb.* on <a loan>.

defect, *n.* of <quality; legal status [form; parties; substance]>; in <a product>.

defect, *vb.* from <one side>; to <the other side>.

defend, *vb.* against *or* from <a charge>; by <a strategy>; [~ oneself] to <an authority>.

defendant, *n.* in <a lawsuit; a prosecution>.

defense, *n.* in <a lawsuit; a prosecution>; of <a defendant; a cause>; against *or* to <a charge>; in ~ of <a person>.

defer, *vb.* to <a person>; in <an option>.

deference, *n.* to <a person; a situation>.

defiance, *n.* of <authority>; toward <a person; an institution>.

deficiency, *n.* of <an amount>; in <an account; a policy>.

defraud, *vb.* into <doing something>; of <a thing; an amount>.

degree, *n.* of <a quality>; in <a field of study>; [awarded a ~] by <an institution>; [earn a ~] from *or* at <an institution>; to some ~.

deliberate, *vb.* over, on, *or* about <a decision>.

delinquent, *adj.* in <payment>.

delivery, *n.* of <a thing>; to <a person>; for <a purpose>; at <a place; a time>; by <the deliverer>; from <the sender>; in ~ of <a thing>; on *or* upon ~.

demand, *n.* on *or* to <a person>; by *or* from <the demander>; of *or* for <a thing; an action>; against <an estate; a corpus>; on ~; in ~.

demur, *vb.* at *or* to <an objectionable suggestion>.

denial, *n.* of <a charge; a request>; by <an accused; a provider>; to <a questioner; a customer>; in ~.

deplete, *vb.* of <all contents>.

deposition, *n.* in *or* for <a lawsuit>; of *or* from <a witness>; by <the deposer>.

derivative, *adj.* of *or* from <a thing>.

descent, *n.* from <a parent>; of <progeny>; pass by ~ to *or* from.

despoil, *vb.* of <a possession>.

destitute, *adj.* of <resources; hope>.

detract, *vb.* from <the whole; a more important aspect>.

detriment, *n.* to <a person; an enterprise>; to one's ~.

detrimental, *adj.* to <an interest [esp., a legal or financial interest]>.

devise, *n.* of <property>; to <a beneficiary>; from *or* by <a testator>; in <a will>; through <a will; an estate>; <pass> by ~.

devise, *vb.* to <a beneficiary>; between *or* among <beneficiaries>.

devolve, *vb.* upon <a successor; an appointee>; into <a worsened condition>; to <a successor>.

dictum, *n.* in *or* from <a judicial opinion>; of *or* by <a judge; a judicial opinion>; about <the content>; in ~.

differ, *vb.* from <something else>; on, about, *or* over <an opinion>; with <another person>.

digest, *n.* of <cases>.

digress, *vb.* from <the main subject>.

diligent, *adj.* in *or* about <a responsibility>.

disability, *n.* of <a person; a legal incapacity>; to <perform a life function; take a legal action>.

disabuse, *vb.* of <an idea; an opinion>.

discharge, *n.* of <an obligation or position; a lawsuit; a gun>; from <a debt; an obligation or position; an institution, esp. a hospital or military service>; by <a creditor; a judge; one in authority>; for <a reason>; in ~ of <an obligation>.

discharge, *vb.* from <an obligation; a position; an institution, esp. a hospital or military service>; for <a reason>.

disclaimer, *n.* of <a legal right or duty; a warranty>; by <a manufacturer, seller, service provider, or other party to a contract>; in <a contract; a notice>.

discovery, *n.* of <information>; by <a party>; from <a witness>; under <rules of procedure; a court order>.

discretion, *n.* to <*inf.*>; of *or* with <a decision-maker>; of, by, toward, *or* from <a confidant>.

discriminate, *vb.* against <a class of people>; by <a means>; between *or* among <two or more things>; <one thing> from <another>.

discriminating, *adj.* in, about, *or* with <taste, fashion, etc.>.

discrimination, *n.* against <a class of people>; of *or* by <one who discriminates against a class of people>.

discriminatory, *adj.* toward <a class of people>.

disfavor, *n.* of <a person>; <earn> ~ by <doing something>; in ~ with.

dismissal, *n.* [*lawsuit*] of <a lawsuit>; with *or* without <prejudice>; for <a reason [e.g., want of prosecution, cause]>; by <a judge>; from <prosecution>.

dismissal, *n.* [*employment*] of <an employee>; for <cause>; by <an employer>; from <employment>.

dispense, *vb.* with <a thing>; to <people>.

dispose, *vb.* of <a thing>; for <a person>; by <a means>.

disposed, *adj.* toward <a person>; to <*inf.*>.

disposition, *n.* of <property [esp., in an estate]; character>; toward <a person>.

dispossessed, *adj.* of <a thing>.

dissent, *n.* from <a dominant opinion; a policy>; in <a case>; by <a judge; a protester>; over, against, with, *or* toward <a policy>; in ~.

dissent, *vb.* from <a dominant opinion; a policy>.

dissociate, *vb.* from <a person; an organization>.

dissuade, *vb.* from <doing something>.

dissuaded, *adj.* by <a person; a reason>.

distinct, *adj.* from <something else>.

distinction, *n.* between <two things>; of <an accomplishment>; <serve> with ~; <person> of ~.

distinguish, *vb.* between *or* among <two or more things>; <one thing> from <another>; by <a difference>.

distinguishable, *adj.* from <something else>; by <a difference>.

distinguished, *adj.* for *or* by <an accomplishment>.

distribution, *n.* of <property [esp., by intestacy]; money [esp., net earnings to shareholders]>; to, between, *or* among <heirs; people [esp., shareholders]>; by <an estate's administrator; a funding organization; a corporation>; for <a purpose>.

diverge, *vb.* from <a central point; a main path>.

diversity, *n.* of <a thing [e.g., interests, opinions, citizenship]>.

divert, *vb.* from <one place>; to <another place>; for <a purpose>.

divest, *vb.* of <an asset>; by <a means>.

divorce, *n.* from <a former spouse>; of <a person>; over <a situation>.

docket, *n.* of <a court>; on the ~.

docket, *vb.* for <a trial or hearing date>.

documentation, *n.* of <an event; a fact>; for <a claim; an allegation>; by <a means>; from <a source>.

dominion, *n.* over <a possession>; of <a realm>.

draft, *n.* on <a bank>; for <an amount; a person>; of <a writing>; from <a maker; a writer>.

due, *adj.* to <a reason; a creditor>; for <a change>; on, by, *or* before <a time>; from <a debtor>; to <*inf.*>; come ~.

duress, *n.* of <a threat>; from <a person>; under ~.

duty, *n.* to <*inf.*>; to *or* toward <a person>; of <care>; on <an import>; on *or* off ~; in the line of ~.

easement, *n.* on, in, through, across, *or* over <property>; by <type [e.g., necessity, estoppel]>; for <a purpose [e.g., ingress–egress]>; from <a grantor; a predecessor in interest>; to <a grantee; a successor in interest>.

ejectment, *n.* of <an occupant; an owner>; from <property>; by <the person ejecting the occupant>; for <a reason>.

elicit, *vb.* from <a person>.

embargo, *n.* on <a product; a nation; a news story>; by <the one imposing the embargo>; against <another nation>; lift an ~ from <another nation>; under ~.

embezzle, *vb.* from <an employer; a client>.

embezzlement, *n.* of <an employer's money or property>; by <the embezzler; the means of embezzlement>; from <the embezzler's employer>.

emigrate, *vb.* from <an old home country>. Cf. IMMIGRATE.

employment, *n.* of <an employee>; by <an employer>; for <a position; a term>; at <will>; under <contract>; to <*inf.*>.

encroach, *vb.* on *or* upon <another's property or rights>.

encumber, *vb.* with <a burden>; by <a debt>.

encumbrance, *n.* on <a title>.

endorsement, *n.* of <a candidate; a product>; by <a person>; for <an office>. Cf. INDORSEMENT.

endow, *vb.* with <an asset; an advantage; a talent>.

endowment, *n.* of *or* for <an institution; a field>.

enjoin, *vb.* from <an action>; to <*inf.*>; on *or* upon <a person to *inf.*>.

entice, *vb.* into <doing something>; with *or* by <an inducement> ~ into <an act>.

entitled, *adj.* to <a thing>; to <*inf.*>.

entrapment, *n.* of <a person>; by <police; a means>; into <a crime>; by ~.

entrust, *vb.* to <a person>; with <a thing>.

equal, *adj.* to <a thing; a person; a task>; in <size; number; ability>; of <a person>.

equality, *n.* between *or* among <people>; in <a field>.

equate, *vb.* with *or* to <another thing>.

equity, *n.* of *or* through <a remedy>; for <an injustice>; from <a court>; toward <a person>; in <a situation>; in <property>; in ~.

escheat, *vb.* to <the state>.

escrow, *n.* for <a purpose; a person>; of <an account>; by <a depositor; a depositary>; in ~.

estate, *n.* of <a deceased>; at <will>; for <years>; in <reversion>; on <limitation>; by <curtesy>.

estopped, *adj.* from *or* to <an assertion; an action>; by <one's own contradictory assertion or action; contract>; on <legal principle>; under <a statute; a contract>.

estranged, *adj.* from <a former companion [esp., a spouse]>.

estrangement, *n.* from <a former companion [esp., a spouse]>; between <two people>; over <a situation>.

eviction, *n.* of <an occupier of property>; from <occupied property>; by <the owner>; for <a reason>.

evidence, *n.* of <an alleged fact>; for *or* against <a side in a trial>; by *or* from <a provider; a witness>; in <a trial>; plant ~ on; <piece, shred, scintilla, etc.> of ~; in ~; into ~.

examination, *n.* of <a person; a situation>; about <a situation>; by <an examiner; a lawyer>; on *or* in <an academic subject>; on *or* upon closer ~.

exception, *n.* to <a rule; a ruling>; for <a person>.

exchange, *vb.* of <things>; for <another thing>; with <another person>; by <a person>.

exclusion, *n.* of <evidence; income>; for <a reason>; by <a judge; the tax code>; from <evidence; taxation>.

exculpate, *vb.* from <an accusation>.

excuse, *n.* for <an action>; of <a reason>; by *or* from <an accused>; to <*inf.*>.

execution, *n.* of <a person; a will; a contract; a court order; a money judgment>; for <a capital crime; enforcement of a judgment>; by <a person>.

executioner, *n.* of <a condemned person>.

executor, *n.* of <a deceased person's estate>.

exemplar, *n.* of <a person's handwriting, voice, or other identifying characteristic>.

exempt, *adj.* from <an obligation>.

exhaustion, *n.* of <options>; from <an effort>; state of ~; to ~.

exhibit, *n.* of *or* in <evidence>; for <viewing>; by <a party>; on ~.

exonerate, *vb.* from <an accusation>.

expert, *n.* in *or* on <a field>; at <a skill>; with <the tools of a skill>.

explicit, *adj.* about <a meaning; an intention>.

expostulate, *vb.* about, upon, *or* on <a topic>; with <another person>.

exposure, *n.* to <the elements; the public>; of *or* about <a scandal>; by <a person>; in <the media>; die of ~.

expound, *vb.* on *or* upon <a weighty subject>; to <a person>.

expropriate, *vb.* from <a property owner>; for <a public use>.

expungement, *n.* of *or* from <a record>; by <a court>.

extortion, *n.* from <a person>; of <a thing of value; an act; a public official>; by <a person; a public official>; to <*inf.*>; by ~.

extradition, *n.* of <a suspect>; to *or* from <another state or nation>; in <a prosecution>; by <the foreign jurisdiction>.

extraneous, *adj.* to <the thing itself>.

extrapolate, *vb.* from <known data>; to <*inf.* [esp., make an assumption about an unknown thing]>.

extricate, *vb.* from <a situation>; by <a means>.

extrinsic, *adj.* to <the thing itself>.

eyewitness, *n.* to <an event>.

faithless, *adj.* to *or* toward <a person [esp., an employer]>.

familiar, *adj.* to <a person>; with <a fact; a person>.

fastidious, *adj.* about <details; a personal habit>.

feasible, *adj.* to <*inf.*>.

fee, *n.* for <a service>; of <an amount>; from <the charger>; to <do something>.

fiat, *n.* to <*inf.*>; from <a court; an executive>; by ~.

fiduciary, *n.* of <a client, trust beneficiary, shareholders, etc.>.

finder, *n.* of <fact>.

fine, *n.* for <an offense>; on <a person>; of <an amount>; by *or* from <a magistrate>.

fixture, *n.* of <property>; in <a place>.

foreclosure, *n.* of *or* on <mortgaged property>; by <a lender; a governmental entity>.

forfeiture, *n.* of <assets>.

forgery, *n.* of <a check; a signature; a work of art>; by <a forger>.

franchise, *n.* of <a business>; to <*inf.*>.

fraud, *n.* on <a person; the community; a court, agency, etc.>; in <the inducement; the factum>; by <the actor>.

freedom, *n.* of <speech, religion, etc.>; from <oppression, censorship, etc.>; to <*inf.*>; grant ~ to <a person>; secure ~ for <a people>; gain ~ from <a tyrant>.

frustration, *n.* of <purpose>; over *or* toward <a situation>; in ~.

fundamental, *n.* to <a higher-order right or principle>; [*pl.*] of <a discipline>; for <advancement>.

furlough, *n.* to <*inf.*>; on ~.

garnishment, *n.* of <wages; assets>; for <a debt; execution of a judgment>; by <a court>.

generalize, *vb.* about <a conclusion>; from <observations>.

generous, *adj.* with <money, help, advice, etc.>; in <doing something>; to *or* toward <a person>; that was ~ of <a person> to <*inf.*>.

germane, *adj.* to <an issue>.

gibe, *n.* at <a person>; about <an incident; a person>; [*pl.*] of <others>; for <a reason>.

glean, *vb.* from <an experience>.

gloat, *vb.* over <a success>.

goad, *vb.* into <doing something>; to <*inf.*>.

grant, *n.* of <a right; money>; for <a purpose>; to <a person>; by *or* from <a grantor>; to <*inf.*>.

grapple, *vb.* with <an issue>; for <an object>; onto *or* with <a larger object, for safety>.

grievance, *n.* against <a person>; about <a situation>; of <an aggrieved person>.

grieve, *vb.* for, after, *or* over <a lost loved one>; with <another person>; at <a loss>.

gross, *n.* a ~ of <things>; easement in ~.

grounds, *n.* for <taking action>; to <*inf.*>; on [what] ~; on ~ of <reason>.

grouse, *vb.* about <a situation>.

guarantee (guaranty), *n.* of *or* about <security>; against <defects>; for <performance of an obligation>; by *or* from <the guarantor>; to <the person being assured>.

guard, *vb.* against <something happening>; from <attack>; stand ~ for <a protected person>; stand ~ over <a protected thing>.

guardian, *n.* of <a dependent>; for <a purpose>.

guest, *n.* of <a host>; in *or* at <a place>; on <the premises>.

guilt, *n.* for <a crime>; by <association>.

guilty, *adj.* of <a crime>; feel ~ for *or* about <doing something>.

habit, *n.* of <doing something>; by ~; in, into, *or* out of <the ~ of>; force of ~.

haggle, *vb.* over *or* about <a thing; an issue; a price>; with <a person>.

hail, *vb.* from <a place>; as <a champion, a great thinker, etc.>.

hale, *vb.* into *or* to <a place [esp., court]>; before <a person [esp., a judge]>.

haul, *vb.* into *or* to <a place [esp., court]>; before <a person [esp., a judge]>; to, from, around, across, etc. <a place>; between <two places>; at, on, *or* upon <a rope; reins>; on, upon, *or* to <the wind [naut.]>.

hazardous, *adj.* to <health; well-being>; to <*inf.*>.

hearing, *n.* on, for, *or* about <a purpose>; by <a court; a regulatory agency>; in <a case>; ripe for ~.

heat, *n.* of <passion>.

hedge, *vb.* against <a possible loss>.

hegemony, *n.* of <one nation; one power>; over <other nations [esp., in a region]; other powers [esp., in a field]>.

heir, *n.* to <an estate>; of <a deceased person>.

hesitant, *adj.* about <doing something>; to <*inf.*>.

hesitate, *vb.* over, about, *or* in <taking action>; for <a period of time>; to <*inf.*>.

hinder, *vb.* in <doing something>; from <accomplishing something>; for <a reason>; by <a means>.

hindrance, *n.* to *or* of <a person; an enterprise>; from <an adversary; an adverse condition>; without ~.

holder, *n.* in <due course>; for <value>; of <commercial paper>.

holding, *n.* of *or* by <a court>; on <a question of law>; in <a case>.

holdover, *n.* from <a lease>.

hostile, *adj.* to *or* toward <a person; a group; a nation>; about *or* over <a situation>.

hypothesize, *vb.* about <a posited situation>.

identify, *vb.* as <a particular person>; to <a person [esp., police]>; with <another person>; by <a distinctive characteristic>.

immaterial, *adj.* to <an issue>.

immigrate, *vb.* into *or* to <this country>. Cf. EMIGRATE.

immunity, *n.* from *or* to <liability; a sanction; a disease>; of <a person; a cause of immunity>; by <authority granting immunity>; on *or* in <a lawsuit>; under <a law; a doctrine>; grant ~ to <a person>; grant of ~ for <a person; liability>.

immunization, *n.* against <disease>.

impeachment, *n.* of <an official; a witness>; on *or* for <a charge>; by <a legislature; a questioner>.

impel, *vb.* to *or* into <action>; to <*inf.* [esp., take action]>.

impelled, *adj.* by <a force; an obligation>; to *or* into <action>; to <*inf.* [esp., take action]>.

impinge, *vb.* on, upon, against, *or* at <a thing; a person; a right>.

implicated, *adj.* in <a crime; an enterprise>; with <others involved>.

implicit, *adj.* in <another idea>.

implied, *adj.* in <law>; by <a suggestion>.

import, *vb.* from <another country>; to <this country>.

impose, *vb.* on *or* upon <a person>; for <a favor>; to <*inf.*>.

improvement, *n.* of *or* to <a thing>; on *or* upon <property>; in <a condition; an area>; by <a means>; over, on, *or* upon <a previous condition>.

impulse, *n.* to <*inf.*>; on ~.

impute, *vb.* to <a person>.

inadmissible, *adj.* into, to, *or* as <evidence>; for <a purpose>.

inaugurate, *vb.* as <an official>.

incapacity, *n.* to <*inf.* [perform; take legal action]>; of <a person>.

incident, *adj.* to <an event>.

incite, *vb.* to *or* into <action, esp. violence>; by *or* with <words; action>; against <another>; to <*inf.*>.

incompetence, *n.* at <a skill>; in <a field>; of <a person>; to <*inf.*>.

incompetency, *n.* of <a person>; to <*inf.* [esp., stand trial; testify]>.

inconsistent, *adj.* with <another statement, activity, etc.>.

incorporation, *n.* of *or* by <a company>; for <a purpose>; into <another thing>; articles of ~.

inculcate, *vb.* in, on, *or* into <a person>.

incumbent, *adj.* on *or* upon <a person>; to <*inf.*>.

indecency, *n.* of <a person>; toward <another person>.

indemnify, *vb.* from *or* against <loss; liability>; for <damages>; under <a contract; a judgment>; in <a lawsuit>.

indemnity, *n.* from *or* against <loss; liability>; under <a contract; a judgment>; seek ~ from <an insurer>.

independent, *n.* of *or* from <another person; one reason>.

indicative, *adj.* of <a conclusion>.

indictment, *n.* on *or* for <a crime>; in <a prosecution>; of <an accused>; by <a grand jury>; under ~.

indigenous, *adj.* to <a place>.

indignant, *adj.* toward *or* to <a person>; about, at, *or* over <a situation>.

indistinguishable, *adj.* from <something else>.

indorsement, *n.* of <a negotiable instrument>. Cf. ENDORSEMENT.

inducement, *n.* to <a person> to <*inf.*>.

inequality, *n.* between <two groups of people; two things>.

infer, *vb.* from <a statement>.

influence, *n.* of, by, *or* from <a person>; on *or* over <another person>; for <good or evil>; about, in, on, *or* against <a decision>; to <*inf.*>; under the ~.

inform, *vb.* on *or* against <a person>; to <another person [esp., the police]>; of *or* about <information>.

infringement, *n.* of, on, *or* upon <a right>; by <a person>; under <a law; a doctrine>.

inheritance, *n.* of <property; money>; by <an heir>; from <a deceased person>; pass by ~.

inhibit, *vb.* from <doing something>.

injunction, *n.* against *or* on <a person>; to <*inf.* [do something]>; of <an action>; from <a court>; under ~.

injury, *n.* to *or* of <a person>; by *or* from <a person; a means>; in <an incident>; inflict ~ on <a person>.

innocent, *adj.* of <a charge>.

innuendo, *n.* about <a person; an allegation>.

inquest, *n.* into <a crime; a death; a situation>; by <an authority>.

inquire, *vb.* about *or* into <a matter>; after <a person>; of <the person being asked>.

inquisitive, *adj.* about <a matter>.

insinuate, *vb.* into <a situation>; to <a person>.

instill, *vb.* in *or* into <a person>.

insulate, *vb.* from *or* against <an adverse condition>.

insurance, *n.* against <loss; liability>; from <an insurer>; on <property>; for <an enterprise>.

intent, *n.* to <*inf.*>; of <a person; doing something>; with ~ to <*inf.*>.

intercede, *vb.* for <a person>; with <another person>; in <a dispute>.

interest, *n.* of <a person; a principle>; on <an investment>; for <an investment; an investor>; from <a depositary>; at <a rate>; in <an enterprise; an activity>; in <a person's> ~ [to <*inf.*>]; of ~ to <a person>.

interference, *n.* in *or* with <an activity; a relationship>; of, by, *or* from <a person>.

interpleader, *n.* petition in ~.

interrogatory, *n.* to <a party>; from <an adversary>; about <an issue>.

intervention, *n.* in *or* into <a lawsuit; a dispute>; of, by, *or* from <an intervenor>; for <a purpose>; against <an action>; to <*inf.*>.

intimidate, *vb.* into <doing something>.

intolerance, *n.* against, of, *or* toward <a group of people; a religious or political group; a behavior>; to <a medication; a food>.

intolerant, *adj.* of *or* toward <a group of people; a religious or political group>.

intrude, *vb.* into <a place>; on or upon <a right or privilege>.

inure, *vb.* to <a person's benefit>.

invasion, *n.* of <an interest [e.g., privacy]; a country>; by <a person; an invading country>; for <a purpose>; from <a place>; against <a country>; under ~.

inveigh, *vb.* against <an enemy; a doctrine>.

inveigle, *vb.* into <doing something>; out of <a possession>; into, in, out of, away from, etc. <a place>; by <guile>.

invest, *vb.* in <a security; a venture>; with <authority; a covering>.

investigation, *n.* into, of, *or* about <a situation>; of <a person; a situation>; by <an investigator>; on closer ~; under ~.

irreconcilable, *adj.* with <a contradictory thing>.

irrelevant, *adj.* to <an issue>.

issue, *n.* of *or* about <a question>; at *or* in ~; take ~ with.

jibe, *vb.* with <another person's opinion; another set of facts>.

joinder, *n.* of <another party; another claim; remedies>; in <pleading>; to <*inf.* [esp., defeat jurisdiction]>.

judgment, *n.* of *or* from <a court>; for <the winning party>; against <the losing party>; on *or* in <a case>; about <an issue>; concur in a ~; dissent from a ~; sit in ~; in <a person's> ~.

jurisdiction, *n.* over <a person; a subject matter>; of <a court; an agency>; to <*inf.* [e.g., review a judgment, adjudicate a claim, impose a penalty]>; on *or* over <a place [e.g., an Indian reservation]>; under <a statute; Article III>; under <a court's; an agency's> ~; confer ~ upon *or* on <a court; an agency>; outside *or* within <a court's> ~.

jury, *n.* of <peers, 12, 6, etc.>; in <a trial>; trial by ~.

justice, *n.* of <the peace>; for <a wrong>; by <a means>; to <a person>; bring to ~.

justification, *n.* for <an action>; with *or* without ~.

justified, *adj.* in <doing something>; by <mitigating circumstances>.

kidnapping, *n.* of <a victim>; for <a reason [esp., ransom]>; by <a perpetrator>; from <a place>.

landlord, *n.* of <a rental property>.

lapse, *n.* in *or* of <e.g., time, subscription, judgment, concentration>; time ~ between <two events>; mental ~ by <a person>.

lapse, *vb.* into <e.g., unconsciousness, a coma, a bad habit>; will ~ on <a date>.

larceny, *n.* of <a thing>; by <a perpetrator; a means>; over *or* under <an amount>.

law, *n.* of <a legal area; a jurisdiction>; in <a jurisdiction>; by ~; under the ~ of <a jurisdiction>; within the ~; against the ~; above the ~; get around the ~; attorney at ~.

lawsuit, *n.* over <a dispute>; by <one party>; against <the other party>; in <a jurisdiction>.

lawyer, *n.* for <a client>; with, at, *or* of <a firm>; in <a lawsuit>.

lease, *n.* of *or* on <property>; as *or* for <a purpose>; by <the tenant>; from <the landlord>; under ~.

leave, *n.* of <absence; the court>; by <a court>; on ~.

leave, *vb.* for *or* from <a place>; by <a means>; with *or* without <a thing; a person>; at, before, after, *or* during <a time; an event>.

legacy, *n.* of <a person; an accomplishment or notable quality>; from <a deceased person>; to *or* for <a beneficiary>.

lenient, *adj.* toward, on, *or* with <a person [esp., a criminal defendant]>; in <setting punishment>.

letter(s), *n.* of <e.g., administration, intent, credit>; from <the sender>; to <a person>; about <a subject>; in a ~; by ~.

levy, *n.* on <a taxpayer; a thing that is taxed>; of <property>; to <*inf.* [e.g., fund a project]>; for <a purpose>.

levy, *vb.* on <a taxpayer>.

liability, *n.* for <a tort>; of <a tortfeasor>; to <another person>.

liaison, *n.* between <two people or groups>; from <one group>; to <another group>; with <a paramour>.

libel, *n.* of *or* against <a person>; by <the defamer>; in <a publication>.

license, *n.* of <intellectual property>; from <the owner of an intellectual-property right>; by <the licensee>; for <a use; a royalty>; through <a clearinghouse>; to <a person>; to <*inf.*>.

lien, *n.* on *or* against <property>.

liquidated, *adj.* by <agreement; litigation>.

liquidation, *n.* of <assets>; by <the owner; a bankruptcy trustee>; in ~.

litigation, *n.* of *or* over <a dispute>; by <the parties>; against <a defendant>; to <*inf.*>; in ~.

loan, *n.* of <a thing; money>; for <a purpose>; from <a lender>; to *or* by <a borrower>; on ~.

loss, *n.* of <bargain; consortium>; by <a person>; to <a person; a situation>; at a ~; for a ~.

magistrate, *n.* of, for, *or* in <a jurisdiction>.

maintenance, *n.* of <a thing; a person; a lawsuit>; on <a thing>; for <a purpose>; by *or* from <a person>.

majority, *n.* of <people; things>; for *or* against <a proposal; an opinion>; in <a group; an assembly>; in the ~; age of ~.

maker, *n.* of <a promissory note>.

malice, *n.* toward <a person; a group of people>; act with *or* without ~.

mandamus, *n.* to <*inf.* [e.g., vacate, rescind, review]>; of, from, *or* by <a court>; writ of ~.

master, *n.* of <a servant; an art>; at <an art>; over *or* in <a domain>.

material, *n.* to <an issue>.

mediation, *n.* of, over, *or* about <a dispute>; by *or* through <a neutral third party>; between <parties>; to <*inf.* [e.g., reach a settlement]>; in ~.

memorandum, *n.* of <law; content; a person; a date>; from, by, *or* to <a person>; about *or* on <content>.

merger, *n.* of, by, *or* between <companies>; with <another company>.

merits, *n.* of <a case>; on the ~.

militate, *vb.* against *or* in favor of <severity of punishment>.

misrepresentation, *n.* of *or* about <a fact>; by *or* to <a person>; in <a dealing>; by *or* through ~.

mistake, *n.* of <fact; law>; by <a person>; about <a fact>; in <doing something>; it was a ~ to <*inf.*>; by ~.

mistaken, *adj.* about *or* in <a fact; a belief>; for <another person>; by <a person>.

mitigation, *n.* of <damages; culpability>; by <an action; a person>.

monopoly, *n.* of, on, over, *or* in <a market; an industry>; by <a company; a means>.

mortgage, *n.* on <a property>; for <a property; an amount>; to, from, *or* with <a lending institution>.

motion, *n.* for <a court order [e.g., to quash an indictment, for a new trial]>; in <limine>; to <*inf.* [e.g., strike, suppress, transfer venue]>.

motive, *n.* for *or* behind <an action>; of <an actor>; to <*inf.*>; in <taking action>.

mulct, *vb.* of <money; a possession>.

muniment, *n.* of <title>.

murder, *n.* of <a person>; for *or* over <a motive>; by <a perpetrator; a means>; with <a weapon>; in *or* on <a place>.

necessity, *n.* of <life; an activity>; for <an activity>; of ~.

neglectful, *adj.* of *or* toward <a person; a condition>; in <performing a duty>.

negligence, *n.* of *or* by <a person>; for <an injury>; in *or* about <conduct>; with <an instrumentality>; toward <another person>.

negotiable, *adj.* for <money>; by <a bearer; a payee>.

nonsuit, *n.* of <a claim; a defendant>; by <a plaintiff; a judge>; for <a reason>.

notice, *n.* of <a legal action; a condition>; to <an adverse party>; by *or* from <a person; a court>; on ~.

novation, *n.* of <a contract>; by <a new party>; in <a new agreement>.

nuisance, *n.* of, in, *or* over <a situation>; for *or* to <a person>; by <a person creating the nuisance>.

oath, *n.* of <office; allegiance>; by <a person taking an oath>; from <a person administering an oath>; administer an ~ to <a person>; to <*inf.*>; under ~; by ~; on ~.

objection, *n.* to <an act; a question; admission of evidence>; of, by, *or* from <the objector>; against, about, *or* over <a subject>; without ~; despite ~; over ~.

objective, *adj.* about *or* in <a perception; an opinion>.

objective, *n.* in *or* of <taking an action>.

obligation, *n.* to <a person>; to <*inf.*>; under [no] ~.

obstruction, *n.* of <justice; an investigation; an enterprise>; to <a flow; a process>.

obtrude, *vb.* upon *or* on <a person>; ~ <oneself> into <an affair>.

offense, *n.* of <a crime>; by <a perpetrator>; against <a victim>; take ~ at <an act; a comment>.

> "If the word following the verb really is a preposition, then the two do not form a phrasal verb. 'Please stand in the corner' and 'Get up to five pounds free' are not phrasal verbs, but 'Please stand in for me while I'm gone' and 'What are you getting up to?' consequently are."
>
> —*W.F. Bolton*

offer, *n.* to <*inf.*>; of <a deal; assistance>; for *or* on <a thing; a service>; from, by, *or* to <a person>.

officer, *n.* of <the court; the law; an organization>.

omission, *n.* of <an act; a fact>; by <a person>; from <a record>; <crime; act; sin> of ~.

operation, *n.* of <law; an enterprise>; by <a person>.

opinion, *n.* from, of, *or* by <a judge>; in <a case>; about *or* of <a situation>.

option, *n.* of <choices>; on <a thing for sale>; to <*inf.*>; on ~.

order, *n.* of <a court>; for <a thing>; by *or* from <a person>; to <*inf.*>; on ~; in ~ to <*inf.*>.

ordinance, *n.* of <a municipality>.

panel, *n.* of <people [e.g., jurors, judges, experts]>; on <a subject>.

pardon, *n.* of <an accused or convicted person>; by *or* from <a chief executive>; for <a crime>; grant a ~ to <a person>.

parity, *n.* with, between, *or* among <another person; another nation>; of *or* in <things; status>; [of currency and stocks] at, above, *or* below ~; on ~ with.

parole, *n.* of <a prisoner>; by *or* from <a parole board>; grant ~ to <a person>; on ~.

partner, *n.* of <another partner; a firm>; in <an enterprise>; at <a law firm>.

partnership, *n.* of, by, between, *or* among <all the partners>; with <another partner>; for <a purpose>; in <an enterprise>; by <estoppel>; under <a statute>; to <*inf.*>; in ~ with <other partners>.

party, *n.* in <a lawsuit>; to <a lawsuit; an enterprise; a conversation>.

patent, *n.* on *or* for <an invention>; from <the patent office>.

patented, *adj.* by <an inventor>.

payment, *n.* of <a debt; a cost>; to <a creditor; a seller>; by *or* from <a debtor; a buyer>; on *or* against <an account>; for <a thing>; into <a savings plan>; in ~ of *or* for.

penalty, *n.* of <a punishment>; for <an offense>; from <a court; an adjudicator>; on *or* to <an offender>; under <a statute or regulation>.

performance, *n.* [*art*] of <a work of performing art>; by <an artist>; with <another artist>; for *or* before <an audience>; in <a venue>; as <a role>.

performance, *n.* [*contract*] of <an obligation>; by *or* from <a promisor>; for <a promisee>; in ~ of <an obligation>.

perjury, *n.* of *or* by <a witness>; in *or* during <testimony>; on <the witness stand>.

perpetuity, *n.* in ~.

petition, *n.* for <legal action [e.g., bankruptcy, removal, review]>; of, by, *or* from <a petitioner>; to <a court>; to <*inf.* [e.g., change name]>; in <bankruptcy; admiralty>.

plaintiff, *n.* in *or* of <a lawsuit>.

plea, *n.* of <guilty; not guilty; nolo contendere; a defendant; type of plea [e.g., privilege, release]>; to <a charge; type of plea [e.g., the jurisdiction, the writ]>; in <a prosecution; type of plea [e.g., abatement, equity]>; for <court action [e.g., leniency]>.

plead, *vb.* to <a charge; an adversary's pleading>; for <a remedy>; in <response to a pleading>; with <a person>.

pleading, *n.* of <a party; a defendant>; for <a remedy>; by *or* from <a defendant>; in <a lawsuit; a prosecution>; to <a court>.

pledge, *n.* of <security; a promise>; for <a debt>; to <a creditor>; from *or* by <a surety>; against <default>; to <*inf.* [esp., perform]>.

plurality, *n.* of <people; things>; for *or* against <a proposal; an opinion>; in <a group; an assembly>; in the ~.

point, *n.* of <law; fact; procedure [e.g., error]>; about <an issue>; to <*inf.*>; on ~; ~ by ~.

possession, *n.* of <property>; by <a person>; take ~ from <a previous possessor>; charged with ~; in ~ of.

power, *n.* of <an authority [e.g., attorney, the press]>; for <a purpose [e.g., good or evil]>; from <a source>; over <an underling>; under <legal authority>; to <*inf.*>; in ~; by the ~ vested in me.

prayer, *n.* for <relief>; to <a court; a deity>.

precedence, *n.* over <something else>; of <a criterion for ordering>.

precedent, *adj.* to <an event>.

precedent, *n.* of <a case>; for <a decision>; from <a case; a jurisdiction>.

preclude, *vb.* from <doing something>; by <a means>.

precursor, *n.* of *or* to <something else>.

predicated, *adj.* on *or* upon <a ground>.

predispose, *vb.* to <a type of action; a quality>; to <*inf.*>.

predominance, *n.* of *or* by <a person; an idea>; over <someone else; something else>; in <a field>.

preeminence, *n.* of <a person>; over *or* in <a field>.

preemption, *n.* of *or* from <a legal action>; by <a legal doctrine>; under <legal authority>.

preference, *n.* for <one choice>; to <a person>; in ~ to <another choice or person>.

preferred, *adj.* over <an alternative>; by <a person>; in <a situation>.

prejudice, *n.* against, toward, *or* to <a class of people>; with *or* without ~.

prejudicial, *adj.* to <one side of a dispute>.

preliminary, *adj.* to <an event>.

premeditation, *n.* with ~.

premises, *n.* of <an occupant>; for <a use>; on *or* off the ~.

premium, *n.* on <a charge>; at a ~.

preoccupation, *n.* with <a thing; a quality; a person>.

preparatory, *adj.* to <an event>.

preponderance, *n.* of <evidence>.

prerequisite, *n.* to *or* for <a more advanced thing>.

prescription, *n.* for <a medicine; an outcome>; of <a person>; by ~.

presumption, *n.* of <a fact [e.g., innocence, undue influence]>.

pretext, *n.* for <another action>; to <*inf.*>; on, under, *or* at any ~.

prevail, *vb.* over *or* against <a person>; in <a contest>; on *or* upon <a person [to do something]>.

principal, *n.* of <an institution [e.g., a school]; an agent; an investment>.

principle, *n.* of <a belief system; a science>; with *or* in <a person>; against <an unethical act>; on ~; in ~.

priority, *n.* over <another person; another thing>; in <a field>; as <a status>.

privilege, *n.* of <a legal advantage [e.g., immunity]; good fortune [e.g., meeting an esteemed person]>; to <*inf.*>.

privity, *n.* of <a legal relationship [e.g., contract]>; with <another person>; between <two people>; in ~.

probate, *n.* of <a will; an estate>; in <a court>; to *or* into ~; at ~.

probation, *n.* of <a jail or prison term>; in <a sentence>; for <a conviction; a convicted person>; by *or* from <a judge>; on ~.

probative, *n.* of <the truth or falsity of an assertion>.

procedure, *n.* for <doing something [esp., conducting a lawsuit]>.

proceed, *vb.* against <a person [esp., in a lawsuit]>; to *or* from <a place>; with <an activity>; by <a means>.

proceeding, *n.* of *or* in <a tribunal; an assembly>; against <an accused>; for <a purpose>; to <*inf.*>.

proceeds, *n.* from <an event; insurance; a sale>.

proclivity, *n.* for, to, *or* toward <a quality; an activity>; to <*inf.*>.

procure, *vb.* for <a person>; by <a means>; at *or* in <a place>; from <another person>.

proffer, *n.* of <a thing [esp., evidence]>; to <a court; a person>; by, of, *or* from <the offeror>; against <the other party>.

proficient, *adj.* at *or* in <an activity>; in <a foreign language, mathematics, medicine>.

progress, *n.* in <an undertaking>; against <an adversary>; toward <a goal>; by <a means>; in ~.

prohibit, *vb.* from <doing something>; by <a means>; under <an authority>.

prohibition, *n.* on *or* against <doing something>; of *or* against <a thing>.

promise, *n.* to <*inf.*>; of <a performance; the promisor>; by *or* from <the promisor>; to <the promisee>.

proof, *n.* of *or* about <a fact>; by <a means; a person>; from <a person>; in <a trial; a proceeding>; burden of ~.

propensity, *n.* for, to, toward, *or* of <an activity; a quality>; to <*inf.*>.

propinquity, *n.* to <a place>; of <blood [closeness of relationship]>.

prosecution, *n.* of <a criminal case; a patent application; an enterprise>; for <a charge>; by <a prosecutor>; against <a defendant>; in <a case>; under <a penal statute>.

protection, *n.* of <a person; a thing>; against *or* from <a threat>; by <a means>; under ~.

protective, *adj.* of *or* toward <a person>.

provoke, *vb.* into <an emotion [esp. anger]; doing something>; to <*inf.*>.

proximate, *adj.* to <a nearby thing>.

proxy, *n.* for <another person>; to <*inf.* [do something on someone else's behalf]>; by ~.

punish, *vb.* for <an offense>; as <an offender>; by <a means>.

punishable, *adj.* by <a means>.

punishment, *n.* of *or* to <an offender>; for <an offense>; by *or* of <a means>; from <a court; an authority>.

purport, *vb.* to <*inf.* [esp., be something]>.

qualified, *adj.* for <a task; a position>; as <a position>; by <a condition>; to <*inf.* [do something]>.

rancor, *n.* of <a person>; toward *or* against <another person>; over <a situation>; with *or* without ~.

ratification, *n.* of <a compact [esp., a contract, a charter, a constitutional amendment, or the like]>; by *or* from <the parties to the compact>.

reasonable, *adj.* for <a person in some position>; about <a situation>; to <*inf.* [esp., act in a certain way]>; under *or* in <the circumstances>.

rebuttal, *n.* of *or* to <an assertion; a presumption>; by, of, *or* from <an adversary>; in <an exchange>; on ~; in ~.

receipt, *n.* of <a thing>; for <a payment>; by <the receiver>; from <the payee>; in ~ of <a thing>; on *or* upon ~.

receiver, *n.* of *or* for <a thing [esp., the subject matter of litigation]>; under <legal authority>.

reciprocate, *vb.* for <an act>; with *or* by <another act>.

reciprocity, *n.* between <two people; two organizations; two governments>; for <an act>; from <another person, organization, or state>.

recital, *n.* of <facts [esp., preliminary expository clauses in a contract or deed]>; in <a contract or deed>.

recklessness, *n.* of *or* by <a person>; in *or* about <an act>; toward <another person>.

reconcile, *vb.* with <another person>; to <a situation>.

record, *n.* of <a proceeding>; for <an appeal>; from <a prior proceeding>; on *or* off the ~; for the ~; of ~.

recourse, *n.* to <a court; a remedy; an alternative>; for <a person; a dispute>; against <an injustice; a person>; in <a situation>; under <a statute; a doctrine>; without ~.

recusal, *n.* of *or* by <an adjudicator>; from <a proceeding>.

redemption, *n.* of <commercial paper [e.g., stock, bond, coupon]; an oppressed people>; by <a company; a liberator>; from <oppression>; in <forgiveness; restitution>.

reformation, *n.* of <a contract>; by <a court>; to <*inf.* [e.g., carry out the parties' intent]>.

regard, *vb.* as <stature>; with <emotion [esp., contempt>.

rehabilitation, *n.* of <a criminal; a drug or alcohol abuser; a witness; a bankrupt's financial affairs>; by *or* through <a means>.

release, *n.* from <an obligation; custody>; of <a person; a thing>; by *or* from <a person granting release>; into <custody of another person>; under <legal authority>; upon <habeas corpus>; deed of ~.

release, *vb.* from <an obligation; custody>; into <custody; an environment>.

relegate, *vb.* to <a lesser position; another decision-maker>.

relevant, *n.* to <an issue>.

reliance, *n.* on <another person's promise>; of *or* by <a person>; in ~ on.

relief, *n.* for <an inequity; a party>; of <type of equitable remedy>; by *or* from <a court>; under <legal authority>; from <a bad situation>; to <a person>.

remainder, *n.* of <an estate; an amount>; to *or* in <a remainderman>.

remand, *vb.* to <a lower court>; from *or* by <an appellate court>; for <further proceedings>; with <instructions>; of *or* in <an appeal>; on ~.

remedy, *n.* for <an injury; infringement of a legal right>; of <type of remedy>.

removal, *n.* of <a thing; a state-court lawsuit>; to <a place; a federal court>; from <a place; a state court>.

renege, *vb.* on <a promise>.

renowned, *adj.* as <a master in some field>; for <an accomplishment>; by <the public>.

renunciation, *n.* of <a right; a criminal undertaking>; by *or* from <a person>; for <a purpose>.

repatriate, *vb.* from <a country of exile or immigration>; to <a former home country>.

replete, *adj.* with <things; a quality>.

reply, *n.* to <an accusation; a communication; a person>; by *or* with <an answer>; from <a person>; through <an intermediary>; in ~ to; by way of ~.

representation, *n.* of <a client; a thing; a condition>; as <attorney>; in *or* for <a legal problem>; before <a tribunal; an agency>; to *or* by <a person>.

reprove, *vb.* for <a fault>.

repudiation, *n.* of <a contract; a debt; a statement; a relationship>; by *or* from <a person>; over <a situation>.

reputation, *n.* as <one of a particular character>; for <deeds; character>; by ~; stake one's ~ on.

rescission, *n.* of <a contract>; by <a party>; for <a good reason>.

respite, *n.* from <a bad situation>; without ~.

restitution, *n.* for <damage; injury>; of <an amount>; from *or* by <a person>; to <an injured person>; in <a sentence>.

restraint, *n.* of <a thing [e.g., trade]>; on <a right [e.g., alienation]>; by *or* from <a person>; toward <another person>; in <conduct>.

reversion, *n.* to <a grantor; a prior state>; of <an estate; a thing>; from <an intermediate estateholder>.

revocation, *n.* of <an act; a power; a trust>; by <the revoker>.

right, *n.* of <legal benefit [e.g., privacy, survivorship, way]>; under <a source of legal right>; of ~; by all ~.

robbery, *n.* of <a person>; by <a perpetrator>.

royalty, *n.* for <a license>; to <the owner of an intellectual-property right>; from <a licensee>.

rule, *n.* of <type of rule [e.g., law, reason, capture]; a sovereign>; in <source of rule [e.g., Shelley's Case]; a territory>; against <a practice [e.g., perpetuities, accumulations]>; for <doing something [e.g., distributing an intestate estate]>; by <a sovereign>; over <a dominion>.

rulemaking, *n.* by *or* of <a regulatory agency>; in <an area of jurisdiction>.

ruling, *n.* of, by, *or* from <a court; a regulatory agency>; for <a winning party>; against <a losing party>; in <a case>; on *or* about <an issue>.

sale, *n.* of <a good; a service>; for <a price>; by <the seller>; to <the buyer>; through <an intermediary>; on <a discounted item>; on ~; for ~.

sanction, *n.* [*endorsement*] of, from, *or* by <an authorizing agency>; for <an approved act or event>; to *or* on <an approved action or event; a person responsible for an approved act or event>.

sanction, *n.* [*penalty*] [*usu. pl.*] against, on, *or* upon <a hostile nation; a person, esp. a member of a profession or an institution>; by, of, *or* from <a court or disciplinary agency>; for <a condemned act>; under <a law; a rule>; under ~.

satisfaction, *n.* of <a debt; a promise; a promisee>; for <a debt; a promise>; by *or* from <an alternative performance; a promisor>; at *or* in <a performance>; with, in, over, *or* about <a situation>; give ~ to <a creditor; a promisee>; to one's ~; in ~ of <a promise>.

schism, *n.* between <two people; two factions>; over <an issue>.

scintilla, *n.* of <evidence>.

scope, *n.* of <employment; authority>.

scrutiny, *n.* of <an argument>; by <a court>; under ~.

search, *n.* of <a place; a person>; by <a person [esp., a police officer]>; for <a thing [esp., evidence, contraband]; a wanted person; a lost person or thing>; in, inside, at, *or* through <a place; a container>; with *or* without <a warrant>; in ~ of.

secured, *adj.* by *or* with <a surety; collateral; physical protection>; for <a person>; from *or* against <loss; damage>.

segregate, *vb.* from <one group from another>; into <separate groups>; for <a purpose>.

seised, *adj.* of <property>.

seisin, *n.* in <deed; fact; law>; covenant of ~; livery of ~.

seizure, *n.* of <a thing; a person>; by <a person [esp., a police officer]>; for <evidence; arrest>; at, from, *or* in <a place; a container>; with *or* without <a warrant>.

sentence, *n.* of <a punishment>; by *or* from <a judge; a jury>; for <an offense>; to <a convicted person>; in <a prosecution>; under <a statute>.

sequestration, *n.* of <a jury; property or funds in legal dispute; property owed to an enemy nation>; by <a court; a government>; for <security pending the outcome of a dispute>; from <outside influence>; in *or* inside <a place>.

setoff, *n.* for, of, *or* against <a counterclaim; a credit>; by <a party; the amount owed by the other party>; under <a statute; a doctrine>; right to a ~.

settlement, *n.* of, on, *or* in <a dispute; a lawsuit; an estate>; by, between, *or* among <the parties>; for <a sum of money; a performance; an acceptable distribution>; with *or* from <the adverse party>.

settlor, *n.* of <a trust>.

share, *n.* of *or* in <the whole>.

share, *vb.* in <the whole>; with, among, *or* between <others>.

shelter, *vb.* from *or* against <a threat>; by *or* with <a means>.

shield, *vb.* against *or* from <a danger>; by *or* with <a means>.

situs, *n.* of <property; an event>; law *or* court of the ~.

skeptical, *adj.* of *or* about <something>.

slander, *n.* of <title>; by <a defamer>; about, toward, *or* against <a person>.

smuggle, *vb.* into *or* out of <a place>; past, through, *or* by <customs>; across <a border>.

solicitation, *n.* of <a thing; a potential customer or client; someone to commit a crime; prostitution>; from *or* by <a person>; to <*inf.* [esp., donate something or do something]>.

speculate, *vb.* about *or* on <a possibility>; in *or* on <an investment>.

speculation, *n.* in <goods; a commodity; land; an investment>; over *or* about <an outcome; a mystery>; by, of, *or* from <a person>; on ~.

spoliation, *n.* of <evidence; goods in transit>.

standard, *n.* of <care; proof; living>; for <a decision>; in, for, *or* throughout <an industry>.

standing, *n.* to <*inf.* [esp., bring suit]>; in <a community>; with <another person>.

state, *n.* of <condition [e.g., mind, shock, disrepair]>.

statement, *n.* of <facts; financial affairs>; to *or* for <an intended audience>; by *or* from <the speaker>; on *or* about <a subject>; against <a person; an issue; interests>; through <a spokesperson>.

statute, *n.* of <type of statute [e.g., frauds, limitations, wills]>; by ~; under ~.

stay, *n.* of *or* in <type of stay [e.g., execution, trial]>; by *or* from <a court; an executive>.

stipulation, *n.* by *or* from <a party>; of *or* on <a fact>; by ~.

stock, *n.* in *or* of <a corporation>; take ~ in *or* of.

subjective, *adj.* about <a perception; an opinion>.

sublease, *n.* of <a rental property>; from *or* by <a tenant>; to <a third party>; for <a term; a purpose>; under ~.

subpoena, *n.* of <a person; a document>; for <a trial; a hearing; discovery>; by *or* from <a party; a court>; to <*inf.* [esp., appear in court]>; under ~; serve a ~ on <a person>.

subpoena, *vb.* as <a witness>; to <*inf.* [esp., appear in court]>; for <a trial; a hearing; discovery>.

subservient, *adj.* to <another person; a thing>.

subsidy, *n.* for <a purpose; a project>; to <a person; an organization>; of <an amount>; from *or* through <a funding organization; the government>.

succession, *n.* of <people; events>; to <a position; a legal right>; from <a seller; an assignor; a testator>; by ~; in ~.

summons, *n.* to <a person>; to <*inf.* [esp., testify]>; from *or* by <a court>; in <a trial; a hearing>; with <notice>; under ~; serve a ~ on <a person>.

suppression, *n.* of <evidence>.

surcharge, *n.* on <an item>; of <an amount>; for <a purpose>.

surety, *n.* for <the obligation [esp., debt] of another person>.

taint, *n.* of <a negative quality; an illegal activity>.

taint, *vb.* with *or* by <a negative quality; an illegal activity>.

tainted, *adj.* with *or* by <a negative quality; an illegal activity>.

taking, *n.* of <property; game>; for the ~.

tangential, *adj.* to <a main topic>.

tantamount, *adj.* to <a crime; another type of thing>.

tariff, *n.* on <an import; an export>; of <a rate>.

tax, *n.* on *or* against <a person; a thing; a transaction>; for <a purpose>; from <a taxpayer>; to <a government>; of <a rate>.

teem, *vb.* with <things>.

tenancy, *n.* for <a term>; by <the entireties>; in <common>; from <period to period>; at <sufferance; will>.

tendency, *adj.* to <*inf.* [do something]>; toward <a quality; a type of action>.

tender, *n.* of <money; performance of an obligation>; by <a debtor; a promisor>; for <an offer; a bid>; in <cash; check; other means of payment>.

testament, *n.* of <a person [by a will]>; to <a meaning>.

testation, *n.* of <property [by disposition according to a will]>.

testify, *vb.* about *or* on <a subject>; for *or* against <a party>; to <an assertion>; under <oath>; in <a trial>; before <a judge; a jury>.

testimonial, *n.* to <success against obstacles>; of *or* by <an endorser>.

testimony, *n.* of, by, *or* from <a witness>; for *or* against <a party>; on *or* about <a subject matter>; in, during, *or* before <a trial; discovery>.

theft, *n.* of <a thing>; by <a thief>; from <a victim>; over *or* under <an amount>.

threaten, *vb.* to <*inf.*>; with <harm>; by <a means>.

thwart, *vb.* in <an attempt>; by <a means>.

title, *n.* to <property>; of <a writing; record>; <abstract; chain; muniment> of ~.

tort, *n.* of <type of tort [e.g., battery, negligence]>; an action in ~.

trademark, *n.* of *or* on <a product>.

tradename, *n.* of <a company>.

traffic, *vb.* in <contraband [esp., drugs]>.

trample, *vb.* on <rights>.

transcript, *n.* of <a trial>.

transfer, *n.* of <venue; funds>; from *or* to <a place; an account>.

transform, *vb.* from <one form>; into *or* to <another form>.

transgress, *vb.* against <a person; a limit>.

transmute, *vb.* into <another form>.

treatise, *n.* on, about, *or* in <a subject>; of, by, *or* from <an author>.

trespass, *n.* to <chattels; real property>.

trespass, *vb.* on *or* onto <property of another>; against <another person>.

trial, *n.* of <an accused; a lawsuit>; for <a charge>; in <a lawsuit>; on <the merits>; to <the bench>; by <jury; one's peers>; before <a judge>; over <an issue; a dispute>; on ~; at ~; ready for ~; go to ~; bring to ~.

trust, *n.* [*a legal entity*] for <a beneficiary>; of *or* by <a settlor>; hold in ~.

trust, *n.* [*confidence*] of *or* by <a person>; in *or* toward <another person>; about <a matter>; to <*inf.*>.

trust, *vb.* in <a belief>; with <a thing; information>; to <a person>; ~ someone to <*inf.*>.

trustee, *n.* of <a trust; a school; a beneficiary>; for <a settlor>; over <the corpus of a trust>.

unanimous, *adj.* in <agreement; opposition>.

unbecoming, *adj.* in, to, *or* of <a person in some position>.

unbiased, *adj.* toward <a person; a class of people>; about <a subject>.

unburden, *vb.* ~ <someone> of <a liability; a secret>.

unconcerned, *adj.* over, about, *or* at <an event>; with <doing something>.

uncooperative, *adj.* toward *or* with <a person>; in <a process>; about <doing something>.

unequal, *adj.* to <something else>; in <amount; number; a quality>.

unequaled, *adj.* at <a skill>; in <a field>; by <any other>.

unfair, *adj.* to, with, *or* toward <a person>; about <a subject>; in <dealings>.

unfaithful, *adj.* to <a person; a cause>; in <a responsibility>; by <a means>.

unfit, *adj.* to <*inf.* [fill a role]>; as <a person in some capacity>; for <a position>.

union, *n.* of <people [esp., workers], factions, or nations; things>; for <a purpose>; by <a uniting principle or entity>; against <an enemy>; with <another person, faction, or nation>.

unique, *adj.* in <a field; itself>; to <a place; a class>; among <the nations; the cities>.

unity, *n.* of <requirements for a joint tenancy [e.g., interest, possession, time, title]>; in <diversity; variety>; with <the world>.

unjustified, *adj.* in <doing something>; under *or* in <the circumstances>; to <*inf.*>; by <the facts; the evidence>.

unleash, *vb.* on *or* against <an adversary>.

unprepared, *adj.* for <an occurrence>; to <*inf.*>; caught ~ by <the enemy; war>.

unqualified, *adj.* for <a position>; to <*inf.*>.

unreasonable, *adj.* of <a person>; to <*inf.*>; in <doing something>; for <someone to do something>.

usage, *n.* of <trade; custom>; in <a field; a population>; English ~.

use, *n.* of <a thing>; by <a person>; for <a purpose>; against <an adversary>; with <another thing>; as <a means>; in <an undertaking>; in ~; of ~ to.

vacillate, *vb.* between <positions>; in *or* on <a decision; policy>; from <one thing>; to <another thing>; with <changing influences>.

variance, *n.* with <a pleading; a charging instrument>; from <a zoning restriction>; at ~ with; of <a centimeter [or other measure]>; to <*inf.* [esp., allow, permit, construct, establish]>.

vengeance, *n.* on *or* upon *or* against <an enemy>; for <an injustice>; of <heaven; the people>; in <the name of somebody>; with a ~.

verdict, *n.* of <outcome [e.g., guilty, not guilty]>; for *or* against <an accused; a party>; by *or* of <a jury; a judge>; in <a case>.

verification, *n.* of <a fact>; from *or* by <a confirmer>; in <the laboratory; history>.

vest, *vb.* in <a person>; with <authority>; by <statute; Congress>.

veto, *n.* of <a bill>; by <a chief executive>; for *or* over *or* on <an issue>; in <a given case>.

void, *adj.* of <legal effect>; for <a legal infirmity>; by <reason of a legal doctrine; court order>.

voidable, *n.* by <one party>; for <a legal doctrine>; at <someone's discretion>; for <fraud; duress>; in <equity; bankruptcy>; on <specific grounds>.

> "The endeavor to keep bad English out of the Law Reports . . . is a harder task than one would think at first sight, for it has to be performed against a persistent enemy."
>
> —*Sir Frederick Pollock*

vouch, *vb.* for <a person; a fact>.

waiver, *n.* of <a legal right>; by *or* from <a person>; to <*inf.* [esp., permit an activity; extend a deadline]>; on <a particular basis>.

ward, *n.* [*a minor*] of <a guardian; the state>.

ward, *n.* [*a place*] of *or* in <a municipality>; with <patients>; for <certain types of patients>.

warrant, *n.* for <a search; an arrest>; to <*inf.* [esp., search a place; seize a thing or a person]>; in <an investigation>; of <arrest>; with *or* without ~; swear out a ~ against <a person>; serve a ~ on <a person>.

warranty, *n.* of <a covenant [e.g., title; habitability]>; of, by, *or* from <a seller>; to <a buyer>; for *or* on <a product>; against <a defect>; under ~; in ~.

weigh, *vb.* against <an argument; a person; a standard>; on <one's mind>; in <for a flight or a fight>; in *or* out <for a contest>; out <a measure for use or sale>.

weight, *n.* of <the evidence>; on <the other side; one foot>; carry ~ with <the public; the jury>.

wheedle, *vb.* into <doing something>; <information> from *or* out of <a person>; into, out of, away from, etc. <a place>.

withdraw, *vb.* from <a position; a community; an account>; to <another position; seclusion>; in <the night; silence; haste; confusion>.

witness, *n.* to *or* of <an incident; a scene>; for *or* against <a party>; in <a lawsuit>; on <the stand; someone's behalf>; bear ~ to.

wrangle, *vb.* with <a person; a question>; over *or* about <a dispute>; among *or* between <people>; for <power; precedence>.

wrest, *vb.* from <a person>.

writ, *n.* of <type of writ [e.g., certiorari, error, habeas corpus, mandamus]>; for <doing something [e.g., electing, summoning]>.

yield, *vb.* to <a person; an order>; in <a case or matter>; up <the ghost; the soul; a position of superiority>.

zone, *n.* of <a given type [e.g., privacy; danger]>; in <a geographical area>.

zoning, *n.* of <property>; for *or* against <a land use>; by <a municipality>; in <a place>.

13.5 Avoid needlessly offending readers with your word choices.

(a) *Characteristics.* Avoid references to a personal characteristic such as sex, race, ethnicity, disability, age, religion, sexual orientation, or social standing if such a characteristic is irrelevant to the matter at hand. When a characteristic is relevant to the facts, law, issues, or analysis, refer to it as neutrally as the circumstances allow.

(b) *Professional conduct.* Rules governing professional conduct often include admonitions against bias and prejudice. For example, Rule 8.4(d) of the ABA Model Rules of Professional Conduct states: "It is professional misconduct for a lawyer to . . . engage in conduct that is prejudicial to the administration of justice." Comment 3 of this rule states: "A lawyer who, in the course of representing a client, knowingly manifests by words or conduct, bias or prejudice based upon race, sex, religion, national origin, disability, age, sexual orientation or socioeconomic status, violates paragraph (d) when such actions are prejudicial to the administration of justice." State rules contain similar provisions.

(c) *Ineffective advocacy—and worse.* Comments that betray a writer's conscious or unconscious biases or ignorance may cause readers to lose respect for the writer, diminish the writing's persuasiveness, and evoke a response opposite to that intended. Avoid direct quotations that use offensive or outdated terms; paraphrase them in plain English. If the quoted writer's prose is too distinctive to paraphrase, consider editing slightly by inserting a neutral term or descriptive phrase in brackets in place of the antiquated language. Also, an insult or sarcastic remark, no matter how wittily or subtly expressed, will detract from your point. How bad can it get? Courts may use a judicial sanction such as a fine or even the striking of a pleading. Harsher disciplinary actions are also possible. For example, in *In re Vincenti*, 704 A.2d 927, 929–34, 938–44 (N.J. 1998), an attorney was disbarred to end a long history of abusive, intimidating, and contemptuous behavior. And in *Hoeffer v. Florida*, 696 So. 2d 1265, 1265–66 (Fla. Dist. Ct. App. 1997), an attorney was held in contempt of court for using profane language and threats against the opposing counsel.

(d) *Unwarranted distinctions.* Referring to a personal characteristic, such as sex, race, or disability, suggests that the distinction is relevant to what's being discussed. Such a reference may imply that the person's situation is unusual or unexpected. It may sound limiting or patronizing. For example, the statement *Ruth Bader Ginsburg is perhaps the greatest female judge of all time* implies that she is a great judge "for a female," but maybe not so good if compared to male judges. If you did not mean to limit the scope of the comparison, *female* should be deleted or the whole sentence recast. Another example: writing *Barbara Jordan was an outstanding black representative* suggests that she stands out only among black representatives as a group, and also that it is unusual for a black person to hold high office. But when writing *Barbara Jordan was the first black woman to represent a southern state since Reconstruction*, the function of the racial reference is clearer. Also, a reference may imply that the characteristic has some bearing on a legal issue or credibility. For example, needlessly mentioning a criminal defendant's race may suggest that race is somehow related to and predictive of behavior. And a pointless mention of a witness's physical disability (e.g.,

> "We'll not soon excise the *-man-* syllable from words like *penmanship*."
> —*Kenneth G. Wilson*

blindness) may invoke a reader's biases (e.g., a presumption of diminished mental capacity).

(e) *Person, not characteristic.* When mentioning a person's race, nationality, physical characteristic, appearance, or other trait is warranted and relevant, do so using an adjective rather than a noun. That is, instead of referring to someone as *a black*, *a gay*, or *a deaf-mute*, emphasize the person over the characteristic by referring to *a black woman*, *a gay man*, *a deaf and mute person*.

(f) *Labels.* People are sensitive about how they're described, so try to use the term that is currently preferred by the affected individual or group. Labels change. For example, by the mid-1980s, *disabled* had been widely adopted to describe people with disabilities, replacing *handicapped*. By the mid-1990s, *disabled* seemed insensitive and the common label became *challenged*. But by 2001, *disabled* was widely acceptable again and *challenged* was discarded as a "politically correct" euphemism. The racial designation preferred by African-Americans evolved through the twentieth century from *colored* <National Association for the Advancement of Colored People> to *Negro* <National Negro College Fund> to *black* <National Black Law Students Association> to *African-American*. The preference of American Indians shifted to *Native Americans* and back again. In some instances, labels may have subtly different denotations (e.g., *Eskimo*, *Inuit*, *Tlingit*), or more than one acceptable label may be in use simultaneously (e.g., *black*, *African-American*), or a label may be accepted or preferred in one geographic area but not another (e.g., *Hispanic*, *Latino/Latina*, *Chicano/Chicana*). Be aware of what's current—and appropriate.

(g) *Euphemisms.* Although they are meant to avoid unpleasantness, euphemisms tend to be broad, vague, and sometimes inaccurate, so use them with great care. A euphemism such as *mobility-impaired* might be useful if referring to an entire class of people who share a broadly defined characteristic (i.e., difficulty walking). But it is meaningless when applied to an individual. Few disabilities are absolute; rather, they come in many degrees. An impairment may be relatively slight (e.g., walks with a limp) or substantial (e.g., uses a wheelchair). Not all euphemisms should be avoided. At times, a direct or explicit term might divert the reader's attention from the issue; a softer substitute is desirable then. For example, the terms *bastard* and *illegitimate child* historically attach to an innocent person. *Nonmarital child* and *child out of wedlock* convey the same meaning without offense.

(h) *Equivalence.* When writing about more than one group, use equivalent labels whenever possible. Distinctively labeling only one group implies that it is to be regarded as superior or inferior to the other, or that one group is normal and the other is not. Instead of *blacks and Asian-Americans*, write *African-Americans and Asian-Americans*. Some labels, although equivalent, are not commonly used and could make your prose sound awkward. People of

European descent are usually labeled *white*. Many find *European-American* stuffy, and *Anglo* (commonly heard in the Southwest) inaccurate. If a specific label doesn't apply, then use the common label, even if it is not equivalent (e.g., *whites and Chinese-Americans*). Sometimes there is no reasonably equivalent label. For example, one is or is not a disabled person; only one distinguishing label exists. Don't invent a label just to achieve balance.

(i) *Slang.* The extreme informality of slang can diminish the authority of your writing and destroy any sense of objectivity. Slang terms may have additional connotations that expand or restrict their meanings. For example, the slang terms *bro* (for *brother*), *craziness* (for *excitement*), *cray* (for *crazy*), *dank* (for *excellent*), *dude*, *fam* (for *closest friend*), *gonna*, *hundo* (for *100% certain*), *hey*, *insane* (for *excellent*), *lit* (for *excellent*), *probs* (for *probably*), *totes* (for totally), *yas* (for *yes*), *you guys*, and many another evanescent term may make you feel au courant (or hip-to-the-know), but they're sure to strike many readers as unprofessional.

(j) *Inflammatory hyperbole.* The casual use of inflammatory terms, such as referring to the police as *gestapo* or an objectionable law in terms of *genocide*, is for shock entertainers, not professional writers. The writer seeks to inflate an issue by linking it to a historic enormity or injustice. But the tactic is bound to backfire. The irritated reader may discount the issue to less than its true importance.

(k) *Jargon.* Using outdated and offensive jargon shows poor research and a lack of knowledge. No responsible writer should misuse another field's current technical language. For example, until the 1970s, some popular medical terminology, such as *mongolism* and *Siamese twins*, had racial and ethnic roots. These terms have been replaced with more accurate and ethnically neutral equivalents (i.e., *Down syndrome*; *conjoined twins*). Similarly, until the 1960s, shipping and engineering jargon commonly included a highly offensive racial slur (*see, e.g.*, *State v. Hamilton*, 141 S.E.2d 506, 508 (N.C. 1965); *Weigel v. The Belgrano*, 189 F.Supp. 103, 105 (D. Or. 1960) (referring to some undefined portion of a winch)). The terms have long since been replaced with neutral phrases.

(l) *False friends.* Some legitimate words are similar in appearance to (and sometimes sound like) slurs. If you think a word or phrase might be questionable, consult a dictionary. There is almost always a neutral substitute that serves exactly the same function. Just a few words that have created problems are *niggardly* (having an ancient Old Norse derivation, and meaning *stingy*), *yellow* (when used in a negative sense, e.g., *coward*), *welsh* (meaning *to break a promise* or *to avoid payment*, and unrelated to the Welsh people), *blackguard* (meaning *rascal* and unrelated to skin color), and *chicanery* (meaning *trickery*, apparently of French origin and dating to 1609, whereas *Chicano* is thought to have come from the Mexican-Spanish *mexicano* and did not appear until 1947). Of course, if a word is the best choice for a particular writing, use it. It isn't reasonable to purge your vocabulary of every good word that might conceivably be misperceived. But if the word will predictably engender resentment, avoid it.

(m) *Suitability.* Some labels are acceptable for a thing but not a person. For example, one can say that a rug is Oriental (a rug of particular style and manufacture) or mention an Asiatic bear (a species of bear), but Asian-American people consider it offensive to say that a person is Oriental or Asiatic instead of Asian.

(n) *Capitalization.* Labels for race, ethnicity, and religion are capitalized in some circumstances.

- Labels drawn from geographic origins are always capitalized and hyphenated <African-American> <Asian-American> <Mexican-American> <Swedish-American>.
- Labels naming an ethnic origin are usually capitalized <Berber> <Celtic> <Hispanic> <Inuit> <Tutsi>.
- Labels based on color <black> <white> <brown> are rarely capitalized unless placed at the beginning of a sentence or included in a title <National Black Law Students Association>.
- Labels naming a religious faith and its members are always capitalized <Buddhism> <Buddhist>. When used as an adjective, a religious name is capitalized if it retains its religious basis <Protestant work ethic> <Shinto temple>. Several words, such as *catholic*, *protestant*, and *methodist*, are similar or identical to religious names but have nonreligious meanings; these are never capitalized unless they are part of a title or at the beginning of a sentence.

(o) *Gender-neutral language.* Masculine pronouns (e.g., *he*, *him*) should be avoided unless you're writing only about men. Below are eight techniques for gender-inclusive writing.

- Use a plural noun as the antecedent instead of a singular noun. This allows you to use plural pronouns.

  Not this: *A lawyer* must affirm that *he* has truthfully advised *his* client.

  But this: *Lawyers* must affirm that *they* have truthfully advised *their* clients.

- Rework or replace a phrase or clause to eliminate the need for a personal pronoun altogether.

  Not this: If *a man or woman* dies without a will, *his or her* property will be disposed of under the laws of intestate succession.

  But this: If *a person* dies without a will, *the decedent's* property will be disposed of under the laws of intestate succession.

- Rewrite the sentence.

  Not this: Either the angry father or the mother will have to change *her* attitude before the custody hearing starts.

  But this: The father and the mother are both angry; at least *one of them* must calm down before the custody hearing starts.

- Use an article instead of a pronoun.

  Not this: An accused person must actively waive *his* right to speak to *his* lawyer.

  But this: An accused person must actively waive *the* right to speak to *a* lawyer.

- Rephrase the sentence using an indefinite pronoun, preferably without a personal pronoun.

  Not this: An indigent defendant without an attorney can ask the court to appoint one for *him*.

  But this: An indigent defendant *who* needs an attorney can ask the court to appoint one.

- Repeat the noun, but only if you can keep repetition to a minimum.

  Not this: If a creditor has in *his* possession some property belonging to the debtor, *he* may be entitled to retain possession until *she* repays the debt.

  But this: If a creditor has possession of some property belonging to the debtor, *the creditor* may be entitled to retain possession until *the debtor* repays the debt. (If you have to repeat the noun more than twice, it may be better to recast the sentence.)

- If it's appropriate, use the imperative mood to eliminate the need for explicit pronouns.

  Not this: Before the trial of a case, a lawyer shall not communicate with anyone *he* knows to be a member of the venire.

  But this: Before the trial of a case, do not communicate with anyone you know to be a member of the venire.

- Use the phrase *he or she* instead. This is a last-resort option because the phrase usually sounds stilted. Used in excess, it becomes obnoxious. Never use it twice in the same sentence.

  Not this: Each plaintiff must file *his* suit separately, or else *he* will not be allowed to complain about the disparate treatment *he* has suffered.

  But this: If a plaintiff does not file an individual suit, the court will not hear *his or her* claim of disparate treatment.

- If you're comfortable doing so, if no imprecision results, and if you're willing to risk a raised eyebrow from some readers, use *they* as a gender-neutral singular (see 11.10(o)).

  Ex.: If a petitioner raises a due-process argument for the first time in a high court, they deprive the lower courts of the opportunity to address the question in the first instance.

(p) *Titles.* When possible, avoid using titles that have increasingly archaic feminine suffixes (such as *-ess*, *-ette*, or *-ix*) or that use *man* as a suffix or prefix. Many words have ready substitutes.

Instead of this:	**Try this:**
administratrix	administrator
anchorman	anchor
aviatrix	aviator
businessman	businessperson; executive; entrepreneur
cameraman	camera operator; photographer
chairman	chair
congressman	representative; senator; member
craftsman	craftworker; crafter; artisan
draftsman	drafter
executrix	executor
fireman	firefighter
foreman	supervisor; manager
foreman of the jury	presiding juror
housewife	homemaker
layman	nonlawyer; layperson
maid	housekeeper
mailman	mail carrier; letter carrier
mankind	humanity; humankind
manpower	workforce; staff; human resources
newsman	reporter
ombudsman	ombuds
policeman	police officer
postman	mail carrier; postal worker
prosecutrix	prosecutor
repairman	repairer; servicer; technician
salesman	sales clerk; salesperson
spokesman	representative
testatrix	testator
tribesman	tribe member
venireman	veniremember
watchman	guard; security officer
workman	worker

(q) *Gender-specific language.* When writing about something that concerns a matter related to only one gender (e.g., women's rights; men's health) or referring to an institution that is inherently single-sex (e.g., a convent or sorority), use sex-specific language. In these circumstances, trying to write in gender-neutral language is likely to produce peculiar or even absurd prose (e.g., "If a prospective member of a sorority experiences hazing, he or she may sue for personal injuries.").

(r) *Age references.* Consider how specific an adjective of age is—or is not—before using it. It's better to specify age without qualification (e.g., *Mr. Ali is 72 years old*), by using modifiers sparingly and cautiously (e.g., *an older teenager*), or by substituting a different adjective (e.g., *an inexperienced bank teller*). Describing someone as *young* isn't necessarily complimentary: depending on the context, it may describe an infant or a 30-year-old, or it may connote immaturity or vigor. Consider: *The young lawyer prepared the appellate brief.* If this sentence appeared in a negative passage, perhaps about how an appeal was mishandled, *young* may take on the sense of *inexperienced* or *incompetent*, and may subtly shift blame onto the brief-writer's shoulders. Consider also: *The young judge adjourned the court and answered the defense attorney's question the next morning.* The phrasing implies that the judge's youth (leading to indecision born of inexperience) might be the reason for the delay in answering the question. Likewise, something *old* may be either useless or venerable. And the adjective is imprecise because it broadly refers to something from the past, either the recent past <do you still have that old newspaper, the one dated yesterday?> or the distant past <that old book belonged to Henry VIII>. Applied to people, *old* suggests at least a degree of physical infirmity and age-related restrictions, especially weakness and senility. Because the connotations of *old* may be inaccurate, many people prefer the less restrictive label *senior citizen* to *old person*. The phrase *senior citizen* isn't of recent coinage (it's been around since 1938). It's not a euphemism for *old* because its denotation isn't restricted to age but encompasses political and social contexts as well. The term is usually applied to a person who has attained or is close to attaining retirement age, but has not necessarily retired.

(s) *Sexual orientation.* When writing about a person's sexual orientation, avoid using adjectives that connote choice (e.g., *avowed*). And avoid using adjectives that imply a disclosure against the person's will or an element of shame, unease, or guilt (e.g., *acknowledged*, *admitted*, and *confessed*).

(t) *Religious references.* Unless the subject or issue is one that plainly intertwines law and religion (e.g., freedom of religion), a legal writer who uses religious imagery, quotations, parables, and analogies will always sound biased to a reader whose spiritual background is dissimilar. And a reader who is unfamiliar with the sources of the writer's religious allusions will miss the writer's point. Or a reader might perceive an attempt to evoke unwarranted sympathy, or to sanctify a person or thing, or to unfairly legitimize an argument with theology rather than law.

> "It is clear that the writer exists for the sake of the reader, not the reader for the sake of the writer."
>
> —*Thomas DeQuincey*

§ 14
Editing and Proofreading

14.1 Review your work closely and systematically to improve the style.

(a) *Two readings necessary—three desirable.* No matter how good an editor you become, you will never do your best work until your second or third read-through and markup. Always have a pen in hand to make the most obvious corrections, but during your first read-through, try restricting yourself to low-level editing. Only after you read and understand the entire piece will you be able to make your best edits. They will be more detailed, more substantive, and more effective at achieving the goals of the writing. They will look beyond the immediate word or sentence to the fuller context and structure of the piece.

The point about tenacity is worth reiterating: never, never give up on a piece of work if you can think of some way—any way—to improve it before the deadline.

(b) *Worsening the piece.* Ineffective self-editors often say that their first draft is their best, and that every time they edit, their prose gets worse. An editor can indeed worsen a piece of writing, as by unintelligently applying unintelligent "rules." (One example is changing every sentence-starting *But* to *However.*) But this is like saying that a beginning golfer gets worse after a lesson: although often true, it's because the golfer must first learn and practice something new before improving. The solution is not to stop taking lessons, but to keep working toward a higher level of proficiency.

If a piece is truly getting worse with every edit, then it was probably bad to begin with. The writer is probably unskillful, and the self-editor even worse.

14.2 Habitually ask yourself Orwell's six questions.

(a) *Orwell's questions.* In one of the most famous essays ever written, "Politics and the English Language," George Orwell wrote that a scrupulous writer, while writing each sentence, asks these crucial questions:

(1) What am I trying to say?
(2) What words will express the idea?
(3) What image or idiom will make it clearer?
(4) Is this image fresh enough to be effective?
(5) Could I put it more shortly?
(6) Have I said anything that is avoidably ugly?

(b) *Applicability to editing.* Orwell's questions apply as much to self-editors and (with a change to the third person in #1, #5, and #6) to editors as they do to writers. In fact, they might apply with even greater force to second and third drafts, since one of the goals of the first draft is simply to get words down freely on paper. If posing these questions stifles you unduly—if they bring on writer's block—then you're best off posing them while revising.

14.3 Tighten the style by ridding the draft of verbosity.

(a) *Tightening generally.* Verbosity is like dust: each time you write, it reappears. It may be just a few extra words here, a few there. But the cumulative effect dulls the prose, which becomes a little heavier and slower and (typically) less clear. The comments that follow explain several good techniques to tighten writing. Although these techniques may seem simple, you will acquire them only through diligent effort.

(b) *Minimizing the passive voice.* Look for passive-voice constructions that might better be active (see 11.27, 11.44(c)). Instead of *The documents were then signed by Jillson*, try *Jillson then signed the documents.* Besides yielding a more engaging sentence, a passive-to-active edit usually saves two words: the auxiliary verb and the preposition *by*.

(c) *Converting zombie nouns.* Search for abstract nouns that hide actions (see 11.44(a)). These are sometimes called *zombie nouns* or *nominalizations.* For example, you can often turn an abstract noun ending in *-ion* back into an action verb; instead of *is in violation of*, try *violates.* Other suffixes that signal zombie nouns include *-ment* (instead of *make an investment*, try *invest*), *-ence* and *-ance* (instead of *provide assistance to*, try *assist* or, even better, *help*), and *-ity* (instead of *establish the identity of*, try *identify*).

(d) *Trimming prepositional phrases.* Cut down on prepositions, especially *of*-phrases (see 11.44). Instead of writing *at the time of the execution of the documents by Jillson* (*execution* here being a fancy equivalent of *signing*), try *when Jillson signed the documents.* Instead of *the decision of the court*, try *the court's decision.* You can often turn a prepositional phrase into a single word (instead of *after a while*, try *later*) or even eliminate it altogether without sacrificing anything. Watch particularly for distracting chains of prepositional phrases (instead of *participation by the plaintiff in the collection of the debt was in violation of § 1692*, try *the plaintiff's participation in collecting the debt violated § 1692*, trimming five prepositional phrases down to one).

(e) *Replacing wordy phrases.* Edit down the typical multiword phrases that displace more straightforward words (see 12.2(c)). Instead of *a number of*, write *many* or *several*; instead of *bring an action against*, write *sue*; instead of *prior to the time when*, write *before*; instead of *until such time as*, write *until.* Edits like these become mental habits. Ultimately they should become second nature.

(f) *Eliminating redundancy.* Avoid saying the same thing twice, whether in phrases such as *near and proximate to*, or in consecutive sentences or paragraphs. Condense where you can.

Not this: Masri, an unpaid intern at a medical college, reported multiple alleged violations of medical ethics to the Department of Surgery Administrator. After reporting multiple violations, she was fired from her unpaid internship at the medical college. [36 words]

But this: Working as an unpaid intern at a medical college, Masri reported several alleged medical-ethics violations to the Department of Surgery. She was then fired. [25 words]

14.4 Sharpen the writing by reducing abstractions.

(a) *Sharpening generally.* Vagueness can result from uncertainty (all you know is that it was a *motor vehicle*), from the mental haze of abstract thought (you know that it was an *SUV*, but you've come to prefer generic words like *motor vehicle*), or from a worm in the brain that makes one yearn for official-sounding prose (so that you prefer to say *the pedestrian sustained injuries consequent to a motor-vehicle collision*).

To sharpen prose is to combat vagueness. If you can say that it was an *SUV* or *car* or *tractor-trailer* or *pickup truck* or *motorcycle*, then do. If you can name the pedestrian and the driver, then do. If you can give a down-to-earth description, you'll be writing better: *Peter Grabowski, driving his SUV, hit Jill Bartson from behind as she was crossing the street.* Or: *As Jill Bartson crossed the street, Peter Grabowski rounded the corner in his SUV and struck her from behind.* Do your homework and get your facts right, but make your writing as concrete and vivid as you reasonably can. Try to convey a mental image of what you describe. Even if you've tried to do just that in your first draft, read later drafts with an eye to sharpening the image.

Similarly, avoid saying *for several reasons* (or worse, *for a number of reasons*—which is both vague and wordy). Say *for two reasons*, *for three reasons*, etc. Your readers will perk up a bit to see what they are. Give specific numbers if they'll add interest. *The club has lots of members* isn't nearly as memorable as *The club has about 100 members.*

(b) *Two red-flag adverbs.* Two terms to be especially wary about are *subsequently* and *recently*: they often signal a cagey vagueness. For example: "The company was incorporated in 2018. *Subsequently*, its affairs were wound up." What? Was that two weeks after incorporation? Two years? A decade? Was it ever a going concern? And of course, *subsequently* is just a high-flown equivalent of *later.* But *later*, if the writer had used it, would more immediately point up the preposterousness of the vague idea expressed: it doesn't tell us the *when* of who-what-when-where-how, which is what interests readers. The same problem plagues *recently*. Some inkling of time is typically desirable, without superabundant information. Hence "last fall" is probably better, under normal circumstances, than "at 10:02 a.m. on October 17, 20—, [etc.]."

(c) *Nouns and verbs*. It's often said that writers should rely on nouns and verbs to carry the message, shunning adjectives and adverbs. As the examples above show, that's sometimes good advice. But it often goes too far: fresh adjectives and adverbs can add spice to almost any writing. What makes for bad writing—and especially bad legal writing—is to just declare, for example, that your adversary's conduct was "unconscionable" rather than explaining the specific facts that make it so. Avoid this sort of conclusory use of descriptive words.

14.5 In editing your own prose, try a phased approach, making several passes through the document: begin by reconsidering the structure you've used (your arrangement of material); then read for edits at the paragraph level; then read closely sentence by sentence for clarity and correctness.

(a) *Systematic approach*. When editing, you can work at any of various levels. You might reorganize the whole document. You might improve the flow from paragraph to paragraph. You might correct word choices (as when the first draft misuses *principal* for *principle*, or *infer* for *imply*), misspellings and word-processor "auto-corrections" (such as *statue* for *statute*, or *trail* for *trial*), or the correct use of plural and possessive forms. You might correct punctuation. You might shorten your average sentence length. You might ensure that your headings will be useful to readers who want to skim the document. Or you might double-check the citations to make them perfectly consistent and fully accurate. But you will never be able to do all these things at the same time. For maximal effect, each type of edit will probably require a separate sweep through the document. So systematize your editing into several steps.

(b) *Stage one: macro edits*. Check to see whether (1) the central point emerges quickly and clearly; (2) the logic is both explicit and sound; (3) every strong counterargument has been rebutted; (4) the arguments fit together and flow one into the next; and (5) the tone is relaxed but forceful.

(c) *Stage two: basic micro edits*. Check to see whether you can revise, edit, or delete (1) passive voice where active voice would be better; (2) *be*-verbs where an active verb is possible; (3) prepositional phrases that prop up wordy constructions; (4) legalisms; and (5) faults in word choice, grammar, punctuation, and citations.

(d) *Stage three: advanced micro edits.* Challenge yourself to cut each sentence by 25%. Collapse sentences into clauses, clauses into phrases, and phrases into single words. When you can, replace long words with shorter ones, and fancy words with simpler ones. If you find a *which* that has neither a preposition nor a punctuation mark before it, change it to a *that*; if the result doesn't make sense, recast the sentence.

(e) *Stage four: polishing.* Read through again, asking yourself whether you can clarify each point with an example or an analogy. Be sure that in every passage, you've been clear about who is doing what to whom. Be objective about whether the ideas flow smoothly and whether a sense of momentum carries the reader through. Ensure that you've quoted only as much as necessary, that you've woven every block quotation into your narrative rather than dumping it on the page and hoping that it will do your work for you, and that you've supplied each block quotation with an informative lead-in before the colon.

(f) *Stage five: distanced editing.* If you can, give yourself some time away from the document before performing a final edit. This distance will lower the chance of your "reading" what you intended to say instead of what you actually said. This final distanced edit must leave you enough time to address any problems you find. Alternatively, you can give the document to someone else to look over with fresh eyes. Or try reading it anew as if you were a stranger to the document.

14.6 When editing someone else's prose, begin by assessing the context in which you're working and then mark the manuscript appropriately.

(a) *Editing someone else's prose vs. your own.* Editing another's writing is fundamentally different from editing your own. Why? You will be unfamiliar with someone else's piece, and therefore you'll need to read closely to grasp the argument and its structure. Meanwhile, if you're knowledgeable about the mechanics of writing, you'll find it all but impossible to read past errors without correcting them as you go. Doing so will detract from your concentrating on structure. That's to be expected, and it's quite all right. So embrace the focus on "micro" edits at the outset. Focus on overall structure and flow only after making some basic edits in your first read-through. By contrast, with your own prose, you'll probably be thinking continually about structure (which you will have devised) in many read-throughs before

> "Alexander Pope wrote 'To err is human, to forgive divine.' Nevertheless, when proofreading the writer should take the attitude that there is not a forgiving soul in the world."
> —*Kenneth S. Rothwell*

checking small points for correctness. Be that as it may, in what follows the assumption is that you will be editing someone else's prose. Your basic mindset as an editor is that you're looking at a manuscript that has something wrong with it. Your job is to spot the problems and fix them—reliably.

(b) *An admonition.* As an editor, do no harm. Never, never introduce errors into a document or mar a good style by making it less good. Know what you're doing. Your fact-checking must be impeccable. You should be able to justify every edit you make by citing either this book or a sound dictionary of usage. You mustn't rely merely on half-remembered untruths about writing that you think you recall from your childhood.

(c) *Context.* If you're editing a peer's prose by invitation, you might use a freer editorial hand than you would if, for example, you're a student editor on a law journal who has been assigned a famous law professor's article. In the latter context, you might confine yourself to correcting only errors and inconsistencies. Ideally, your edits will be self-explanatory, and they will be reflected in the next draft. If your edits aren't accepted, then you haven't edited well for present purposes. You've somehow misgauged your mission. Rethink what you're doing.

(d) *Selling your edits.* One technique for making your edits palatable is to ensure that they aren't threatening, sarcastic, or otherwise negative. They should have no unnecessary sting. The best way to sell your edits is to write a brief note to the writer, usually at the top of the first page if doing so seems appropriate in the situation. It must be honest and sincere, yet it must also be at least moderately laudatory. For example, you might say: "R— Thank you for letting me see this. Your first and third arguments strike me as *really* strong and well researched. I trust that my edits will be self-explanatory. Let me know if you have any follow-up questions or if you'd like me to review a further draft. It would be a pleasure." Then sign your first name.

14.7 Use single-minded focus in editing the different parts of documents.

(a) *Generally.* Certain editing approaches may help you when editing particular parts of a document. For instance, in a research memo, be sure that you've included all the relevant facts in the statement of facts and that you've addressed all these relevant facts in the discussion. In your issue statement, you want to be sure that you don't state as a fact a conclusion that the court needs to reach to decide the issue. Thus, you should create and use particular editing tools when editing these parts of the document. A couple of pointers are listed below.

(b) *Revisiting the issue presented.* Once you've completed your memo or brief, reconsider your issue statement. Make sure that it (1) avoids improper conclusory statements, (2) includes the key facts on which resolution of the issue will be based, and (3) phrases the question properly. Which key facts to include can vary with the type of document. Don't state as a fact any legal or factual conclusion that the court or fact-finder must decide to resolve the issue.

(c) *Reconciling facts and discussion.* Check your statement of facts and your discussion twice. First, highlight the facts mentioned in the discussion and confirm that they are introduced (preferably in their chronological place) in the statement of facts. If they aren't, add them. Then, in the fact section, highlight those facts mentioned in the discussion; for any fact not highlighted, decide whether to (1) add it to the discussion section, (2) delete it, or (3) leave it in as relevant background.

(d) *Combing out argumentative and reasoning words from fact sections.* Regardless of what type of document you're preparing—whether predictive or persuasive—don't allow argumentative words (such as *clearly* or *obviously*) or reasoning words (such as *therefore* or *thus*) to invade the statement of facts. Because such words amount to editorializing, they destroy your credibility when they appear in the "fact" section.

14.8 When proofreading, limit your marks to corrections or necessary improvements.

(a) *Minimal discretion.* A proofreader is typically limited to fixing outright errors or inarguable mistakes. It is inappropriate, for example, to insert discretionary commas into someone else's writing at this stage—marks that might justifiably be either included or omitted. (See 1.2.) But if you see *attorney's fees*, then *attorneys' fees*, then **attorneys fees*, or the like, you must regularize all instances of the phrase.

(b) *Hands-off attitude unacceptable.* Although writers end up receiving the discredit occasioned by errors, a proofreader is chargeable with the blame for any errors that escaped his or her attention. So proofread with great vigilance. As with editing, the ideal proofreader approaches the task with a lifetime's experience as an attentive reader, a thorough knowledge of English usage, and the ability to focus closely on the manuscript to be cleaned up.

> "The question 'Is this correct written English' can be more specifically phrased: 'Would a copy editor pass this?' 'Does this accord with the style books of the publishing houses?' "
> —*Paul Roberts*

*An invariably inferior form.

14.9 Learn and use the standard proofreaders' marks.

(a) *The necessity of editing on paper.* Although you can accomplish a great deal on the computer screen, the time inevitably comes when you will need to edit a printout. This is especially so in team editing, when several people mark up a draft and then the various edits are collated into a single document. But it's also true of a document edited by a single person. When you hold the paper, as opposed to reading copy on a computer screen, you will see further opportunities for improvement.

(b) *The value of standard marks.* Proofreaders' marks are a kind of visual jargon: in printing, they constitute shorthand ways of telling the typographer what changes to make on a manuscript page. But even outside the print shop, the use of the standard marks is a skill that everyone who edits papers should master. As with every other form of communication, editing is more efficient if everyone speaks the same language—how to mark deletions, insertions, and corrections; how to designate punctuation marks; and how to correct a misspelling. Everyone should know that a circled "stet" (with accompanying dots below the altered text) means that the original should stand without the errant edits, that backward bracket-like marks indicate how type should be aligned on the page, and that different types of underlining show that the designated type should be changed to italics or boldface. Otherwise, misunderstandings mean wasted time, and as lawyers know, time is money. It's well worth the small investment of time it takes for everyone in a law office to become familiar with proofreaders' marks.

(c) *List of proofreaders' marks.* For a complete set of proofreaders' marks, see the table inside the back cover.

14.10 For all court filings, be sure to comply with court rules.

(a) *Court rules.* Most courts publish court rules or local rules addressing, among other things, restrictions and specifications for formatting, deadlines, word and page limits, content, and procedure. Verify—both at the outset and again as a final editing step—that your document complies with the most current rules. The earlier you complete your final check, the more time you will have to cure any noncompliance. Failure to comply with these rules could cause the court to reject your filing; and if your failure prejudices your client's case, you could be subject to disciplinary proceedings or a malpractice action.

(b) *Checklists.* Some courts provide checklists of parts they require for particular documents. If so, use the court's checklist to review your document for compliance. If not, make your own.

Part 3: Specific Documents

§ 15
Case Briefs

15.1 Understand the main goals of a case brief.

(a) *Generally.* A case brief serves as a memory aid for preparing a legal memo or a course outline, making a last-minute review, or refreshing your memory during a trial. A good case brief succinctly and clearly summarizes the relevant facts, the legal issue presented, and the reasoning the court used to reach a decision. The audience for a case brief is usually someone who needs a quick summary of the case.

(b) *Orderly format.* Styles vary, but all case briefs include the name of the case, the weight of the authority (court and date), a brief statement of the relevant facts, the issue, the court's holding, and the court's reasoning. Other elements might be helpful, especially when briefing many cases in preparation for writing a memo or opinion letter. So you might include a concise statement of the rule of law, the procedural nature of the case, notes on concurring or dissenting opinions, your own comments, and perhaps a quotation you'd like to use later. Recording all this information in a structured format makes the case brief more valuable as a shared tool in joint research efforts and as part of a growing resource collection for later use.

(c) *Critical thinking.* The most important task in preparing a case brief is to study the analytical process that the court used to support or derive the legal rule that it applied to the facts. You must analyze the parts of the opinion, understand its structure, and recognize any fallacies in its reasoning. Although the case brief is a summary of the court's opinion, you should add a section of notes containing your own observations and criticisms of the court's analysis and conclusions. Include a short statement of how this case matches or differs from the facts or law involved in your own case. Approached this way, case briefing becomes more than a scrivener's task. It becomes a valuable exercise in critical analysis of the legal problem you're researching.

(d) *Comprehension.* Because a case brief breaks the opinion down into its components, you can focus on each aspect of the opinion. Focus especially on the facts that guided the court to choose a particular law or legal principle over another. In essence, the case brief is a road map of the court's legal analysis that shows how the court arrived at its decision. For the law student, a case brief makes it easier to discuss the case in class and analyze how changes in the facts might have affected the holding. For the practicing lawyer, a case brief makes it easier to compare and distinguish cases and argue their applicability to the facts of a client's case.

(e) *Time management.* If you create a good case brief, you won't have to read the case repeatedly; you'll have a concise but thorough summary at hand.

15.2 Think about the specific goals of your case brief.

(a) *Preparing to answer questions.* Briefing helps you winnow out irrelevant facts and isolate the relevant ones, identify the law, frame the main issues, and explain their answers. These skills are invaluable when you have limited time to address a judge's question about a case you've relied on or to analyze a set of facts and answer a professor's or a client's question. In short, case-briefing hones your most important skill: the ability to think like a lawyer.

(b) *Mastering a new development in the law.* Many changes in the law come from appellate-court decisions. The only way to quickly become familiar with a new development is to read and analyze the case. Summarizing it will help you focus on exactly what has (and hasn't) changed and what ripple effects the new ruling may have later.

(c) *Finding an argument for your client.* Whether you're in law school preparing for moot court or in practice working for a client, a case brief can help you formulate an argument. With a case that supports your client's goal, the court's reasoning may form the basis of your argument. Even with a contrary case, you may find something useful in dicta or in a dissenting opinion, such as indications that a change in certain facts or looking at them differently might have led to a different outcome. Briefing the case with your goal in mind will help you focus on useful information.

(d) *Building a foundation for your research.* A well-written case brief reduces a case to a size that can be easily read and understood. When you've phrased the question you need to answer in a memo and reduced your research to case briefs, you can readily compare the facts of your client's case with those in the cases you've read and quickly identify the facts and issues that are most similar. If you make additional notes about each case, such as why it is a well-reasoned or badly reasoned decision, you will have a head start on points to develop in your memo.

15.3 Avoid the common faults of case briefs.

(a) *Accepting the court's opinion as gospel.* Writing a case brief requires you to focus on the opinion's logical structure and the court's thought processes—to understand what factors led to the decision and how. The analysis may contain logical flaws and fallacies. Or the facts, issues, and reasoning may be similar to those in another case, yet lead to a different outcome. Question the court's opinion. A reader who simply accepts a court's statements as gospel won't be able to use the case briefs effectively or be a good advocate.

(b) *Mistaking dicta for law.* Dicta are statements that aren't part of the court's holding. Common signs that statements are dicta include words or phrases such as *if*, *for example*, *suppose*, or other language indicating that statements are analogies, generalizations, hypotheses, illustrations, or mere passing observations. In such statements a judge may, for any number of reasons, expound on irrelevant or nonexistent facts or a theory of law that was not applied. Dicta have no authority, so don't rely on them. But they may offer insight into how the court might rule given a different set of circumstances.

For the subtle delineation between holdings and dicta, see Bryan A. Garner et al., *The Law of Judicial Precedent* § 4, at 44–75 (2016).

(c) *Writing without reading the case thoroughly.* To extract the essential elements of the court's opinion, you must read it all—and think about it. The relevant facts aren't always clear, especially on the first reading. Underlying policy or social considerations may play more of a role in the outcome than a statute or common-law principle, yet be hard to identify from the text of the opinion. And a court's opinion isn't necessarily correct or unassailable merely because it has been published and may be cited as authority. In reaching its decision, the court may have made certain presumptions without recording them. The court may have distorted precedent or ignored some facts. There may even be logical fallacies in the court's reasoning. Read the whole case carefully several times. You can't write clearly until you understand clearly.

(d) *Skimping on the court's reasoning.* A case that seems to have similar facts and an issue similar to those presented by your client is useful only if your case brief makes clear the reasoning that led to the holding. The court's decision may have turned on a particular fact or a law that doesn't apply or isn't available in your case. If your analysis of the court's reasoning is shallow, you could damage your credibility by using an opinion improperly—such as citing the holding to support your argument when, in fact, the court considered and rejected an argument similar to yours in its reasoning.

(e) *Including too much detail.* As a rule, if your case brief is more than one single-spaced typewritten page, it is probably too detailed. Boil it down. Reexamine the facts and the issues. Eliminate trivial details, such as exact dates and irrelevant personal information about the parties. Although some details may be interesting, they don't belong in your case brief if they have no bearing on the court's reasoning or decision. State the issues in no more than 75 words. If you've woven dicta into the reasoning, delete them; if the dicta are useful for some other purpose, make notes in your observations. If there is a significant concurrence or dissent, summarize the key points of difference in two or three sentences. A very long and complex case may require two pages to brief, but three is almost always too much.

(f) *Using weak briefing methods.* To save time, some researchers don't prepare thorough case briefs. They make a few terse notes of the facts and holding and omit an analysis or review of the reasoning. But unless the user understands how or why the court made its decision, the case brief isn't a help in deciding whether the case is similar to another or whether it can be cited as supporting or contrary authority. Other researchers just highlight passages that seem relevant. But many cases don't clearly identify the issues, state the law, or explain the law's application. Unless you make notes about why the highlighted passage is important, a review of the case requires going back and forth over pages and paragraphs to weave the highlighted threads into a coherent cloth. A third weak method is to skim the syllabus and headnotes of a case. The syllabus is only a terse rendition of the case that is largely, if not entirely, free of analysis. Headnotes are often formulaic rather than analytical; they usually don't reveal factual or legal nuances that led the court to its conclusion. No time is actually saved and much is wasted by relying on any of these common shortcuts.

(g) *Ignoring concurrences and dissents.* Concurring and dissenting opinions may help you understand a decision. Concurring opinions are partial disagreements with the majority opinion and may suggest limits to the majority's reasoning. Dissenting opinions often reveal weaknesses in the majority's reasoning or facts that the majority ignores (for a good example, see *Smith v. Pittsburgh Rys. Co.*, 175 A.2d 844 (Pa. 1961)). The points raised in these types of opinions may warrant development in a memo, depending on the facts of your case.

15.4 Study effective case briefs.

(a) *Further guidance.* Several books explain the elements of a case brief in depth and suggest useful styles. Some good ones are:

- Charles R. Calleros, *Legal Method and Writing* (7th ed. 2014).
- Veda R. Charrow et al., *Clear and Effective Legal Writing* (5th ed. 2013).
- John Delaney, *How to Brief a Case* (1983).
- Bryan A. Garner, *Legal Writing in Plain English* (2d ed. 2013).
- Bryan A. Garner, *The Winning Brief: 100 Tips for Persuasive Briefing in Trial and Appellate Courts* (3d ed. 2014).
- Nancy L. Schultz & Louis J. Sirico Jr., *Legal Writing and Other Lawyering Skills* (6th ed. 2014).
- William P. Statsky & R. John Wernet Jr., *Case Analysis and Fundamentals of Legal Writing* (4th ed. 1994).

(b) *Examples.* The first case, from the Louisiana Supreme Court, includes a dissent that argues against the reasonableness of the majority position.

That might give you either a basis for arguing against legal tradition or some thoughts about how to defend it. In the second, from the Ninth Circuit, you can see how different facts might have changed the outcome. What if the dog had barked loudly instead of yipping, or had barked during the performance? You might add a note on your thoughts about how the answers to those questions could alter the outcome.

> "First, you have to go through hell to know exactly what you're writing about, inside and out. Then you have to leave most of it out. Just keep in mind a variation of Thoreau's great imperative: 'Summarize, summarize.' "
>
> —*Tom Shroder*

Gallo v. Gallo
861 So.2d 168 (La. 2003)

Facts: Husband and Wife divorced when Child, born during the marriage, was five years old. Husband paid child support for six years, then asked the court's permission to stop paying because he had discovered that he was not Child's biological father. A DNA test confirmed Husband's claim. Husband asked to be reimbursed for his child-support payments.

Issue: A husband whose wife bears a child during the marriage is presumed to be the child's father. Child was born while Husband and Wife were married. After divorcing, Husband paid child support until proving that he was not Child's biological father. Is Husband entitled to be reimbursed for his child-support payments?

Holding: No. By statute, a presumptive father has only one year to disavow paternity. Child support paid before a successful disavowal cannot be recovered. Also, child support is not an obligation that can be recovered from the parent who receives the payments even though the payments are made under a mistaken belief.

Reasoning: State law expressly prohibits recovery of child-support payments made before a payor's obligation is terminated, regardless of the circumstances for termination. The child-support payments cannot be recovered from the custodial parent as a mistakenly paid debt because child support is owed to the child, not the custodial parent. Because the custodial parent is only a conduit for the money paid and expended for the child's benefit, that parent cannot be required to reimburse the other despite the mistake.

Dissent: The laws declaring a husband to be the presumed father of a child born in wedlock were settled long before paternity could be reliably established by scientific means. DNA testing makes it unnecessary to perpetuate this legal fiction.

Lentini v. California Center for the Arts
370 F.3d 837 (9th Cir. 2004)

Facts: Lentini brought a service dog to several concert-hall performances. The dog yipped during intermission on two occasions when people got too close to Lentini's wheelchair. No patrons complained about the dog, and it made no audible sounds during the performance. The hall's managers did not tell Lentini that the dog was a problem. But the hall's director told the staff not to admit Lentini again. When Lentini returned for another performance and was told the dog would not be admitted, she entered with the dog anyway. When the manager called the police and demanded her arrest, she left.

Issue: The ADA requires places that are open to the public to allow service animals access to the premises, unless the accommodation or modification is unreasonable or unnecessary or if it would fundamentally alter the nature of the services provided. Lentini's dog yipped only during intermissions, to warn Lentini that people were near her wheelchair. Unlike many of the people present, the dog was silent during the performance. Did the dog's behavior warrant permanent exclusion?

Holding: No. Allowing the dog into the concert hall was reasonable and necessary. The dog's behavior did not disrupt the performance.

Reasoning: Lentini showed that she needed the dog's support. The dog did not make more noise than an occasional cough from a human would. When it did yip, it did so only to alert Lentini to a possible danger. The dog's yips produced no complaints from patrons, and the dog never made a sound while performers were on stage, so it did not fundamentally alter the services provided at the concert hall.

§ 16
Research Memos

16.1 Understand the main goals of a research memo.

(a) *Generally.* The primary purpose of a research memo (also called an *objective* or *predictive memo*) is to analyze a legal problem—usually a particular client's legal problem—and to educate and inform the reader. The memo summarizes the relevant facts, states the applicable law, applies the law to the facts, and predicts how a court would rule on the issue. A memo is primarily practical, not theoretical. It answers one or more specific questions posed and memorializes how current law stands on certain points. It's not a law-review article, balancing policy questions and weighing them from various angles. It's a practical analysis of what would happen in court, based on the current state of the law as applied to the facts presented. Although the memo may deal with novel or creative arguments, it must assess them candidly. If no court has ever ruled on those arguments, then the memo should say so, focus on what the courts have done in similar cases, assess the strengths and weaknesses of the client's case, and predict the likely outcome.

(b) *To help readers.* There may be many intended readers of a research memo: the assigning attorney, the client, other lawyers involved in the case, and future readers within the organization who may someday deal with a related problem. Before writing the memo, try to find out who the intended audience might include. Even if you're writing solely for the immediate benefit of an assigning attorney who is familiar with the facts and issues the memo addresses, always look beyond that immediate reader and assume that other readers may need to understand the analysis. The purpose and gist of the memo should be clear at a glance. And remember that none of your readers will be as familiar as you are with the specific information you've read.

(c) *To summarize issues.* The most important part of the memo is the front-page summary, which lets busy readers see quickly what your memo concerns. Start on the first page with an issue statement that almost any reader could understand, not just those familiar with your case. Tell the reader the key facts behind the question. Follow the issue with a brief answer to that question and summarize the reason for the answer. Headings such as *Question Presented* (or *Issue*) and *Brief Answer* are helpful. If there are several issues, the summary should contain the issues, the answers, and the reasons—all presented in an orderly way. Keep the brief answer with the question it answers: that is, instead of stating questions 1, 2, and 3, followed by answers 1, 2, and 3, present question 1 and its answer, question 2 and its answer, and question 3 and its answer. When you summarize your main findings on the first page, the rest of the memo should fall neatly into place. Follow this summation with the *Discussion* (or *Support*) sections. State the relevant facts as part of this discussion or in a separate section.

(d) *To anticipate problems.* Readers use memos as planning and decision-making tools. A good memo identifies and analyzes both supporting and contrary authority and discusses all the foreseeable outcomes—even the less likely ones—so that the reader can weigh the risks of a possible course of action. Even if you're confident about your predicted outcome, you must still account for other possible lines of reasoning. If a matter goes to litigation, a good memo may help a brief-writer anticipate and rebut the other party's position.

16.2 Think about the specific goals of your research memo.

(a) *Needs of the assigning attorney.* Find out the assignment's purpose: the assigning attorney may be preparing an opinion letter, a pleading, a motion, or some other document. Learn all you reasonably can about the facts of the case; unless you connect the facts and the applicable law, the research will be less useful—maybe even useless. Once you know the purpose of the memo and the facts, you'll be in a position to conduct research and report your findings more clearly, precisely, and reliably.

(b) *Needs of the client.* Although many memos are written for internal purposes only, assigning attorneys often share them with the client or otherwise use them when corresponding with the client. So report your research in a focused way, being sure to tie your analysis to the client's particular problem. Identify the determinative facts and any missing facts that might be important. When the law or facts seem unfavorable to the client, you may suggest arguments or strategies to deal with the potential problems. But make certain that your analysis is sound, thorough, and supportive of your suggestions. Don't write just what the client wants to hear.

(c) *More research necessary.* Your research may well raise issues that aren't part of the assigned question. When that happens, either clarify the question with the colleague who assigned the memo or put your thoughts into a separate memo suggesting another line of research. If your factual information is so incomplete that you can't give a reliable answer, make a list of things you still need to know before you can give one. Consider adding a final section recommending areas where further research is needed. But if a germane point is readily resolvable, then resolve it.

16.3 Avoid the common faults of research memos.

(a) *Omitting the up-front summary.* Summarize your main points—the issues and conclusions—on the first page. These are what the reader wants to see. Don't sprinkle your conclusions throughout the middle of the memo or save them for the end (thinking, erroneously in this circumstance, that the "conclusion" must come at the end). Nor should the statement of facts precede the deep issue and brief answer. The result wastes readers' time (inducing the question, "Why are you telling me this?") and makes the memo less useful in future research on related points. The IRAC (issue-rule-application-conclusion) model from law-school exams is inappropriate for structuring memos and briefs because it relegates the answer to the end of the document. In practice, your readers want to see the question and the answer at the outset.

(b) *Parroting an ill-phrased question.* Don't assume that a great deal of thought has gone into the phrasing of the question or questions assigned to you. So don't assume that you must state the question verbatim as originally posed. One part of your research task is to refine the questions presented. What had been posed as a single question may turn out to be two quite distinct issues. Or the question may have been put in a way that only an insider to the case would understand. Your job, as the writer of the memo, is to phrase the question in a way that will make the issue best understandable to any reader. Perhaps most important, rephrasing the question in this way will help *you* understand it. Don't hesitate to ask whether your rephrased question better addresses the relevant issue. The assigning attorney is relying on you to improve and sharpen the question based on your tailored research.

(c) *Using surface issues.* A superficial, incomplete statement of the question ("Whether Micrologistics is estopped by the 2014 consent decree?") will be useful at most to only a few readers for only a short while. This type of one-sentence *whether*-issue is unfortunately common in "insider" memos. A more delicately structured issue statement, with separate sentences that contain the crucial facts in chronological order, will be more transparent to all types of readers ("In 2014, Micrologistics Corp. and Spamster Co. signed a consent decree in which Micrologistics admitted the validity and infringement of three Spamster patents. In 2016, Micrologistics significantly changed its product designs but faces another infringement claim from Spamster under the same patents. Under the 2014 consent decree,

> "An intelligent statement of the problem is one of the most important parts of your presentation. It is the 'why' of your [memo]: why are you writing it, why you are concerned, why someone should read it."
>
> —*Ernst Jacobi*

can Micrologistics challenge the validity of the Spamster patents in the current lawsuit?"). Keep each issue to no more than 75 words, and present the factual premises within it. Then give the brief answer immediately afterward.

(d) *Waffling in the answer.* Sometimes the brief answer must be "probably" or "it depends" rather than "yes" or "no." If that's the case, explain what your answer depends on and why. Weigh in with your best judgment on the issue ("X is likely because . . . . But A, B, and C are possible because . . . ."). Give your best answer backed up with solid reasons supported by your analysis. Don't hedge with vague reservations, but if you must hedge in any way, say why the answer isn't clear-cut.

(e) *Meandering.* The most common problems with research memos are organizational ones. The legal analysis must be logically organized and methodically presented. This always requires outlining—a step that too many writers of all types omit. Disorganized thinking results in a stream-of-consciousness writing style that is sometimes comprehensible only to the writer. Chart a course through the material and stick to it. And don't repeat parts of an argument that have already been covered in another part of the discussion.

(f) *Losing focus.* Avoid going off on tangents. Answer the question raised thoroughly, but avoid the temptation to dump all your research into the memo. No matter how interesting the facts of some case you read may be, if the holding or the reasoning doesn't advance your discussion or present useful information, leave it out. Ask yourself, "Does my reader need to know this to understand the question presented?" Usually, the shorter a memo is, the more helpful it is.

(g) *Beginning with lengthy facts.* To put a statement of facts at the beginning is to begin in the middle. It's a way of refusing to summarize the issues at the outset. Although professors write law-school exams this way—with an intricate statement of facts followed by a series of brief questions—this isn't a sound strategy in writing for one's colleagues. The issues and answers should come before a detailed statement of facts, and the crucial facts for each issue should be set out in the statement of the issue itself. You may want to *write* the detailed facts first to make certain that you've mastered them, but you should place them after the summary.

(h) *Omitting headings.* Even in a short memo, a few headings will serve as important guideposts for the reader. In a longer memo, headings become obligatory. They will help the reader see the logical development and direction of the analysis as it draws toward a conclusion.

(i) *Overquoting.* Don't blindly copy lengthy, unmemorable, and obtuse passages from your sources. Try to paraphrase or summarize their meaning. Extensive quoting is no substitute for analysis. In fact, it more often obscures the point you're trying to make: the reader must work to figure out the quoted text's meaning and how you think it relates to the memo's issue. Although a passage may strike you as insightful when you read it, another reader may find nothing there worthwhile when it's taken out of context. If it's really stated so brilliantly or succinctly that it can't be improved on—and if it's directly on point—then a direct quotation may be valuable. But far more often, you'll find that the effort spent paraphrasing is valuable in itself. It helps you analyze and distill the reasoning. After all, if you don't fully understand the issue yourself, how can you explain it to the reader and project an outcome?

(j) *Poor citation form.* Because memos are often used to prepare other legal documents, such as briefs and letters, your citations must be accurate. Use citations that your reader or another researcher can easily follow to the source. Always use a source's long-form citation the first time you discuss it, even if it was cited earlier in a footnote. If you use only an abbreviated name, the next researcher will have to flip through the pages looking for the full citation. Follow the standard conventions of legal citation, using *The Bluebook* or *ALWD*, and observing any applicable local rules (see § 9).

16.4 Study effective research memos.

(a) *Where to find them.* Consult senior colleagues or peers who have written memos for the assigning attorney or other lawyers in the firm. Outside a law office, well-written research memos are hard to come by, even in legal-writing books. But an excellent example of a research memo, written by a highly successful lawyer at a major firm, is reproduced in Bryan Garner's *Legal Writing in Plain English* 193–201 (2d ed. 2013).

(b) *Examples.* These samples are both internal memos. The first discusses a single legal question that is well settled. The second is more complex; the law is less clear.

> "Student writers frequently lament pathetically, 'I know what I want to say, but I can't seem to get it down.' The odds are that they really have only the fuzziest idea of what they want to say and are too lazy to work it out."
>
> —*John E. Jordan*

Single-Issue Memorandum

Memorandum

To: PARTNER

From: ASSOCIATE

Re: Irwin & Nancy Brown, #01-523-5: Calculating Days in Real-Estate Option

Date: 22 May 2006

An excellent deep issue: see 16.3(c) & 25.1(d).

Question Presented

Our clients the Browns contracted to buy a piece of residential property in Dallas. Under § 7(D)(1) of the earnest-money contract, the Browns paid a $250 option fee for "the unrestricted option to terminate the contract for 7 days after the effective date." The contract became effective on Saturday, November 17, so that seven days later was another Saturday, with Thanksgiving intervening. In the absence of any contractual definition of "day," how are the days calculated?

Brief Answer

For contract purposes, a day is a calendar day. Intervening Sundays and legal holidays are usually treated as calendar days. So the calculation begins with the first day after the effective date and ends on the seventh calendar day. Counting November 18 as the first day, the seventh and final day for exercising the option was Saturday, November 24.

Discussion

No statute defines "day" for contract purposes. But Texas common law provides that a day is a calendar day, unless otherwise defined by the parties.[1] A day begins at midnight and ends at the following midnight.[2] When the instrument provides that time is to be computed from or after a certain day or date, then the designated day is excluded, and the last day of the period is included.[3] Because the language of the clause quoted above provides for the period to begin

1 *Long v. Wichita Falls*, 176 S.W.2d 936, 938 (Tex. 1944); *City of Amarillo v. York*, 167 S.W.2d 787, 790 (Tex. Civ. App.—Amarillo 1943); *Dallas Cty. v. Reynolds*, 199 S.W.2d 702, 703 (Tex. Civ. App.—Dallas 1918).

2 *York*, 167 S.W.2d at 790; *Reynolds*, 199 S.W.2d at 703.

3 *Home Ins. Co., N.Y. v. Rose*, 255 S.W.2d 861, 862 (Tex. 1953).

"after the effective date," November 17 is not included as a calendar day.[4] If the last day for a contract's performance falls on a Sunday or legal holiday, that day is not counted.[5] But there is no authority holding that an intervening Sunday or legal holiday is not counted as a calendar day unless the contracting parties so specify.[6]

There is no Texas law expressly on point. But there are two cases concerning option contracts for real estate and time of performance. The contractual periods in both cases overlapped with intervening Sundays and legal holidays.

In *Gaut v. Dunlap*,[7] the parties executed a contract for a real-estate sale. The agreement provided for the delivery of an abstract of title "within 10 days from the 18th day of December, 1915." The parties did not define "day." Citing the general rule that the contract's date of execution is excluded, the court held that the 10-day period began on December 19 and lasted through December 28.[8] The court took no notice of the fact that both a Sunday and a legal holiday (Christmas) had fallen between December 18 and 28. Both days were treated as ordinary calendar days and included in the 10-day period.

Similarly, in *Wilbanks v. Selby*,[9] the real-estate sale contract stipulated a 60-day period for exercising the option. The contract was executed on May 17. It contained no definition of "day." *Wilbanks* included the date of execution in his calculation of the 60-day period. But the court declared that the date of the contract must be excluded when calculating the last day for performance, and decided that the period had ended on July 16, exactly 60 calendar days after May 17.[10] At least eight Sundays and three holidays, Memorial Day, Flag Day, and Independence Day, fell within the 60-day period. The court must have regarded the holidays and Sundays as ordinary calendar days and included them in calculating the option period.

---

4 *Id.*

5 *Ley v. Patton*, 81 S.W.2d 1087, 1090 (Tex. Civ. App.—Beaumont 1935) (Sunday); *Glover v. Glover*, 416 S.W.2d 500, 502 (Tex. Civ. App.—Eastland 1967) (legal holiday).

6 See *Home Ins. Co.*, 255 S.W.2d at 862 (suggesting that parties can expressly choose to override common-law rule and include or exclude certain days from consideration).

7 188 S.W. 1020, 1021 (Tex. Civ. App.—Amarillo 1916).

8 *Id.* at 1021–22.

9 227 S.W. 371 (Tex. Civ. App.—Amarillo 1921).

10 *Id.* at 373.

One case, *Minor v. McDonald*, suggests that Sundays (and presumably holidays) are not counted as days and are excluded from the period when there is inadequate time to act.[11] But the period in question was 20 days, and the case's holding rested on statutory law, not a contract. *Minor* has been cited to support other statutory subject matter,[12] but it has never been applied to a common-law situation. The period in *Gaut* was shorter (10 days), but the case was decided five years after *Minor*, and the *Gaut* court apparently found that the intervening Sunday and legal holiday had no effect on the parties' ability to act. So the court counted the days as ordinary calendar days. A court today would be unlikely to apply *Minor* in the contractual situation here presented.

Conclusion

The precedents here cited strongly suggest that (1) a "day" means a calendar day, and (2) the seven-day option period was not extended by the intervening Sunday or Thanksgiving holiday. The period began on Sunday, November 18, and expired at midnight, Saturday, November 24.

---

11 140 S.W. 401, 402 (Tex. 1911).

12 E.g., *Fidelity & Cas. Co. of N.Y. v. Millican*, 115 S.W.2d 464, 465–66 (Tex. Civ. App.—San Antonio 1938).

Multiple-Issue Memorandum

MEMORANDUM

Notice how the concrete issues and answers on page one amount to a highly informative summary—much more efficient than most misnamed "summaries."

To: Harold H. Jillofson

From: Katherine G. Pilchen

Date: April 2, 2002

Re: Rillerton Group Insurance Litigation, File No. 02-5949-234;
Insurer's possible communications with Rillerton's former employees.

Summary of Issues and Answers

1. **Ex parte communication with former employees.** Our client Rillerton, Inc. has sued its former insurance carrier for bad-faith denial of coverage. Rillerton is concerned that the insurer might attempt to contact Rillerton's former employees in their pretrial investigation. Are ex parte communications between a litigant and the former employees of its adversary permitted under Maryland law?

   Short Answer: Maryland law probably allows ex parte communication between a litigant and a former employee of its corporate adversary, unless the former employee is represented by counsel in the litigation. The out-of-state and federal courts that have considered the question allow ex parte contact. And the Committee on Ethics of the Maryland State Bar Association has concluded that such communications are generally permissible.

2. **Rules governing ex parte communications.** If such communications are allowed, what rules govern the communications?

   Short Answer: Professional Conduct Rules 4.3 and 4.4 protect Rillerton's unrepresented former employees. An opponent's attorney must make certain disclosures to the person contacted, including the client's identity and the attorney's role in the litigation. Also, the lawyer cannot induce a breach of the attorney–client privilege by asking about what a former employee said to corporate counsel. But the attorney may ask about the facts underlying the communication.

Discussion

1. Permissibility of Ex Parte Communications

This question is undecided in Maryland. But a Maryland court would most likely follow the court decisions and bar-association opinions and comments that uniformly permit ex parte communications between an opposing party's attorney and the former employees of a corporate adversary.

A. Ethical Limitations Under Rule 4.2

In Maryland, Rule of Professional Conduct 4.2 (Rule 4.2) now controls an attorney's ability to contact parties and affiliated persons, such as employees, who are represented by lawyers. Historically, Maryland's bar association has advised us that under Rule 4.2 and its predecessor,[1] an attorney's ex parte contact with a corporate party's former employee is permissible as long as the former employee is not represented by counsel.[2]

Maryland's Rule 4.2, which has never been judicially interpreted, is patterned on Rule 4.2 of the ABA Model Rules of Professional Conduct (the Model Rule). The Model Rule is designed to govern an attorney's right to contact an opposing party. Its plain language does not prohibit ex parte contact with a corporate party's former employees, managerial or otherwise.[3] The comment explains that the rule applies to anyone known to be represented regarding the litigation, not just to those named as parties.[4] Paragraph 4 of the comment explains the limits of an attorney's ex parte communications with a corporate party's current agents and employees. In a formal opinion, the ABA refused to extend the Model Rule's interpretation to cover former employees because such a liberal interpretation would unduly restrain discovery.[5] Maryland courts regard the ABA's opinions on its Model Rules as highly persuasive authority.[6]

Many courts have addressed the Model Rule and its applicability to former corporate employees. The majority have held that the Model Rule applies

---

1 Md. Code Prof. Resp. DR 7-104(A)(1) (1985). See Md. R. Prof. Conduct 4.2 cmt. (2001) (comparing rule and code).

2 Md. State Bar Ass'n Op. 86-13 (1986); Md. State Bar Ass'n Comm. on Ethics Op. 90-29 (1990).

3 ABA Comm. on Ethics & Prof. Resp. Formal Op. 91-359, at 3 (1991).

4 ABA Comm. on Ethics & Prof. Resp. Formal Op. 95-396, at 9 (1995).

5 ABA Formal Op. 91-359, at 3, 5; see also ABA Model R. Prof. Conduct 4.2 cmt. (1985).

6 *Brown & Sturm v. Frederick Road L.P.*, 137 Md. App. 150, 180 (2001).

only when there is an ongoing agency or employment relationship, and hence attorneys may contact a corporate party's former employees.[7] A few courts have held that an attorney may not contact a corporate party's former employee if the information obtained from that person could result in liability to the former employer, e.g., by respondeat superior; all but one of these cases predate the ABA's opinion refusing to extend the coverage of the Model Rule.[8] Only a few courts interpreted the Model Rule as forbidding any ex parte contact with former employees; all those cases have been vacated or superseded.[9]

The federal district court in Maryland has considered the permissibility of ex parte communication with former employees and decided that Maryland law allows contact only with former employees who have not been extensively exposed to confidential information.[10] At that time, Maryland's Rule 4.2 was nearly identical to the Model Rule.[11] Although the court discussed and analyzed Rule 4.2, the court applied proposed section 162 of the preliminary draft of the Restatement (Third) of the Law Governing Lawyers, which would impose a no-contact rule with regard to "a person whom the lawyer knows to have been extensively exposed to relevant trade secrets, confidential client information, or similar confidential information of another party interested in the matter."[12] The court cites no Maryland law in support of its decision, and no other court has adopted the proposed section.

In 2001, Maryland's Rules of Professional Conduct were amended. The first sentence of Rule 4.2(a) is substantively identical to that of the Model Rule.[13]

---

7 *See, e.g., Cram v. Lamson & Sessions Co.*, 148 F.R.D. 259, 262 (S.D. Iowa 1993); *In re Domestic Air Transp. Antitrust Litig.*, 141 F.R.D. 556, 561 (N.D. Ga. 1992); Shearson Lehman Bros., Inc. v. Wasatch Bank, 139 F.R.D. 412, 418 (D. Utah 1991).

8 *See Valassis v. Samelson*, 143 F.R.D. 118, 123 (E.D. Mich. 1992); *PPG Indus., Inc. v. BASF Corp.*, 134 F.R.D. 118, 121 (W.D. Pa. 1990); *Chancellor v. Boeing Co.*, 678 F.Supp. 250, 253 (D. Kan. 1988); *Amarin Plastics, Inc. v. Md. Cup Corp.*, 116 F.R.D. 36, 39–41 (D. Mass. 1987).

9 *See Curley v. Cumberland Farms, Inc.*, 134 F.R.D. 77, 86 (D.N.J. 1991) (noting vacation and withdrawal of opinions in the Ninth Circuit and a New York federal district court); *Pub. Serv. Elec. & Gas Co. v. Assoc. Elec. & Gas Ins. Servs., Ltd.*, 745 F.Supp. 1037, 1039 (D.N.J. 1990), *superseded by Klier v. Sordoni Skanska Constr. Co.*, 766 A.2d 761, 769 (N.J. 2000); *see also Andrews v. Goodyear Tire & Rubber Co.*, 191 F.R.D. 59, 69–73 (D.N.J. 2000).

10 *Camden v. Maryland*, 910 F.Supp. 1115, 1122 (D. Md. 1996).

11 *Compare* ABA Model R. Prof. Conduct 4.2 (1986) (using word person) *with* Md. R. Prof. Conduct 4.2 (1987) (substituting party for person).

12 *Camden*, 910 F.Supp. at 1121 (quoting Restatement (Third) of the Law Governing Lawyers § 162 (Prelim. Draft No. 10, 1994)).

13 *Compare* Md. R. Prof. Conduct 4.2(a) (2001) *with* ABA Model R. Prof. Conduct 4.2 (1985).

It clearly prohibits ex parte contact with individuals who are represented by counsel. The rule's new comment states that the "no contact" provision extends to a corporate party's "(1) *current* officers, directors, and managing agents and (2) *current* agents or employees who supervise, direct, or regularly communicate with the organization's lawyers concerning the matter or whose acts or omissions in the matter may bind the organization for civil or criminal liability."[14] Additionally, an attorney must not contact a "*current* agent or employee of the organization" if that person is in either of the two categories mentioned above.[15] The emphatic repetition of "current" strongly points to an intention to make the rule inapplicable to former employees. The comment also expressly refers to Rule 4.4(b) as covering communications with former employees.

B. Application to Rillerton's Former Employees

If a former employee is not represented by counsel in this litigation, a Maryland court will probably allow the insurer's attorney to make ex parte contact. The ABA's comments that unrepresented former employees are not included in the scope of Rule 4.2 are persuasive authority. The majority of courts have found no basis for limiting contact with former employees under Rule 4.2. And the comment to Maryland's version of Rule 4.2 makes it clear that Rule 4.2 is intended to cover only current employees. The court would probably not be persuaded by the reasoning of the courts that have found limitations in Rule 4.2 because those limits are not explicit in Rule 4.2 and may be covered by other rules and privileges.

2. Rules Governing Ex Parte Communication Between a Party and the Former Employees of an Opposing Party

If Rule 4.2 does not limit ex parte communications with Rillerton's former employees, then Rules 4.3 and 4.4, as well as the evidentiary rules of attorney-client privilege and work-product privilege, may still impose some restraints.

A. Rule 4.3

Rule 4.3, which covers communications with an unrepresented person, has never been construed by Maryland courts, but the language of the rule and the comment are plain. Maryland's rule and comment are identical to ABA Model

14 Md. R. Prof. Conduct 4.2 cmt. (2001) (emphasis added).

15 *Id.* (emphasis added).

Rule 4.3. Only one court has interpreted Model Rule 4.3, but the court held that the Model Rule and local rules based on it apply to contacts with former employees.[16] An opposing attorney cannot properly contact any former Rillerton employee unless the attorney identifies the client, reveals that the client is an adverse party to Rillerton, and explains the nature of the lawyer's role in the litigation.[17] This restrains an attorney from taking advantage of a person who has not retained a lawyer.

B. Rule 4.4

The ABA comment to Model Rule 4.4 prohibits an attorney from asking a former employee to disclose privileged information.[18] Maryland expressly incorporates this prohibitory language into Rule 4.4 itself.[19] Hence, an opposing party's lawyer must be careful not to induce the former employee to violate the attorney-client privilege when asking questions that may relate to communications between the former employee and the former employer's counsel.[20] The Maryland rule's comment expressly restricts a lawyer from *knowingly* inducing a waiver of privilege:

> Third persons may possess information that is confidential to another person under an evidentiary privilege or under a law providing specific confidentiality protection . . . . [P]resent or former organizational employees or agents may have information that is protected as a privileged attorney-client communication or as work product. A lawyer may not knowingly seek to obtain confidential information from a person who has no authority to waive the privilege.[21]

C. Attorney-Client Privilege

Attorney-client privilege is recognized as a rule of evidence in Maryland.[22] This privilege restricts ex parte communications to some extent, especially when coupled with Rule 4.4. The attorney-client rule is not an absolute protection since it protects only communications with an attorney, not the facts underlying

---

16 *DuBois v. Gradco Sys., Inc.*, 136 F.R.D. 341, 347 (D. Conn. 1991).

17 ABA Formal Op. 91-359, at 5

18 ABA Model R. Prof. Conduct 4.4 cmt. (1986); see ABA Formal Op. 91-359, at 5.

19 Md. R. Prof. Conduct 4.4(b) (2001).

20 *Id.*; see ABA Formal Op. 91-359, at 5.

21 Md. R. Prof. Conduct 4.4 cmt. (2001).

22 *Blair v. Maryland*, 747 A.2d 702, 720 (Md. 2000) (attorney-client privilege).

those confidential communications. So an opponent's counsel may still ask about those facts.[23]

Conclusion

Unless a former Rillerton employee is represented by a lawyer, a court will probably allow ex parte communications with the employee by the insurer's attorney. The contact is limited only by the ethical rules that protect unrepresented people and the privilege protecting confidential communications.

Perhaps we should talk with Rillerton's general counsel about interviewing whichever former employees the company is most concerned about. Either in-house counsel or we could do this. But the practical problems here relate as much to maintaining good relations with former employees as they do to what the Maryland court might end up doing.

23 *Upjohn Co. v. United States*, 449 U.S. 383, 395 (1981).

§ 17
E-mail Messages

17.1 Be direct—but not abrupt.

(a) *Pithiness.* Your goal in writing an e-mail should be to convey the necessary information as succinctly as possible. The longer your message, the less likely it is to be read and the more likely its details will be overlooked, lost among verbose clutter. Instead, keep it tight: tell your recipients only what they need to know—using no more words than necessary. (But don't tighten by omitting necessary *that*s and articles, such as *a* and *the*; doing so only impairs clarity.)

(b) *Directness.* Always state the purpose of your e-mail within the first few sentences. (But avoid such throat-clearing filler phrases as *I'm writing to inform you that . . .* and *I just wanted to ask . . . .*) Your e-mail is just one of many—possibly hundreds—that your recipients receive each day, so show respect for their time by being direct. If you waste a paragraph or more before getting to the point, readers will be prone to abandon your message for more concise correspondence.

(c) *Politeness.* It's possible to be too direct. Come to your point quickly, but not so quickly as to seem curt or brusque. Observe the pleasantries of professional correspondence, and consider opening with a brief compliment—particularly when making a request. On the whole, it's better to be understated here than overblown; attempts to ply your recipient with saccharine praise will be transparently insincere.

> Not this: Send me your comments.
>
> Not this: You're always so insightful and erudite that I am certain to be enlightened by any grains of wisdom you might be willing, despite your busy schedule, to scatter my way.
>
> But this: Please give me your thoughts, for which I'll be grateful.

(d) *Specifics.* Set out deadlines and other important details clearly. Be specific: provide only the information the recipient needs to act on your message—no more and no less. And place those details where they can't be missed—for instance, at the beginning of the second paragraph, immediately after stating your purpose. You might even state in the subject line that a response is needed at a particular time <Urgent: comments on draft motion needed by 4:00 p.m. today>. If a project involves multiple tasks or steps, consider using bullets or a numbered list. But never use all caps, which are abrasive and difficult to read, to get your reader's attention.

17.2 Choose your recipients carefully—on a need-to-know basis.

(a) *Addressing.* Use discretion when addressing your e-mails. Recipients to whom the mail is addressed—those named in its salutation—belong in the *To* line. Add any other recipients to the *Cc* (carbon copy) line. Be wary of overinclusion: copy only those who actually need the information and will immediately know why you've copied them.

(b) *Reply all.* Before clicking *Reply All*, first review the list of recipients and consider whether all of them actually need to see your response. It may be that the original sender copied more people than necessary; or that an e-mail was addressed to your whole department, but only the sender needs your response. By continuing to include all recipients in irrelevant conversations, you only increase their irritation and the surfeit in their inboxes.

(c) *Bcc.* The *Bcc* (blind carbon copy) feature, available in most e-mail programs, copies a given person on an e-mail without informing the other recipients. While this can occasionally be appropriate—for instance, when you need to inform someone in your office who is not a proper party to the conversation—use it sparingly. Though *Bcc* recipients are invisible to the others, people you blind-copy on one e-mail may wonder whom you're silently including in your correspondence with *them*. If you make this a habit, you may gain a reputation for indiscretion.

17.3 Make your subject lines specific and concise.

(a) *Specificity.* Your subject line should clearly state the subject or purpose of your e-mail. Be specific: generic—or worse, blank—subject lines are counterproductive. E-mails with such subjects will not catch the recipients' attention and will likely get buried in their inboxes. If a recipient needs to find the e-mail later, a generic subject line such as "Deposition" will force your colleague to dig through identically titled e-mails you've probably sent in the last year. An e-mail with a blank or irrelevant subject line will probably never be unearthed. To make it easier to find all correspondence related to a given case or client, consider including either the docket number or whatever designation your firm uses to identify the matter internally. Whatever you choose, use it consistently. Encourage your colleagues to do the same.

Not this: Here you go.
Not this: Deposition
But this: Transcript of Richard Wright deposition 7/29/13 (13-0521)

(b) *Conciseness.* Be concise with your subject lines. A full sentence around ten or fewer words is acceptable. But a short phrase is usually better if it clearly identifies your message's import. Your recipients should always be able to read your entire subject line in their inboxes so that they know the e-mail's topic without having to open it.

(c) *Updating.* If the topic of an e-mail chain switches abruptly, try to remember to change the subject line. Otherwise, a hopelessly dated subject line will be perpetuated well past its utility. Stay aware.

17.4 Adhere to normal writing conventions.

(a) *Professionalism.* Though it may seem easier and more efficient to abandon the conventions of formal prose when dashing off a quick reply or tapping out a message on a mobile device, the result is sure to appear rushed and sloppy. The recipient will likely think you careless at best, and may even question your professional judgment. A client may wonder whether you really gave the issue your full consideration. So always follow the standard rules of grammar, punctuation, and style in your e-mails—just as you would in a research memo or brief.

(b) *Clarity.* An abbreviated, highly colloquial style with lax punctuation or capitalization is likely to hinder the reader's comprehension. While such a style may be clear enough in spoken language, written prose relies on standard style elements to convey ideas clearly without the vocal and visual cues that aid speech.

(c) *Two caveats.* First, avoid relying on formatting elements such as italics and boldface to get your meaning across. Most e-mail services can handle these, but some receive only plain text, meaning that you cannot exactly know how your message will appear on your recipient's device. Second, be wary of the autocorrect and autocomplete functions on smartphones and other mobile devices. While these can save time when typing common words, they may incorrectly replace terms of art and other specialized words with more common alternatives spelled similarly—e.g., *refilled* for *refiled.* So always proofread your messages before sending, and don't expect your message to look the same on your recipient's screen as it does on yours.

17.5 Follow your messages with a simple, professional signature block.

(a) *Purpose.* Use your signature block to identify yourself and to give your recipients alternative means of contacting you should they need to. The block should begin with your name, title, and organization. Below these should be your relevant contact information: your e-mail address and phone number, at a minimum. Include a fax number or mailing address as well if recipients are likely to use these. A company website may also be appropriate, particularly if you work for a small firm or business. But as with the body of your message, include only the information that people will need. Your signature block should not outbalance your message.

(b) *Professional appearance.* Your signature block represents your professional identity in e-mails. It should be no longer than necessary. Use the same font, size, and color as the body text—no decorative or novelty fonts. These may be fine (if distracting) for personal e-mails, but business correspondence is not the place to highlight your unique personal charm. Likewise, leave out any clip art or other images, as well as favorite movie quotations, one-liners, and other unnecessary text. One exception is the name of your company or firm, which may prefer that you use a particular font and color—or even logo image—in your signature block. If so, add this after your name and contact information so that it doesn't interrupt the signature block. And remove any footers that your e-mail, antivirus, or other programs may add to your e-mails. Footers added by a mobile device are acceptable, however, because they can explain why your response may be briefer or less polished than it might otherwise be (but see 17.4). But consider using a generic wording <"Sent from a mobile device"> instead of a device-specific version such as "Sent from my iPhone," which may seem more like a status statement and obscure its real purpose.

Not this: *David Johnson*

David G. Johnson
BOARD-CERTIFIED PROBATE ATTORNEY

Johns Brensen LLC
3279 S. Nat'l Hwy
Hollywood, FL 33020
954.555.1759

View my biography **here**.
Read my blog **here**.
Find me on **Facebook**.
LinkedIn.
Favorite saying: "The world is not enough!"

But this: David G. Johnson
Board-Certified Probate Attorney | Johns Brensen LLC
3279 S. Nat'l Hwy | Hollywood, FL 33020
(954) 555-1759 | dgjohnson@johnsbrensen.net

(c) *Privilege notices.* There are two basic schools of thought on privilege notices attached to e-mails: One holds that they are little more than useless boilerplate language whose only effect is to bloat law-firm e-mails with their addition to each successive reply. In truth, this is probably right 99.9% of the time. But the other .1% is what matters: when it gives you an argument in court. So even though the notice may be irrelevant or unnecessary most of the time, it is safer to include the privilege notice on every e-mail. (Of course, the message itself needs to satisfy the elements of attorney–client privilege.) Your goal, then, should be to make the notice as succinct and unobtrusive as possible while retaining its efficacy.

Not this: ***** **PLEASE NOTE** *****

This e-mail/telefax message and any documents accompanying this transmission may contain privileged and/or confidential information and is intended solely for the addressee(s) named above. Should the intended recipient forward this e-mail/telefax to another person or party, that action could constitute a waiver of the attorney/client privilege. If you are not the intended addressee/recipient, you are hereby notified that any use of, disclosure, copying, distribution, or reliance on the contents of this e-mail/telefax information is strictly prohibited and may result in legal action against you. Please reply to the sender advising of the error in transmission and immediately delete/destroy the message and any accompanying documents. If you are not an existing client, do not construe anything in this e-mail/telefax to make you a client unless it contains a specific statement to that effect and do not disclose anything in reply that you expect to be held in confidence. Thank you.

But this: This e-mail may contain confidential or privileged information. If you believe you've received it in error, please notify the sender immediately and delete this message without copying or disclosing it. No waiver of privilege is intended by such an error.

17.6 Use an automatic out-of-office reply when you know you will be away from e-mail for a day or more.

(a) *Content.* If you plan to be out of the office and will be unable (or unwilling) to check your e-mail, prepare an automatic out-of-office reply so that correspondents know when they can expect a response. The message should plainly state when you left and when you will return. (If you're uncertain about your return, give a date when you know you will be back. And it is never a bad idea to provide a date that is a day or two after your actual return, building in some catch-up time before people begin demanding responses.) Also include an urgent-contact number, the contact information of your assistant or someone else who can get in touch with you, or the information of a colleague who has agreed to handle urgent matters in your absence. Mention whether you will have e-mail access while away. And use a simple subject line that gives readers the essential information at a glance <Re: Out of Office until 5/21/18>.

The message should be succinct and professional—double-check it for typos and other errors. As an automatic response, it will go out to anyone who sends you an e-mail, so you never know who might see it. And always remember to turn the auto-reply off when you return. An outdated out-of-office message will leave senders guessing whether you're actually still gone.

Ex.: I will be out of the office May 14–21 and will not have regular e-mail access while away. I will respond to your e-mail as soon as possible when I return. If you need help, please contact Colleen Beale at (210) 555-0291 or cbeale@franklinjohnson.com.

(b) *Unnecessary detail.* A common—sometimes unfortunate—tendency is to include too much information in an out-of-office message. Resist this urge: tell correspondents only what they need to know. For instance, leave out your travel plans unless they are somehow professionally relevant. Most correspondents don't need to know your itinerary. (Would you really want them to?) And those who do already should.

Many absences result from some misfortune—typically illness, death, or crisis. In these cases, undue specificity may leave correspondents—especially those who don't know you well—uneasy, wondering whether the appropriate response is to express sympathy or respect your privacy. Medical details in particular may make some recipients uncomfortable. Instead, use generic phrases such as *a death in the family*, *a family matter*, *illness*, or *medical leave*, which will adequately explain your absence while avoiding such pitfalls.

(c) *Receipt confirmation.* Some lawyers use this auto-reply feature all the time as an automatic receipt confirmation, thanking senders for their message and telling them that it will be returned within a given time frame. This is unnecessary: senders should expect a reasonable delay for nonurgent e-mails, and you should give timely responses as a matter of course. The autoreply serves only to clog inboxes. It is especially burdensome in ongoing conversations, when your correspondent's every reply is answered by the same meaningless message. By the same token, request read receipts from your addressees only when necessary—e.g., for urgent information requiring immediate action. Otherwise, you risk annoying your recipients and filling your inbox with useless confirmation messages.

17.7 When reporting research in an e-mail message—in lieu of a research memo—be sure to state both the question and the answer clearly.

(a) *E-mails as surrogate memos.* In the rushed exigency of modern law practice, with the expectation of nearly immediate responses to all manner of queries, e-mails are overtaking formal memos as the standard method for communicating your research both to senior colleagues and to clients. Before hitting *Send*, you should step back and ask yourself just how clear you're being. Avoid answering in a way that begets follow-up queries. You might be well advised to make your summary at least as clear as it would be in a formal memo. For that matter, perhaps you should review all of § 16 to become more adept at reporting your research in any format. But especially for e-mails, see the examples under (c) and (d) below.

(b) *Undue succinctness.* Say that a question is posed to you. The temptation is to answer it "directly," given all that has been said here about directness as a virtue. The problem with reporting research in reply is that piecing together the question and answer becomes a matter of reading an entire e-mail chain. Further, you may be tempted to answer lazily and superficially if you're simply hitting *Reply* and reporting your findings without restating the question.

(c) *An illustration.* You've been working with a senior colleague on behalf of a bar owner who has been sued under Connecticut's dram-shop act. A patron who had consumed liquor at the bar drove while intoxicated and was injured. Your senior colleague writes you an e-mail:

> Re: **Meaning of "Sale" Under the Act**
>
> Please look into whether a "sale" actually took place on the evening of May 19.

The easy thing, after you've concluded your research, is to reply laconically:

> Re: **Meaning of "Sale" Under the Act**
>
> Almost certainly. Although McKnight may not have given the drinks directly to the inebriated person, the sale is imputed because he sold to a member of the party. Conn. Gen. Stat. Ann. § 30–102 (West 2011).

Note that the e-mails themselves (devoid of the background) are not illuminating. One may legitimately wonder just how sound the analysis is and, for that matter, just how well you've understood the question.

By contrast, look what happens when you take the time to lay out the problem so clearly that anyone could follow:

> Re: **Meaning of "Sale" Under the Dram Shop Act**
>
> Question
>
> The Connecticut Dram Shop Act requires a "sale" from bartender to patron. Our client, Jeff Burton, is the owner of a one-room bar; he sold rounds of beer to a group of eight, one of whom four witnesses have said was visibly intoxicated. Did the rounds of beer constitute a "sale" to all eight guests?
>
> Answer
>
> Almost certainly. Connecticut courts have interpreted "sale" in this context to mean "the purveying or furnishing of alcohol" to a person or group, any one of whom is visibly intoxicated. Specifically, the Connecticut Supreme Court held last year that circumstantial evidence alone can be enough to prove a sale—on facts much more tenuous than we have here. On the facts as we understand them, a sale occurred.
>
> Attached are the three most relevant cases. I'll be happy to write a more formal memo if you like.

> "To find out someone's meaning you must . . . know what the question was (a question in his own mind, and presumed by him to be in yours) to which thing what he has said or written was meant as an answer."
>
> —*R.G. Collingwood*

(d) *Another illustration.* Sometimes the cryptic nature of an e-mail exchange results from unstated premises that the correspondents have exchanged conversationally. In other words, the e-mail messages are mystifying to an outsider—and may well mystify even the correspondents after a short time has passed. Once again, a senior colleague asks you to look into a point that you've already spoken about briefly:

> Re: **Impact of Refiling**
>
> Please let me know how the timing of the refiling of the amended complaint against the Horchows affects our ability to serve valid proposals. Research this.

You answer laconically:

> Re: **Impact of Refiling**
>
> A new proposal can be served 90 days after the newly refiled complaint. Fla. R. Civ. P. 1442.
>
> Anything else?

Again, your senior colleague might well question the accuracy of your response—even whether there has been a meeting of the minds about the problem. The blame lies partly with the elliptically phrased assignment and partly with the equally elliptical reply.

Notice what an improvement it makes if you spell out the problem more fully—again, so that anyone can understand your answer.

> Re: **Impact of Refiling**
>
> George, here are my findings:
>
> Question
>
> The Horchows, who had previously filed and dismissed a state lawsuit against our client Allied Mutual, have now filed an "amended complaint" naming Allied Mutual as a defendant. Does the amended complaint commence a new lawsuit, restarting the 90-day clock for the service of a proposal for settlement?
>
> Answer
>
> Yes. Under Florida law, a complaint refiled after a voluntary dismissal commences a new lawsuit, even if that pleading includes the descriptor "amended" in the title. The dismissal ended the earlier lawsuit. A new lawsuit begins upon the filing of either a new complaint or an amended one. Under Florida Civil Rule 1442, the 90-day rule on timing for valid proposals for settlement is also restarted.

This type of concrete explicitness is highly desirable because it earns more credibility, shows a greater command of the material, and confers on the writing something approaching universal comprehensibility.

§ 18
Business Correspondence

18.1 Understand the main goals of business correspondence.

(a) *Communicating effectively.* Correspondence is all about communicating. And effective communication takes attention to detail. To connect with your reader, you must pay attention to the nature of your business relationship. Ideally, you should know something about your reader personally. Effective business correspondence reads like simple, direct talk—not a page laden with legalisms and commercialese. It is always concise because time really is money. It is straight to the point, immediately stating the nature of the business and staying focused on that purpose. And it had better not be vague, lest you convey a message you did not intend to convey.

(b) *Making an impression.* You'll be judged by the content, style, and appearance of your correspondence, especially by people who haven't yet met you face to face. A handsome letter or a polite e-mail is a nice introduction, as is an opening that acknowledges the reader with a *you*-statement ("Thank *you* for" or "*You* might enjoy") instead of one acknowledging yourself ("*I* wanted to thank you for" or "*I* thought you might enjoy"). Although your letter is unlikely to win the adoration of a stranger, it can easily lower that person's opinion of you. And those who do know you, especially your clients and colleagues, expect your correspondence to meet a certain level of competence. In business, nothing is more important than your reputation. Every letter you send is a commentary on you—your degree of professionalism and care, and perhaps also your knowledge, taste, discernment, discretion, and tact.

(c) *Providing a record.* Business correspondence often finds renewed importance months or even years after it has been exchanged. When disputes arise, lawyers often consult past correspondence to determine what actions were taken and what agreements or understandings were made among clients, counsel, and third parties. Sometimes these writings can be simple reminders of a forgotten agreement or valuable evidence in a motion to compel. Regardless, every piece of correspondence must clearly identify the subject and, if it is a response to another party, the correspondence it refers to. This makes it easier for all parties to file and retrieve messages.

> "Let not your letters be penned like English statutes."
> —*Ben Jonson*

In addition to any of these identification tags, however, the correspondence must contain enough context to be clear about what subject it's addressing. Remember that your business correspondence may later be read by a larger, more critical audience.

18.2 Think about the specific goals of your correspondence.

(a) *Being reader-friendly.* Good business correspondence is always reader-friendly, with every aspect designed to make your reader's job easy. The format, content, and language should all strive for clarity. A letter or memo should be arranged in a standard format and appear organized at first glance. If you're responding to a letter, mention who sent it and when, either in the subject line or in the first sentence. Get right to the point with your first words so that your reader doesn't have to work to find it. Write as plainly and clearly as if you were talking with your reader.

(b) *Projecting your personality.* The tone of your business correspondence often creates the most lasting impression on your reader. Make yours friendly and helpful. Keep your letters as short as possible, and your sentences and paragraphs concise. Strive for a conversational tone that's courteous and to the point but that also reveals your personality. If a letter is too abrupt, you'll seem gruff; if it's too colloquial, you'll sacrifice professionalism. Let your style be relaxed, not wooden.

(c) *Exuding professionalism.* Strive for professionalism in every aspect of your business correspondence. Stick to standard formats, respond quickly and completely to incoming correspondence, and always keep your reader's needs in mind. If you're addressing a problem, do it tactfully. Proofread your letter so that there are no grammatical or formatting mistakes. And take just as much care with e-mails: avoid the tendency to be less formal in electronic correspondence.

18.3 Avoid the common faults of business correspondence.

(a) *Lacking focus.* Don't let your recipient's attention stray from your main point. State the gist of your business quickly. The worst thing you can do is to spend a few paragraphs explaining the background of your request and then spring the main point at the end of a paragraph tucked somewhere in the middle or end of the letter. The harder your purpose is to find, the less chance you stand to get the results you want.

(b) *Making multiple requests.* Keeping the reader focused becomes complicated when you make multiple requests in a single letter. That's why it's best to limit each letter to one instruction or request. When that's simply not possible, give your reader a list of everything you're asking for in the first paragraph, perhaps in a bulleted list. Bullets work well because they make each item stand out, and the reader can use the list to make sure that everything you've asked for has been addressed. After that introductory summary, you might continue by explaining each request in more detail, as needed.

(c) *Using inappropriate style.* Keep your letters as short as possible. Work hard to say whatever you need to say in one page. For clarity, keep your sentences and paragraphs short. Shun the commercialese that plagues business correspondence, such as starting with *Enclosed please find* . . . . (Instead, write *Here are* or the like.) Use legal terms when necessary, but *only* when necessary. Avoid all jargon. Never use bloated words or phrases when simple ones would suffice. You don't want your tone to become stilted. On the other hand, keep it businesslike: don't be breezy or slangy.

(d) *Blundering.* As in any writing, mistakes in grammar and usage in a letter reflect badly on the writer. They undercut how the reader evaluates the writer's competence and credibility. Errors in form suggest a sloppy writer and therefore a sloppy thinker. Pay particular attention to careful usage: meanings must be clear and precise (see § 13). Avoid words that are commonly misused (such as *comprise*) because whether they are used correctly or not, they're likely to distract some readers.

(e) *Hiding information.* When setting out a series of items, don't string them together in the text. Break them out into a list. This creates a graphical element that stands out.

(f) *Omitting information.* Make sure that every piece of correspondence contains all the information the reader needs. When responding to correspondence that asks several questions, be sure to reply to all of them. Of course, use some discretion—your reader doesn't always need to know every last detail. But give all the information that's immediately relevant and necessary.

> "Some business letters are sadly down at heel. Some seem to say things that do not need saying, in a way that shows the writer to have no interest in saying them. Others look all right on the outside, being carefully typed on good paper and with the proper margins, but they are as indigestible as a gaudily iced cake filled with concrete."
>
> —*Royal Bank of Canada*

18.4 Use a standard format for business letters.

(a) *Modified-block style.* Most law offices and businesses use the modified-block format with indented paragraphs. The date, the complimentary close, the signature, and the writer's identification all begin about the middle of the page. The other elements of a letter start at the left margin. Indent paragraphs and separate them by an extra line space.

(b) *Date.* The standard American format is month–day–year, as in December 31, 2018. Europeans and the U.S. military use the day–month–year format, as in 31 December 2018. The latter flows more logically and saves a comma, but you risk being perceived as a Europhile. Firms also generally have a standard style; if so, always use that.

(c) *Margins and type.* Set your margins to 1.2 inches on all documents and use at least 13-point type. The extra margin space helps prevent text from getting lost on photocopies, and the slightly larger type is vastly more legible. Type should be set flush left, not right-justified.

(d) *Titles.* If you're writing to a person with an M.D., a J.D., or another professional degree, or to someone in public office like a senator or judge, include the appropriate title in the inside address. If the recipient is a professor, you might use *Prof.* For lawyers, the American practice of appending *Esq.* to others' names is entirely acceptable, but no other titles may be used in conjunction (*Mr. John Doe, Esq.* is unacceptable). If you prefer not to use *Esq.* (some consider it pretentious), a mere *Mr.* or *Ms.* will suffice. For judges, put *The Honorable* before the full name, and specify the court or office on the next line. (**Hon. Reavley* is a solecism for *Hon. Thomas M. Reavley.*) British lawyers often have titles or affiliations that should be included after their names, such as *Q.C.* (Queen's Counsel) and *F.B.A.* (Fellow of the British Academy). Some other countries, such as Germany, refer to their lawyers as doctors, so be sure to determine the local custom.

(e) *Subject line.* You might include a subject line to state precisely the subject of your letter. If you do, position it two lines below the introductory address and center-align it. Both *Subject:* and *Re:* are appropriate captions in the subject line. Some writers prefer *Subject:* because it's plain English, while others prefer *Re:* because it's shorter and is universally understood.

(f) *Appropriate salutation.* The traditional *Dear Mr. Jackson* or *Dear Ms. Burke* is still standard. Even if you know that a woman is married, stick to *Ms.* unless you're certain she prefers *Mrs.* If you don't know the gender of the recipient, use *Dear Sir or Madam* or, more plainly, *Dear Friend* (or *Friends*). For recipients under 18, *Miss* is appropriate for young women and *Mr.* is appropriate for young men (*Master* is also acceptable but rarely used). A salutation in a business letter is always followed by a colon, not a comma. A semicolon after a salutation is always wrong. Under appropriate

*An invariably inferior form.

circumstances, you may use the recipient's first name in the salutation (e.g., *Dear Sarah:*). If you do that, sign only your first name (although the signature block will have your full name).

(g) *The corporate and legal "we."* Use the pronoun *we* when speaking on behalf of your company or firm in correspondence or when referring to it in the text. Resist the temptation to repeat the name of your company or firm every time you make reference to it. *We* is usually a perfectly clear substitute in correspondence as well as in memos.

(h) *Complimentary closes.* Depending on how formal the letter is, there are many standard closes to choose from. For very formal letters, *Respectfully (yours)* and *Very respectfully (yours)* are options. For less formal letters, *Very truly yours*, *Yours very truly*, and *Yours truly* are all acceptable. For general use, *Sincerely (yours)* and *Yours sincerely* do nicely. For informal letters, *With best wishes*, *Best wishes*, *With best regards*, *Best regards*, and *Kindest personal regards* are just a few possibilities.

(i) *Modifying your identification as appropriate.* If you're using company stationery, don't repeat the information given there as an element of your letter. You may identify your position (e.g., *Deputy General Counsel*) or your role in the relevant proceedings (e.g., *Counsel for the Defendant*). But if the letterhead is personalized with your name and title, don't repeat that identification below your signature.

(j) *Copies.* When sending multiple copies of the same letter to separate people, identify the list by using *Copies:* or *cc:*. The former is better because it is plain English, but the second is short. *Cc:* was formerly disfavored as an antiquated convention, but because of e-mail, its meaning (though not what the abbreviation stands for, *carbon copy*) is universally recognized. Position the list of copy recipients two lines below the signature block, and make it left-aligned.

18.5 Study effective business correspondence.

(a) *Further guidance.*

- L. Sue Baugh, *How to Write First-Class Letters* (1998).
- Dianna Booher, *To the Letter: A Handbook of Model Letters for the Busy Executive* (1988).
- Helen Cunningham & Brenda Greene, *The Business Style Handbook* (2d ed. 2012).

- L.E. Frailey, *Handbook of Business Letters* (3d ed. 1998).
- Bryan A. Garner, *HBR Guide to Better Business Writing* (2012).
- Andrea B. Geffner, *Business Letters the Easy Way* (2d ed. 1991)
- Bernard Heller, *The 100 Most Difficult Business Letters You'll Ever Have to Write, Fax, or E-Mail* (1994).
- *Merriam-Webster's Guide to Business Correspondence* (2d ed. 1996).
- Prentice-Hall Editorial Staff, *Director's and Officer's Complete Letter Book* (3d ed. 1991).
- Robert L. Shurter & Donald J. Leonard, *Effective Letters in Business* (3d ed. 1984).

(b) *Examples.* Everything about the two examples that follow is true to form but the margins, which are smaller here only because of the page design of this book. Remember to use 1.2-inch margins.

> "Style, in its finest sense, is the last acquirement of the educated mind; it is also the most useful. It pervades the whole being. Style is the ultimate morality of mind."
>
> —*Alfred North Whitehead*

Randall A. Langen
Attorney at Law
Fortescue Plaza, 5949 Pensacola Lane
Suite 888
Dallas, Texas 75201
Telephone (214) 212-8888
Fax (214) 212-7777

27 July 2018

Ms. Melanie Wanamaker
Clerk, Fifth District Court of Appeals
Second Floor, Dallas County Courthouse
600 Commerce St.
Dallas, TX 75202-4658

One blank line.

Re: ***Firth v. State Insurance***, No. 06-92-00291-CV

Dear Ms. Wanamaker:

Enclosed for filing are seven originals of the brief of Paula Firth, an appellee in this case. Please return three file-stamped copies with our courier.

Many thanks.

Sincerely yours,

No typed name because it appears in the letterhead.

Copies: Michael W. Higgleson, Esq.
Bruce Walters, Esq.
Joseph Paderewsky, Esq.

Blind copy: Ms. Paula Firth

Bilston & Boyd

Attorneys at Law

Sac and Fox Plaza, 311 Appalachia Lane
St. Cloud, MN 56301

Telephone (320) 992-8788
Fax (320) 992-9797

May 11, 2018

One blank line.

Commissioner Ramey N. Boxer
Overnight Delivery
National Indian Gaming Commission
1441 L Street NW, 9th Floor
Washington, DC 20005

Re: Amended and Restated Gaming Ordinance for the Erawan Tribe of South Dakota

Dear Commissioner Boxer:

We represent the Erawan Tribe of South Dakota. As you know, on March 13, 2018, the Tribe submitted its amended and restated gaming ordinance for the Commission's review and approval. Because the Tribe decided yesterday to reconsider the ordinance over the next six months, I hasten to withdraw the March 13 request. Please treat it as null. We will resubmit in due course. Thank you.

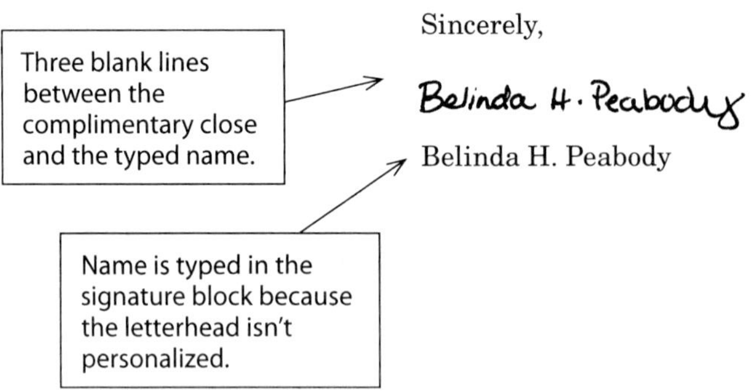

Sincerely,
Belinda H. Peabody
Belinda H. Peabody
Three blank lines between the complimentary close and the typed name.
Name is typed in the signature block because the letterhead isn't personalized.

§ 19
Letters Relating to Engagement*

19.1 Document your communications with a client or prospective client to eliminate misunderstandings.

(a) *The lawyer–client relationship.* When someone seeks legal advice or services from a lawyer, a lawyer–client relationship may form intentionally or accidentally. When a lawyer plainly shows consent to represent the person, it's intentional. But what if the lawyer merely fails to show a *lack* of consent and knows (or reasonably should know) that the person is relying on him or her to provide legal services? A lawyer–client relationship may still form, even without the lawyer's explicit consent.

(b) *Importance of documentation.* A formal letter documents the relationship with a client or prospective client and, if done properly, leaves little room for misunderstandings. By clearly stating what the relationship is and what it entails, that the relationship has been established or has ended, or that no relationship has yet formed at all, you minimize your chances of discipline for an ethical breach and litigation. An engagement or nonengagement letter is the clearest way to expressly form—or avoid forming—a lawyer–client relationship. And a disengagement letter is the clearest way to end one.

19.2 Send an engagement letter when you agree to represent a client, and ask for the client's express consent.

(a) *Purposes of an engagement letter.* Forming the lawyer–client relationship depends on the client's consent, which is typically documented by the client's signature on an engagement letter. When you decide to represent a client, you need to explain the representation clearly and document the client's consent as well as your own. The engagement letter defines and sets out what services the client should expect from you, what you expect from the client, the scope of your representation, fee arrangements, and other specifics particular to the situation. Talk to the client before sending the letter and invite the client to ask questions before signing. Explicitly asking for the client's consent also shows your belief that the client hasn't yet placed any reliance on you as a lawyer.

(b) *Contents.* Because this letter is a contract or part of a contract's terms, the contents need to be carefully drafted to ensure that all the necessary elements are included. The letter should call for the client's signature,

---

*Randall M. Tietjen of Minneapolis made major contributions to this chapter.

which is required in some circumstances (e.g., when the fee is contingent). Generally, a long-form engagement letter should include the following information:

- the identity of your client or clients (when necessary to avoid misunderstanding, also identify who is not your client);
- the identities of the adverse parties and related parties;
- the engagement's beginning date;
- the scope of the engagement, with any appropriate but reasonable limitations described in detail, including the point at which the engagement is expected to end;
- the goals for the representation;
- a detailed description of your responsibilities and authority, as well as the client's;
- proposed staffing, including your and the client's agents;
- if you have more than one client in the same matter or related matters, a description of the effects of the multiple representation on confidentiality and privilege and potentially on settlement;
- the client's consent to waive any potential conflicts associated with the engagement;
- the acceptance and effect of any outside-counsel guidelines or policies that would govern the lawyer–client relationship;
- preferred and alternative means of communication, and the associated risks;
- the fee and expense agreement and billing schedule;
- if the fee is contingent on the outcome, the method by which the fee will be calculated and a description of any division of the fee with another law firm;
- the client's immediate obligation to preserve any related documents or other potential evidence if litigation is at least anticipated;
- the client's right to terminate the representation any time, with or without reason, although remaining obligated to bring accounts current;
- grounds for your withdrawal from representation;
- methods for resolving disputes between you and the client; and
- your policy on file retention.

19.3 Be aware of the common mistakes in preparing an engagement letter. Although you and your client can mutually agree to amend the terms of engagement if circumstances change, you must know as much as possible before preparing the engagement letter.

(a) *Failing to talk with the client.* In most instances, a letter should be the culmination of the lawyer's communications with a prospective client about engagement terms—not the beginning and end of all communications on the subject. One of a lawyer's goals should be to ensure that the client understands the letter's terms, and this often requires a conversation and an opportunity for questions by the lawyer and the client. If some aspect of the engagement requires the client's "informed consent confirmed in writing"—which is often how the rules of professional conduct phrase the form of agreement required—the need for a conversation is implied in the word *confirmed.*

(b) *Inadequately identifying the client's goals.* If the engagement letter doesn't state what the client wants to achieve, the lawyer may later become aware of related issues that will require more work than originally agreed to or that the lawyer wasn't retained to work on. Is the object to renegotiate a lease? Does the client want an injunction against the defendant? Is the purpose of the engagement to defend against the claim of infringement? Discuss the client's goals as thoroughly as possible before taking on additional responsibilities.

(c) *Failing to identify the client.* When you are engaged by multiple parties, by an organization, or by an individual who is closely involved with or related to other persons who may have an interest in the matter, clearly state in the engagement letter precisely who you represent—and who you do *not* represent. Nonlawyers likely won't understand, for example, that (1) if you represent a corporation, you don't necessarily represent individual board members or employees; (2) if you represent a corporate board's special-litigation committee, you can't represent the board as a whole, much less the corporation; (3) if you represent a closely held corporation, you don't necessarily represent any of the individual owners; (4) if you represent one spouse, you might not represent the other spouse; and (5) if you represent a child, you might not represent the parents. It's easy for a closely related or involved person to think that you also represent that person, so you must carefully avoid using any ambiguous language suggesting that you do.

(d) *Inadequately identifying the scope of the engagement.* Along with identifying the client's goals in an engagement letter should go a description of the extent of your expected involvement in trying to achieve those goals. If the matter involves litigation, for example, will you be representing the client in court as well as in any related administrative proceedings? Will you represent the client in an appeal, or only in the trial court? Questions of the scope of representation are always important for a client to understand. A well-defined scope can become especially important in matters involving flat or alternative fees or contingent fees because it can affect your expected profitability.

19.4 Send a nonengagement letter when you decide not to represent a client—to remove any contrary impression. Because the formation of the lawyer–client relationship depends on the *client's* perception of your consent to representation, a nonengagement letter is an important tool to refuse representation unequivocally.

(a) *Purposes of a nonengagement letter.* The chief goal is to make it clear that you have not agreed to represent this person and are not acting as the person's lawyer. It's necessary in at least three common circumstances. The most common is after a consultation with a potential client, when the decision is made to refuse representation. A second occurs when a client doesn't respond to your requests to return a signed engagement letter or pay the initial retainer; presumably, the client doesn't want to employ you. By sending a nonengagement letter, you will make it clear that you are not representing the person because the written contract (engagement letter) is not in effect. The third occurs when an existing or former client in a separate legal matter might be misled to believe that your representation extends beyond the scope of the original engagement letter.

(b) *Contents.* A nonengagement letter will typically be fairly short—it must be straightforward and plainly state that you are not representing the person. You don't need to give a reason for declining representation, but if the reason is that you haven't received the client's signed engagement letter or retainer or advance, you may include a friendly reminder to the client that you can't act on the legal matter until the client signs the engagement letter or pays the retainer or advance. This way, you don't give the impression that you aren't interested in representing the client if the client wants to use your services. Always send the letter by a means that includes proof of delivery, such as an overnight-courier confirmation, certified mail with a return receipt requested, or an e-mail service that provides acknowledgment of receipt. Generally, the letter should include:

- a clear statement that you haven't been engaged by and don't represent the person in the matter discussed;
- a clear statement that you haven't assessed the merits of the case and aren't making any comment on them;
- optionally, the reason why you can't represent the person (e.g., the need for a signed engagement letter, or the subject matter's being

outside your area of practice)—but never a reason based on the case's merits;

- a reminder that a deadline, such as a statute of limitations, may affect the person's case (but don't give advice about it);
- a recommendation that the person consult with other lawyers (optionally including a referral to another lawyer or to the appropriate state bar association or other body that offers lawyer-referral services);
- as enclosures, the originals of all documents belonging to the client;
- a statement that you haven't kept any copies of the client's documents except for a copy of the nonengagement letter; and
- a statement that all confidences remain private.

(c) *No legal advice.* In a nonengagement letter, don't give any kind of legal advice—not even on the date a statute of limitations might expire. If the letter's recipient relies on that advice, a lawyer–client relationship has formed. You're responsible for the quality of that advice and subject to discipline if it turns out to be incorrect. Choose your words with care to distinguish between information (which you may freely give) and legal advice (which you must not).

19.5 Send a disengagement letter when your representation of the client ends.

(a) *Purposes of a disengagement letter.* A disengagement letter, also called a *closing letter* or *end-of-engagement letter*, is primarily a risk-management tool. Even when it seems intuitive that the lawyer–client relationship is over, the client may believe that the representation is continuing. A disengagement letter can legally end the lawyer–client relationship. And if done properly, it can help you avoid conflicts or other risks that may arise from misunderstandings about the continuation of the relationship.

A disengagement letter should always be sent when you have finished providing the agreed-on services for a specific matter. But you should also send the letter anytime you've determined—before the client's matter is completed—that you should or must withdraw from the representation. This withdrawal decision could follow from a variety of circumstances, including when you close your practice or join another law firm. The disengagement letter should assure the client that the matter is concluded or—if unfinished and if possible—that you will protect the client's interests while new counsel is engaged and work to minimize any disruption.

(b) *Contents.* You need to clearly inform your client that your representation is at an end. If your representation is ending while the client's matter is still active, you may want to offer to help the client find other counsel, if necessary, and promise to make reasonable efforts to protect the client's interests and smoothly transfer responsibility to new counsel. A disengagement letter should generally state:

- the subject matter of the representation;
- the termination of your representation of the client;
- the reason for ending (e.g., the case has ended or you must for some reason withdraw from representation);
- the implications of disengaging;
- the date when the lawyer–client relationship ended;
- if the matter has not been concluded, what work remains unfinished and what time limits exist or deadlines are in the future;
- if you are transferring your responsibilities to another lawyer, when your duties to the client end; and
- your policy on file retention.

(c) *Give the client critical help.* In a disengagement letter, you must give the client all pertinent information and explain what duties you still have before your representation is over. If ending the representation will have an effect on the client's matter—especially if you withdraw before the matter is concluded—tell the client what steps you will take to avoid a problem, such as taking reasonable steps to extend or comply with an imminent deadline, or continuing to represent the client until he or she can engage new counsel. Legally, you may not be permitted to end your representation until those steps are taken. If the matter is in litigation and there is no substituting lawyer, the steps required might include obtaining the court's permission before you terminate the relationship.

19.6 Study effective letters relating to the lawyer–client relationship.

(a) *Further guidance.* The requirements or recommended contents and layouts for engagement, nonengagement, and disengagement letters vary by jurisdiction. Check your local rules and state-bar publications for the specifics and additional samples that comply with those rules.

(b) *Examples.* The first two examples are engagement letters, one with additional terms of representation attached. The third example is a nonengagement letter. The fourth example is a disengagement letter.

A word of caution is in order. Requirements for engagement letters vary from jurisdiction to jurisdiction: do your homework before adapting to your own purposes any of the forms that follow.

Sample Engagement Letter #1

Havermeyer & Goshen
223 Normandy Blvd., Suite 1515
Orlando, Florida 32801
(321) 407-4545

December 1, 2018

Mr. William Gregson
3700 Melba Grove Ave.
Salsa, Florida 32832

Re: Claim of Food Poisoning on Exploring Fjords Cruise

Dear Mr. Gregson:

Thank you for your interest in engaging our firm to represent you individually in this matter. The terms of representation are set forth below.

1. Client

You are our client for purposes of this representation. We will not represent any of your family members or friends without a signed conflict-of-interest waiver from each party. We cannot communicate through any third parties without your express consent. You understand that if you ask us to speak with someone other than those listed, or if you reveal our discussions with you to a third party, the communication may waive attorney–client privilege and be discoverable by the opposing party.

2. Scope of representation

We agree that the scope of work to be performed is to represent you in connection with Exploring Fjords Cruise's food-poisoning issue. Unless we agree otherwise, the representation will be limited to this matter. The terms of this agreement will apply only to extensions of the scope of representation on which we both agree. This agreement concerns only legal services rendered and costs and expenses for the matter expressly stated in this agreement. It does not concern any other matter for which you may seek representation.

3. Fees

Because this is a pro bono case, we agree to waive our normal fees.

4. Costs

As this is a pro bono case, we will cover all reasonable expenses necessary to resolve this matter before the complaint is filed. You will be responsible for any fees and expenses related to taking this case to trial, beginning with filing the Complaint. Examples of these costs are filing fees for court papers, online research, court-reporter's fees, transcripts, delivering court papers to the opposing party, copying charges, long-distance telephone charges, and postage.

5. Invoices due and payable upon receipt

Each month you will receive via e-mail an invoice from the firm. (We may send the invoice on a bimonthly or quarterly basis at our discretion.) The invoice will state the costs that you must cover as described in paragraph 4: for work performed and any out-of-pocket costs. Our invoices are due and payable upon receipt. We will be unable to perform work on your matter if your account is delinquent.

6. Interest on unpaid balances; referral to collections

Any statement that is not paid within 30 days of its date is considered past due. We reserve the right to charge interest on past-due billings at the rate of 1.4% per month compounded (18% per annum) until paid. You understand that this debt may be referred to collections and you agree to pay for the reasonable costs and attorneys' fees associated with any collection efforts. If we perform the collection work ourselves, then our fee rate would be $125 per hour.

7. Billing disputes and choice of forum

If you have any questions regarding a bill, please call me to discuss the matter. If you dispute the amount stated as due under any billing statement that we issue to you, then please notify us in writing about your disagreement within 30 days of the billing statement's date. If we do not receive a timely written communication about the amount billed, we assume that you have agreed to the amount of the statement and that you will pay that amount within 30 days of the statement's date. You agree that any disputes regarding billing will be decided in courts located in Orange County, Florida.

8. Termination of agreement

Both you and the firm are otherwise free to terminate the engagement at any time for any reason by written notice, subject on our part to the relevant rules of professional conduct. If court permission for withdrawal is required, we will promptly apply for permission and you agree to engage successor counsel to represent you. If we terminate the engagement, we will take steps as reasonably practicable to protect your interests and cooperate as necessary with any successor counsel.

9. Files and electronic records

We retain many file documents in electronic format only. Accordingly, unless you instruct us that you prefer to receive only a paper copy in the mail, or that you would like to receive both an electronic and paper copy, we will send you each document that is relevant to your case by e-mail as a scanned document in PDF format.

You are responsible for providing us with a secure e-mail address that you want us to use for correspondence related to the representation. You should check that e-mail address regularly. We will assume that third parties do not have access to that e-mail address and, therefore, that you can receive confidential correspondence from us at that address. We will also assume that you are receiving and reviewing our e-mails at that address unless you alert us to an issue. Please be certain that your e-mail filters do not block e-mails from our office and that the allowable size of incoming e-mails is sufficient to accept e-mails from us with attachments.

During the course of the representation, we will provide you with copies of correspondence, research, and pleadings that we receive or generate on your behalf (other than our own notes). At the representation's conclusion, we will return any original documents that you send to us. Please keep copies of all e-mails sent to or received from us; these are your file. You are responsible for maintaining your own copy of your file. The firm will assume that you have a complete copy of your file and we will retain our copy of your file for at least five years, at which time it may be destroyed without further notice under our document-retention policy.

10. No promises or guarantees

In any legal matter there is a possibility of a disappointing outcome despite the attorneys' best efforts. You understand that the outcome of negotiations and litigation is subject to many factors that cannot always be foreseen. You understand that we have not made any promises or guarantees (written or verbal) to you concerning the outcome of this representation and cannot do so. Nothing in this agreement can be construed as a promise or guarantee of the outcome.

11. Consent to resolution

No resolution of your matter may be made without your consent.

12. Communications

You acknowledge that we can achieve the best results in this matter if you provide us with full and complete information about this case. Your signature on this fee agreement attests that the information you give us will be truthful and accurate to the best of your knowledge. If there are any changes in material information or contact information, you must promptly notify us.

13. Client responsibilities

Your role and responsibility as the client are crucial. You agree to be accessible and to timely respond to requests. Most importantly, we need you to give us any and all requested information fully and promptly. Your timely giving us all documents and information enables us to fully prepare your case. You agree to notify us of any changes in material facts, and to keep us informed about your contact information, including your address, telephone numbers (work, home, and cell), e-mail, and emergency contact.

14. Communication policies

You understand that you should not use work e-mail addresses, work computers, or public computers (such as those at a public library or hotel) to communicate with us. This policy is intended to protect the confidentiality of our discussions. Please also tell us if we should not communicate with you by e-mail or even regular mail because of a risk that those communications might be intercepted. We will not waive the attorney–client privilege without your written consent.

15. Responsible attorneys

I will be the primary attorney responsible for representing you in this matter. I also may use other attorneys, paralegals, litigation/clerical assistants, and law clerks as appropriate. I will be your primary contact.

16. No tax advice

You understand that you will need to seek separate tax counsel, accounting assistance, and advice for any recovery. We will not provide you with any tax advice.

17. Notice requirement before filing for bankruptcy

You agree that you will give us 14 day's advance written notice before filing for bankruptcy protection.

18. Electronic signature

We agree that my electronic signature below is a valid substitute for my hand signature. Thank you for giving us the opportunity to try to help you with this difficult situation. If you are in agreement, please sign and return this letter to me. The hallmark of our practice is strong and consistent communication with, and responsiveness to, our clients. Please feel free to contact me with your questions, concerns, and any information you feel would be valuable to this matter.

If you agree, please return this signed letter.

Very truly yours,

Irene Goshen

AGREED:

____

Date:

____

Sample Engagement Letter #2 (terms attached)

EAKINS–CALDER LLP
1623 Wilshire Boulevard
Suite 1420
Los Angeles, CA 90017
213-555-1212

14 July 2018

Mr. James Butler
874 East Tappan Rd.
Fresno, CA 93704

Dear Mr. Butler:

We welcome you as a client of Eakins–Calder. For convenience, I'll refer to you as "you" and "your" in this letter, and our firm as "we," "us," and "our."

We have agreed to represent you in your personal-injury case against Lassiter Manufacturing, Inc. and its employee, Nathaniel Post. You were injured by Mr. Post while he was driving a truck for his employer and failed to stop at a red light before making a right turn at the intersection of Division Boulevard and Channel Way in Tucson, Arizona. He struck you as you were crossing the street. We will initiate contact with Lassiter Manufacturing, Mr. Post, and all the applicable insurance companies; follow your medical treatment and progress; and attempt to settle your claim in an amount sufficient to cover your medical bills, lost wages, and pain and suffering. If we cannot reach a satisfactory settlement, we will file suit against the appropriate parties.

We will keep you informed about the progress of our representation in this matter and any legal processes it involves. We welcome your questions about it and will timely respond to each question. You will cooperate in our efforts by giving us complete and accurate information about the matter, keeping us informed of relevant developments, and cooperating with us in planning how to proceed at each stage of the matter.

This engagement letter, together with the enclosed Terms of Representation, is a contract between you and us, so it's important that you read and understand this letter and the Terms, and that you keep a copy of the contract in your files. If any related matters arise during our representation, the contract will also apply to our services in those matters.

Fees and Billing

We will send you a statement each month for services rendered and expenses incurred during the previous month, including hourly fees and out-of-pocket expenses. Generally, we charge for legal services based on the actual time that individual professionals devote to the matter. But other factors may also affect the charges, as explained in the Professional Fees section of the attached Terms of Representation.

Advance Payments

As we discussed, you will return with this signed engagement agreement an advance payment of $10,000 to be held in a dedicated account. We will apply that balance against our fees and expenses on each monthly statement. You will promptly pay any fees and expenses exceeding the account's balance, plus any amount necessary to maintain the account's balance of $10,000.

Confirmation of Agreement

The attached Terms of Representation are fully incorporated into this engagement agreement. If these documents accurately reflect your understanding of our agreement, please sign and return to me the enclosed copy of this letter, along with the requested advance payment.

If you have any other questions, please feel free to call me. We look forward to a mutually fulfilling relationship.

Very truly yours,

Joseph W. Saldana
Senior Partner
Eakins–Calder LLP

Approved and Agreed:

By: ______________________

James Butler

Date: ______________________

Terms of Representation
Eakins & Calder

Except as modified in writing, these terms will apply to the relationship between us (Eakins & Calder LLP) and you, as identified in the accompanying letter agreement and in paragraph 1.1:

1. **Limited scope of representation.** Unless we and you expressly agree otherwise in writing, we will represent you as stated below.

   1.1 **Identity of client.** We represent only you, not your spouse, children, or any other persons.

   1.2 **Matters represented.** We represent you only in your personal-injury action against Lassiter Manufacturing, Inc. and its employee, Nathaniel Post. If you want us to expand our representation of you in this matter or represent you in a different matter, you and we must agree in writing and sign another letter agreement and terms of representation.

   1.3 **Services outside scope of representation.** We will not render any tax advice.

2. **Professional fees.** We will bill you for our services based on the actual time spent, the complexity of the matter, the time limitations imposed, the novelty and difficulty of the issues posed, the amount involved, the results obtained, and the experience, reputation, and ability of the legal, paralegal, or other staff performing services on your behalf. The billing rates of our attorneys and paralegals vary, depending generally on their experience and ability, and we adjust these rates from time to time. Unless otherwise agreed in writing, we will charge you for their services at their assigned rates. Your matter is currently assigned to attorney Angel Juarez ($450/hour) and paralegal Dwayne Hodgins ($175/ hour). If we adjust these rates or reassign your matter, the rates charged to you may change. Other attorneys and paralegals may also perform services for this engagement, and you will also be responsible for their billings.

3. **Expenses; ancillary-services costs.** You are responsible for reimbursing us for all reasonable out-of-pocket expenses and ancillary-services costs actually incurred in rendering our services. We normally advance such expenses and costs on your behalf and bill you for them monthly. But for significant expenditures, we may ask you to prepay the expenses or to pay the expenses directly to a third-party vendor. Whenever practical,

discounts received from vendors will be passed on to you. The primary ancillary services and our specific policies for billing are set forth below. We may render other services during the engagement that will also be billed to you. Our charges for these costs and ancillary services are subject to change from time to time.

3.1 **Word processing.** We do not charge for the use of our equipment or word-processing time.

3.2 **Secretarial time.** We do not charge for routine secretarial time. We bill $40 per hour for overtime secretarial services only under unusual circumstances, such as:

(a) your demands necessitate work beyond regular business hours; or

(b) the complexity of your matter necessitates dedicated secretaries to be assigned to it.

3.3 **Copying services.** We charge 10 cents per copy for in-house copying services. If you ask, we will use outside copying services and charge you the amount that we are billed.

3.4 **Telephone.** We do not charge for local telephone service. We charge a fixed per minute rate for long-distance calls. The rate is based on our actual cost and is revised periodically.

3.5 **Faxes.** We do not charge for incoming faxes. Our charges for outgoing faxes are the same as our long-distance telephone charges.

3.6 **Legal research.** Online legal research is available at attorneys' desks and in each office's library. The vendors bill us for actual time doing research time and for documents delivered. We bill you for these charges.

3.7 **Postage and special deliveries.** We do not charge you for routine postage. We do charge for large-volume mailings, based on our actual costs. We also charge you our actual costs for overnight deliveries and local deliveries by outside courier services.

3.8 **File storage.** We do not charge you for file storage except in extraordinary circumstances, and only after consulting with you about your needs. We may, at our discretion, choose to store files electronically rather than by hard copy.

3.9 **Office supplies.** We do not charge you for routine use of office supplies. If your needs become unusually excessive for a particular matter, we may charge you our actual costs.

3.10 **Travel expenses.** If our attorney must travel to render services, other than routine local transportation to and from our office, we will bill you for the attorney's actual expenses for lodging, meals, and other travel costs. We instruct all our attorneys to keep those costs as reasonable as possible, including seeking the lowest fares reasonable within time constraints.

3.11 **Other costs.** We will bill you for other costs we incur for your benefit (such as filing fees and expert-witness fees) at our actual cost.

3.12 **Third-party vendors.** You may need services that we cannot provide. If so, we may contract with a third-party vendor for those services, pay for them, and bill you the actual amount we paid. But if those services will be substantial or expensive, we will notify you and offer you the option to either (1) pay the costs before we contract for the services, or (2) contract with a third-party vendor yourself. You indemnify us for any claim made against us by any outside vendor for services rendered in connection with our representing you.

4. **Estimates.** At your request, we will give you a written estimate of the time, fees, and expenses involved in preparing for and handling the dispute. Because we cannot foresee all the possible circumstances that may affect the actual amounts we bill you, our estimate is not guaranteed by or binding on us.

5. **Advance payments.** The amount of the advance payment is a partial payment of the total charges we may incur. At the end of our representation, we will refund to you any remaining portion of any advance payment.

6. **Statements; payment.**

6.1 **Timing.** We will send you an itemized statement each month. A statement is payable upon receipt and is past due 30 days after the statement's date. We may, at our discretion, charge a late fee of 1% per month on past-due balances.

6.2 **Your review; objections.** You are responsible for reviewing our statements within 30 days of receipt and raising any questions about amounts or items billed. If you object to a portion of the charges on a statement, you are still responsible for paying the undisputed portion. That payment will not waive your objection.

6.3 **Our right to cease services.** If billed amounts are not paid when due, we have the right to suspend additional services or to withdraw from representing you, subject to any applicable legal-ethics constraints. If we withdraw, we will advise you in sufficient time for you to find other counsel.

7. **No guarantee of outcome.** We do not guarantee the outcome in any matter. Our comments about the outcome of your matter are expressions of opinion only.

8. **Electronic Communications.** We intend to use electronic communications such as e-mail, cell phones, faxes, and document transfer by computer. If you tell us that you are concerned about security for any given communication, we will mutually agree on a nonelectric means for that particular communication.

9. **Related proceedings and activities.** You agree to pay us for any resulting costs, including for our time, calculated at the hourly rate for the particular individuals involved, even if we no longer represent you, if (a) any claim is brought against us or any of our personnel based on your negligence or misconduct; (b) we are asked to testify as a result of representing you; or (c) we must defend the confidentiality of your communications in any proceeding.

10. **Termination of representation.**

10.1 **Termination by you.** You may terminate our services at any time. You will still be obligated for all services rendered and costs or expenses paid or incurred on your behalf up to the time of termination, as well as any costs or expenses that are reasonably necessary afterward. If we are attorneys of record in any proceeding, you agree to execute and return to us any documents necessary for our withdrawal.

10.2 **Termination by us.** If we must withdraw from this representation, you will take all steps necessary to free us from any obligation to perform further services and will sign any documents necessary to complete our withdrawal. After termination, you will still be obligated for all services we provided and costs and expenses we paid or incurred on your behalf. We must withdraw from this representation if:

(a) you fail to honor the terms of our engagement letter and these Terms of Representation; or

(b) anything happens that would, in our view, render our continued representation unlawful or unethical.

10.3 Date of termination. Our representation of you will end at the earliest of

(a) your termination of our representation;

(b) our withdrawal from representing you; or

(c) the completion of our work for you.

10.4 Duties upon termination. When our involvement in the matter for which you engaged us ends, we will have no duty to inform you of future developments or changes in law that may be relevant to that matter. Further, unless we mutually agree in writing to the contrary, we will have no obligation to monitor renewal or notice duties or similar deadlines that may arise relating to the matters for which you engaged us. If your matter involves obtaining a judgment and the judgment is obtained, we will be responsible for only those postjudgment services (such as recording abstracts, filing judgment liens, and calendaring renewals of judgments) that we have expressly agreed to in writing and for which you will be obligated to pay.

11. Document retention and destruction. While representing you, we are likely to come into possession of documents or other materials belonging to you or others. Once the matter that those materials relate to has been concluded, we will make arrangements to return them to you, retain them in our storage facilities, or dispose of them. Unless you make some other arrangement with us, our retention policy provides that five years after the matter has been closed, all materials in the file may be destroyed or discarded without notice to you. So if there are any materials that you wish to retrieve from your file, you must ask for them to ensure that they are not destroyed. Our own files pertaining to the matter — such as our administrative records, time and expense reports, personnel and staffing materials, credit and accounting receipts, and internal lawyers' work product — remain our property and may be stored, disposed of, or destroyed at our discretion.

12. Dispute resolution.

12.1 Waiver of right to jury or court trial. You and we are waiving our right to a jury or court trial.

12.2 Waiver of right to punitive damages. To the maximum extent allowed by law, you and we waive any right to an award of punitive damages.

12.3 Arbitration of all disputes, claims, or controversies. Any dispute, claim, or controversy arising out of or relating to this agreement, our relationship created by it, or services performed under it must be determined exclusively by confidential, final, and binding arbitration as follows:

(a) The matters submitted to arbitration must be heard and determined by a single arbitrator in the principal city of the federal jurisdiction in which this agreement is entered into, in accordance with the then-existing rules for commercial arbitration of the Judicial Arbitration and Mediation Services (JAMS).

(b) Any party to the arbitration may request JAMS to identify panels of retired or former judges qualified and able to sit as arbitrators of the matters submitted for arbitration, and the arbitrator determining the subject matters must be selected from those panels under the JAMS rules.

(c) Disputes, claims, and controversies subject to final and binding arbitration under this agreement include, without limitation, all those that otherwise could be tried in court to a judge or jury in the absence of this agreement. These disputes, claims, and controversies include, without limitation, claims for professional malpractice, disputes over fees and expenses, disputes over the quality of services that we render, claims relating to or arising out of your or our performance under this agreement, and any other claims arising out of any alleged act or omission by you or by us.

(d) Unless the arbitrator specifies otherwise, the fees of the arbitration will be paid equally by you and us.

(e) Section 1283.05 of the California Code of Civil Procedure ("Manner of Taking Deposition") is incorporated into this arbitration agreement.

(f) The arbitrator may determine all issues in arbitration as if the arbitrator were sitting as a judge without a jury, and the arbitrator must render a written, reasoned award with findings of fact and conclusions of law sufficient to support any judicial review provided by applicable statutes governing arbitrations.

(g) Any arbitration award will be final, binding, and conclusive upon you and us, subject only to judicial review provided by statutes governing arbitration, and a judgment rendered on the arbitral award may be entered in any state or federal court having appropriate jurisdiction.

12.4 State Bar of California fee arbitration. In a dispute over fees or costs, you have the right to choose arbitration under the fee-arbitration procedures of the State Bar of California. Those procedures permit a trial after arbitration unless the parties agree in writing, after the dispute has arisen, to be bound by the arbitral award.

13. Amendments. This Agreement may be amended only by a writing signed by your duly-authorized representative and by us.

14. Entire agreement. These Terms of Representation constitute the sole agreement between you and us. They supersede any earlier written or oral agreements or communications between you and us. They cannot be modified except in a writing signed by both you and us.

15. Severability. If any part of this agreement is for any reason held to be unenforceable, the rest of it remains fully enforceable.

16. Applicable law. California law applies to this Agreement without regard for any choice-of-law rules that might direct the application of the laws of any other jurisdiction.

Sample Nonengagement Letter

Adler, Drissel & Cardwell
48 Central Park South
New York, NY 10019
212-555-1212

25 August 2018

Ms. Adelie Gable
62 Roosevelt Drive, Suite G
Emerson, NJ 07676

Dear Ms. Gable:

Thank you for the opportunity to meet you earlier this week to discuss the possible appeal of your libel suit. After reviewing the materials that you provided, we have decided not to represent you. Please understand that our decision is not an opinion about the merits of your case.

You may have a deadline for the appeal approaching. Because time is always important in legal matters, you may want to contact another law firm about your appeal. The New York State Bar Association offers a lawyer-referral service that can help you.

Because we have declined to represent you and express no opinion on the merits of your case, we are returning with this letter all the materials you gave us. We have not kept any copies of your materials except for a copy of this letter.

We wish you all the best and hope you resolve the matter to your satisfaction.

Sincerely,

Rashad Adler
Senior Partner

Sample Disengagement Letter

Hughes & Branston LLP
3177 Tinley Gardens Plaza
Chicago, Illinois 60605

18 April 2018

Ms. Gracia Armin
806 West 15th Street
Arlington Heights, Illinois 60004

Re: Your estate-planning documents

Dear Ms. Armin:

Enclosed are the original documents that were signed and witnessed in my office on April 7 and a CD with one electronic copy of each document:

1. Will.
2. Medical Durable Power of Attorney.
3. General Durable Power of Attorney.
4. Designation of Guardian.

As we discussed, I've also enclosed an unsigned original Memorandum for Disposition of Personal Property with instructions on its use.

Under no circumstances should you attempt to change or mark anything in these documents without consulting a lawyer. Generally, to make any changes effective, you'll need to make an amendment to the document with all the formalities involved in signing the original document.

You should keep the original documents in a secure place, such as a safe-deposit box or another secure place. I must remind you that if you keep your will in your home and it can't be found after your death, there could be a strong presumption that you revoked the will, which would cause your property to be transferred under intestacy laws rather than to the heirs you chose. I recommend that you tell your executor and designated successors where you are keeping your will. This would also be a good time to talk with your personal representative and family members about these documents and what they need to know in case of your disability or death. These matters would include the location of your safe-deposit box, the contact information for your accountant or broker or other financial advisors, the location of life-insurance policies, the passwords to electronic accounts, a list of your physical and digital assets, and so on.

It's been a pleasure to work with you in this matter. As of the date of this letter, our lawyer–client relationship has ended. I'll keep electronic copies of your signed estate-planning documents in my file. Unless you engage me to perform additional legal services for you in the future, I won't be taking any further action on your behalf. If you have any questions or your circumstances change, please contact me again. Because tax laws change over time, I recommend that you periodically contact me or another estate-planning lawyer to determine whether and how the changes may affect your situation.

Yours truly,

Allison Branston

§ 20
Opinion Letters

20.1 Understand the main goals of an opinion letter.

(a) *Purpose.* The phrase *opinion letter* denotes a broad category encompassing many types of letters with various purposes and formats. Usury opinions in loan transactions, title opinions in real-estate transactions, closing opinions in securities offerings, and coverage opinions in insurance matters are just a few examples. As it's used here, *opinion letter* means a lawyer's written opinion of law—and perhaps other considerations—regarding a decision to be made or plan of action to be taken. An opinion letter should prepare the client to make an informed decision. Don't lull the client into a false sense of security: your opinion alone can't guarantee success. While relying on the letter should put the client in the best legal posture against any future dispute, this reliance can't ensure that the client will stay out of court or win any resulting litigation. Another party can sue no matter how good an opinion letter is, and no matter how carefully the client has relied on it. Although relying on the letter should insulate the client against litigation as effectively as possible, the letter doesn't mean that the client will never need a court's help to make someone else comply with the law. And the letter doesn't protect against someone else's lawsuit.

(b) *Format.* A reasoned opinion letter—one that contains legal analysis—should begin much as a research memo does, with a summary of the issue and your conclusion. Typically, this summary is less formal than in a research memo; that is, it need not have a *Question Presented* and *Brief Answer* so labeled. The opening should set forth every assumption on which the opinion is based, the basic facts (woven into the issue), and the conclusion (with a brief statement of its basis). Then, after the summary, a full statement of facts may appear. Some opinions don't require a lengthy facts section; others, such as those concerning possible patent infringement or insurance coverage, do require one. After the summary and facts sections, the body of the opinion letter explains what legal principles apply, their sources, and how they apply to the facts. The conclusion then restates the main findings, preferably in a slightly different form. Don't simply repeat the summary. You should introduce each of these parts—summary, facts (if any), explanation, and conclusion—with a flush-left heading.

(c) *Answering the question.* Clients who seek your opinion want to know their rights, obligations, and potential risks and what possible legal consequences they may face in a given situation. Don't meander before answering a client's questions. Although legal analysis of the situation is essential, an opinion letter isn't a treatise or law-review article. Focus narrowly on the specific facts presented and the particular legal issues they raise. Assess the controlling legal principles; then state your conclusions and advice as clearly as possible. Explain the costs and benefits associated with the different available approaches. Avoid giving a broad answer that could be applied to a different question or to the same question but with significantly different facts. Use plain English. Explain any legal terms that the client may not understand.

(d) *Alternatives.* No one likes getting bad news. If possible, suggest alternative ways to achieve the client's goals, or measures that might avoid or minimize the harm. If you can't avoid a negative conclusion, at least avoid unduly harsh statements such as "claims like yours are flatly rejected by all courts." Find a softer way to relate a disappointing conclusion (e.g., "none of the cases based on facts similar to this one have succeeded"). But also make sure that your conclusion cannot be read equivocally. If something is illegal or risky, say so clearly and immediately.

(e) *Limitations.* An opinion letter doesn't create legal rights. State in the letter that your conclusion and advice apply only to the facts, the law, and the jurisdiction at the time. An opinion letter may have other limitations as well. If the law isn't entirely clear—and that is typically the situation when an opinion is sought—include a statement like this one: "It is impossible to predict with certainty what a court would hold. But given the facts as you presented them, a court in this state would probably . . . ." Or: "In a lawsuit, these questions would ultimately be decided by a fact-finder (perhaps a jury), and a fact-finder can be unpredictable." Be explicit about every assumption you make in rendering the opinion. And if relevant, explain how a different assumption might lead to a different conclusion.

(f) *Who may issue the opinion.* Many law firms have strict guidelines about legal opinions. Some firms have an opinions committee. Typically, only a partner of the firm may issue an opinion, and often even the partner must have the approval of a member of the opinions committee. An opinion is typically rendered in the firm's name, not in a partner's name, and the firm name is signed at the end by an authorized partner. Know the guidelines where you work.

20.2 Think about the specific goals of your opinion letter.

(a) *Particular client with particular needs.* Make sure that you understand the entire business context of the question. Consult senior lawyers to determine whether the letter addresses every necessary issue. A client may not be sure what to ask. Work with the client to learn everything you can about the problem and to help the client see it from a lawyer's perspective. Doing this will help you focus your research and develop a satisfactory answer. By letting the client participate this way, you'll make the client more confident in you and your firm.

(b) *Written vs. oral opinion.* You may conclude that a client's practices or intended acts violate the law, and you can't recommend a legal alternative. If your written opinion is potentially discoverable, you may consider delivering the opinion orally—at least initially, allowing the client to respond to bad facts. Keep in your file a detailed record of the conversation, your conclusion, and the basis for your conclusion. For a client who may have trouble understanding a written opinion, you may want to supplement the opinion with an oral presentation and answer the client's questions. The two versions—oral and written—should be substantively identical. A written opinion should be marked with a legend stating that it is subject to the attorney–client privilege or the work-product doctrine, or both, as appropriate.

(c) *Legal effects.* Although an opinion letter doesn't create legal rights, it usually contains a statement of a particular person's legal position. A client who relies on the opinion may be liable for mistakes it contains. And although an opinion is not a guarantee, the drafting attorney may be subject to a malpractice lawsuit or disciplinary action if the attorney has been negligent (a question often decided with keen hindsight). This is one of the reasons that law firms have detailed procedures on drafting and reviewing opinion letters.

20.3 Avoid the common faults of opinion letters.

(a) *Failing to answer the question.* An opinion letter is ineffective if it doesn't both pose a clear issue and answer it. Not every issue has a firm yes-or-no answer, but an unambiguous conclusion should be stated with only specific and necessary qualifications or reservations.

> Ex.: You've informed me that your horse occasionally roams onto the farm-to-market road next to your pasture. And because of increasing traffic on the road, you've asked me whether you have a legal duty to prevent your horse from doing this.
>
> I conclude that you do not owe motorists a statutory or common-law duty to do so. The Texas legislature has not passed any law requiring a fence around a horse pasture, and there is no applicable city ordinance. The Texas Supreme Court has said that Texas does not follow the rule mandating fences to control livestock. The Court has also said that Texas is "traditionally a free-range state where cattle may roam unrestrained."

Reaching an unnecessarily tentative conclusion hedged with general reservations and qualifications won't deliver an answer that your client can use—or worse, understand. And it won't boost your client's confidence in relying on your advice.

(b) *Trying to use a formula.* Although there are common formats for opinion letters, no such thing as a "form" or "fill-in-the-blank" opinion is possible. You might be able to update a previous letter, but be extremely careful that (1) it's still based on good law, (2) dissimilar facts don't change what law will apply, and (3) the old opinion is readable to a nonlawyer and not full of legalese. Adjust the letter's tone to suit your own style and your relationship with the client.

(c) *Leaping to a conclusion.* Answers must be supported by precedent and reasoning. But a broad or general discussion of the law isn't necessary or desirable; just explain how and why, based on the current law, the facts and their specific legal effects lead to your conclusion. Adjust the depth and detail of your analysis, but remember that the client must understand how and why you reached the conclusion, as well as any inherent limitations.

20.4 Study effective opinion letters.

(a) *Review good examples.* Samples of good opinion letters are hard to find outside a law office. Many legal-writing texts and books on practical legal drafting describe opinion letters but don't fully illustrate them. Ask senior colleagues for samples of their opinion letters written for different types of clients, especially for questions in the same area of law. Note the tone used and how much depth and detail are provided in the analysis. Follow your firm's format, but freely adapt it as needed if doing so produces a better letter.

(b) *Further guidance.* Perhaps the most important document for opinion-givers to examine is the American Bar Association's *Legal Opinion Project*, published at 47 Bus. Law. 168 (1991). Also valuable is the *Report of the Legal Opinions Committee Regarding Legal Opinions in Business Transactions*, 29 Bull. of Bus. Law Section, State Bar of Texas (Nos. 2 & 3, June–Sept. 1992); this report has been supplemented in 31 Bull. of Bus. Law Section, State Bar of Texas (No. 4, Dec. 1994) (regarding usury) and in 37 Tex. J. Bus. Law 1 (2001) (regarding business transactions generally). Two other recommended guides are *Drafting Legal Opinion Letters* (M. John Sterba ed., 2d ed. 1999) and Mary Barnard Ray & Barbara J. Cox, *Beyond the Basics* 350–70 (3d ed. 2012). A timeless essay on the subject, well worth reading, is Mortimer Levitan, *Dissertation on Writing Legal Opinions*, 1960 Wis. L. Rev. 22.

(c) *Examples.* The first example that follows was issued by a large California firm for a client who was dissatisfied with another law firm's services and was considering a malpractice lawsuit. The second is a transactional opinion, showing that counsel has verified the client's compliance with various legal requirements; lenders often condition their willingness to make a loan on their receipt of an opinion letter containing such assurances.

Belton, Forbes, Renshaw & Mitford

Attorneys at Law

666 Los Robles Avenue, Suite 1500
Pasadena, California 91101

Telephone (213) 212-8888
Fax (213) 212-7777

25 May 2018

Mr. Forsythe H. Howard
Biltmore Credit Corporation
850 E. Colorado Blvd., Suite 1000
Pasadena, CA 91101

Re: Evaluation of Weingarten & Pierce's
Representation of Biltmore Credit Corporation

Dear M. Howard:

You have asked Belton, Forbes, Renshaw & Mitford to review the performance of your prior counsel, Weingarten & Pierce ("W&P"), and its representation of Biltmore Credit Corporation concerning title issues in connection with Lot 2 of the Montrobles Tract, San Marino, Los Angeles County, California (commonly known as "Parcel 3"), and the actions of USMore Title Company.

Specifically, you have asked whether any of W&P's advice fell below the standard of care expected of the legal profession and, if so, whether Biltmore can now sue W&P for legal malpractice. In brief, we conclude that (1) at least some of W&P's advice fell below the level of skill and diligence that other members of the legal profession possess and would use in a similar situation, but (2) an action based in malpractice would probably fail because Biltmore will have great difficulty proving that it has incurred actual damages.

Of course, in discussing the actions and the advice of W&P, we have the benefit of examining the actions of W&P in hindsight. We have attempted to form our opinion on W&P's actions and advice without making unfair use of the perspective of hindsight. Moreover, a more detailed knowledge of the totality of the communications between the individuals at W&P and those at Biltmore might change the facts and assumptions on which this letter is based.

Although in many respects W&P did not provide the advice that we believe would have been appropriate to the situation, most of the matters on which we differ with W&P are those where competent lawyers could disagree.

Yet in one particular area, we believe that W&P failed to exercise the level of skill and diligence that other members of the legal profession possess and would use in a similar situation. Specifically, we believe that W&P's advice to Biltmore at the time of the settlement agreement between Biltmore and USMore Title was deficient. This conclusion is based on our understanding that W&P failed to discuss with Biltmore the potential scope of the release that Biltmore was to sign and failed to take the necessary steps to identify other claims that might have existed against USMore Title — claims that appear to have been released under the language of the agreement.

With the information provided to us, we understand that when Biltmore acquired the Montrobles Tract though foreclosure, the property description attached to the deed of trust included only five of the six parcels of land at issue. Despite this, the title insurance issued by USMore Title erroneously issued the deed of trust's lien as a first-priority lien against all six parcels. This error gave rise to a claim by Biltmore against USMore Title, and the parties settled. The settlement agreement contained a release that arguably released all claims, including future claims, that Biltmore had or may have against USMore Title.

Biltmore has informed us that when the settlement and release were being negotiated, W&P did not inform anyone at Biltmore about the possible scope of claims that it was potentially relinquishing under the language of the release. In other words, Biltmore did not understand the release's effect in possibly surrendering more claims against USMore Title than the claim at issue here. We believe that W&P should have discussed with Bilmore the possible scope of claims that Biltmore may have against USMore Title and the effect of the release on those potential claims, This failure, if it occurred, falls below the minimum standard of care required of attorneys.

In settling the case against USMore Title, Biltmore relied on additional information concerning Parcel 3 provided by USMore Title that proved erroneous. Specifically, USMore Title stated that the title search had been completed but failed to inform Biltmore that judgment liens had been recorded against the prior owners of the property. This misinformation had given rise to a potential claim by Biltmore against USMore Title. But in light of the language of the release contained in the settlement agreement, it is possible that Biltmore has no further legal recourse against USMore Title.

Further, before recommending that Biltmore sign the settlement agreement and release, W&P apparently failed to investigate the additional information provided by USMore Title and failed to inform Biltmore that it had not investigated that information. We believed that, at a minimum, W&P should have informed

Letter to Forsythe H. Howard of
Biltmore Credit Corporation
25 May 2018
Page 2

Biltmore that it was relying solely on the information provided by USMore Title. In light of USMore Title's previous errors, we conclude that W&P should have independently verified the information provided by USMore Title. This failure, if it occurred, falls below the minimum standard of care required of attorneys.

Based on the information we have received, we find fault with the actions and advice of W&P in not fully advising Biltmore as a releasing party. But as explained more fully below, we do not believe that W&P's actions give rise to a claim for legal malpractice, since it is uncertain that all the elements for a malpractice claim can be shown.

A legal-malpractice claim arises if (1) the attorney has a duty to the client to use at least the level of skill and diligence that other members of the legal profession possess and use; (2) the attorney fails to use the appropriate level of skill and diligence in connection with the client's work; (3) this failure proximately causes injury to the client; and (4) the client suffers actual loss or damage as a result of the attorney's failure to act appropriately. *Nichols v. Keller*, 15 Cal. App. 4th 1672, 1682 (1993).

One of the primary duties of an attorney to the client is to advise the client of his or her rights. The standard of care owed by an attorney to a client "may be breached where the attorney fails to inform a client about his or her rights and the alternatives available under the circumstances." *Considine Co. v. Shadle, Hunt & Hagar*, 187 Cal. App. 3d 760, 765 (1986). *See also Ishmael v. Millington*, 241 Cal. App. 2d 520 (1966) (the attorney's failure to advise his client, and failure to disclose pertinent information to his client, could constitute legal malpractice). Indeed, "[n]ot only should an attorney furnish advice when requested, but he or she should also volunteer opinions when necessary to further the client's objectives." *Nichols*, 15 Cal. App. 4th at 1683–84. The attorney especially has an obligation to provide advice concerning matters "that may result in adverse consequences if not considered." *Id.* at 1684.

As discussed above, we believe that W&P had a duty to explain to Biltmore the fact that the release could be construed as releasing *all* future claims against USMore Title, whether or not those claims had arisen. The failure of W&P to advise Biltmore of the potential effect of the release could arguably give rise to a claim against W&P for legal malpractice.

But to maintain a malpractice claim, the alleged malpractice must have caused the client to suffer actual damages: "The mere breach of a professional duty, causing only nominal damages, speculative harm, or the threat of future harm—not yet realized—does not suffice to create a cause of action" for the attorney's negligence

Letter to Forsythe H. Howard of
Biltmore Credit Corporation
25 May 2018
Page 3

or legal malpractice. *Albino v. Starr*, 112 Cal. App. 3d 158, 176 (1980). If any one of the four elements of a malpractice claim is absent, the claim will fail. *Nichols*, 15 Cal. App. 4th at 1682.

Biltmore has informed us that it is not certain whether Biltmore would have settled if it had been informed by W&P that, by signing the release, Biltmore would be releasing all future claims against USMore Title. The facts show that Biltmore potentially has a claim against USMore Title. But even if Biltmore had not signed the release, the chance of recovery from USMore Title would be speculative at best. If no damages were suffered by Biltmore, any claim for legal malpractice would be likely to fail.

In conclusion, we do not believe that the advice given by or the actions taken by W&P give rise to a claim by Biltmore against W&P for legal malpractice. Although W&P failed to advise Biltmore of the potential effect of the release on any future claims that Biltmore may wish to bring against USMore Title, it is uncertain whether Biltmore has suffered any damage as a result of W&P's practice. This uncertainty of actual damages would make a claim for legal malpractice difficult to prove.

Please contact us if you have any questions about the matters here discussed, or any other issue.

Very truly yours,

Belton, Forbes, Renshaw & Mitford

Letter to Forsythe H. Howard of
Biltmore Credit Corporation
25 May 2018
Page 4

Sobleski & Ohego
Attorneys at Law

1900 Pacific Coast Hwy., #175
Cairngorm, CA 97117-4782
416-460-4600

July 7, 2018

Mr. Edwin S. Grimbley
Elenchus Affiliates, Inc.
1700 First City Center
Klamath, OR 97211-8888

Dear Mr. Grimbley:

We are counsel for the Irmak Rancheria Tribe of California (the "Tribe"), which is a nonprofit, public-benefit corporation organized under § 501(c)(3) of the Internal Revenue Code seeking to confirm its status as a federally recognized Indian tribe. We have represented the Tribe as it entered into various agreements with Elenchus Affiliates, including (1) an interim-funding, exclusive-agency, and dispute-resolution agreement; (2) a real-estate development agreement; and (3) a permanent-loan agreement (collectively, the "Agreements") to finance certain costs related to confirming the Tribe's federally recognized status, acquiring Indian Lands, negotiating and entering into a tribal–state compact, and eventually developing and operating a Class II and Class III Gaming Facility in the State of California. Elenchus requires the opinions expressed in this letter as a condition to entering into the Agreements.

In preparing this opinion, we have reviewed the following documents (each of which the Tribe has certified as an accurate copy of the original):

1. The Tribe's articles of incorporation, adopted in October 2002 and accepted by the California Secretary of State on July 26, 2003.

2. The Tribe's articles of organization as an Indian tribe, adopted May 1, 2000.

3. Resolution No. A19-2006 (the "Approving Resolution") of the Tribe's General Council, which:

   (a) approved the Agreements;
   (b) approved the Tribe's limited waiver of sovereign immunity; and
   (c) repealed conflicting tribal laws.

4. Resolution No. A20-2006, enacting the Tribal Secured Transactions Code.

In addition, we have reviewed executed counterparts of the Agreements.

Finally, we have reviewed provisions of the Indian Gaming Regulatory Act, 25 U.S.C. §§ 2701–2721, and regulations of the National Indian Gaming Commission as currently in effect (collectively, "IGRA"), as well as a certificate of the Tribe's chair dated today. We have also made other legal and factual examinations as necessary and appropriate for this opinion.

Based on our review and analysis, our opinion is that:

1. The Tribe is a nonprofit, public-benefit corporation and is an Indian tribe seeking to confirm its federally recognized status. The Tribe's articles of incorporation and articles of organization are in full force as the Tribe's governing documents.

2. Under the Tribe's articles of organization, the supreme governing body of the Tribe is its General Council. It has the full power and authority to undertake all governmental actions, including:

   (a) enacting laws for the Tribe such as the Approving Resolution and the Tribal Secured Transactions Code; and

–2–

(b) approving the Agreements and binding the Tribe to them without further action of the tribal membership or any instrumentality of the Tribe.

3. The Tribe's General Council has duly adopted the Approving Resolution according to all procedures required by the Tribe's articles of incorporation, its articles of organization, and all applicable traditions, customs, laws, and other regulations. The Approving Resolution therefore constitutes a valid action of the General Council.

4. The Approving Resolution duly authorizes a representative to take all actions contemplated by the General Council.

5. The Tribe has full power and authority to enter into, deliver, and perform the Agreements.

6. The Tribe's General Council adopted or took each governmental action specifically mentioned in paragraph 2, and each action is in full force as law of the Tribe without any amendment or repeal. No action to cause an amendment or repeal of all or any part of any governmental action is pending, nor, to the best of our knowledge after due inquiry, is any such action threatened or proposed by any person with the power to initiate a proceeding to amend or repeal.

7. The Tribe has duly signed and delivered each of the Agreements. Assuming that all other parties to the Agreements have duly authorized, signed, and delivered them, each agreement is valid and enforceable according to its terms, except as enforcement may be limited by general equitable principles or by bankruptcy, insolvency, reorganization, moratorium, or other legal occurrence that may affect creditors' rights generally.

8. No lawsuit, proceeding, inquiry, or investigation is pending that could affect the Agreements before any tribunal, agency, or other governmental entity. And to the best of our knowledge after due inquiry, none is threatened. No pending lawsuit, proceeding, inquiry, or investigation:

(a) contests or puts in issue in any manner the Tribe's membership or its governance;

–3–

(b) has as a party the Tribe or any Affiliate (as defined in the Interim Loan Agreement);
(c) affects any of the Tribe's or an Affiliate's properties by:
  (1) challenging or putting in issue any powers of the Tribe as a nonprofit corporation or as an Indian tribe; or
  (2) seeking to restrain, enjoin, prevent the consummation of, or otherwise challenge the signing, delivery, or performance of any of the Agreements or any transactions required or contemplated by the Agreements; or
(d) could reasonably be expected to result in an unfavorable decision, ruling, or finding with a Material Adverse Effect (as defined in the Interim Loan Agreement) on:
  (1) the validity, enforceability, or security of the loan from Elenchus to the Tribe;
  (2) the Tribe's ability to timely pay in full all amounts due from any or all sources or contemplated in the Interim Loan Agreement; or
  (3) the Tribe's performance of its obligations under any Agreement.

9. To the best of our knowledge after due inquiry, neither the Tribe nor any Affiliate is in violation of or in default under any contract, agreement, deed, indenture, mortgage, instrument, or agreement of any other nature other than violations or defaults that could not, singly or in the aggregate, have a Material Adverse Effect.

10. To the best of our knowledge after due inquiry, neither the Tribe nor any Affiliate is violating any federal, state, or tribal law, or any regulation or order—whether created in writing or by custom or tradition, including IGRA—applicable to:
(a) the Tribe or any Affiliate;
(b) any of the operations of the Tribe or any Affiliate; or
(c) any properties of the Tribe or any Affiliate.

–4–

11. The Tribe has obtained all authorizations, approvals, licenses, orders, registrations, and qualifications with state, federal, and tribal governmental authorities required for or as a condition to signing, delivering, and performing the Agreements or consummating the transactions contemplated by the Agreements (the "Transactions").

12. The signing and delivery of any Agreement and the consummation of any of the Transactions will not:

(a) require any consent other than those consents already obtained; or
(b) result in a lien or other encumbrance being imposed on any property of the Tribe or any of its Affiliates; or
(c) accelerate indebtedness.

13. None of the Agreements conflicts with or violates any law. The signing and delivery of any agreement and the consummation of any of the Transactions will not under any agreement of the Tribe:

(a) constitute a breach or a default;
(b) accelerate any performance; or
(c) cause any lien or other encumbrance to be imposed.

14. The Tribe holds all permits, licenses, and approvals (collectively, "Permits") required to perform under the Agreements unless the failure to obtain Permits would not, individually or in the aggregate, have a Material Adverse Effect. To the best of our knowledge after due inquiry, the Tribe has not received any notice of any proceeding relating to revoking or modifying any permit unless the revocation or modification would not, individually or in the aggregate, have a Material Adverse Effect. The Tribe's signing, delivery, and performance of the Agreements will not cause any permit in favor of the Tribe to be terminated, revoked, or suspended.

15. The Interim Loan Agreement does not violate any usury law or any limitation on interest or returns applicable to obligations of the Tribe.

16. The choice-of-governing-law provisions in the Agreements comply in all material respects with applicable federal, state, and tribal law. The Agreements constitute valid and binding agreements of the Tribe, enforceable against the Tribe according to their terms.

–5–

17. The Tribe has duly and irrevocably waived its sovereign immunity subject and according to each of the Agreements. Each waiver is valid and enforceable against the Tribe under all laws of the Tribe, the State of California, and the United States.

18. Each term in the Agreements relating to arbitration, forum-selection, and jurisdiction constitutes the law of the Tribe. It binds the Tribe and is valid and enforceable in all respects. Any court convened by the Tribe is obligated to give full faith and credit to any arbitration award rendered under the contractual terms.

19. None of the Agreements (individually or collectively) constitutes a "management contract" or an agreement that is a "collateral agreement" to a management contract relating to a gaming activity regulated by IGRA, so none of the Agreements require approval by the Chair of the National Indian Gaming Commission under IGRA.

20. The requirement that the Secretary of the Interior approve certain agreements under 25 U.S.C. § 81, as amended, does not apply to any of the Agreements.

21. The Agreements are currently effective and will be effective after the Tribe has succeeded in confirming its federal recognition.

This opinion letter may be relied on only by Elenchus and its affiliates, counsel, successors, and assigns, and only for purposes related to the transactions this letter identifies. The letter must not be used by any other person or entity for any purpose whatsoever without our prior written consent in each instance.

Sincerely,

Paulette V. Ohego
Attorney for the
Irmak Rancheria Tribe

cc: Irmak Rancheria Tribe of Indians

–5–

§ 21
Demand Letters

21.1 Understand the main goals of a demand letter.

(a) *Gauging the reader.* A demand letter may serve various purposes. Typically, it should attempt to goad the adversary to capitulate—to do whatever is demanded. To this end, it should be reasonable and realistic, but it should convey the threat of litigation and its attendant costs and headaches if the adversary isn't reasonable and realistic in turn. As a writer, you must get inside the recipient's head to understand what type of approach will succeed.

(b) *Meeting statutory requirements.* Sometimes a demand letter is sent only to comply with a statutory prerequisite for filing suit. The demanding party may be seeking to recover double or even treble damages; to make such a demand, the demander may have to attach the letter to the initial pleading (usually either a complaint or a petition). In this situation, there may be no real possibility of resolving the dispute before legal proceedings begin. But the demanding party must send a letter that adequately alleges harm, requests a remedy, and allows time for a resolution.

(c) *Meeting contractual requirements.* If the parties have a contract in place, you'll need to ensure that your demand letter meets its requirements. The contract's Notice clause sets out the procedure for sending a demand letter. It gives the name and address of the person (or persons) who must receive notice of a breach and who should receive a copy. One or more means of contact should be stated. If you have a choice, consider which means best suits your client's needs. For example, an e-mail is the fastest means of contact, but it is less secure than others and may not provide for proof of receipt. But never use a means that isn't specified in the contract. In your demand letter, plainly refer to the breached contract section, state the specific facts, and weave in some of the contract language (e.g., *Under § 8 of the Lease, you agreed to pay rent of $1,500 per month by cash or cashier's check, due on the third day of each month. You breached § 8 of the Agreement by sending late personal checks for the rent payments due on June 3 and July 3, 2018*). In figuring out the "drop-dead" date for complying with the demand, consider what the contract says on the point. The language of Notice provisions varies greatly on when a Notice becomes effective.

(d) *Documenting efforts to resolve the dispute.* Demand letters are often attached to pleadings or discovery responses to demonstrate that the plaintiff tried to avoid litigation. Courts generally don't favor litigants who fail to respond to such good-faith efforts or fail to try to negotiate a resolution short of a lawsuit. Also, a simple, thoughtful demand letter can form the basis for a later request that the other party pay your client's legal fees.

21.2 Think about the specific goals of your demand letter.

(a) *Strategy.* You must talk with your client about what you specifically hope to accomplish with the demand letter. Although you may hope to resolve the matter without filing suit, don't lead your client to expect such a favorable (and relatively inexpensive) outcome. (For that matter, never project an unduly optimistic attitude about what you might accomplish.) Work with the client to develop a clear understanding of what it would take to resolve the dispute to the client's satisfaction short of litigation: returning property, paying money, acknowledging a right, or whatever it might be. And remember that a demand letter is often the initial volley in a negotiation, so think strategically about what you demand. Your demand should amount to something less than what you would ask for in court—so that the adversary will have an incentive to settle early. But be careful not to harm your litigation position by assigning too low a value to your claim.

(b) *Specificity and tone.* The purpose of a demand letter is almost always to get someone to do something that he or she is reluctant to do. You must be clear about what that something is, why it's in the recipient's best interests to do it, and what will happen if the recipient doesn't comply. Specifically, you must clearly communicate (1) your client's position, (2) your client's specific demand, (3) your assessment of the recipient's essential position as wholly or partly meritless, (4) the recipient's deadline for complying (e.g., "by 4 p.m. (CST) on Wednesday, March 24"), and (5) your intentions if your client's demands aren't met. Take special care with that last statement because you seek satisfaction only to the extent that the adversary's position lacks merit. The tone should reflect the message that this is a firm statement of position and intention; it should not be that of a bully. Nor should it overstate your position, since the letter could become an exhibit if litigation becomes necessary.

(c) *Allowing an independent assessment.* Include enough information for the recipient to understand the claim. The letter must include enough facts (and have documents attached) so that the adversary may make an independent assessment of your position.

(d) *Collection letters.* Consumer-debt collection letters need to be especially clear and crisp. A collection letter must give all the warnings and include all the information required by federal and state law. Be sure to research the current state of the law. *See, e.g.*, Fair Debt Collection Practices Act § 809(a), 15 U.S.C. § 1692g(a).

(e) *Deciding on the recipient.* If you're writing to a company or association, make sure you send the demand letter to the right person. If your client has been dealing unsuccessfully with a midlevel manager, you might consider directing your letter to someone more senior—perhaps the owner or the president, or perhaps the general counsel (if there is one). You may want to have your client call the company to find out the name of a person with the authority to handle your demand. Get the full name (with the correct spelling) and title. There are two other possibilities. You can send the letter to the corporation at its corporate headquarters, where the mailroom should route the letter to the appropriate decision-maker. Or if you really want to get the recipient's attention and signal your seriousness, you can send the letter to the corporate agent for service of process, whose address most states require to be filed with the secretary of state or other governmental department in charge of licensing corporations. If there is an insurer or a superior affiliate company, consider sending the letter—or at least a copy—to someone in a position of responsibility there.

(f) *Sending the letter.* Be sure that the letter reaches its intended recipient by sending an original by registered or certified mail, whichever is customary within your jurisdiction, and sending a copy by regular U.S. mail or overnight mail. You can also send a copy by e-mail—but that should never take the place of registered or certified mail. If you're writing to an individual on behalf of a client and you know the individual's home address and work address, you may decide to send copies by both methods to both addresses—four letters in all. Your seriousness will not be lightly questioned. Also send a copy to your client (noting that fact with a *cc:* or *Copies*: in the letter), but don't send copies to lots of other people on either side.

21.3 Avoid the common faults of demand letters.

(a) *Typical shortcomings.* Demand letters often fail on several counts. They may be downright unintelligible to the lay recipient. They may be filled with hyperbole and therefore needlessly inflammatory, achieving just the opposite of the desired result. They may state the facts incorrectly. (Before writing, you must get reliable information from your client, preferably using documents to establish names and dates.) They may even misstate the law. (Avoid this by performing basic research into your putative cause of action.) They may be vague about how the client wants to resolve the matter without litigation. They may get bogged down in minutiae. Avoid all these common pitfalls, any one of which might lead the recipient to question your seriousness or even your competence. After a few cases, your reputation for such carelessness diminishes the impact of any future demands.

(b) *Two caveats.* First, never seek civil restitution by threatening criminal punishment. This is unethical and often illegal. The Model Code of Professional Responsibility prohibits a lawyer from threatening to present "criminal charges solely to obtain an advantage in a civil matter." DR 7-105(A). Second, never, never, never send a demand letter to someone who you know has retained a lawyer in the matter. If the adversary has a lawyer, the demand must go to the lawyer—not to the adversary. If you don't know whether the recipient is represented by a lawyer, you might include this statement as a postscript: "I am writing to you without knowing whether you are represented by an attorney in this matter. If you are, then please let me know and I will communicate through your attorney."

21.4 Study effective demand letters.

(a) *Collect good examples.* Ask senior colleagues to share some model demand letters with you. If you're allowed to, photocopy or keep computer files of the ones that strike you as particularly persuasive. Develop a file of good demand letters. Most jurisdictions have some characteristic variations here and there. In Georgia, for example, demands typically end with the sentence, "Govern yourself accordingly." Whether you make these types of phrases habitual in your own demands is for your supervisor (if you have one) to decide in the short run and for you to decide in the long run. But before you can decide, you must know what effective demand letters look like. What you're looking for is a hard-to-achieve balance: pithy treatment yet with adequate detail; a threatening tone yet with a sensible suggestion for resolving the dispute; formal distance yet with the sense that a forceful, persistent human being (not an automaton) has written the letter. The successful demand letter requires adequate preparation, a fair amount of self-assurance, and a command of tone.

(b) *Examples.* In the first example here, a lawyer has written to a publisher in a borderline situation: an academic author appears to have misappropriated the title of another academic's work, with the false implication that the new work is a continuation of the old. Nothing has been published yet, and the letter seeks to ensure that no real misappropriation will take place. In the second example, the wrong is more clear-cut and the demand is considerably more forceful.

David X. Sterling
Attorney at Law
Callinghast Plaza, 6040 Sherry Lane
Suite 1400
Dallas, Texas 75225
Telephone (214) 212-8888
Fax (214) 212-7777

5 December 2018

Ms. Phyllis Torping
Editor, Marginalia Publishing, Inc.
717 Avenue of the Americas
New York, NY 10028

Re: Daniel Martin Schimmelman Copyright Protection
By Certified and Regular Mail

Dear Ms. Torping:

I represent Professor Daniel Martin Schimmelman, with whom you have corresponded about Bertrand Katt's annotated bibliography of articles on the English Renaissance. As you know, Professor Schimmelman's work, *The English Renaissance (1475–1525): An Annotated Bibliography* (published in 1995), is an important work of scholarship that has become the standard in the field. Now Mr. Katt has tried to appropriate this title by calling his book *The English Renaissance (1525–1575): An Annotated Bibliography.*

Before we even get into the law, you should concede that this matter has been handled very poorly. Mr. Katt didn't bother to check with the author of the seminal work he sought to update. Marginalia apparently did the same back in 2006. At the very least, these are serious breaches of academic courtesy.

More than that, though, Professor Schimmelman has been legally harmed. First, the fact that Mr. Katt and Marginalia have made it possible for *Books in Print* to record that Mr. Katt's book already exists seriously limits the marketable possibilities for Professor Schimmelman's own updating of his work. Second, this misrepresentation in the marketplace—apparently an attempt to forestall competition—suggests to reasonable observers that Mr. Katt's book is somehow an "official" updating of Professor Schimmelman's work. Third, it suggests that Professor Schimmelman himself isn't engaged in that work or perhaps is no longer capable of doing the work. And all this is seriously exacerbated by the fact that Mr. Katt has used the same title in *Books in Print*—regardless of what you now intend to call the book.

Given the harm to Professor Schimmelman's reputation, your actionable conduct could easily lead to a substantial award of damages, possibly including an assignment of all profits from the sale of Mr. Katt's book, a published apology, and attorney's fees. I therefore request that you immediately:

- Ensure that Mr. Katt's book in no way infringes my client's rights.
- Ensure that, if you do publish a noninfringing work, you include a full acknowledgment of Professor Schimmelman's seminal work dealing with 1475–1525, which was the germ of Mr. Katt's idea.
- Send two copies to Professor Schimmelman and two to me so that we can evaluate for ourselves whether any infringement has occurred.
- Take immediate corrective action with *Books in Print* and any other source that may have disseminated your misrepresentations about the existence and title of Mr. Katt's work.

These are reasonable demands. If I do not hear from you by December 19, my client will assess what legal recourse he should take against Marginalia and Mr. Katt.

Very truly yours,

David X. Sterling

Copy to Mr. Bertrand Katt (by certified and regular mail)

Potsdam, Herald & Schiffering

Attorneys at Law

419 Crystal Avenue, Suite 500
Detroit, MI 48801

Telephone (517) 212-8888
Fax (517) 212-7777

Bertrand R. Frankelshouse
Partner

5 January 2018

Francis B. Bolling, M.D.
Medical Associates of Dearborn
32345 Dearborn Parkway, #745
Dearborn, MI 48951

Re: Account #5214-1829-93
By Hand Delivery, Certified Mail, and Regular Mail

Dear Dr. Bolling:

Our firm represents the Michigan Commercial Bank, N.A., where you have several accounts. I write to demand immediate repayment of the $350,000 erroneously posted to your savings account.

On November 15, 2017, through clerical error at the Bank, a deposit of $350,000 was credited to your account 5214-1829-93. At the time, you had a little more than $12,000 in that account. Two weeks later, the Bank mailed out account statements, and then on December 5, you withdrew $362,519 and closed the account.

The Bank discovered the error in mid-December 2017 and has tried repeatedly to work with you to correct it. Specifically, Vice President Laura S. Diller spoke with you on the morning of December 16, asking for only the return of $350,000, without interest. You told her that you intend to keep the money, to which you have no legal entitlement.

Unless you deliver cash or a cashier's check (payable to the Bank) for $350,000 to my office by 3 p.m. on Friday, January 19, 2018, we will promptly institute legal proceedings against you, seeking damages significantly in excess of $350,000, together with interest, attorney's fees, and punitive damages.

Very truly yours,

Bertrand R. Frankelshouse

§ 22
Pleadings

22.1 Understand the main goals of a pleading.

(a) *What a pleading is.* A pleading is a formal document in which a party to a lawsuit sets out or responds to allegations, claims, denials, or defenses. In federal civil practice, the only pleadings allowed are a complaint, an answer, a reply to a counterclaim, an answer to a cross-claim, a third-party complaint, and a third-party answer. Fed. R. Civ. P. 7(a). In other jurisdictions, the names may vary to include declarations, demurrers, general denials, replications, rejoinders, surrejoinders, rebutters, surrebutters, and the like. Unfortunately, the term *pleading* is sometimes misused to cover papers that are definitely not pleadings. Among these are process (a summons to appear in court, at a deposition, etc.), motions (an application for a court order), and discovery requests and responses (even when written). None are properly classified as pleadings.

(b) *Complaints generally.* A complaint initiates a lawsuit, describes the harm suffered by the plaintiff, identifies the party responsible, and requests a remedy. A complaint should provide the defendant with adequate notice of the plaintiff's claim. Make sure you know the requirements of the courts in which you file a complaint. In some jurisdictions, the plaintiff alleges only the facts necessary to support the claim. In others, the plaintiff must give adequate notice of a claim's nature, concisely state the grounds for each claim, and request relief; the elements of the claim need not be established by a statement of fact or law.

(c) *Complaints in federal court.* Under the Federal Rules of Civil Procedure (and many states with similar rules), the plaintiff's claim may be dismissed if it fails to state a claim on which relief may be granted. *See* Fed. R. Civ. P. 12(b)(6). So the complaint must state facts that, if proved, would entitle the plaintiff to some relief. You'll need to research the elements of the claim you're pleading. And certain "special matters"—such as capacity, fraud, conditions precedent, and admiralty and maritime claims—have additional pleading requirements. *See* Fed. R. Civ. P. 9. For example, despite the general notice-pleading requirements of the Federal Rules, allegations of fraud or mistake must be "stated with particularity." Fed. R. Civ. P. 9(b).

(d) *Answers.* The defendant must admit or deny each of the plaintiff's allegations and may also raise defenses and assert compulsory counterclaims. If the defendant cannot admit or deny an allegation for lack of information, the defendant customarily disclaims knowledge of its truth or accuracy. Except for special forms, such as affirmative defenses and objections to jurisdiction, defenses can usually be stated in general terms. In some jurisdictions, it's possible to file an answer that simply denies all of the plaintiff's claims categorically (in an answer called a *general denial* or a *general demurrer*). Most affirmative defenses and compulsory counterclaims must be raised in the answer or they are lost. *See* Fed. R. Civ. P. 8. Consult local practice guides (such as Siegel's *New York Practice*, *Moore's Federal Practice*, and Schwing's *California Affirmative Defenses*) for lists of potential affirmative defenses.

(e) *Focusing the dispute.* The pleadings should alert the court to the nature of the dispute, state the facts that give rise to the issues, and frame the issues to be tried.

22.2 Think about the specific goals of your pleading.

(a) *Protect your client's interests.* Filing pleadings can help preserve trial strategy, aid discovery, and stop the running of a statute of limitations. They may even help your client avoid going to trial.

(b) *Essential and additional claims.* In state-court actions, always assert the claims that are most important to the client in the initial pleading. Additional claims can usually be added later, after the advantages and disadvantages of litigating them have been considered. In federal-court actions, there are limited times to amend pleadings as a matter of course, after which amendments may be made only by leave of court (which is freely but not automatically granted) or by written consent of the adverse party. If time allows, include all potential claims in the initial complaint.

(c) *Answer.* Brief, precise responses to the plaintiff's claims may narrow the issues for trial to only those that are disputed. If the plaintiff's allegations are general or ambiguous, repeated denials may broaden the issues that will be tried but may make the plaintiff's case look weak. They also invariably lead to interrogatories asking the basis for the denials and seeking related documents. A longer response that recites supporting facts may promote settlement discussions, but it could also aid the plaintiff's preparation for trial. To avoid inadvertently failing to address some alleged fact, an answer may deny all allegations contained in the complaint, except as admitted, qualified, or otherwise responded to.

(d) *Available defenses.* Present any specific or affirmative defenses that can or should be made against a claim; these defenses must be pleaded in the answer or else they are waived. A general defense or simple denial alone may be inadequate because it doesn't include a specific or affirmative defense. The best practice is to assert all available defenses in your answer: some jurisdictions will not allow additional defenses later.

22.3 Avoid the common faults of pleadings.

(a) *Violating pleading rules.* Most jurisdictions have explicit rules for both the form and the substance of pleadings. Plead as the rules require by, for example, timely asserting all specific and affirmative defenses, pleading facts that show how venue is proper, or stating that the court has subject-matter jurisdiction over the claims and personal jurisdiction over the parties.

(b) *Overpleading.* Pleading too elaborately may backfire: what you plead, you must prove. Your opponent may argue that a failure of proof on some trivially or unnecessarily pleaded fact undermines your whole position.

(c) *Omissions in complaints.* Include every piece of essential information. The essential elements for a complaint are usually (1) a succinct statement of the grounds for the court's jurisdiction, (2) a succinct statement of the claim showing that the party is entitled to relief, and (3) a request for relief. The most common failing of complaints is not alleging all facts necessary to state a claim. A necessary element may have been overlooked, or the drafter may have omitted facts that establish an element because the facts are undisputed. As a result, the incompletely alleged claim may be dismissed because no relief can be granted. Another common failing is to neglect asking for relief. Some jurisdictions don't allow requests for specific dollar amounts, but general relief—such as a demand for damages—must still be requested.

(d) *Omissions in answers.* The most common mistake that lawyers make in drafting an answer is failing to respond to every fact set out in the complaint. Unless the answer expressly denies a fact or alleges a lack of knowledge about a fact, the fact is admitted. A second common error is failing to assert an affirmative defense or to raise a compulsory counterclaim in the answer. In most jurisdictions, defenses are waived if not asserted in the answer. The same is true of compulsory counterclaims. Moreover,

> "Pleadings perhaps do not ordinarily mean much to the Court . . . [;] nevertheless the lawyer who drafts his pleadings with meticulous care and skillful art is well paid for his efforts. Well-written pleadings may serve to require the opposite party to state his position exactly and clearly, as to issues which he would prefer not to have exposed. Also, well-written pleadings are often conducive to advantageous pretrial settlements. If the lawyer can make his case look particularly strong on the pleadings, the other side may be driven to the conclusion that it cannot risk a trial."
>
> —*Frank E. Cooper*

an amended answer cannot undo an admission (even by omission) in the answer.

(e) *Reliance on boilerplate forms.* Looking at sample forms may be a good start. But whether the forms are commercial or in-house, they can provide only general guidance. The facts will always be different. Laws change; so do courts' pleading requirements. And older pleadings are typically written in stuffy legalese. Draft pleadings in plain English and tailor them to the facts of your case, the specific claim, the current state of the law, and the local rules.

(f) *Verbosity.* Pleadings should be written concisely and with particularity. Judges don't want to read lengthy arguments in pleadings and may strike nonconforming pleadings, sometimes with prejudice. For examples of abuses and sanctions, see *McHenry v. Renne*, 84 F.3d 1172, 1176 (9th Cir. 1996) (rejecting a "novelized form" complaint); *Gordon v. Green*, 602 F.2d 743, 744–45, 745 nn.6–7 (5th Cir. 1979) (refusing to struggle with pleadings totaling 4,000 pages and filling volumes).

22.4 Study effective pleadings.

(a) *Model forms.* Standardized forms are most helpful as formatting templates but should never be used as fill-in-the-blank pleadings. In other words, don't follow an illustrative form mindlessly; make certain to tailor the form to your facts. The appendix to the Federal Rules of Civil Procedure contains many types of model pleadings for federal court. Sample pleadings are also available in Charles Alan Wright, Arthur R. Miller & Mary Kay Kane, *Federal Practice and Procedure* vol. 12A, app. D (2001), and in Michol O'Connor's *Federal Trial Forms* (updated annually). Most states also have formbooks illustrating acceptable pleadings for their courts. Before you begin to draft, check the local court rules to see precisely what requirements apply.

(b) *Further guidance.* Three recommended guides for drafting pleadings are Irwin Alterman, *Plain and Accurate Style in Court Papers* (1987); Mary Barnard Ray & Barbara J. Cox, *Beyond the Basics* 248–72 (3d ed. 2012); and Celia C. Elwell & Robert Barr Smith, *Practical Legal Writing for Legal Assistants* 308–75 (1996). You might also consult the most current treatises on causes of action and affirmative defenses. *See, e.g.*, Michol O'Connor, *O'Connor's Texas Causes of Action* (updated annually); Ann Schwing, *California Affirmative Defenses* (5th ed. 2014).

(c) *Examples.* The first example below is a notice pleading seeking recovery of a debt and avoidance of a fraudulent conveyance of the debtor's property. The statement of jurisdiction and the facts are terse, yet clearly outline the basis of the dispute. The second example is an answer to the complaint that complies with the requirements of Federal Rule of Civil Procedure 12(b).

Earl Jowitt Bouvier,	§	United States District Court
	§	for the Northern District
Plaintiff,	§	of Illinois
	§	
vs.	§	
	§	
Webster Tomlinson and	§	
Burrill Stroud, Inc.,	§	
a Colorado Corporation,	§	
	§	
Defendants.	§	Civil Action No. 02-C-2247

Complaint on Claim for Debt and to Set Aside Fraudulent Conveyance Under Rule 18(b)

1. Earl Jowitt Bouvier is a citizen of the State of Illinois. Webster Tomlinson is a citizen of the State of New Mexico. Burrill Stroud, Inc. is a business incorporated under the laws of Colorado with its principal place of business also in Colorado. The amount in controversy, exclusive of interest and costs, is more than the minimum specified by 28 U.S.C. § 1332.

2. On April 21, 2012, Tomlinson executed a promissory note for $158,000 with interest at the rate of 8% per year, payable in full to Bouvier on April 21, 2014.

3. Tomlinson did not make the promised payment on April 21, 2014.

4. Bouvier demanded payment from Tomlinson on at least five dates between April 21 and October 15, 2014.

5. Tomlinson has not paid any part of the $158,000 or the accrued interest.

6. On or about October 15, 2014, Tomlinson conveyed all his property, real and personal, to Burrill Stroud, Inc.

7. There was no legitimate purpose for Tomlinson's conveyance to Burrill Stroud, Inc.

8. Tomlinson's sole purpose for making the conveyance was to defraud Bouvier and to impede Bouvier's efforts to collect Tomlinson's debt.

Bouvier asks the Court to:

- Enter judgment against Tomlinson for $158,000 plus interest.
- Declare Tomlinson's conveyance to Burrill Stroud, Inc. void and impose a judgment lien on the conveyed property.
- Order Tomlinson to pay Bouvier's costs.

Respectfully submitted,

____

Lawrence M. Humsberger
Illinois State Bar #57249310
Humsberger, Shiffen & Albers
316 W. Randolph St., Suite 3200
Chicago, IL 60606
(312) 476-8888

Earl Jowitt Bouvier,	§	United States District Court
	§	for the Northern District
Plaintiff,	§	of Illinois
	§	
vs.	§	
	§	
Webster Tomlinson and	§	
Burrill Stroud, Inc.,	§	
a Colorado Corporation,	§	
	§	
Defendants.	§	Civil Action No. 18-C-2247

Tomlinson's Answer to Bouvier's Complaint

First Defense

1. The complaint fails to state a claim against Webster Tomlinson on which relief can be granted.

Second Defense

2. If Tomlinson owes Earl Jowitt Bouvier any money, Tomlinson owes the debt jointly with Jacob Chadman Wharton.

3. Wharton is alive, a citizen of Nebraska, and subject to the jurisdiction of this Court as to both service of process and venue.

4. Wharton is not a party to this suit, but can be made a party without depriving this Court of jurisdiction.

Third Defense

5. The statute of limitations requires that suits to collect a debt be filed within four years of the date when the debt became payable.

6. Bouvier alleges that the debt became payable on April 21, 2014.

7. Brewer filed this suit on August 6, 2018.

8. Tomlinson admits the allegations in paragraphs 1 and 2 of the complaint, alleges a lack of knowledge or information sufficient to admit or deny the allegation in paragraph 4, and denies each remaining allegation contained in the complaint.

Respectfully submitted,

____

Matthew Avant
Illinois State Bar #47748320
Avant & Carlisle
25 S. Wacker Dr.
Chicago, IL 60606
(312) 594-6666

I certify that on September 17, 2018, I served a copy of this answer by regular U.S. mail, postage prepaid, on Lawrence M. Humsberger, Humsberger, Shiffen & Albers, 316 W. Randolph St., Suite 3200, Chicago, IL 60606.

____

Matthew Avant

§ 23
Affidavits and Declarations

23.1 Understand the main goals of an affidavit.

(a) *Terminology.* An affidavit is a written statement prepared by or on behalf of a person (known as the *affiant*) who swears that what it contains is true and accurate. It usually recites facts based on the affiant's personal knowledge (or that are otherwise admissible, such as under a hearsay exception) or states an opinion that the affiant professes to be qualified to state. It must be sworn to before someone authorized to administer oaths, such as a notary public, who validates the signature and affirms that an oath or affirmation was administered.

A declaration is similar to an affidavit in content, but it doesn't have to be sworn to. A declaration may be adequate for some nonlitigation purposes, and in some circumstances it may be admissible in court.

A federal statute, 28 U.S.C. § 1746, allows an unsworn statement to be used in the place of an affidavit if it states that it is true under penalty of perjury and is dated and signed. Most states have similar statutes. It's astonishing how many practitioners fail to heed the particular requirements of § 1746 or a comparable state rule. Don't be one of them.

The advice in this chapter applies to both affidavits and declarations, even though for convenience the word *affidavit* is used alone.

(b) *General purposes.* An affidavit serves as evidence. Although affidavits are used most often in litigation, especially to support motions with evidence, they may also be used to support documents unrelated to litigation—for example, to prove a will, supplement an application, or correct a record.

(c) *Basic format.* A typical affidavit identifies the affiant, attests to the affiant's qualifications for making the statement, and records the affiant's statement of facts or opinion. It should also include a clear statement of the affidavit's purpose, such as to support a motion or to serve as evidence. Traditional affidavits place each statement in a separate, numbered paragraph. An alternative style uses headings to identify a set of facts, particularly if the affidavit is long. Litigators use paragraph numbers and sometimes headings to cite statements in affidavits.

(d) *Presenting evidence.* Affidavits should include only specific factual statements—not conclusions unless the statement is made by an expert witness. An affidavit is usually attached to another document. Some sworn documents that may be inaccurately referred to as affidavits make promises and acknowledge facts as true, rather than recite and swear to the truth of personally known facts. But these documents are really oaths, warranties, or contracts; they're not truly affidavits.

23.2 Think about the specific goals of your affidavit.

(a) *Purpose.* Before drafting an affidavit, think about how it will be used. Because only relevant facts are admissible, decide which facts are relevant and which ones aren't. For example, if your client wants to obtain a mechanic's lien against a customer who didn't pay for car repairs, the affidavit would contain facts about when the customer agreed to pay for the repairs, what work was done, and the value of the work. Leave out details that are clearly unimportant or inadmissible.

(b) *Helping the reader make a decision.* The usual audience for an affidavit is a decision-maker, such as a judge, arbitrator, or other official. Don't write an affidavit to make an argument. Your specific purpose for using the affidavit will guide what facts you include and how you present them. For example, an affidavit attached to a loan application may detail how the borrower will spend and repay the money, reassuring a prospective lender that the borrower is trustworthy. An affidavit attached to a motion for summary judgment will serve the same purpose as in-court testimony, presenting facts to show why the judge should grant summary judgment. Although no argument may appear and facts must not be slanted, the facts should be set out so that the reader comes to the desired conclusion. But be careful: a reader may view an affidavit as self-serving and discount or disregard it if contradictory facts emerge.

23.3 Avoid the common faults of affidavits.

(a) *Failing to show personal knowledge.* Because an affidavit is a form of evidence, an affiant must have direct, personal knowledge of a concrete fact. Courts usually won't accept an affidavit that merely expresses a belief, although some may accept a statement of belief if the affiant also states the grounds for that belief. Generally, an affidavit that contains language suggesting that the affiant lacks personal knowledge will carry no weight with a reader who is deciding whether to grant an application or motion.

(b) *Using stiff language, archaic legalisms.* Lawyers often draft affidavits on behalf of laypeople. Yet the language may end up sounding very formal and contrived, especially if it contains legal jargon. Don't substitute your voice for the affiant's. An affidavit sounds better when written the way the affiant speaks. Use plain English and adjust the style and diction to reflect the affiant's level of sophistication. If possible, have the affiant or someone else read the affidavit aloud; listen to how natural or contrived it sounds to you, since it will likely sound the same way to a reader.

Obsolete language also plagues the openings and closings of affidavits. To give but one example, the hoary introduction "who, being duly sworn, deposes and says" adds nothing. It doesn't even establish that the affiant has, in fact, been sworn—that information appears at the bottom of the affidavit. And the traditional conclusion "further affiant sayeth naught" may have been good form in the 18th century but became obsolete in British legal usage long ago. It should become obsolete in American usage, too.

(c) *Using third person instead of first.* An affidavit is supposed to be a personal statement, not a set of responses to an interrogation, so it should never be written in the third person. Even if you draft the affidavit using notes from an interview with the affiant, remember who the speaker is and use first-person pronouns.

(d) *Rambling.* Statements in an affidavit are supposed to support a specific point in another document or to assert a specific position. Long-winded, rambling sentences are open to misinterpretation. They're ineffective.

(e) *Tweaking or "improving" facts.* The statements in an affidavit are facts, not arguments or conclusions. While it's perfectly acceptable to choose a word for its connotation (e.g., the plaintiff might use *collision* and the defendant might use *accident* for the same incident), it isn't all right to distort the facts (e.g., using emotion-charged words such as *malicious* and *heartless*). Nor is it acceptable to slant or omit facts so that the decision-maker might be misinformed.

(f) *Neglecting to label an evidentiary affidavit as an exhibit.* Sometimes a litigator will submit a document that refers to an affidavit as a specific exhibit, but the drafter of the affidavit has neglected to mark it to be clearly identifiable as the one referred to (e.g., "Exhibit A to Plaintiff's Motion; Affidavit of John Brown"). Readers understand that an affidavit is prepared with a specific purpose in mind. Adding that purpose to the title doesn't make it seem contrived.

(g) *Common shortcomings of federal-court affidavits.* Violating 28 U.S.C. § 1746, many affidavits in federal court refer to a state law instead of federal law or fail to specify the date on which an affidavit was signed. Avoid putting a federal judge in the position of having to decide whether an affidavit that is insufficient under § 1746 nevertheless satisfies some other legal requirement for the filing of an affidavit, such as Federal Rule of Civil Procedure 56.

23.4 Follow rules of evidence.

(a) *Admissibility.* When an affidavit is being used in place of in-court testimony—for example, to support a summary-judgment motion—it must comply with the rules of evidence. A witness giving a factual account must ordinarily testify on personal knowledge only, so the affidavit must contain a section that explains the basis for admitting the evidence. For example, if the affidavit is offered to tell how a traffic accident happened, the affiant should explain how he or she witnessed it, whether as a driver, a passenger, or a bystander. A bystander should state how far he or she was from the accident, whether the view was obstructed in any way, what the weather conditions were, and that he or she saw the collision.

(b) *Hearsay.* In the American legal system, hearsay isn't admissible unless it falls within one of several exceptions. An affidavit that contains hearsay must lay a foundation for its admissibility. To continue the example of a traffic accident, if the affiant wants to say that another passenger warned the driver by saying "red light" just before the collision, the affidavit must include facts from which the court could find that the statement "red light" was an excited utterance or fit within another hearsay exception.

(c) *Expert witnesses.* Rules of evidence require an expert witness to be qualified, so the affidavit must include not just the opinion but also the expert's qualifications and the basis for reaching the conclusions stated. It should state the witness's education, training, and experience. In a personal-injury suit to recover money damages, a physician's affidavit about the injuries should identify his or her medical training, licenses, and other relevant experience such as publications. It should also state the basis for the witness's conclusions, including when and where the witness examined the injured person.

(d) *Standard for expert testimony.* If complex or cutting-edge scientific or technical evidence appears in the affidavit, the affiant must comply with whatever standard the court uses to determine the reliability of that evidence, such as the general-acceptance test.

(e) *Writings, business records, photographs, things.* For a court to consider something other than human testimony as evidence, the affiant must establish personal knowledge of the thing's authenticity. For example, an affidavit accompanying a business record must establish that the affiant knows this to be a record kept in the ordinary course of business. Similarly, in an affidavit accompanying a photograph, the affiant must state that the photograph was taken at a certain scene at a certain time or that it accurately depicts the place or person.

23.5 Study effective affidavits.

(a) *Further guidance.* Form affidavits for specific purposes can be found in statutes or formbooks. But form affidavits don't fit every case, and there is no generic affidavit for all purposes. Of necessity, the contents will always vary because every affiant will swear to different facts in different ways. For sound advice on how to make an affidavit more effective, see Wayne Schiess, *Writing for the Legal Audience* 82–89 (2d ed. 2014); Kamela Bridges & Wayne Schiess, *Writing for Litigation* 121–31, 207–10 (2011).

(b) *Examples.* The first affidavit below uses the traditional format, laying out facts in short numbered paragraphs. This format tends to hide the critical point in the middle, and the language often sounds more like the affiant is reciting someone else's words rather than attesting to personal knowledge. But the format is acceptable for a short affidavit with clear facts. The second affidavit uses a modified format. It opens with a summary, labels each section with a heading, and uses the affiant's own words to produce a relaxed, personal tone.

> "Preparing an affidavit presents the litigation writer with ample opportunities to use legalistic terminology, archaic verbiage, and insider legal jargon. But remember: The affiant will quite often be a nonlawyer who is unfamiliar with legal language. And more to the point, the affiant is the one actually 'speaking' through the affidavit, even if the lawyer wrote it. . . . No matter how you prepare an affidavit, avoid the excesses of legalese."
>
> —*Kamela Bridges & Wayne Schiess*

Traditional format

Affidavit of Robert Wood to Prove Use of an Opposition Mark

ROBERT WOOD, being duly sworn, stated:

1. My name is Robert Wood. I am over 21 years of age, I am of sound mind, and I have personal knowledge of the facts stated below.

2. I am the Marketing Director for Unicorn Books. I started work at Emperor Penguin Books as a design artist in 1994 and helped design the company's logo.

3. The company's logo features a black silhouette of a unicorn with a gold horn and details of the mane and tail picked out in silver. A sample of the logo is attached.

4. Every book published by Unicorn has the unicorn mark at the top of its spine and at the bottom of the title page. Samples of the logo's use are attached.

5. Books with the Unicorn mark have been sold in the states of Jefferson, Terlingua, and East Columbia continuously since 1994.

6. I personally suggested that the company use distinctive pink and pale-blue covers for girls' and boys' books, respectively. The company has used the unicorn logo on pink-covered and blue-covered books since 1994. Samples of the logo and of the pink and blue covers are attached.

7. Unicorn sells about 500,000 books and has sales revenue over $1 million each year.

____

Robert Wood

[*notarial verification*]

Modified format

Affidavit of Mike Martinez in Support of Motion for Summary Judgment

This affidavit, by Erika Pettigrew's supervisor Michael Martinez, explains that Ms. Pettigrew was fired because she lied about the reason for an absence and abused a credit card belonging to Aircraft Maintenance, Inc. Ms. Pettigrew was not fired because she is female.

The Affiant

My name is Mike Martinez. I am over 21 years of age and of sound mind. I have personal knowledge of the facts stated below. I am the assistant manager for Aircraft Maintenance, Inc. (AMI), located at York Regional Airport in York, Texas.

The Employee

Janet Greene, AMI's general manager, hired Erika Pettigrew as an assistant manager on March 16, 2017. Ms. Pettigrew was scheduled to work Mondays through Fridays from 8 a.m. to 3 p.m. She began work on March 23, 2017.

Events Surrounding Ms. Pettigrew's Firing

On November 28, 2017, Ms. Pettigrew didn't show up for work. I called her home around 9:30 a.m. and got no answer. She called me at AMI about 11 a.m. to say she had to leave town for an emergency and wouldn't return to work until December 14. She said her brother had died, and she had to arrange for his burial and help settle his estate. I said she could have the time off.

Reasons for Ms. Pettigrew's Firing

I got the contact information for Ms. Pettigrew's parents from her personnel file and called them on December 2, 2017, to express my condolence's on their son's death. I was surprised to hear that Ms. Pettigrew is an only child.

Then on December 3, 2017, I received AMI's credit-card statement. I discovered that dozens of charges had been made plus cash advances. I didn't authorize most of the charges or advances, which dated back to April

2017. A lot of the charges were made at jewelers and high-end clothing stores. I asked for and received copies of the credit-card slips. When I saw that most of them were signed by Ms. Pettigrew, I contacted the police.

When Ms. Pettigrew was extradited from Mexico in February 2018, she could not explain why the charges or advances had been made and or where the cash and merchandise had gone. I fired her because she was dishonest. She lied about her reason for suddenly failing to report for work, lied to get time off, and abused a company credit card.

No other AMI employee has ever been allowed to return to work after taking time off without permission and without a good reason. No AMI employee has been retained after abusing a company credit card. I didn't fire Ms. Pettigrew because she's a woman. That had nothing to do with my decision.

____

Mike Martinez

[*notarial verification*]

§ 24
Motions

24.1 Understand the main goals of a motion.

(a) *Purpose.* A motion is simply a formal request directed to a court. If your client needs something from the court, move for it. You will be asking the judge to enter an order—for example, to compel discovery, to quash an indictment, to suppress evidence, to continue a trial date, to grant a summary judgment, or to change the venue. Although courts often decide motions without oral arguments, based solely on written documents, filing a motion usually means that you're asking for a hearing on some issue.

(b) *Strategic advantages.* A motion may preserve your client's procedural rights (as with a motion requesting submission of a particular question to the jury) or substantive rights (as with a motion for a preliminary injunction). It may also serve to inform the court about an issue and to advance your legal theory. For example, a motion to strike irrelevant portions of the complaint may direct the court's attention to the real issues and reduce the number of issues for trial. Unmeritorious claims and defenses may be disposed of by a motion for summary judgment on those issues. Because most judges manage extensive dockets, the strategic use of motions may help educate the judge about the merits of your case—or the lack of merit in your opponent's case.

24.2 Think about the specific goals of your motion.

(a) *Goals.* What advantage do you seek? While planning your litigation strategy, consider what types of motions may help you. For example, if the opponent's physical or mental condition is an issue, you may need to move for an examination that could produce valuable evidence. A successful motion (to certify or decertify a class, for example, in a class action) may prove so advantageous that your opponent will settle out of court.

(b) *Proposed order.* Most jurisdictions require an advocate to submit what is called a *proposed order* or *form of order* with the motion. This is simply a draft of the order that the advocate would like entered, with blanks for the date and the judge's signature. Even if the jurisdiction in which you file the motion doesn't require a proposed order, you should prepare and present one: it will focus your mind on the precise relief that you're requesting, and it will let the court know how to rule in your favor. Don't write an order that simply "grants the motion"; rather, make the order specific (e.g., "the trial is continued until July 24, 2018" or "the expert designation of Garrett Hobart is struck").

(c) *Cross-motions.* It may become necessary, by motion, to counter an adverse party's previous motion. Cross-motions are appropriate when you need a court not only to deny the other side's motion but to do more as well. For example, your opponent may file a motion to compel discovery; you might file an objection to the motion combined with your own motion for a protective order. But not every motion that your opponent files calls for an equal and opposite motion on your part. As in everything else, use judgment and discretion.

24.3 Avoid the common faults of motions.

(a) *Violating rules.* Federal and state courts have rules controlling both the substantive and the procedural aspects of motion practice. In some jurisdictions, the motion is separate from the memorandum in support of it, but in others the two documents are combined; learn the rules—including any local rules—that govern the courts you appear before. Rules also control vital details such as time limits for filing various types of motions and their supporting documents, as well as for any prehearing conferences. Some motions must be prefaced by a formal "notice of motion"—that is, a document stating that the motion is attached and setting out the date and time when the motion will be heard or submitted. The court may have a meet-and-confer requirement; if so, the movant's counsel must attach a certificate attesting that the attorneys for both sides have conferred about the subject of the motion, that they have been unable to come to an agreement, and that the movant's counsel now seeks the court's involvement. Some courts require an explicit request for oral argument if a party desires it. And most courts have length limits on motions and supporting memorandums. A violation of court rules may result in the denial of a motion or possibly sanctions.

(b) *Not getting to the point.* A good motion begins by clearly stating the point to be decided. Don't recite case history until you've made your request. The burden of most courts grows year by year, and judges have only limited time to consider motions. So regardless of the jurisdiction, include a preliminary statement in which you synopsize the issue, say how you think it should be resolved, and briefly explain why. Leave less important details for the main body. You should try to win a motion in the first page and a half.

(c) *Overreliance on forms.* Although some courts have fill-in-the-blank motions for routine matters, many cut-and-paste forms just waste your time. If you don't take the time to redraft the form to fit the particular facts of your case, you may inadvertently leave in irrelevant material or omit material that you should have included. Besides wasting the court's time, a sloppy motion suggests that the writer is sloppy in other ways as well (in analyzing legal problems, in preserving clients' rights, and so on).

(d) *Failing to cite authority.* No order may issue without legal authority. Apart from preliminary procedural motions that are purely discretionary (asking the judge, for example, to let a party change lawyers), a motion must include the authority by which the judge can legally order the specific relief you've asked for. You may cite a statute or a case (preferably both), but you generally shouldn't just assume that the judge will know the grounds for your motion. Cite the authority, or else your motion may never even get a hearing on the merits. If the relief you're seeking isn't a routine matter, attaching a copy of the authority may sometimes bolster your client's position.

(e) *Incorrect or frivolous contents.* Failing to double-check facts and authority is a common blunder. An erroneous citation or a misstatement of fact will reflect poorly on your competence and waste the court's time. While you should describe the law and facts persuasively, always use precise, accurate language so that the court can trust your representations. Don't overstate them. The court won't look favorably on this motion or on your future motions if you lose credibility in this way (and possibly faces sanctions).

(f) *Churning.* A lawyer who files many motions with little success may well lead the court to suspect that the lawyer's real purpose is delay and perhaps harassment. The client may begin to suspect that the lawyer is simply padding the bill. The court might even levy sanctions.

(g) *Educating your adversary.* Motions often educate the other side without gaining the movant any advantage. For example, a motion to dismiss for inadequate pleading often results in a court's allowing the defect to be cured. Likewise, a motion for summary judgment often sets out for the other side precisely what facts must be proved. Think hard before making a motion. Is it likely to be granted? Or will you simply be helping your opponent do whatever is necessary to defeat you in the end? If the latter, you may also lose a ground for appeal.

24.4 Study effective motions.

(a) *Models.* Some excellent model motions appear in the appendix to the Federal Rules of Civil Procedure and in Michol O'Connor's *Federal Trial Forms* (updated annually). These forms exemplify clarity and simplicity. For a good before-and-after example, the "before" version being typically slow and legalistic and the "after" version being much more succinct and powerful, see Bryan A. Garner, *The Winning Brief* 699–716 (3d ed. 2014).

(b) *Further guidance.* Good discussions of motion-drafting appear in Mary Barnard Ray & Barbara J. Cox, *Beyond the Basics* 273–91 (3d ed. 2012), and in Celia C. Elwell & Robert Barr Smith, *Practical Legal Writing for Legal*

Assistants 379–402 (1996). A detailed checklist for drafting motions appears in Barbara Child, *Drafting Legal Documents* 80–82 (2d ed. 1992).

(c) *An example.* Unlike many motions, the following sample omits the deadwood at the beginning and encapsulates the main reasons that the court should grant summary judgment. The supporting memorandum goes into greater depth with a statement of the precise issue, followed by a more detailed argument based on the undisputed facts and the law.

> "Perhaps the trick of successful argumentation is to steer a course between oversimplification and overelaboration. Most questions are more complex than they appear on the surface, and any effective arguments concerning them must recognize that complexity. Complexity and confusion, however, can be near akin, and they are likely to be so in the hands of a writer who cannot distinguish valid qualifications and necessary defensive maneuvers from all manner of tangentially related ideas. We have all had a painful experience, particularly in conversation, with an arguer who is continually being led away to elaborate the structure of the substrata of the foundation of some flying buttress on his thesis. The first law of argumentation is to keep to the point."
>
> —*John E. Jordan*

In the Court of Common Pleas
Franklin County, Ohio

JOYCE WARREN,	§	Case No. 18CVC-04-1588
	§	
Plaintiff,	§	
	§	
and	§	
	§	
AMERICAN AMARANTHUS INSURANCE COMPANY,	§	
	§	
	§	Hon. Jerre Williams
Intervenor,	§	
	§	
v.	§	
	§	
JAY FINDLAY,	§	
	§	
Defendant.	§	

American Amaranthus Insurance Company's
Motion for Summary Judgment

In accordance with Rule 56 of the Ohio Rules of Civil Procedure, American Amaranthus respectfully moves the Court for summary judgment on the claims contained in its complaint for declaratory judgment. Although Mr. Findlay's insurance policy with American Amaranthus excludes coverage for his intentional acts, all the allegations against Mr. Findlay are for intentional acts. After

18 months of litigation, there are no genuine issues of any material fact relating to this point. American Amaranthus is therefore entitled to judgment as a matter of law.

Respectfully submitted,

____

Barbara L. Hull
State Bar No. 444444444
Marina H. Johnston
State Bar No. 555555555
HULL, BRIM & JOHNSTON
500 Park Place Ave.
Suite 1900
Cleveland, Ohio 44114
(216) 566-7777

ATTORNEYS FOR AMERICAN
AMARANTHUS INSURANCE
COMPANY

American Amaranthus Insurance Company's Memorandum in Support of Its Motion for Summary Judgment

An excellent deep issue: see 25.1(d). Deep issues work superbly in motion practice as well.

1. Preliminary Statement

In deciding this motion, the Court is presented with a single issue:

> Jay Findlay's homeowner's insurance policy with American Amaranthus specifically excludes coverage for Findlay's intentional acts. Last spring, while the policy was in effect, Findlay hosted Joyce Warren at his house, where she claims that he physically abused her and attempted to kill her. She has now sued. Must American Amaranthus defend Findlay against these claims of assault and attempted murder?

Although Warren has now amended her complaint to allege that Findlay "negligently and recklessly assaulted her," this count fails to state a claim under Ohio law and should not influence the Court's decision on the critical issue posed above.

2. Background

On April 20, 2017, Warren filed suit against Findlay, claiming that he had "knowingly, intentionally, and maliciously assaulted" her at his house earlier that month. (Complaint ¶ 2.) Specifically, she alleges that he injured her left eye and left cheekbone, that he cut and bruised her mouth, and that she suffered bruises and scrapes on her neck, arms, and chest. (*Id.*) She also alleges that Findlay "knowingly, intentionally, and maliciously" attempted to murder her. (*Id.* ¶ 4.) Five months later, she amended her complaint by adding a count alleging that he "negligently and recklessly assaulted her." (*Id.* ¶ 5.)

American Amaranthus moved to intervene in the case on October 26, 2017, in order to obtain this Court's determination whether the insurer should be required to defend Findlay against Warren's claims. As fully explained below, American Amaranthus is entitled to a declaratory judgment stating that because of the terms of Findlay's insurance policy and because of the allegations contained in Warren's complaint (as amended), American Amaranthus has no duty to defend against Warren's claims.

3. Law and Argument

Two procedural points arise at the outset. The first is the standard for granting summary judgment. The Ohio Supreme Court favors summary judgment when a party fails to establish the existence of an element essential to that party's case.[1] In responding, a nonmoving party must demonstrate that there is a genuine issue of material fact.[2] This is just such a case. The second point is that American Amaranthus has properly sought declaratory relief. The Ohio Supreme Court has held that an insurer is entitled to intervene in a lawsuit brought against its insured so that it may raise questions about its potential liability.[3] This is precisely the question that American Amaranthus now raises.

Although an insurer's duty to defend may arise even when a claim is false or fraudulent,[4] the specific policy at issue here explicitly states that

---

1 *See, e.g.*, *Nelson v. Takoka*, 82 Ohio App. 3d 101, 107 (1992); *McKay v. Cutlip*, 80 Ohio App. 3d 487, 492 (1992).

2 *McKay*, 80 Ohio App. 3d at 492.

3 *Howell v. Richardson*, 45 Ohio St. 3d 365, 367 (1989) (relying on Ohio Revised Code ch. 2721); *Preferred Risk Ins. Co. v. Gill*, 30 Ohio St. 3d 108, 112 (1989) (same).

4 *Gill*, 30 Ohio St. 3d at 114.

this is so only "if the allegations, if true, would be covered." (Ins. Pol. ¶ 2.) All that matters is the language of the complaint—not an assessment of the insured's underlying acts or the results of those acts.[5] As the Supreme Court noted in *Gill*: "[T]he insurer has no duty to defend or indemnify its insured where the insurer demonstrates in good faith in the declaratory-judgment action that the act of the insured was intentional and therefore outside the policy coverage."[6] Hence the insurer need not defend against claims that would not be covered even if they were true.

Warren has made no allegations that, if true, would cause American Amaranthus to be liable. Although she has alleged various bodily injuries, the insurer would have liability only if these resulted from an "accident." (Ins. Pol., Defs. §, at 2.) There are only three counts in Warren's complaint, and none of them alleges the kind of unintentional circumstance or carelessness that would fit any accepted meaning of the word *accident.*[7]

In count one ("Civil Assault"), Warren alleges that Findlay "*knowingly, intentionally, and maliciously* assaulted the Plaintiff, causing injuries to her left eye, left cheekbone, lacerations and contusions to her mouth and face, and bruises and scrapes on her neck, arms, and chest." (Amended Complaint ¶ 2 (emphasis added).) She never alleges that these bodily injuries resulted from an accident. Yet the tort of civil assault centers on actions

---

5 *Id.*

6 *Id.* at 114–15.

7 *See Black's Law Dictionary* 15 (Bryan A. Garner ed., 7th ed. 1999) (defining *accident* as "[a]n unintended and unforeseen injurious occurrence" and quoting insurance treatises); *Webster's New World Dictionary* 8 (3d coll. ed. 1994) (defining *accident* as either "an unforeseen event that occurs without anyone's fault or negligence" or "a happening that is not expected, foreseen, or intended").

intended to cause harm—not on accidental actions.[8] For this reason, Findlay is not entitled to a defense on the first count.

In count two ("Murder"), Warren alleges that Findlay "knowingly, intentionally, and maliciously attempted to murder the Plaintiff, thereby causing the injuries described in Count One." (Amended Complaint ¶ 4.) There can be no argument that this allegation is entirely inconsistent with the idea of an "accident." Hence Findlay is not entitled to a defense on the second count.

In count three ("Negligent and Reckless Assault"), Warren alleges that Findlay "negligently and recklessly assaulted" her. (Amended Complaint ¶ 5.) This count fails not only to state a claim that would be covered under Findlay's insurance, but also to state a claim under Ohio law. There is no cause of action for "negligent and reckless assault." Under Ohio law, a claim for assault (tortious or criminal) requires intent.[9] And an intentional act of the type here alleged is inconsistent with an "accident."

Warren's placing the words "negligently and recklessly" before the word "assault" does not make the assault an "accident" under the meaning of the insurance policy. The amended complaint is a transparent attempt to bring Findlay's alleged acts within insurance coverage, but Warren's position is not supported by precedent, and "negligent and reckless assault" remains an oxymoron in Ohio law. So Findlay is not entitled to a defense on this count.

---

8 *See Smith v. John Deere Co.*, 83 Ohio App. 3d 398, 406 (1993) ("An essential element of the tort of assault is that the actor knew with substantial certainty that his or her act would bring about harmful or offensive contact.").

9 *See De Lisa v. Scott*, 47 Ohio App. 503, 510 (1934); *Williams v. Pressman*, 113 N.E.2d 395 (Ohio Ct. App. 1953); *Jones v. Wittenberg Univ.*, 534 F.2d 1203 (6th Cir. 1976).

4. Conclusion

American Amaranthus should prevail in its declaratory-judgment action because Warren's allegations of assault, attempted murder, and "negligent" assault are not covered by Findlay's policy. Regardless of whether any of the claims might be true, they are not covered because they allege intentional acts that could not possibly be "accidents." American Amaranthus should not be required to defend Findlay because (a) its duty to defend arises solely from the allegations of the complaint, and (b) Warren has failed to allege an "accident" covered under the policy. American Amaranthus asks this Court to grant judgment as a matter of law.

Respectfully submitted,

____

Barbara L. Hull
State Bar No. 444444444
Marina H. Johnston
State Bar No. 555555555
HULL, BRIM & JOHNSTON
500 Park Place Ave., Suite 1900
Cleveland, Ohio 44114
(216) 566-7777

ATTORNEYS FOR AMERICAN AMARANTHUS INSURANCE COMPANY

CERTIFICATE OF SERVICE

I certify that on January 15, 2018, I served a copy of this motion by regular U.S. mail, postage prepaid, of the foollowing counsel of record:

Keith Fargo, Esq.
297 South High St., Suite 2700
Calumbus, Ohio 43215

Melanie H. Trew, Esq.
444 Walnut St., Suite 1580
Cincinnati, Ohio 45202

____

Barbara L. Hull

§ 25
Appellate Briefs

25.1 Understand the main goals of a brief.

(a) *Purpose.* The purpose of an appellate brief is to persuade a panel of impartial readers—extremely busy readers—to decide a dispute in your client's favor by holding that a lower tribunal's judgment or decision is or isn't erroneous. To do this, you must efficiently convey your points, preferably by summing up their essence in a short preliminary statement at the very outset of the brief. By reading the first page and a half, each judge should have a clear sense of what will follow in the remaining pages. The up-front summary is crucial to your persuasiveness.

(b) *Tone.* Your tone should be calm, forthright, and unflinching. It shouldn't be heated, accusatory, defensive, or hyperbolic. You'll persuade by forcefully stating—but never overstating—the legal and factual support for your position. Ideally, you should set all this out in an interesting, engaging way. The only way to do that is to have developed your prose style long before sitting down to write a particular brief.

(c) *Reliability.* Because you must in the end be viewed as a thoroughly reliable source, you should keep three things constantly in mind while preparing a brief. First, whenever you state a fact, ask yourself whether you're fairly representing the record. Second, whenever you state the law, ask yourself whether you're fairly representing both what the statutes provide and what the relevant cases say. Third, whenever you make an argument, ask yourself whether it is fair. If your answer is ever no, or you're uncertain, don't write what you were thinking of writing.

(d) *Identifying the issues with great clarity.* Tell the judge what the deep issue or issues are, and do it coolly and logically. You should state the problem in a way that leads the judge to an answer before he or she begins reading your argument. In no more than 75 words, present the core law, facts, and question to be answered. Begin a deep issue with a concise statement of the controlling law or legal principle—in about 25 words. Then you'll have 45 or so words for the who, what, when, where: the determinative facts in chronological order. Then present a short question—perhaps four to seven words, introducing nothing new. The answer should be clear from the premises. From the first page of your brief, before you present your full argument, the judge will know how you're framing the issue on appeal and what your suggested answer is. Following are three properly framed deep issues—multisentence statements that culminate in a question mark by the 75th word.

Ex.: The U.S. Supreme Court has held that Title VI of the Civil Rights Act of 1964 does not confer a private right of action under the statute or its implementing regulations. The plaintiffs here are a class of California schoolchildren who allege that the Department of Education has violated Title VI and its implementing regulations. Can these plaintiffs sue the Department for violating Title VI or its implementing regulations? [69 words]

Ex.: Under New Jersey law, to recover for fraud a plaintiff must prove detrimental reliance on a deliberate misrepresentation. In a meeting with Perkins, Dedman allegedly misrepresented the price of his goods, saying that they were competitively priced when they were not. Perkins sued for fraud. But in his deposition, Perkins testified that he had made no decision based on anything said at that meeting. Can Perkins recover against Dedman for fraud? [71 words]

Ex.: Delaware courts have consistently held that Delaware's blue-sky laws do not apply to securities transactions that take place out of state. All the transactions between Balancio Securities and Ellsmere before April 2018 occurred outside Delaware—in Kansas, Nebraska, and South Dakota. Should this Court dismiss Ellsmere's claims under the blue-sky laws for the transactions completed before April 2018? [60 words]

If you'd like more examples, dozens are supplied in Garner, *The Winning Brief* 97–103; 108–09; 116–19; 124–26 (3d ed. 2014).

(e) *Killer point headings.* Many appellate judges, probably having realized how insufficient single-sentence "issue statements" are (and how pervasive they have become), look first to the table of contents. There they find the point headings, which should give the argument at a glance. The best ones are full-sentence headings throughout the argument section, ranging from 15 to 35 words and progressing from the law to the facts, first on main points and then on points in refutation. They are printed as down-style sentences—preferably not in initial capitals (see 2.19(c)). Here's a great set of point headings from the U.S. Solicitor General's Office:

> "A brief should be brief and concise, while elaborating in written form the propositions laid out in your pleading. Skill in presentation and in arguing those propositions, first in writing and then on your feet, will challenge and command the attention of the court."
>
> —*Sherman Minton*

Argument

Petitioner's detention incident to the execution of a search warrant was valid under the Fourth Amendment.

A methodical explanation of the law.

A. Under *Michigan v. Summers*, police officers executing a search warrant for contraband may detain departing occupants a short distance from the premises when reasonably necessary.

1. The reasonableness of a warrantless seizure is determined by balancing the law-enforcement interests against the intrusion on personal liberty.
2. Balancing those concerns, *Summers* held as a categorical rule that officers executing a search warrant may detain occupants who leave the premises.
3. *Summers* and later cases confirm that the manner in which officers conduct such a detention must be objectively reasonable under the circumstances.

A refutation of the Petitioner's position.

B. A strict geographic limit on detention would be inconsistent with *Summers*.

1. When officers see an occupant leave premises subject to a search warrant, they have an identifiable and individualized basis to detain him.
2. Sum*mers* rejected a strict geographic limit on where an occupant may be detained.
3. No federal court of appeals has adopted petitioner's strict geographic limit on detention.

A detailed account of policy points underlying the *Summers* case.

C. Substantial law-enforcement interests justify detaining an occupant away from the premises as soon as reasonably practicable.

1. An occupant who has left the premises may flee from officers.
2. An occupant who has left the premises may return to harm officers or interfere with the search.
3. A detained occupant who has been taken from the premises may be returned to help in the orderly completion of the search.
4. Detaining an occupant away from the premises prevents needlessly alerting others inside to the police presence.
5. Detaining an occupant away from the premises prevents needlessly forcing officers to begin the search prematurely.

Further reasons to reject the Petitioner's arguments.

D. Detaining an occupant a short distance from the premises is not substantially more intrusive, and may be less intrusive, than detaining him in the immediate vicinity of the premises.

E. Petitioner's geographic limit is artificial, unnecessary, and impractical.

Conclusion

Headings should never be an afterthought. You should write them before composing any other passage in your brief—apart from the issue statements.

For an informative essay on point headings, see Garner, *Final Grades on Point Headings for the 2016 Term*, 44 Litig. 19 (Winter 2018).

(f) *Marshaling the pertinent facts.* Even if the only question before the court is one of law, you must acquaint the court with the relevant facts. Never force a judge's clerk to dig through the record. Clearly, fully, and succinctly tell the court what the facts are before arguing about what the law is and how it applies to the facts. Although you must never misstate the facts, or omit the facts that cut against your position, part of the advocate's art is to present the facts in the light most favorable to your client. After reading your fact section—even before getting to the legal discussion—the judge's reaction should be, "This side wins."

(g) *Standard of review and governing law.* In at least one section of the brief, cite the appropriate standard of review for the issues on appeal: de novo, clearly erroneous, abuse of discretion, etc. *See* Fed. R. App. P. 28(a)(9)(B). And always address the standard in your argument. Demonstrate why it applies to the case. (This point is particularly important with an erroneous finding of fact: appellate judges are generally loath to second-guess a trial court in matters lying within its purview.) On the merits, cite the applicable statutory or decisional law and explain why it is persuasive. Avoid merely stating general legal principles without tying them to specific facts. Instead of "A motion to dismiss lies where the complaint fails to set forth facts constituting a claim upon which relief can be granted," for example, write "Wilfong's complaint did not state a claim for slander because it never denied the truth of Stelzer's statement."

25.2 Think about the specific goals of your brief.

(a) *Appellant seeking reversal.* The appellant's chief goal is to persuade the appellate court that the lower court misinterpreted or misapplied controlling law—and that its doing so substantially changed the outcome. Sometimes, you must ask the court to adopt or even devise a favorable principle that was unavailable in the lower court. This usually entails persuading the court that adopting a legal principle applied to factually similar cases in other jurisdictions would be legally sound. Occasionally, a case's facts may require a novel proposition of law to achieve justice. If such a proposition is supported solely by logic rather than precedent, you should explain why no citations are given in direct support. If you analogize from other areas of the law, supporting citations should be included.

(b) *Appellee seeking affirmance.* An appellee seeks to persuade the appellate court to uphold the lower court's decisions of law. You'll need to defend what the lower court has done. Sometimes, however, an appellee who isn't satisfied with the relief granted below may seek to increase it as a result of an error affecting the relief. Or the appellee may seek to have counterclaims restored and tried (if dismissed) or retried. This is usually done in a cross-appeal, for which a slightly different set of briefing rules may apply; the appellee becomes a cross-appellant, and part of the appellee's brief functions as an appellant's brief.

(c) *Client's interests.* Open with your strongest argument. Drop implausible or weak points: they detract from your strong ones. If you cannot achieve a complete victory, focus on achieving a partial victory, especially on the points of vital importance to the client (e.g., a client may be more concerned with having a right to privacy recognized than with preserving an award of damages).

(d) *Your reputation.* Make a good impression on your judicial readers. Ask for no more than what your client is legitimately entitled to. Advance your client's case while also being respectful of your opponent, fair in stating the facts and the law, and ethical in every particular. Double-check everything in the brief: inaccurate citations, arguments, or statements of fact or law can torpedo your credibility. Be meticulous in following the court's briefing rules. Even details such as the color of the brief cover matter. Proofread your brief for misspellings, grammatical lapses, and other distractions. The attention you pay to details reflects your degree of care and professionalism.

25.3 Avoid the common faults of briefs.

(a) *Omitting the standard of review.* An appellate court typically reviews procedures, judgments, and decisions for errors. Whereas a trial court weighs evidence, assesses credibility, and finds facts, an appellate court determines only whether the trial court applied the correct law correctly. The appellate court reviews questions of law de novo, but the standard for reviewing findings of fact is much narrower. In the federal system, a circuit court may reverse a factual finding made during a bench trial if it is clearly erroneous, but it may reverse a jury's factual finding only if no reasonable juror could have so found. So the initial question on an appellate judge's mind is, "What is the proper standard of review for each issue on appeal?" Given this frame of mind, the brief-writer must focus on the standard and build it into the arguments for reversal or affirmance—never attempting to retry the case. Remember: an appellate court's affirmance doesn't necessarily mean that the appellate judges agree with the trial's outcome, but that the lower court has followed the law.

(b) *Ignoring statutes and rules.* Some brief-writers either research their briefs inadequately or choose to ignore applicable statutes and rules. Either approach is a gross lapse. Statutes affecting appellate briefs and the appellate court's briefing rules both prescribe limitations on filings, such as time periods and the form and substance of briefs. If a writer violates a rule, the court may refuse to accept the brief.

(c) *Using a shotgun approach.* Judges dislike briefs that present every possible issue (meritorious or not), detail every fact (relevant or not), and argue points without making a concentrated analysis, establishing a logical progression, or citing adequate authority. Never waste time and space arguing obvious or noncontroversial points (e.g., "the burden of proof on a motion for summary judgment is on the moving party"). Avoid boring the reader by putting a weak argument early in the brief; leave it until the end or, better yet, omit it entirely. The best briefs are as short and clear as they can be, covering only the critical issues in the appeal.

(d) *Misstating facts.* Never exaggerate or omit pertinent facts to make them more favorable to the client. Don't dramatize facts with hyperbole. A sentence such as this one might be acceptable in a third-rate novel: "It was a dark and stormy night when John Doe recklessly decided to drive without headlights and without windshield wipers, not caring that an innocent young bicyclist, intent on reaching home, was sharing the rain-drenched road." But it is unacceptable in a brief. Consider a more straightforward approach: "One night last fall, Dan Jordan was driving home in the rain. Although his headlights and windshield wipers did not work, Jordan drove west down Fibble Road around 10:30 p.m. He struck Paul Brown, who was riding his bicycle in the westbound lane." Never ignore pertinent facts, even those that work against your client. Your opponent will make sure that the court hears about them (e.g., "Brown, with a blood-alcohol content of .09%, was cycling down the middle of the wrong lane against oncoming traffic."). Misstatements of fact are wholly counterproductive—sometimes even sanctionable.

(e) *Misstating the law.* Never misrepresent the relevant law. Several problems may arise. Most serious of them is a breach of your duty to disclose adverse binding authority if the opposing party doesn't raise it first. "Sitting on" that information is tantamount to misleading the court. Lawyers are required to know the law and are duty-bound to cite adverse controlling authority if the other party seems to be unaware of it. In fact, it's good practice to cite that authority *before* your opponent raises it because then you seize the opportunity to frame the relevant question. You will have to answer the problems created for your client's position anyway, but confronting those problems head-on lets you lead off that discussion with an argument about why the adverse authority shouldn't apply or control in your client's case—for example, because the facts differ or the precedent is being applied too broadly. If you let your opponent raise the authority first—or, worse, leave it for the court to discover on its own—you'll have to not only defend your position but also explain why you didn't cite it. Another serious problem is citing authority that is irrelevant to the argument or that you've misinterpreted to support your point. The consequences of misstating the law may include sanctions, disciplinary actions, and malpractice lawsuits. A third, less serious, problem is omitting authority that isn't binding but that may be persuasive. But regardless of how persuasive it may be, your best approach is still to raise and answer it first.

(f) *Not being brief.* Be concise. Appellate judges read thousands of words every week, and they understandably place a high value on their time. They appreciate a brief that gets straight to the point. Show some consideration in sparing your reader the usual verbiage, redundancies, and irrelevant details that bloat most briefs—probably including your adversary's. Just remember, though, that brevity's ultimate purpose is enhancing clarity: don't get so carried away in cutting words that you mangle your meaning. It won't matter how brief your brief is if the judge can't make sense of it.

(g) *Not being clear.* Above all, your argument must be lucid. First, judges don't have time to labor over convoluted sentences or unduly long paragraphs—and simply saying that a point is clear doesn't make it so. Use simple language, short sentences, and manageable paragraphs intelligently connected to advance your line of argument. Second, judges as a rule are generalists; they hear cases in a wide range of practice areas. You're the specialist: you know the case, the facts, and probably even the relevant law better than the judge will. In your brief, you must assume the role of the teacher, explaining the core concepts well enough that a nonspecialist can understand them. Guide the reader over potential points of confusion. A judge who simply can't follow your arguments won't be inclined to rule in your favor.

(h) *Showing disrespect.* No matter how you feel personally toward the court, the opposing party, or the opposing counsel, you must always disagree respectfully. Disrespect is shown, among other ways, by using insulting language; by overusing italics, boldface type, and underlining; by using "scare" quotes; and by resorting to inappropriate slang. Attacking the court's or an opponent's integrity instead of arguing the case's merits never succeeds.

(i) *Relying on quotations.* Arguments made up solely of strings of quotations look and sound weak. Using too many quotations can make a writer sound hesitant and unconfident, as if hiding behind someone else's words and thoughts rather than daring to make an assertion and backing it with authority and reasoning. Quotations that are genuinely memorable, strictly on-point, and so well phrased that an effective paraphrase is impossible are helpful. But quotations from unrelated and distinguishable cases almost never are. Consciously or subconsciously, the reader may feel that the writer isn't confident about the argument and is propping it up essentially by dropping names. See 8.2.

(j) *Failing to address weaknesses.* Few cases are free of exploitable weaknesses, yet many brief-writers ignore or overlook their own weaknesses until an opponent has seized on them. By being the first to point out and discuss a weakness in your own case, you avoid starting the discussion on the defensive and deny your opponent that first-strike advantage. You get to frame the issue involved and force your opponent to counter those arguments before trying to exploit the weakness. Another benefit not to be overlooked is that your candor will enhance your credibility as an advocate.

25.4 Study effective briefs.

(a) *Models.* Model briefs are relatively easy to find. Although some older texts contain well-written briefs, recently published books are the best resources because the briefs are usually shorn of legalese and written in plain English. An especially good collection is *The Great Advocates Legal Briefs* (Steven D. Stark ed., 1994). See also Bryan A. Garner, *Legal Writing in Plain English* 211–25 (2d ed. 2013); Linda Holdeman Edwards, *Legal Writing* 377–86 (1996).

(b) *Further guidance.* Some useful guides are:

- *Appellate Practice Manual* (Priscilla Anne Schwab ed., 1992).
- *Classic Essays on Legal Advocacy* (George Rossman ed., 2010) (earlier published as *Advocacy and the King's English*).
- Judith A. Fischer, *Pleasing the Court: Writing Ethical and Effective Briefs* (2d ed. 2011).
- Bryan A. Garner, *The Winning Brief* (3d ed. 2014).
- Bryan A. Garner, *The Future of Appellate Advocacy*, 54 Duquesne L. Rev. 311 (2016).
- Ross Guberman, *Point Made: How to Write Like the Nation's Top Advocates* (2d ed. 2014).
- Noah Messing, *The Art of Advocacy: Briefs, Motions, and Writing Strategies of America's Best Lawyers* (2013).
- Antonin Scalia & Bryan A. Garner, *Making Your Case: The Art of Persuading Judges* (2008).
- Frederick Bernays Wiener, *Briefing and Arguing Federal Appeals* (rev. ed. 1967) (reprinted with a new introduction in 2001).

(c) *An example.* The following appellee's brief, written by a distinguished Louisiana practitioner, addresses a question of constitutionally protected rights. It was the winning brief in the appeal.

> "Successful argumentation . . . not only advances positive proof in support of its proposition, but meets all weighty objections that either are, or may possibly be, urged against it."
>
> —*Edward Fulton*

In the

Louisiana Supreme Court

For the State of Louisiana

Docket No. 2000-C-2812

Bernard Poitier et al.,
Plaintiffs/Respondents,

vs.

Parish of Debevoise,
Defendant/Petitioner.

Opposition to Debevoise Parish's Application for Supervisory Writs
from the Third Circuit Court of Appeal
Docket No. 99-01334

Brief for Respondents

Richard R. Kennedy
P.O. Box 3243
309 Polk Street
Lafayette, LA 70502-3243
Phone: (337) 232-1905
Fax: (337) 232-1906

Attorney for Bernard Poitier et al.

It's a good idea to include the issue statement—in the form of a deep issue (see 25.1(d))—in the table of contents.

Table of Contents

i

Notice that the point headings—those appearing between "Argument" and "Conclusion"—are down-style. See 2.19(c). And they're complete sentences.

ii

Table of Authorities

Cases

iii

Constitutions, Statutes, and Rules

iv

Poitier's Brief Opposing Debevoise Parish's Writ Application

Reasons for Denying the Writ

Under Louisiana Supreme Court Rule X, § 6, the Poitiers oppose Debevoise Parish's writ application. The Third Circuit's decision is consistent with court rulings on the same routine legal issues since 1855, and its decision does not conflict with any decision by the Louisiana appellate courts, this Court, or the U.S. Supreme Court on the same legal issue. This Court should therefore deny the Parish's writ application.

An excellent deep issue: see 25.1(d).

Issue

Louisiana courts do not apply substantive laws retroactively to divest a person of a vested property right. Because this Court held a 1985 damages-cap statute to be unconstitutional, a plaintiff could recover unlimited general damages from a public entity until a new statute was enacted in 1996. Poitier was injured in 1991 and sued the next year. Should this Court give the 1996 statute retroactive effect?

Introduction

The retroactive application of a substantive law divesting or limiting a person's vested property right violates the due-process clauses of both the United States and Louisiana Constitution. Louisiana courts have steadfastly refused to commit the constitutional error that the Parish here urges. The Parish offers this Court no legally acceptable reasons why it should now reverse this 150-year-old precedent. Such a decision would create chaos by ushering in a new era in which constitutionally vested rights could be rendered meaningless and unprotected.

1

Actions of the Lower Courts

The State of Louisiana and the Parish filed a declaratory-judgment petition asking the district court to find that the 1996 amendment to § 5106(B)(1), imposing a $500,000 statutory cap on general damages in suits against the State and its entities, applied retroactively. The district court held that the 1996 amendment was a substantive law and that the legislature had not made it retroactive.

The State did not join with the Parish in appealing the district court's ruling. The Third Circuit unanimously affirmed the district court's ruling for three reasons. First, the 1996 amendment is a substantive law that affects a person's vested property right. Second, the legislature did not expressly make the law retroactive. Third, the wording *all cases* as used in the 1996 amendment is not a legislative or constitutional term that signifies legislative intent to apply a substantive law retroactively. One circuit-panel member noted an additional reason for denying the Parish's appeal: retroactively applying a law that divests a person of a vested property right is unconstitutional.

Summary of the Facts

The narrow issue here is whether the Third Circuit and the trial court correctly denied the Parish's petition for declaratory judgment asking the lower courts to apply a 1996 substantive amendment retroactively to a June 1, 1991 motor-vehicle crash at a rural Debevoise Parish intersection formed by a State road and a Parish road. Poitier contends that the crash happened because dense plant growth in front of the stop sign prevented him from seeing the sign until after passing the vegetation. By then it was too late for him to stop, and the crash occurred as a southbound SUV on the State road struck Poitier's westbound

2

truck in the intersection, causing his pickup truck to overturn. Because of injuries suffered as a result of the accident, Poitier became a quadriplegic.

When this 1991 crash happened and when in 1992 the Poitiers sued the State and the Parish, no valid law limited the amount of general damages that a party could recover from the State, its agencies, or its political subdivisions.

Argument and Authorities

I. A law that retroactively divests a person of a vested property right violates the due-process clauses of the United States and Louisiana Constitutions.

A. The retroactivity canon has been consistently applied in this state since 1855.

In nearly 150 years Louisiana courts have never retroactively applied a law that deprived a party of a vested property right. In 1855, this Court held in *Municipality No. One v. Wheeler & Blake* that "retrospective laws in civil matters do not violate the Constitution, unless they tend to divest vested rights or to impair the obligations of contracts."[1] Just seven months ago, in *Walls v. American Optical Corp.*,[2] this Court held that an amendment to Louisiana Revised Statute 23:1032 extending tort immunity to executive officers applied only to claims that arose after the amendment became effective because the parties had a vested property right to sue the executive officers before the amendment and because the negligent act giving rise to the claim occurred before the amendment.

Many modern authorities follow the 1855 precedent. For example, in *Lott v. Haley*, this Court refused to retroactively apply Louisiana Revised Statute 9:5628—a statute of limitations—to a claim that arose before this law was

1 10 La. Ann. 745 (1855).
2 740 So. 2d 1262, 1268–69 (La. 1999).

3

enacted because "to do so would divest a plaintiff of his vested right in his cause of action in violation of the due process guarantees under the state and federal constitutions."[3] So the medical-malpractice plaintiff, who had sued more than three years before the new limitations statute became effective, was not bound by that later-enacted limitations period because the statute disturbed a preexisting right.

To the same effect was *Gilboy v. American Tobacco Company*,[4] in which this Court held that the legislature's elimination of a theory of recovery from the Products Liability Act—abolishing the category of things unreasonably dangerous per se—altered a substantive right and thus did not apply retroactively. Two years later, in 1993, this Court again refused to apply a substantive statute retroactively, this time holding that a 1989 amendment to Louisiana Revised Statute 23:1103 was not retroactive because that statute abolished the employee's right to recover general damages and created a right in the employer's favor to be paid out of any damages the employee recovered in a third-party suit.[5]

B. Recent decisions of this Court continue to rely on the retroactivity canon.

This Court soon had yet another opportunity to reaffirm this principle, holding in *Aucoin v. State*[6] that amendments to Louisiana Civil Code Articles 2323 and 2324 were substantive and nonretroactive because they shifted liability obligations—thereby changing the amount of recoverable damages. In particular, the Court refused to retroactively apply a 1996 amendment to Article 2324(B), which adopted pure comparative fault, to a 1990 accident that would

3 370 So. 2d 521, 524 (La. 1979).
4 582 So. 2d 1263, 1264-65 (La. 1991).
5 *St. Paul Fire & Marine Ins. Co. v. Smith*, 609 So. 2d 809, 822 (La. 1993).
6 712 So. 2d 62, 67 (La. 1998).

4

have reduced the Department of Transportation's liability from 50% to 15%. The amendment was found to be substantive in that it changed the amount of recoverable damages.[7]

The same broad holding obtained in four other recent cases: *Segura v. Frank*[8] ("[E]ven where the legislature has expressed its intent to give a substantive law retroactive effect, the law may not be applied retroactively if it would impair contractual obligations or disturb vested rights."); *Graham v. Sequoya Corp.*[9] (refusing to retroactively apply a statutory amendment giving parties the right to contract for fees exceeding the standards set by the Code of Professional Responsibility because suit was filed before the statute became effective); *Burmaster v. Gravity Drainage District No. 2*[10] ("Where an injury has occurred for which the injured party has a cause of action, such cause of action is a vested property right which is protected by the guarantee of due process."); and *Terrebonne v. South Lafourche Tidal Control Levee District*[11] ("[T]he legislature simply cannot take away an existing cause of action based upon substantive rights which had clearly been granted by the legislature during the preceding session and had become vested on the effective date of the legislation.").[12]

---

7 *Id.* at 67–68.
8 630 So. 2d 714, 721 (La. 1994).
9 478 So. 2d 1223, 1226 (La. 1986).
10 366 So. 2d 1381, 1387 (La. 1978).
11 445 So. 2d 1221 (La. 1984).
12 *Id.* at 1224. Circuit courts have also applied the rules against retroactivity to a substantive law. *See, e.g.*, *Jamison v. Hilton*, 721 So. 2d 494, 497 (La. Ct. App. 1998), *writ denied*, 730 So. 2d 871 (La. 1999) (refusing to retroactively apply a statute barring a plaintiff's suit against the state unless the plaintiff requested that the petition be served within 90 days after filing suit); *Batiste v. Capitol Home Health*, 699 So. 2d 395, 398 (La. Ct. App. 1997) (refusing to retroactively apply a 1995 amendment giving an employer 60 days to pay a claimant's medical bills to a 1993 accident, a time when the law required payment within 14 days, because the 14-day rule was a "vested constitutional right").

5

From this long and unbroken line of distinguished cases, certain immutable legal principles may be derived:

- Both the United States and the Louisiana Constitutions prohibit the retroactive application of a substantive law that deprives a person of a vested property right or impairs a contractual obligation.[13]
- "Once a party's cause of action accrues, it becomes a vested property right that may not constitutionally be divested."[14]
- A cause of action accrues when the party has the right to sue.[15]
- An amendment that changes the amount of damages is a substantive law.[16]
- "An injured party's cause of action is a vested property right which is protected by the guarantee of due process."[17]
- The parties' rights and duties are determined when the suit is filed.[18]
- Even when the legislature expressly states that a substantive law applies retroactively—which, as explained below, is not true here—the courts refuse to do so if its retroactive application disturbs a vested right.[19]

C. The Parish offers this Court no reason to abandon this ancient principle.

Though the Parish cannot and does not point to any contrary authority, it is surprising that its brief to this Court fails to cite (much less to distinguish) any of these controlling precedents. The Parish offers no reason for this Court to abandon this precedent.

13 U.S. Const. amend. XIV, § 1; U.S. Const. art. I, § 10, cl. 1; La. Const. art. I, § 2; La. Const. art. I, § 23; *Cole v. Celotex Corp.*, 599 So. 2d 1058, 1063 n.15 (La. 1992); *Segura*, 630 So. 2d at 733.

14 *Cole*, 599 So. 2d at 1063; *see also Walls*, 740 So. 2d at 1268–69 (La. 1999); *Aucoin*, 712 So. 2d at 67.

15 *Terrebonne*, 445 So. 2d at 1224; *Cole*, 599 So. 2d at 1063; *Abate v. Healthcare Int'l, Inc.*, 560 So. 2d 812, 819 (La. 1990).

16 *Aucoin*, 712 So. 2d at 67; *Socorro v. City of New Orleans*, 579 So. 2d 931, 944 (La. 1991); *St. Paul Fire & Marine Ins. Co.*, 609 So. 2d at 817.

17 *Davis v. Willis-Knighton Med. Ctr.*, 738 So. 2d 1191, 1194 (La. Ct. App.), *writ denied*, 751 So. 2d 254 (La. 1991) (citing *Burmaster*, 366 So. 2d at 1387).

18 *Graham*, 478 So. 2d at 1226.

19 *Segura*, 630 So. 2d at 721; *Long v. Ins. Co. of N. Am.*, 595 So. 2d 636, 639 (La. 1992) (quoting *Plebst v. Barnwell Drilling Co.*, 148 So. 2d 584, 588 (La. 1963)).

6

Both the Louisiana Revised Statutes and the Louisiana Civil Code prohibit the retroactive application of a substantive law in the absence of a contrary legislative expression.[20] But this Court has never wavered from its prohibition against even the express retroactive application of a substantive law if it disturbs vested rights or impairs contractual obligations.[21] The reason for this bedrock legal principle is simple: the courts cannot give substantive laws retroactive effect without implicating the due-process and contract clauses of the United States and Louisiana Constitutions.[22]

Hence this Court does not have to waste its valuable time addressing the Parish's two red-herring issues: (1) whether an unconstitutional 1985 general-damages-cap law was viable in 1991 because it was not until 1993 that this Court declared the law unconstitutional; and (2) whether the 1996 amendment to § 5106(B) applies retroactively, because the Parish knows that it is a substantive law that diminishes a party's pre-1996 vested property right to fully recover general damages. This Court need only follow its 150-year-old precedent in denying the Parish's writ application and affirming the lower courts' decisions holding that this 1996 substantive amendment creating a $500,000 general-damages cap does not apply retroactively to a 1991 motor-vehicle crash.

As discussed in the following sections, this Court has still more reasons to deny the Parish's writ application.

20 La. Rev. Stat. Ann. § 1:2 (West 1987); La. Civ. Code Ann. art. 6 (West 1993).
21 *See Keith v. U.S. Fid. & Guar. Co.*, 694 So. 2d 180, 183 (La. 1997).
22 *Burmaster*, 366 So. 2d at 1387.

7

II. Louisiana did not have a general-damages cap until 1996.

A. This Court held in 1993 and 1994 that the legislature's 1985 attempts to limit general damages and prejudgment interest in suits against public entities violated the 1974 Constitution.

Louisiana's 1974 Constitution—which provides in Article I, § 1 that government originates with the people and is founded on their will alone—placed no limit on general damages. Because the legislature lacked constitutional authority to limit the State's liability on its own, this Court held that the legislature unconstitutionally passed two laws in 1985.

In 1993, this Court held in *Chamberlain v. State*[23] that the amendment to Louisiana Revised Statute 13:5106(B), imposing a $500,000 cap on general damages awarded in suits against the State, its agencies, and its political subdivisions, was unconstitutional because it contravened the Constitution's Article XII, § 10 proscription against sovereign immunity.[24]

The next year, relying on *Chamberlain*, this Court held in *Rick v. State*[25] that the legislature had unconstitutionally enacted Louisiana Revised Statute 13:5112(C), limiting prejudgment interest to 6% on judgments against state entities, because this law also violated the Constitution's prohibition against sovereign immunity.[26]

Against this backdrop, Poitier asks for nothing more than reaffirmation of what this Court has already decided: that the 1995 and 1996 laws creating a general-damages cap are substantive laws that are not retroactive.

23 624 So. 2d 874 (La. 1993).
24 *Id.* at 888.
25 630 So. 2d 1271 (La. 1994).
26 *Id.* at 1277.

8

B. Although a 1995 constitutional amendment permits the legislature to limit general damages on existing and future claims in suits against public entities, this Court has held that this permissive, non-self-executing amendment requires that the legislature clearly express any retroactivity for a general-damages cap.

By 1995, the legislature realized that it needed a constitutional amendment before it could limit general damages and change the legal interest rate for judgments against the State and its political subdivisions. Reacting to *Chamberlain*, the people amended constitutional Article XII, § 10(C); only then was the legislature free to validly reenact Louisiana Revised Statute 13:5106(B).

A constitutional amendment and two laws became effective on November 23, 1995. First, amended constitutional Article XII, § 10(C) provided that the legislature may limit the amount of recoverable damages in suits against the State and its political subdivisions to existing as well as future claims.[27] Second, contingent upon the passage of this constitutional amendment, the legislature amended Louisiana Revised Statute 13:5106(B) to create a $750,000 general-damages cap, and Louisiana Revised Statute 13:5112(C) to provide for 6% prejudgment interest.

After the 1995 vote of the people, the legislature now had constitutional permission to retroactively impose a general-damages cap on judgments against the State and its political subdivisions. But the Second Circuit refused, in *Holt v. State* to retroactively apply the 1995 general-damages cap to a 1985 automobile accident because the legislature did not make the 1995 amendment applicable to existing claims and because *Chamberlain* had held that the 1985 statutory cap was unconstitutional.[28]

27 La. Const. art. XII, § 10

28 671 So. 2d at 1174.

9

Then in May 1999, a unanimous Supreme Court further clarified the effect of the constitutional amendment by holding in *Jacobs v. Town of Bunkie*[29] that the language and functions of Article XII, § 10(B) and (C) were not self-executing and thus required the legislature to provide supplemental legislation to limit the liability of the state or any public entity.[30] As the Court noted, subdivision (C) uses permissive language: "the legislature by law may limit . . . the . . . liability of the state."[31] *Jacobs* narrows the focus to whether the legislature, in its 1996 amendments to § 5106, clearly and expressly made that substantive law retroactive.

III. An unconstitutional law is void *ab initio*: it is not law, it confers no rights, and it imposes no duties.

A. The Parish's argument that a general-damages cap existed in 1991 is unsound.

The Parish posits an unusual thesis for its argument that a general-damages cap existed in 1991 to support its contention that the 1996 amendment applies to this 1991 crash. The incorrect syllogism goes like this:

Major Premise: An otherwise unconstitutional law is constitutional until the date on which the Supreme Court declares it unconstitutional.

Minor Premise: This Court did not declare the 1985 damages-cap law in suits against public entities[32] unconstitutional until *Chamberlain* in 1993, two years after Poitier's crash.

Conclusion: The unconstitutional 1985 $500,000 damages cap applies to Poitier's 1991 crash.

29 737 So. 2d 14 (La. 1999).
30 *Id.* at 19.
31 *Id.* at 18 (emphasis added).
32 Effective September 6, 1985, the legislature amended § 5106(B)(1) to impose a $500,000 general-damages cap in suits against public entities. *See Dubois v. State Farm Ins. Co.*, 571 So. 2d 201, 206 (La. Ct. App. 1990), *writ denied*, 575 So. 2d 367 (La. 1991).

10

Understandably, the Parish cites no authority for its proposition, and this Court can quickly dispose of this curious argument. First, *Chamberlain* merely confirmed what Article XII, § 10(A) of the 1974 Constitution made clear: sovereign immunity does not exist in Louisiana. Second, nearly 60 years ago this Court negated the Parish's argument in *Flournoy v. First National Bank of Shreveport.*[33] In dealing with unconstitutional tax legislation, *Flournoy* quoted from a United States Supreme Court decision in holding:

> An unconstitutional act is not a law; it confers no rights; it imposes no duties; it affords no protection; it creates no office; it is, in legal contemplation, *as inoperative as though it had never been passed.*"[34]

That constitutional-law rule applies here with equal vigor. The Parish's implausible argument must suffer the same fate as did the *Flournoy* unconstitutional tax law, because the Parish simply cannot breathe life into a law that this Court has declared unconstitutional. In sum, no general-damages cap existed in 1991; the 1985 cap was a legal nullity.

In refusing to apply the 1985 general-damages cap to a 1987 accident, *Chamberlain* made it clear that constitutional Article XII, § 10(C) provides that the State is not immune from tort damages: "Limiting recoverable tort damages thus flies directly in the face of the constitutional proscription that the state waive sovereign immunity from liability for injury to person or property."[35]

33 3 So. 2d 244 (La. 1941).

34 *Id.* at 248 (emphasis added) (quoting *Norton v. Shelby Cty.*, 118 U.S. 425, 442 (1886)). *See also Vieux Carre Prop. Owners & Assocs., Inc. v. City of New Orleans*, 167 So. 2d 367, 371 (La. 1964) (citing *City of New Orleans v. Levy*, 64 So. 2d 798 (La. 1953)).

35 624 So. 2d at 883 (internal quotations omitted).

11

The Parish thus wrongly asserts that Poitier was burdened by a 1985 general-damages cap that this Court later ruled unconstitutional; taken together, *Chamberlain* and Louisiana law on the effect of unconstitutional laws are far more than the mere nuisance that the Parish would implicitly have them be. The Parish wrongly asserts that the 1996 law merely reaffirmed an unconstitutional 1985 general-damages cap.

B. In 1993, when *Chamberlain* held that the 1985 general-damages cap was unconstitutional, the Poitiers' claim was pending.

The Parish evidently misconstrues the narrow exception to the general rule that an unconstitutional law is void. *Flournoy* recognized that the general rule cannot apply to a final decision because "'[t]he past cannot always be erased by a new judicial declaration.'"[36] The Poitiers concede that if their case had become final before the *Chamberlain* decision, and if the issue of the unconstitutionality of § 5106(B)(1) had not been raised—something the Parish speculatively assumes that Poitier would not have done[37]—and if this Court had imposed the general-damages cap, then Poitier would have been bound by that decision. But this *if*-ridden surmise does not apply to the facts here. This is a pending case, and Poitier contends that no general-damages cap applies to this 1991 crash.

36 3 So. 2d at 249 (quoting *Chicot Cty. Drainage Dist. v. Baxter State Bank*, 308 U.S. 371, 374 (1940)).

37 Parish Brief at 9–10. This is not only purely speculative but also wrong: Poitier indeed contends that the general-damages cap does not apply to this 1991 crash, and there is no reason to suppose that he would, pre-*Chamberlain*, have meekly acceded to the statute's obvious unconstitutionality.

12

That is precisely what the First Circuit decided in *Magee v. Landrieu*,[38] in which the issues were whether *Chamberlain*'s anti-cap decision and *Rick v. State*'s[39] anti-prejudgment-interest limitation applied to pending actions. Following an earlier Supreme Court decision, *Magee* held that both *Chamberlain* and *Rick* applied to the pending claims because no final judgment had been rendered on the dates on which those decisions were rendered. In the Court's own words: "[T]he holding in Chamberlain is applicable to any and all judgments that were not final, definitive and executory as of the date of rendition of Chamberlain, September 3, 1993. The same is true for the holding in *Rick*, which had a rendition date of January 14, 1994."[40]

The courts consider three factors in deciding whether a decision should be applied retroactively.[41] First, the courts do not retroactively apply a decision that establishes a new legal principle, either by overruling clear past precedent on which the litigants may have relied or by deciding an issue of first impression whose resolution is not clearly foreshadowed. This factor does not apply here because *Chamberlain*, in declaring the 1985 act unconstitutional, simply upheld the 1974 Constitution's sovereign-immunity prohibition. Second, the courts weigh the merits and faults in each case by looking to the history of the rule in question, its purpose and effect, and whether retrospective application will further or retard its operation. Again, applying *Chamberlain* retroactively furthers the meaning of the 1974 Constitution's waiver of sovereign immunity. Third, the courts weigh the inequity that a retroactive application may impose. Again, the

38 653 So. 2d 62, 64 (La. Ct. App.), *writ denied*, 654 So. 2d 319 (La. 1995).
39 630 So. 2d at 1277.
40 *Magee*, 653 So. 2d at 68.
41 *Lovell v. Lovell*, 378 So. 2d 418, 421–22 (La. 1979); *Magee*, 653 So. 2d at 66.

13

inequity in failing to retroactively apply *Chamberlain* would be to deprive Poitier of a vested property right, something prohibited by the due-process clauses of both the federal and state constitutions.

The Parish tries for two equity-like arguments in suggesting that the Poitiers' only expectation when suing in 1992 could have been to recover $500,000, based on the 1985 cap; and that vast liabilities might ensue if this Court affirms the decisions below. As for the first, what the Poitiers expected was that the legislature would adhere to the Constitution; since it did not, a rational litigant would expect that in some case—whether his or someone else's—this Court was bound to eventually undo an unconstitutional law.[42] The "vast liabilities" argument simply fails as a point of equity: the Poitiers' case is bound to be one of only a few still pending that were filed when an unconstitutional statute was technically on the books but had yet to be declared unconstitutional.

The Court's holding in *Chamberlain* that the 1985 general-damages cap was unconstitutional applies to Poitier's 1991 crash. Because the 1985 cap was void, it did not exist in 1991.

C. Contrary to the Parish's argument, the 1985 general-damages-cap law was not a "defect" and Poitier is not seeking a "windfall."

Undaunted, the Parish would have this Court believe that in 1985 general-damages-cap law was problematic simply because of a "defect" in Louisiana's Constitution.[43] *Chamberlain* did not use the word "defect" to declare the 1985 act unconstitutional. Rather, it classified the law as unconstitutional because it violated the 1974 Constitution's prohibition against any limitation on the State's

42 *Chamberlain* was already pending when the Poitiers sued.
43 Parish Brief at 7, 9, 10.

14

waiver of sovereign immunity. The Parish correctly notes that the people have the right to amend the Constitution,[44] and they did that in late 1995, by amending Article XII, § 10(A) to give the legislature permission to limit the State's liability. (The vote could, of course, have gone the other way, a possibility that the Parish implicitly ignores by characterizing the 1985 law as merely based on a defect.) Although even in the face of *Chamberlain*, the Parish contends that Poitier seeks a "windfall,"[45] it is hardly a windfall to assert a constitutional right to recover full general damages unencumbered by an unconstitutional 1985 law or by a 1996 substantive law that constitutionally cannot apply retroactively to deprive Poitier of a vested right to recover his full damages.

Interestingly, the Parish cites *Walls v. American Optical Corp.*,[46] from which Poitier quotes because it nicely summarizes his position that his right to recover his full damages vested when he was injured in 1991:

Once a party's cause of action accrues, it becomes a vested property right that may not constitutionally be divested. Therefore, statutes enacted after the acquisition of such a vested property right . . . cannot be retroactively applied so as to divest plaintiff of his vested right in his cause of action because such a retroactive application would contravene the due process guarantees.[47]

Having acknowledged this constitutional proposition, the Parish then concedes that Poitier's right vested on June 1, 1991—the date on which he became a quadriplegic.[48]

44 *Id.* at 8.
45 *Id.* at 7.
46 740 So. 2d 1262 (La. 1999).
47 *Id.* at 1268-69 (internal citations omitted)
48 Parish Brief at vii, 5.

15

To conclude, this Court should reject the Parish's arguments because they would require the Court to:

- Find that Chamberlain merely found that the 1985 general-damages-cap act was a "defect," thus ignoring this Court's holding that the act was unconstitutional.
- Ignore the minor "defect" of its 1993 declaration that the 1985 general-damages-cap law was unconstitutional and now apply the unconstitutional 1985 law to this 1991 crash.
- Overturn a 150-year-old constitutional proposition that an unconstitutional act is void ab initio.

Conclusion

The outcome of the Parish's writ application rests on eight legal doctrines, all of which show that the Parish's position is folly:

- Both the United States and Louisiana Constitutions prohibit the retroactive application of a substantive law that deprives a person of a vested property or impairs a contractual obligation. So even when the legislature expressly states that a substantive law applies retroactively, the courts refuse to do so if its retroactive application disturbs a vested right.
- Once a party's claim accrues, it becomes a vested property right that may not be constitutionally divested.
- A claim accrues when the party has the right to sue.
- An amendment that changes the amount of damages is a substantive law.
- An injured party's claim is a vested property right that is protected by the guarantee of due process.
- The parties' rights and duties are determined when the suit is filed.
- The 1996 amendment to § 5106(B) imposing a $500,000 general-damages cap is a substantive law.
- The word "all" is not a term that the legislature uses to clearly signal its intent to apply a substantive law retroactively.

16

The Parish cannot avoid the simple fact that since 1855 Louisiana courts have consistently refused to apply a substantive law retroactively if it deprives a party of a vested property right. A damage claim is a vested property right. A law limiting a party's damages recovery is a substantive law. In 1991, when Poitier became dead from the neck down in a motor-vehicle crash, the State imposed no lawful limitation on general damages in suits against public entities. The Parish has not given this Court one reason to overturn a nearly 150-year-old rule prohibiting the retroactive application of a law that deprives a person of a vested property right.

Surely this Court has more pressing business than to take the time to affirm yet again such a bedrock, unremarkable rule of law. It should therefore deny Debevoise Parish's petition for writ of certiorari.

Respectfully submitted,

____

Richard R. Kennedy
P.O. Box 3243
309 Polk Street
Lafayette, LA 70502-3243
Phone: (337) 232-1905
Fax: (337) 232-1906

Attorney for Bernard Poitier et al.

17

§ 26
Judicial Opinions

26.1 Understand the main goals of a judicial opinion.

(a) *Purposes.* Judicial opinions serve three major functions: (1) to help the writing judge think through the problems raised by the case; (2) to justify the outcome to parties and counsel, especially to the losing litigant and losing counsel; and (3) with an appellate court, to serve as a source of precedent. There are other purposes as well: to persuade colleagues on the court to join in the ruling, to alert the legislature to inadequacies in statutory law, and to publish the law and ensure its acceptance in society generally.

Trial judges have an additional audience to consider seriously: the reviewing appellate court. Because losing litigants typically have a right to appeal, trial judges must "make the record" for appellate purposes. Their job doesn't normally require them to struggle through difficult legal questions. Instead, trial judges often describe their role as performing a more mundane assembly-line type of work: applying the law to the facts before them. When an appellate panel reviews their orders, it's scrutinizing whether appropriate consideration and analysis took place in the court below. Hence trial judges must show their work, since a primary goal of every trial-court order is to make a record of the judicial decision-making.

(b) *An extraordinary challenge.* Opinion-writing is an especially hard task, different from ordinary discursive or persuasive writing. The decision must generally be consistent with previous judicial decisions and must at the same time conform to the judge's notions of how law is to be applied. Often, and especially in difficult cases, the doctrine of stare decisis plays tug-of-war with conscientious fairness. The dilemma is especially acute because some of the most complex problems of society and of individual human lives must be reduced to the simplest of dichotomies: yea or nay. Not all the uncertainties can be plumbed by the judge writing the opinion; the task is to justify the court's determination sensibly and clearly, while not slighting or even ignoring the merits on the losing side.

26.2 Write for as broad an audience as possible.

(a) *Many possible readers.* In various polls, state and federal judges have cited all sorts of different readers that they have in mind when writing judicial opinions. Among these are judicial colleagues; the bar; future judges; the legislature; the losing litigant; the losing lawyer; law students; newspaper readers; oneself; a higher court; advertisers (e.g., in a prospective opponent's campaign); and the general intelligent reader.

(b) *"Ordinary reader" as a useful fiction.* Some of the most effective judicial writers have a person of average intelligence and average education in mind as their reader. Many judges acknowledge that people other than lawyers or law students might actually read their opinions. In his Supreme Court confirmation hearings, Justice Stephen Breyer said that as an appellate judge, he wanted his opinions to be understandable to a high-school student. This approach helps law serve the sense of fairness and decency in society by making judicial decision-making as accessible as possible to all members of society. The judge who writes plainly, clearly, and straightforwardly helps instill confidence in our legal system and respect for the judiciary.

26.3 Develop a good protocol for working on opinions.

(a) *Working habits.* Although judges take various approaches to working on opinions, all start by grasping the issues in the case. Some judges read through the briefs sequentially—in the order in which the parties have filed them. Others read the briefs in reverse order (reply brief first), on the theory that the reply brief will have the most focused discussion of the complaining party's issues. One common approach is to read in this order: (1) the trial court's opinion; (2) the appellant's reply brief; (3) the appellee's brief; and (4) the appellant's main brief. It is certainly acceptable (and common) to switch #2 and #4. Many judges sketch out each party's contentions, together with the opposing party's answers to those points. This practice helps the judge develop a good understanding of the dispositive points. Some judges do all this in a routine way. Others claim to have no set pattern for approaching cases. But a good routine fosters efficiency. And by no means does it result in predictable, cookie-cutter opinions. It simply suggests a level of discipline that professional writers in any field should have.

(b) *Deficiencies in law-clerk style.* Judges' practices vary with law clerks. A few judges draft all their own opinions from scratch and use their law clerks to amplify and verify the research. Others delegate opinion-drafting to their clerks—typically with detailed directions about how to write the opinion, but sometimes with little more direction than advising which party wins. The law clerk then drafts the opinion for the judge, and perhaps others in chambers, to edit. The rise of clerk-drafted opinions in recent years has brought these attendant problems: (1) a law-review style in judicial writing, with excessive citation of authority; (2) a certain immature grandiloquence as fledgling lawyers reach for the rhetorical heights they imagine to be appropriate to judicial writing; and (3) a structurally diffident approach in which every point is considered ad nauseam, including all the facts in detail, because the writer isn't confident about what really matters and what doesn't. Unless the judge has a heavy editorial hand—and a surefooted way to train new clerks shortly after they arrive—the judge's style will probably be infected to some degree with such flaws. The greater the judge's involvement, of course, the better.

(c) *Advice to law clerks.* If you clerk for a judge who expects you to draft opinions, your role is to give the opinion the judge's voice—not yours. Do your best to learn your judge's style. Study the judge's tone—especially at its best. You'll be trying to create the best opinion that the judge would write given the time to do so. Once the judge accepts a draft opinion, it is the judge's—not yours. If the judge has a heavy editorial hand and seems not to accept the draft that you've prepared, learn from the experience. Study what changes were made, and figure out why. Even if the judge has a light editorial hand—or accepts the draft as you prepared it—remember that it's still the judge's opinion, not yours.

26.4 Understand the paramount importance of style.

(a) *Pure vs. impure.* A "pure" opinion style has an up-front summary: it gives the outcome as part of the opener. An "impure" style delays the outcome to the end; it's been called a mystery-novel approach. Most American judges prefer the pure style, but not all. Two of the most influential writers on the American bench—Chief Justice John G. Roberts of the U.S. Supreme Court and Judge Frank H. Easterbrook of the U.S. Court of Appeals for the Seventh Circuit—prefer the impure style. Whichever approach one takes, the essential ingredient is logic. With the pure style, the challenges are (1) to state the problem clearly (preferably in separate sentences—not one long, convoluted sentence that begins *This case presents the question whether . . .*), (2) to capsulize the reasoning, and (3) to state the result. Few openers are more embarrassing than one that says, essentially, *This is a torts case. We affirm.* Although that's a gross non sequitur, it's fairly common. Instead, the opener should be truly informative and comprehensible, like this:

> In May 2015, Andrew McNair pleaded guilty to burglary in order to receive deferred adjudication, but he now regrets that decision because he has been charged with violating the terms of his plea agreement and may face harsher punishment. We must decide whether McNair can now change his initial plea to avoid the harsher punishment. Because Ohio criminal procedure prohibits a defendant from withdrawing a guilty plea after being sentenced, we hold that he cannot.

The structure of this type of pure-style opener can be stated in syllogistic terms for those with a smattering of formal logic:

1. [Minor premise stated briefly in narrative form.]
2. We are asked to decide whether [conclusion].
3. Because [major premise], we hold that [outcome].

(b) *Only the necessary facts.* Three points. First, there is a balance to be struck with facts. Enough of them need to be included for the reader to understand what has given rise to the legal problem. But don't simply summarize all the facts in the record—as many lawyers do in their briefs. Rarely can a lawyer's statement of the facts be adapted into a judge's—only when the advocate has done an exceptional job of laying out all the pertinent facts fairly and without argumentation. Some judicial writers set out all the facts as a starting point. This overinclusiveness tends to make the opinion muddy, exceedingly dull, and so detailed as to become readily distinguishable from other cases. Second, overspecificity in facts is deathly. Precise dates, in particular, can be quite distracting. If you say *On January 4, 2016, X happened*—as writers so often do—you're suggesting that there is something significant about the date, as if it matters that it wasn't the 3rd or the 5th of January. The best practice is to include specifics (such as *5 grams of heroin* or *48 hours after the deadline*) only when they matter. Don't crowd the reader's mind with needless detail. Third, it's important to understand how opinions are typically found and used—electronically, with a mere screenful of an opinion to be read at once. In other words, most opinions today are not read linearly. So the best practice is to give a bare-bones statement of facts toward the outset (after a good summary paragraph) and then to incorporate some of the factual discussion as it bears on the legal analysis. If all the facts come before the analysis and are never again mentioned—or only glancingly—the opinion becomes much harder for researchers to use. Key facts, the ones that make a difference in the outcome, can and should be introduced during the analysis of the relevant point.

(c) *Mandate.* As a practical matter, judges must learn to worry about the clarity of their orders. If the case is on appeal, is the court reversing? Reversing and remanding—and, if so, remanding for what purpose? What is the trial court to do? Is the court affirming in part and reversing in part? Precisely which parts? Among the vaguest mandates are *So ordered* and *Ordered accordingly*—especially if the opinion itself has been unclear. Even with a more specific direction in the mandate, the judicial writer should word it fastidiously. For example, writing **The trial court is affirmed* is careless because the appellate court cannot act on the trial court—only on its judgment. In the most careful judicial usage, an appellate court may affirm, reverse, or modify a judgment or order; it may agree with, approve, or disapprove an opinion or decision; and it may remand cases and actions. For more guidance on drafting mandates, see *Garner's Dictionary of Legal Usage* 497–98 (3d ed. 2011).

26.5 Avoid the common shortcomings of judicial opinions.

(a) *Verbosity.* In 1940, the ABA president, Charles A. Beardsley, campaigned for shorter judicial opinions and plain language in the law. Long opinions, he said, waste time in four ways. First, they waste the writer's time. Second, they waste the time of the other judges on the court. Third, they waste the time of the editorial staff at legal publishers, which prepare headnotes and digests. Finally, they waste the time of every lawyer who ever needs

*An invariably inferior form.

to consult the opinions. The cumulative effect of this waste, Beardsley said, is immeasurable. Yet judicial opinions have gotten longer and longer since Beardsley's day. The best judicial writers know that shorter is better. Everything you add that doesn't help positively hurts. Think of this analogy: a fifth leg wouldn't help a gazelle move more swiftly and gracefully.

(b) *Wigmore's six complaints.* In his great treatise on the law of evidence, the scholar John Wigmore noted six recurrent shortcomings in American judicial opinions. They are still telling points. (1) Judges cite authority without enough discrimination. He said that modern judges need to be well grounded in legal history and legal literature. (2) Judges often show unfamiliarity with controlling precedents. This problem, Wigmore believed, has three causes: the brief tenure of most appellate judges; the crush of work; and the lack of a body of capable appellate advocates to help judges reach the highest standards of research. The problem might also be traced to unnecessarily complex law. But the problem is surely less pronounced today than it was in Wigmore's day, especially because of the widespread use of electronic research. (3) Judges often tend to treat judicial questions mechanically. Too much of our law, Wigmore said, is "dead bark." Reasons can be lost from sight. (4) Judges often misconceive the doctrine of precedent. Wigmore complained of the constant "loose resort to the law of other states," which he said makes the doctrine "optional," since decisions of other states are not binding precedents. (5) Judicial writers often overwrite—they consider far too many points in dicta. This habit, wrote Wigmore, "tends to remove the decision from the really vital issues of each case and to transform the opinion into a list of rulings on academic assertions." (6) Too many judges think of opinions as being single-judge opinions as opposed to full-court or full-panel opinions. As Wigmore put it: "All the law of every opinion should be affirmed by the whole court."

(c) *Tone.* The tone of a judicial opinion should be judicial: controlled, calm, assured, and dignified—yet it can also be relaxed and idiomatic. It needn't be stuffy, and it shouldn't be. A good opinion is, as much as possible, in plain English. And for those who take a contrary view, it shouldn't be sarcastic and unpleasant.

26.6 Develop a sensible approach to concurrences.

(a) *Origin of concurrences.* A concurring opinion is really a vestige of the old seriatim-style opinion common in the American federal courts in the 1790s. It means that an individual appellate judge is having his or her say separately from the rest of the court.

(b) *Reasons for proliferation.* Court-watchers have offered any number of reasons for the growth of concurrences and dissents in American law. Some believe that they reflect our increasingly complex and ideologically charged legal atmosphere. Others say that they are the practical outcome of a divided court. On the federal level, Chief Justice William H. Rehnquist attributed the rise of separate opinions to the sharp jump in the percentage of cases in which a constitutional issue is involved.

(c) *A cynical view of Frankfurter.* Justice Felix Frankfurter was known as the "concurringest" of the Supreme Court Justices when he served. In the 1955–1956 term, when 94 opinions were handed down, there were 21 concurrences—two-thirds by Frankfurter. Noting that Frankfurter's concurrences have almost never been cited by anyone since, some commentators have said that Frankfurter might just as well have folded his concurrences into paper airplanes and thrown them out a Supreme Court window.

(d) *Concur with caution.* The "opinion of the court"—a development originally instituted by Chief Justice John Marshall of the Supreme Court—should be viewed as an important ideal in American law. A concurring opinion can reduce a majority opinion to a plurality, thereby making its authority questionable. For the sake of clarity and desirable simplicity, judges would do well to write concurring opinions as seldom as possible. And when they do, it would be advisable to explicitly join the main opinion so that a clear ruling remains.

26.7 Develop a sensible approach to dissents.

(a) *Dissents generally.* Over a century ago, one scholar compared the dissenter to a kid who makes faces at a tougher kid across the street. Chief Justice Charles Evans Hughes, in his 1928 book on the Supreme Court, described the idea with more dignity—and surely with more accuracy: "A dissent in a court of last resort is an appeal to the brooding spirit of the law, to the intelligence of a future day, when a later decision may possibly correct the error into which the dissenting judge believes the court to have been betrayed."

(b) *Purposes.* Dissents have five main purposes: (1) to set forth the argument that did not convince a majority of the court, but did convince a minority; (2) to attract the attention of a higher court; (3) to avoid stretching out a compromise opinion that, in the end, reads unclearly; (4) to speak to future judges in hopes of persuading them someday to change the legal rule; and (5) on courts of last resort—mostly on the Supreme Court of the United States—to complete the picture of a Justice's philosophy of constitutional jurisprudence and to mark the roadmap of constitutional history.

(c) *The old view.* Through the mid-20th century, many legal scholars argued that dissents had no place in our justice system because they are unnecessary and divisive. The view was that dissents shouldn't be filed unless it was reasonably certain that a public gain, as distinguished from a private one, would result. Chief Justice John Marshall's approach typified the judicial practice of his day: in 35 years on the U.S. Supreme Court, he dissented only nine times. The modern view of dissenting opinions is generally much more tolerant, though we still hear laments that unanimity on high courts is no more common than it is in our intermediate appellate courts. Some modern scholars believe that Justice Oliver Wendell Holmes, the "Great Dissenter," made dissents fashionable. Whether that is true or not, few judicial writers today carry off their dissents with anything approaching his level of eloquent panache.

(d) *The voice of a dissenter.* Dissenting judges aren't constrained by the voice or language of precedent. While majority opinions generally purport to interpret the law objectively, dissents can be more passionate. As Justice J. William Brennan Jr. has said, dissents often "seek to sow seeds for future harvest." These tend to be separate opinions that have the ring of rhetoric, and they can, in Brennan's words, "straddle the worlds of literature and law." The judge's word choice, tone, and structure of presentation are crucial. Avoid clichés such as "I vigorously dissent." If you're going to dissent, be vigorous about it; but don't call yourself vigorous.

26.8 Study effective judicial writing.

(a) *Widely admired judicial writers.* What follows is something of a pantheon of federal judicial writers whose work may be studied to good effect: Justice Robert H. Jackson (1892–1954) of the U.S. Supreme Court; Justice Antonin Scalia (1936–2016) of the U.S. Supreme Court; Judge Richard S. Arnold (1936–2004) of the Eighth Circuit; Judge Henry J. Friendly (1903–1986) of the Second Circuit; Judge Thomas Gibbs Gee (1925–1994) of the Fifth Circuit; Judge Learned Hand (1872–1961) of the Second Circuit; Judge Spottswood W. Robinson (1916–1998) of the D.C. Circuit; Judge Alvin B. Rubin (1920–1992) of the Fifth Circuit; and Judge John Minor Wisdom (1905–1999) of the Fifth Circuit. Among the living judges whose shorter opinions might be carefully studied are:

- Chief Justice John G. Roberts of the U.S. Supreme Court.
- Justice Elena Kagan of the U.S. Supreme Court.
- Justice Neil Gorsuch of the U.S. Supreme Court.
- Judge Thomas L. Ambro of the Third Circuit.
- Judge Carlos Bea of the Ninth Circuit.
- Judge José A. Cabranes of the Second Circuit.
- Chief Judge Ed Carnes of the Eleventh Circuit.
- Judge Morgan Christen of the Ninth Circuit.
- Judge Frank H. Easterbrook of the Seventh Circuit.
- Chief Justice Nathan Hecht of the Texas Supreme Court.
- Judge Sandra L. Lynch of the First Circuit.
- Judge Kevin C. Newsom of the Eleventh Circuit.

- Judge Jill A. Pryor of the Eleventh Circuit.
- Judge William H. Pryor Jr. of the Eleventh Circuit.
- Judge Sri Srinivasan of the D.C. Circuit.
- Judge Jeffrey S. Sutton of the Sixth Circuit.
- Judge J. Harvie Wilkinson III of the Fourth Circuit.
- Chief Judge Diane P. Wood of the Seventh Circuit.

(b) *Books on judging.* Among the very best books on the art of judging are:

- Erwin N. Griswold, *The Judicial Process* (1973).
- Robert E. Keeton, *Keeton on Judging in the American Legal System* (1999).
- Karl N. Llewellyn, *The Common Law Tradition: Deciding Appeals* (1960).
- David Pannick, *Judges* (1987).
- *Judicial Decision-Making* (Glendon Schubert ed., 1963).

Also useful—and highly amusing—are R.E. Megarry's three books: *Miscellany-at-Law: A Diversion for Lawyers and Others* (1956); *A Second Miscellany-at-Law: A Further Diversion for Lawyers and Others* (1973); and *A New Miscellany-at-Law: Yet Another Diversion for Lawyers and Others* (Bryan A. Garner ed., 2005).

(c) *Further guidance.* The following publications will prove helpful:

- Bryan A. Garner et al., *The Law of Judicial Precedent* (2016).
- Bryan A. Garner, "Opinions, Style of," in *The Oxford Companion to the Supreme Court of the United States* (2d ed. 2005).
- Walker Gibson, *Literary Minds and Judicial Style*, 36 N.Y.U. L. Rev. 915 (1961).
- Ross Guberman, *Point Taken: How to Write Like the World's Best Judges* (2015).
- Joseph Kimble, *The Straight Skinny on Better Judicial Opinions*, 9 Scribes J. Legal Writing 2 (2003–2004).
- Glen Leggett, *Judicial Writing: An Observation by a Teacher of Writing*, 58 Law Libr. J. 114 (1965).

(d) *Examples.* Three examples follow. First is a trial-court opinion by Judge Jennifer Dorsey of the District of Nevada. Second is a rewritten appellate opinion in the pure style. For an interesting contrast, see the original opinion, which appeared as *Israel v. Allen*, 577 P.2d 762 (Colo. 1978). Third is an opinion by Chief Justice Nathan Hecht of the Supreme Court of Texas.

Sample Trial-Court Opinion

It's commendable to summarize reasoning in the opener. This is a "pure" judicial opinion.

Bradley ROBERTS, Plaintiff

v.

CLARK COUNTY SCHOOL DISTRICT, Defendant

2:15–cv–00388–JAD–PAL

United States District Court, D. Nevada.

Order Granting in Part Bradley Roberts's Motion for Partial Summary Judgment, Denying the School District's Countermotion for Partial Summary Judgment, and Granting Roberts's Motion for Leave

[ECF Nos. 54, 89, 143 [1]]

Jennifer A. Dorsey, United States District Judge

Plaintiff Bradley Roberts is a transgender police officer with the Clark County School District ("CCSD") who identifies as a male officer. When CCSD prohibited Roberts from using either the men's or women's bathrooms, Roberts sued for discrimination, retaliation, and hostile-work environment.

The basic story is presented in a pithy summary.

The parties cross-move for partial summary judgment, and I am asked to decide whether this bathroom ban violated Title VII, which prohibits employers from discriminating on the basis of "sex." CCSD argues that Title VII only prohibits discrimination based on biological sex, not gender identity. But Title VII prohibits discrimination based on sex stereotypes, too, and the record shows that the district's bathroom ban was based on precisely the sort of stereotyping that the Ninth Circuit has found Title VII to prohibit. So I grant Roberts partial summary judgment on the school district's discrimination liability under both Title VII and Nevada law. Because neither party has demonstrated an absence of material fact on the remaining issues in this case, however, I otherwise deny their motions and refer this case for a mandatory settlement conference.

The question presented occurs second—as a separate sentence.

The Factual Record

The Clark County School District hired Bradley Roberts as a campus monitor in 1992. At that time, he was known as Brandilyn Netz and aspired to be a police officer.[2] In 1994, Roberts graduated from the Northern Nevada Law Enforcement Academy and was hired by CCSD as a police officer.[3] Roberts held that position without incident for seventeen years.

Footnoted record citations keep the text uncluttered.

2. ECF No. 55–1 at ¶ 2.

3. *See id.*

A. Brandilyn Netz becomes Bradley Roberts.

In 2011, Roberts began dressing for work like a man, grooming like a man, and identifying himself as a man. And he started using the men's bathroom at work.[4] When others complained that a woman was using the men's bathroom, Roberts's commanding officers, Sgt. Anthony Jones and Lt. Young, scheduled a meeting with him.[5] Roberts confirmed that it was him and explained that he was transgender and in the process of transitioning into a man.[6] He also told them that he wants to be known as Bradley Roberts and use the men's bathroom.[7]

But Roberts's commanding officers told him that he could not use the men's rooms and that he should confine himself to the gender-neutral restrooms "to avoid any future complaints."[8] In response, Roberts sent a letter to his superiors again explaining that he was changing his name to Bradley J. Roberts, wanted his coworkers to use male pronouns to reference him, and that he would comply with the men's grooming code.[9]

B. CCSD officially bans Roberts from both the men's and women's bathrooms.

The district responded to Roberts's letter by holding a second meeting on November 14, 2011, with Capt. Anthony York, Lt. Young, Roberts, and his union representative.[10] Roberts repeated his requests: he wanted his coworkers to refer to him as a man, and he wanted to use the men's restrooms.[11] Capt. York said no: as far as CCSD was concerned, Roberts would not be referred to as a man or allowed to use the men's restroom until he could provide official documentation of a name and sex change.[12]

Two days later, Capt. York asked Roberts to appear for a third meeting.[13] York explained that the purpose of the meeting was to "discuss the issues in [Roberts's] memo to the department" and "facilitate . . . department action as soon as possible."[14] Capt. York and Clark County's General Counsel Jon Okazaki told Roberts that they had decided he could informally use a man's name for the time being, but that "all official and formal documents" would contain his female name until he obtained a court order and a name-change packet from human resources.[15] Okazaki further explained that Roberts was banned

4. *Id.* at ¶¶ 3–4.

5. *Id.*

6. *Id.*

7. *Id.*

8. ECF No. 89–1 at ¶ 6.

9. ECF No. 55–4 at 1.

10. ECF No. 55–5; ECF No. 55–6.

11. ECF No. 55–5; ECF No. 55–6.

12. ECF No. 55–5.

13. ECF No. 55–7.

14. *Id.*

15. *See* ECF No. 56–9; ECF No. 56–10.

from the men's restrooms until he had a documented sex change.[16] Okazaki told Roberts that he was required "to use a gender-neutral or single occupancy restroom," not the female restrooms.[17]

After the meeting ended, Capt. York sent Roberts, Chief Ketsaa, Lt. Young, and Okazaki proposed language for a memo regarding Roberts's name change:

> Officer Netz, P# 183 is in the final process of a name change to Brad Roberts. In order to assist Officer Netz with this transition, effective immediately, the department will be recognizing him as Brad and using male pronouns in our interaction with him. As soon as Officer Netz's official name is changed to Brad Roberts, he will be using that name on a legal basis.[18]

Roberts responded, "[t]hat's great and to the point."[19] He also asked Capt. Young to "include the [Nevada Equal Rights Commission] document or parts thereof, that you feel should be included" so that his coworkers and commanding officers understand that asking "below the belt" questions may constitute sexual harassment.[20] Capt. York responded: "I am in receipt of your request and have forwarded it to the Legal Department for input."[21]

C. Clark County circulates an email informing Roberts's coworkers that they should refer to him as a man.

A few days after their third meeting with Roberts, Capt. York, Chief Ketsaa, Lt. Young, and Okazaki emailed the entire department that Roberts was changing his name; that everyone should recognize him by his new name, Brad, and use male pronouns when referring to him; and that discriminating on the basis of gender identity violates Nevada law.[22] Roberts claims that this email "blindsided" him;[23] he thought his name change would be treated like any other personnel matter and that the announcement would be sent to supervisors and managers only—not to the entire department.[24]

In early December, Roberts's name-change petition was granted.[25] He immediately updated his driver's licence to identify his gender as male and submitted a completed name-change packet to human

14. *Id.*

15. *See* ECF No. 56–9; ECF No. 56–10.

16. ECF No. 56–10 at 2.

17. *See* ECF No. 56–9. Okazaki also memorialized the meeting in an email to various officials. He confirmed that "Netz shall not be allowed to use the men's restroom on CCSD property until CCSD receives appropriate documentation evidencing his anatomical change to male. Netz shall also be directed to not use the women's restroom on CCSD property, since he looks like a male." ECF No. 138–4 (emphasis original).

18. ECF No. 55–8.

19. ECF No. 55–9.

20. *Id.*

21. ECF No. 55–12.

22. ECF No. 55–16 at 1.

23. ECF No. 55–1 at ¶¶ 20–22.

24. *See id.*

25. ECF No. 55–18.

resources.[26] Once again, Clark County issued a department-wide email explaining that Roberts had changed his name and that now his name change would take effect for purposes of his official department records.[27] But Roberts's records were apparently never updated, because in January 2012, he received a new insurance card listing his gender as "female."[28]

D. Roberts files administrative charges and CCSD lifts the bathroom ban.

Roberts filed an administrative charge with the Nevada Equal Rights Commission ("NERC") that same month.[29] He alleged gender-identity discrimination on account of the bathroom ban, and harassment during the November meetings with CCSD officials.[30]

Capt. York and Okazaki responded to NERC that "Officer Netz's name was legally changed to Bradley Joseph Roberts [and] CCSDPD has changed Officer Roberts'[s] name in its records accordingly had acknowledge his identity with the male gender."[31] The next day, NERC notified Roberts that his administrative charge would not be mediated because the school district refused to participate.[32]

But no records had been updated. In February, Roberts contacted human resources and asked them to update his gender.[33] In March, however, a secretary reported to Capt. York that "Officer Roberts'[s] gender in the HR records still appears as a female."[34] And the bathroom ban remained in effect.

In May, NERC issued a probable-cause finding and informed Roberts that CCSD likely discriminated against him.[35] NERC then set Roberts's case for a public hearing.[36] But a month before the hearing, the department issued a new bathroom policy so that Roberts was no longer singled out and required to use the gender-neutral bathrooms.[37]

CCSD's general counsel emailed Chief Ketssa, Capt. Young, and others to inform them that Roberts had been notified of the new bathroom policy and "that as of this date he was no longer directed to use single occupant/gender neutral bathrooms at non-school District sites."[38] He also wrote "that the notice of hearing be withdrawn and this case closed as it is moot."[39] A week later, NERC did just that—it issued a three-line notice of withdrawal that closed Roberts's case because the school district had allegedly "taken measures" that rendered his complaint "moot."[40]

Roberts responded by filing a second administrative charge that alleged sex discrimination based on the bathroom ban, offensive comments made by coworkers,

26. ECF No. 55-1 at ¶ 24.
27. ECF No. 55-20.
28. ECF No. 55-1 at ¶¶ 26-27.
29. ECF No. 55-24.
30. *Id.*
31. ECF No. 56-3 at 2.
32. ECF No. 56-4.
33. ECF No. 56-5.
34. ECF No. 56-26 at 1.
35. ECF No. 56-11.
36. *See* ECF No. 56-18.
37. ECF No. 55-1 at ¶ 38 (citing ECF No. 56-16).
38. ECF No. 56-17.
39. *Id.*
40. ECF No. 56-18.

and the department-wide emails.[41] He also alleged that the district retaliated against him and subjected him to a hostile-work environment because he filed the NERC complaint [42] and various coworkers asked prying questions and made crude gestures and remarks to Roberts.[43]

By February of 2012, CCSD still had not updated Roberts's gender in his personnel records.[44] Two years later, the Equal Employment Opportunity Commission sent Roberts a right-to-sue letter [45] and he commenced this action.[46]

E. The lawsuit and cross-motions for partial summary judgment

Roberts alleges that the department subjected him to discrimination, harassment, and retaliation, and he asserts six claims: gender discrimination and harassment under Title VII; gender-identity expression and harassment under Nevada's Anti–Discrimination Statute, NRS 613.330; and retaliation under Title VII and NRS 613.340.[47]

While discovery in this case was ongoing, Roberts moved for partial summary judgment and requested a finding that he was subjected to discrimination, harassment, and retaliation during the period that the department banned him from the men's room.[48] He is joined by amici curiae Lambda Legal Defense and Education Fund.[49] CCSD filed a countermotion seeking partial summary judgment in its favor on the same claims.[50] Recognizing the complex nature of this case and the various legal arguments raised by the parties, I deferred ruling on these motions until after discovery closed and the parties had an opportunity to brief me on the impact of that discovery.[51] I also granted the parties leave to file two supplemental briefs and responses.[52] I now consider the parties' fully briefed arguments.

Discussion

A. Summary–judgment standards.

The legal standard governing the parties' motions is well settled: a party is entitled to summary judgment when "the movant shows that there is no genuine issue as to any material fact and the movant is entitled to judgment as a matter of law."[53] An issue is "genuine" if the evidence would permit a reasonable jury to return a verdict for the nonmoving party.[54] A fact is "material" if it could affect the outcome of the case.[55]

41. ECF No. 56–20.

42. *Id.*

43. *See id.*

44. *See* ECF No. 55–25.

45. ECF No. 89–2.

46. *See* ECF No. 1–1 (dated October 16, 2014).

47. Roberts also alleged a claim for negligent training and supervision, which I dismissed. *See* ECF No. 49.

48. ECF No. 54 at 6:15–20.

49. ECF No. 105.

50. ECF No. 89 at 9.

51. ECF No. 131.

52. *Id.* Roberts seeks leave to exceed the ten-page limit I set for these briefs because a transcription error pushed his motion into the eleventh page by three lines. ECF No. 143. Good cause appearing, I grant this request.

53. Fed. R. Civ. P. 56(a); *see also Celotex Corp. v. Catrett*, 477 U.S. 317, 330, 106 S.Ct. 2548, 91 L.Ed.2d 265 (1986) (citing Fed. R. Civ. P. 56(c)).

54. *Anderson v. Liberty Lobby, Inc.*, 477 U.S. 242, 249, 106 S.Ct. 2505, 91 L.Ed.2d 202 (1986).

55. *Id.* at 248.

When considering a motion for summary judgment, I view all facts and draw all inferences in the light most favorable to the nonmoving party.[56] The purpose of summary judgment is "to isolate and dispose of factually unsupported claims"[57] and to determine whether a case "is so one-sided that one party must prevail as a matter of law."[58] It is not my role to weigh evidence or make credibility determinations.[59] If reasonable minds could differ on material facts, summary judgment is inappropriate.[60]

If the moving party shows that there is no genuine issue as to any material fact, the burden shifts to the nonmoving party, who must "set forth specific facts showing that there is a genuine issue for trial."[61] The nonmoving party "must do more than simply show that there is some metaphysical doubt as to the material facts"; the nonmoving party "must produce specific evidence, through affidavits or admissible discovery material, to show that" there is a sufficient evidentiary basis on which a reasonable fact finder could find in his favor.[62] When reviewing the parties' papers, I only consider properly authenticated, admissible evidence.[63]

In their cross-motions for summary judgment, the parties focus on two overarching issues: (1) whether Roberts properly exhausted his administrate remedies; and, (2) if so, whether either party is entitled to summary judgment on the merits of Roberts's discrimination, harassment, or retaliation claims. I consider the exhaustion issue first.

Full sentence headings—in proposition form—show an orderly mind at work.

B. Roberts adequately exhausted his administrative remedies.

The school district raises two arguments for why Roberts did not properly exhaust his administrative remedies: (1) Roberts's charges did not provide Clark County with sufficient notice, and (2) Roberts's claims are untimely.[64] Neither has any merit.

1. Roberts's administrative charges provided CCSD with adequate notice.

The district argues that Roberts's administrative charges did not provide adequate notice because they did not contain explicit citations to Title VII or NRS

56. *Kaiser Cement Corp. v. Fischbach & Moore, Inc.*, 793 F.2d 1100, 1103 (9th Cir. 1986).

57. *Celotex Corp.*, 477 U.S. at 323–24, 106 S.Ct. 2548.

58. *Anderson*, 477 U.S. at 252, 106 S.Ct. 2505.

59. *Id.* at 249, 255.

60. *Warren v. City of Carlsbad*, 58 F.3d 439, 441 (9th Cir. 1995); *see also Nw. Motorcycle Ass'n v. U.S. Dep't of Agric.*, 18 F.3d 1468, 1471 (9th Cir. 1994).

61. *Anderson*, 477 U.S. at 256, 106 S.Ct. 2505; *Celotex*, 477 U.S. at 323, 106 S.Ct. 2548.

62. *Orr v. Bank of Am.*, 285 F.3d 764, 783 (9th Cir. 2002) (internal citations omitted); *Bhan v. NME Hosps., Inc.*, 929 F.2d 1404, 1409 (9th Cir. 1991); *Anderson*, 477 U.S. at 248–49, 106 S.Ct. 2505.

63. Fed. R. Civ. P. 56(c); *Orr*, 285 F.3d at 773–74.

64. CCSD also argues that Roberts's state-law claim is barred by NRS 233.170(2) because it "agreed to cease the unlawful" bathroom ban. But NRS 233.170(2) requires the parties to mediate and then to reach an agreement that addresses all of the issues in the charge. And the district cites no evidence to show that an official agreement was reached.

613.330.[65] But plaintiffs are not required to list specific laws or causes of action in a charge. "[A] charge is sufficient when the Commission receives from the person making the charge a written statement sufficiently precise to identify the parties, and to describe *generally* the action or practices complained of."[66] And I must construe charges "with utmost liberality since they are made by those unschooled in the technicalities of formal pleading."[67]

Roberts's administrative charges were more than sufficient to put CCSD on notice. Indeed, I remarked during the motion-to-dismiss hearing in August 2015 that Roberts's administrative charges are "possibly the most fact intensive that I have seen."[68] They describe the parameters of the bathroom ban, the series of meetings in November that were used to justify it, the email regarding Roberts's name charge, the department's failure to update his personnel records, and the alleged offensive comments made by CCSD employees.[69] I thus find that CCSD was provided with adequate notice of Roberts's claims.

2. ***Roberts's claims are timely.***

CCSD next argues that Roberts's state-law claims are untimely. It reasons that NERC withdrew Roberts's first charge (which is the only charge that explicitly mentioned Nevada law), and that this means that the statute of limitations has since expired on these claims.

To toll Nevada's statute of limitations, an administrative charge merely needs to be "pending" before NERC.[70] And here, regardless of what happened to Roberts's first charge with NERC, CCSD does not dispute that Roberts filed a second charge that was still pending with the agencies leading up to the EEOC issuing its right-to-sue letter. While it is true that Roberts's second charge did not mention Nevada law explicitly, as I explained above, it didn't need to.

Even if the limitations period were not tolled statutorily, I would equitably toll it. The statutory period for a discrimination claim can be equitably tolled if a plaintiff diligently pursues his claims with the administrative agency, prejudice to the defendant is slight, and justice favors tolling.[71] In *City of North Las Vegas v. State Local Government Employee–Management Relations Board*, for example, the Nevada Supreme Court tolled the statutory period because the plaintiff diligently filed a charge with NERC as soon as he realized he was supposed to, and there was no indication that the defendant would be severely prejudiced.[72] Here, Roberts filed two administrative charges, he cooperated

65. *See generally* ECF No. 89 at 23–26; ECF No. 115 at 12–13.

66. 29 C.F.R. § 1601.12(b) (emphasis added).

67. *B.K.B. v. Maui Police Dep't*, 276 F.3d 1091, 1100 (9th Cir. 2002), as amended Feb. 20, 2002 (quoting *Kaplan v. Int'l All. of Theatrical & Stage Emp. & Motion Picture Mach. Operators of U.S. & Canada*, 525 F.2d 1354, 1359 (9th Cir. 1975)).

68. ECF No. 117 at 25:1–2.

69. ECF No. 55–24 at 5–6.

70. NRS 613.420 states that the statute of limitations period is tolled "during the pendency of the complaint before [NERC]."

71. *City of N. Las Vegas v. State Local Gov't Employee–Mgmt. Relations Bd.*, 127 Nev. 631, 261 P.3d 1071, 1077 (2011).

72. *City of N. Las Vegas*, 261 P.3d at 1077; *see also State Dep't of Taxation v. Masco Builder Cabinet Grp.*, 127 Nev. 730, 265 P.3d 666, 672 (2011) (limitations period tolled where agency apprised of allegations and plaintiff merely failed to file the proper form).

fully in the agency investigations, and any prejudice to CCSD is slight given that the federal discrimination claim—based on the same facts as the Nevada claim—would go forward anyway. I thus find that Roberts's claims are timely.[73]

C. Roberts is entitled to summary judgment on the school district's discrimination liability, but neither party is entitled to judgment on the other issues in this case.

1. Title VII protects against gender discrimination.

Nevada law broadly prohibits "gender" discrimination,[74] but Title VII prohibits only discrimination "because of . . . sex."[75] CCSD argues that this is an important difference, and that Title VII does not prohibit *gender* discrimination. Thus, as long as it treated Roberts like any other person of his biological sex, it did not discriminate against him under Title VII. To resolve this dispute, I must first answer the threshold question: does Title VII's protection against "sex" discrimination include gender-identity discrimination?

a. The weight of authority suggests that Title VII's use of the word "sex" encompasses protections for discrimination against gender identity.

Our jurisprudential understanding of Title VII's prohibition against discrimination based on sex has evolved considerably since the statute's enactment in 1964. When Title VII was amended in 1972, courts understood the phrase "because of sex" to prohibit only discrimination that impeded women from attaining "equal footing with men."[76] This had the unfortunate effect of allowing employers to offer health-benefit packages that denied coverage for pregnancy-related expenses.[77] And it triggered the Seventh Circuit's decision in *Ulane v. Eastern Airlines*, in which the Court held that Title VII does not "prohibit discrimination against transsexuals" because "Congress had a narrow view of sex in mind when it passed [Title VII]."[78]

When the Supreme Court decided *Price Waterhouse v. Hopkins* in 1989, it broadened the notion of discrimination "because

73. Further, the bathroom ban was enforced through at least October 2012, which would have given Roberts until July 2013 to file.

74. Nev. Rev. Stat. § 613.330(1) ("it is an unlawful employment practice for an employer: (a) . . . to discriminate against any person with respect to the person's . . . terms, conditions or privileges of employment, because of his or her race, color, religion, sex, sexual orientation, gender identity or expression, age, disability or national origin; or (b) To limit, segregate or classify an employee in a way which would deprive or tend to deprive the employee of employment opportunities or otherwise adversely affect his or her status as an employee, because of his or her race, color, religion, sex, sexual orientation, gender identity or expression, age, disability or national origin.").

75. 42 U.S.C. § 2000e–2(a) (making it unlawful for an employer "to discriminate against any individual with respect to his compensation, terms, conditions, or privileges of employment, because of . . . sex . . .").

76. *Holloway v. Arthur Andersen & Co.*, 566 F.2d 659, 662 (9th Cir. 1977) (discussing the legislative history of Title VII), *overruling recognized in Schwenk v. Hartford*, 204 F.3d 1187, 1201 (9th Cir. 2000).

77. *See Gen. Elec. Co. v. Gilbert*, 429 U.S. 125, 128, 97 S.Ct. 401, 50 L.Ed.2d 343 (1976).

78. *Ulane v. Eastern Airlines*, 742 F.2d 1081, 1086–87 (7th Cir. 1984).

of sex" under Title VII.[79] Hopkins was a senior manager up for partnership at a national accounting firm.[80] Everyone agreed that Hopkins was great at her job, but some of the partners disliked the fact that she did not act like "a lady."[81] Hopkins was told that she should not use profanity, that she "overcompensated for being a woman," and that her chances for partnership would be improved if only she could "walk more femininely, talk more femininely, dress more femininely, wear make-up, have her hair styled, and wear jewelry."[82]

The High Court held that Title VII prohibited Hopkins's employer from making employment decisions based on these sorts of gender stereotypes.[83] The Court explained that Title VII does not operate merely to keep men and women on an "equal footing," it protects people from all forms of "sex stereotyping."[84] It noted that "Congress'[s] intent to forbid employers to take gender into account in making employment decisions appears on the face of the statute," and these words "mean that gender must be irrelevant to employment decisions."[85]

Some circuits read *Price Waterhouse* differently. In *Etsitty v. Utah Transit Authority*, the Tenth Circuit applied *Ulane* and held that transgender people are not a protected class under Title VII.[86] And the Seventh Circuit recently held that Title VII does not protect against discrimination based on sexual orientation under its own precedent, including *Ulane*.[87]

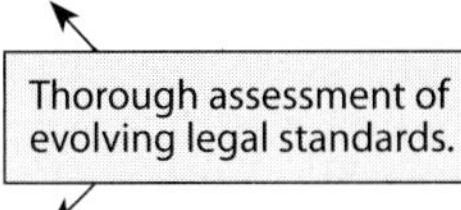

But the Ninth Circuit disagrees with the Tenth and Seventh Circuits' approach. In *Schwenk v. Hartford*, the Ninth Circuit wrestled with questions about gender under the Gender Motivated Violence Act.[88] The defendant contended that the Act does not extend to conduct motivated by a person's gender, and that—like Title VII—it extends only to conduct motivated by a victim's biological status as a male or female.[89] The panel extensively discussed the issue in the context of Title VII, explaining that " 'sex' under Title VII encompasses both sex—that is, the biological differences between men and women—*and gender*."[90] Early cases, the *Schwenk* court noted, had refused "to extend protection of Title VII to transsexuals because discrimination against transsexuals is on the basis of 'gender' rather than 'sex.' "[91] These early cases distinguished between "[t]he term 'sex,' " which referred to "an individual's distinguishing biological or anatomical

79. *Price Waterhouse v. Hopkins*, 490 U.S. 228, 109 S.Ct. 1775, 104 L.Ed.2d 268 (1989).
80. *Id.* at 234.
81. *Id.* at 234–35.
82. *Id.*
83. *Id.* at 250–53.
84. *Id.* at 251.
85. *Id.* at 240; *see also Smith v. City of Salem, Ohio*, 378 F.3d 566, 572 (6th Cir. 2004) ("The Supreme Court made clear that in the context of Title VII, discrimination because of 'sex' includes gender discrimination: 'In the context of sex stereotyping, an employer who acts

86. *Etsitty v. Utah Trans. Auth.*, 502 F.3d 1215, 1222 (10th Cir. 2007).
87. *Hively v. Ivy Tech Cmty. Coll.*, 830 F.3d 698, 699–702 (7th Cir. 2016).
88. *Schwenk v. Hartford*, 204 F.3d 1187, 1202 (9th Cir. 2000).
89. *Id.* at 1201–02.
90. *Id.* at 1202 (emphasis in original)
91. *Id.* at 1201 (citing to *Holloway v. Arthur Andersen*, 566 F.2d 659 (9th Cir. 1977)).

characteristics," and the "term 'gender,' [which] refers to an individual's sexual identity, or socially-constructed characteristics."[92] The unanimous panel then reasoned that this sex/gender distinction was overruled by *Price Waterhouse* and that Title VII applies both to discrimination based on concepts of sex and discrimination based on other stereotypes about sex, including gender identity:

> In *Price Waterhouse*, which was decided after *Holloway* and *Ulane*, the Supreme Court held that Title VII barred not just discrimination based on the fact that Hopkins was a woman, but also discrimination based on the fact that she failed "to act like a woman"—that is, to conform to socially-constructed gender expectations. . . . Thus, under *Price Waterhouse*, "sex" under Title VII encompasses both sex—that is, the biological differences between men and women—*and* gender. **Discrimination because one fails to act in the way expected of a man or woman is forbidden under Title VII.**[93]

The Ninth Circuit's unpublished decision in *Kastl v. Maricopa County Community College District* leaves little doubt which way the circuit is leaning in transgender Title VII cases.[94] Kastl, a transgender community-college teacher, identified as a woman.[95] But Kastl's employer banned her from the women's bathroom, stating that she would only be allowed in if she proved she had biologically changed her sex to female.[96] The Ninth Circuit panel held that these facts stated a prima facie case of gender discrimination.[97] It reasoned that, after "*Schwenk*, it is unlawful to discriminate against a transgender (or any other) person because he or she does not behave in accordance with an employer's expectations for men or women."[98] And it found that "gender stereotyping is direct evidence of sex discrimination prohibited by Title VII."[99]

Other circuits have reached conclusions consistent with *Schwenk's* reasoning. The Sixth Circuit held that "[s]ex stereotyping based on a person's gender non-conforming behavior is impermissible discrimination, irrespective of the cause of that behavior," and it found that the City of Cincinnati violated Title VII by discriminating against a male police officer who dressed like a woman.[100] The Eleventh Circuit held that the Georgia General Assembly's Office of Legislative Counsel violated Title VII when it terminated a person because he was transitioning into a woman.[101] And just this year, the Fourth Circuit held that the Gloucester County School Board violated analogous Title IX provisions by segregating transgender students from their peers based on the students' "biological sex."[102]

92. *Id.*

93. *Id.* at 1202 (italicized emphasis original; bold emphasis added).

94. *Kastl v. Maricopa Cty. Cmty. Coll. Dist.*, 325 Fed.Appx. 492 (9th Cir. 2009).

95. *Id.* at 493–94.

96. *Id.*

97. *Id.*

98. *Id.*

99. *Id.* The panel ultimately upheld summary judgment for the employer because it provided unrebutted evidence that Kastl was banned from the bathroom for safety reasons.

100. *Barnes v. City of Cincinnati*, 401 F.3d 729, 737 (6th Cir. 2005) (quoting *Smith v. City of Salem, Ohio*, 378 F.3d 566 (6th Cir. 2004)).

101. *Glenn v. Brumby*, 663 F.3d 1312, 1316–17 (11th Cir. 2011).

102. *G.G. ex rel. Grimm v. Gloucester Cty. Sch. Bd.*, 822 F.3d 709, 722–23 (4th Cir. 2016).

The EEOC has joined this growing majority.[103] In *Macy v. Holder*, the Commission concluded that intentional discrimination against a transgender person "is, by definition, discrimination 'based on . . . sex,' and such discrimination therefore violates Title VII."[104] The Commission reasoned that "[a] person is defined as transgender precisely because of the perception that his or her behavior transgresses gender stereotypes."[105] In *Lusardi v. McHugh*, the Commission considered a bathroom ban on a transgender employee. It applied *Price Waterhouse*, its progeny, and *Macy* to hold that "[e]qual access to restrooms is a significant, basic condition of employment, and [ ] denying transgender individuals access to a restroom consistent with gender identity discriminates on the basis of sex in violation of Title VII."[106]

103. The EEOC's decisions should be deferred to when persuasive. *Nat'l R.R. Passenger Corp. v. Morgan*, 536 U.S. 101, 111, 122 S.Ct. 2061, 153 L.Ed.2d 106 (2002) (citations omitted). *See also Fabian v. Hosp. of Cent. CT*, 172 F.Supp.3d 509, 518 (D. Conn. 2016) (collecting authority and noting, "though most of the earliest cases held that Title VII does not protect gender identity, the weight of authority has begun to shift the other way, especially (though not uniformly) after the Supreme Court's decision in *Price Waterhouse*").

104. *Macy v. Holder*, No. 0120120821, 2012 WL 1435995, at *11 (E.E.O.C. Apr. 20, 2012).

105. *Id.* at *9 (quoting *Glenn*, 663 F.3d at 1316–17).

106. *Tamara Lusardi v. John McHugh, Sec'y, Dep't of the Army*, No. 0120133395, 2015 WL 1607756, at *9 (E.E.O.C. Apr. 1, 2015).

This passage exemplifies the trial judge's work-showing function. See 26.1(a).

b. I join the weight of authority and hold that discrimination against a person based on transgender status is discrimination "because of sex" under Title VII.

I realize that the Ninth Circuit's reasoning in *Schwenk* is merely persuasive, as is the reasoning of the many other tribunals I have cited to. But because it appears that the Ninth Circuit would hold that gender-identity discrimination is actionable under Title VII, I see no reason to depart from the heavy weight of this authority. Nothing in the few contrary decisions cited by the school district persuades me otherwise. The contrary Seventh and Tenth Circuit decisions provide no cogent analysis of Title VII's language or Supreme Court caselaw. They rely heavily on *Ulane*, a case that predates *Price Waterhouse* and which the Ninth Circuit recognized in *Schwenk* retains questionable precedential value.[107] I thus conclude that discrimination "because of sex" under Title VII includes discrimination based on a person's gender.

107. *See, e.g., Schroer v. Billington*, 577 F.Supp.2d 293, 308 (D. D.C. 2008) (questioning whether *Ulane* is still good law because *Price Waterhouse* "eviscerated" the anatomical or chromosomal understanding of "sex"); *Schwenk*, 204 F.3d at 1201–02 (stating that what matters is not the victim's biology but what is "in the mind of the perpetrator"); *see also Hively v. Ivy Tech Comty. Coll.*, 830 F.3d 698, 701–18 (7th Cir. 2016) (conceding that "the writing is on the wall" and "our society

2. ***Roberts is entitled to judgment on his gender-discrimination claims because CCSD discriminated against him based on his transgender status.***

To survive summary judgment in the context of Title VII, a plaintiff must establish a prima facie case of discrimination by presenting evidence that "gives rise to an inference of unlawful discrimination."[108] This may be established with direct or circumstantial evidence of discriminatory intent or through the *McDonnell Douglas* burden-shifting framework.[109]

Direct evidence establishes the department's discriminatory intent here. It banned Roberts from the women's bathroom because he no longer behaved like a woman. This alone shows that the school district discriminated against Roberts based on his gender and sex stereotypes. And the department also admits that it banned Roberts from the men's bathroom because he is biologically female. Although CCSD contends that it discriminated against Roberts based on his genitalia, not his status as a transgender person, this is a distinction without a difference here. Roberts was clearly treated differently than persons of both his biological sex and the gender he identifies as—in sum, because of his transgender status.

Even if I apply the *McDonnell Douglas* framework, Roberts is still entitled to summary judgment on the school district's discrimination liability. Under this framework, Roberts carries the initial burden of establishing a prima facie case of discrimination.[110] Then the burden shifts to the school district to articulate a legitimate, nondiscriminatory reason for its conduct.[111] If the defendant provides a justification, the burden shifts back to Roberts to show that the justification is a mere pretext for discrimination.[112]

To state a prima facie claim for discrimination, Roberts must show that (1) he belongs to a protected class, (2) he performed his job satisfactorily, (3) he suffered an adverse employment action and, (4) the employer treated him differently than a similarly situated employee who does not belong to the same protected class.[113] I apply the same framework to Roberts's gender-identity discrimination claim under NRS 613.330.[114] CCSD only

can[not] continue to condone a legal structure in which employees can be fired, harassed, demeaned, singled out . . . based on who they date, love, or marry," but recognizing that the court was nevertheless bound by its precedent, including *Ulane*, to hold that sex-based discrimination under Title VII does not include sexual-orientation discrimination).

108. *Cordova v. State Farm Ins. Companies*, 124 F.3d 1145, 1148 (9th Cir. 1997); *see also McDonnell Douglas Corp. v. Green*, 411 U.S. 792, 802, 93 S.Ct. 1817, 36 L.Ed.2d 668 (1973).

109. *See Metoyer v. Chassman*, 504 F.3d 919, 931 (9th Cir. 2007).

110. *McDonnell Douglas*, 411 U.S. at 802, 93 S.Ct. 1817.

111. *Id.*

112. *Id.* at 804.

113. *Cornwell v. Electra Cent. Credit Union*, 439 F.3d 1018, 1028 (9th Cir. 2006) (citing

114. *See Apececche v. White Pine Cty.*, 96 Nev. 723, 615 P.2d 975, 977–78 (1980).

Again, the footnoted citations allow the full text to be read—without the reader's skipping through the text.

disputes the third and fourth elements—that Roberts suffered an adverse employment action and was treated differently than similarly situated employees.

a. The bathroom ban was an adverse employment action.

Adverse employment actions include any decision by an employer affecting "compensation, terms, conditions, or privileges of employment."[115] As the EEOC explained in *Lusardi*, "[e]qual access to restrooms is a significant, basic condition of employment."[116] The Commission reasoned that restroom access is a basic condition of employment because it is mandated by OSHA.[117] And it concluded that segregating bathroom access based on a person's transgender status constitutes a significant harm because it provides one set of terms and conditions of employment for transgender individuals and another set for male and female individuals.[118] I find the Commission's reasoning in *Lusardi* persuasive, and I adopt it. The school district's bathroom ban was an adverse employment action.

b. CCSD treated Roberts differently than similarly situated employees.

The school district contends that Roberts was not treated differently than similarly situated employees because his anatomy made him a female, and other females were not permitted to enter the men's restroom. But Roberts was not allowed to use the female bathroom either—so he was treated differently than other females.[119]

c. CCSD failed to articulate a legitimate nondiscriminatory reason for the bathroom ban.

Because of the direct evidence that CCSD discriminated against Roberts on the basis of gender, I need not proceed with the *McDonnell Douglas* burden-shifting analysis.[120] Had I, I would have noted that, although the department contends that the bathroom ban was implemented to protect "the privacy rights of other CCSD employees and its students,"[121] there is no evidence to support this contention. CCSD cites to Okazaki's deposition, but Okazaki said nothing about privacy rights. Nor did

114. *See Apececche v. White Pine Cty.*, 96 Nev. 723, 615 P.2d 975, 977–78 (1980).

115. 42 U.S.C. § 2000e–2(a)(1); *Fonseca v. Sysco Food Servs. of Ariz., Inc.*, 374 F.3d 840, 847 (9th Cir. 2004).

116. *Lusardi*, 2015 WL 1607756, at *9.

117. *See id.* (citing 20 C.F.R. 1910.141 § (c)(1)(i) (requiring that employers provide access to toilet facilities so that all employees can use them when they need to do so)).

118. *Id.*

119. CCSD cites *Kastl* for the proposition that the Ninth Circuit has "held that enforcing restroom use practices based on biological gender is not unlawful." ECF No. 89 at 17 (emphasis original) (citing *Kastl*, 325 Fed. Appx. at 492). But that is not what *Kastl* holds. The Ninth Circuit found that the plaintiff stated a prima facie case for gender discrimination under Title VII and *Price Waterhouse* but failed to put forward sufficient evidence that the bathroom ban was motivated by her gender.

120. *Cordova*, 124 F.3d at 1148.

121. ECF No. 136 at 10.

he say that the department based its policy on those rights as opposed to Roberts's gender and anatomy.[122]

I therefore grant partial summary judgment in Roberts's favor and against CCSD on the question of whether it discriminated against Roberts under Title VII and NRS 613.330. I leave for trial the question of Roberts's damages because they remain genuinely disputed.

3. ***Neither party is entitled to summary judgment on Roberts's harassment claims.***

Title VII's prohibition against discrimination "because of sex" encompasses the right to be free of a hostile-work environment and be "free from discriminatory intimidation, ridicule, and insult."[123] Roberts's hostile-work environment claim requires him to prove not only that he was subjected to unwelcome harassment, but that this harassment was sufficiently severe or pervasive.[124] "Severe and pervasive" harassment is harassment that a reasonable person would find frequent, severe, or abusive enough to alter the conditions of the workplace.[125] Petty harassment, even "singling [someone] out

121. ECF No. 136 at 10.

122. *See* ECF No. 136-11 at 3–4.

123. *McGinest v. GTE Serv. Corp.*, 360 F.3d 1103, 1112 (9th Cir. 2004) (quoting *Meritor Sav. Bank v. Vinson*, 477 U.S. 57, 65, 106 S.Ct. 2399, 91 L.Ed.2d 49 (1986)).

124. *Craig v. M & O Agencies, Inc.*, 496 F.3d 1047, 1055 (9th Cir. 2007) (quoting *Fuller v. City of Oakland*, 47 F.3d 1522, 1527 (9th Cir. 1995) (internal quotation marks omitted)).

125. *Id.*

for unfavorable treatment," is not necessarily enough.[126] I must consider the totality of the circumstances, including: "[the] frequency of the discriminatory conduct; its severity; whether it is physically threatening or humiliating, or a mere offensive utterance; and whether it unreasonably interferes with an employee's work performance."[127]

None of the incidents cited by Roberts is frequent, severe, or abusive enough for me to rule that he was "severely and pervasively" harassed as a matter of law. Roberts mainly points to the various emails that the department sent regarding his transition. But Roberts was told about these emails ahead of time—and he even agreed to the wording in at least the initial one. There is conflicting evidence about whether Roberts was told that the email would be sent out to the entire department. CCSD provides evidence that department staff were not rude or disrespectful to Roberts.[128] And Roberts's other allegations about the delays in processing his personnel records and the comments made by coworkers are not so severe that a reasonable juror must conclude they were "severe or pervasive."
erts's sexual identity. It invited Roberts's coworkers to ask questions about his transition. And Roberts has introduced evidence that department staff made inappropriate remarks about his genitalia, among

125. *Id.*

126. *Swenson v. Potter*, 271 F.3d 1184, 1195 (9th Cir. 2001).

127. *Nichols v. Azteca*, 256 F.3d 864, 871–72 (9th Cir. 2001).

128. *See* ECF No. 89-1 at 5–6.

priate remarks about his genitalia, among other things. With evidence on both sides, I thus deny summary judgment to either party on Roberts's harassment/hostile-work-environment claim.

More work-showing.

4. Neither party is entitled to summary judgment on Roberts's retaliation claims.

To succeed on his retaliation claim, Roberts must prove that (1) he was engaged in protected activity, (2) he suffered an adverse employment action, and (3) there was a causal link between the protected activity and the adverse employment action.[129] Causation is a "but for" test: would the retaliatory act not have happened but for the plaintiff's protected activity. Roberts contends that his protected activity was requesting to use the men's bathroom and refusing to provide medical documentation to the department. CCSD then allegedly retaliated by banning Roberts from the bathroom.[130]

[21] Roberts has not established beyond genuine dispute that the bathroom ban was motivated by his request or refusal to provide documents, rather than simply a response to the complaints the department received about a woman using the men's bathroom. Roberts must prove that, but for his request or refusal to provide documents, CCSD would never have instituted the ban. But there is little direct evidence that the department was retaliating against Roberts for protected activity and not just implementing a policy in response to complaints. I thus deny summary judgment on Roberts's retaliation claim.

Conclusion

Accordingly, IT IS HEREBY ORDERED that plaintiff Bradley Roberts's motion for partial summary judgment **[ECF No. 54] is GRANTED in part and denied in part. I grant summary judgment in Roberts's favor on the issue of the school district's liability for discrimination in violation of both Title VII and NRS 613.330; the motion is denied in all other respects**.

IT FURTHER IS ORDERED that Clark County School District's countermotion for partial summary judgment **[ECF No. 89] is DENIED**.

IT IS FURTHER ORDERED that Roberts's motion for leave to file excess pages **[ECF No. 143] is GRANTED** nunc pro tunc.

IT IS FURTHER ORDERED that **this case is referred to the magistrate judge for a mandatory settlement conference**.

129. *Villiarimo v. Aloha Island Air, Inc.*, 281 F.3d 1054, 1064 (9th Cir. 2002) (citation omitted).

130. Roberts also contends that the adverse action was that CCSD allowed him to be harassed. But I would not grant summary judgment on this ground for the same reason that judgment is inappropriate on Roberts's harassment claim itself.

Sample Appellate-Court Opinion (pure style)

Supreme Court of Colorado, En Banc

Martin Richard ISRAEL and Tammy Lee Bannon Israel,
Plaintiffs-Appellees

v.

Norman C. ALLEN, County Clerk and Recorder of Jefferson County,
Defendant-Appellant

No. 27823

April 24, 1978

This "pure" style of judicial opener summarizes the court's decision at the outset.

PRINGLE, Chief Justice

Summary

Martin and Tammy Israel, who are siblings only by adoption, were denied a marriage license because the Colorado Uniform Marriage Act[1] prohibits marriage between adoptive siblings. The trial court declared the prohibition unconstitutional because it found that marriage is a fundamental right, and subject to equal protection. We find that the prohibition is unconstitutional because it does not meet minimum rationality requirements. On that basis, we affirm the judgment.

The Two Siblings

Before they married in 1972, Raymond Israel and Sylvia Bannon each had a child from a previous relationship. Raymond Israel legally adopted his wife's daughter, Tammy. She thus became his son Martin's adoptive sister.

Martin Israel and Tammy Bannon Martin Israel applied for a marriage license. Their application was denied because the Colorado Uniform Marriage Act prohibits "marriage between an ancestor and a descendant or

1 C.R.S. § 14-2-101 et seq. (1973).

between a brother and sister, whether the relationship is by the half or the whole blood *or by adoption*; . . . .[2]

The couple sought declaratory relief. The trial court decided that marriage is a fundamental right, and applied an equal-protection standard of review, which requires a compelling state interest to support barring a marriage between a brother and sister related only by adoption. Finding no such interest, the court held that the prohibition was unconstitutional. The court severed the words "by adoption" from the statute.

Why the Act Is Unconstitutional

The basic test of constitutionality is the minimum rationality standard or rational-basis test. A law or a provision in a law must have some reasonable relationship to a legitimate state interest, and it must serve to further that interest. If it doesn't, the we must find the law unconstitutional.[3]

The only argument offered to support the prohibition is that the state has an interest in preserving family harmony and that prohibiting the marriage between this adoptive brother and sister furthers this interest. But the proposed marriage does not threaten the Israel family's harmony. Raymond Israel and Sylvia Bannon are in favor of the marriage. Also, Bishop Evans of the Roman Catholic Archdiocese of Denver funds no religious bar to the marriage.

There are other reasons for a state to forbid marriages between a brother and sister, but they do not apply when the man and woman are related only by adoption.

Society objects to marriages between blood relative because they are considered more likely to product children with serious genetic defects. This does not apply to people related only by marriage.[4] Like marriage, adoption into a family does not change blood relationships. So while there is a rational basis to prohibit siblings of the full or half blood from marrying, it doesn't logically extend to brothers and sisters related only by adoption.

Colorado law recognizes that adoptive siblings are different from siblings related by blood. In some statutes, the legislature makes adopted and

2 C.R.S. § 14-2-110(1)(b) (1973) (emphasis added).

3 *Stevenson v. Indus. Comm'n*, 545 P.2d 712, 716 (Colo. 1976). *See also Dandridge v. Williams*, 397 U.S. 471, 484–87 (1970).

4 *See* 1 Vernier, *American Family Laws* 183 (comparing English, ecclesiastical, and American law regarding marriage between people related only by affinity).

natural children equal, such as in matters of inheritance and parental duties. But the legislature exempts adoptive siblings from other statutes that affect families. For example, the criminal-incest statute does not forbid sexual relationships between an adoptive brother and sister.[5] If such a relationship is not forbidden outside of marriage, it is illogical to forbid it within.

We hold that the portion of the statute forbidding marriage between a brother and sister related only by adoption is unconstitutional because there is no rational basis for the prohibition.

Severability of the Provision

Language in a statute may be declare unconstitutional and severed if the severance has no effect on the remaining provisions.[6] The provision against marriage between a brother and sister related by blood is independent of the words "or by adoption,"[7] so the rest of the statute is still effective. The trial court did not err in holding that this statute was severable and striking the unconstitutional provision.

Disposition

Although the trial court held that the statute infringed a fundamental right, and the rational-basis test usually applies only when no fundamental right is implicated, we have found that prohibiting marriage between a brother and sister related only by adoption does not satisfy minimum rationality requirements. So we need not decide whether marriage is a fundamental right in Colorado.

Affirmed.

---

5 C.R.S. § 18-6-301 (1973).

6 *Shroyer v. Sokol*, 550 P.2d 309, 311 (Colo. 1976).

7 *See* C.R.S. § 14-1-110(1)(b) (1973.

Sample Appellate-Court Opinion (impure style)

36 S.W.3d 119
Supreme Court of Texas.
In re The TEXAS SENATE and The Honorable Rodney Ellis, Relators.
No. 00–1321.

Dec. 28, 2000.

JUSTICE HECHT delivered the opinion of a unanimous Court.

Yesterday, five newspapers and a magazine[1] sued the Texas Senate and the Honorable Rodney Ellis, president *pro tempore* of the Senate, contending that the Senate is prohibited by the Texas Open Meetings Act[2] from electing one of its members to perform the duties of Lieutenant Governor except by *viva voce* vote in open session. The office of Lieutenant Governor became vacant on December 21, 2000, when its holder, the Honorable Rick Perry, was sworn in as Governor,[3] following the resignation of the Honorable George W. Bush, President Elect of the United States. The defendants have stipulated that the election of a Senator to perform the duties of Lieutenant Governor is to be by secret ballot of the Committee of the Whole Senate at a meeting scheduled for today at 1:30 p.m. After a nonevidentiary hearing, the district court issued a writ of mandamus prohibiting the election by secret ballot. Relators filed a petition for mandamus with the court of appeals, requesting that the district court's order be vacated. The court of appeals denied the relators' petition.

This "impure" style of judicial opener explains the problem but doesn't state the court's resolution.

Section 551.003 "prohibit[s] secret meetings of the legislature, committees of the legislature, and other bodies associated with the legislature, except as specifically provided in the constitution."[4] This provision clearly covers the Committee of the Whole Senate. Thus, its meeting and

1 The real parties in interest, the plaintiffs in the trial court, are the *Austin American-Statesman,* the *Bryan-College Station Eagle,* the *Houston Chronicle,* the *San Antonio Express-News, Texas Monthly,* and the *Waco Tribune-Herald.*

2 Tex. Gov't Code §§ 551.001–.146. All statutory references are to the Texas Government Code.

3 Tex. Const. art. XVI, § 40.

4 Tex. Gov't Code § 551.003. *See also* Tex. Gov't Code § 551.102.

votes cannot be secret "except as specifically provided" by the Texas Constitution.

Article III, section 41 of the Texas Constitution states: "In all elections by the Senate and House of Representatives, jointly or separately, the vote shall be given viva voce, *except in the election of their officers.*" (Emphasis added.) This provision authorizes the Senate to elect its officers by secret ballot, should it choose to do so.[5] This specific provision is therefore an exception to section 551.003. The question, then, is whether the election of a Senator to perform the duties of the office of Lieutenant Governor is an election of a Senate officer within the meaning of article III, section 41.

The person to be elected will be the presiding officer of the Senate,[6] but he will also be performing the duties of a State official in the Executive Department of the government with duties beyond those as a Senate officer.[7] The real parties in interest concede as they must that the person to be elected will be in part a Senate officer, but they contend that his additional duties remove him from the category of Senate "officers" as that term is used in the Constitution. We disagree.

This opinion is short enough and direct enough that headings aren't necessary.

In the first place, the Constitution defines the Lieutenant Governor to be a Senate officer. Article IV, section 16 states: "The Lieutenant Governor, shall by virtue of his office, be President of the Senate, and shall have, when in Committee of the Whole, a right to debate and vote on all questions; and when the Senate is equally divided to give the casting vote."[8] Although section 16 also gives the Lieutenant Governor the powers and authority of Governor in specified circumstances, these do not detract from the express reference to the Lieutenant Governor as a Senate officer.

Moreover, article III, section 9 contemplates that the Lieutenant Governor is a Senate officer. Article III, section 9 requires that certain legislative officers be elected. Section 9(a) provides for the election of the president *pro*

---

5 *See also* Tex. Const. art. III, § 11 (authorizing each House of the Legislature to determine the rules of its own proceedings).

6 *See* Tex. Const. art. III, § 9; art. IV, § 16.

7 Tex. Const. art. IV, §§ 16–17.

8 There are two provisions in article IV labeled section 16, both proposed by the 76th Legislature and ratified by the people in November 1999. *See* Tex. H.R.J. Res. 44, 76th Leg., R.S. (1999); Tex. H.R.J. Res. 62, 76th Leg., R.S. (1999). The two provisions are different in some respects, but the language quoted here is essentially the same in both.

tempore of the Senate, who will perform the duties of the Lieutenant Governor in certain circumstances. Section 9(a) also provides that in the event the office of Lieutenant Governor becomes vacant, the Committee of the Whole Senate "shall elect one of its members to perform the duties of the Lieutenant Governor in addition to the member's duties as Senator until the next general election." Section 9(b) requires the House of Representatives to elect a Speaker. Section 9(c) then states: "Each House shall choose its *other* officers." (Emphasis added.) Reading these provisions together, section 9 clearly contemplates that the member of the Senate elected to perform the duties of the office of Lieutenant Governor is an "officer" of the Senate. We see no reason to read the word "officer" differently in article III, section 41.

Section 41 clearly gives each House of the Legislature the authority to elect its officers by means other than a *viva voce* vote. The Senator elected to perform the duties of Lieutenant Governor is, by the plain language of the Constitution, a Senate officer. Indeed, he remains a member of the Senate. If the framers and ratifiers intended that the exception clause in section 41 apply to Senate officers except those whose duties could extend beyond the Senate—the Lieutenant Governor and president *pro tempore*—then they could easily have said so. We decline to make exceptions for these officers ourselves.

The parties have argued policy reasons for and against an election by secret ballot. These arguments are not for us to consider; the Constitution, by allowing but not requiring a secret ballot, commits that choice to the Senate.

Article IV, section 3 of the Constitution provides for the election of certain executive officers by the Legislature in the event of a tie in the popular vote. We express no opinion whether that vote could be by secret ballot if the tie was in the election for Lieutenant Governor.

Concededly, this opinion uses several Latinisms: *instanter*, *pro tempore*, and *viva voce*. Perhaps those were thought to contribute to the *gravitas* (so to speak) of the opinion, which is otherwise plain-spoken and admirably clear.

Accordingly, without hearing oral argument, the Court directs the district court to vacate *instanter* its order issued December 27, 2000, in Cause No. GN-00-3659, and to notify the Clerk of this Court by 1:30 p.m. today that it has done so. We are confident that the district court will comply. If it does not, the Clerk shall issue a writ of mandamus immediately thereafter.

§ 27
Contracts

27.1 Understand the main goals of a contract.

(a) *Creating a legal relationship.* A contract, the most general type of transactional document, creates reciprocal duties between the parties. It may be anything from a lease to a license to a land sale to a settlement. A lawyer drafting a contract or advising a client about a contract must remember the simple truth that whenever someone asks someone else to sign a document, the signer may someday regret having signed. The contractual terms matter most if that day comes. While a contract may begin a relationship that all the parties are pleased with or close a deal that they are optimistic about, the drafter must look toward the chance that the satisfaction and optimism may fade. The document must serve well in that future day as well as in the present.

(b) *Making terms clear.* On the one hand, a contract should be readable so that the parties will understand their rights and duties. On the other hand, it must be unmistakable in its meaning, since whenever a disagreement arises each party will interpret the contract in its own favor. Unlike most other documents, contracts can be subjected to willful perversions of meaning. So the wordings must be so clear that they foreclose frivolous positions about what they mean.

27.2 Think about the specific goals of your contract.

(a) *Accuracy, completeness, and precision.* As a drafter, you must understand exactly what the parties wish to accomplish. This means that you must truly understand the practical character of the business transaction. You must express this accurately, completely, and precisely.

(b) *Protecting the client.* You must foresee situations that your client has not necessarily thought about. If the relationship sours, or if goods turn out not to be as represented, or if one of the parties goes bankrupt, what happens then? The central question is always the same: How can you protect the interests of your client in advance? The answers to this question (there will always be more than one answer) will vary from contract to contract, but it is precisely the question that you will have to pose again and again. In a publishing agreement in which you represent the author, what happens if the publisher goes out of business? What happens with later editions if the author dies? Are the heirs protected, and for how long? Can you retain the copyright in your client's name (as opposed to granting it to the publisher)?

Can you have escalating royalties after the sale of a few thousand copies? Can you negotiate a commitment from the publisher to promote the book and related computer products? Depending on the type of contract you work on, the provisions that you need to think about require great creativity and insight.

(c) *Getting the deal done.* Although you want to protect your client's interests, you'll never be able to reduce your client's risk to zero. Undertaking contractual obligations always entails some element of risk. After offering your advice, you must let your client make business judgments about what level of legal risk is acceptable. If you draft an agreement that is so lopsided that the other party scoffs at it or (worse) gets offended by it, you've failed in an essential element of good drafting. Even though your draft will invariably protect your client more than the other party, you should always approach the deal with an eye toward reasonableness and the type of business relationship that your client hopes to cultivate. It is an inexperienced transactional drafter who always begins with the most extreme positions. The best deal is good for both parties at the inception; the contract memorializes the deal so that if the context changes, the parties' interests are defined. The contract must be fair.

27.3 Avoid the common faults of contracts.

(a) *Patchwork style.* Contracts are often the product of many generations of drafters, each of whom had a slightly different style. Duties are often inconsistently stated (*shall*, *shall have the duty to*, *agrees to*, *is required to*, *must*, *will*, *understands that it is her sole responsibility to*, *is to*, *promises to*, etc.). Sometimes as many as four ways of stating a duty will appear on a single page. The modern drafter must reconcile these inconsistencies, preferably using ordinary English (preferably *will* or possibly *agrees to*).

(b) *Ambiguous "shall."* Although every drafter seems to have heard that *shall* is a mandatory word, contracts often use the word in as many as four or five different senses. Sometimes its sense is indeed mandatory (*the employee shall send notice*); sometimes it means "may," especially after a negative (*neither party shall disclose*); sometimes it means "is entitled to" (*the corporate secretary shall be reimbursed for all expenses*); sometimes it is merely a future-tense verb (*if any partner shall become bankrupt*); and courts have often held that it means "should." Generally speaking, contractual promises are well expressed with *will* <Grogan will pay $25,000 to Jensen upon delivery of the piano>. Where a mandatory word is needed for a non-duty-bearing subject, use *must* <each order must be signed>.

(c) *Overreaching.* A contract that demands too much from the other party can defeat the contract's very purpose. Even if you have a legitimate protection or right at stake, a provision that's unfair to the other party gives the contract an unpleasant odor and makes negotiations more difficult. It may even break the deal. And if an overreaching clause leads to litigation, it could jeopardize any claim asserted under that clause and might be struck altogether.

(d) *Density.* Wall-to-wall type can put off any reader—lawyer and client alike. Yet it's all too common among legal drafters. Use headings to divide the contract into related terms (see 4.21–4.23). Set out lists in subparts so readers can easily find and understand the terms. Use a numbering system so anyone can cite any provision in the document (see 4.21(b)). Cut the verbiage, especially the doublets and triplets that don't add meaning (see 12.2(f)): then you'll be able to use a larger, more reader-friendly font (see 4.5), more generous page margins (see 4.7), white space with headings (see 4.6), and hanging indents (see 4.9).

(e) *Awkward numbering.* One possible reason for density is that the drafter has not adopted a workable numbering system. Some documents are misguidedly sprinkled with romanettes, which make for awkward tabs once they are set out in separate subparts. For maximal readability and consistency, the following system is recommended:

1. Compensation

- 1.1 Salary. --:
    - (A) --:
        - (1) --; or
        - (2) --:
            - (a) ---------------------------; and
            - (b) --; and
    - (B) --:
        - (1) ---------------------------------; or
        - (2) ---.
- 1.2 Signing Bonus. --:
    - (A) --:
        - (1) -------------------------------------; and
        - (2) --:
            - (a) ----------------------------------; or
            - (b) ---------------------------------; or
    - (B) --.

Imposing this kind of numbering system on an old form will typically lay bare both stylistic and substantive problems.

(f) *Uncritical use of forms.* Experienced lawyers know that forms are a better guide to content than they are to form. They will help you think through the kinds of issues that you will need to address, but they will probably be of

family members, as well as by anyone that the Contractor invites onto the Property.

7.6 **Owners' Joint and Several Liability.** Each person signing the Agreement as an Owner is responsible for all Owner obligations under the Agreement. Their liability is joint and several.

8. Miscellaneous Provisions

8.1 **Entire Agreement.** This Agreement constitutes the sole agreement of the Parties with respect to its subject matter. It supersedes any prior written or oral agreements or communications between the Parties. It may not be modified except in a writing signed by the Parties.

8.2 **Assignments.** Neither party may assign the Agreement without the other party's prior written consent, which must not be unreasonably withheld. A party's entering into contracts with subcontractors is not considered an assignment.

8.3 **Waiver.** If either party fails to require the other to perform any term of the Agreement, that failure does not prevent the party from later enforcing that term. If either party waives the other's breach of a term, that waiver is not treated as waiving a later breach of the term.

8.4 **Successors and Representatives.** The Agreement binds and inures to the benefit of the Parties and their respective heirs, personal representatives, successors, and (where permitted) assignees.

8.5 **Notices.** All notices and other communications required or permitted under the Agreement must be in writing and must be sent to the party at that party's address set forth below or at whatever other address the party specifies in writing.

8.6 **Severability.** If any part of the Agreement is for any reason held to be unenforceable, the rest of it remains fully enforceable.

8.7 **"Including."** Unless the context requires otherwise, the term "including" means "including but not limited to."

8.8 **Headings.** Headings are for convenience only and do not affect the interpretation of the Agreement.

8.9 **Applicable Law.** Texas law applies to the Agreement without regard for any choice-of-law rules that might direct the application of the laws of any other jurisdiction.

8.10 **Counterparts.** The Agreement may be signed in counterparts, each one of which is considered an original, but all of which constitute one and the same instrument.

CONTRACTOR:

TRIPOD LLC, d/b/a Hershey Custom Homes

By: ______________________________

Bruce Hershey
Managing Member

OWNERS:

____

Bertrand A. Renrag

____

Karo H.C. Renrag

IMPORTANT NOTICE: You and your contractor are responsible for meeting the terms and conditions of this contract. If you sign this contract and you fail to meet the terms and conditions of this Agreement, you may lose your legal ownership rights in your home. Know your rights and duties under the law.

§ 28
Statements of Work

28.1 Understand the main goals of a statement of work.

(a) *Definition.* A statement of work (SOW*) is a contractual document—usually contained in an attachment and incorporated by reference into a broader master agreement (sometimes called a "frame agreement")—defining precisely what one party, such as a supplier or service provider, will do for the other to further a particular project. It typically covers such items as the nature of and standards for deliverables, quality assurance, inspection, and acceptance. An SOW is crucial to making a contract workable, and a good one will save managers time and companies money.

SOWs can run the gamut from simple one-page sets of requirements for building a website to exceedingly long and detailed specifications for building a spacecraft. In what follows, the assumption is that the SOW is a stand-alone attachment to a contract, as opposed to a provision or set of provisions within a contract.

(b) *Objectives.* An SOW must clearly and concisely explain the work to be accomplished. Its broad goal is to provide enough concrete detail to convey what must be done by whom and when, without so much detail as to plunge the reader into the technical weeds. It should outline with reasonable specificity the work to be done, the expected product or result, the employees who are to be involved in the project, the various parties' responsibilities, and so forth. It should be in plain English: a nontechnician (e.g., a contract manager or a judge) should be able to understand what's essential to a successful contractual performance. It should also be accurate: grammatical, consistent, and correct in all cross-references, both internally to the SOW and externally to the master agreement.

(c) *Subordination to agreement.* Nothing in the SOW should change—or purport to change—the master agreement's terms. The SOW must remain subordinate to the master agreement: it just sets forth what must be done and when. The contract itself should contain language making the SOW binding on the burdened party and enforceable by the benefited party. Of course, if there's a seeming discrepancy between the master agreement and the SOW, anyone interpreting the two should, if possible, try to read them harmoniously. Ideally, the contract and the SOW should expressly refer to each other.

---

*The term generally used is the initialism *SOW*, normally pronounced /ess-oh-**dəb**-əl-yoo/. The term is sometimes (much less commonly) pronounced as an acronym (/soh/, not /sow/).

Like a contract, an SOW should provide that it can be changed only by amendment or by a written change order. Any amendment or change order should refer explicitly to the clause being changed.

28.2 Think about the specific goals of your SOW.

(a) *The basic elements: who, what, when, where.* Begin by identifying the parties. Refer at the outset to the master agreement to which the SOW is attached. Specify the SOW's effective date. Then describe the ultimate goal of the work to be performed: the expected end result by a specified date. Specify the responsibilities of each party: the language must clearly allocate responsibility for each task to one party or the other. Arrange the SOW to progress from a big-picture description to narrower specifics. For example, a tech company might want a contractor develop a component with certain features. State that, and then break it down into the following project-specific elements:

- A recitation of the parties involved (mirroring the parties to the contract).
- The names of organizational representatives, so that lines of responsibility are clear.
- A high-level description of the project.
- A brief chronological list of the work to be performed.
- The timing (milestones) for completion for each task, whether by relative times (e.g., within 60 days of some event) or hard deadlines (e.g., 5:00 p.m. EDT on May 1 of a specific year).
- Explicit identification of any tasks that are interdependent, and how they are interdependent.
- The cost of each task, broken down as appropriate—payments being earned according to milestones reached (consider making a table for milestones).
- Specific limitations or exceptions.
- The criteria for the acceptance of each deliverable—preferably objective criteria subject to verification.
- A change-order procedure that allows flexibility for changes that become necessary.
- An escalation path for any technical problems encountered.
- Project-level breach provisions aligning with overarching breach provisions within the master agreement.

You may want to consider additional terms for on-site visits while the work is ongoing. Other possibilities might involve additional expenses for travel, additional training requirements, and visa requirements for foreigners.

(b) *Things to exclude.* Avoid including legal provisions such as warranties and limitations of liability: these should be in the master agreement itself, not the SOW, which shouldn't contain any hidden legal provisions.

(c) *Consistency with master contract.* Review the SOW carefully for how it aligns with the master agreement—and any other attachments to that agreement. Ensure that nothing in the SOW conflicts in any way with the master agreement. Don't attempt to override the master agreement in the SOW; instead, that would require an amendment to the master agreement.

28.3 Avoid the common pitfalls in SOWs.

(a) *Failing to set forth clear goals.* Sometimes a service provider will have a "form SOW" that describes in vague language various actions it plans to take but never really says, from the counterparty's viewpoint, what the ultimate objective is. That's a poor approach. If the goal, for example, is editorial software that uses artificial intelligence to translate suboptimal documents into plain-English equivalents without substantive change, then say so with some specificity.

(b) *Failing to apportion responsibilities clearly.* Don't make parties jointly responsible for deliverables. There must be a clear delineation of who is to deliver what by when.

Not this: The block must not contain more than . . .
But this: Customer will ensure that the block does not contain more than . . .

Not this: Vendor's contract is required to . . .
But this: Vendor will require that its contractor . . .

Not this: The logic library will be designed with the architectural features to allow it to be interoperable with Acme 10nm 12DG library.
But this: Vendor will design the logic library with architectural features allowing it to be interoperable with Acme 10nm 12DG library.

Not this: The patent block must meet the following requirements: . . .
But this: Vendor will ensure that the patent block meets the following requirements: . . .

Not this: The schedule will set forth . . .
But this: The parties will agree to a schedule setting forth . . .

Keep in mind that because you're so intimately involved in the project, some points may seem obvious to you that may not be so clear to an outsider. The allocation of responsibility must be explicit and fully understandable to a stranger to the deal. For the same reasons, avoid language that merely expresses wishes or desires. Don't use *should*, *would like to*, *wants*, or *wishes*: these so-called *precatory words* create uncertainty about whether an action is required.

Not this: The flowchart should be able to show the relevant criteria for generating design collaterals.
But this: Customer will ensure that the flowchart shows the relevant criteria for generating design collaterals.

Not this: The qualification schedule should feed into the overall project schedule.
But this: The parties will create a qualification schedule comporting with the overall project schedule.

(c) *Rehashing topics already covered in the master agreement.* If you start repeating things that are covered in the master agreement, you're performing not only an unnecessary task but a dangerous one: you're creating the very real possibility of introducing inconsistencies. You're also complicating the process of amendment. Plus, you're not recognizing the limited purposes of an SOW as opposed to the broader legal purposes of the master agreement. In any event, all substantive questions such as ownership, as well as assurances and guarantees, belong in the master agreement, not in the SOW.

An SOW shouldn't address who owns or is entitled to use the outcome of the work performed—or, for that matter, any of the parties' other legal rights. But the question of ownership is sometimes muddied in an SOW using the word *owns* in the colloquial sense of "is responsible for" or "has responsibility for developing." Don't say *Acme owns the design block* if you mean *Acme is responsible for developing the design block.*

(d) *Failing to distinguish hard vs. soft deadlines.* Some deadlines are more important than others. You can use the terms *hard deadline* and *soft deadline* to distinguish them. Consider the difference between "Acme will deliver the block by December 4, 2018" and "Acme will target early December for delivery of the block." You may want to give yourself some flexibility. For example, a company and its contractor may prefer to complete a project before the end of the third quarter of the year even though for legal purposes, the project need only be completed before year's end. The parties could say: "Contractor must use commercially reasonable efforts to complete the project before September 30, 2018, and in any event must complete the project on or before December 31, 2018." Alternatively, if the parties want to give the soft deadline more "teeth," the same sentence could be restyled to offer an incentive for achieving the earlier deadline (or to impose a disincentive for failing to do so): "Contractor must complete the project no later than December 31, 2018. If Contractor completes the project before September 30, 2018, the overall contract price will be raised by 10%."

(e) *Lacking specificity.* If you want to buy an oak tree and you ask to buy a "tree," it's hard to complain when the seller delivers a pine. Similarly, if you want a 2,500-square-foot house with three bedrooms and two and a half bathrooms, you surely wouldn't sign a contract with a builder to erect a "reasonably sized house, with adequate plumbing." You'd be much more specific, whether buying goods or services. If service is an important aspect of the deal, make sure that you're specific about the timing of various levels of services. Some will be more important than others. The point is to avoid vagueness when you know the specifics of what you require. Specificity, as opposed to generality, will make both parties happier because it fosters real understanding and performance standards. Contractors want to know what they're expected to do, and customers want to know what they're getting.

(f) *Failing to have adequate drafting safeguards.* Writing unmistakably, in an SOW or elsewhere, is a challenge. Many SOWs fail for too much generality, vagueness, or downright ambiguity. You must take enough time to be clear about what's expected, and then have a second or third set of eyes review important parts. Listen sympathetically (and gratefully) to constructive comments. Whatever you do, don't insulate yourself from criticism and think that something that you've drafted solo, without others' critical review, is likely to succeed. If you're a contract manager at a company, don't wait until the last minute to review your SOW with in-house counsel; discuss your questions in advance.

28.4 Study models of exemplary SOWs, as well as explanatory literature.

(a) *Finding exemplars.* Because SOWs can be so varied in length and content, it's a good idea—if you work with them routinely—to build your own collection for the types of contracts you're working with. Although this may take some time, you shouldn't overlook it. Critically study the SOWs you encounter and constantly upgrade your selection of the most admirable ones relevant to your work: explicit, well worded, to the point, and streamlined.

(b) *Further guidance.* For more on on drafting effective SOWs, recommended books are:

- Peter S. Cole & Michael G. Martin, *How to Write a Statement of Work* (6th ed. 2012).
- Michael G. Martin, *The Government Manager's Guide to the Statement of Work* (2014).
- Stanley E. Portny et al., *Project Management: Planning, Scheduling, and Controlling Costs* (2008).
- James Taylor, *Project Scheduling and Cost Control* (2008).
- Glenn J. Voelz, *Contractors in the Government Workplace* (2010) (appendix D).

(c) *An exemplar.* The following SOW ("Annex A") is one of many types. It has to do with wind-farming.

Annex A

Statement of Work

This Statement of Work (this "SOW") is effective as of January 29, 2018 and is made by Financial Advisers, Inc. ("Contractor") and Client Corporation ("Client") in connection with that certain Master Agreement, dated January 29, 2018 (the "Agreement"), between Contractor and Client and to which this SOW is attached.

Except as otherwise set forth in this SOW, this SOW incorporates by reference, and is treated as a part of, the Agreement. Capitalized terms used but not otherwise defined in this SOW have the meanings assigned them in the Agreement.

Scope of Services

Contractor will provide a cost-segregation study to support Client's federal income tax computed with regard to building, land improvements, and tangible personal property at Client's wind-farm project located in Canyon, Texas. This cost-segregation study will also serve as the basis for determining which costs are eligible to include in calculating the Internal Revenue Code Section 48 Investment Tax Credit.

Contractor's Obligations

In providing these services, Contractor will:

- Meet with appropriate personnel of Client to discuss the project's overall scope and gather the required data for use in Contractor's analysis.
- Determine the project deliverables with Client to ensure that the analysis provides the level of detail required for federal-tax-depreciation purposes.
- Analyze the available cost data (provided by Client) that includes the general contractor's application for payment, change orders, Client-incurred costs, and indirect costs.
- Review the full set of construction drawings to develop proper asset classifications for federal-income-tax purposes.
- Estimate the land improvements and tangible personal property by performing quantity "take-offs" (engineering estimates) from the

construction drawings and specifications for items not readily identified on the cost information, as needed.

- Allocate for federal-tax purposes the Client's and Contractor's indirect costs (provided by the Client), such as architect fees, permits, general-contractor fees, and engineering fees when appropriate.
- Issue, no later than June 1, 2018, a final report to Client including the following: overview and scope of study; property description; income-tax provisions; summary of the expenditures classified into their proper recovery periods; detailed schedules supporting the summary; description of the methods undertaken and tasks performed; and photographs of specified assets.

Contractor undertakes the services subject to the following key assumptions:

- Contractor's scope of work does not include issuing any interim reports or schedules. Contractor's fee will increase by $5,000 for each additional report or schedule Contractor issues at Client's request.
- The anticipated in-service date for the project is June 1, 2018. If the project spans multiple in-service years because of a delayed schedule or changes in the project's phasing, Contractor and Client will mutually agree on additional fees because of the change in scope.
- Contractor's scope of services includes considering authority related to depreciation and the applicable tax credits as of the date of this SOW. If tax law changes before June 1, 2018, Contractor will notify Client of the impact on the study and the parties will mutually agree on additional fees or a modified deadline if a change in scope is necessary.

Client's Obligations

Client personnel will be responsible for the following during this engagement:

- Gathering and organizing project data.
- Providing the total cost to be capitalized for the project, with supporting detail.
- Coordinating a site-visit representative who knows the building and the construction costs and can walk through the facility with Contractor's team.

- Making available a representative familiar with construction costs whom Contractor can contact with questions about the analyzed project costs.
- Determining whether bonus-depreciation treatment applies to self-constructed and acquired assets.
- Uploading project data into Client's fixed-asset system.

Client will not, and will not permit others to, quote or refer to any reports—or any portion, summary, or abstract of their reports—in any document filed or distributed in connection with (1) a purchase or sale of securities to which United States or state securities laws ("Securities Laws") apply; or (2) periodic reporting obligations under Securities Laws.

No Warranty

The services Contractor provides are advisory in nature. Contractor will not render an assurance report or assurance opinion under the Agreement, nor will Contractor's services constitute an audit, review, examination, or other form of attestation, as those terms are defined by the American Institute of Certified Public Accountants. Contractor will not conduct a review to detect fraud or illegal acts.

Contacts

Client has identified Joe Smith as the contact with whom Contractor should communicate about the services Contractor will provide under this SOW. Contractor's contact will be Jane Doe.

Fees

The General Terms and Conditions of the Agreement address Contractor's fees and expenses generally.

Client will pay Contractor a $40,000 fee for the services. Client will also pay any potential value-added taxes, sales taxes, and other indirect taxes and direct expenses incurred in connection with Contractor's performing the services, including any such taxes and related administrative costs resulting from billing arrangements that Client specifically requests. Direct expenses include reasonable and customary out-of-pocket expenses such as travel, meals, accommodations, and other expenses specifically related to this SOW.

Contractor will bill Client monthly for its fees, expenses, applicable taxes, and any other charges. Payment is due upon receipt of Contractor's invoice, and in no event later than 10 business days after the date of the billing statement.

Client may request Contractor's assistance in presenting the results of Contractor's report to the Internal Revenue Service to support cost-recovery deductions consistent with the report. But Contractor's fees for any such assistance are not included in this SOW and would need to be covered under a separate statement of work.

§ 29
Legislation, Rules, and Regulations

29.1 Understand the main goals of a governmental prescription.

(a) *The nature of governmental directives.* As with almost all other writing, legislative drafting has as its touchstones clarity, accuracy, and brevity—clarity being foremost. The purpose and result of a governmental directive should always be evident from its very words. Generally, a statute or regulation (1) imposes a duty, (2) creates a right, (3) confers a power, (4) grants a privilege, or (5) prohibits specific behavior. Often a governmental directive is subject to conditions, limitations, qualifications, or exceptions; ideally, these are set forth clearly and explicitly.

(b) *Achieving clarity.* A governmental prescription must accurately reflect what the enactors want it to mean and how they want it to function. It must be clear enough to be consistently interpreted and applied. Two of the greatest aids to clarity are consistent word usage and economical expression. Consistent usage means using one word or phrase to denote an idea throughout the text, without variation, because to vary the wording is presumably to vary the meaning. Economical expression means using no more words than necessary to express the idea—in the shortest sentences that reasonably convey the idea. These two aids to clarity have been formalized in legal interpretation as the presumption of consistent usage and the surplusage canon. *See* Antonin Scalia & Bryan A. Garner, *Reading Law: The Interpretation of Legal Texts* 170–79 (2012).

29.2 Determine precisely what you're trying to accomplish.

(a) *Your client's objectives.* Drafting is a collaborative process between the client and you, the drafter. The client should know what he or she ultimately wants the document to do but won't necessarily know how best to achieve it. Begin by interviewing your client to obtain as much information as possible about the document's purposes and policies, its limitations, its consequences, and what the client ultimately wants to achieve. You must learn, for example, whether agencies or instruments to implement the text already exist and need to be granted power, or whether these agencies or instruments need to be created.

(b) *Your audience's understanding.* Statutes, rules, and regulations identify the behavior that is or is not required or permitted, and they usually prescribe the consequences for not complying. Their provisions are designed to produce or inhibit actions and to have an identifiable legal effect. Because governmental prescriptions are normally directed to laypeople as well as lawyers and judges, they must be clear. The harder they are for the public to understand, the less effective they will be.

(c) *Your plan and first draft.* When drafting a statute, you need to (1) know your client's policy objectives, (2) educate your client about possible means of achieving the desired result, and (3) research legal issues that may be raised by the impending changes in the law. Once you've clarified your client's objectives, then, like an architect, you must plan how to fit them into the existing legislative framework. There is no standard way of planning, but you may begin by making a list of the important legal concepts that form the text's basis. You will identify gaps and other problems that require more legal research and further policy decisions by the client. Note them, but begin drafting the text as soon as you grasp the basic ideas. Don't wait until you have a complete understanding. Your understanding will arrive only through trying to produce a workable draft.

(d) *Feedback.* Once you have a clean full draft, have colleagues review it. Solicit their comments, suggestions, and questions. Invite them to pick it apart and find loopholes or "technicalities" that you might not have seen. Invite them to consider whether the draft will work in practice. Invite them also to make stylistic improvements. Accept all comments with gratitude and good humor.

29.3 Attain a command of the precepts of legislative style.

(a) *Simplicity and naturalness.* The structure of legislative sentences should comport with that of good idiomatic English. Word placement should track that of normal language—hence *Unless § 3.2 specifies otherwise, . . .* , not *Unless § 3.2 otherwise specifies, ...* (In normal English, you write or speak the words *Unless you say otherwise, let's . . . ,* not putting *otherwise* before the verb.) The language you use should lend itself to oral utterance.

(b) *The subject of the sentence.* Generally, the grammatical subject should be the agent that bears the duty that the sentence imposes, that is prohibited from acting, or that is granted discretion. This placement of the agent tends to avoid the use of passive voice, which is largely undesirable in legislative style.

Duty

Not this: Notice must be sent (by the petitioner) within 30 days.
But this: The petitioner must send notice within 30 days.

Prohibition

Not this: Extraneous materials must not be included (by the applicant).
But this: An applicant must not include extraneous materials.

Grant of discretion

Not this: Waiver may be applied for (by the employee).

But this: An employee may apply for a waiver.

In each set of parentheses above, the actor appears after the passive-voice construction. Omitting the parenthetical language leads to what is known as the *truncated passive*—often the source of inexplicit ambiguity in governmental prescriptions.

(c) *Sentence structure.* Keep your sentences short, and limit them to a single main thought. Break down parallel provisions and present them in subparts. When you have a list of subparts, put it at the end of the sentence. Number them, if possible, and offset them with hanging indents. Never put the sentence's main verb after a sizable list—put it early in the sentence so that readers can more easily see the sentence's structure. Avoid using a long list of subjects followed by the main verb. This so-called left-branching structure puts complex information at the beginning of the sentence. When the subparts are enumerated, the verb and any additional language are left dangling, unnumbered, and uncitable. Aid the reader's interpretation by instead composing the sentence so that the verb comes before the subparts and nothing is left dangling beyond them.

Not this:

3.2 Except as may otherwise be provided herein—

(a) every order required by its terms to be served;

(b) every pleading subsequent to the original complaint unless the court orders otherwise because of numerous defendants;

(c) every paper relating to the discovery required to be served upon a party unless the court orders otherwise; and

(d) every written notice, appearance, demand, offer of judgment, designation of record on appeal, or similar paper

—must be served on each of the parties to the action.

[Note that the action of the sentence—the predicate (*must be served on each of the parties to the action*) can't be cited as the earlier parts of the sentence can be.]

But this:

3.2 Except as these rules provide otherwise, the following papers must be served on every party:

(a) an order required by its terms to be served;

(b) a pleading filed after the original complaint, unless the court orders otherwise because of numerous defendants;

(c) a discovery paper required to be served on a party, unless the court orders otherwise; and

(d) a written notice, appearance, demand, offer of judgment, designation of record on appeal, or similar paper.

(d) *Tense.* A law in force is always speaking now. So two tenses are most common in governmental prescriptions: present and present perfect. Facts and conditions that are concurrent with a legal action should be in present tense <if the vehicle's owner cannot be located, the vehicle must be

impounded>. When facts or conditions must occur before a legal action, use present perfect <when the council has met and determined that more peace officers are needed to preserve the peace, the chief of police may recruit prospective candidates>. What has traditionally been called the future tense (with *will*, normally) may be appropriate when an act cannot be performed before a specific time <one month after the applicant files the requested document, the clerk will send notice for the applicant to attend the hearing>. The simple past tense is seldom needed except in recitals or purpose clauses.

(e) *Mood.* Moods indicate how a verb expresses an action or state of being. The two that are most relevant to drafting are the *indicative* and the *imperative* moods. The indicative expresses facts and policies <only a judge may set bail>. The imperative expresses authority and commands <do not stand in the door well>.

(f) *Number.* Use the singular unless the sense is undeniably plural. Under the rules of statutory interpretation, the singular includes the plural (but not necessarily vice versa). *See* Antonin Scalia & Bryan A. Garner, *Reading Law: The Interpretation of Legal Texts* 129–31 (2012). For example, if a prohibition states that *No person may shoot bullets outside the firing range*, and someone has shot 30, how many infractions have there been? The singular number is preferable: *No one may shoot a bullet* . . . . Then you inarguably have 30 infractions.

(g) *Consistency.* Variety isn't desirable in legal drafting. Concision is. Every word or phrase ideally has only one plain meaning, and it consistently expresses that meaning. Repetition may seem dull, but it is both desirable and essential in legal drafting. Courts presume that different words have different meanings. The drafter who ignores this presumption creates interpretive problems.

(h) *Mandatory vs. permissive.* Select words of authority that plainly express whether something is mandatory or permissive. For duties and requirements, preferably use *must* (*is required to*) or *must not* (*is required not to*). To indicate a choice, use *may* (*has discretion to*, *is permitted to*, *has a right to*). To express a right, use *is entitled to* or *has a right to.* For a directory, precatory, or aspirational provision, use *should.* And for a future contingency, use *will.* Avoid *shall.* Even though it's traditional, its multihued meanings cause many interpretive problems. For the rationale explaining these words of authority and examples of their uses and misuses in drafting, see Garner, *Guidelines for Drafting and Editing Legislation* 43–48 (2016); *Garner's Dictionary of Legal Usage* 952–55 (3d ed. 2011); Garner, *Legal Writing in Plain English* 125–26 (2d ed. 2013).

(i) *Formulating and placing definitions.* Overuse of definitions is a common fault in legal drafting. Provide them only when necessary to clarify terms or to give a common term a narrower or broader meaning than it would ordinarily have. But avoid wildly counterintuitive definitions, as by defining "milk" to include all citrus fruits. If more than a few defined terms are used, collect them in a definitional section. A term that appears in and affects only a portion of a governmental prescription may be best defined in that section.

Use care in formulating a definition. A good, useful definition may not be short, but it should be precise and clear enough to eliminate as far as possible the need for judicial interpretation. Think before using a term that needs a definition, and then think harder about drafting the definition.

29.4 Master the structure and format of governmental prescriptions.

(a) *Arrangement of provisions.* Organize provisions so that they are logical and clear. Set forth broad provisions before narrow ones, and the general before specific ones. Place important items closer to the beginning, ahead of less important ones. Describe or list exceptions after the main provision, not before and not in the middle. Group similar provisions together and use parallel headings and subheadings to make the connections clear. Arrange steps chronologically if possible.

(b) *The ideal numbering system.* You may have little discretion in numbering, but a one-level decimal-numbering system with hanging indents enhances clear thinking for both the drafter and the interpreter. The system should proceed in this format, with a hanging indent used at each sublevel: 1, 1.1, (A), (1), (a), (i). Use romanettes only as a last resort. For the first-level number and each decimal number, provide a short, descriptive heading to help guide the reader through the subparts. See 27.3(e).

(c) *Subenumerating.* Use subenumerations only when you have at least two subparts, such as a list of items, conditions, or exceptions. Presume that all lists will be set off in subparts.

(d) *Amendments.* If the statute, rule, or regulation is amended, the draft amendment should preserve the deleted language by using strike-out type and show the new language by underlining it. To make the text easier to read, overstrike or underline the entire amended unit, not part of it.

Not this: A government agency acting under § 3-16(A)~~(1)~~(2)
But this: A government agency acting under § ~~3-16(A)(1)~~ 3-16(A)(2)

In the final draft, the amendment should be explained and the original language preserved in a brief, precise note beneath the text.

Ex.: The 2016 amendment, effective January 1, 2017, clarified when the curfew for underage drivers begins by replacing the phrase "at sunset" with "at 8 p.m."

(e) *Repeals.* When a statute, rule, or regulation repeals another, the repealing section should appear toward the end of the instrument. Keep the repealing language short and precise.

> Ex.: The Tropical Fruits Exclusion Act of 1979 is hereby repealed.
>
> Ex.: Section 24 of the Bicycle Lanes Ordinance of 2011 is hereby repealed.

(f) *Enactment history.* Beneath the statute, rule, or regulation should appear a concise list of dates and citations showing when and where the law was first enacted, any amendments or repeals, recodifications, changes in numbering, and similar information.

29.5 Consider the desirability and effect of standard provisions.

(a) *Application and construction.* An application clause specifies to whom or what the governmental prescription applies, such as schools, highways, or police officers. As for construction clauses, there is no standard form. Some are elaborate, others spartan. The preferable approach depends on the intended purpose. A construction clause may establish the rules for interpreting a text or dictate the effects of interpretation. For example, you may write *Nothing in this subchapter limits or repeals any provisions of the Railroad Inspections Code.* Or *The provision of services to the mentally disabled under this chapter will be carried out subject to the provisions of the Mental Hygiene Code.*

(b) *Saving clauses.* A saving clause provides that rights and duties existing when the statute takes effect remain effective and applicable to transactions already completed or still in progress. The clause ensures that the statute's effect is prospective.

(c) *Severability.* A severability clause allows an unconstitutional or otherwise unenforceable section of a statute to be effectively removed from the rest of the governmental prescription. Without such a clause, the entire text might be rendered unenforceable.

(d) *Repeals and conforming amendments.* A conforming amendment changes an existing law so that it is consistent with a new law. When such an amendment replaces language, it effectively repeals it. A repealer isn't mandatory, but as an aid to interpretation, it may be helpful to clarify that the repeal of the particular language and of its previous effects was intentional.

(e) *Effective date.* In many jurisdictions, standard laws may prescribe when a statute will take effect. If so, an effective date might not be needed. But if a different date is desired, you might write, for example, *This section takes effect on September 6, 2018.*

29.6 Avoid the common faults of statutes and regulations.

(a) *Redundant words and phrases.* Different words and phrases are presumed to have different meanings. Even words commonly recognized as synonyms will not be read synonymously by a judicial interpreter unless all efforts to distinguish them fail. So think carefully before using expressions in which words are conjoined, as with *unless and until*, *alter or amend*, *full and complete*, or *order and direct*. Use only the word that most accurately reflects your intent. Sometimes, however, there will be a real distinction between the terms, as with *sell or lend*.

(b) *Legalese vs. terms of art.* The term *legalese*, properly speaking, doesn't embrace terms of art. A term of art is a word or phrase that has a precise, specific meaning in a given specialty—a term that would otherwise require a lengthy, perhaps detailed, explanation (*habeas corpus*). But legalese is simply jargon for which plain, precise English substitutes are available. Legalese is difficult to interpret. For example, what does *and/or* indicate? Bad-faith readers can argue and support whatever perspective serves their interests best. *Here-* and *there-* words (e.g., *hereafter*, *thereunder*) often produce ambiguity because the terms' boundaries are unclear. For example, does *herein* mean *in this subsection*? *in this chapter*? *in this statute*? Even "time-honored" phrases should be retired and replaced with plain words. For example, *provided that* can mean *if*, *except*, or *also*. And *pursuant to* can always be replaced with a preposition (*under*) or a more precise phrase (*in accordance with*—concededly longer, but universally intelligible in a way that *pursuant to* is not).

(c) *Excessive particularity.* By focusing too much on detail, a drafter may descend into verbosity and decrease clarity. For example, if a statute forbids homeowners from leaving metal cans, cardboard boxes, plastic crates, plastic cartons, and similar trash receptacles in front of their homes on certain days, does the statute allow wooden barrels to be left out? The clause would probably be clearer (and shorter) if it simply forbade "trash receptacles."

(d) *Overvagueness.* A client may want some vagueness or generality in a text, particularly in a statute, if the competing interests cannot agree on specifics. Vagueness may be unavoidable because terms such as *reasonable*, *as soon as practicable*, and *fair* don't have more precise equivalents. But vagueness predictably results in litigation, so make your drafting as specific as possible. If you can say *within 30 days*, you will afford people much more certainty than if you say *within a reasonable time*.

(e) *Separating verbs or parts of verbs.* As explained in § 29.3(c), left-branching sentences create unreasonable gaps between the subject and the verb. Auxiliary verbs may be grossly separated from the main verb in poorly drafted sentences.

Not this: If the trustee does not promptly and with all due care for the beneficiaries' interests provide an inventory . . . . (Ten words separate *does not* from *provide*.)

But this: Taking all due care for the beneficiaries' interests, the trustee must promptly provide an inventory . . . .

(f) *Overpacking sentences.* A sentence should contain only one main thought. Too often, though, drafters add provisos to create conditions or exceptions and produce a sentence with several distinct thoughts, not variations on one. Also, instead of redrafting the text to incorporate new or revised provisions, drafters simply tack on the material at the end, introducing this material with a phrase such as *provided that* or *subject to.* What was formerly a readable sentence of, say, 22 words can quickly grow to 100.

Not this: "False or misleading ways to collect a debt" include communicating by telephone without disclosure of the name of the debt collector and without disclosure of the personal name of the individual making such communication; provided, however, that any such individual utilizing an alias shall use only one such alias at all times and provided that a mechanism is established by the debt collector to identify the person using such alias; the debt collector shall submit a list of all such aliases and the persons using same to the director.

But this: "False or misleading ways to collect a debt" include communicating by telephone without disclosing the name of the debt collector and without disclosing the name of the person making the communication. If the person uses an alias, only that one alias may be used. The debt collector's employer must know the person's real name and the alias used, and must give that information to the director.

(g) *Unusual word order.* Inversion is unnatural in speech and in most other forms of writing, including legal writing. Even lawyers find inverted phrases and sentences increasingly difficult to understand. Some examples are *as in this chapter provided*, *such documents as the injured person may be required by section 42.45(A)(1)(a) to furnish*, *therein appearing*, and *being then a licensed driver.* All can, and should, be stated in plain, concise, modern English.

29.7 Study models of exemplary legislative drafting, as well as explanatory literature.

(a) *Two excellent sources.* Although their work is occasionally impeachable, both the American Law Institute and the National Conference of Commissioners on Uniform State Laws consistently produce legislation of a high caliber. Their model acts are well worth your study.

(b) *Further guidance.* For more on drafting governmental prescriptions and judicial interpretation of them, recommended books are:

- Martin Cutts, *Lucid Law* (2d ed. 2000).
- Reed Dickerson, *The Fundamentals of Legal Drafting* (2d ed. 1986).

- Bryan A. Garner, *Guidelines for Drafting and Editing Court Rules* (1996).
- Bryan A. Garner, *Guidelines for Drafting and Editing Legislation* (2016) (written under the auspices of the Uniform Law Commission).
- Robert J. Martineau & Michael B. Salerno, *Legal, Legislative, and Rule Drafting in Plain English* (2005).
- Antonin Scalia & Bryan A. Garner, *Reading Law: The Interpretation of Legal Texts* (2012).
- Sandra Strokoff & Lawrence E. Filson, *The Legislative Drafter's Desk Reference* (2d ed. 2007).
- Helen Xanthaki, *Thornton's Legislative Drafting* (5th ed. 2013).

(c) *An exemplar.* What follows is the Plain Writing Act of 2010 (Public Law 111-274, 111th Cong.), signed into law on 13 October 2010. The version presented here has been gently edited to improve the style. One unusual feature of the statute is that it does not confer a right of action or indeed any means of enforcement; in fact, it expressly disclaims enforceability. When passed, the statute was nevertheless hailed as a milestone in the centuries-old effort to reform and streamline government communications.

> "Writers of legislation often take refuge, like compilers of a thesaurus, behind a barricade of more or less synonymous words, which is much as if one should nail up a number of 'No trespassing' signs on a post in the center of his property but none along the borders. Thus, the New York State Penal Law places sanctions against materials that are 'obscene, lewd, lascivious, filthy, indecent, sadistic, masochistic, or disgusting' or that appeal to 'the prurient interest' of the average members of the community; but just what kinds of materials these are . . . is defined or redefined only each time a court decides a case involving a specific book, magazine, play, moving picture, or statue."
>
> —*Louis B. Salomon*

Sample Statute

Public Law 111-274
111th Congress

An Act

To enhance citizen access to Government information and service by establishing that Government documents issued to the public must be written clearly, and for other purposes.

Be it enacted by the Senate and House of Representatives of the United States of America in Congress assembled,

1. **Short Title.** This Act may be cited as the "Plain Writing Act of 2010."
2. **Purpose.** The purpose of the Act is to improve the effectiveness and accountability of Federal agencies to the public by promoting clear Government communication that the public can understand and use.
3. **Definitions.**

   (A) ***Agency.*** The term "agency" means an Executive agency, as defined under § 105 of title 5, United States Code.

   (B) ***Covered document.*** The term "covered document":

   (1) means any document that:

   (a) is necessary for obtaining any Federal Government benefit or service or filing taxes;

   (b) provides information about any Federal Government benefit or service; or

   (c) explains to the public how to comply with a requirement the Federal Government administers or enforces;

   (2) includes (whether in paper or electronic form) a letter, publication, form, notice, or instruction; and

   (3) does not include a regulation.

   (C) ***Plain writing.*** The term "plain writing" means writing that is clear, concise, and well organized, and that follows other best practices appropriate to the subject or field and to the intended audience.

4. **Responsibilities of Federal Agencies.**

4.1 *Preparation for implementation of plain-writing requirements.*

(A) *In general.* No later than 9 months after the date of enactment of this Act, the head of each agency must:

(1) designate one or more senior officials within the agency to oversee the agency implementation of this Act;

(2) communicate the requirements of this Act to the employees of the agency;

(3) train employees of the agency in plain writing;

(4) establish a process for overseeing the ongoing compliance of the agency with the requirements of this Act;

(5) create and maintain a plain-writing section of the agency's website as required under § 4.1(B) that is accessible from the homepage of the agency's website; and

(6) designate one or more agency points of contact to receive and respond to public input on:

(a) agency implementation of this Act; and

(b) the agency reports required under § 5.

(B) *Website.* The plain-writing section described under paragraph 4.1(A)(5) must:

(1) inform the public of agency compliance with the requirements of this Act; and

(2) provide a mechanism for the agency to receive and respond to public input on:

(a) agency implementation of this Act; and

(b) the agency reports required under § 5.

4.2 *Requirement to use plain writing in new documents.* Beginning no later than one year after the date of enactment of this Act, each agency must use plain writing in every covered document of the agency that the agency issues or substantially revises.

4.3 *Guidance.*

(A) *In general.* No later than 6 months after the date of enactment of the Act, the Director of the Office of Management and Budget will develop and issue guidance on implementing the requirements of this section. The Director may designate a lead agency, and may use interagency working groups to assist in developing and issuing the guidance.

(B) *Interim guidance.* Before the issuance of guidance under paragraph (A), agencies may follow:

(1) the writing guidelines developed by the Plain Language Action and Information Writing Network; or

(2) guidance provided by the head of the agency that is consistent with the guidelines referred to in subparagraph (1).

5. Reports to Congress.

5.1 ***Initial report.*** No later than 9 months after the date of enactment of this Act, the head of each agency will publish on the plain-writing section of the agency's website a report that describes the agency plan for compliance with the requirements of this Act.

5.2 ***Annual compliance report.*** No later than 18 months after the date of enactment of this Act, and annually afterward, the head of each agency will publish on the plain-writing section of the agency's website a report on agency compliance with the requirements of this Act.

6. Judicial Review and Enforceability.

6.1 ***Judicial review.*** There will be no judicial review of compliance or noncompliance with any provision of this Act.

6.2 ***Enforceability.*** No provision of this Act creates any right or benefit, substantive or procedural, enforceable by any administrative or legislative action.

7. **Budgetary Effects of PAYGO Legislation for this Act.** The budgetary effects of this Act, for the purpose of complying with the Statutory Pay-As-You-Go Act of 2010, must be determined by reference to the latest statement titled "Budgetary Effects of PAYGO Legislation" for this Act, submitted for printing in the Congressional Record by the Chairman of the House Budget Committee, if the statement has been submitted before the vote on passage.

Approved October 13, 2010.

§ 30
Resolutions*

30.1 Understand the main goals of a resolution.

(a) *Expressing a consensus.* A resolution is a declaration formally expressing the sentiment, will, or action of a deliberative assembly, such as a legislative body or an organization's board. It might authorize a particular act, transaction, or appointment, or express the consensus of the assembly adopting it. It serves as a record of the body's action and as proof that the action has been officially approved.

(b) *Enabling activities.* A resolution is subordinate to (and easier to amend than) an organization's articles of incorporation, constitution, bylaws, or other governing documents, but may provide for the activities that those documents contemplate. It might be necessary to carry out certain functions in a corporation's administrative business or other activities. A resolution can be used for many business purposes: to standardize steps for seeking or making bids for contracts; to make major purchases (e.g., of real estate); to enter into leases; or to delegate, certify, approve, or rescind someone's authority to make decisions on the corporation's behalf. But resolutions aren't typically used or required for the general operation of an organization or to exercise routine powers that have been delegated to officers and senior management.

(c) *Authoritativeness.* Because an oral decision or agreement is less formal than a resolution—and hence subject to being recalled differently by the individuals involved—a written resolution stands as a definitive and reliable record. It may be designed to avoid conflict by providing exact advice or direction to management about a business's operations, or it may help to avoid litigation by settling concerns about the way in which a corporation has been doing business or by directing how the business will be conducted in the future. A resolution can become valuable documentation for third parties who are performing due diligence before a major transaction such as a merger or a venture-capital investment.

(d) *Tone.* Although most resolutions use a tone similar to legislation, the language is normally less complex. A resolution should ordinarily get straight to the point, and it can often express its point in a sentence or two. Some resolutions are more involved, as when the resolution is adopting a policy or procedure that covers a broad or knotty topic. But not all resolutions

*Brian Melendez of Minneapolis made major contributions to this chapter.

need to be dry: a resolution of commendation, congratulation, or gratitude often works better with a lighter or even more florid tone.

(e) *Referring to documents outside the resolution.* A resolution may refer to an external document, such as legislation, to express an organization's viewpoint about that document. That external document exists regardless of the resolution, which may react to the document but can't act directly on it. But a resolution may also refer to a document within the control of the assembly considering it—for example, a proposed conflict-of-interest policy for a company's employees—in which case the distinction between the resolution and the other document becomes less clear. When a resolution addresses such an internal document, the drafter should consider incorporating the internal document into the resolution, so that the document itself can be amended if necessary as part of the process of considering the resolution.

30.2 Master the structure and format of resolutions.

(a) *Resolving clause.* Many legislatures are constitutionally or statutorily required to use an enacting formula such as "Be it enacted by the Senate and House of Representatives of the United States of America in Congress assembled . . . ." If it's not required, a resolution doesn't need an enacting or resolving formula beyond the word *Resolved* (always italic), which is followed by the resolving clause itself. A resolution that consists of multiple resolving clauses may introduce each clause with the words *Resolved* or *Further Resolved*, or may simply use a single *Resolved* followed by numbered paragraphs.

(b) *Preamble.* A preamble (sometimes called a *recital* or the *whereas clauses*) is a clause or series of clauses—each traditionally beginning with the word *Whereas*—that introduces the resolution using language that is primarily declarative rather than operative. Although most resolutions don't need a preamble, one may be useful if (1) the resolution depends on conditions precedent having occurred, in which case the resolution may recite the facts that satisfy those conditions; or (2) the resolution is likely to circulate beyond the adopting organization, in which case the organization can spell out the background and reasons for making the resolution. A resolution of commendation, congratulation, or gratitude may likewise set forth the circumstances giving rise to its adoption, such as the history of a retiring member's long service to the organization. But instead of the legalistic *whereas* language, use a simple heading such as *Background* or *Purpose.*

(c) *Report.* Although a report is not a part of a resolution, it may accompany a resolution and advocate the resolution's adoption. An accompanying report is often a better vehicle than a preamble for positing the argument in favor of its passage, since argumentative (and therefore possibly controversial) propositions in the preamble may dissuade prospective supporters who are otherwise comfortable with the resolution's operative clauses.

(d) *Platforms and policies.* Some organizations, especially political organizations, trade associations, and interest lobbies, may adopt a platform or a statement of policies that the organization supports or opposes. If so, then the resolutions stating the organization's views usually take a slightly different form from ordinary resolutions. The resolving clause often begins with a verb that expresses the organization's view (*supports*, *opposes*, *approves*, *commends*, *condemns*) instead of the word *Resolved*, and the preamble's clauses often begin with a participle or other adjective that expresses the organization's state of mind leading up to the resolution (*believing*, *recognizing*, *recalling*, *grateful*).

30.3 Determine precisely what your client wants to accomplish.

(a) *Persuading decision-makers to approve or ratify an action.* Depending on a statute or the organization's bylaws, the validity of some resolutions rests on approval by a governing board. The resolution itself is written as a fact. But the preambular explanation for the resolution is written to persuade the decision-makers to approve it. A standard corporate resolution, for example, may include:

- A heading, including the organization's legal name, the name of the governing body, and the place and date of registration.
- The date and location of the meeting, and a statement that a quorum was in attendance (a list of names is optional).
- A statement about what led to the need for a resolution.
- A statement of the resolution's purpose.
- A list of the steps necessary to carry out the purpose.
- A legal attestation that the document's contents are true.
- Signature spaces, with the signers' names beneath.

(b) *Identifying who is authorized to act.* If a resolution calls for an action to be taken, it should also state who will carry it out. It may be adequate for this purpose to state an office or department, or it may be necessary to identify individuals. For example, to open accounts with banks and securities brokerages or to engage in corporate real-estate transactions with title companies or to execute contracts, the names of individuals authorized to act on the corporation's behalf should almost certainly be provided.

(c) *Documenting the basis of a past action.* A resolution may be drafted retroactively, as when a corporation must record the basis for a past decision or an action already taken. Sometimes, for example, if the board of directors had decided to extend a loan to another corporation, a resolution might be drafted to record the board's meeting date and detail the negotiated terms of the loan.

30.4 Avoid the common faults of resolutions.

(a) *Legalese.* Resolutions are drafted for laypeople who are typically not familiar with legalisms, including *here-* and *there-* words, *whereas*, and *in witness whereof.* Use plain English. For example, instead of using *whereas*, use a heading such as *Background* or *Purpose* and then clearly state what circumstances led to proposing or adopting the resolution.

(b) *Stilted or archaic language.* Many resolutions use a "Resolved, That . . ." formula, such as "Resolved, That the Treasurer be directed to open a bank account." This traditional formula comes from the days when the English Parliament enacted statutes using the subjunctive mood: *Resolved* is short for *Be it resolved*, and was often followed by a subjunctive clause in the passive voice, which sounds odd to the modern ear. Instead, use a heading such as *Resolved* and list the clearly stated action or actions agreed on to accomplish the purpose. For example:

Resolved:

(1) The Company will open a business checking account at Rogers National Bank.

(2) The Company Treasurer will deposit $100,000 in that account with a check drawn on the Company's account at Winthrop Bank.

(c) *Misstating or omitting information.* When a client needs a resolution drafted in a very short time, the drafter might misstate or omit critical information. For example, an incorrect date for an action or an improper description of a step to be taken could invalidate the approval. And failing to identify who is authorized to act on behalf of the corporation could delay performance.

(d) *Overrelying on forms.* There are books filled with standardized resolutions that companies can use for routine matters. Before using a form, make sure it's updated to reflect current law. Then, of course, revise it to reflect the client's specific purpose. Standard forms never include the details that underlie a resolution, so don't use them if a thorough record is needed to explain why the resolution was made.

(e) *Failing to do research or consult with experts.* A resolution may have effects, such as financial, legal, and preparatory (e.g., environmental-impact studies), that are not immediately apparent. Because the people responsible for making or approving a decision or action might not be aware of these effects beforehand, they can be listed and explained in an attachment to the resolution (and incorporated into it before passage).

(f) *Failing to determine who must approve the action.* A corporation's bylaws—and sometimes state law—provide for decision-making powers. Some actions may require the approval of shareholders, and that approval may take a supermajority or even a unanimous vote. If a resolution is not approved according to mandatory procedures, it may be invalid or may provoke unnecessary litigation.

(g) *Overpacking.* A resolution should be limited to a single action, especially if it requires multiple steps. This will avoid confusion about the resolution's purpose and the means of its accomplishment.

(h) *Mimicking legislation.* While resolutions are a species in the same genus as legislation (indeed, some legislative acts are accomplished by resolution), a resolution seldom requires the same level of formality or detail as a legislative act. A resolution rarely needs an effective date because it takes effect upon adoption. And while a resolution can (and often should) define any terms whose meaning is open to interpretation, a resolution seldom needs a declaration of intent, a severability clause, or other interpretive guidance for a constitutionally distinct executive or judiciary. In contrast to legislation, the leaders who will implement and interpret a resolution are usually members of the adopting body, or at least people working closely with the adopting body itself, so they will often have had a hand in the resolution's adoption and will need less interpretive guidance than would legislation being interpreted by a separate branch of government.

(i) *Fleshing out unclear terms by discussion rather than by amendment.* An assembly cannot control how a resolution will be interpreted or applied, except by the words that it adopts. When an assembly debates a resolution, its members are often tempted to ask the presiding officer, or the resolution's mover, to say how he or she expects or intends the resolution to be interpreted or applied by the present or a future administration. The kind of subjective expectation or intent elicited by such a question may sound authoritative (especially if it comes from the chair), but it is mere nonbinding speculation—a poor substitute for carefully drafted and clearly worded text. A member who wants a resolution to mean something that it does not clearly say cannot rely (or mislead others into relying) on speculation by the mover or the chair, but must instead offer an amendment that properly clarifies the resolution.

(j) *Imaginary "legislative history."* When an assembly debates a resolution, members may make statements or ask questions "for the record" in the hope that the statement or answer will somehow supplement the resolution's meaning for all time. A member may even insist that the minutes reflect the statement or answer, in the hope of creating a "legislative history" that will fix the putative meaning. But unless the assembly is an actual legislative body, its resolutions do not have a "legislative history"—and even an actual legislative history would not ordinarily come into play unless the legislation is ambiguous. The minutes are a poor place to record how a problem was solved. The best place to fix a resolution's meaning is in its text, the only language that future members and other readers are likely to see.

30.5 Study effective resolutions.

(a) *Further guidance.* The classic guide for action by deliberative assemblies, including the procedure and form for resolutions, is Henry M. Robert III et al., *Robert's Rules of Order Newly Revised* (11th ed. 2011). Good advice on preparing corporate resolutions in particular may be found in Anthony Mancuso, *The Corporate Records Handbook: Meetings, Minutes, and Resolutions* (7th ed. 2017) and Clifford R. Ennico, "Drafting Corporate Minutes and Resolutions," in *Closely Held Corporations: Forms and Checklists* § 5:2 (2016).

(b) *Models.* The best-drafted resolutions are usually those passed by Congress (or one house of Congress) or a state legislature, since those bodies have staff who are experienced in perfecting each resolution's form and drafting. Congressional resolutions are available on Congress's website, congress.gov, by searching for "Resolutions," "Joint Resolutions," or "Concurrent Resolutions." Resolutions by nonpublic bodies, such as corporate boards, are harder to find, but may nevertheless be modeled after resolutions by public bodies.

(c) *Examples.* Because of the great variety of types of resolutions, what follows is a copious sampling. The examples show (1) a corporate resolution authorizing a signatory for a bank account; (2) a policy resolution by a trade association; (3) a procedural resolution by a trade association; and (4) a congressional resolution.

Sample Resolution #1

Resolution to Authorize Signatory for Bank Account

Purpose

A proposal was placed before the Board to authorize an additional individual signatory for the Company's business-checking account and as an additional joint signatory for the Company's trust account. The change is expected to make it easier to conduct day-to-day financial transactions.

After discussions, the Board unanimously agreed on the following.

Resolved:

1. Teague Harmon, Deputy Treasurer, is an individual authorized signatory for the business-checking account and a joint authorized signatory of the trust account jointly with Gayle Allico, Treasurer. Both accounts are with First National Bank of Jefferson.

2. The bank will be instructed to accept and act on any instructions signed by the Company's authorized signatory and relating to the account kept in the Company's name or relating to any of the Company's transactions with the bank.

3. The bank will be instructed to accept receipts for money, deeds, securities, other documents or papers, property, or any indemnities given on the Company's behalf, if they are signed by the Company's authorized signatory or signatories.

4. The bank will be informed about this resolution, which will remain in force until rescinded. When it is rescinded, any director of the Company may give the bank written notice of the rescission.

5. The authority granted to Harmon is valid and effective and exercisable as long as Harmon remains in his present position—unless the Board revokes his authority.

6. The Board will not be responsible for any of Harmon's acts that are beyond the scope of the granted authority. Such acts will not in any manner bind the Company against any third party or before any authorities.

Sample Resolution #2

Minnesota State Bar Association Assembly Resolution on Judicial Selection

Resolved, That the Minnesota State Bar Association supports and prefers the method of judicial selection proposed in the first minority report to the final report and recommendations from the Citizens Commission for the Preservation of an Impartial Judiciary (commonly known as the "Quie Commission") dated March 2007. But the Association also finds acceptable, and does not oppose, the Quie Commission's majority report.

§ 1. **Features of a performance-evaluation commission.** The Association supports and seeks the following features in any commission that evaluates judges with respect to their qualifications, performance, reappointment, or retention:

(a) The commission must focus strictly on public and professional considerations without regard to partisan or other political concerns.

(b) The commission must not second-guess or otherwise evaluate the correctness of a judge's rulings, which is the proper province of appellate review. But the commission may take into account a judge's abuse of discretion or improper conduct that an appellate court or a disciplinary body identifies.

(c) The commission will evaluate each judge eligible for reappointment according to criteria that the commission develops and publishes, and any other criteria as may be established by law. These criteria should include factors like the ones that the merit-selection commission now considers: integrity, maturity, health if job-related, judicial temperament, diligence, legal knowledge, ability, experience, and community service.

(d) The commission may gather information from lawyers who practice before a judge being evaluated, from litigants over whose cases the judge has presided, from direct observation, from public hearings, and in any other appropriate way. The judge being evaluated should have the chance to review and respond to any information that the commission considers.

(e) The commission should be subject to the open-meeting law. Any information that the commission receives or considers should be a matter of public record.

§ 2. **Composition of a performance-evaluation commission.** The Association believes that any commission that evaluates judges with respect to their qualifications, performance, reappointment, or retention should consist of members chosen in a diverse manner, by multiple appointing authorities that check and balance each other (such as the executive and legislative branches, the bench, and the Association), so that no single appointing authority controls a majority or nearly a majority of the commissioners. The Association also believes that any such commission should include lawyers and at least some judges along with other citizens, so that the commission as a whole more fully appreciates the judicial office whose tenants it evaluates. The Association therefore opposes the Quie Commission's recommendation of a commission "the majority of whom will be nonattorney members of the public."

Adopted June 29, 2007.

Sample Resolution #3

AMERICAN BAR ASSOCIATION
YOUNG LAWYERS DIVISION
ASSEMBLY

REPORT WITH RECOMMENDATIONS
RENEWABILITY OF MOTIONS

Resolved, That the bylaws are amended by inserting the following new section after § 4.4:

4.5 Renewability of motions

(A) ***Meeting and session.*** The Assembly's meetings from the call to order of the annual meeting until the call to order of the next annual meeting will constitute a single session for parliamentary purposes.

(B) ***Renewing motions.*** A resolution of which the Assembly has finally disposed, or a resolution that presents the same or a substantially similar question, will not be in order again until a whole annual or midyear meeting has intervened. This rule does not prohibit a motion that brings the question again before the Assembly at the same meeting where it was disposed of, nor does it prohibit a motion to rescind or amend something previously adopted.

(C) ***Suspension.*** The Assembly may suspend § 4.5(B) by a motion to suspend the rules.

(D) ***Executive Council.*** This § 4.5 likewise applies in the Executive Council unless the Council by a two-thirds vote adopts a different rule.

Report

This recommendation addresses the question of how often the Assembly can consider the same or a substantially similar question. It proposes a new bylaw that limits how often the Assembly may or must consider the same or a substantially similar question.

The myth of the "ten-year rule"

First, this recommendation should dispel the mythical ten-year rule (sometimes known as the *six-year rule*) that allegedly already limits how often the Assembly can consider the same or a substantially similar question. The mythical rule, in one of its more egregious forms, states that the Assembly cannot address any subject that the Assembly has addressed within the last ten years—that is, once having voted a question up or down, the Assembly has settled it irrevocably for a decade. ***There is no such rule.***

The ten-year rule does not apply to the Young Lawyers Division. There is a basis in fact for the myth of the ten-year rule: the ABA House of Delegates does follow a ten-year rule, although the myth has metamorphosed that rule into a barely recognizable form. The actual rule provides that

> A report . . . that contains a recommendation to be considered by the House of Delegates may be considered only if:
> (1) the recommendation proposes new policy or a change of policy, or reaffirms existing Association policy that has not been approved within the last ten years . . . .[1]

That rule by its terms applies only to the ABA House of Delegates. The Association's authority does not extend the rule to the Division. The Division's authority does not incorporate the rule.[2] The ten-year rule does not apply to the Division in any form.

The ten-year rule applies only to an adopted resolution, never to a defeated one. The ten-year rule has been cited to the effect that the Assembly, having voted down a controversial resolution, cannot revisit that issue for a decade. Not only does the ten-year rule

1 ABA, *Rules of Procedure of the House of Delegates* § 45.2(a). The rule formerly provided a six-year limit, hence the occasional reference to a "six-year rule."

2 There is an argument that the Division, being "a constituent of the Association, whose constitution and bylaws (and action taken under their authority) control and supersede [the Division's] bylaws and action taken under their authority," YLD Bylaws § 1.3.1, can consider only resolutions that are suitable for consideration by the ABA House of Delegates. If that argument succeeded, however, then the Division could never adopt a policy that is *consistent* with the Association's policy, being already bound by the existing policy and unable (as the ABA House would be unable) to reaffirm it. That argument would thereby dictate the absurd result that the Division could not encourage its delegates to oppose the repeal of an existing policy.

not apply to the Division, but even if it did, the rule would apply only to an adopted resolution, never to a defeated one. The rule explicitly authorizes a resolution that "proposes new policy or a change of policy." A defeated resolution never became policy and will thus always "propose new policy or a change of policy" within the rule's meaning.

The ten-year rule prohibits only affirmation, not reversal, of an existing policy. The ten-year rule was intended to prohibit the repeated reintroduction of a popular policy for the purpose of reaffirming it at each session, since such a policy is already in force with or without such reaffirmation. The rule was never intended to prohibit the reversal or modification of a controversial policy; indeed, it implicitly encourages resolutions to that effect, by preventing the policymaker from wasting its time on matters that have already been resolved in preference over matters on which a consensus is still being sought.

The ten-year rule applies only to the same resolution, not the whole subject that the policy addresses. Finally, the ten-year rule applies only to a recommendation, not to a whole subject. That the policymaker has adopted one policy does not mean that it cannot then consider a supplementary or otherwise related policy.

The recommended rule. Having debunked the Division's mythical ten-year rule, the question remains: What is the best rule for the Division? Ought the Division to incorporate the ten-year rule? adopt its own counterpart? adopt some different rule? take no action?

The status quo. As the rules now stand, and as things will stand if no action is taken, any delegate can introduce any resolution at any meeting, even if the next preceding meeting adopted or defeated the same resolution. The 1997 annual meeting in San Francisco, California, established the principle that any delegate can introduce a resolution.[3] The parliamentary authority defines

3 *See* Resolution No. 4YL (seditious fraud). The resolution was introduced by one delegate whose "title as a delegate is mentioned . . . only for the purpose of identification" and whose "affiliate does not necessarily share any of the views that this

each annual and each midyear meeting as one *session*[4] and establishes the principle of the "freedom of each new session":

> The principal significance of the session as a complete unit of an assembly's engagement in proceedings lies in the freedom of each new session, as contrasted with the limitations placed upon a session in progress by decisions it has made. . . .
>
> **Freedom of each new session.** As a general principle, one session cannot tie the hands of the majority at any later session, or place a question beyond the reach of such a majority, except through the process of adopting a special rule of order or an amendment to the bylaws . . . .
>
> . . .
>
> **Relation of session's freedom to the renewability of motions.** The conditions under which a motion can be renewed—that is, can be introduced as if new after having previously been made and disposed of without adoption—are closely related to the freedom of each new session, and to the distinction between a meeting and a session. As stated . . . , the same or substantially the same question cannot be brought up a second time during the same session except by means of the parliamentary motions that bring a question again before the assembly. At any later session, on the other hand, any motion that is still applicable can normally be renewed unless it has *come over from the previous session* as *not finally disposed of.*[5]

Redefining "session." As the parliamentary authority recognizes, "any society has the right to define, in its bylaws, what constitutes a session of the organization."[6] Rather than accept the parliamentary default that each annual and each midyear meeting constitutes its own session, this recommendation defines a *session* as "[t]he

---

resolution expresses." *Id.* n.13 at 3.

4 *See* Henry M. Robert, *Robert's Rules of Order Newly Revised* § 8 at 82–83 (Sarah Corbin Robert ed. 1990) (explanation of terms); *see also id.* at 85 ("In the case of a state or national organization that holds annual or biennial conventions, each convention constitutes a session of the organization").

5 *Id.* at 88 (citations and parentheses omitted).

6 *Id.* at 84 (number of meetings in a session).

Assembly's meetings from the call to order of the annual meeting until the call to order of the next annual meeting."

This definition recognizes that the Assembly's delegates are allocated, distributed, and selected between the midyear meeting and the annual meeting[7] for the ensuing year. Likewise, the bylaws organize the Assembly through annual officers, who "will serve for a term of one year beginning with the adjournment of the annual meeting of the Assembly at which they are elected and ending with the adjournment of the next annual meeting of the Assembly . . . ."[8] Therefore, if there is any implicit principle that the Assembly consists of the two sessions within one *Division year*, then it is likely that the Division year runs concurrently with the officers' terms.[9] This definition ensures that the same delegates, having disposed of a question at the annual meeting, need not revisit the same question when they attend the midyear meeting six months later.

Limiting renewability. Likewise, lest the Assembly dispose of a question at the midyear meeting and then face the same question again at the annual meeting six months later, this recommendation provides that "[a] resolution of which the Assembly has finally disposed, or a resolution that presents the same or a substantially similar question, will not be in order again until a whole annual or midyear meeting has intervened." This provision effectively means that a question, having been disposed of, can be renewed a year later.

Yet this recommendation does not limit renewability beyond that one-year period, so that each session (now lasting for one year, rather than only for an annual or a midyear meeting) can eventually consider whatever it wants. Limiting renewability over any period longer than one year may enshrine an error that the Assembly could not correct even if every affiliate elected every delegate with a clear mandate to do something that the preceding meeting failed to do. Furthermore, the recommendation explicitly does not prohibit the

7 YLD Bylaws §§ 4.6-.8.

8 *Id.* § 3.3 (term of office).

9 *Cf.* ABA Const. § 2.1 (defining "Association year" as "the period beginning with the adjournment of an annual meeting and ending with the adjournment of the next annual meeting").

reversal or modification of a controversial policy, no matter how recently it may have been adopted.

Flexibility. Finally, this recommendation preserves flexibility by letting the Assembly (and, to the extent that the same rules apply, the executive Council) suspend the rules relating to the renewability of motions "by a motion to suspend the rules." Such a motion is not debatable,[10] and so will not take up too much time; and takes a two-thirds vote,[11] so a suspension will not occur unless a substantial supermajority so desires.

Conclusion

Recommendation. The Bylaws Subcommittee respectfully recommends that the foregoing recommendation be adopted.

Finance. This recommendation will not result in any direct costs.

Respectfully submitted,

Kathleen J. Hopkins
Rew Goodenow, Assembly Clerk
Brian Melendez, Parliamentarian,
on behalf of the
Bylaws Subcommittee,
Resolutions Committee.
[Date.]

10 Robert, *supra* note 4, § 25 at 260.

11 *Id.*

Sample Resolution #4

One Hundred Fifteenth Congress of
The United States of America

AT THE FIRST SESSION

Begun and held at the City of Washington on Tuesday, the third day of January, two thousand seventeen

Concurrent Resolution

Resolved by the House of Representatives (the Senate concurring):

§ 1. Authorization of Use of Capitol Grounds for D.C. Special Olympics Law-Enforcement Torch Run.

On October 6, 2017, or on another date that the Speaker of the House of Representatives and the Committee on Rules and Administration of the Senate may jointly designate, the 32d annual District of Columbia Special Olympics Law-Enforcement Torch Run may be run through the Capitol grounds to carry the Special Olympics torch to honor local Special Olympics athletes.

§ 2. Responsibility of Capitol Police Board.

The Capitol Police Board will take appropriate actions to carry out the event.

§ 3. Conditions Relating to Physical Preparations.

The Capitol Architect may prescribe conditions for physical preparations for the event.

§ 4. Enforcement of Restrictions.

In connection with the event, the Capitol Police Board will provide for enforcement of the restrictions contained in 40 U.S.C. § 5104(c) concerning sales, advertisements, displays, and solicitations on the Capitol grounds, as well as other applicable restrictions.

Attest:

Clerk of the House of Representatives

Attest:

Secretary of the Senate

[This resolution has been lightly edited.]

Part 4: Scholarly Writing

§ 31
Student Research Papers and Law-Review Notes*

31.1 Understand the chief aims of student research.

(a) *Purpose.* A research paper or law-review note (also termed a *lawnote*) is a student-authored work of academic writing that analyzes in some depth a legal issue or problem, especially a novel one. It's typically relatively short and may address the effects (or projected effects) of a single case or set of related cases. Because it scrutinizes and critiques a judicial decision or suggests a new direction for a specific legal field, it may well (if published) inform practicing professionals, the judiciary, and academia alike.

(b) *Chief distinctions.* Because a published lawnote is really just a highly successful research paper, the term *lawnote* will appear throughout the rest of this chapter as a broad term that also embraces research papers. But even within the spectrum of published student pieces, there are several varieties. For example, a *casenote* is an extended, ambitious case brief (see § 15): it takes usually 500 to 2,000 words to methodically explain the holdings and reasoning of a case, often distinguishing dicta from holdings and remarking on the case's likely implications for future litigation. A lawnote, by contrast, normally analyzes a line of cases, or two contradictory lines of cases, and elaborates a specific thesis about their reasoning or implications. Somewhat more ambitious is a *comment*, which examines a narrow area of law, focusing on specific issues, cases, and legislation. It might develop a thesis about a particular trend in the law, and a good one always contains a well-supported argument. By still further contrast, a *law-review article* is broader in scope and analysis and is often, though not always, written by an expert in a particular field. For related discussions, see § 32 on law-review articles.

(c) *Expectations.* For a lawnote, you're expected to make some small contribution or provide some new insight into the law. You're usually competing with fellow second-year law students, so the bar is set accordingly. (By contrast, when a law student wants to write a full-length law-review article, he or she will be competing with the entirety of the legal academy.

*Contributors to this chapter include Professor David A. Anderson of the University of Texas at Austin; Professor Josh Blackman of the South Texas College of Law; Dean Ward Farnsworth of the University of Texas at Austin; Professor Kenneth S. Klein of California Western School of Law; Dean Stephen M. Sheppard of St. Mary's University School of Law; and Professor Steven R. Smith of California Western School of Law.

Of course this bar is much, much higher.) Yet the lawnote's role has grown in importance over the years. Today lawnotes are more widely accepted as a source of fresh legal analysis and criticism. And having one published is certainly a significant asset on any law student's résumé.

(d) *Publication.* If you're on a law-review staff, your first objective should be to have your piece published; just writing something to fulfill a requirement is a fruitless exercise. Time spent selecting a topic (see 31.2) is time well spent. Study the notes your target journal has published in recent years and try to determine what the editors like: Simple casenotes about recent decisions? Notes synthesizing a line of cases? Notes that identify an emerging issue? If your note editor tells you what he or she is looking for, so much the better.

(e) *Coping with edits.* Be prepared for the editorial process to be an intellectual and emotional challenge. It will probably result in some changes that you don't particularly like, but these will doubtless improve your lawnote—and you're unlikely to help matters by resisting too much the help of editors. Aim for perfection, but don't expect to achieve it. Remember: this is the first thing you will have to say about the law—not the last.

31.2 Find your topic.

(a) *Hitching your cart.* The most important part of writing a lawnote is picking the right topic. Usually, your adviser or, if you're on a journal, your editorial board will ask you to identify several possible topics so that, at the appropriate time, you can select the best from among several options. Although you may receive some good advice, you alone must come up with your topic. So choose wisely. After you think you've picked a topic, ask yourself, "What am I going to say about it?" If you find that all you can say is "I'm going to describe this, and then describe that," do some more thinking. Even the least ambitious journal wants notes that do more than describe. Even if your journal doesn't, you want to showcase your abilities. Ask yourself, "What can I say about this that hasn't been said before?" If the answer is "Nothing," pick another topic.

(b) *Your interests.* Focus on something you enjoy—better still, something that evokes deep curiosity or that you're passionate about. You may be stuck with it for the better part of a year, and even longer if it is ultimately selected for publication. After many hours of researching, writing, and editing, you may begin to hate the topic. Writing a lawnote about something you don't enjoy—perhaps because a professor or editor recommended it to you—is painful. If the Commerce Clause puts you to sleep, don't choose to live and breathe it for the next six months while writing your lawnote. Pick a subject you love—or at least one you find some stake in.

(c) *Your knowledge.* Choose something you know. It's tough enough to write an excellent lawnote without having to teach yourself a whole new discipline. Help yourself by selecting a subject with which you're at least somewhat familiar. Think about your first-year classes. What did you do well in? What classes interested you? What did you easily grasp? What piqued your interest unexpectedly? These are good starting points.

(d) *A little help from your professoriate.* Don't be afraid to ask your professors for possible areas to write about. But don't just walk into your professor's office and ask, "What should I write about?" Invariably, your professor will want you to have narrowed it down to a few topics before giving you advice. The points discussed in (b) and (c) should serve as prerequisites before talking to faculty. Professors naturally tend to recommend topics in their areas of expertise, though, so remember that when asking for their advice.

(e) *Keep it simple.* Law students tend toward overambitiousness by trying to develop a single unifying theory to resolve everything. Don't make this mistake. If you're writing a note, pick a discrete, concrete legal point that is unclear, and try to address it. If you're writing a comment for publication and decide to address a circuit split, try to narrow your inquiry to a single aspect of the dispute. (This strategy can be risky since a cert grant by the Supreme Court may preempt your topic.) The lawnote's minimum word limit may seem daunting. But don't worry: the bulk of the lawnote will consist of background information and discussion of the existing literature. Hitting the word limit should not be a problem—if anything, your lawnote will probably be too long. If you make your topic too broad, you must invariably narrow it down at the end. There is nothing wrong with this—and often focusing the topic will teach you a great deal. But this takes, and potentially wastes, a lot of time—a scarce commodity in law school.

(f) *Intellectual enjoyment.* Enjoy the process. Depending on your future career, writing a lawnote may be your only opportunity to engage in deep thinking about a legal issue through your writing. Who knows? It may spur an interest that will lead to future opportunities. It's an experience unlike any other.

31.3 Think about the specific goals of your lawnote.

(a) *Limiting your material and finding your thesis.* If your research entails expansive thinking and purposely casting your net wide, developing a thesis demands that you contract your thinking and focus on a central point. Your writing must have a central point, probably with several subpoints. You might think of it as filling in this lengthy blank: "I intend to prove that——."

(b) *Focusing.* Having done the reading, resist the temptation to report it all to the reader in endless footnotes or a long literature review. By all means acknowledge prior work, but the fact that it took you a long time to learn about something doesn't mean your readers should have to retrace your journey. Your goal is to synthesize your research so that readers can follow your argument. More generally, most academic writings get read by very few people. If you want a better fate for your article, keep it concise and keep it moving. Most writers labor under the illusion that long articles are more likely to command attention than short ones. But you should know better than most that this is an illusion: When doing your own research, did you read the shorter or longer articles first? Like most people, you probably favored the shorter ones. So put yourself in your readers' shoes and ask whether anything important would really be lost by cutting your discussion in half—assuming that you will still have met the arbitrary word or page limits.

Let's say you're writing about statutory construction. You might set out to prove many things. The narrower, more tightly focused your thesis, the narrower your research will have to be. Perhaps you're writing about the desuetude canon—the doctrine that statutes cannot become defunct by the mere passage of time or a change of circumstances (see generally Antonin Scalia & Bryan A. Garner, *Reading Law: The Interpretation of Legal Texts* 336–39 (2012)). A state supreme court has just held, perhaps without so much as a nod to the existing literature, that the passage of a century meant that a statute had become defunct. Perhaps you'll argue this as your thesis (the example is fictitious):

> Although the Supreme Court of California has held that statutes can fall into desuetude and become defunct, this anomalous pronouncement is belied by Anglo-Saxon legal history and some of the Court's own earlier decisions.

You might connect that decision to a 2013 decision of the United States Supreme Court in which, in a unanimous holding, the Court didn't even raise desuetude as a possible rationale for holding an obscure 1789 statute to be inapplicable.[1]

Or perhaps you would find a different thesis on the same subject:

> Given the anomaly of the California Supreme Court's holding on desuetude—and the seemingly unknowing error of the decision supporting that holding—the state legislature should explicitly repeal the outdated statute at issue.

Or again, still a different thesis (much more challenging):

1 *Kiobel v. Royal Dutch Petroleum Co.*, 569 U.S. 108 (2013).

> The Supreme Court of California has boldly held that statutes can obsolesce, and the time has come to reverse the age-old desuetude canon in other jurisdictions as well, given the way it has shackled courts in the field of wills and trusts. The California case is a prime example of the benefits to be gained.

Or again, yet a different tack:

> The Supreme Court of California has held an 1857 statute to be obsolete by the mere passage of time, without an express or implied repeal, and without a declaration of unconstitutionality. Because many other pre–Civil War statutes in the field of wills and trusts are likewise vulnerable, the courts should hold them obsolete by reason of desuetude—and should explicitly declare the anti-desuetude canon inapplicable in California generally.

Better yet, perhaps the holding was by an intermediate appellate court, and you might write something that could affect the outcome of a pending appeal:

> The California Court of Appeal has held an 1857 statute to be obsolete by the mere passage of time, without an express or implied repeal. Given that this holding contradicts earlier holdings of the California Supreme Court—as well as the almost universal anti-desuetude canon—the California Supreme Court should accept review and reverse the judgment.

Whatever the case, your piece must argue a position.

(c) *Thesis.* Consider what effect you want your note to have and how it will be helpful to others. Do you want to present a new standard for applying a statute? Are you trying to discover and explain the unspoken reasoning underlying a court's decision? Are you trying to alert people to a new statute's potentially negative effects? If your lawnote focuses on one case, what is your thesis: Does the opinion provide a clear standard for future guidance? Does it create a complex standard that impairs predictability of the outcome in future cases? Did the court apparently rely on unstated assumptions? Did the court reach the right decision but not for the reason it expressly stated? Whatever your thesis is, consider your audience. Write with a particular reader in mind—a specific person. Are you writing to your school's faculty? Scholars in the field? Practitioners and judges? Or simply the student editors on the law journal? Choose your audience generally, and then write with one member of it—preferably a somewhat skeptical reader—as your primary reader. Tailor your technique to your audience.

(d) *Devising a good title.* Although you will find an embarrassing variety of lawnote titles—many too clever by half—your best strategy is to play it pretty straight, with at most a slight degree of cleverness. Forget *Whatever Happened to the Owl and the Pussycat?* Embrace *Inlaws vs. Outlaws: The Status of Illegal Aliens in Family Law*. (*Inlaw* is an old antonym of *outlaw*—so the restrained pun in this fictitious title works.) For more on titling law-review notes and articles, see Bryan A. Garner, *The Elements of Legal Style* 75–77, 158–59 (2d ed. 2002).

31.4 Be systematic and efficient.

(a) *Time management.* Learn the skill of using small units of time productively—to run down a citation, or rewrite a paragraph, etc.—because if you wait for large blocks of time to do your work, you'll never do it.

(b) *Venturing a title and an opener.* Devise a working title at once and write an introductory section to your article early. This will not be your final title or your real introduction, but it will help define the boundaries for your work. It will give you focus.

(c) *Researching effectively.* Use all the tools at your disposal: not just Westlaw and LEXIS, but also Google Books (with the advanced-search function)—and don't forget to consult all the relevant treatises (hard copies) and to spend time using their indexes. You should approach every research project on two fronts: by electronic searches and by turning to old-fashioned paper books. You will almost certainly find relevant materials using each method—materials that would otherwise have eluded you.

Take notes systematically, being careful to note all the proper bibliographic information that you might later need, including page numbers. Make all your references exact. Develop a note-taking system that suits you, and stick to it so that you follow the system automatically.

(d) *Necessary research paraphernalia.* Always have two things in your possession—your laptop computer and your *Bluebook.* On your laptop have your working document. Every time you read anything remotely interesting, capture it in your document, with a footnote in correct *Bluebook* form. There will be plenty of time later to make sense of it all, but not enough human memory to find it all a second time. If you're old-fashioned, keep notecards always at the ready. Never assume that another writer used a cited primary source correctly (or even used the source at all), or wrote without bias. Always check the originals yourself.

(e) *Primary sources.* Don't forget about primary sources. Law places so much value on published appellate decisions and earlier scholarly articles that we often forget about telephones, e-mails, and interviews. If you're writing a casenote, talk to the lawyers who worked on the case. You might even write to the judge (never call), but only if the decision has become final.

(f) *Reading aloud.* When you think you're done, read your work aloud to a friend or loved one (or even just to yourself)—you will hear edits that you wouldn't otherwise see on the page.

(g) *Your mindset throughout.* Be patient and rigorous with your thinking and writing. Understand that you'll encounter obstacles—seemingly insuperable ones. That is part of the writing process. Set your mind to work, ask lots of questions, talk with others who are interested in the problem, and you should be able to work through frustrations.

(h) *Précis.* Some law reviews, such as *Columbia Law Review*, include a précis (that is, a synopsis or summary) for each article and lawnote. Study them. Write a similar précis for your own piece before, during, and after composing it. You'll find that it clarifies precisely what it is you're saying. In other words, in writing the note, start with what you've decided you wanted to say about your topic. It's usually a mistake to start with descriptive material and then get to your thesis only at the end. The reader wants to know where you're headed. State your thesis up front, and then keep relating your descriptive material to the thesis as you proceed.

31.5 Avoid the common faults of lawnotes.

(a) *Poor openers.* An essay—and yes, a lawnote is a type of essay—is doomed if it gets off to a bad start. Study examples that strike you as having particularly strong opening paragraphs. Then read the end to see whether it ties up with something in the opener. Once you've found a couple of good examples, try this technique yourself.

(b) *Cumbersome roadmapping.* One of the most lamentable habits of law-review writing is the tendency to say, "In Part I, this note will . . . . In Part II, this note will . . . . In Part III, ..." Imagine if a *Sports Illustrated* account of a basketball game proceeded in this manner. The better approach is to signal the organization more subtly, without the ham-fisted enumerations, or to be even less subtle about it by providing a table of contents. But the prosaic table of contents—one presented through sentences and paragraphs—is a sleeping pill on paper.

(c) *Analytical unsoundness.* Your thesis may be wrong or it may be incompletely analyzed because you've focused too much on a particular scenario. Before submitting the work, review it thoroughly for loose ends, weak arguments, and faulty reasoning.

(d) *Impracticality.* Law reviews are often criticized for having no real practical application in the field. The more highly ranked the law school where the law review is located, the more "theoretical" the articles and lawnotes are likely to be. A law review with pretensions to "national" standing is likely to proffer articles of broad scope and to reject articles of a state-specific nature. Examining the journal's previous issues will give you a good idea about the nature of its editors' perspective. But whatever your subject, you'll want to keep an eye on practicality. Why does your article matter? What real-world significance could it have? Why might someone want to consult it—or cite it?

(e) *Abstractitis.* At first it may feel more impressive to make your note long, to use terminology you found in the literature, and to speak in abstractions. But it's more impressive to understand your subject so well that you can explain it simply—in clear English—and in concrete words that a nonlawyer would use and understand. Abstraction is usually a sign of uncertainty. The author might prefer to feel like part of an in-crowd than engage readers who aren't part of it, or the author worries that the underlying idea is weak and will be revealed as such if seen naked. This isn't an appeal for plain and dull writing. It's an appeal for writing that is attractive because the words are well chosen, put into perfect order, and never wasted. Think like an architect at the beginning, but like a sculptor at the end.

(f) *Plagiarism.* Claiming the credit for someone else's mental work, whether to make money from it or merely to get a better grade or to seem smarter, is a serious academic offense. The most outright instances involve stealing chunks of a paper or article word for word and adopting them as if you had produced them. While the Internet makes this kind of theft easier than ever, it also makes the detection of it easier than ever. Whenever you're using a fact that isn't easily found in myriad reference works (the birth date of a famous author, for example), or you're using someone else's words or opinions, you should cite the source. Students most often get into trouble over four basic mistakes: (1) omitting attributions, so that sources are not properly identified; (2) missing quotation marks, so that another's words are claimed as one's own; (3) close paraphrasing at length, so that the essence of an extended passage derives from an unnamed source; and (4) inadequate citation, so that the reader cannot tell the extent of reliance on a given source, or what parts the researcher has relied on. There is much more to be said about this subject, but the upshot is to take notes carefully so that you fastidiously record quoted words, with due attribution, and to paraphrase by truly using your own words (not just changing a key word here and there), again being careful to supply all necessary attributions.

31.6 Study effective lawnotes and the literature on producing them.

(a) *Exemplars.* Each year, the American Society of Legal Writers, known as Scribes, bestows an award for the outstanding lawnote of the year. For a list of winners, go to www.scribes.org.

(b) *Further guidance.* See Elizabeth Fajans & Mary R. Falk, *Scholarly Writing for Law Students* (5th ed. 2017); Eugene Volokh, *Academic Legal Writing* (5th ed. 2016).

§ 32
Law-Review Articles*

32.1 Understand the main goals of a scholarly article.

(a) *The nature of scholarship.* Scholarly articles serve various purposes—from influencing courts and commentators on matters of legal doctrines or reforms to providing practitioners with trial strategies they might not have thought of or arguments they might otherwise find difficult to support. Legal scholarship is a complex set of disciplines, and its readers are a diverse group. Scholars approach their material in many different ways. Some are relentlessly concrete in their approach to cases and historical legal materials; others are unfailingly abstract and philosophical in their approach. Some try to remain as objective as possible, drawing a conclusion only if it has been carefully supported and proved; others engage in thoroughgoing advocacy in which there is no pretense of objectivity (they even dispute whether objectivity is humanly possible). Still others, in recent years, have approached scholarship through personal narrative—in which individuals' stories (sometimes accounts of the authors' own experiences) are recounted. Although the individual styles will vary, what all scholars have in common is an abiding belief in writing as an important tool of inquiry, critical thinking, and communication.

Because the ideas in this section overlap with the more basic information in § 31, you might want to review that section as well.

(b) *The basic approaches.* Law school teaches you to be descriptive. But in scholarly work, that approach is generally unhelpful. Every article should take this tack: I am comprehensively familiar with the following area of law, and here is what I have to add. There are three basic approaches to the scholarly article:

#1: Present a problem or conundrum and propose a solution.

#2: Present another writer's solution to a legal problem and show how and why it's flawed—preferably suggesting a better solution.

---

*Contributors to this chapter include (the late) Professor Monroe H. Freedman of Hofstra University; Professor Stephen Gillers of NYU Law School; and (the late) Professor Geoffrey C. Hazard Jr. of U.C. Hastings.

#3: Present research findings on a topic that otherwise receives scant attention and suggest preliminary conclusions and further avenues of inquiry.

Be willing to challenge conventional thinking. If you aren't willing to do so in this context, who will—and when? The law is a vast, dynamic set of disciplines and subdisciplines. Because scholars are continually posing new questions, we continually see the law in new ways. Nuances arise. Orthodoxies change. The best way to enter the world of legal scholarship is the same way you learn about a case that you're working on: ask as many questions as you can about the issues you're studying, from as many vantage points as you can. As you seek answers, remain vigilant to the new and even more complicated questions that your answers raise, and let these new questions guide your further exploration.

(c) *Close reasoning.* Don't get ahead of yourself. Deal with the issues methodically—step by step. Be as concrete as you can, citing instances and providing examples. Try to be so straightforward that a smart high-school student could follow your analysis.

32.2 Canvass the literature.

(a) *Background digging.* The first step in scholarly writing of any sort is to know all that has preceded—*all*, to the extent you realistically can. You must research thoroughly. "A man may turn over half a library to write one book," Samuel Johnson once quipped. It's true.

(b) *An example.* Let's take an example from a field you're unlikely to be writing about: legal philosophy. If you were to produce anything of even moderate importance in the field, you'd need a thorough knowledge of modern legal philosophers—say, from 1800 to the present day: Jeremy Bentham, James Fitzjames Stephen, Oliver Wendell Holmes, Roscoe Pound, Drucilla Cornell, John Salmond, Ruth Gavison, H.L.A. Hart, Hannah Arendt, Lon Fuller, Tony Honoré, Neil MacCormick, Anita Allen, Joseph Raz, and many others. You'd read about them, and you'd read much of their own writing. You'd need to know a great deal about all the different schools of jurisprudence, including the so-called outsider jurisprudence of critical legal studies and feminist scholars. To write in ignorance of this work would be to produce a kind of naive, pseudo-profound writing. Although you might well react negatively to some of your predecessors' work, at least you'd *know* it. And scholarship entails knowing as well as demonstrating and arguing convincingly.

(c) *A more mundane example.* To change the subject to something far more mundane—mechanic's liens—you'd need to read at least 20 and consult perhaps hundreds of articles on mechanic's liens if you hoped to produce a passably good article on one subdoctrine of mechanic's liens in one particular state. That's the nature of scholarship.

(d) *The moral.* So start by reading. You need an idea that is worth both your time and your reader's time. You're most likely to generate one by thinking hard about what courts and scholars have said, not by staring out the window (though the staring is useful when the reading is done). And yet it's best to begin writing, at least informally, before you finish reading everything on earth. Otherwise, you never will start, or once you do, your creativity will get smothered and you will just write about things that others have said. It's best to read and write and read and write.

32.3 Avoid the common flaws of law-review articles.

(a) *Undue length.* In recent years, law-review articles have grown longer and longer on average. One sometimes suspects that legal scholars are rechanneling failed book manuscripts—tedious, bloated affairs—and submitting them as law-review articles. One advantage for them is that armies of student editors will clean up the footnotes, correct all the quotations and citations—and often even supply footnotes where none existed before. But the biggest advantage to the scholars who proceed in this way is that their material actually gets published, an outcome that would probably be impossible otherwise.

Many leading law reviews have begun to curb this practice by imposing flexible word limits—25,000 words at most, except in special circumstances, or sometimes as low as 15,000 words. The trend is to be encouraged. If you're preparing to submit an article, you might try keeping it to 15,000 words, including footnotes. Trim away all the fat you can.

(b) *Stylistic flaws.* A poorly written article is a chore to read. Readers get distracted by misused phrases and overused emphatic fonts. They grow tired when forced to plow through extremely long paragraphs. And they may give up when confronted with long sentences containing double and triple negatives. Try emulating the prose style of *The New Yorker* or *The Economist.*

(c) *Overusing block quotations.* Occasionally you'll find an expression that can't be improved on, or one so well known that it should be repeated verbatim. Such quotations are rare and almost always short. Block quotations, used sparingly, may help to advance your own expressions if they are too good to paraphrase. But when they appear repeatedly, they overwhelm your prose and obscure your expression. You should be writing, not compiling.

(d) *Overabundant footnotes.* Too often, writers use footnotes to dwell on sidebar ideas and tangential thoughts rather than just to cite sources. Some footnotes become so swollen that a law review can fit only one line of text on a page above the footnotes. This phenomenon typifies excess.

For the opposite kind of footnote—the substantive footnote that illuminates and entertains—see 10.9(d).

(e) *No table of contents.* Law-review articles are typically long because they cover many aspects of a topic. Without a table of contents, readers can't see the logical structure of your writing or find the points of most interest and relevance to them.

(f) *Long sections with no subheadings.* Headings are guideposts for readers. They signal the progression of your discussion and keys to your analysis, etc. They also serve as rest stations, where a reader can pause and think about what you've said before continuing. Without them, readers may get lost or just distracted from fatigue. Make your headings both informative and interesting.

(g) *Writerly narcissism.* Many writers, usually those with well-founded insecurities, avoid seeking critical commentary on their work. The resulting work is flawed in any number of fixable ways. No matter how good you think you are, you will need reviewers as you go. For the most part, lawyers and academics are generous with their time and suggestions. Once you have a good draft, have as many smart people as you can read successive versions and offer suggestions. Ask them to identify holes in your research or arguments that need strengthening. People who aren't knowledgeable in your field are often as useful as people who are. Credit every reader in your first footnote, but be dignified about it—not gushy or effusive.

32.4 Take the advice of some established scholars.

(a) *Stephen Gillers of NYU Law School.*

The rules for good law-review writing are the rules for good writing.

Appreciate the importance of word choice, voice, syntax, metaphor, simile, signal words, the concrete over the general, rhetorical questions, and paragraphs and sentences of varying length. Find a voice of your own. Read your drafts aloud to learn how they will sound in a reader's head. Read and reread Strunk & White.

Know your argument well and state it clearly in a paragraph or two in your introduction. This ensures that you will not confuse the reader or yourself. An argument that cannot be described simply implies trouble. Then say why your argument is important. What turns on it? Why should readers care?

But before all, begin with a title and a sentence that entices the reader. Good writing seduces. Here are first lines from two of my articles:

Ex.: Today, the store at 27 West Eighth Street in Greenwich Village sells shoes.

Ex.: In 2009, after thirty-five years of lingering questions, I went looking for Leonard Garment.

Of course, the first line is but an outer wrapper, intended to spark curiosity, to bait the reader. (What happened at 27 West Eighth Street before today? Who is Leonard Garment and what were the lingering questions?) It may do so, but you must then have something of value to say. Say it and be done. Edit and rewrite until it makes you sick. Then put the draft away for a week or two and edit again. Less is more, here as in all other creative work. Prune your drafts. Delete the extraneous. Expunge jargon and cliché. You will be tempted to disperse your brilliant insights in footnotes, however superfluous to your claim. Resist. Resist. It is self-indulgent. Be lean. Respect the reader. Make your case and stop. —S.G.

(b) *The late Geoffrey C. Hazard Jr. of U.C. Hastings.*

First, focus on the points or propositions you're advancing. No more than three; if more, reorganize to no more than three.

Second, although you've labored long to formulate these points, spare the reader that agony. Explain the confusion you're clearing up and expound the clarification in detail.

Third, conclude with a brief summation. —G.C.H.

(c) *The late Monroe H. Freedman of Hofstra University.*

First, scholarly doesn't mean stuffy or arcane. Show mastery of your subject, and develop a thesis that opens up new ways of thinking about it. But don't smother your argument in pseudo-scholarly language. Your goal is to communicate, not obfuscate.

Second, the shorter your article, the better. Scholarly doesn't necessarily mean long. Repetition and digression detract from the thesis and turn away readers. The shorter the article, the more likely it will be read, cited, and discussed, and the more likely it will be reprinted. About two dozen articles I have written have been reprinted in casebooks and other publications; they average under 20 pages. As the Red King told the White Rabbit: "Begin at the beginning . . . and go on until you come to the end: then stop."

Third, use a title that tells researchers what the article is about. Clever titles please authors, but it's best to use a title that says simply what the article is about. "The Unconstitutionality of Electing State Judges" is not likely to be missed by later authors researching the issue of the unconstitutionality of electing state judges. For one article, however, I used "What Ever Happened to the Search for the Truth?" because it seemed clever to me. Unfortunately, nobody researching the subject of that article—the ethics of accessing metadata in an adversary's document—has ever found the article without additional help from me.

Finally, everyone needs a good editor. So find one or more good editors, including one who isn't an expert in your field. Well, yes, I'm generalizing from my own experience. When we know what we mean to say, we sometimes express it in a way that isn't immediately clear to readers. An editor can help to clarify the meaning. My colleague and frequent coauthor, Professor Abbe Smith, has a sharp eye for verbiage and for awkward phrasing, and never fails to improve what I think is a final draft. I reciprocate by trying to curb her propensity for clichés. My granddaughter, Ana Izquierdo, isn't a lawyer, but as a former major in English at Barnard, she often helps make my writing more readable. One more thought: re-edit your own work after setting it aside for a while. There's a good chance you'll make significant improvements. —M.H.F.

32.5 Study examples of effective law-review articles.

(a) *Sources generally.* Unsurprisingly, the top-ranked law schools typically boast the top-ranked law reviews. So generally speaking, the higher the ranking of the law school, the better its primary journals will be. Spend time perusing them.

(b) *Authors.* Many of the classic law-review articles were by noted scholars of the mid- to late 20th century. If you're serious about the genre, you will find it profitable to consult pieces by these scholars:

David A. Anderson	W. Page Keeton
Hans W. Baade	John H. Langbein
Alexander Bickel	W. Barton Leach
Charles L. Black	Arthur Allen Leff
Vincent Blasi	Warren Lehman
John E. Coons	Sanford Levinson
Brainerd Currie	Charles T. McCormick
David P. Currie	Frank I. Michelman
John P. Dawson	Roscoe Pound
Ronald M. Dworkin	Thomas Reed Powell
Frank H. Easterbrook	William L. Prosser
Henry Friendly	Max Radin
Lon Fuller	Charles A. Reich
Grant Gilmore	Ernest F. Roberts
Ruth Bader Ginsburg	Antonin Scalia
Leon Green	Jacobus tenBroek
H.L.A. Hart	Herbert Wechsler
Henry M. Hart	Glanville Williams
Judith Kaye	Charles Alan Wright

(c) *Anthologies.* The most foundational law-review articles aren't difficult to come by. In 1984, the Legal Classics Library published a hefty volume entitled *Great American Law Reviews*, edited with commentary by Robert C. Berring. It contains 22 seminal articles published from 1890 to 1964 by many of the authors listed just above. Far more dated, but equally fascinating to the legal historian, is the three-volume anthology entitled *Select Essays in Anglo-American Legal History* (1907–1909), compiled and edited by the Association of American Law Schools. This set reflects the modern heritage of legal scholarship; it would be a mistake to labor in ignorance of it. Meanwhile, many leading law reviews have occasionally collected the most influential articles to have appeared in their pages—a notable example being *Essays on Jurisprudence from the Columbia Law Review* (1962). The essays in a few similar compilations, such as *Harvard Legal Essays* (1967) and *Stanford Legal Essays* (1975), appear never to have actually appeared in law reviews, although the pieces are of the same type.

(d) *A humorous anthology.* For those wishing to see that law reviews aren't always dry-as-dust intellectual mortuaries, see *Amicus Humoriae* (2003), compiled by Robert M. Jarvis, Thomas E. Baker, and Andrew J. McClurg.

(e) The Green Bag, *Second Series.* If there is a model from which modern law reviews could benefit by emulation, it is Ross Davies's *The Green Bag,* established in 1997. The articles are short, erudite, and often witty. The editorial standards are nonpareil. Each piece is strictly limited to 50 footnotes. A personal subscription is highly recommended.

> "The first rule in writing is to sit down and spend time. Stay at the desk. Keep going."
>
> —*Richard Marius*

§ 33
Book Reviews

33.1 Understand the main goals of a book review.

(a) *Selection.* Book reviews help readers decide which of the many new publications in their field merit closer attention. In this way they help readers keep up with recent developments in a field of interest and provide new ways of looking at the current lay of the land. They also provide a place for readers to scan through new offerings within their own specialties and to broaden their vistas by letting them see what issues and ideas are developing in other fields. This intellectual cross-pollination is somewhat like roaming the aisles of an old-fashioned bookstore, but with more than the self-serving information found on dustjackets. The selection is narrower than a bookstore's offerings, but this is an advantage of book reviews, not a shortcoming. Selecting books for review gives editors—and, to a lesser extent, writers—a gatekeeper role. The goal is that the books selected will be the ones that in fact merit further study (or, perhaps, the ones that don't but will be high-profile additions in the field anyway).

(b) *Description.* Every review must give basic citational information about the book: title, author, publisher, and year of publication. The page count and list price are normally included. As a reviewer, you will want to include the author's credentials for writing this book: certainly the author's current position and perhaps a mention of previous writings or other achievements. Readers expect a short report on the scope of the book's contents. Although the description should be kept brief, out-of-the-ordinary content in the book—photographs, artwork, helpful appendixes, and the like—probably deserves mention.

(c) *Evaluation.* Any competent book reviewer will go beyond mere description to make a fair statement of the book's overarching themes and assess its importance in the field. This can be a big goal, and one that can be impossible to fully achieve within most book reviews' word limit. A major contribution to the field may be given the space needed to develop the substantive assessment more thoroughly—but that is the exception rather than the rule. The reader has every right to expect some guidance about what this book promises in the way of new insights, and the reviewer's informed opinion about whether or how well the author delivers on those promises.

33.2 Think about the specific goals of your book review.

(a) *Audience.* As with any other writing, you must keep the reader in mind. Will this review attract the attention of specialists in one field of law only, or will it address a more general audience? Consider the publication in which your review will appear and its likely readership. Then gauge how you might best inform and be helpful to that readership.

(b) *Scope.* Book reviews generally fall into two categories, which may be thought of as short form and long form. The short-form review is something of an expanded book notice. It gives the title, author, publisher, and other citational data, and adds a brief description of the content and the reviewer's evaluation of that content. The long form studies the book—and perhaps other new publications—in greater detail, typically with a view toward evaluating what the book contributes to the current literature in the field.

33.3 Avoid the common faults of book reviews.

(a) *Overdescribing.* Although you will always want to briefly describe the book and its contents, readers will quickly tire of an unduly elaborate exposition. Summarize efficiently. Avoid a chapter-by-chapter or section-by-section narrative, or a fleshed-out recitation of the table of contents. A review that is all summary and no analysis is little help to the reader.

(b) *Ultracrepidarianism and lack of disinterestedness.* It's a mistake to expect a reviewer to give a first-rate assessment of a book outside the reviewer's field of expertise. More often than not, insiders will catch on to the reviewer's ignorance about some aspect of the specialty. If you're assigned a review and the subject seems beyond your ken, you might either (1) give yourself a crash course in the field if you're a quick study, or (2) decline the assignment if the circumstances allow. Ideally, you should have no personal interest in the book or its author. In the small world of specialized fields of study, however, this point can be tricky. Any bias the reviewer has—for or against the author—will detract from the review's credibility in the minds of readers who are aware of the personal or professional relationship between the two.

(c) *Glib evaluations.* Standing alone, a conclusory rating ("excellent," "good," "fair," "poor") tells the reader nothing. You must justify any such subjective grading with examples from the book and with a supporting analysis. If the book has merits or shortcomings, point them out with some specificity.

(d) *Cheerleading.* Some reviewers cannot seem to bring themselves to say a negative word. Often they haven't done their homework, and they assume that the safe course is unmitigated praise. But if the praise is being lavished unknowledgeably—with no critical understanding of works that have preceded the one under review—then it's a disservice to your readers. You must try to assess the book's significance within the existing literature—a challenging task. To do this, you might try assuming the role of omniscient narrator, tending toward kindness and courtesy but never failing to be honest in your evaluation.

(e) *Bushwhacking.* If uncritical praise is a fault in a book review—and it certainly is— then so is nitpicking and uncivil sniping. Criticism that is unjust may give the reviewer's ego a temporary boost, but it does a disservice to the readers, the author, and the public. It's one thing if the prose is unidiomatic, pretentiously contrived, or unbearably dull throughout, or if the book is rife with misspellings, typographical errors, or other mistakes. These things do distract readers from the author's message and are worth pointing out. But to dwell on an uncharacteristic gaffe (at the cost of giving the book a serious evaluation) reflects far more poorly on the reviewer than on the author. And if you're going to call something a mistake, be sure it really is one: an erroneous allegation of error is despicable.

For a funny account of untoward bushwhacking—a satirical one—see Stephen Potter, *Lifemanship* (1950) in the chapter "Book Reviewmanship."

33.4 Study effective book reviews.

(a) *Past reviews.* One way to find fascinating reviews and to weigh their merits is to take an important book from 50 to 75 years ago—say, Glanville Williams's *Learning the Law* (first published in 1945), Karl Llewellyn's *The Common Law Tradition: Deciding Appeals* (1960), or Grant Gilmore's *The Ages of American Law* (1977)—and compare what contemporary reviewers said about it soon after it first appeared. Another good source is the *Law Quarterly Review*, a British journal whose book reviews have long been among the best in law-related English-language periodicals.

(b) *General periodicals.* Never forget that you can learn invaluable techniques from such modern sources as these:

- *The Atlantic.*
- *Bookforum.*
- *Claremont Review of Books.*
- *Harper's Magazine.*
- *The London Review of Books.*
- *The New Yorker.*
- *The New York Review of Books.*
- *The New York Times Book Review.*
- *The Times Literary Supplement* (*TLS*).

Word Index

*An invariably inferior form.

*An invariably inferior form.

*An invariably inferior form.

*An invariably inferior form.

*An invariably inferior form.

*An invariably inferior form.

*An invariably inferior form.

*An invariably inferior form.

*An invariably inferior form.

*An invariably inferior form.

*An invariably inferior form.

*An invariably inferior form.

*An invariably inferior form.

*An invariably inferior form.

*An invariably inferior form.

*An invariably inferior form.

*An invariably inferior form.

*An invariably inferior form.

*An invariably inferior form.

*An invariably inferior form.

*An invariably inferior form.

*An invariably inferior form.

*An invariably inferior form.

General Index

Colophon

The pages of *The Redbook* were created in-house at the LawProse offices in Dallas. This fourth edition uses the typeface Equity for its main text, a change from the Times New Roman used in earlier editions. Equity was designed by Matthew Butterick, a Los Angeles lawyer and typographer. The author of *Typography for Lawyers*,* Butterick crafted the typeface with legal writers in mind. It gives roughly the same word count per page as Times New Roman, which is widely used in law offices.

Butterick based the design of Equity on Monotype's font Ehrhardt, which gets its name from influences in the Dutch and German printing industry of the late 1600s. The first version originated there at the Ehrhardt Foundry in Leipzig, Germany. Monotype modernized that face in the 1930s—shortly after the company introduced its popular Times New Roman. Ehrhardt and Equity both feature a slightly condensed letterform and a larger x-height that remains legible in smaller type sizes.

The Redbook's running headers use Concourse, a font also designed by Butterick as a complement to Equity. The section numbers in the headers are Futura Bold, which is also used for section heads and injunctions. Futura was designed by Paul Renner and the Bauer Type Foundry of Frankfurt, Germany, in the 1920s. It features hard—some think strident—geometrical shapes, especially circles, triangles, and lines, for a minimalist feel. In boldface it is especially stark, as perhaps appropriate for a manual of instruction.

---

*Jones McClure Publishing (2d ed. 2015).